Contents

PART **III** **Economics and Society**   143

7   **Economic Behavior and Rationality**   145

8   **Consumption and the Consumer Society**   158

Microeconomics
in Context

Microeconomics
in Context THIRD EDITION

NEVA GOODWIN
Tufts University

JONATHAN HARRIS
Tufts University

JULIE A. NELSON
University of Massachusetts Boston

BRIAN ROACH
Tufts University

MARIANO TORRAS
Adelphi University

With contributions by
Frank Ackerman • Synapse Energy Economics
Thomas Weisskopf • University of Michigan, Ann Arbor

M.E.Sharpe
Armonk, New York
London, England

The EuroSlavic fonts used to create this work are © 1986–2014 Payne Loving Trust.
EuroSlavic is available from Linguist's Software, Inc.,
www.linguistsoftware.com, P.O. Box 580, Edmonds, WA 98020-0580 USA
tel (425) 775-1130.

Library of Congress Cataloging-in-Publication Data

Goodwin, Neva R.
  Microeconomics in context / Neva Goodwin, Jonathan Harris, Julie Nelson, Brian Roach, and
Mariano Torras. -- Third edition.
      pages cm
  Includes index.
  ISBN 978-0-7656-3878-6 (pbk. : alk. paper)
  1. Microeconomics. 2. Microeconomics--Social aspects. I. Title.
  HB172.G632 2014
  338.5--dc23   2013038499

Printed in the United States of America

The paper used in this publication meets the minimum requirements of
American National Standard for Information Sciences
Permanence of Paper for Printed Library Materials,
ANSI Z 39.48-1984.

∞

EB (p)   10   9   8   7   6   5   4   3   2   1

Brief Contents

Introduction

Microeconomics in Context provides a thorough introduction to the principles of microeconomics. Too often, introductory microeconomics textbooks have taught students a few useful concepts and have given them plenty of practice in theoretical curve shifting, without encouraging students to critically evaluate the applicability of these models to real-world issues. While this book incorporates the theoretical content expected in a principles text, it also delves deeper, offering a fresh understanding of the economic complexities of the twenty-first century.

From the start, *Microeconomics in Context* dispels the traditional notion that economics is primarily a positivist discipline, by recognizing that the ultimate objective of economics is to enhance human well-being—a fundamentally normative goal. Further, the "in Context" approach continually emphasizes that economic analysis must be embedded in a rich social, environmental, historical, and political context.

At the same time that this book introduces the many applications of economic theory, it provides a variety of viewpoints. A full treatment of standard neoclassical market theory and related topics is complemented by integral discussions of history, institutions, gender, ethics, ecology, and inequality throughout the book. Thus, this comprehensive and up-to-date text offers all the benefits of a standard microeconomic course together with greater depth and realism, and a more interesting and accessible presentation.

Students will find this textbook readable, interesting, and relevant throughout. Whether this class will represent their only formal exposure to economics, or they plan to study the subject further, *Microeconomics in Context* will equip them with the standard tools *and* the contemporary knowledge that they need to succeed.

Microeconomics in Context is the companion textbook to *Macroeconomics in Context* (2nd ed.) also published by M.E. Sharpe.

CONTENT AND ORGANIZATION

Some of the innovative features of this text are apparent in a quick scan of the Table of Contents or the material in "Chapter 0." The "in Context" approach we take in this text diverges from most economics textbooks in four crucial ways:

- First, what are commonly thought of as purely economic issues more appropriately are viewed as questions about human well-being. Rather than confining "economic thinking" to maximizing efficiency, this book addresses deeper issues. What do we want in life? How do we get it? What conflicts may exist between what I want and what you want? Must there always be winners and losers?
- Second, this book reflects a more comprehensive understanding of what constitutes economic activity. Production, distribution (or exchange), and consumption form three

essential economic activities, but no less important than these is a fourth: resource maintenance. If an economic system fails to maintain factories, roads, schools, and homes; the physical and mental health of the people who make up the system; or the farmland, forests, fisheries, and other aspects of the natural environment on which these people depend, the economic activities of production and consumption become difficult, or in some cases even impossible. Explicit discussion of the economic activity of resource maintenance updates economics to include twenty-first–century concerns about environmental and social sustainability.

- Third, the economy is not portrayed as an autonomous system. Instead, it is understood as fully integrated with and crucially dependent on the social contexts of history, psychology, institutions, culture, and ethics, as well as the context of the natural world. The economic system also affects these contexts in many ways: The success of an economy in producing wealth may—or may not—produce increased well-being. Whether or not an economy is considered successful, it can be seriously disruptive to the ecological or social contexts. Citizens need to understand these interconnections in order to support an economic system that contributes to the health of the social and ecological contexts on which it depends.

- Finally, this book looks at the full spectrum of economic activities, not only at those that occur in the "business sphere." It also examines the ways in which economic activities are carried on in the "core sphere" of households and communities and in the "public purpose sphere" of governments and nonprofits.

We have organized the material in this book into five major parts in an effort to offer a comprehensive picture of economic theory and analysis.

- Part I begins with the innovative "Chapter 0," which provides background information on many key economic statistics, as well as on some ecological and socioeconomic measures. The purpose of Chapter 0 is to get students thinking about well-being more broadly than they would if working with a traditional economics text. The other two chapters in Part I introduce the major themes of the book, as well as the principal actors in the economy.

- Part II introduces basic supply and demand analysis, elasticities, and welfare analysis. It also includes a chapter on international trade. For many users, this part of the book will contain the "meat" of the introductory course. While most of this material will appear familiar to teachers of microeconomics, this text gives greater recognition to the limitations of traditional welfare analysis and provides greater emphasis on real-world market institutions than is typical in microeconomics textbooks.

- Part III considers the economic roles that will be familiar to all readers throughout their lives, both as workers and as consumers. These roles are illustrated with examples that depart from the standard models—for example, household production is recognized throughout. This part of the book is introduced by a chapter on economic behavior, incorporating knowledge that has come from the latest studies in behavioral economics. It also includes a chapter on the topic of consumerism, and one on labor markets.

- Part IV puts the economy in a social context with one chapter on distribution, inequality, and poverty, and another on government roles, with an emphasis on the impact of taxes. The ecological context for the economy is then examined in two chapters that take up issues such as pollution, externalities, common property, and public goods.

- Part V goes into more depth on market topics by describing the idealized model of perfect competition, presenting models of market power, and analyzing various resource markets.

Note that instructors who wish to cover the standard microeconomic topics of production and market organization early in the semester may wish to assign Part V after Part III, or even move directly to Part V from Part II.

WHAT MAKES THIS BOOK DIFFERENT FROM OTHER TEXTS?

This text covers the traditional topics that most microeconomics texts include but examines them from a broader, more holistic perspective. The following chapter-by-chapter synopsis explains how this book manages both to be "familiar enough" to fit into a standard curriculum and "different enough" to respond to instructors' and students' commonly expressed needs and dissatisfactions with other approaches.

Chapter 0, "Microeconomics and Well-Being," is a unique element, offering visual presentations of interesting data on a number of topics. The variables have been selected for intrinsic interest, as well as for relevance to the material covered in the rest of the book. Instructors and students may choose to use this statistical portrait in a variety of ways, including as an introduction to later topics, as a reference for use in other chapters, or as material to draw on in designing research projects. The majority of the variables illustrated in Chapter 0 are given only for the United States, but several of the graphs present data for different countries to provide international context.

As in other textbooks, Chapter 1, "Economic Activity in Context," opens with a discussion of what economics is all about. If you have taught this subject using another textbook, you will find familiar topics here, including discussions of the basic questions of economics (what, how, and for whom), efficiency, scarcity, opportunity cost, and the Production Possibilities Frontier. However, we immediately set these topics in the broader context of concern for human well-being. We define economics as "the study of how people manage their resources to meet their needs and enhance their well-being," and discuss the important difference between intermediate goals and final goals. We introduce concepts such as externalities in this chapter—much earlier than in most other texts—in order to emphasize that markets, though very effective in a number of areas, are not on their own sufficient to organize economic life in the service of well-being. To the familiar three essential economic activities (production, distribution, and consumption) we add an essential fourth: resource maintenance. In a discussion of modes of economic analysis, the standard circular flow diagram, illustrating exchange between households and firms, is used as an example of a simple model. This is followed by a broader circular flow model showing the different spheres of economic activity and their social and ecological contexts.

Chapter 2, "Markets and Society," points out that the economy may be understood as existing within "three spheres" of activity: not only the sphere of businesses (estimated at 58 percent of the economy), but also the core sphere, comprising economic activity that occurs within households and communities (32 percent), as well as the public purpose sphere, of government and not-for-profit activity (10 percent). This chapter supplements the rather abstract treatment of markets that appears in most textbooks with discussion of how markets came about and what they require in terms of legal and social supports. It also draws on contemporary research regarding institutions and the design of market mechanisms in order to give students insight into the complexity and variety of real-world markets.

Chapter 3, "Supply and Demand," includes supply and demand presentations that will be familiar from other textbooks, such as the slopes of the curves, factors that shift the curves, equilibrium and market adjustment, and the signaling and rationing functions of prices. Unlike many books that present equilibrium analysis as "the way the world works," however, we explicitly introduce supply and demand analysis as a *tool* whose purpose is to help disentangle the effects of various factors on real-world prices and quantities. Rather than concentrating solely on the potential efficiency of markets, our contextual approach demands that distributional consequences and power issues also be raised.

Chapter 4, "Elasticity," presents traditional definitions and discussions of price elasticities of demand and supply, income elasticity of demand, and the income and substitution effects of price changes.

Chapter 5, "Welfare Analysis," is new for this edition. It presents standard welfare analysis, including the topics of consumer and producer surplus. This chapter also includes a close examination of different ways of understanding efficiency. Consideration of what is efficient—and for whom—is followed by a first look at policy conclusions that have been drawn from this approach and at the requirements for "perfect markets" that underlie traditional welfare analysis.

Chapter 6, "International Trade and Trade Policy," is another new chapter for this edition. Among the familiar topics covered is the gains-from-trade story that is now so important in discussing topical issues of global commerce. (The formal theory of comparative advantage and the gains from trade is spelled out in the appendix to this chapter.) We also discuss some contemporary vulnerabilities from trade as they may affect both developed and developing countries. These issues are put these in the context of the globalized world, as it differs from the historical example of trade between England and Portugal.

Chapter 7, "Economic Behavior and Rationality," elaborates on the topics of individual choice, rationality, and self-interest, which were discussed briefly in Chapter 2 of the previous edition. This expanded text updates and amplifies standard expositions, drawing on studies of human economic behavior by scholars such as Herbert Simon and Daniel Kahneman, and introduces issues of organizational structure and behavior. The result is an accurate picture of the complex motivations and institutions underlying real-world economic activities.

Chapter 8, "Consumption and the Consumer Society," begins by presenting the traditional utility-theoretic model of consumer behavior. We explain the notion of consumer sovereignty, show students how to graph a budget line, and discuss the rule for utility maximization derived from marginal thinking. We also discuss the historical development of the "consumer society" and the psychological models of consumer behavior used in marketing research. We present views and evidence regarding the relationship between consumption/consumerism and happiness. Public policy is discussed in reference to the personal and ecological impact of high-level consumption patterns. The Appendix presents a formal theory of consumer behavior, using budget lines and indifference curves to illustrate utility maximization in the standard model.

Chapter 9, "Markets for Labor," includes the traditional derivation of profit-maximizing labor demand by a perfectly informed and perfectly competitive firm. Topics include the upward-sloping and backward-bending individual paid labor supply curves. We also discuss additional ways of understanding how wages are influenced, including theories of compensating wage differentials, market power, worker motivation, and labor market discrimination. Instead of focusing only on market equilibrium and efficiency, we note that in view of strong norms and the frequent lack of good information about worker productivity, historical and social factors can have persistent effects on wage and employment patterns. The Appendix sets out in formal terms the standard theory of a firm's hiring decisions.

Chapter 10, "Economic and Social Inequality," introduces Part IV of this book, moving from definitions and measurement of inequality to data on inequality trends in the United States and other countries. The second half of the chapter focuses on what is known about the underlying causes of economic inequality, and discusses possible policy responses.

Chapter 11, "Taxes and Tax Policy," starts out, like many of the other chapters, with standard theory—in this case, taxes in the supply-and-demand model. Referring back to the chapter on welfare analysis, it shows how economists may demonstrate the inefficiency of most taxes. Moving then to discuss taxation specifically in the United States, data are presented on the structure of various federal taxes and their impacts.

Chapter 12, "The Economics of the Environment," reveals how an understanding of externalities makes supply-and-demand analysis more relevant. However, this discussion also raises the problem of the valuation of externalities. We draw a distinction between standard and ecological views of the value of natural capital, raising the question of whether a standard cost-benefit framework can reasonably be applied to issues with unpredictable effects over the very long term (given the complexity of natural systems). A section on approaches to nonmarket environmental valuation is followed by a survey of various policy options for dealing with externalities. The Appendix offers a formal analysis of negative externalities.

Chapter 13, "Common Property Resources and Public Goods," differentiates between private and public goods. It relates recent work on this important topic to environmental considerations, contrasting Garrett Hardin's "tragedy of the commons" analysis with Elinor Ostrom's work on common property management. These analyses are then applied to a discussion of the challenges posed by global climate change.

Chapter 14, "Capital Stocks and Resource Maintenance," is the first of two chapters on production. It begins with a discussion of the activity of resource maintenance—that is, the importance of taking into consideration the impact of flows created by economic activity on the stocks of productive resources that will be available for future use. In a departure from treatments in other texts, this chapter examines the crucial contributions of natural capital (environmental resources), human capital, and social capital to economic activity and human well-being. It also considers treatments of manufactured capital (machinery and physical infrastructure) and financial capital.

In Chapter 15, "Production Costs," the discussion of production continues with a focus on the costs of production. We present the standard model of a firm's cost structure, with a focus on marginal costs, and a traditional discussion of fixed and variable inputs; diminishing, constant, and increasing returns; and short-run versus long-run issues. The student learns to graph total product curves and total cost curves and is introduced to the concept of marginal cost. We set this model in context in two important ways: First, the chapter encourages students to reflect on the idea that because of externalities, private and social net benefits from production may not be equivalent. Second, the chapter offers examples of cases where other economic actors (besides firms) make production decisions, and cases where other methods of decision-making are necessary.

Chapter 16, "Markets Without Power," focuses on the concept of a perfectly competitive market. Its theoretic characteristics are described, and the zero-economic-profit and efficiency outcomes are discussed. Continuing the discussion from the previous chapter, we explain the profit-maximizing decisions of a perfectly competitive firm. Rather than simply concluding that perfectly competitive markets are always efficient, this chapter contextualizes the material with a discussion of efficiency and equity, including the topics of path dependence and network externalities. The Appendix offers a formal model of perfect competition.

Chapter 17, "Markets with Market Power," covers traditional models of monopoly, monopolistic competition, and oligopoly. The different market structures are presented along a competitiveness continuum, with perfect competition and pure monopoly (the "ideal types") representing the opposite extremes. Abundant examples are provided of the different market structures, including a separate section on agriculture and health care.

SPECIAL FEATURES

Each chapter in this text contains many features designed to enhance student learning.

- Key terms are highlighted in boldface type throughout the text, and defined in marginal notes.
- Discussion Questions at the end of each section encourage immediate review of what has been read, and link the material to the students' own experiences. The frequent appearance of these questions throughout each chapter helps students review manageable portions

of material, and thus boosts comprehension. The questions can be used for participatory exercises involving the entire class or for small-group discussion.

- End-of-chapter Review Questions are designed to encourage students to create their own summary of concepts. These questions also serve as helpful guidelines to the importance of various points.
- End-of-chapter Exercises encourage students to work with and apply the material, thereby gaining increased mastery of concepts, models, and analytical techniques.
- Throughout all the chapters, boxes enliven the material with real-world illustrations drawn from a variety of sources.
- In order to make the chapters as lively and accessible as possible, some formal and technical material (suitable for inclusion in some but not all course designs) is carefully and concisely explained in chapter appendices.

A glossary at the end of the book contains all key terms, their definitions, and the number of the chapter in which each is defined.

SUPPLEMENTS

The supplements package for this book provides a complete set of resources for instructors and students using this text. All supplements are available in electronic format, for free download, at www.gdae.org/micro.

Verified instructors will be granted access to the *Instructor's Resource Manual.* For each chapter, the *Instructor's Resource Manual* includes a statement of objectives for student learning, a list of key terms, a Lecture Outline, and answers to all Review Questions and end-of-chapter Exercises. In addition, the "Notes on Text Discussion Questions" provide not only suggested answers to these questions but also ideas on how the questions might be used in the classroom. For some chapters, sections entitled "Web Resources" and "Extensions" provide supplementary material and links to other materials that can be used to enrich lectures and discussions.

Also available to verified instructors, the *Test Bank* includes a full complement of multiple-choice and true/false questions for each chapter. PowerPoint slides of figures and tables from the text are also freely available.

For students, an electronic *Study Guide* provides ample opportunity to review and practice the key concepts developed in the text, and includes practice questions with answers. The *Study Guide* is available for free download at www.gdae.org/micro.

Additional supplementary material is also available for students and faculty at www.gdae. org/micro. Among these supplements are:

- Expanded data for Chapter 0, including additional data for the United States along with international comparisons.
- Chapter-length modules on each of the three economic spheres: the business, core, and public purpose spheres.
- Text updates and policy briefs that address up-to-date issues and present the latest data. Such updates will continue to be added to the site in the future.

HOW TO USE THIS TEXT

The feedback we have received from instructors who used this text in its First and Second Editions has been enthusiastic and gratifying. We have found that this book works in a variety of courses with a wide range of approaches, and we would like to share some of these instructors' suggestions on tailoring this book to meet your own course needs.

Even if you are among those rare instructors who normally get their students all the way through a microeconomics principles text in a semester, you may find that, with a text that is quite different from those you have used before, it is harder to anticipate which chapters will require the most time. Other instructors (perhaps the majority) do not expect to cover all of the material in the textbook. In either case, it is wise to plan in advance how to deal with the possibility that you may not be able to cover the entire text.

On pages xxv–xxvii you will find several possible course plans based on different emphases (such as neoclassical, ecological, and public policy). We hope that these topically arranged outlines will help you plan the course that will best suit your and your students' needs.

NOTES ON DIFFERENCES FROM THE SECOND EDITION

A Second Edition of this text was published by M.E. Sharpe in 2009. If you were one of the users of that edition, you will want to note the following changes which have been made in response to user feedback. The following chapters are either completely new or largely recomposed, using sections of chapters from the Second Edition:

- Chapter 0: Microeconomics and Well-Being
- Chapter 5: Welfare Analysis
- Chapter 6: International Trade and Trade Policy
- Chapter 7: Economic Behavior and Rationality (This replaces, with some overlap, the previous Chapter 2: Economic Actors and Organizations)
- Chapter 11: Taxes and Tax Policy
- Chapter 10: Economic and Social Inequality (This includes some of the material that was covered in the previous Chapter 9: Distribution: Exchange and Transfer)
- Chapter 12: The Economics of the Environment (This picks up some of what had been in the previous Chapter 14: Markets for Other Resources)
- Chapter 13 Common Property Resources and Public Goods

At the same time that new materials have been developed, some material from the Second Edition has been compressed or deleted. Some of the deleted material, such as Chapters 15–17 from the Second Edition (on the three spheres of economic activity) can now be found at www.gdae.org/micro.

ACKNOWLEDGMENTS

Microeconomics in Context was written under the auspices of the Global Development and Environment Institute, a research institute at Tufts University. This text has been a long time in the making, and many people have been involved along the way.

First, we would like to thank the late Wassily Leontief, who initially urged us to write a book on economic principles for students in transitional economies. He provided inspiration and encouragement during those early years. We also are enormously grateful to Kelvin Lancaster, who allowed us to use *Modern Economics: Principles and Policy* (a textbook that he and Ronald Dulany wrote in the 1970s) as a jumping-off point for our work.

An early workshop testing our "contextual approach" through a variety of interactions with students and faculty got us started. We are grateful to David Garman, of the Tufts University Economics Department, who arranged an opportunity for us to class-test a very early draft. Other faculty members who assisted in the developmental stage of this text include Steven Cohn (Knox College), Julie Heath (University of Memphis), and Geoffrey Schneider (Bucknell University).

An early draft of the textbook was prepared in 2000. We would like to thank Robert Scott Gassler (Vesalius College of the Vrije Universiteit Brussels), Julie Matthaei (Wellesley College), and Adrian Meuller (CEPE Centre for Energy Policy and Economics), who, among others, provided helpful comments on that draft.

The early draft also formed the basis for editions designed for transitional economies, which were translated and published in Russia (Russian State University for the Humanities, 2002) and Vietnam (Hanoi Commercial University, 2002). Economists who contributed ideas to the transitional economies texts included Oleg Ananyin (Institute of Economics and Higher School of Economics, Moscow), Drucilla Barker (Hollins College), Raymond Benton (Loyola University), Peter Dorman (Evergreen College), Susan Feiner (University of Southern Maine), Cheryl Lehman (Hofstra University), Robert McIntyre and Andrew Zimbalist (Smith College), and Hoang Van Kinh and Pham Vu Luan (Hanoi Commercial University).

Work on the early U.S. editions, led by Julie Nelson, was greatly facilitated by feedback from Steven Cohn, as well as by careful readings and extensive commentaries on successive drafts from Jonathan Harris and Brian Roach at the Global Development and Environment Institute.

Among the many faculty who provided valuable comments on these editions, we would like to thank Steve Balkin (Roosevelt University), Sandy Baum (Skidmore College), Jose Juan Bautista (Xavier University of Louisiana), Timothy E. Burson (Queens University of Charlotte), David Ciscel (University of Memphis), Polly Cleveland (Columbia University), Will Cummings (Grossmont College), Fred Curtis (Drew University), Dennis Debrecht (Carroll College), James Devine (Loyola Marymount University), Amy McCormick Diduch (Mary Baldwin College), Ernest Diedrich (College of Saint Benedict/Saint John's University), Richard England (University of New Hampshire), Gary Ferrier (University of Arkansas), Ronald L. Friesen (Bluffton College), Judex Hyppolite (Indiana University), Miren Ivankovic (Southern Wesleyan University), Mehrene Larudee (Bates College), Bruce Logan (Lesley College), Valerie Luzadis (SUNY-ESF), Mark Maier (Glendale Community College), Ken Meter (Kennedy School of Government), Eric P. Mitchell (Randolph-Macon Woman's College), Akira Motomura (Stonehill College), Maeve Powlick (Skidmore College), Shyamala Raman (Saint Joseph College), Judith K. Robinson (Castleton State College), Malcolm Robinson (Thomas More College), June Roux (Salem Community College), Sigrid Stagl (University of Leeds), Myra Strober (Stanford University), Marjolein van der Veen (Bellevue Community College), Abu N. M. Wahid (Tennessee State University), and Edward K. Zajicek (Kalamazoo College).

Special thanks go to the many students who provided feedback on previous editions, including Brian Cotroneo and Marc McDunch of Boston College; Castleton State College students Noah Bartmess, Kevin Boucher, April L. Cole, Shawn Corey, Lisa Dydo, Tim Florentine, Roger Gillies, Ashley Kennedy, Nicole LaDuc, Matt Lane, Joesph O'Reilly, Kevin Perry, James Riehl, Jessica Schoof, Josh Teresco, Jennifer Trombey, Monica Tuckerman, Craig Wetzel, and Liza Wimble; Colby College student Eric Seidel; Drew University students Sigourney Giblin, Erin Hoffman, Jennifer Marsico, Leo A. Mihalkovitz, Peter Nagy, and Sofia Novozilova; Catherine Hazzard, a student at Saint Joseph College; Stonehill College student Anthony Budri; Sarah Barthelmes, Kathryn Cash, Aris Dinitraropolous, Jen Hanley, Krista Leopold, Mary Pat Reed, E. Rose, Kaitlyn Skelley, and Ryan Tewksbury from the University of New Hampshire; Rebecca Clausen of the University of Oregon; and students from Will Cummings's class at Grossmont College.

Reviewers who provided valuable comments for the Third Edition were Rachel Bouvier (University of Southern Maine), Armagan Gezici (Keene State College), Dennis Leyden (University of North Carolina, Greenville), and Mark Wenzel (Wayne State University).

Josh Uchitelle-Pierce at the Global Development and Environment Institute coordinated several important tasks for this book, including data research and manuscript preparation. He was ably assisted by Tufts University students Lauren Jayson and Mitchell Stallman. Administrative and outreach support at the Global Development and Environment Institute was provided by Erin Couts and Casey Kennedy.

We also thank the staff of M.E. Sharpe publishing, particularly Irene Bunnell, Patricia Kolb, and Angela Piliouras, for their enthusiasm and meticulous work in getting this book to press on a tight schedule. Our editor, George Lobell, contributed support and helpful suggestions throughout the process.

All contributors of written text materials were paid through grants raised by the Global Development and Environment Institute, and all royalties from sales of the book, by agreement of the authors, support the work of the institute. We are extremely appreciative of the financial support we have received from the following foundations: Barr, Ford, Island, Spencer T. and Ann W. Olin, and V. K. Rasummen.

Finally, we would like to thank the many students we have had the privilege to teach over the years—you continually inspire us and provide hope for a bright future.

Sample Course Outlines

The timespan of an academic term often imposes significant constraints on what material an instructor can cover, requiring choices about which topics to include and how much time to devote to each. *Microeconomics in Context* can be used as the basis for a variety of approaches, depending on how much flexibility you have and which topics particularly interest you and your students.

To help identify the material that makes the most sense for your class, we have put together some ideas for course outlines below. Arranged topically, they are designed to help you choose specific parts of the text when there is not enough time to cover the entire book.

We understand that in many departments a primary objective of the introductory course is to teach in some detail "how (neoclassical) economists think." Instructors focusing primarily on neoclassical content can select the "Base Chapters" (listed below), the "Additional Standard Microeconomic Material," and the "Neoclassical Emphasis" material. While this material does not come close to exploiting fully the richness of *Microeconomics in Context*, contextual discussions (a hallmark of this text) interwoven into the standard material will broaden students' understanding of microeconomic theory by fostering critical evaluation of the assumptions and limitations of neoclassical approaches.

For those instructors seeking to combine coverage of traditional neoclassical ideas with other material, we provide suggestions for particular emphases below. For example, ecological sustainability is an issue of increasing importance to economics; material devoted to this topic is listed below under "Ecological Emphasis." Materials suitable for several other emphases also are listed below.

BASE CHAPTERS

- Chapter 1, "Economic Activity in Context"
- Chapter 2, "Markets and Society"
- Chapter 3, "Supply and Demand"
- Chapter 4, "Elasticity"

ADDITIONAL STANDARD MICROECONOMIC MATERIAL

- Chapter 6, Section 1, "Trade, Specialization, and Productivity," and Section 2, "Gains from Trade"
- Chapter 9, Section 1, "Labor in the Traditional Neoclassical Model," and Section 2, "Labor Supply and Demand at the Market Level"
- Chapter 15, "Production Costs"
- Chapter 16, Section 2, "Perfect Competition," Section 3, "Profit Maximization Under Perfect Competition," and Section 4, "Losses and Exit"

- Chapter 17, Section 1, "The Traditional Models," Section 2, "Pure Monopoly: One Seller," Section 3, "Monopolistic Competition," and Section 4, "Oligopoly"

NEOCLASSICAL EMPHASIS

- Chapter 6, Appendix, "A Formal Theory of Gains from Trade"
- Chapter 7, Section 1, "Economic Understandings of Human Motivations"
- Chapter 8, Section 1, "Economic Theory and Consumption," and Appendix, "A Formal Theory of Consumer Behavior"
- Chapter 9, Appendix, "A Formal Model of a Firm's Hiring Decision"
- Chapter 16, Appendix, "A Formal Model of Perfect Competition"
- Chapter 17, Appendix, "Formal Analysis of Monopoly and Monopolistic Competition"

WELFARE ANALYSIS EMPHASIS

- Chapter 5, "Welfare Analysis"
- Chapter 11, Section 1, "Economic Theory and Taxes"
- Chapter 12, Section 1, "The Theory of Externalities," and Appendix, "Formal Analysis of Negative Externalities"

EMPHASIS ON CRITIQUES OF NEOCLASSICAL ECONOMICS

- Chapter 1, Section 2, "The Goals of an Economy," and Section 5, "Microeconomics in Context"
- Chapter 2, Section 4, "Advantages and Limitations of Markets"
- Chapter 3, Section 5, "Topics in Market Analysis"
- Chapter 6, Section 3, "Drawbacks of Free Trade"
- Chapter 9, Section 5, "Wages and Economic Power"
- Chapter 16, Section 1, "Understanding Market Power and Competition," and Section 5, "Production, Efficiency, and Equity"

ECOLOGICAL EMPHASIS

- Chapter 8, Section 4, "Consumption in an Environmental Context"
- Chapter 12, "The Economics of the Environment"
- Chapter 13, Section 3, "Common Property Resources," Section 4, "Public Goods," Section 5, "Climate Change"
- Chapter 14, Section 2, "Natural Capital"

POLICY/APPLIED EMPHASIS

- Chapter 5, Section 5, "Policy Inferences from Welfare Analysis"
- Chapter 6, Section 4, "Globalization and Policy"
- Chapter 8, Section 5, "Consumption and Well-Being"
- Chapter 9, Section 3, "Changes in Jobs and in the Labor Force," and Section 4, "Alternative Explanations for Variations in Wages"
- Chapter 10, Section 4, "Responding to Inequality"
- Chapter 11, Section 2, "The Structure of Taxation in the United States," and Section 3, "Tax Analysis and Policy Issues"
- Chapter 12, Section 2, "Valuing the Environment," and Section 3, "Environmental Policies in Practice"
- Chapter 17, Section 5, "Imperfect Competition in Agriculture and Health Care"

BEHAVIORAL ECONOMICS EMPHASIS

- Chapter 7, Section 2, "Economic Behavior," and Section 3, "Economic Rationality"
- Chapter 8, Section 3, "Consumption in a Social Context," and Section 5, "Consumption and Well-Being"

INEQUALITY/SOCIAL JUSTICE EMPHASIS

- Chapter 8, Section 3, "Consumption in a Social Context,"
- Chapter 9, Section 4, "Alternative Explanations for Variations in Wages," and Section 5, "Wages and Economic Power"
- Chapter 10, "Economic and Social Inequality"

Microeconomics
in Context

PART

I

The Context for Economic Analysis

0 Microeconomics and Well-Being

What comes to your mind when you think of the word "economics"? Perhaps you think about things like money, the stock market, globalization, and supply-and-demand. These things are definitely important to our study of economics, and we will spend much of our time in this book studying these concepts.

But the goals of economics are about much more than these. As we will see in Chapter 1, economics is: *the study of how people manage their resources to meet their needs and enhance their well-being.* The term "well-being" can mean different things to different people. We take an inclusive approach to well-being in this book. Well-being depends on traditional economic indicators like our income and material standard of living. But our well-being also depends on many other issues, such as the quality of our environment, our leisure time, and our perceptions of fairness and justice. Our study of microeconomics will help you better understand many of the outcomes that we observe and think about ways that we might be able to improve things. Many of the topics that we will study relate to current economic and political debates, such as economic inequality, the environment, taxes, and globalization.

The purpose of this introductory chapter is to provide an overview of some of the topics that we cover in more detail later in the book. We believe that good data are essential for informed debates about how to enhance well-being in our communities. In this chapter, for each topic we provide a graphical representation of important data. We have tried to be as objective as possible by presenting a wide range of data from reliable sources. You may find some of this information surprising, as the results may differ from common perceptions and media representations.

We focus on the United States here, and in much of the rest of the book, as this book has been written by American authors and is designed primarily for use in the United States. If you live in a different country, we encourage you to locate similar data for your own country. For international context, we present some international comparisons here, but such comparisons are mostly a topic for macroeconomics. In fact, our companion textbook (titled, not surprisingly, *Macroeconomics in Context*) includes a Chapter 0 that provides only international comparisons. In the following list of the graphs included in this chapter, those that include international data are identified by italics.

1. Income Inequality
2. Unequal Income Growth
3. *Income Inequality: International Comparisons*
4. Gender-Based Earnings Inequality
5. Educational Attainment
6. Taxes as a Percentage of GDP
7. *Taxes: International Comparisons*
8. *Global International Trade*
9. Stock Market Performance
10. Median Home Prices
11. Median Worker Earnings vs. Corporate Profits
12. *CEO Pay vs. Worker Pay: International Comparisons*
13. Industrial Concentration Ratios
14. Global Carbon Dioxide Emissions
15. *Carbon Dioxide Emissions per Capita: International Comparisons*

1. INCOME INEQUALITY

What it is: The graph below shows the average household income for different income groups in the United States, based on 2011 data. Each group represents one-fifth of American households, except for the last group, which includes only the top 5 percent.

The results: For households in the bottom fifth of Americans, average income in 2011 was only about $11,000. For those in the middle fifth, household income averaged about $50,000. Those in the top fifth had an average household income of nearly $180,000. Average household income was more than $300,000 for the top 5 percent. Note that these are average values, so some households in each group made less than these income values, while some made more. We discuss income inequality, including its causes, in more detail in Chapter 10.

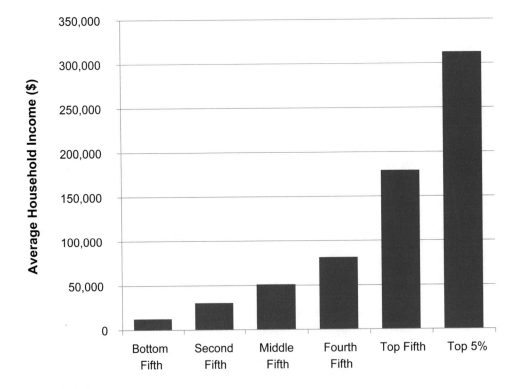

Source: U.S. Census Bureau, Historical Income Tables: Income Inequality, Table H-3.

2. UNEQUAL INCOME GROWTH

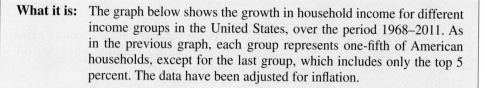

What it is: The graph below shows the growth in household income for different income groups in the United States, over the period 1968–2011. As in the previous graph, each group represents one-fifth of American households, except for the last group, which includes only the top 5 percent. The data have been adjusted for inflation.

The results: You have probably heard the saying: "The poor get poorer and the rich get richer." That is close, but not quite true. We see that those at the bottom of the income distribution did see small income gains in recent decades. Those in the middle did a little better. But the largest gains, by far, were obtained by those at the top, particularly those in the top 5 percent. The graph tells us that income inequality has increased considerably in recent decades. We discuss trends in income inequality in more detail in Chapter 10.

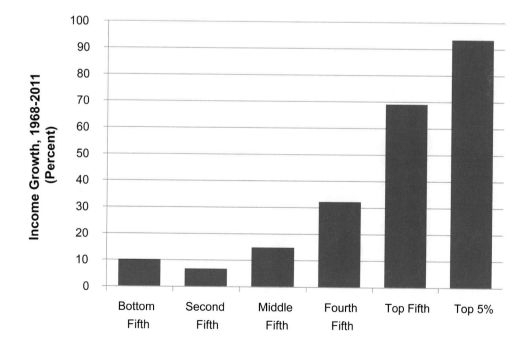

Note: We use 1968 as the starting year in this analysis because it is the year in which income inequality in the United States started to increase, as we will discuss in Chapter 10.

Source: U.S. Census Bureau, Historical Income Tables: Income Inequality, Table H-3.

3. INCOME INEQUALITY: INTERNATIONAL COMPARISONS

What it is: A Gini coefficient is a measure of economic inequality in a country, as we
discuss in Chapter 10. It can range from 0 (everyone in the country has the
same income) to 1 (one person receives all the income in a country).

The results: Scandinavian countries, such as Finland, Norway, and Sweden, tend to
be the most equal countries in the world, by income. Other countries
with low Gini coefficients include Germany, Hungary, and Iceland. The
United States is the most economically unequal developed country and
has a Gini coefficient similar to China's and Mexico's. Several African
countries, including Botswana, Lesotho, Sierra Leone, and South Africa,
are the most unequal countries in the world.

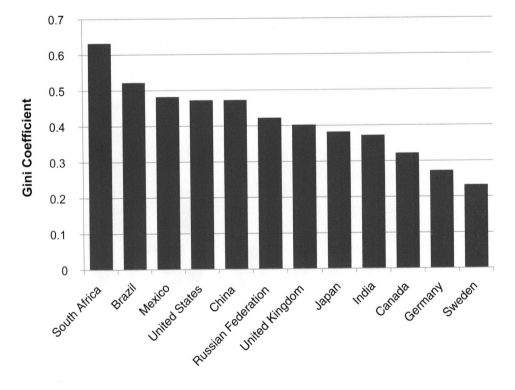

Source: U.S. Central Intelligence Agency, CIA World Factbook.

4. GENDER-BASED EARNINGS INEQUALITY

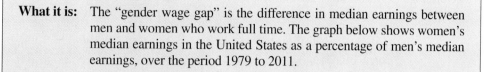

What it is: The "gender wage gap" is the difference in median earnings between men and women who work full time. The graph below shows women's median earnings in the United States as a percentage of men's median earnings, over the period 1979 to 2011.

The results: In 1979, women working full time in the United States earned only 62 percent of what men earned. During the 1980s the gender wage gap closed considerably. By the early 1990s, women working full time earned more than 75 percent of what men earned. Since then, the wage gap has continued to close, but more slowly. In 2011, women earned 82 percent of what men earned. Is this clear evidence of gender discrimination? We discuss this topic in more detail in Chapter 9.

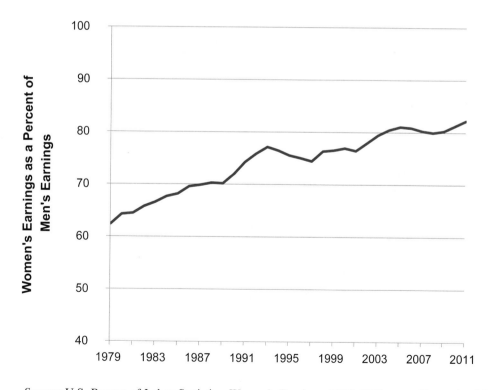

Source: U.S. Bureau of Labor Statistics, Women's Earnings, 1979–2011, www.bls.gov/opub/ted/2012/ted_20121123.htm.

5. EDUCATIONAL ATTAINMENT

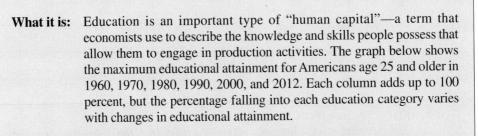

What it is: Education is an important type of "human capital"—a term that economists use to describe the knowledge and skills people possess that allow them to engage in production activities. The graph below shows the maximum educational attainment for Americans age 25 and older in 1960, 1970, 1980, 1990, 2000, and 2012. Each column adds up to 100 percent, but the percentage falling into each education category varies with changes in educational attainment.

The results: In 1960, about 58 percent of Americans age 25 and older had not graduated high school, and less than 10 percent had a college degree or higher. We see that educational attainment has increased each decade but still only about 30 percent of adult Americans have a college degree or higher. We discuss the relationship between education and wages in Chapter 9 and education as a form of human capital in Chapter 14.

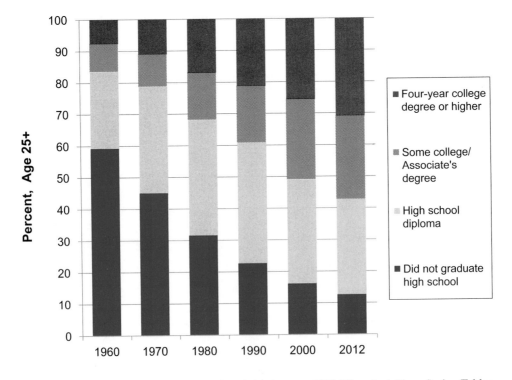

Source: U.S. Census Bureau, Educational Attainment, CPS Historical Time Series Tables, Table A-1.

6. TAXES AS A PERCENTAGE OF GDP

What it is: The graph below shows tax collections in the United States over the period 1950–2012, measured as a percentage of gross domestic product (GDP). Total taxes are divided into federal taxes and state and local taxes.

The results: Total tax collections in the United States gradually increased from about 25% of GDP in the 1950s to close to 35% of GDP in the late 1990s. Since then, state and local tax collection has remained relatively constant, while federal tax collection has generally declined. Although in surveys many Americans say they believe taxes have increased in recent years (particularly federal taxes), the opposite is true. We discuss taxes in more detail in Chapter 11.

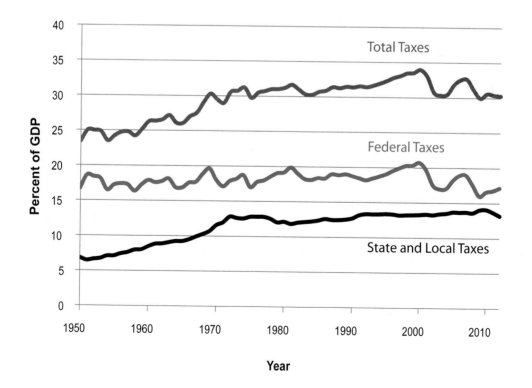

Source: U.S. Bureau of Economic Analysis, online database.

7. TAXES: INTERNATIONAL COMPARISONS

What it is: The graph below shows total tax collections in 2011, as a percentage of GDP, for various member countries of the Organisation for Economic Co-operation and Development (OECD). The OECD has 34 members, most of them developed countries, and promotes policies to improve economic and social well-being.

The results: Tax collections, as a percentage of GDP, vary considerably across countries. Taxes tend to be relatively high in European countries. Among high-income countries, the United States has one of the lowest overall tax rates in the world. This is not necessarily the perception of many Americans. We discuss international comparisons of taxes further in Chapter 11.

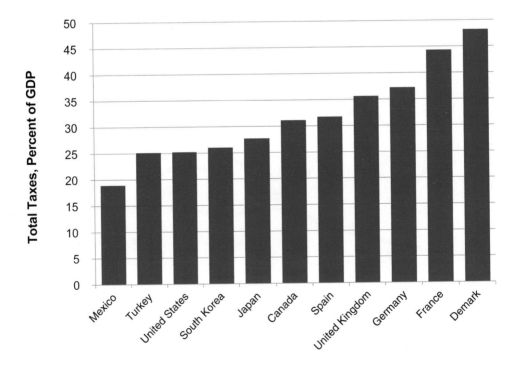

Source: Organisation for Economic Co-operation and Development, online tax statistics database.

8. GLOBAL INTERNATIONAL TRADE

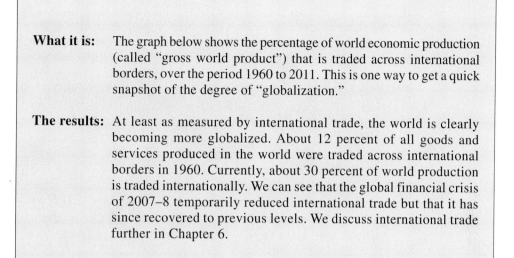

What it is: The graph below shows the percentage of world economic production (called "gross world product") that is traded across international borders, over the period 1960 to 2011. This is one way to get a quick snapshot of the degree of "globalization."

The results: At least as measured by international trade, the world is clearly becoming more globalized. About 12 percent of all goods and services produced in the world were traded across international borders in 1960. Currently, about 30 percent of world production is traded internationally. We can see that the global financial crisis of 2007–8 temporarily reduced international trade but that it has since recovered to previous levels. We discuss international trade further in Chapter 6.

Source: World Bank, World Development Indicators database.

9. STOCK MARKET PERFORMANCE

What it is: Media stories about the economy often focus on the performance of the stock market. Several common stock indices, such as the Dow Jones Composite, the Nasdaq Composite, and S&P (Standard & Poor's) 500 Index, provide a broad overview of stock market prices. The graph below shows the value of the S&P 500 Index from 1965 to mid-2013. The S&P 500 Index is calculated based on the stock prices of 500 large, mostly American, companies.

The results: From 1965 to 2000, the S&P 500 Index rose from about 100 to more than 1,500. Since 2000, two major "crashes" have taken place in the U.S. stock market. In each crash, the S&P 500 lost about half its value and then recovered to previous levels over several years. Although we do not discuss the stock market in much detail in this book, we spend considerable time discussing how markets operate, including the factors that lead to price fluctuations.

Source: St. Louis Federal Reserve Bank, S&P 500 Stock Price Index (SP500), http://research. stlouisfed.org/fred2/series/SP500/downloaddata.

10. MEDIAN HOME PRICES

What it is: The "median" price of home sales is the price at which half of homes sell for more than this price, and half sell for less. The graph below shows median home price in the United States over the period 1987 to mid-2013. The prices have not been adjusted for inflation.

The results: The median price of houses in the United States increased by a factor of three between 1987 and 2007. Then the housing bubble burst, and home prices fell by about one-third. Since then home prices have remained relatively low. Our discussion of markets, beginning in Chapter 2 and covering many of the chapters in this book, will help you understand how markets operate.

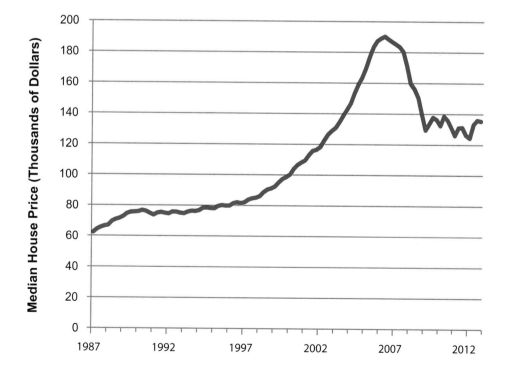

Source: S&P Dow Jones Indices, Case-Shiller Home Price Index, National; www.spindices.com/indices/real-estate/sp-case-shiller-us-national-home-price-index.

11. MEDIAN WORKER EARNINGS VS. CORPORATE PROFITS

What it is: The graph below shows the change in two variables over the period 1980 to 2012 in the United States:

1. Total corporate profits, measured in billions of dollars
2. Median weekly earnings for American workers, measured in dollars

The data for both variables have been adjusted for inflation. Note that the vertical axis is measured in dollars for median worker earnings and billions of dollars for corporate profits.

The results: Corporate profits have fluctuated based on the health of the overall economy, but we see that profits reached a record high in 2012. Corporate profits in 2012 were over three times the level they were at in 1980. Meanwhile, the median wages of U.S. workers have essentially not changed at all since 1980. We will discuss wages in more detail in Chapter 9, including the reasons why wages have not risen in proportion to corporate profits.

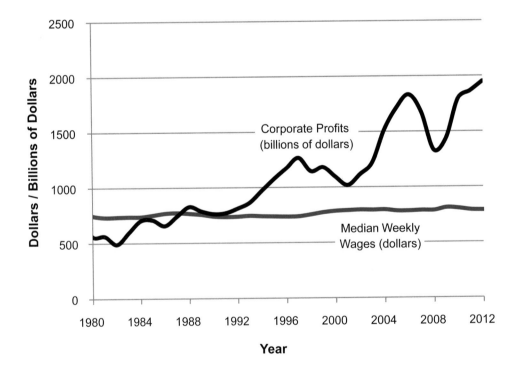

Sources: U.S. Bureau of Economic Analysis, National Income and Product Accounts Tables; U.S. Bureau of Labor Statistics, Weekly and Hourly Earnings Data from the Current Population Survey.

12. CEO Pay vs. Worker Pay: International Comparisons

What it is: In addition to comparing corporate profits to worker pay, we can look at the pay difference between chief executive officers (CEOs) and workers. The graph below shows the ratio of average CEO compensation to the average pay of "rank-and-file" workers, in several industrialized countries. The ratios are based on data from 2011 and 2012.

The results: In the United States, average CEO pay is more than 350 times higher than average worker pay. (This difference has rapidly increased in the past 50 years—in the mid-1960s average CEO pay was only about 20 times that of the average worker.) In other industrialized countries, CEOs today make significantly more than rank-and-file workers, but pay differences are not as pronounced. For example, in France CEOs make, on average, 100 times more than workers, while in Denmark CEOs make about 50 times worker pay.

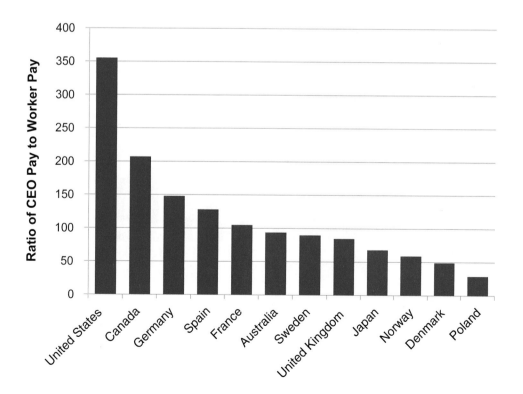

Source: AFL-CIO, Executive Paywatch, CEO-to-Worker Pay Ratios Around the World.

13. INDUSTRIAL CONCENTRATION RATIOS

What it is: An industrial concentration ratio measures the percentage of all sales in a particular industry that are received by the largest firms in that industry. The figure below shows four-firm concentration ratios—the percentage of all sales received by the largest four firms in each industry. Industrial concentration ratios provide information about the degree of market power held by large firms in a particular industry.

The results: Some industries in the United States are dominated by a few firms, while other industries are more competitive. Examples of industries with a few dominant firms include discount department stores (e.g., Walmart and Target) and home centers (e.g., Home Depot and Lowe's). Examples of industries that are not dominated by a few firms include convenience stores and gasoline stations. We discuss market power in more detail in Chapter 17.

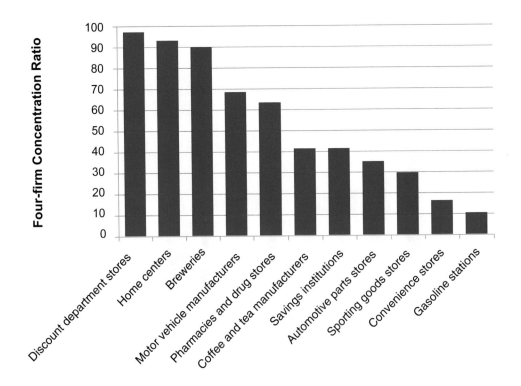

Source: U.S. Census Bureau, 2007 Economic Census.

14. GLOBAL CARBON DIOXIDE EMISSIONS

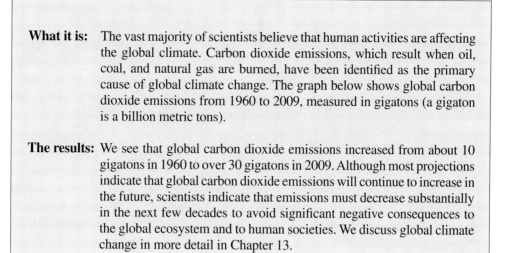

What it is: The vast majority of scientists believe that human activities are affecting the global climate. Carbon dioxide emissions, which result when oil, coal, and natural gas are burned, have been identified as the primary cause of global climate change. The graph below shows global carbon dioxide emissions from 1960 to 2009, measured in gigatons (a gigaton is a billion metric tons).

The results: We see that global carbon dioxide emissions increased from about 10 gigatons in 1960 to over 30 gigatons in 2009. Although most projections indicate that global carbon dioxide emissions will continue to increase in the future, scientists indicate that emissions must decrease substantially in the next few decades to avoid significant negative consequences to the global ecosystem and to human societies. We discuss global climate change in more detail in Chapter 13.

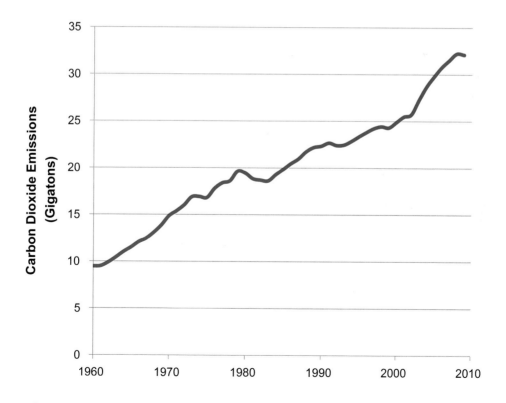

Source: World Bank, World Development Indicators database.

15. CARBON DIOXIDE EMISSIONS PER CAPITA: INTERNATIONAL COMPARISONS

What it is: The graph below shows carbon dioxide emission per capita (the average per person) for several countries, measured in tons. The data are from 2011.

The results: Carbon dioxide emissions per capita vary significantly across countries. In general, emissions per capita rise with higher incomes, but this is not always the case. The highest per-capita emissions are found in oil-producing countries. Emissions per capita are quite high in the United States, at around 18 tons. Per-capita emissions are about 9 tons in Germany, 7 tons in China, and 4 tons in Mexico. Carbon dioxide emissions per capita are much lower in the world's poorest countries. We discuss carbon dioxide emissions and global climate change in Chapter 13.

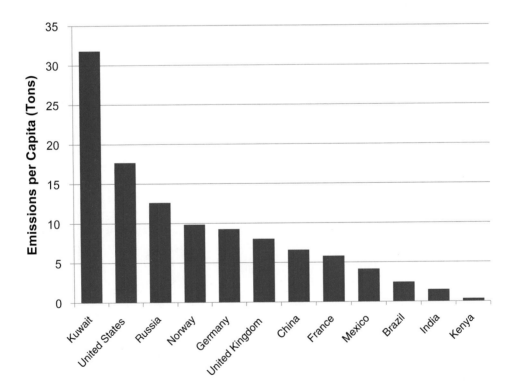

Source: U.S. Energy Information Administration, International Energy Statistics.

1 Economic Activity in Context

There are many reasons to take an introductory economics course, beyond just needing to satisfy a course requirement. Some knowledge of economics, for example, may help you get a rewarding job. Studying economics can help you understand important policy debates on issues such as the environment, taxes, and health care. More broadly, economics can provide insights into how we all make decisions—as consumers, as employees or businesses owners, and as citizens.

The decisions that we make every day are guided by various goals. Sometimes these goals conflict with one another. You surely want to get good grades, but you also want to have spare time to spend with your friends and family. As a society, we may want better health care, but we also probably want a clean environment and national security. Economics has much to teach us about how we negotiate the tradeoffs among the many things that matter to us. Some of these things are measured in dollars, but as we will soon see, economics is about much more than money.

Whatever your reasons for taking an economics course, we hope that by the end of it you will be better able to define your goals and to understand how to move toward them in the ever-changing economy.

1. Our Starting Point

economics: the study of how people manage their resources to meet their needs and enhance their well-being

Economics is the study of how people manage their resources to meet their needs and enhance their well-being. This may sound a little vague, so let's discuss this definition a bit.

Our "resources" include natural resources such as trees, coal, and air, as well as human-made productive resources such as factories, vehicles, computers, and roads. Our resources also include our knowledge and skills, financial resources, and even the social relationships that improve the quality of our lives.

Our "needs" obviously include our basic requirements for food, shelter, and physical security. Beyond that, different people may have different views about what constitutes a "need." Some people may think that having their own car is a "need," while others may see it as a luxury. We discuss this issue in more detail below.

well-being: a term used to broadly describe a good quality of life

Finally, we use the term **well-being** to broadly describe a good quality of life. Beyond meeting our "needs," virtually everyone desires such things as a decent income, sufficient leisure time, good friends, and the freedom to express one's opinions. All of these are part of what economics is about.

People manage their resources by engaging in four essential economic activities:

1. resource maintenance
2. production of goods and services
3. distribution of goods and services
4. consumption of goods and services

Economists study how people engage in these activities, both as individuals and as a society. We discuss these activities in more detail a little later in the chapter. First, however, we briefly address the issue of how an understanding of economics can be useful—to you as an individual and to society.

Economics can be applied to help people meet personal, business, and social goals. For example, suppose that you are especially concerned with issues of social justice. You might, for instance, have questions about how wages and taxes are determined, how corporations make decisions about where to locate and how many people to hire, or whether people are able to meet their basic needs. Economics will not fully answer all these questions, but it will give you a good start on understanding the tradeoffs faced by societies and individuals. It will help you to grasp what is possible now—and what changes might be required to create better options in the future. It will give you some insights into people's motivations (modern economics is increasingly using insights from psychology). And it can help you anticipate how your participation in the economy, as a worker, family or community member, employer, or policymaker, can relate to your goals—whatever they may be.

We recognize that your personal goals will always be significant motivators in what interests you about this subject. Now, however, we move on to the more general topic of social goals. In recent history, economic beliefs, advice, and policies have been very influential in shaping the kind of world in which we live. It is important to understand what goals, overt or hidden, economists pursue. That topic raises the question: What is the goal, or the purpose, of the economy?

Discussion Questions

1. In which social issues are you most interested? How do you think that economics might help you understand these issues?
2. Thinking further about the social issues in which you are interested, do you see economics as part of the problem or part of the solution? Is it possible that economics can be both—responsible for social problems yet also potentially part of a solution?

2. THE GOALS OF AN ECONOMY

positive questions: questions about how things are

normative questions: questions about how things should be

Social scientists often make a distinction between two kinds of questions. **Positive questions** concern issues of fact, or "what is." **Normative questions** have to do with goals and values, or "what should be." For example, "What is the level of poverty in our country?" is a positive question, requiring descriptive facts as an answer. "How much effort should be given to poverty reduction?" is a normative question, requiring analysis of our values and goals. In our study of economics, we often find that positive and normative questions are inevitably intertwined. For example, both of the questions just posed require that we start with a definition of poverty. To achieve this, we need to combine facts about income and wealth with a normative assessment of where to draw the poverty line. Life rarely offers us a neat distinction between "what is" and "what ought to be." More often, we have to deal with a combination of the two.

Positive statements also sometimes carry normative implications. Consider the statement: "The total share of federal taxes paid by the top 1 percent of households, by income, has risen from 14.2 percent in 1980 to 22.3 percent in 2009."[1]

This is a positive statement, but it seems to suggest that taxes on the top 1 percent have increased rather dramatically and that further tax increases might be unfair. But is this really true? As we discover in more detail in Chapter 11, a more complete analysis reveals that the main reason that the share of taxes paid by the richest 1 percent has risen so much is that this group is now receiving a much larger share of all income. So we need to be careful about coming to normative conclusions based on incomplete or misleading positive statements.

Although much of this textbook is concerned with positive issues, we have, in defining the objective of economics as enhancing well-being, begun with a normative statement. People disagree about what it means to "enhance well-being." Economic actions that we take are all significantly affected by our goals and values. When we study, for example, how business decisions are made, we need to understand what might motivate all the people involved—business owners, workers, and their customers. Thus it is helpful for us to think further about our goals.

2.1 INTERMEDIATE AND FINAL GOALS

intermediate goal: a goal that is desirable because its achievement will bring you closer to your final goal(s)

final goal: a goal that requires no further justification; it is an end in itself

A useful way to look at goals is to rank them in a kind of hierarchy. Some are **intermediate goals**—that is, they are not ends in themselves but are important because they are expected to serve as the means to further ends. Goals that are sought for their own sake, rather than because they lead to something else, are called **final goals**. For example, you might strive to do well in your courses as an intermediate goal, toward the final goal of getting a good job. Of course, we might also think of the goal of "getting a good job" as itself intermediate to other final goals, such as satisfaction, status, or well-being.

2.2 TRADITIONAL ECONOMIC GOALS

Before taking this course, you probably thought that economics is mostly about money and wealth. Although it is true that many economists spend their lives studying these topics, in this book we take the position that these are intermediate, as opposed to final, goals. We first consider the goals that economics has traditionally emphasized and then go on to consider how those relate to our final goals.

Adam Smith and the Goal of Wealth

wealth: the net value of all the material and financial assets owned by an individual

Adam Smith (1723–1790) emphasized the word *wealth* in the title of his famous book *An Inquiry into the Nature and Causes of the Wealth of Nations* (published in 1776). **Wealth** is often defined as the net value of all the material and financial assets owned by an individual. Is wealth really what economics is about? Those who seek to enhance their country's wealth generally do so because they have a notion that a wealthier country is in some way stronger, better, safer, or happier. Here, the relevant final goals might be strength, virtue, safety, or happiness. Similarly, an individual might seek wealth, or a good job, as an intermediate goal leading to such final goals as security, comfort, power, status, or pleasure.

The variety of final goals held by different individuals is sometimes used as a reason for viewing the accumulation of wealth as the sole purpose of economics. Implicitly or explicitly, this position rests on the normative argument that material wealth is a nearly universal intermediate goal because it can be used to pursue so many final goals.

economic efficiency: the use of resources, or inputs, such that they yield the highest possible value of output or the production of a given output using the lowest possible value of inputs

In Smith's time, the vast majority of people lived in conditions of desperate poverty. Although about a billion people on earth still struggle with poverty on a daily basis, economic advancement in the past couple of centuries allows many people to focus on goals other than acquiring more wealth. Moreover, we are coming to recognize that the continual expansion of human economies in a finite material world has costs as well as benefits. Looking at the complex fallout of our achievements—including environmental degradation, stresses felt by families, and other social ills—it is clear that promotion of material wealth without concern for the ends to which wealth is used, or for the consequences of the manner in which wealth is pursued, may in fact work *against* the final goals that we most desire to achieve.

Recent Trends and the Goal of Efficiency

Most economists have focused on **economic efficiency** as a key goal in economic policy-making. An efficient process is one that uses the *minimum value of resources* to achieve a desired result. Or to put it another way, efficiency is achieved when the *maximum value of output* is produced from a given set of inputs. Given this focus, many economists have seen their role as advising policymakers on how to make the economy as efficient as possible.

One appealing aspect of the goal of efficiency is that apparently everyone can agree on it. Who in his right mind would argue for using more resources than necessary or having less of something good when more is possible at the same cost? Because it seems so obvious that efficiency is a good thing, aiming for it is often thought of as a purely technical and scientific exercise, one based on positive analysis. This is not actually the case, however, because regarding efficiency as a goal involves a very important normative judgment: A standard of *value* must be adopted before the definition of efficiency can be applied.

Money is the standard of value that has traditionally been used in economics. Specifically, the commonest economic definition of value has been that of *market* value— that is, price. Using this standard, an economist would say that resources are being used most efficiently when the market value of the resulting outputs is maximized. "More is always better," it is assumed, where the "more" is composed of things that people are willing to pay for.

This definition of efficiency is not a simple matter of positive fact; when examined, it clearly includes some normative assumptions. First, it is based on an implicit acceptance of the current distribution of wealth and income. Because a person's *willingness* to pay for something is obviously influenced by his or her *ability* to pay, in general those with the most money will disproportionately determine what is an economically "efficient" allocation of resources. For example, if the aggregate willingness to pay of high-wealth households for luxury cars exceeds the willingness to pay of lower-income households for basic health care, then the efficient allocation would tilt toward production of luxury cars over provision of basic health care.

Second, this definition of efficiency assumes that nothing has value unless humans are willing to pay for it. In other words, nothing has intrinsic value and should exist for its own sake regardless of whether people place monetary value on it. But perhaps certain things should have intrinsic value, such as the right of nonhuman species to exist or goals like freedom or fairness.

Other standards could be used instead to measure value. Many things that we value are *not* bought and sold in markets: Health, fairness, and ecological sustainability are examples. Policies directed toward producing the highest value of *these* outputs from given inputs may be quite different from policies designed simply to maximize the market value of production. Likewise, focusing only on minimizing the monetary costs of inputs may lead to actions with high social and environmental costs. Thinking of efficiency only in terms of market value can lead to neglect of other, perhaps more urgent considerations (see Box 1.1).

2.3 COMPONENTS OF WELL-BEING

We define economics in terms of enhancing well-being, but what exactly do we mean by this? We have mentioned that well-being is about a good quality of life, recognizing that this concept has many normative components. But we suggest that some components of well-being are common to all living things. Evolution has instilled in all living creatures a preference for survival, along with an aversion to pain, hunger, thirst, and other sensations that signal a threat to survival.

Evolution has operated not upon individuals but upon gene pools. Thus the survival imperative works to motivate behavior that will enhance group, as well as individual, survival. In the human species, the group survival imperative is expressed through culture, values, and goals. Thus it is normal for human beings to hold values that would lead us to preserve the health of the society in which we live as well as the health of the environment, on which, ultimately, the future survival of our species depends.

We can distinguish between the things that make life possible (our true "needs," or survival issues) and the things that we feel make life worth living (quality-of-life, or well-being, issues).

BOX 1.1 GOALS BEYOND EFFICIENCY

The point that efficiency defined in terms of market value is rarely the only important goal is vividly illustrated in a story that a now-eminent economist always tells at the first session of a new class.

After he finished graduate school, this young man's first job was to advise the government of a rice-growing country where it should put its research efforts. He was told that two modern techniques for rice milling had been developed elsewhere and was asked to calculate which of these two technologies should be selected for development. The young economist analyzed the requirements for producing a ton of rice under each of the two competing technologies. Each of them used a mixture of labor, machinery, fuel, and raw materials. He calculated the monetary costs for these inputs, and, finding that Technology A could produce a ton of rice at slightly less cost than Technology B, he recommended that the government invest in the more "efficient" Technology A.

Returning a few years later, the economist was horrified to discover what had happened when the country implemented his suggestion. It turned out that the traditions of that country included strict norms for the division of labor: specifically, what work women were allowed to do and what was defined as men's work. Technology B would have been neutral in this regard, maintaining the same ratio of "male jobs" to "female jobs" as had existed before. Technology A, however, eliminated most of the women's work opportunities. In a society where women's earnings were a major contributor to food and education for children, the result was a perceptible decline in children's nutrition levels and school attendance.

Charged with determining which technology was best, the young economist had not asked, "Best for what?" Instead, he made an implicit assumption that the only final goal was maximizing output and that the only intermediate goal he had to worry about was efficiency in resource use. He has subsequently told several generations of economics students, "Nobody told me to look beyond efficiency, defined in terms of market costs—but I'll never neglect the family and employment effects again, even when my employer doesn't ask about them."

Even this distinction involves some normative judgments. Some evidence indicates that when the things that make life worth living are removed, many individuals go against the dictates of survival and even risk their own lives for a higher purpose (see Box 1.2).

In Table 1.1, we present one possible list of the final goals of economic activity, summarizing the careful reflection of a number of thinkers but not attempting to represent a final consensus. The first five goals on the list are related to individual concerns; the last five are related to social concerns. Some of the goals (such as the first one) involve making life possible, some (such as the third) involve making life worthwhile, and yet others involve both types of concerns. You may believe that some of the elements on this list are less important than others or could even be omitted, or you may believe that other important goals should be added. Normative analysis is not something that is set in stone forever; rather, it develops with reflection, discussion, experience, and changing circumstances. In any case, it is clear that any reasonable discussion of the quality of life must go beyond the simple notions of wealth or efficiency.

BOX 1.2 GOALS BEYOND SURVIVAL

A simple view of evolution might suggest that the individual survival imperative would always prevail over any other motives. Yet even among animals this is not true, as illustrated by stories of dogs that lie down and die when they have lost their master or of birds courting danger as they try to lure a predator away from the young in their nest.

Many famous stories of human heroism also illustrate human choices for quality of life over life itself or the sacrifice of present survival for the sake of future generations. A true story of such a choice occurred during World War II, when Leningrad (now St. Petersburg) was under siege and starvation was widespread. A researcher at the university who had been developing improved strains of seeds locked himself in his laboratory. At the end of the war, his starved body was found there, among the containers of seed corn that he had protected for future generations.

Table 1.1 **A Potential List of Final Goals**

Satisfaction of basic physical needs, including nutrition and care adequate for survival, growth, and health, as well as a comfortable living environment

Security: assurance that one's basic needs will continue to be met throughout all stages of life, as well as security against aggression or unjust persecution

Happiness: the opportunity to experience, reasonably often, feelings such as contentment, pleasure, enjoyment, and peace of mind

Ability to realize one's potential in as many as possible of the following dimensions of development: physical, intellectual, moral, social, aesthetic, and spiritual

A sense of meaning in one's life—a reason or purpose for one's efforts

Fairness in the distribution of life possibilities, and fair and equal treatment by social institutions (fairness is a universal goal despite cross-cultural differences in how it is defined or assessed)

Freedom in making personal decisions (limited by decision-making capacity, as in the case of children); also, not infringing on the freedom of others

Participation: opportunity to participate in the processes in which decisions are made that affect the members of one's society

Good social relations, including satisfying and trustful relations with friends, fellow citizens, family, and business associates, as well as respectful and peaceful relations among nations

Ecological balance: preserving natural resources, and where needed, restoring them to a healthy and resilient state

2.4 ECONOMICS AND WELL-BEING

Economic activity is not, of course, the only ingredient that goes into creating well-being. Economics cannot make you fall in love, for example, or prevent you from being in a car accident. But economic factors can help to determine whether your job leaves you with the time and energy to date, whether your car has advanced safety features, and whether you have access to medical treatment. A well-functioning economy is one that operates to increase the well-being of all its members.

In Table 1.1, we have suggested for your consideration one plausible list of final goals to be taken into account in guiding economic activity. Economic activities are often necessary to promote our final goals, but economic activities can also sometimes create "ill-being" instead of well-being, whether because of conflicts among goals or because of unintended consequences. However, some economic activities directed toward one goal have consequences that *enhance* the achievement of other goals. For example, doing work that is believed to contribute something positive in the world can add significantly to people's happiness and their ability to realize their potential, at the same time as it brings in the income that permits the satisfaction of their basic needs.

Conflicts Among Goals

If the goal of immediate enjoyment is given too much emphasis, economic activity can actually decrease health and long-term happiness. A supermarket checkout counter offers a good example. Appealing displays of unhealthy snack foods may offer short-term satisfaction, but the temptation of immediate gratification may lead us, even if we are fully informed about the consequences, to make decisions that are unhealthy in the long term.

economic actor (economic agent): an individual or organization involved in the economic activities of resource maintenance or the production, distribution, or consumption of goods and services

In addition to tradeoffs between immediate and longer-term impacts, we often also face conflicts among our goals. For example, a current public health debate concerns whether people with contagious, antibiotic-resistant tuberculosis or dangerous new illnesses such as bird flu should be *required* to accept hospital services—in locked wards, if necessary. In this case, we see that the social goal of a physically healthy population and the goal of freedom seem to demand opposite approaches. Likewise, an employer may need to decide between trying to pressure workers to produce the largest possible quantity of some product and wanting to help employees realize their intellectual and social potential on the job.

Unintended Consequences: An Introduction to Externalities

negative externalities: harmful side effects, or unintended consequences, of economic activity that affect those who are not directly involved in the activity

positive externalities: beneficial side effects, or unintended consequences, of economic activity that accrue to those who are not among the economic actors directly involved in the activity

An **economic actor**, or **economic agent**, is an individual or organization engaged in one or more of the four economic activities listed at the beginning of this chapter—resource maintenance, and the production, distribution, or consumption of goods and services. Although aimed at achieving a goal, such activity may also produce unintended side effects. Some of the impacts are harmful, such as air pollution that is emitted in the course of production. Negative consequences of an economic activity that affect those who are not directly involved in the activity are called **negative externalities**. In the case of a negative externality like air pollution, neither the firm emitting the pollution nor the consumers buying its products is likely to take the externality into account. But as economists, we need to consider the impacts of the externality on the broader well-being of society. We discuss negative externalities, particularly in relation to environmental issues, in more detail in Chapter 12.

Some of the unintended consequences of economic activity increase well-being. **Positive externalities** are the beneficial effects of an economic activity that accrue to those who are not directly involved in the activity. A college education is an example of an economic activity that generates positive externalities. Although education can be viewed as an economic transaction between the educational institution and the student, society as a whole benefits because college-educated people are likely to be more productive and more informed as citizens in the democratic process.

Discussion Questions

1. You have evidently made a decision to dedicate some of your personal resources in time and money to studying college economics. Which of the goals listed in Table 1.1 was most important to you (and perhaps to your family or community, if they were involved) in making this decision? Did any of the other goals figure in this decision? If you were to write up a list of your own final goals, how would it differ from Table 1.1?
2. Certain drugs such as heroin act on the brain to produce intense, temporary feelings of euphoria or pleasure. Some of them are physically addictive and cause people to lose interest in everything except getting another dose of the drug. Do these drugs add to well-being? Discuss.

3. THE ISSUES THAT DEFINE ECONOMICS

In discussing goals, we have addressed the question of what economics is *for*—what its purpose is. Now we summarize what economics is *about*: what activities it covers, and which questions it addresses.

3.1 THE FOUR ESSENTIAL ECONOMIC ACTIVITIES

We think of an activity as "economic" when it involves one or more of four essential tasks that allow us to meet our needs and enhance our well-being.

**resource mainte-
nance:** preserving
or improving the re-
sources that contrib-
ute to the enhance-
ment of well-being,
including natural,
manufactured, human,
and social resources

Resource maintenance means preserving or improving the resources that contribute to the enhancement of well-being. As we mentioned earlier, these resources may be physical, as in the case of natural resources and manufactured products, but they also include the knowledge and skills of individuals and the social relations and institutions that underpin economic activity. Forestry projects that plant trees for future use are one common example of resource maintenance, but there are many others. Child care and education prepare people for future economic activity as well as directly improving well-being. Other examples of resource maintenance include figuring out how much oil to extract from an oil field now and how much to leave for later; maintaining the transportation infrastructure (subways, roads, etc.) of a city; and, in a factory, keeping the machinery in good repair and maintaining the necessary knowledge, skill levels, and morale of the employees.

production: the con-
version of resources
into goods and
services

Production is the conversion of some of these resources into usable products, which may be either goods or services. Goods are tangible objects, such as bread and books; services are intangibles, such as TV broadcasting, teaching, and haircuts. Popular bands performing music, recording companies producing CDs and MP3s, local governments building roads, and individuals cooking meals are all engaged in the economic activity of production.

distribution: the
sharing of products
and resources among
people

exchange: the trad-
ing of one thing for
another

transfer: the giving
of something, with
nothing specific ex-
pected in return

Distribution is the sharing of products and resources among people. In contemporary economies, distribution activities take two main forms: **exchange** and **transfer**. When you hand over money in exchange for goods and services, you are engaging in exchange. People are generally much better off if they specialize in the production of a limited range of goods and services and meet most of their needs through exchange than if they try to produce everything that they need themselves. (We study this in more detail in Chapter 6 of this book.) Distribution also takes place through one-way transfers, in which something is given with nothing specific expected in return. Local school boards, for example, distribute education services to students in their districts, tuition-free (although public education is, of course, supported by tax revenues). Parents are engaged in transfer when they provide their children with goods and services.

consumption: the
final use of a good or
service

Consumption is the process by which goods and services are, at last, put to final use by people. In some cases, such as eating a meal or burning gasoline in a car, goods are literally "consumed" in the sense that they are used up and are no longer available for other uses. In other cases, such as enjoying art in a museum, the experience may be "consumed" without excluding others or using up material resources.

Most real-world economic undertakings involve more than one of the four economic activities. The trucking industry, for example, can be seen as "producing" the service of making goods available, physically distributing produced goods, and consuming large amounts of fuel—as well as a variety of mechanical inputs required to keep the trucks on the road.

Resource maintenance in particular often overlaps with production, consumption, and distribution. For example, the production of paper using recycled materials can be classified as both production, because a good is being produced, and resource maintenance, because the impact on natural resources is minimized. As another example, you may decide to distribute a memo to your coworkers via e-mail to save on paper, thus engaging in resource maintenance as part of the distribution process.

Of course, not all production, consumption, and distribution activities can also be classified as resource maintenance. Consuming unhealthful food does not aid in maintaining human resources. Printing out e-mail for a quick reading on single-sided paper with no recycled content would not be considered a resource-maintaining activity.

A final point on the relationship between resource maintenance and the other economic activities is that sometimes resource maintenance means *not* engaging in production, consumption, or distribution. For example, people who make voluntary decisions to minimize their unnecessary consumption are maintaining resources. Although this may look like *inactivity*, including resource maintenance as an economic activity implies that minimizing some kinds of consumption can contribute to well-being. As another example, deciding not to distribute a minor memo to your coworkers may save everyone involved valuable time resources.

3.2 THE THREE BASIC ECONOMIC QUESTIONS

The four economic activities that we have listed give rise, in turn, to the three basic economic questions:

1. *What* should be produced, and *what* should be maintained?
2. *How* should production and maintenance be accomplished?
3. *For whom* should economic activity be undertaken?

For example, a family faces the problem of how much of its economic resources (money, credit, and so on) to use now and how much to preserve for future use. Suppose that members of a family decide to spend some of their money on a dinner party. They will have to decide "what" foods to prepare. The "how" question includes who is going to cook and what recipes to use. Answering the "for whom" question means deciding who will be invited for dinner and how to take into account the food preferences and needs of the various individuals.

The complexity of decision making and the number of people involved rise steeply as we move to higher levels of economic organization, but the questions remain the same. Businesses, schools, community groups, governments, and international organizations all have to settle the questions of *what, how,* and *for whom.*

Discussion Questions

1. The admissions office at your college decides who will be admitted and who will not be. Is this an economic activity? Of what kind? (There may be more than one correct answer.)
2. Imagine that an engineer, an artist, and an economist are all observing the construction of a new office building. What aspects of the process might the economist notice, and what words might she use to describe what is going on? How will her description differ from that of the engineer and that of the artist?

4. ECONOMIC TRADEOFFS

Tradeoffs are a central concept in economics. When we have limited resources, we have to decide how to allocate them to meet competing goals. If we allocate more resources toward one objective, then less are available to meet other goals.

4.1 ABUNDANCE AND SCARCITY

When you think of all the abundant natural resources in our world, all the human knowledge that exists, all the investments that have been made in organizing human societies, and the massive stock of machinery and other productive resources that have accumulated, you realize that the world is wealthy indeed. When you are well fed, comfortably warm, engaged in interesting activities, and close to those you care about, you can appreciate these benefits. Although the distribution of resources is far from even, either across countries or among people within countries (a topic that we take up again in a later chapter), contemporary human society as a whole still has a rich resource base on which to build. It is no wonder that many world religions and ethical teachings encourage gratitude for life's abundance.

It may seem odd, then, that when discussing society's choices concerning *what, how,* and *for whom,* many economists emphasize the notion of **scarcity**—that is, the notion of insufficiency. What this really means is that even with all the available resources, not all of our goals can be accomplished, at least not at the same time. The current capacity of a particular hospital, for example, may allow it to increase the number of heart transplants that

scarcity: the concept that resources are not sufficient to allow all goals to be accomplished at once

are performed there *or* increase the amount of care that can be provided there for the severely mentally ill, but not both. If a given resource, such as an hour of your time, is dedicated to one activity, such as studying, then it will be unavailable for certain other activities, such as relaxing with your friends. Choices have to be made.

This book presents some key tools and language that can be helpful in understanding how choices can best be made about what to produce, how, and for whom, when current resources are insufficient for meeting all possible current well-being goals, and also when choices need to be made between meeting well-being goals now and meeting them in the future.

4.2 SOCIETY'S PRODUCTION-POSSIBILITIES FRONTIER

production-possibilities frontier (PPF): a curve showing the maximum amounts of two outputs that society could produce from given resources, over a given period

Economists use the model of a **production-possibilities frontier** (PPF) to illustrate several important economic concepts. To make matters simple, let us assume that society is considering only two possible choices of what to produce over the coming year from its available resources. The classic example is to take "guns" as one output and "butter" as the other. In more general terms, the guns-versus-butter tradeoff can refer to the general choice of a society between becoming more militarized ("guns") and becoming more civilian- or consumer-oriented ("butter").

Figure 1.1 shows a PPF for this case. In this graph, the quantity of "butter" produced over a year is measured on the horizontal (or *x*-) axis. The quantity of "guns" is measured on the vertical (or *y*-) axis. The points on the PPF curve illustrate the maximum quantities of guns and butter that the society could produce. For example, point A, where the curve intersects the *x*-axis, shows that this society can produce 120 units of butter if it does not produce any guns. Moving up and to the left, point B illustrates production, over the year, of 100 units of butter and 5 units of guns. (At this level of abstraction, it is not necessary to be specific about what is meant by "units." You may imagine these as kilos of butter and numbers of guns, if you like.) Point C illustrates that the society can produce 9 units of guns if it decides to produce no butter. While it may seem odd to think about a society that only produces two goods, this figure is nevertheless helpful for illustrating several important economic concepts.

Scarcity. Point D in Figure 1.1 represents a production combination (80 units of butter and 8 units of guns) that is not attainable given existing resources (or, as we will see, the present state of technology). To produce at that point would take more resources than the society currently has. The PPF is specifically defined so that only those points on or inside it (the shaded region) represent outputs that can actually be produced.

opportunity cost: the value of the best alternative that is foregone when a choice is made

Tradeoffs. All the points that lie on the PPF illustrate the important notion that scarcity creates a need for tradeoffs. Along the frontier, one can get more of one output only by "trading off" some of the other. Figure 1.1 illustrates the important concept of **opportunity costs**. Opportunity cost is the value of the best alternative to the choice that one actually

Figure 1.1   **Society's Production Possibilities Frontier**

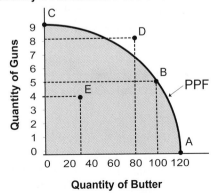

As you select different points along the PPF, you see that the more you get of one good, the less you can have of the other.

makes. In this case, the cost of increasing gun production is less butter. For example, suppose the economy is at Point A, producing 120 units of butter and no guns, but then decides that it needs to produce 5 guns. Point B illustrates that after some resources have been moved from butter production into producing the 5 guns, the maximum amount of butter that can be produced is 100 units. The gain of 5 guns comes at a "cost" to the economy of a loss of 20 units of butter. Likewise, starting from a point where the economy is producing only guns, the "cost" of producing more butter would be fewer guns.

Efficiency. Resources are used efficiently as long as the process by which they are used does not involve any waste. Points that lie *on* the PPF illustrate the maximum combinations that a society can produce from its given resources, if these are used efficiently. But what about points *inside* the frontier, such as point E? At point E, the economy is not producing as much as it could. It is producing 30 units of butter and 4 guns, even though it *could* produce more of one or the other, or even more of both. Some resources are apparently being wasted at point E. This could occur for at least three reasons:

1. The resources may be wasted because they are being left idle. For example, workers may be left unemployed, or cows could be left unmilked.
2. Even if resources are fully employed, the technology and social organization applied to the resources may not be optimal. For example, suppose that the gun factory is poorly designed, so a lot of the workers' time is wasted moving parts from one area to another. In this case, a better, more efficient organization of the work flow could increase production, with no increase in resources.
3. The allocation of resources between the two production activities (i.e., guns and butter) might not be optimal. For example, if gun factories are built on the best pasture land when they could just as well be built on poorer land, the ability of the economy to graze cows and produce butter would be hampered.

When an economy is imagined to be *on* the PPF, and thus producing efficiently, the only way to produce more of one good is to produce less of the other. If an economy is *inside* the PPF (producing in the shaded region), however, it is producing inefficiently, and improvements in the employment of resources, the application of available technology and social organization, or allocation of resources among production activities could allow it to move toward the frontier (i.e., to produce more of both goods).

The bowed-out shape of the curve comes from the fact that some resources are likely to be more suited for production of one good than for the other. We can see, for example, that the society can get the first 5 guns by giving up only 20 units of butter production. Workers, for example, can be pulled out of butter production and set to work on relatively plentiful supplies of the materials most suited for guns, such as easily tapped veins of iron ore and minerals for gunpowder. Gun manufacturing plants can—if allocation decisions are made wisely—be built on land unsuitable for pasture. To produce 4 more guns (to go from point B to point C along the PPF), however, comes at the cost of the remaining 100 units of butter! Why is this? In order to produce more guns, we must pull workers off of the most productive dairy land and direct them toward increasingly less-accessible veins of mineral ores or to the now-crowded gun assembly lines.

Of course, we could put on the axes many other pairs of outputs, besides guns and butter, and still illustrate these concepts. We could look at soda and pizza, cars and bicycles, or health care and highways. This classic example, however, is a good one. In the real world, such guns/butter or militarization/peacetime tradeoffs can be crucially important (see Box 1.3).

What precise combination of outputs, such as guns versus butter or health versus highways, should society choose to produce? The PPF does *not* answer this question. All points along the PPF are efficient, in the sense that there are no wasted resources. But among the different efficient points, such as A, B, or C, which one would produce the most social well-being? To

BOX 1.3   THE OPPORTUNITY COST OF MILITARY EXPENDITURES

What do military buildups and wars really cost? One way to look at this is to consider what else could have been bought with the money spent on armaments.

World military expenditures in 2013 totaled $1.75 trillion, or 2.5 percent of world GDP. The United States is by far the biggest spender, accounting on its own for 46 percent of the global total. The United Kingdom, France, China, and Japan are the next biggest military spenders. Smaller and poorer countries spend less, but some of the poorest countries—including Eritrea and Burundi—spend more on the military than they do on public services such as health care and education. Where do such countries get their weapons? The United States and Russia are the leading suppliers of military goods to international markets.

Meanwhile, about 10 million children every year—over 27,000 every day—die before they reach the age of 5, most of them from malnutrition and poverty. The Millennium Development Goals set out by the United Nations include eradicating extreme poverty, achieving universal primary education, reducing child mortality rates, and improving maternal health, gender equity, and environmental sustainability in the poorest areas of the world. All this comes at a cost, of course. The amount of money that would be needed to achieve these goals has been estimated to be in the range of $145 to $270 billion per year, that is, about 8–15 percent of what is currently spent on arms. This level of funding has not been forthcoming, however, and indications are that some of the goals will not be met.

As U.S. president Dwight D. Eisenhower said in 1953, "Every gun that is made, every warship launched, every rocket fired, signifies in the final sense a theft from those who hunger and are not fed, those who are cold and are not clothed."

Sources: Stockholm International Peace Research Institute, *SIPRI Military Expenditures Database,* www.sipri.org/; United Nations Millennium Project, www.unmillenniumproject.org/reports/costs_benefits2.htm.

determine this, we would have to know more about the society's requirements and priorities. Is civilian satisfaction a high priority? Then the society would lean toward production of butter. Does the society fear attack by a foreign power? Perhaps then it would choose a point closer to the guns axis. For good social decision making, this production question would have to be considered alongside a full array of questions of resource maintenance, distribution, and consumption, because all have effects on well-being. In a society with free speech and democratic discussion, there is wide room for disagreement about what the best mix of goods might be. The PPF provides a rubric for thinking about scarcity, tradeoffs, and efficiency but does not, itself, tell us how to choose among the various economically efficient possibilities.

4.3 TRADEOFFS OVER TIME

We have said that a PPF reflects possible production combinations for a given set of resources. This idea deserves more investigation. Do we mean that society should look at *all* the resources it has at a point in time and then strive to employ them to produce the *maximum quantity* of valued outputs over the coming year?

If we consider that achieving well-being also involves questions of *how* and *for whom,* as well as activities of resource maintenance, distribution, and consumption, then the question becomes more complex—and more interesting. For example, we generally want to conserve resources so that we can produce goods not only right now but also later in our lives. And we have an obligation to future generations to include them in our considerations of *for whom.*

Some production activities are also resource maintenance activities, of course, and these activities can add to the stock of resources available for the future. Investments in plant and equipment can provide productive capacity not just for a few months but, often, for years. Production of goods and services that protect the environment or that encourage the development of new forms of knowledge and social organization also lead to an improved resource base. **Technological progress**, in which new methods are devised to convert resources

technological progress: the development of new methods of converting inputs (resources) into outputs (products or services)

Figure 1.2   **An Expanded Production Possibilities Frontier**

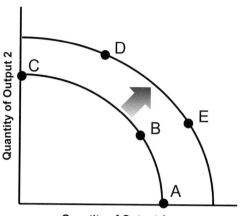

Quantity of Output 2

Quantity of Output 1

Figure 1.3   **Society's Choice between Current Production and Resource Maintenance**

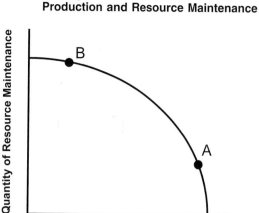

Quantity of Resource Maintenance

Quantity of Current Production

When the PPF moves "out" (away from the origin), we can obtain previously unattainable production choices, such as points D and E.

Society also faces a tradeoff between current production and resource maintenance for the future.

into products, can lead to long-run improvements in efficiency and productive capacity. Thus some kinds of production can *add* to the production possibilities for the future. The PPF may expand over time, out and to the right, making previously unobtainable points obtainable, as shown in Figure 1.2. With the initial PPF, points A, B, and C are attainable, but points D and E are unattainable. With technological progress and an expanded PPF, points D and E could become attainable.

Some productive activities create an ongoing flow of outputs without drawing down the stock of capital resources, such as organic farming that maintains the nutrient levels in soil. Many other productive activities, however, lead to resource depletion or degradation. The intensive use of fossil fuels is now depleting petroleum reserves, degrading air quality, and contributing to global climate change. Production processes that destroy important watersheds and wildlife habitats are also resource depleting. Mind-numbing drudgery, work in dangerous circumstances, or excessively long hours of work can degrade human resources by leaving people exhausted or in poor mental or physical health. These kinds of productive activities are at odds with resource maintenance.

Taking a longer-term view, then, it is clear that getting the absolute most production, right now, out of the available resources is not an intelligent social goal. Decisions such as our guns versus butter example need to be accompanied by another decision about *now* versus *later.* What needs to be currently produced, what needs to be maintained, and what investments are needed to increase future productivity?

The choice between current and future production can be presented in terms of a different PPF, as shown in Figure 1.3. In this case, the tradeoff is between current production and resource maintenance for the future. If society chooses point A, current production is high but resource maintenance for the future is low. However, choosing point B reduces current production but results in significantly higher resource maintenance.

The consequences of choosing between points A and B are illustrated in Figure 1.4, where once again we portray a two-output PPF (such as that for guns versus butter). Now, however, the graph illustrates how future conditions are affected by the current choice between A and B. As Figure 1.4 shows, a decision to maintain more for the future, by choosing point B in Figure 1.3, leads to a larger set of production possibilities in future years. A decision to

Figure 1.4   **Possible Future Production Possibilities Frontiers**

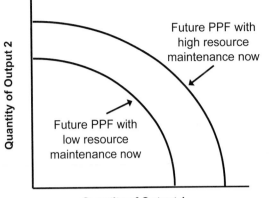

Future PPF with
high resource
maintenance now

Future PPF with
low resource
maintenance now

Quantity of Output 2

Quantity of Output 1

Current decisions about how to
produce will affect our options for
future production.

engage in less resource maintenance in Figure 1.3 leads to the smaller future PPF shown in
Figure 1.4.

Of course, some will argue that advances in technology will *always* push out the PPF (as
in Figure 1.2) and make up for low current resource maintenance. But this is no more than
an assertion of belief. If this belief turns out not to be warranted, then acting on the basis of
it may lead to large-scale, unfortunate, and irreversible consequences.

Discussion Questions

microeconomics:
the subfield of economics that focuses
on activities that
take place within and
among the major economic organizations
of a society, including
households, communities, governments,
nonprofit organizations, and for-profit
businesses

1. Suppose that your "resources" for studying can be devoted to either or both of two "outputs": knowledge of economics and knowledge of the subject matter of another class you
   are taking. Would the PPF for your "production" have the shape portrayed in Figure 1.1?
   Discuss.
2. Consider the following possible productive activities. Which ones do you think will tend
   to expand the PPF in the future? Which ones will tend to contract it? (There may be room
   for disagreement on some points.)
   a. Increasing educational opportunities
   b. Manufacturing lawn mowers
   c. Building a nuclear power plant
   d. Restoring wetlands
   e. Building a new interstate highway
   f. Expanding Internet capacity

5. MICROECONOMICS IN CONTEXT

macroeconomics:
the subfield of economics that focuses
on the economy as a
whole

Microeconomics is the subfield of economics that focuses on activities that occur within
and among the major economic organizations of a society. Households and communities,
governments and nonprofit organizations, and for-profit businesses are all involved in the four
essential economic activities: resource maintenance and the production, consumption, and
distribution of goods and services. **Macroeconomics**, the other main subfield of economics,
adopts an overview, focusing on understanding national and international trends and fluctuations in economic activity taken as a whole.

5.1 ECONOMIC MODELS

In order to study economics, we need a shared background and vocabulary, along with various analytical tools for exploring economic behavior.

Some parts of this book deal with history, explaining how economic institutions came to be the way they are. Other parts are analytical and, when necessary, use specialized language to help you to think clearly and communicate effectively about economic topics. It is sometimes useful temporarily to isolate certain aspects of economic behavior from their larger historical and environmental context, in order to examine more closely the complex elements involved. Many chapters use models to explain economic concepts. A **model** is an analytical tool that highlights some aspects of reality while ignoring others. It can take the form of a story, a description, an image, an illustration, a graph, or a set of equations, and it always involves assuming away many real-world details and complications. Models can be useful for building understanding, even though they require temporarily neglecting many complications and much of the larger context.

model: an analytical tool that highlights some aspects of reality while ignoring others

As an example of a simple economic model, we present the traditional model of economic activity. In this model, the economy includes just three economic activities (resource maintenance is excluded), and limiting assumptions are made about the relationships between activities and actors:

- Production, it assumes, is performed only by firms.
- Exchange is performed in markets.
- Consumption is done only by households.

circular flow diagram: a graphical representation of the traditional view that an economy consists of households and firms engaging in exchange

This model, referred to as the **circular flow diagram**, is shown in Figure 1.5. The two actors (households and firms) are represented by rectangles, the activity of exchange by arrows. Flows of goods or services create the clockwise flow of the outer circle. Households are considered the ultimate owners of all assets, including land (or natural resources), physical capital (such as factories and machinery), and financial capital. They supply the services of these assets, along with their labor, to firms via **factor markets**. (We'll discuss exactly what we mean by "markets" in the next chapter.) Firms use these to produce goods and services, which return to the households via **product markets**. Households are consumers, buying and using these products. Flows of monetary funds, exchanged for these goods and services, move in the opposite direction around the inner circle.

factor markets: markets for the services of land, labor, and capital

product markets: markets for newly produced goods and services

Figure 1.5   The Circular Flow Diagram

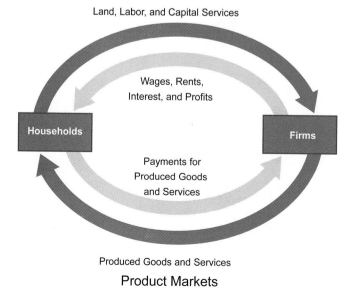

The circular flow diagram presents a simple model of economic activity with only two kinds of economic actors interacting in the types of markets.

This diagram is useful in portraying in a very simplified way two of the major actors (households and firms) and three of the major activities (production, exchange, and consumption) involved in economic life. However, it is important to recognize that the model leaves out some key actors and activities.

For example, while "land" is included as a factor of production, the fact that natural resources can be used up or polluted is not portrayed. Because of this, the circular flow diagram is a little like a "perpetual motion machine"; the economy it portrays can apparently keep on generating products forever without any inputs of materials or energy. The necessity of resource maintenance activities is not included.

Also, the diagram only takes into account flows of goods or resources that are paid for through the market (the inner, gray arrows show these payments). This ignores unpaid work and free use of natural resources, among other things. You will also notice that there is no role for government in this diagram. While this oversimplification has some value, in allowing us to focus only on the workings of specific markets, we also want to present a broader picture.

5.2 THE CONTEXTUAL APPROACH

We titled this book *Microeconomics in Context* because it discusses how economic activities take place within *environmental* and *social contexts*. Thus we need a more inclusive, and more realistic, model than the one presented in Figure 1.5. This is illustrated in Figure 1.6.

Because all economic production entails some processing of raw materials, the economy operates in a *physical system*. The physical context for economic activities includes the built environment as well as the natural world, but its fundamental processes are ecological: Economic activity brings natural resources into the economy and transforms them for human use. In the process, pollution and waste materials are generated, and these in turn affect the flow of natural inputs that are available.

Figure 1.6   **Microeconomics in Context**

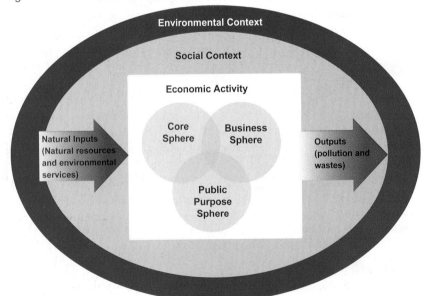

Economic activity always occurs within a broader social and environmental context.

The economy also operates in a *social system*, one that is created and operated by human beings, even when they are not consciously designing it as a system. The social context that shapes the institutions and norms of any economy includes history, politics, culture, ethics, and other human motivations. In Figure 1.6 we show the social context as existing inside the environmental context because all human activities—not only those of the economic system—are ultimately completely dependent on the environmental context.

Instead of showing economic activity as occurring between just two actors, households and firms, as in Figure 1.5, our contextual approach presents economic activity as occurring within three "spheres." These spheres provide a basic classification of the major types of economic actors.

core sphere: households, families, and communities

business sphere: firms that produce goods and services for profitable sale

public purpose sphere: governments as well as other organizations that seek to enhance well-being without making a profit

1. The **core sphere** includes households, families, and communities. Traditionally, economists have focused on the core sphere as consumers and workers, in their interactions with businesses. But important economic activity occurs *within* the core sphere. For example, the core sphere is where people generally raise children, prepare meals, maintain homes, organize leisure time, and care for mildly ill individuals.
2. The **business sphere** includes firms that produce goods and services for profitable sale. It is often thought that businesses operate only to obtain profits. But the final goals of many businesses may extend beyond simply maximizing profits.
3. The **public purpose sphere** includes governments as well as other organizations that seek to enhance human well-being without making a profit. These may be anything from the United Nations down to a local homeless shelter.

Individuals may move among these three spheres in their economic activities. A woman may be a wife and mother in the core sphere, a business executive in the business sphere, and a volunteer for an environmental group in the public purpose sphere.

Economic activity within and between these three spheres always occurs within the social and environmental contexts. At the same time, our economic actions often have important impacts on the larger physical and social contexts. A useful understanding of economics must take into account the most critical interactions between the economy and its contexts, showing how the economy is in various ways enabled and constrained by the contexts in which it is embedded, and how these environmental and social influences *on* the economy are in turn affected *by* the economy. One important feature of this context relates to the primary actors in the economy and how they are organized. Perhaps the most important way that economic activities are organized for our purposes is through "markets." We turn our attention to them in Chapter 2.

Discussion Questions

1. Describe three situations in which economic behavior could affect its physical context and three ways in which economic behavior could affect its social context. How might these influences that the economy exerts on its contexts result in changing how the contexts, in turn, affect (either support or constrain) economic activity?
2. Model building is sometimes compared to map making. If you wanted to give people directions for reaching the place where you live, what would you put on the map that you drew for them? What would you put on the map you drew if someone asked you about good places to go hiking, where the highest point is, or how close you are to your town boundary? Is it possible for a single, readable map to answer every possible question? Does your goal for the map affect what you put on it?

REVIEW QUESTIONS

1. What is the definition of economics?
2. Name the four essential economic activities.
3. What is the difference between positive and normative questions? Give a couple of examples of each.
4. What is the difference between final and intermediate goals?
5. Is the attainment of wealth a final goal?
6. What is the goal of efficiency?
7. What are some examples of final goals?
8. What is an economic actor?
9. Define negative and positive externalities, and give examples of each.
10. How do abundance and scarcity create the possibility of, and the necessity for, economic decision making?
11. Draw a societal PPF, and use it to explain the concepts of tradeoffs (opportunity cost), attainable and unattainable output combinations, and efficiency.
12. What kinds of decisions would make a PPF expand over time? What kinds of decisions would make it contract over time?
13. What is the relationship between a society's PPF and resource maintenance?
14. What is a model?
15. What is the circular flow model of economic activity?
16. How can we classify economic actors into three spheres?
17. What do we mean when we speak of economic activity "in context"?

EXERCISES

1. In each of the following, indicate which of the four essential economic activities is taking place, and in which sphere.
   a. Ms. Katar, an executive at Acme Manufacturing, directs the cleanup of one of the company's old industrial waste dump sites.
   b. Mr. Ridge plants a garden in his yard.
   c. Ms. Fuller hands an unemployed worker a bag of groceries at a local food pantry.
   d. Private Hernandez, a recent recruit, eats lunch at an army base.
2. The notion of scarcity reflects the idea that resources cannot be stretched to achieve all the goals that people desire. But what makes a particular resource "scarce"? If a resource seems to be in greater supply than is needed (like desert sand), is it scarce? If it is freely open to the use of many people at once (like music on the radio), is it scarce? What about resources such as social attitudes of trust and respect? Make a list of a few resources that clearly *are* scarce in the economic sense. Make another list of a few resources that are *not* scarce.
3. How is the concept of efficiency related to the concept of scarcity? Consider, for example, your own use of time. When do you feel that time is more, and when less, scarce? Do you think about how to use your time differently during exam week than you do when you are on vacation?
4. Suppose that society could produce the following combinations of pizzas and books:

Alternative	Quantity of pizzas	Quantity of books
A	50	0
B	40	10
C	30	18
D	20	24
E	10	28
F	0	30

   a. Using graph paper (or a computer program), draw the PPF for pizza and books, being as exact and neat as possible. (Put books on the horizontal axis. Assume that the dots define a complete curve.)
   b. Is it possible or efficient for this society to produce 25 pizzas and 25 books?
   c. Is it possible or efficient for this society to produce 42 pizzas and 1 book?
   d. If society is currently producing alternative B, then the opportunity cost of moving to alternative A (and getting 10 more pizzas) is _____ books.
   e. Is the opportunity cost of producing pizzas higher or lower moving from alternative F to E than moving from alternative B to A? Why is this likely to be so?
   f. Suppose that the technologies used in producing both pizzas and books improve. Draw one possible new PPF in the graph above that represents the results of this change. Indicate the direction of the change that occurs with an arrow.

5. Match each concept in Column A with an example in Column B.

Column A	Column B
a. Negative externality	1. You should spend more time studying economics.
b. An essential economic activity	2. A fair and just society
c. A final goal	3. If you spend more time studying economics, you will have less time to sleep.
d. An intermediate goal	4. The current unemployment rate is 7 percent.
e. A normative statement	5. You are studying economics in order to get a good job.
f. A positive statement	6. Producing this book resulted in pollution.
g. An opportunity cost	7. Resource maintenance

NOTE

1. Data from tax reports published by the Congressional Budget Office, www.cbo.gov.

2 Markets and Society

1. THE THREE SPHERES OF ECONOMIC ACTIVITY

As we mentioned last chapter, economic activity takes place in three major spheres, which we designated as the core, public purpose, and business spheres. In other economics writings, the terms used are "household," "government," and "business." In this text, we use the term "core" instead of "household" to emphasize the importance of communities, in addition to households, in the "core" activities described below. (Think of the maxim "It takes a village to raise a child.") We use the term "public purpose" instead of "government" to include both government organizations and the nongovernmental nonprofit organizations whose activities are of growing importance in modern societies. Many economic activities are conducted through markets, but some activities, especially in the core sphere, take place outside of markets. In this chapter, we give an overall view of the three spheres and then focus on the nature and workings of markets, which we also analyze in more detail in Chapter 3.

1.1 THE CORE SPHERE

Long before the invention of money, organized markets, and systems of government, human societies organized themselves along lines of kinship and community to undertake the economic activities essential to maintaining and improving the conditions for human life. The **core sphere** is made up of household, family, and community institutions that undertake economic activities, usually on a small scale, and largely without the use of money. Even in modern societies, the core sphere is still the primary site for raising children, preparing meals, maintaining homes, taking care of the mildly ill, and organizing activities among family members, friends, and neighbors.

core sphere: households, families, and communities

One distinguishing characteristic of the core sphere is how work activities are rewarded: Instead of earning money, work tends to be rewarded directly by what it produces. For example, work in a home garden is rewarded with tomatoes, and the reward of good child care is a happy and healthy child. People may volunteer their services to their community because they recognize that living in a healthy community is important. People play cards, softball, or music together because they find these activities intrinsically enjoyable. Another distinguishing characteristic is that activities in the core sphere are organized to respond not only to *wants* but also, importantly, to *needs*—unlike market activities, which respond to what people are able and willing to pay for (regardless of need).

The core sphere is obviously critical for subsistence economies, where extended families and villages may raise or make for themselves most of what they consume, with little outside trading. Although reliance on the core sphere has to some extent been reduced in the United States and many other countries by the increasing use of prepared foods, child-care centers, restaurants, commercial forms of entertainment, nursing homes, housecleaning services, and the like, it remains of central importance for the maintenance and flourishing of any economy.

Core sphere activities, however, have been—and sometimes still are—often described as noneconomic or nonproductive because they generally do not produce goods and services for trade through a market. However, consider just one activity that takes place in the core sphere: the help provided by relatives, friends, and neighbors that enables seniors to remain in a home setting rather than entering a nursing facility. If we were to value the actual unpaid time invested in these activities in the United States at a low wage of $8–$9 an hour, we would find that each year about $300 billion to $400 billion worth of elder care is provided in the core sphere—without being recorded in gross domestic product (GDP) statistics.* For comparison, this amount exceeds the total annual expenditures on nursing-care services, including both private and public spending.

According to one estimate, between a third and half of all economic activity in industrialized countries consists of unpaid labor that is not counted in GDP.[1] Recognizing the value of unpaid work is important if we are to make a comprehensive assessment of well-being. To quote from a recent report:

> Unpaid work contributes not only to current household consumption (e.g., cooking) but also to future well-being (e.g., parental investments in raising children) and to community well-being (e.g., voluntary work). In all countries, women do more of such work than men, although to some degree balanced—by an amount varying across countries—by the fact that they do less paid work.[2]

When the core sphere is working effectively to support the quality of life, important goods and services are provided to many people, even if the scale of production in each specific case is quite small. Because most core sphere activities involve face-to-face interaction, the core sphere is the primary location in which the ability to form good social relations is developed.

Of course, core spheres can also work badly or inadequately. For example, responsibilities for children, the elderly, and ill people may be inequitably assigned between women and men. Such responsibilities may also overwhelm the personal resources of impoverished families and communities. There are limits to what can be accomplished within small-scale, largely informal networks of personal relations. For many economic goals, more formal and larger-scale organizations are also needed. The public purpose sphere is uniquely capable of meeting certain well-being needs.

1.2 THE PUBLIC PURPOSE SPHERE

public purpose sphere: governments as well as other organizations that seek to enhance well-being without making a profit

The **public purpose sphere** includes governments and their agencies, as well as nonprofit organizations such as charities, religious organizations, professional associations, and international institutions such as the World Bank and the United Nations. They may be as large as a national government or an international scientific organization or as small as a Cub Scouts group or an organization whose only goal is the protection of a landmark building. The distinguishing characteristic of these institutions is that they exist for an explicit purpose related to the public good—that is, the common good of some group larger than a household or informal community—and they do not aim at making a profit. Some of the larger ones, often associated with a level of government, are charged with purposes such as defending a country's borders, relieving poverty, providing formal health care and education, protecting the natural environment, and stabilizing global financial markets. Religious organizations are other well-known public purpose organizations, associated

*Estimates of unpaid elder care in "Valuing the Invaluable: A New Look at the Economic Value of Family Caregiving," AARP Policy Brief, http://assets.aarp.org/rgcenter/il/ib82_caregiving.pdf.

with governments in some countries but not in the United States. Small nonprofits may be found working on local issues such as the preservation of a particular park or providing homeless people with shelter.

Organizations in the public purpose sphere tend to be more formally structured than those in the core sphere, and usually they are more monetized, though a public purpose organization can lie anywhere on a spectrum of those that rely entirely on voluntary work to those that pay for all work done to achieve their ends. Even in the latter case, however, people will often accept pay for jobs in the public purpose sector that is lower than the going wages for comparable work in the business sphere.

The reason for this is twofold. First, public purpose organizations are often scraping by with financial resources too small to achieve their goals and are therefore more careful to watch every dollar than is necessary in some businesses. In addition, many people are willing to accept lower salaries in public purpose work because they receive an additional psychic benefit in the feeling that their work is meaningful.

In some instances public purpose organizations offer goods and services for sale as businesses do, but this is generally not their primary focus. They usually raise much of their support by soliciting monetary contributions or, in the case of governments, requiring such contributions in the form of taxes or fees. Your college or university, for example, may be either a nonprofit or government entity (i.e., operated by the city, county, or state). As another example, public (that is, government-supported) hospitals in the United States provide emergency medical care to the poor and uninsured.

The public purpose sphere is able to provide goods and services that cannot, or would not, be adequately provided by core sphere institutions and businesses alone. Some of the goods and services that it provides are what economists call public goods. A **public good** (or service) is freely available to anyone (or some people could be excluded from using it only with difficulty), and use of a public good by one person does not diminish the ability of another person to benefit from it.

public good: a good whose benefits are freely available to anyone, and whose use by one person does not diminish its usefulness to others

For example, when a local police force helps to make a neighborhood safe, all the residents benefit. Public roads (at least those that are not congested and have no tolls) are also public goods, as is national defense. Education and quality child care are in a sense public goods because everyone benefits from living with a more skilled and socially well-adjusted population. A system of laws and courts provides the basic legal infrastructure on which all business contracting depends. We discuss public goods in more detail in Chapter 13.

The public purpose sphere is a substantial contributor to U.S. economic activity. In 2010, the value of the production by nonprofit organizations was 5.5 percent of GDP, and federal, state, and local governments contributed 12.3 percent of GDP—for a total share of about 18 percent.[3]

The main strength of public purpose institutions is that (like core institutions) they provide goods and services of high intrinsic value, but (unlike core institutions) they are big enough to take on jobs that require broader social coordination. The provision of goods and services itself, and not the financial results of these activities, remains the primary intended focus of public purpose organizations, in contrast to the business sphere.

Overall, a larger amount of the work that is undertaken by governments in other industrialized countries is taken care of by either the business or the nonprofit sector in the United States. Canada and countries in most of Europe, for example, put more government resources into health and social welfare than is the case in the United States. However, the United States has traditionally been a leader in charitable and philanthropic support for private, nonprofit organizations in this sphere.

The public purpose sphere has its weaknesses, of course. Compared to the core sphere, the government, in particular, is often criticized as cold and impersonal. Some parents prefer to home school, for example, rather than accept what they characterize as "one size fits all" public education. Compared to for-profit businesses, not-for-profit institutions and governments are sometimes accused of being rigid, slow to adapt, and crippled by inefficiency through impenetrable regulations and a bloated bureaucracy. Organizations can lose sight of the goal of providing "public service" and become more interested in increasing their own organizational budgets. Public purpose organizations are commonly supported by taxes or donations that are often not tightly linked to the quality of their services. For this reason, they may not have a *financial* incentive to improve the quality of what they provide. Many current debates about reforms in both governments and nonprofits concern how efficiency and accountability can be improved without eroding the commitment of these organizations to providing valuable goods and services.

Public purpose organizations respond to the demands of their "public," whether voters, members, or other participants. Nonprofit organizations frequently offer services related to religion, education, health, and welfare. Sometimes, they offer these services only within a particular community (such as to members of a certain religion); at other times, they work more widely and may receive subsidies from the government. Some such organizations may have goals that are directly at odds with other public purpose organizations; for example, organizations working to support gay families seek outcomes that differ from those sought by organizations that aim to maintain exclusively the traditional family headed by a married man and woman.

Because definitions of the public good vary, some people will reject the "public purpose" of some of these organizations. For example, a few nonprofit organizations are thinly disguised hate groups. Trade organizations and labor unions promote the interests of (some of) their own members, while other members of society may disagree with their agendas. A continuing issue with government institutions is the question of *whose* interests are represented. Majority groups? Outspoken minority groups? Special interests who donate money to campaigns? Yet, because of the nature of public goods and the general interests of social welfare, the question cannot be *whether* to have a public purpose sphere but only *how* to allow it to function well.

1.3 THE BUSINESS SPHERE

business sphere:
firms that produce
goods and services
for profitable sale

The U.S. government defines businesses as "entities that produce goods and services for sale at a price intended at least to approximate the costs of production."[4] The **business sphere** is made up of such firms. A business firm is expected to look for opportunities to buy and manage resources in such a way that, after their product is sold, the owners of the firm will earn profits.

It is sometimes thought that maximizing profits is the *only* goal of businesses. But firms may not always aim for the highest profit for two main reasons.

First, some business managers cite being a good "corporate citizen," with regard to their workers, communities, or the environment, as a motivation for some of their actions. Businesses organized on a cooperative model (including large food-marketing organizations such as Land O'Lakes for dairy products and Ocean Spray for cranberries) explicitly state their purpose in terms of providing services to their members, rather than in terms of profit. Still, making enough profit to stay afloat is a goal of all well-run businesses. Some businesses may set a certain goal for profits while also pursuing other goals. Mindless profiteering, however—going after the last bit of profit at all costs, neglecting social and even ethical concerns—need not be how businesses are run.

Second, within a modern business corporation of any size, the activities of "the firm" are made up of the activities of many people, including its stockholders, board of directors, chief executive officer (CEO), mid- and top-level managers, and employees. The interests of the various individuals and suborganizations may be in conflict. Sometimes, top officers and managers may act, for example, not in the profit-making interest of the owners but according to their *personal* self-interest. That is, they may seek to maximize their own prestige and incomes, even when this goes against the interests of everyone else involved in the firm, including those who have invested in it. Profits, and even the long-term survival of the company itself, may be sacrificed in a race for individual high salaries and lucrative bonuses.

Whereas the core sphere responds to direct needs, and the public purpose sphere responds to its constituents, business firms are responsive to demands for goods and services, as expressed through markets by people who can afford to buy the firms' products.

One strength of business organizations is that because they have at least one clear goal—making a profit—their efficiency in operating to reach that goal may be greater than the efficiency of activities in the other two spheres. A profit orientation is commonly thought to drive firms to choose the most (market) valuable outputs to produce and to produce them at the least possible cost—where, again, costs are determined by the forces of the market. (In Chapter 3 we begin a much closer look at how markets determine prices; ability to pay is just one of the relevant forces.)

Another advantage of the profit motivation is that it encourages *innovation:* People are more motivated to come up with clever new ideas when they know that they may reap financial rewards. We all benefit, in terms of our material standard of living, from business efficiency and from innovations when they bring us improved products at lower prices.

The relative weakness of the business sphere comes from the fact that business interests do not necessarily coincide with overall social well-being. Firms *may* act to enhance social well-being—for example, by making decisions that consider all the needs of their customers and their workers and take into account externalities, including those that affect the natural environment. They *may* be guided in these directions by the goodwill of their owners and managers, by pressure from their customers or workers, or by government regulation.

Production for market exchange, however, has no *built-in* correction for market externalities; this is, indeed, a way to remember the meaning of the term "externalities"—it refers to things that are external to the interests of the firm (or of any other economic actor in question). We will discuss externalities in more detail in Chapter 12. Moreover, sometimes "innovation" can take a perverse form. In the late 1990s, for example, Enron boosted its reported earnings primarily by inventing unusual and "innovative" accounting practices, which served to hide the extreme weakness of its financial situation from investors. In fields such as health care and education, where it can be difficult to define clear goals, businesses may increase profits by "innovatively" cutting corners on the less-measurable and less-often-marketed aspects of quality of life.

The potential for social harm grows when firms gain excessive market power—that is, when they come to dominate the market in their area. They may then be able to charge socially inefficient prices (as we discuss in Chapter 17) or to squelch socially advantageous innovations by competing firms. Industrialized countries also have considerable power to harm the natural environment on which they ultimately depend. Thus market economies today face a major conundrum: How can societies continue to benefit from the strengths of the business sphere while ensuring that this sphere supports the kind of world that will sustain the livelihoods and the well-being of future generations? For one example of the debate over the allocation of certain economic activities to the business sphere, see Box 2.1.

1.4 THE SIZE OF THE THREE SPHERES

Figure 2.1 presents estimates of the monetary value of the annual production of goods and services in the United States by the three spheres in 2010, in dollar and percentage terms. The business sphere contributed 58 percent of production, the core sphere contributed 32 percent, and the public purpose sphere contributed 10 percent. The dollar figures add up to more than GDP in that year ($14.7 trillion) because an estimate of the value of unpaid household labor as equal to one-third of the value of GDP has been included. This differs from government estimates of GDP, which do not currently include the value of household production.

BOX 2.1   PRIVATE PRISONS

The United States has more prisoners than any other country, not only in absolute numbers but also on a per-capita basis. Up until the 1980s, prisons in the U.S. were operated exclusively by state and federal government agencies. But since 1984, a growing share of U.S. prisons are being operated by for-profit companies. Currently, around 130,000 prisoners in the United States, or 9 percent of the prison population, are housed in prisons operated by private companies. The main argument in favor of prison privatization is that for-profit companies will have an incentive to identify economic efficiencies, and thus reduce prison operation costs to taxpayers.

However, a 2011 report on private prisons reported that most studies indicate little or no cost savings when prisons are turned over to for-profit companies. Analysis of private prisons in Arizona found that per-prisoner costs were actually *higher* in private prisons. The report concluded that:

> the supposed benefits (economic and otherwise) of private prisons often fail to withstand scrutiny. The view that private prisons save taxpayer money, fuel local economies, and adequately protect the safety of prisoners helps to feed mass incarceration by making privatization appear to be an attractive alternative to reducing prison populations. But the evidence for such benefits is mixed at best. Not only may privatization fail to save taxpayer money, but private prison companies, as for-profit institutions, are strongly incentivized to cut corners and thereby maximize profits, which may come at

the expense of public safety and the well being of prisoners. (ACLU, 2011, p. 18)

For example, a 2007 audit of a private prison in Texas found deplorable conditions, with prisoners denied medical care, refused access to their lawyers, and forced to live in their own wastes due to a lack of toilets. One study found that private prisons hire fewer guards than public prisons, leading to higher rates of violence.

Another implication of prison privatization is that companies that operate prisons lobby legislators for higher incarceration rates and longer prison terms. The largest prison company, Corrections Corporation of America, hired 199 lobbyists in 32 states between 2003 and 2011. Prison companies are normally paid on a per-prisoner basis, so they have an incentive to house as many prisoners as possible. A 2013 article on private prisons concluded that:

> unless authorities implement significant changes, including regular inspections and holding private institutions to humane standards, private prisons are not a solution. Corporations which benefit from longer prison stays must also be removed from discussions of sentencing and drafting legislation.

Sources: American Civil Liberties Union, *Banking on Bondage: Private Prisons and Mass Incarceration* (New York, 2011); Paul, Samakow, "Private Prisons: The Worst of the American Dream," *The Washington Times*, July 7, 2013.

Figure 2.1   **Estimated Size of the Three Spheres of Economic Activity in the United States, 2010**

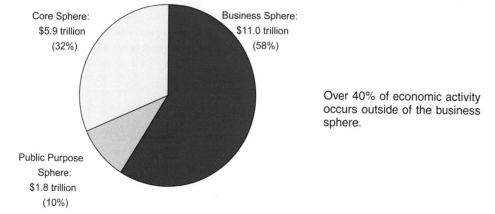

Core Sphere:
$5.9 trillion
(32%)

Business Sphere:
$11.0 trillion
(58%)

Public Purpose
Sphere:
$1.8 trillion
(10%)

Over 40% of economic activity occurs outside of the business sphere.

Sources: U.S. Census Bureau, *Statistical Abstract of the United States, 2012* (Washington, D.C.: GPO, 2011); Katie Roeger, Amy S. Blackwood, and Sarah L. Pettijohn, *The Nonprofit Almanac 2012* (Washington, D.C.: Urban Institute Press, 2012); and authors' calculations.

1.5 A COMPARATIVE NOTE: LESS INDUSTRIALIZED COUNTRIES

informal sphere:
businesses operating
outside government
oversight and regula-
tion. In less industri-
alized countries, it
may constitute the
majority of economic
activity

Many less industrialized countries have large **informal spheres** of small market enterprises operating outside government oversight and regulation. Although this sphere could be classified as business because it involves private production for sale, it is also similar to the core sphere in that the activities are very small-scale and often depend on family and community connections. Like activities in the core sphere, informal business activities are often excluded from government-compiled accounts. In the United States, illegal drug trades and house-cleaning services provided "off the books" are two examples of the informal sphere. In less industrialized countries, however, it is sometimes the case that *most* people are employed in small-scale agriculture, trade, and services, which often go uncounted.

If this textbook were being written for use in developing countries, it would be necessary to pay a great deal more attention to the complicating reality of informal economic activity and perhaps to discuss it as a fourth sphere. However, in a text for use in industrialized countries, we can deal with this issue by simply noting, as we have just done, that informal economic activity could legitimately be classified as occurring within either the business sphere or the core sphere, leaving open the question of which of these classifications is more appropriate.

Discussion Questions

1. Education is sometimes provided within the core sphere (at-home preschool activities and home schooling), is often provided by the public purpose sphere (public and nonprofit schools), and is occasionally provided by for-profit firms ("charter schools" or firms offering specific training programs). Can you think of some possible advantages and disadvantages of each of these three ways of providing education?
2. Make a list of several things that, over the past few days, you have eaten, drunk, been entertained by, been transported by, been sheltered by, or received other services from (e.g., "dinner at Gina's," "my apartment," and "the health clinic"). Then, using the definitions in this section, determine which of the three spheres of economic activity provided each item.

2. THE ROLE OF MARKETS

Having discussed the three major spheres of economic activity, we are now ready to move to the more specific economic issue of how markets work. When you think of the word "market," you probably think of a store where you buy groceries. But in economics markets are defined more broadly and represent an important structure to guide many economic activities. We first define precisely what we mean by the term, starting with the most concrete definition and moving toward the most abstract. Then we look at ways to make markets work smoothly. We end the chapter by considering the advantages and limitations of markets as a way to conduct economic activities.

2.1 THREE DEFINITIONS OF MARKETS

Markets as Places to Buy and Sell

**market (first mean-
ing):** a place (physical
or virtual) where
there is a reasonable
expectation of find-
ing both buyers and
sellers for the same
product or service

The most concrete and commonsense definition of a **market** is that it is a place where people go to buy and sell things. Historically markets have been physical locations. For example, the Grand Bazaar in Istanbul, Turkey, is one of the world's oldest and largest covered markets in the world, dating to the fifteenth century. The Grand Bazaar now has more than 3,000 shops and attracts hundreds of thousands of visitors every day. The Grand Bazaar and produce stands in African villages have flourished for ages as meeting places for people who wish to engage in exchange transactions.

In the context of the contemporary world, many different kinds of physical markets have these same functions. They can be a single store, a shopping mall with many retail stores sharing one structure, or a livestock auction. A market, as suggested by these examples, can be defined as a physical place where there is a reasonable expectation of finding both buyers and sellers for the same product or service.

But in modern societies, markets do not necessarily need to be physical places. One can now easily make purchases online that in the past required physically going to a store. Amazon and eBay are modern examples of "places" where buyers and sellers can also come together.

Markets as Social Institutions

market (second meaning): an institution that facilitates economic interactions among buyers and sellers

institutions: ways of structuring human activities based on customs, habits, and laws

The term "market" can also refer to economic activity that is not confined to a single place such as a shopping mall or a Web site. A more general definition is that a market is an "institution" that facilitates economic interactions among buyers and sellers.

To understand this definition of a market, we first have to understand what we mean by an **institution**. Once again, we have a word that can be understood in several ways. An institution can be a physical location, such as penal institutions (prisons), mental institutions (psychiatric hospitals), or institutions for housing parentless children (orphanages). This meaning is, in fact, incorporated into the U.S. Census in a number of instances in which the people being counted are specified as the "noninstitutionalized population"—meaning that they are neither in prisons nor in long-term hospital care.

However, an institution in an economic sense is more than a physical structure. The term refers to the ways of structuring economic activities based on customs, habits, and laws. Thus we can speak, for example, of the institutional structure of health care in the United States as one that is based on private care for many working-age adults, Medicare for older adults, and Medicaid for low-income children, families, and people with disabilities. This institutional structure also includes the federal and state laws regarding health care, the rules of health insurance companies, customary procedures about doctor visits, and so on.

When we view markets as institutions, we can see that they not only bring buyers and sellers into communication with each other but also structure and coordinate their interactions. Specific market institutions come in many types. Credit cards are a type of market institution that facilitates purchases when a consumer does not have enough cash readily available. Consumer protection laws are a market institution that defines certain exploitative business practices and makes them illegal. The ability to return purchased products for a refund can also be viewed as a widely accepted market institution.

Thinking of markets as institutions, rather than places, leads to definitions of markets for particular goods and services or categories of goods and services. For example, we can speak of the "real estate market" in a particular city or even the entire country. We can define the market for used cars, the market for wind turbines, or the market for luxury goods. Speaking of the "stock market" in a broad sense is another common example of a market as an institution, whereas the New York Stock Exchange would be a market according to our first definition, as a place where buyers and sellers come together.

market (third meaning): an economic system (a "market economy") that relies on market institutions to conduct many economic activities

We can define markets at various levels of detail depending on our interests. Thus we can analyze the wheat market or be more specific and study the market for No. 2 dark winter wheat or No. 1 dark northern spring wheat. Or we might delineate a market based on geographic location, such as the New England market for home heating oil.

"The Market" as an Economic System

In the most abstract terms, people sometimes refer to markets as an economic system, for example, describing the United States as having a "**market economy**" or indicating a preference for "free markets." In this macroeconomic sense, a market economy is one that relies on markets (as social institutions) to conduct economic activities, rather than relying on other institutions.

When you think of an alternative to a market economy, you might think of a system that relies on central planning to conduct economic activities, as was the case in the Soviet Union. But we should realize that, even in modern market economies, many economic activities are not structured by markets. For example, decisions about resource maintenance are not always made based on markets, but often on scientific evidence or political preferences. The distribution of economic resources within the core sphere is normally made based on social or family relationships rather than market forces.

The view of markets as an economic system underlies some of the most heated current debates in economics; one side takes a "pro-market" view, and the other side takes an "anti-market" view. Market advocates claim that "free markets" and a **laissez-faire economy** (one with very little government regulation) lead to economic growth and prosperity. Others believe that markets can provide social benefits in many cases, but that unchecked and unregulated markets can contribute to problems such as poverty, inequality, environmental degradation, and an erosion of social ethics. As we examine different issues throughout this book, we frequently refer to these perspectives and this continuing debate.

laissez-faire economy: an economy with little government regulation

2.2 INSTITUTIONAL REQUIREMENTS OF MARKETS

Contemporary markets do an amazing thing: They allow many separate decision makers, acting in a decentralized manner, to coordinate their behavior, resulting in highly complex patterns of economic activity. However, in order for markets to operate smoothly, they depend on a number of even more basic institutions. We classify these in four broad groups:

1. individualist institutions related to property and decision making
2. social institutions of trust
3. infrastructure for the smooth flow of goods and information
4. money as a medium of exchange.

Individualist Institutions of Property and Decision Making

private property: ownership of assets by nongovernment economic actors

Before people can begin to think about making a market transaction, they have to be clear about what belongs to whom. Ownership is usually defined through systems of property rights set out in law and enforced by courts and police. These rights define what is **private property** and how economic actors can manage their property. Markets require that economic actors be free to make decisions about voluntarily trading their private property (including their financial assets) for others' property. Also, prices must not be under the complete control of a central planning agency but are generally determined by the interactions of market participants themselves.

The institutions of private property and individualist decision making exist both formally, in codes of law, and informally, in social norms. For example, some Western economists expected markets to grow quickly in the former republics of the Soviet Union after communism was dismantled and market opportunities opened up. However, many people living in these countries were accustomed to being told by the state where to work and what to do. Norms of individual entrepreneurship, it turns out, do not just arise naturally. Nor did other sorts of market infrastructure appear quickly, and the post-Soviet Russian economy went into a severe decline for some time.

Social Institutions of Trust

A degree of trust must exist between buyers and sellers. When a buyer puts down her payment, she must trust that the seller will hand over the merchandise and that it will be of the expected quality. A seller must be able to trust that the payment offered is valid, whether in the form of currency, personal check, credit card, or online payment. Consider that the online auction site eBay could not operate unless winning bidders were confident that they would receive their products.

One way in which trust is built up is through the establishment of direct, one-to-one relationships. If you have dealt with some people in the past and they treated you fairly, you are likely to choose them when it comes time to trade again. Even in sophisticated contemporary economies, this kind of confidence plays an important role. Companies know which suppliers they can count on to come through on time, and consumers patronize stores where they feel comfortable.

Reputation also can be important in creating trust. A buyer might be fleeced by a seller in a transaction, but if that buyer spreads the word, the seller may suffer a damaged reputation and a loss of customers. Online reviews provide useful information about which products and merchants are reliable. Marketers try to capitalize on the tendency of buyers to depend on reputation by using advertising to link certain expectations about quality and price to a recognizable brand name and thus creating "brand loyalty" among repeat customers.

Cultural norms and ethical or religious codes can also help to establish and maintain an atmosphere of trustworthiness. The functioning of markets is facilitated by having enough members of a society subscribe to a common moral code and not betray one another's trust.

explicit contract: a formal, often written agreement that states the terms of an exchange and may be enforceable through a legal system

In addition to broad cultural ethics, markets depend on specific legal structures. A "contract" is a general set of terms that structure a market exchange. **Explicit contracts** are formal, usually written, contracts that provide a legally enforceable description of the agreed-on terms of exchange. Explicit contracts can be quite complex, including many clauses to cover a multitude of contingencies (such as "If goods are not delivered by June 1, the price paid will be reduced to . . . "). They may involve many parties, as in a contract between a union and an employer. For formal contracts to work, there must be laws that state the parties' legal obligation to honor contracts and establish penalties for those who fail to do so.

implicit contract: an informal agreement about the terms of a market exchange, based on verbal discussions or on traditions and normal expectations

An **implicit contract** is said to exist when the parties have agreed informally about the terms of their exchange. Such agreement may be based on verbal discussions or on traditions and normal expectations.

In modern societies, many market encounters take place between strangers who are unlikely ever to meet again and may not even share the same traditions and moral codes. In such cases, the formal institutions of explicit contracts are often needed. Even with a system of formal contracts, however, social norms are still essential. Detailed formal contracts are costly to write and costly to enforce. It is not practical to police every detail of every contract, and it is impossible to cover every conceivable contingency. The legal system can work smoothly only if most people willingly obey most laws and believe that it is dishonorable to cheat.

Infrastructure for the Smooth Flow of Goods and Information

physical infrastructure: roads, ports, railroads, warehouses, and other tangible structures that provide the foundation for economic activity

A third set of institutions needed for market functioning has to do with making possible a smooth flow of goods and information. Most obviously, a **physical infrastructure** is needed for transportation and storage. Such infrastructure includes roads, ports, railroads, and warehouses in which to store goods awaiting transport or sale. This sort of infrastructure can be most noticeable when it is absent, as in economies ravaged by war.

In addition, an infrastructure must be in place for information to flow freely. Producers and sellers need information on what and how much their customers want to buy. At the same time, consumers need to know what is available and how much of something else they will have to give up (i.e., how much they will have to pay) to obtain the products that are on the market. Ideally, in fact, consumers should be able to compare *all* potential purchases as a basis for deciding what to acquire and what to do without. Access to the Internet, as well as more traditional sources of information such as newspapers and radio, facilitate the flow of market information.

Money as a Medium of Exchange

money: a medium of exchange that is widely accepted, durable as a store of value, has minimal handling and storage costs, and serves as a unit of account

The final basic institution required to facilitate the operation of markets is a generally accepted form of money. Many different things have been used as money in the past. Early monetary systems used precious or carved stones, particular types of seashells, or other rare goods. Gold, silver, and other metal coins were the most common choice for many centuries. More recently, paper currency has become important. Today, the use of checks, credit cards, and debit cards further facilitate making payments for goods and services.

What makes something **money**? Three criteria are necessary for something to be defined as money in a market economy.

1. One obvious criterion is that money must be widely accepted as *a medium of exchange*. In other words, money is whatever everyone accepts as money. In this sense, money is a social institution of trust.
2. Money must provide *a durable store of value*. Imagine the problems that would occur if heads of lettuce were proposed as money. A form of money that starts to rot within a week or two would be difficult to use! The value of money must be relatively stable over time. In addition, money *must have minimal handling and storage costs*. By this criterion, paper currency is generally better than coins, and electronic transactions are better still.
3. Money must be accepted as a *unit of account*. When people say that something is worth $1,000, that does not necessarily mean that they are proposing to buy or sell the item. Money serves as a way of valuing things, even if no market exchange takes place.

In most cases, money is created or sanctioned by national governments. However, this is not essential. For example, cigarettes are often used as a form of money by prisoners. Also, communities smaller than national governments can create their own money. In recent years, local "time-banking" currencies have appeared in some communities in the United States and elsewhere. People earn time dollars by performing valuable services for others or for the community as a whole, such as child care, tutoring, or building repairs. Time dollars can then be used to pay for other services or used instead of "normal" dollars to purchase products from local merchants (see Box 2.2).

Discussion Questions

1. You attend a college or university. In what sense is it an "educational institution"? Can you identify any institutionalized patterns that structure the behavior of students and faculty at your school?
2. In what sense is the term "market" being used in each of the following sentences? "Go to the market and get some bananas." "The market is the best invention of humankind." "The labor market for new Ph.D.s is bad this year." "The advance of the market leads to a decline in social morality." "The market performance of IBM stock weakened last month." Can you think of other examples from your own readings or experience?

3. TYPES OF MARKETS

Markets take a wide variety of forms. They can be classified according to what is sold, how prices are determined, and the period covered.

3.1 MARKETS DEFINED BY WHAT IS SOLD

Recall from last chapter that we defined two basic market types—product and factor markets—in the traditional model of economic activity. In this section we further classify different types of markets.

BOX 2.2 TIME BANKING

Time banking is a core sphere activity that uses a creative system to bring together unused human resources with unmet human needs. It is of interest because it is so closely related to *all* the spheres of economic activity. Time banking is a system of computerized credits operating within a defined location (it might be a hospital or nursing home, or a city, such as Portland, Maine). If you join a time bank system, you are initially issued a small number of credits; each one is a claim on one hour of time offered by someone else in the system. You list, in the central computer, the services that you can offer—from doing errands or cooking to carpentry or music lessons—and whenever you provide an hour of such service to someone else in the system, you receive a credit. Some interesting characteristics of the system include:

- It is a little like barter, only the person who receives your service does not need to be the same one who provides something for you in return.
- It is strictly non-monetized. However, it has been learned that it is usually necessary to have a small amount of money to pay an individual who will ensure that the central computerized system is operating smoothly.
- Some people join time banks who are not keen to do traditional volunteer work, because in the latter they sometimes feel that their time is valued at zero.

Time banks often have to grapple with an unexpected fact: Many people are more eager to give services than to receive them—as long as their service is recognized in some formal way. The resulting "balance of payments" problems have been solved in a variety of ways, such as asking people to donate their excess time dollars to day-care centers (which can call on time bank members to read to the children) or places where the residents are too ill to be able to offer anything in return. However, even in the latter case, there are often examples of receivers finding something that they can offer in return.

Time banks—more than 300 of them—exist in 23 countries. The largest one in New York City is the Visiting Nurse Service of New York Community Connections TimeBank. It has more than 2,000 members and is most active in three places—Upper Manhattan, Lower Manhattan, and parts of Brooklyn. Members come from all over New York City, but exchanges are easiest when people live in the same neighborhood. One example is Elayne Castillo-Vélez, who earns a credit for each hour she spends tutoring immigrant students who are having trouble learning English. She coordinates with the students' teachers to help focus her efforts. The students she has worked with have seen improvements in their grades and even won certificates for academic achievement. She spends her accumulated credits to take art classes.

Source: Tina Rosenberg, "Where All Work Is Created Equal," *New York Times,* September 15, 2011.

---

retail markets: markets where goods and services are purchased by consumers from businesses, generally in small quantities

The most obvious and well-known product markets are those in which people buy goods and services from businesses. Such **retail markets** deal in food, books, clothes, haircuts, and so on. Some retail markets sell, instead of tangible objects, services such as banking or repairs for your car. Retail markets may be supplied directly by producers, but more often they are supplied by distributors and brokers who trade in **wholesale markets,** which act as intermediaries between producers and retailers and tend to involve transactions in larger quantities. For example, Walmart and most other discount retailers don't actually produce the products they sell, but purchase them from suppliers in wholesale markets.

wholesale markets: markets where final goods are purchased by retailers from suppliers, normally in large quantities

We can differentiate between wholesale markets and **intermediate goods markets**, which involve sales of unfinished products between businesses, such as the purchase of sheet metal by an automobile company. **Resale markets** are product markets for items that have been previously owned. Used-car markets are resale markets, as are markets for antique furniture. Most shares traded in stock markets are also being resold, having been previously owned by other investors. In **commodities markets**, raw materials such as agricultural products, minerals, or petroleum are bought and sold.

intermediate goods market: a market for an unfinished product

resale market: a market for an item that has been previously owned

The **labor market** is a type of factor market, defined as the set of institutions through which people who wish to work offer to sell their services to employers: businesses, public agencies, nonprofit organizations, and households other than their own. Unlike a physical object, labor

commodity market: a market for a raw material

labor market: a market in which employers interact with people who wish to work

financial market: a market for loans, equity finance, and financial assets

cannot be produced first and then handed to the buyer; rather, the worker promises to do something in return for a promised payment of wages. Labor markets are sufficiently different from other types of markets that this topic warrants separate treatment (in Chapter 9).

Financial markets, also classified as factor markets, are markets for loans, equity finance, and financial assets such as stocks and bonds. An economic actor who needs money may get a loan from a bank. Businesses may sell shares of stocks—that is, small holdings that represent ownership rights in the firm—as a way to raise funds via "equity financing." Although corporations sometimes issue new shares of their stock to raise funds, as just noted nearly all the activity on stock markets is resale of existing stocks.

Some markets operate outside the law. **Underground markets** (also sometimes called shadow markets or black markets) are illegal markets, normally for a type of product. It might be that the good or service itself is illegal, as are heroin, smuggled antiquities, and murder for hire. Or the markets deal in legitimate goods but in illegal ways. For example, smugglers may sell cigarettes or imported perfume at prices that do not include payment of required taxes.

3.2 MARKETS DEFINED BY HOW PRICES ARE DETERMINED

underground market: a market in which illegal goods and services are sold or legal goods and services are sold in an illegal way

posted prices: prices set by a seller

At first glance, it might seem as if many consumer retail markets violate one of the institutional requirements for markets that we mentioned above: that prices must generally be allowed to be set by the interactions of market participants themselves. In an old-fashioned open-air bazaar or flea market, buyers and sellers haggle about prices. But in a typical retail setting in an industrialized society, you do not "interact" so directly with the retailer to determine the price of bread or a shirt. The price is listed on the shelf, a tag, or directly on the product. Either you pay the **posted price** set by the seller, or you do not buy the item.

Even though you do not haggle with the cashier at The Gap or at the supermarket, the fact that you *can* decide whether to buy is itself a form of interaction. Over time, retailers will take note of what moves off the shelf most quickly and will then order more of it and may also raise its price. They will also take note of what does not sell so quickly and will then reduce their order from wholesalers or mark the items down. The retailers' purchases from the wholesalers, in turn, give the suppliers information that they can use in deciding how much to order or produce and how to set *their* prices.

So while you may not be able to bargain directly, your actions, in combination with the actions of other customers, ultimately affect the prices and quantities offered in the market. These adjustments should tend, at least in theory, to lead posted prices to reflect what economists call the market-determined value, or **market value,** of the item. Market value, discussed in detail in Chapter 3, is the price as freely determined by voluntary interactions of buyers and sellers. The posted price is most likely to move to the market value if markets are competitive, the flow of information is good, the adjustment process is given enough time, and no big changes in market conditions occur in the meantime.

market value: the price for an item as freely determined by the voluntary interactions of buyers and sellers

auction market: a market in which an item is sold to the highest bidder

open auction: an auction in which the opening price is set low and then buyers bid it up

Dutch auction: an auction in which the opening price is set high and then drops until someone buys

Auction markets are markets in which an item is sold to the highest bidder. Auction markets are used when the appropriate price for an item is relatively unknown and there are many possible buyers or sellers. Although in the past auction markets were commonly limited to goods such as antiques and artwork, the advent of online auction sites such as eBay have made auction markets much more prevalent. Real-world auctions offer interesting opportunities to observe how market values are determined.

Auction markets come in different types. In an **open auction,** an opening price is set low, and then potential buyers top one another's bids until only one bidder remains. This is what many people first think of when they think of an auction, and it is the main type of auction used on eBay.

In a **Dutch auction,** an opening price is set high and then drops until a buyer offers to purchase the item. The name comes from its use in the Dutch wholesale cut-flower market.

You can find numerous Dutch auction sites online, and stores that follow the practice of taking an extra 10 percent or 20 percent off the prices of unsold items each week are following a Dutch auction procedure.

sealed-bid auction: an auction in which bids are given privately to the auctioneer

Sealed-bid auctions get their name from the fact that the bids are given privately to the auctioneer, who then selects the winning bidder. In contrast to an open auction, the bidders are not supposed to know how much others value the item. Sealed-bid auctions are often used to sell commercial real estate (where the high-price buyer wins) and to allocate construction contracts (where the low-price seller of construction services wins).

double auction: an auction in which both the buyers and sellers state prices at which they are willing to make transactions

In a **double auction**, both buyers and sellers state prices at which they are willing to make transactions. The New York Stock Exchange is a double auction market. When you see pictures of traders on the stock exchange floor, they are shouting out bids either to buy or sell, and a sale can occur when the "bid" and "ask" prices become the same (although most stock transactions now occur electronically).

bargaining: an activity in which a single buyer and a single seller negotiate the terms of their exchange

Finally, in markets with **bargaining**, a *single* buyer and a *single* seller negotiate the price of an item, for which no definitive market value has been established. Residential real estate, for example, is generally sold by using such negotiated agreements, as are used cars. (Sometimes there is also a posted price, but both parties understand that it is merely a starting point for negotiation.)

Salaries of high-level managers, professionals, and unionized employees—and, notably, of sports and entertainment stars—are commonly set by bargaining. The presence of *potential* other buyers and sellers, however, is obviously important in determining the relative bargaining strength of the two parties. A seller who knows that he can easily find other eager buyers, for example, will quickly walk away from an unfavorable deal. A seller with fewer options will have less ability to hold out for good terms.

Discussion Questions

1. Reviewing the different types of markets outlined in this section, think about whether you have ever directly participated in a market of each type. If so, describe specific instances.
2. The Internet has opened up a whole new set of markets for everything from antiques to airplane tickets. Pool your knowledge with that of others in the class, and, for the types of markets listed in this section, think of as many examples as possible that are online.

4. ADVANTAGES AND LIMITATIONS OF MARKETS

Earlier in this chapter, we talked about the strengths and weaknesses of each of the three economic spheres—core, public purpose, and business. As we conclude this chapter with a discussion of the advantages and limitations of markets, it will be evident that these topics overlap, especially the strengths and weaknesses of the business sphere. The reason for this is obvious: The business sphere operates entirely through markets. But how does this differ from the core sphere, from which are drawn the people who are hired to work in businesses and which must purchase goods and services to serve the needs and wants of families, households, and communities? Or, indeed, from the public purpose sphere, which also hires workers through labor markets and purchases goods and services through other markets?

The essential characteristic that is common to businesses and to markets is the dominant role of the profit motive—as distinct from the motives of the other two spheres. We noted in the earlier discussion that this is not the *only* motive for businesses; however, in individual companies, as in the market as a whole, this motive affects many decisions and outcomes. Let us review the more and less desirable results of this fact.

The many advantages of markets as a way to conduct economic activities include how they allow a steady flow of information, in terms of prices and volumes of sales, that encourages producers to respond flexibly to consumer desires. Profits provide feedback to sellers about whether resources are being transformed in ways that individuals are willing (and able) to pay for. Markets also give people a considerable amount of freedom in deciding which activities to engage in, and they encourage some beneficial forms of innovation and social cooperation.

An important drawback of markets is that they contain no inherent corrections for a tendency toward excessive concentration of economic power. They also cannot on their own address an inequitable distribution of resources, the dependency needs of people with little to offer in the market, or the provision of public goods. For all these reasons, market allocations may not be fair or even efficient.

At the social level, many people have expressed concern about the loss of certain community values when pitted against the individualism that is at the heart of modern markets. Individualism can be a liberating force, especially when it releases less powerful groups in society from traditional relations of subservience. At the same time, individualism has caused a weakening of family ties, creating social, economic, and moral challenges for modern societies. One response to these challenges is for formal institutions and paid labor to play many roles previously performed by families, especially such traditional roles of women as raising children and caring for the sick and the elderly. In some cases, these shifts are liberating, but in others they can cause psychic or financial impoverishment.

Another serious concern is environmental degradation. Like many types of businesses, markets do not do well, on their own, in protecting the environment because the costs of environmental damage are generally external to market transactions—as we noted when talking about the business sphere. But concerns about markets, or about a market system of economic organization, are on quite a different level from concerns about individual businesses. People may agitate, sometimes successfully, about the environmental impact of an individual firm; it is harder to know how we, as individual citizens, should respond to the suggestion made by many ecologists—that the current scale of human economic activity is unsustainable. One measure of our impact on the environment, called our "ecological footprint," suggests that we are using natural resources and emitting wastes at a rate that would require 1.5 planet earths, thus exceeding the capacity of the one earth that we have.[5] Also, the vast majority of scientists contend that global climate change poses a severe threat not only to natural systems but also to human economies, as we discuss in Chapter 13.

In many cases, markets work well as long as the appropriate social institutions are operating smoothly; if families and schools are bringing up children with a strong ethic of responsibility, and governments are creating laws and regulations that represent the long-run interests of the citizens, markets will not be dominated by corrupt or immediately destructive business practices. In other situations, for markets to provide a reasonable basis for conducting economic activity, they must be accompanied by appropriate government involvement in the form of taxes, regulations, and other policies to increase efficiency or promote equity. However, as Albert Einstein is said to have observed, you cannot solve the problem with a whole system from within the system. Sometimes purely, or largely, nonmarket solutions must be found for problems that embrace the entire market.

Many of these knotty issues are taken up throughout this text. In order to understand them, we need to develop a deeper understanding of how markets actually operate. We begin that task in Chapter 3.

Discussion Questions

1. On a sheet of paper, draw two columns. In one column, list some historical and contemporary advantages of market exchanges, and in the other, list some disadvantages. Can you give examples beyond those listed in the text?
2. "Indeed, it has been said that democracy is the worst form of government," said British Prime Minister Winston Churchill (1874–1965), "except all those other forms that have been tried from time to time." Some people make the same claim about more market-oriented forms of economic systems. What do they mean? Do you agree or disagree?

REVIEW QUESTIONS

1. What are some major characteristics of the core sphere?
2. What are some major characteristics of the public purpose sphere?
3. Why do businesses find it difficult to supply "public goods"?
4. What are some major characteristics of the business sphere?
5. Give three different meanings of the term "market."
6. Describe four main categories of institutional requirements for markets.
7. Give several examples of ways in which trust can be established.
8. Give several examples of the infrastructure necessary for markets to function.
9. List eight different types of markets in terms of what is sold.
10. List three major types of markets in terms of how prices are set.

EXERCISES

1. Give an example of each of the following:
   a. A retail market
   b. A commodity market
   c. A resale market
   d. A financial market
   e. An underground market
   f. An auction market
   g. A market with bargaining
2. Imagine trying to run a contemporary market economy without each of the following. What problems do you think would arise? What might people have to do to get around the lack of each one?
   a. Money
   b. The expectation that most people will not cheat
   c. An organized way of keeping people from adulterating foods or selling medicines that do not work
   d. A system of roads, canals, or railways
   e. Phone and computer connections
   f. An expectation that individuals will take the initiative in decision making

3. Match each concept in Column A with an example in Column B.

Column A	Column B
a. Explicit contract	1. Failure to account for environmental externalities
b. A core sphere activity	2. A signed lease for an apartment
c. Implicit contract	3. An auction in which prices start high and go lower
d. A public purpose sphere activity	4. The expectation that roommates will contribute to rent
e. A drawback of markets	5. Police services
f. Dutch auction	6. An auction in which the price is bid up
g. Open auction	7. Home care for the elderly
h. Double auction	8. An auction in which both buyers and sellers state prices

NOTES

1. Miranda Vreel, "Cooking, Caring, and Volunteering: Unpaid Work Around the World," OECD Social Employment and Migration Working Papers, No. 116, 2011.

2. Ibid., p. 30.

3. Katie L. Roeger, Amy S. Blackwood, and Sarah L. Pettijohn, *The Nonprofit Almanac 2012* (Washington, D.C.: Urban Institute Press, 2012); U.S. Census Bureau, *The Statistical Abstract of the United States, 2012* (Washington, DC: GPO, 2011).

4. www.bea.gov/scb/account_articles/national/0398niw/maintext.htm.

5. Based on data from the Global Footprint Network, www.footprintnetwork.org/en/index.php/GFN/page/world_footprint/.

Basic Economic Analysis

3 Supply and Demand

Prices are among the things considered central to any economy. Many people in the United States have been painfully affected by changes in housing prices, as the median price of a new house increased from about $170,000 in 2000 to about $250,000 in 2007, then fell to less than $220,000 at the bottom of the housing bust in 2009—and is now on the rise again, signaling, for many, the beginning of the end of the recent Great Recession (see Box 3.1).

To give a more relevant example for most students, textbook prices have risen over the past three decades, from an average of about $25 for an introductory economics textbook to an average of more than $200 in 2012. In other parts of the world, corn tortilla prices in Mexico doubled over several months in 2006–7, leading to mass protests. Between 2000 and 2002, coffee prices were cut in half, bringing hardship to many coffee growers—since 2005 they have rebounded and in 2012 were higher than in 2000.

Closely related to *prices,* as variables of economic interest, are *quantities* of things that are bought and sold in markets. When people dramatically decrease their purchases of goods and services, the businesses that had hoped to sell those things suffer—and so do the people working for those businesses, as falling sales result in lay-offs and reduced work hours. The U.S. automobile industry went through some miserable years in 2008–9, when employment fell from more than 1 million to only 650,000. China, in contrast, has seen the quantity of new automobile sales increasing from only about 2 million per year in 2000 to more than 20 million in 2012.

To understand fluctuations in prices, and in the quantities of goods and services sold, it is necessary to understand the basics of market functioning. This chapter introduces the famous relationships between supply and demand, which go a long way toward explaining the workings of markets.

The basic concept, as you will see, is quite simple: In general, sellers (on the "supply" side) will want to supply more of what they sell if they can get higher prices, while on the "demand" side, buyers will generally be willing to buy more when prices are lower. Sellers and buyers thus want to see prices move in opposite ways. Some sort of balance, or equilibrium, has to be established between supply and demand.

demand: the willingness and ability of purchasers to buy goods or services

supply: the willingness of producers and merchandisers to provide goods and services

Note that as we continue to discuss this supply/demand relationship we use the term **demand** to indicate the willingness and ability of purchasers to buy goods and services, while **supply** means the willingness of producers to produce, and merchandisers to sell, goods and services.

1. Introduction to the Microeconomic Market Model

In this chapter, we present the basic microeconomic model of how markets operate and adjust. This model forms the foundation for much of our discussion for the remainder of the book, as we extended it (in the next two chapters) and apply it to different types of markets (in later chapters). The basic microeconomic market model is relatively simple,

BOX 3.1   RECOVERY IN THE HOUSING MARKET

The housing market is considered an important indicator of the overall economy. In the wake of the Great Recession, the average house price in the United States fell by about one-third between 2006 and 2011. Finally, in 2012 the housing market began to show signs of recovery. By the end of 2012 prices were rising at an annual rate of over 7 percent.

The rising prices are a function of both supply and demand factors. The number of homes sold nationally in 2012 was up by about 30 percent compared to the previous year. At the same time, the supply of homes for sale reached its lowest level since 2005.

The increase in house prices varied significantly across regions of the country. The biggest gains were found in areas hit the hardest when the housing bubble burst in 2007. Prices increased by 23 percent in Phoenix, 14 percent in Detroit, 13 percent in Las Vegas, and 10 percent in Miami. Of the 20 major metropolitan markets, only New York City saw further declines in house prices in 2012.

The reasons housing prices have increased recently include an improvement in the overall economy, lower unemployment rates, very low mortgage rates, and the tight supply. Richard Green of the USC Lusk Center for Real Estate, said the recovery in housing prices hasn't been even across all the different price segments. He said the upper end of the market has done well as wealthier families' earnings have recovered and foreign buyers have come into the market. The lower end of the market has recovered due to purchases by investors looking for bargains.

"It's the middle market that needs help—particularly in the form of higher income—if it is going to have a sustained recovery," Green said.

Source: Chris Isidore, "Housing Recovery Gains Strength," CNN Money, February 26, 2013.

---

and, therefore, like all simple models, it inevitably misses many of the subtleties of what really happens in the world. As we go on to examine applications of the supply/demand model throughout this book, you will have plenty of opportunities to become an intelligent critic of basic economic theory, noticing when the model does and does not explain or predict events. First, however, it is necessary to go into considerable detail about how the simple model works.

Our model considers two "market outcomes":

market price: the prevailing price for a specific good or service at a particular time in a given market

- **Market price:** the prevailing price for a specific good or service at a particular time in a given market. In our basic model, we assume that the good or service is narrowly defined such that we can speak of "the" current price, without any variation. For example, we could say that the market price for a can of soda on campus is $1.00. In this case, we have defined "the market" as "the market for cans of soda on campus." Although this price can change over time, it does not vary at any single point in time. Of course, in reality, there may be more than one place to buy soda on campus, and different places may charge different prices. We consider the impact of competition in a market in later chapters.

market quantity sold: the number of "units" of a specific good or service sold in a given market during a particular period

- **Market quantity sold:** the number of "units" of a specific good or service sold in a given market during a particular period. In the example above, "units" are cans of soda. Other markets may measure quantity sold in terms of "tons of wheat," "number of haircuts," or "gallons of gasoline." Note that we also need to define a particular time frame and location in our analysis. So we would define the market quantity as, say, "number of cans of soda sold on campus per week." Again, market quantities can vary over time, but we assume that market activity is constant within each time unit. So by defining the market quantity as "number of cans of soda sold on campus per week," we are not concerned about variation in quantity on a daily basis.

The basic microeconomic model involves the interaction of two economic actors, buyers (or consumers) and sellers (or producers and merchandisers). We can think of consumers as individuals, households, or even businesses buying supplies or raw inputs. Sellers are normally thought of as businesses, but this is not always the case. For example, the "sellers" in labor markets are individuals offering their labor services.

Another important feature of our microeconomic model is that both buyers and sellers are acting voluntarily. We assume that potential buyers are acting to enhance their own well-being. Thus you may be willing to voluntarily trade $1 for a can of soda because you believe that the transaction enhances your well-being. We assume that potential sellers are also acting to enhance their well-being, primarily by earning profits. However, sellers may act on the basis of other motivations, even at the expense of lower profits, such as a desire to conduct business with suppliers that treat their workers with certain ethical standards.

We now consider in more detail the behavior of buyers and sellers in markets. Specifically, we look at the relationship between market prices and quantities from each perspective, first from the point of view of sellers and then from the consumer perspective. After that, we see what happens when buyers and sellers interact in markets.

2. THE THEORY OF SUPPLY

About 40 percent of college students drink coffee on a daily basis. With more than 13,000 Starbucks locations in the United States, plus 13,000 McDonald's locations, 7,000 Dunkin' Donuts stores, and numerous other coffee shops and restaurants, there is no shortage of places to buy coffee. We introduce the microeconomic market model by considering how it applies to coffee markets. Coffee is a good example to use because, as you will see as we go through the chapter, we can use it to illustrate several important features about how markets operate.

First, let's define what we mean by "the coffee market" in this example. Let's assume we are looking at the market for a basic cup of regular coffee in the vicinity of your college campus. Although there may be several different locations on and around campus to buy coffee, for simplicity we also assume that all these businesses offer the same basic regular cup of coffee and sell it at the prevailing market price. Of course, in reality each business could set its own price for coffee, but for now we keep our model as simple as possible. Let's define the period of our analysis as a week. We consider how the market changes week to week, but within each week the price does not vary.

At the beginning of each week, each coffee business must make a decision about how much coffee it will offer to sell in the coming week—buying the appropriate quantity of coffee supplies, establishing employee work schedules, and so on. How would we expect changes in the prevailing market price of a cup of coffee to influence the quantity of coffee offered for sale each week? In particular, if the market price rises, would we expect more coffee, or less coffee, to be offered for sale? Or conversely, if market prices are falling, how would we expect the quantity offered for sale to change?

positive (or direct) relationship: the relationship between two variables when an increase in one is associated with an increase in the other variable

It is important to realize that we are asking this question, for now, only from the perspective of coffee sellers. Coffee sellers are most likely either already selling other products, such as hot chocolate, doughnuts, or sandwiches, or could sell these other products if they thought switching would offer more profit than selling coffee. So if coffee prices are rising, it seems reasonable that these sellers will want to sell *more* coffee relative to selling other items. Conversely, if coffee prices are falling, sellers will be less interested in selling coffee and some may decide to stop selling coffee altogether.

individual supply: the supply of one particular seller

Thus common sense tells us that sellers should offer more coffee when prices are relatively high and less coffee when prices are relatively low. We call the relationship between the market price and the quantity supplied a **positive (or direct) relationship**—increases in the value of one variable (price) tend to be associated with increases in the value of another variable (the quantity supplied).

market (or aggregate) supply: the supply from all sellers in a particular market

Note that we can talk about the quantity supplied at the individual level or the market level. The **individual supply** is the quantity supplied by one particular seller. The **market (or aggregate) supply** is the quantity supplied by all sellers in the market.

2.1 THE SUPPLY SCHEDULE AND SUPPLY CURVE

supply schedule:
a table showing the relationship between price and quantity supplied

We have been talking about the relationship between price and the quantity of coffee supplied only in abstract terms so far. Now let's suppose that we have studied the coffee market around campus by speaking with different coffee sellers and can estimate how the quantity supplied will vary with price. We can present our results as shown in Table 3.1. We call a table representing the relationship between price and the quantity supplied a **supply schedule**. In the case of coffee, we have the supply schedule for a physical good. But we can also think of a supply schedule for a marketed service, such as housecleaning, babysitting, or a college education.

As we expect, the quantity of coffee supplied increases with higher prices. For example, at a price of $0.80 per cup, only 400 cups would be supplied per week. But if the price rises to $1.00 per cup, then 600 cups would be supplied. Note that Table 3.1 shows only the cups supplied at $0.10 increments. We can interpolate to estimate, for example, that 550 cups would be supplied at a price of $0.95 per cup.* The supply schedule in Table 3.1 shows the market supply, which is an aggregation of the individual supply schedules in the local coffee market.

supply curve: a curve indicating the quantities that sellers are willing to supply at various prices

From a supply schedule, we can graph a **supply curve**, as shown in Figure 3.1. This is simply the same relationship between price and quantity supplied in graphical form. It is standard in economics to place the quantity on the horizontal axis (also called the *x*-axis) and the price on the vertical axis (also called the *y*-axis). We see, for example, that at a price of $1.00 per cup, coffee sellers are willing to supply 600 cups of coffee per week.

Note that the supply curve in Figure 3.1 slopes upward. This is another illustration of a positive relationship—as price goes up, the quantity supplied also goes up. (Sometimes this positive relationship between price and the quantity supplied is referred to as the "law of supply." Such a choice of words may reflect a somewhat misguided attempt to make economics

Table 3.1 **Supply Schedule for Cups of Coffee**

Price of coffee ($/cup)	0.70	0.80	0.90	1.00	1.10	1.20	1.30	1.40	1.50	1.60
Cups of coffee supplied per week	300	400	500	600	700	800	900	1,000	1,100	1,200

Figure 3.1 **Supply Curve for Cups of Coffee**

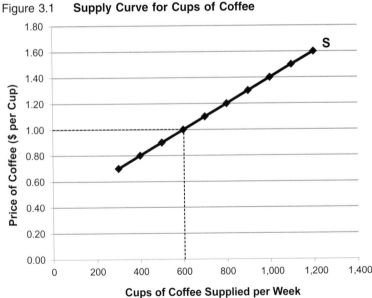

A supply curve shows the same information as the supply schedule. At higher prices, more cups of coffee are offered for sale.

___
* "Interpolate" means to estimate a relationship between known data points.

sound more scientific. As we see in later chapters, especially the one about labor, this "law" does not hold everywhere.)

We now need to introduce an important distinction in market analysis. When price changes, we say that we move *along* a supply curve. So if the price increased from $0.80 to $1.00 per cup, we would move up from a quantity supplied of 400 cups to 600 cups. Another term for movement along a supply curve is a **change in the quantity supplied**. We *would not* say that this is a "change in supply" because that occurs when the entire supply curve shifts—a topic that we address in the next section.

Test yourself by answering this question with reference to Table 3.1 or Figure 3.1: By how much does the *quantity supplied* change when the price changes from $1.20 to $1.40 per cup?*

It is very important when going through this example to imagine that the price is the *only* thing changing. Economists sometimes use the Latin term **ceteris paribus** as shorthand for "all else constant" or "other things equal." This is a basic research technique used in other disciplines as well. For example, when medical researchers try to determine the effect of diet *alone* on a disease, they usually choose as research subjects people whose sex, age, and level of exercise ("all else") are nearly identical ("constant"). If we were to try to estimate a real-world supply curve, we would ideally try to hold everything else in the market constant while varying just the price and observe how the quantity supplied changes. Of course, this cannot be done in the real world, and economists normally have to rely on statistical techniques to try to isolate the effect of price alone. We discuss the issue of estimating actual supply curves in Chapter 4.

change in the quantity supplied: movement along a supply curve in response to a price change

ceteris paribus: a Latin phrase that means "other things equal" or "all else constant"

2.2 CHANGES IN SUPPLY

change in supply: a shift of the entire supply curve, in response to something changing other than price

In contrast to a "change in quantity supplied," which is a response to a price change, we say that there has been a **change in supply** when something else changes and the whole supply curve shifts.

Why might the whole curve shift? In our coffee example, one potential factor that could shift the supply curve is a change in the number of coffee sellers. Starbucks, for example, was founded in 1971 by two college professors and a writer, in Seattle, Washington. If a new coffee seller enters the market, then at any given price, more coffee would be supplied, as shown in Figure 3.2. The addition of a new coffee supplier shifts the entire supply curve from S_1 to S_2. So

Figure 3.2 **An Increase in Supply**

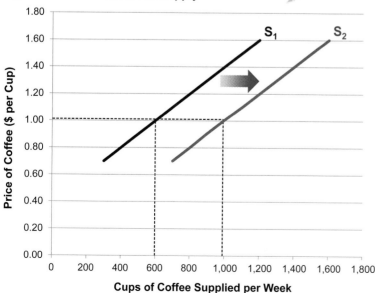

Cups of Coffee Supplied per Week

A supply curve shifts outward (to the right) when sellers decide to offer a higher quantity for sale at the same price (or charge less for a given quantity).

*The quantity supplied increases by 200 cups per week, from 800 to 1,000.

if the prevailing price of coffee was $1.00 per cup, the change in supply would result in 1,000 cups of coffee being offered for sale each week instead of 600, as shown in the graph.

We can describe this increase in supply by saying either that "supply has increased (or risen)" or that "the supply curve has shifted out." (Some students may find it confusing that a supply *increase* shifts the supply curve *down*. Always start by reading across horizontally from the price axis. Then you will notice that the shift goes out toward *higher* numbers on the quantity axis.)

2.3 NONPRICE DETERMINANTS OF SUPPLY

nonprice determinants of supply: any factor that affects the quantity supplied, other than the price of the good or service offered for sale

A change in the number of sellers is not the only factor that can shift the entire supply curve. We can define six potential **nonprice determinants of supply** that would shift the entire supply curve:

1. a change in the number of sellers
2. a change in the technology of production
3. a change in input prices
4. a change in seller expectations about the future
5. a change in the prices of related goods and services
6. a change in the physical supply of a natural resource

Consider, for example, a change in the technology used to make coffee that allows coffee to be produced at lower cost. A decrease in production costs suggests that sellers may be willing to accept a lower price for coffee. In Figure 3.2, we see that with the original supply curve at S_1, sellers would be willing to supply 1,000 cups of coffee at a price of $1.40. Now suppose a decrease in production costs means that sellers would be willing to supply 1,000 cups of coffee at a price of only $1.00 per cup. This technological change would also shift the supply curve to S_2 in Figure 3.2. (Note that in this case it may be easier to think of the supply curve shifting downward because sellers are willing to accept a lower price for their product. But we would still say that "supply has increased" or that "the supply curve has shifted outward.")

A change in input prices (nonprice determinant #3 in our list) includes the price of coffee beans, labor, milk, sugar, coffee cups, electricity, rent, and any other resource that is an input into the coffee production process. Let's suppose that the price of coffee beans increases, which actually occurred in 2010–11 as a result of extreme heat in Brazil and Colombia (two of the top three coffee-producing countries), causing the price of coffee beans to double. In this case, sellers would need to charge higher prices per cup in order to cover the increase in their input costs. We see this in Figure 3.3. With the original supply curve, S_1, sellers were willing to offer 600 cups of coffee at a price of $1.00 per cup. With higher coffee bean prices, sellers now require a price of $1.40 per cup in order to supply 600 cups per week. We would refer to this shift as a "decrease in supply" or that "the supply curve has shifted back."

The effect of seller expectations about the future (nonprice determinant #4) can be tricky. If a coffee seller expects that coffee bean prices will increase soon (perhaps he or she has been following the news on weather conditions in South America), he or she might hold back some coffee bean inventory for now, to sell later when coffee prices increase. However, if he or she hears that a new technology has been adopted by other coffee sellers that lowers production costs, he or she might be eager to sell as much coffee as possible now before the price is driven down.

Suppose that a coffee seller notices that many people are switching from coffee to tea and are willing to pay high prices for gourmet teas. He or she may decide to supply more tea and less coffee. In this case, the price of a related good (nonprice determinant #5) has induced the firm to reduce its output of coffee, causing a decrease in the supply of coffee similar to what is shown in Figure 3.3.

Figure 3.3   **A Decrease in Supply**

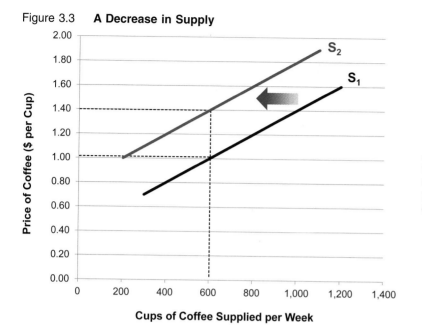

A supply curve shifts backward (to the left) when sellers decide to offer a lower quantity for sale at the same price (or charge more for a given quantity).

Cups of Coffee Supplied per Week

Finally, in markets for natural resources such as agricultural crops, oil, or minerals, the supply curve may shift as a result of physical supply factors like weather conditions or absolute availability. So a drought that decreases crop yields would directly cause a reduction in supply. Supplies of recoverable oil are ultimately limited and may someday lead to reductions in supply. Note that this nonprice determinant differs from nonprice determinant #3 in that supplies are directly reduced as a result of natural factors, rather than indirectly through a change in input prices.

Discussion Questions

1. Verbally explain the difference between a change in "quantity supplied" and a change in supply. Considering the supply side of the market for lawn-mowing services, what kind of change (*increase* or *decrease,* in *quantity supplied* or *supply*) would each of the following events cause?
    a. There is a rise in the price of gasoline used to run power mowers.
    b. There is a rise in the going price for lawn-mowing services.
    c. More people decide to offer to mow lawns.
    d. A new lawn mower is invented that is cheap and makes it possible to mow lawns at a lower cost.
2. Sketch a supply curve graph illustrating a student's willingness to sell his textbooks from all his classes right now. Assume that the student will receive offers of this sort: "I'll give you [a fixed number of dollars] apiece for all the books you want to sell." Carefully label the vertical and horizontal axes. Suppose that, at an original offer of $30 per book, the student will be willing to sell three books, because he knows he can replace these three for less than $30 each at a local bookstore. Mark this point on your first graph. Assume further that at $40 he would be willing to sell four books, at $50 he would supply five books, and so on. Now, on separate graphs labeled (a), (b), and (c), show this line and his offer at $30 and the precise new *point* or an approximate new *curve* that illustrates each of the following changes in conditions. Consider them separately, returning to the condition of no Internet resources in part (c).
    a. He is offered $70 per book instead of $30.
    b. He discovers that the textbook materials for many of his classes are available free on the Internet.
    c. The local bookstore raises its prices substantially.

3. THE THEORY OF DEMAND

We now turn to the coffee market from the perspective of coffee buyers. Unlike sellers, consumers find low prices attractive. So it seems reasonable to expect that people will want to purchase more cups of coffee per week when prices are lower. We now work through the theory of demand using our coffee example. While the consumers in this example are individuals, realize that demand can also arise from, for example, businesses looking to purchase raw materials or government agencies looking to hire employees.

3.1 THE DEMAND SCHEDULE AND DEMAND CURVE

demand schedule: a table showing the relationship between price and the quantity demanded

demand curve: a curve indicating the quantities that buyers are willing to purchase at various prices

Just as with supply, we can present a **demand schedule** showing the relationship between price and the quantity demanded. In Table 3.2, we see that as the prevailing price of a cup of coffee goes up, the quantity demanded goes down.

From the demand schedule, we can graph a **demand curve**, as shown in Figure 3.4, which shows the quantities that buyers are willing to purchase at various prices. So we see, for example, that at a price of $1.40 per cup, consumers would demand 600 cups of coffee per week.

It is important to keep in mind that someone's willingness to buy a good or service is not only a function of his preferences but also of his income or wealth. Economists sometimes use the term "effective demand" to stress that they are talking about demand backed up by enough money to pay the prevailing price. However, you should remember that virtually anywhere that the economic term "demand" is used, it refers to this specific meaning, that is, both a willingness *and* an ability to pay.

Some people who might want to buy a cup of coffee every day may decide not to because they do not believe that they can afford it, and decide instead to make their own coffee. Although the inability of people to pay for daily cups of coffee at a coffee shop may not be a cause for public concern, the inability of people to pay for things such as health care, sufficient nutrition, or a college

Table 3.2   Demand Schedule for Cups of Coffee

Price of coffee ($/cup)	0.20	0.50	0.80	1.10	1.40	1.70	2.00	2.30
Cups of coffee demanded per week	1,000	900	800	700	600	500	400	300

Figure 3.4   Demand Curve for Cups of Coffee

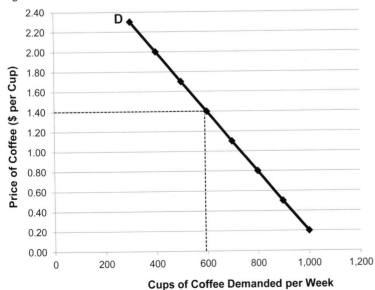

A demand curve shows the same information as the demand schedule. At higher prices, fewer cups of coffee are demanded.

negative (or inverse) relationship: the relationship between two variables if an increase in one is associated with a decrease in the other variable

education may create sufficient motivation for government involvement. Markets do not, by their nature, take into account wants or needs that are not backed up by the ability to pay.

Note that the demand curve in Figure 3.4 slopes downward. Again, this should be common sense that, generally, the higher the price of a good, the fewer that people will want to buy. If a book is very expensive, you might look for it in the library rather than buying it. If an accounting firm raises its rates, some of its clients may consider hiring a different accountant. Price and quantity have a **negative (or inverse) relationship** along a demand curve. That is, when price rises, the quantity demanded falls. (This is sometimes called the "law of demand." Like the "law of supply," it does not always hold. Sometimes, for example, a smart marketer will find that buyers will want more of a good if it is sold as a "prestige" good at a high price.)

market (or aggregate) demand: the demand from all buyers in a particular market

individual demand: the demand of one particular buyer

The curve that we have drawn is the entire **market (or aggregate) demand** curve in our local market for coffee. As was the case with supply, the market demand is obtained by aggregating the **individual demand** of each consumer in the market.

Again we need to differentiate between movement *along* a demand curve and a *shifting* demand curve. Movement along a demand curve is always referred to as a **change in the quantity demanded**. So if the prevailing price of coffee rises from $1.40 per cup to $1.70, we would say that the quantity demanded declines from 600 cups to 500 cups per week.

change in the quantity demanded: movement along a demand curve in response to a price change

Check yourself by answering this question with reference to Table 3.2 or Figure 3.4: By how much does the "quantity demanded" change when the price changes from $1.10 to $0.50 per cup?*

3.2 CHANGES IN DEMAND

change in demand: a shift of the entire demand curve in response to something changing other than price

As with supply, we distinguish between a change in "quantity demanded" and a **change in demand**. When there is a change in demand, the whole demand curve shifts due to a change in some factor other than a change in price.

Why might the whole demand curve shift? Suppose that our demand curve in Figure 3.4 is based on buying patterns at the beginning of a semester. During final exams, we might expect the overall demand for coffee to increase. Such a change in demand is presented in Figure 3.5. Our initial demand curve is D_1, with a quantity demanded of 600 cups per week when price is

Figure 3.5   **An Increase in Demand**

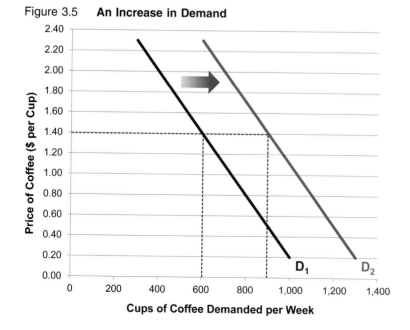

A demand curve shifts outward (to the right) when a higher quantity is demanded at the same price (or people are willing to pay more for a given quantity).

*The quantity demanded increases from 700 cups to 900 cups per week.

$1.40 per cup. But during the final exam period, the demand curve shifts to D_2, with a quantity demanded of 900 cups per week at the same price of $1.40. In this case, we would say that "demand has risen (or increased)" or that "the demand curve has shifted out." (Because of the curve's negative slope, in this case shifting out also means shifting up, but again the normal approach in economics is to refer to curves moving horizontally rather than vertically.)

3.3 NONPRICE DETERMINANTS OF DEMAND

nonprice determinants of demand: any factor that affects the quantity demanded, other than the price of the good or service being demanded

We can identify five **nonprice determinants of demand** that can shift the entire demand curve:

1. changes in buyers' tastes and preferences
2. changes in buyers' income and other assets
3. changes in the prices of related goods and services
4. changes in buyers' expectations about the future
5. a change in the number of buyers in the market

Suppose that a news story comes out that says drinking more than one cup of coffee per day is harmful to your health. This could lead to a decrease in demand as coffee drinkers decide to cut back on their consumption. Such a decrease in demand is illustrated in Figure 3.6. In this case, the demand curve shifts back (to the left) to D_2, and the quantity demanded falls from 600 to 400 per week. Marketers seek to increase demand through advertising campaigns, such as the ads for new Apple products that can lead to many consumers waiting in line to buy something the day that it becomes available.

A change in buyers' income can shift market demand curves. For example, the 2007–9 recession in the United States reduced income for many households and thus their demand for various products such as restaurant meals and new automobiles.

We can define two types of "related" goods and services (nonprice determinant #3). First, there exist **substitute goods** for most market products, that is, a good that can be used in place of another good. For coffee, substitutes include tea and caffeinated energy drinks. If the price of tea were to increase significantly, say as a result of poor weather conditions in tea-exporting countries such as Sri Lanka and India, we would expect the demand for coffee to

substitute good: a good that can be used in place of another good

Figure 3.6　**A Decrease in Demand**

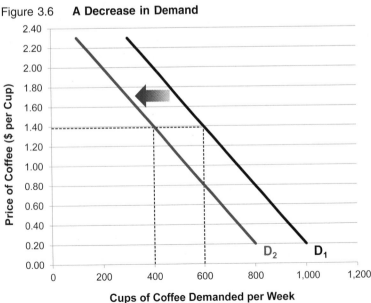

A demand curve shifts backward (to the left) when a lower quantity is demanded at the same price (or people are willing to pay less for a given quantity).

increase. Meanwhile, if the price of tea were to fall, we would expect the demand for coffee to decrease as some coffee drinkers switch to tea instead.

The other type of related goods are **complementary goods**, or goods that tend to be used along with other goods. Examples of complementary goods for coffee include cream and doughnuts. If someone frequently purchases coffee along with a doughnut, a significant increase in doughnut prices may cause that person to reduce his demand for coffee.

complementary good: a good that is used along with another good

Like suppliers, buyers can adjust their behavior based on future expectations (nonprice determinant #4). If you expect several days of late-night studying for final exams in several weeks, you might temporarily reduce your demand for coffee so that it will have a greater effect on you when you really need it to study.*

The last nonprice determinant of demand is the number of potential buyers in the market. Obviously, the demand for coffee will shift depending on whether we are looking at the summer months when many students are away or the normal school months.

Discussion Questions

1. Explain verbally why the demand curve slopes downward.
2. Verbally explain the difference between a change in "quantity demanded" and a change in demand. Considering the demand side of the market for lawn-mowing services, what kind of change (*increase* or *decrease,* in *quantity demanded* or *demand*) would each of the following events cause?
   a. A new office park, surrounded by several acres of lawn, is built.
   b. A drought is declared, and lawn watering is banned.
   c. The going price for lawn-mowing services rises.
   d. A more natural, wild yard becomes the "in" thing, as people grow concerned about the effects of fertilizers and pesticides on the environment.

4. THE THEORY OF MARKET ADJUSTMENT

Now that we have considered sellers and buyers separately, it is time to bring them together. We will see how the interaction of supply and demand can determine what the price of coffee will be and how much coffee will be sold. Remember that with our relatively simple model, we assume that all coffee in our market will sell for the same price. But what will that price be?

4.1 SURPLUS, SHORTAGE, AND EQUILIBRIUM

surplus: a situation in which the quantity that sellers are prepared to sell at a particular price exceeds the quantity that buyers are willing to buy at that price

Using the original supply and demand curves, reproduced here in Figure 3.7, we can look for the answer. Let's suppose, for whatever reason, that the price of coffee is initially $1.40 per cup. As we see in Figure 3.7, at this relatively high price, coffee sellers are prepared to sell 1,000 cups of coffee per week, but buyers are interested in buying only 600 cups. (You can check these numbers in Tables 3.1. and 3.2.) Economists call a situation in which the quantity supplied is greater than the quantity demanded a **surplus**. This is illustrated in the upper part of Figure 3.7, where there is a surplus, or excess supply, of 400 cups of coffee.

If a market is in a situation of surplus, what would we expect to happen? Imagine that at the start of the week, coffee sellers are equipped to sell 1,000 cups of coffee. At the end of the week, they find that they have sold only 600 cups, and they have a large leftover inventory of coffee supplies. Coffee sellers realize that they need to attract more customers, so they will respond to the surplus by lowering their price. Assuming

---

*There is surprisingly little research on whether the consumption of caffeine actually is associated with improved academic performance. It is clear, however, that excessive use of caffeine is associated with several negative health effects including increased blood pressure, seizures, and headaches.

Figure 3.7   **The Market Adjustment Process**

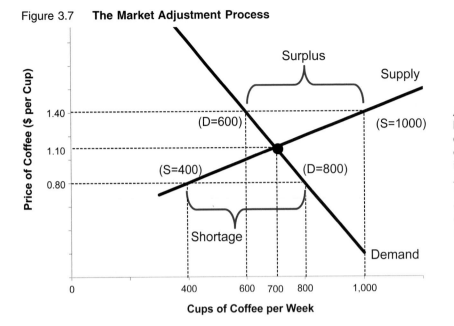

At a price of $1.40 per cup, we have a situation of surplus (the quantity supplied exceeds the quantity demanded), and there is downward pressure on price. At a price of $0.80 per cup we have a situation of shortage (the quantity demanded exceeds the quantity supplied), and there is upward pressure on price.

that all sellers respond equally (which is unlikely in the real world, but it simplifies our model at this point), the prevailing price will be somewhat lower the next week. We do not necessarily know how much lower it will be, but there will be downward pressure on prices whenever there is a surplus.*

Let's say that the next week the prevailing price is lowered from $1.40 to $1.30. Looking at Figure 3.7, we see that there would still be a surplus (the quantity supplied exceeds the quantity demanded), but the surplus would be a little smaller. Thus there would still be downward pressure on prices as long as a surplus existed.

Now let's consider the opposite situation. Assume that the initial price of coffee is relatively low, at $0.80 per cup. As shown in Figure 3.7, at this price sellers are prepared to sell only 400 cups per week while the quantity demanded is 800 cups. A situation in which the quantity demanded exceeds the quantity supplied is referred to as a **shortage**.

shortage: a situation in which the quantity demanded at a particular price exceeds the quantity that sellers are willing to supply

What would we expect to happen in a market with a shortage? Before we even get to the end of the week, the suppliers' inventory will be depleted and they will end up turning away customers who want to buy coffee. Realizing that there is excess demand for coffee, sellers will conclude that they can probably charge a little more for coffee and still have a sufficient number of customers. So whenever there is a situation of shortage, there will be upward pressure on prices.**

So if the prevailing price is "too high" (a surplus), there will be downward pressure on prices, and if the price is "too low" (a shortage), there will be upward pressure on prices. Where will prices be "just right"? Starting from either a surplus or shortage, we see in Figure 3.8 that market adjustments will push the price toward $1.10 per cup. At this price, the quantity demanded equals the quantity supplied at 700 cups of coffee per week. (Check Tables 3.1 and 3.2 to confirm this.)

market equilibrium: a situation in which the quantity supplied equals the quantity demanded, and thus there is no pressure for changes in price or quantity bought or sold

Economists call this a situation in which the "market clears" and a **market equilibrium** is reached. "Equilibrium" describes a situation that has reached a resting point, where there are

---

*If one particular coffee seller lowers his price in response to the surplus, pressure will be created on other sellers to lower their prices as well. Thus the most likely outcome in response to the surplus would be lower prices.

**Because there are many buyers who are willing to pay more than $0.80 for coffee, it is easy for some sellers to raise prices. So even if everyone does not raise prices immediately, the overall tendency will be toward higher prices in a situation of shortage.

Figure 3.8   **Market Equilibrium**

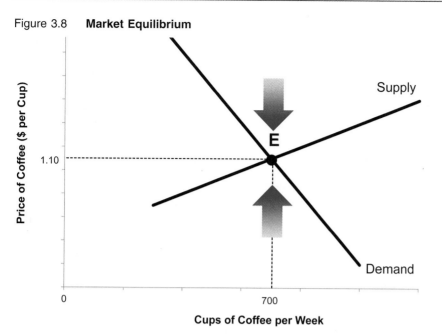

Equilibrium occurs when the quantity demanded equals the quantity supplied. At this point there is no upward or downward pressure on price.

theory of market adjustment: the theory that market forces will tend to make shortages and surpluses disappear

market disequilibrium: a situation of either shortage or surplus

no forces to acting to change it. (Economists borrowed this term from natural science.) In a market situation, equilibrium is reached when the quantity supplied is equal to the quantity demanded. The price will stop falling or rising and the quantity sold will stay constant as long as there are no other changes.

The **theory of market adjustment** says that market forces will tend to make price and quantity move toward the equilibrium point. Surpluses will lead to declines in price, and shortages will lead to rises in price. Surplus and shortage are both instances of **market disequilibrium**. Only at the equilibrium price and quantity is there no tendency to change. In this example, the equilibrium price is $1.10 per cup and the equilibrium quantity is 700 cups per week.

4.2 MARKET FORCES AND OTHER FORCES

We know that market forces will tend to push the price of coffee toward the equilibrium price, but how long will this adjustment process take? Just a couple of weeks, a month, maybe longer? We do not know, as our simple model doesn't address this issue.* In the real world, some markets have adjustment processes that lead rapidly to equilibrium. In highly organized stock markets and other auction-like markets, thousands of trades may take place every minute, as buyers and sellers find each other and quickly negotiate a price. Such a market can probably be thought of as in equilibrium, or moving quickly toward equilibrium, nearly all the time. (When we look at stock markets, it is evident that the price/quantity combinations that constitute equilibrium now may be quite different from the conditions for equilibrium tomorrow—or even 15 minutes from now.)

In other markets, however, adjustment to equilibrium may take months or years—if it happens at all. The market forces that we have just examined are not the only forces in the world. For example, hospital administrators complained for decades about a shortage of nurses. The obvious solution, from the point of view of labor supply and demand, would be for hospitals to offer higher wages, thus increasing the incentives for people to enter (and stay in) nursing careers while also reducing the quantity demanded. As in Figure 3.7, market forces would then move us from shortage to equilibrium.

---

*More advanced market models do consider the period required for adjustments.

If you study the strategies used by hospitals to combat the shortage, however, you will note that offering higher wages is rarely one of them. Instead, larger training programs, signing bonuses, and forced overtime (which reduces the quality of life for workers and the quality of patient care) have often been used to try to fill the gap. Various explanations have been suggested as to why the nursing wage is not rising to clear the market. On the demand side, hospital management may discount the importance of nurses to patient well-being, preferring to devote financial resources to high-tech medicine. On the supply side, unionizing and fighting for higher wages can be emotionally and ethically difficult for health-care personnel, because striking can mean refusing help to people in need.

More generally, the forces that can work against quick movement toward equilibrium include such human characteristics as habit or ignorance. Slow production processes and long-term contracts may also slow down or stop adjustment. A seller may keep a good at its accustomed price long after it has failed to clear, or the back orders have begun to mount up, simply because she is slow to change. A common reason for slow adjustment is a lack of information. To be sure, the corner grocer knows which products are or are not moving; increasingly, sophisticated computerized systems are feeding this information back up the supply chain, to speed up price adjustment. However, in many parts of the world, and in some industries even in industrialized countries, information is slow to get to those who make some of the essential pricing decisions. Consumers, too, often lack information or behave on the basis of habit.

Equilibrium analysis is limited by the reality of constant change in the world, and nonmarket forces may effectively combat the equilibrating tendency of market forces. Market adjustment analysis can, however, tell us what to expect from normal market forces: Most generally, disequilibrium situations create forces that tend to push prices toward an equilibrium level.

4.3 SHIFTS IN SUPPLY AND DEMAND

Our model predicts that after we reach equilibrium, the price will stay the same. In the real world, however, we observe that prices change quite frequently. For example, consider the change in housing prices in the United States over the past few decades, as noted in the introduction to this chapter. Constantly fluctuating prices are also common in fossil-fuel markets, minerals such as gold and copper, and consumer electronics. Even coffee prices have varied significantly over time.

Many price changes can be explained, and in some cases even predicted in advance, by using our microeconomic market model. We can determine how a shift in one (or both) of our curves, as a result of a change in one or more nonprice determinants, will lead to a change in the equilibrium price and quantity.

Returning to our coffee market, let's suppose that a new seller enters the market. As we discussed earlier, this is a change in a nonprice determinant of supply and will shift the supply curve out (to the right). This is shown in Figure 3.9 with the supply curve shifting from S_1 to S_2. Our initial equilibrium is point E_1 with a price of \$1.10 and a quantity of 700 cups per week. But note that with the entry of the new coffee seller shifting the supply curve to S_2, and assuming that initially price stays at \$1.10, we go from equilibrium to a situation of surplus (as shown in Figure 3.9). At a price of \$1.10 per cup, the quantity supplied exceeds the quantity demanded with the new supply curve of S_2.

Just as before, a situation of surplus creates downward pressure on prices. But realize that as sellers lower their prices, the quantity demanded increases as we move along the demand curve. As long as a surplus continues to exist, there is downward pressure on prices, leading to further movement along the demand curve. The surplus is eventually eliminated when we reach point E_2, the new equilibrium. The increase in supply has resulted in:

- a decrease in the equilibrium price
- an increase in the equilibrium quantity

Figure 3.9   **Market Adjustment to an Increase in Supply**

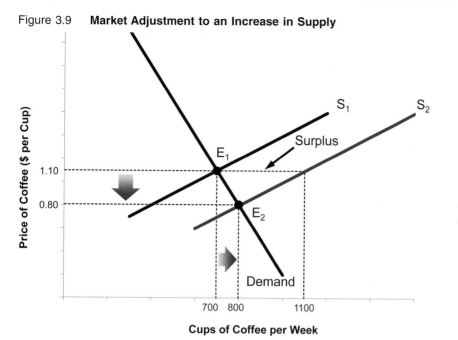

An increase in supply creates a surplus, and downward pressure on price. The new equilibrium occurs at point E_2, with a lower price and a higher quantity sold.

What if, instead, we have a decrease in supply? Suppose one coffee seller decides to stop selling coffee. In this case, the supply curve would shift to the left. The new equilibrium would result in a high price and a lower quantity sold. (Try this yourself by drawing a graph similar to Figure 3.9 but with the supply curve shifting in the opposite direction.)

Now let's consider what happens when the demand curve shifts. Suppose we have an increase in demand as a result of a large incoming freshman class. Figure 3.10 shows an increase in demand (the demand curve shifts to the right) from D_1 to D_2. This creates a temporary situation of a shortage, in which the quantity demanded exceeds the quantity supplied. Sellers perceive the shortage and respond by slightly raising prices. With the higher prices, we move along the supply curve as sellers are willing to supply more coffee.

Figure 3.10   **Market Adjustment to an Increase in Demand**

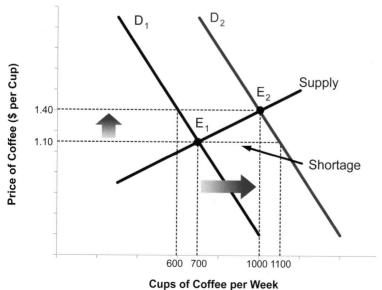

An increase in demand creates a shortage, and upward pressure on price. The new equilibrium occurs at point E_2, with a higher price and a higher quantity sold.

As long as the shortage persists, we have continued upward pressure on prices and further movement along the supply curve. The shortage is eventually eliminated when we reach point E_2, the new market-clearing equilibrium. The increase in demand has resulted in:

- an increase in the equilibrium quantity
- an increase in the equilibrium price

Note that with an increase in supply or an increase in demand, the equilibrium quantity increases. But the effect on price differs—prices rise with an increase in demand but fall with an increase in supply. This should align with your expectations even before you took this class. If people want more of a product, it makes sense that prices should rise. An increase in the availability (supply) of something should drive prices down. Our microeconomic model tells a common sense story about market adjustment, although perhaps in a somewhat complex manner.

What would we expect if demand instead decreases, say due to a news story that indicates that drinking coffee is harmful to your health? The demand curve would shift inward (to the left), and we would expect a lower equilibrium price and a lower equilibrium quantity.

Note that when the supply curve shifts, the resulting change in equilibrium price and quantity are in the *opposite* direction. But when the demand curve shifts, price and quantity change in the *same* direction. We can summarize what happens when one of the market curves shift in Table 3.3 below.

What if *both* curves shift at the same time? What if, for example, there is a concurrent increase in the number of sellers of coffee and an increase in the number of potential buyers of coffee? We analyze this situation in Figure 3.11. Supply increases from S_1 to S_2 and demand increases from D_1 to D_2. The initial equilibrium is E_1, and the new equilibrium, once the market fully adjusts, is E_2. Both shifts tend to increase equilibrium quantity (see Table 3.3), so we can unambiguously state that the overall result will be an increase in the quantity of coffee sold, as shown in Figure 3.11.

But the effect on price is more difficult to discern. Although an increase in demand tends to increase the equilibrium price, an increase in supply tends to decrease prices. Looking at Figure 3.11, we cannot tell whether the net effect is an increase or decrease in price. Although it looks as if price has stayed about the same, note that if we shifted one of the curves a little more, or a little less, the net result could be a price increase or a price decrease.

Whenever both curves shift at the same time, we can make an unambiguous statement about how one of our market variables (price or quantity) will change, but not the other. The net effect on one variable will depend on the relative magnitudes of the shifts in the curves. Table 3.4 summarizes the market results if both curves shift. You should confirm these conclusions based on your own market graphs. See Box 3.2 for a real-world application of our market model to the international coffee market.

Table 3.3 **Summary of the Market Effects of Shifts in Supply and Demand**

Market change	Effect on equilibrium price	Effect on equilibrium quantity
Increase in supply	Decrease	Increase
Decrease in supply	Increase	Decrease
Increase in demand	Increase	Increase
Decrease in demand	Decrease	Decrease

Figure 3.11   **Market Adjustment with an Increase in Both Supply and Demand**

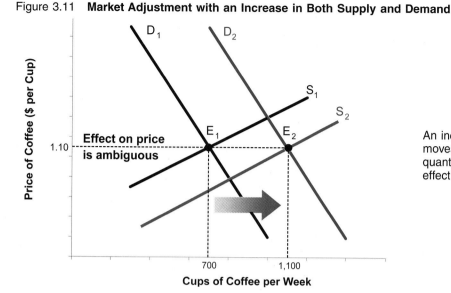

An increase in both supply and demand moves the equilibrium to point E_2. The quantity sold has clearly increased but the effect on price is ambiguous.

Table 3.4   **Summary of the Market Effects When Both Supply and Demand Shift**

Market change	Effect on equilibrium price	Effect on equilibrium quantity
Increase in supply, increase in demand	Ambiguous	Increase
Increase in supply, decrease in demand	Decrease	Ambiguous
Decrease in supply, increase in demand	Increase	Ambiguous
Decrease in demand, decrease in demand	Ambiguous	Decrease

Box 3.2   Coffee Markets in the Real World

After reaching a 14-year high in May 2011, wholesale coffee bean prices began to tumble. By July 2013 prices for arabica beans, the most-consumed coffee in the world, had fallen over 60 percent. How can our market model provide insights into changing coffee prices in the real world?

Our model suggests that falling prices can occur either due to an increase in supply or a decrease in demand, or both. According to data from the United States Department of Agriculture, global coffee supplies increased over this time period. At the same time, consumption in coffee-growing countries and coffee exports both increased. So these data suggest that the main reason prices fell so much over 2011–13 was an increase in the supply of coffee.

In the 2012/2013 growing season Brazil, the world's largest coffee producer, had a bumper crop with production up 14 percent over the previous year. Vietnam, the world's second-largest producer, has been scaling up its coffee production in recent years. Between 2010 and 2012 production there increased nearly 30 percent. Other major coffee-producing countries, including Colombia and Indonesia, also had production gains.

With coffee bean prices so low, you may wonder why in June 2013 Starbucks announced that it was *increasing* its prices. According to a Starbucks spokesman, the reasons for the price increase included higher costs for labor, raw materials, and rent. The cost of the actual coffee beans represents a minor portion of the total cost of producing a retail cup of coffee. So Starbucks raising its coffee prices can be explained by an increase in input prices, which would be modeled as a shift of their supply curve. The price increase could also reflect a response to an increase in the demand for Starbucks coffee.

Sources: U.S. Department of Agriculture, "Coffee: World Markets and Trade," Foreign Agricultural Service, June 2013; Parija Kavilanz, "Next Week You'll Pay More for a Starbucks Latte," CNN Money, June 21, 2013.

Discussion Questions

1. Think about the market for basketballs. In each of the following cases, determine which curve will shift and in which direction. Also draw a graph and describe, in words, the changes in price and quantity. (Treat each case separately.)
   a. A rise in consumers' incomes
   b. An increase in wages paid to the workers who make the basketballs
   c. A decrease in the price of basketball hoops and other basketball gear
   d. The country's becoming obsessed with soccer

2. Have you ever found yourself shut out of a class that you wanted to take because it was already full? Or has this happened to a friend of yours? Analyze this situation in terms of surplus or shortage. Are classes supplied through "a market" similar to what has been described in this chapter?

5. TOPICS IN MARKET ANALYSIS

Now that we understand the basic functioning of microeconomic markets, we can begin to assess markets in terms of their ability to explain real-world economic outcomes and their ability to produce conditions that truly enhance well-being. As we proceed through this book, further developing and analyzing our market model, we seek to gain insights into where markets currently function well, where markets can be made to function better, and where markets do not offer the best way to allocate society's resources.

5.1 REAL-WORLD PRICES

The workings of markets in the real world may differ in some ways from the assumptions in the model constructed above. We discuss this in detail in later chapters, but here are three cases in which individuals or businesses may manage prices in ways that are not predicted by the simple model of supply and demand.

The Cost of Changing Prices

First let's revisit the coffee example, noting that, in reality, the price of coffee in your college's neighborhood probably does not change very often. This contradicts the expectation that the market demand curve should shift at the start of each semester when students return (demand should increase) and at the end of the semester when they leave (demand should decrease). Even though the quantity sold surely fluctuates depending on whether college is in session, prices are rather stable.

One reason is that steady, long-term customers (who are local residents, not students) will be offended by seeing prices "opportunistically" go up when the students arrive. This can give a shop a bad name—and reputation is important for most sellers. Another reason is that changing prices entails costs. For example, a restaurant with printed menus may keep prices fixed even though demand increases because the cost of printing new menus would offset the additional revenue.

markup (or cost-plus) pricing: a method of setting prices in which the seller adds a fixed percentage amount to his or her costs of production

In fact, rather than responding according to each change that might affect them, retailers like the ones where you buy your morning cup of coffee commonly set prices using **markup (or cost-plus) pricing**. Using this method, they determine how much it costs them to make or supply a product and then set its price including a percentage increase over their costs. Markups can vary from as low as 10–15 percent for some goods to 200 percent or more for products such as high-end jewelry or art.

Taking a Loss on One Item to Promote Sales of Other Items

To give another example, during the annual holiday season in December, the demand for electronic products such as televisions and computers increases significantly. According to our model, the increase in demand should lead to an increase in prices. But most retailers *lower* their electronics prices during the holiday season. One reason is that competition among retailers heats up at this time of the year (many retailers in the United States expect that 30–60 percent of total annual sales take place between late November and early January). A retailer that raised the price of its most popular item during this time could lose out if other businesses are lowering theirs. In fact, during the holiday season, some retailers lower their prices on some products so much that they actually lose money on each sale. The rationale is that even though they lose money on sales of those items (called "loss leaders") customers will be attracted to the stores and end up buying other, nondiscounted products so that overall profits will increase.

Taking Advantage of Differences Among Consumers' Willingness and Ability to Pay

A real-world market that seems to follow our predictions more closely in some respects is the market for air travel during the holidays. Here we have an increase in demand that usually produces the predicted price increases: A quick check online reveals that the price of a round-trip ticket between Boston and Los Angeles costs about $250 in early December, but rises to over $700 a few days before Christmas! Why is this different from the electronics case? Why doesn't one airline decide to keep its prices low and increase its ticket sales? One reason is that airlines cannot offer loss leaders because they do not have another product to sell to make up for lower-priced ticket sales. Moreover, as long as an airline can fill its planes at relatively high prices during the holidays, it has no incentive to lower its prices. (We explore the role of competition in markets in more detail in Chapters 16 and 17.) At the same time, however, airlines do attempt to create "brand loyalty" by giving various advantages to "frequent flyers."

5.2 MARKETS AND EQUITY

Markets can be viewed as rationing mechanisms—they determine who gets what. Usually, people think of rationing in terms of government action in times of shortage. For example, during World War II people were issued ration cards indicating how much of certain foods and gasoline they would be allowed to buy.

Freedom of choice is often emphasized as an outstanding characteristic of markets, so it may seem strange to view markets as a way to ration society's resources. But note in our coffee example that there are people who want coffee, (or more coffee) but do not get it. The section of a demand curve to the right of the equilibrium quantity consists of potential consumers who are willing and able to pay prices *lower* than the equilibrium price for the good or service. So if the equilibrium price of coffee is $1.10 per cup, as in Figure 3.8, many people would buy coffee if the price were reduced to, say, $0.70 per cup. Has the rationing function of the market resulted in the "right" amount of coffee being produced and sold?

Of course, this is a normative question, involving one's values and beliefs. In the market for coffee, society probably is not too concerned that some people who want coffee do not buy it at the equilibrium price. Some of these people may simply not like coffee all that much. Others might believe that they cannot afford to buy coffee from a retailer every day, preferring to make their own at a lower cost. Given the availability of alternatives and the fact that coffee is not necessarily an essential good, we may conclude that the amount of coffee sold is approximately the "right" amount.

The view that markets produce about the "right" amount of many goods and services, such as television sets, backpacks, haircuts, and pencils, is a rather amazing accomplishment. No central authority is telling manufacturers how much of these products to offer. Private sellers act in a decentralized, voluntary manner. Motivated by profits and responding to consumer demands, they produce quantities of these goods and services that many would consider about right.

But do markets produce "too much" of some goods and services, and "too little" of others? As mentioned before, markets respond to *effective demand,* backed by a willingness and ability to pay. Billions of dollars are spent every year on luxury yachts, presumably enhancing the

market value: the maximum amount that economic actors are willing and able to pay for a good or service (i.e., effective demand)

well-being of those who buy them. Companies that build yachts are responding to consumer demand. If there were a greater demand for, say, public transportation, then such companies might be making buses or trains instead. But companies will prefer to build yachts as long as they are more highly valued in markets.

But we can differentiate between market value and social value. **Market value** is defined according to effective demand—the maximum amount that economic actors are willing and able to pay for something. Market value can, in theory, be measured positively, without normative judgments. **Social value** is more difficult to define and measure. We broadly define the social value of an outcome according to the extent to which it moves us toward our final goals. So if "fairness" is one of our final goals, then it should be part of how we assess the social value of an economic outcome. But even if we had an accepted way to measure fairness, we would still need to make a normative judgment about how much fairness is appropriate.

social value: the extent to which an outcome moves us toward our final goals

Although yacht production may maximize the market value of production, it may not maximize social value. Devoting yacht-building resources to public transportation, basic health care, or public education may yield greater social value.

5.3 SHORTAGE, SCARCITY, AND INADEQUACY

In thinking about the fairness of market outcomes, it is important to distinguish between conditions of "shortage," "scarcity," and "inadequacy." These different terms have distinct meanings in economic analysis.

We have seen that a *shortage* is a situation in which willing and able buyers are unable to find goods to buy at the going price. We usually think of this as the result of disequilibrium, but it may also be deliberately created. Sometimes producers intentionally choose a production and pricing strategy that will create shortages, such as the one used for selling luxury cars. The shortage could be eliminated, and equilibrium achieved, if producers raised the price enough. However, they have calculated that their long-run profitability will be higher if they permit a shortage to create a mystique around their product.

Economists think of *scarcity* as a more general condition. As we discussed in Chapter 1, a fundamental scarcity of resources relative to everything that people might need or want is what requires individuals and societies to make choices. Scarcity is about an imbalance between what is available and what people would *like* to have, regardless of what they can afford. Perhaps almost everyone would *like* to have a Rolls-Royce, but Rolls-Royces are scarce because not everyone can buy one. But even cups of coffee are scarce in that price acts as a rationing mechanism in which some people decide not to buy all the coffee that they might theoretically want.

inadequacy: a situation in which there is not enough of a good or service, provided at prices people can afford, to meet minimal requirements for human well-being

Not all kinds of scarcity are alike. We tend to feel differently about the scarcity of Rolls-Royces (there are still plenty of other cars that people can purchase to meet their transportation needs) and the scarcity of affordable housing. We use the term **inadequacy** to refer to scarcity when it involves something that is necessary for minimal human well-being but is not obtainable by everyone who needs it. Food, shelter, and basic health care, for example, can be in inadequate supply relative to needs.

While markets can eliminate shortages, and general scarcity is a fact of life, markets normally do not address problems of inadequacy. However, if economics is truly about meeting needs and enhancing well-being, then we need mechanisms to supplement markets to reduce problems of inadequacy, such as provision of some goods and services by governments or other public purpose actors.

5.4 PRECISION VERSUS ACCURACY

Returning one last time to our coffee example, recall that the initial equilibrium price was exactly $1.10 per cup (Figure 3.8). We assumed that this price would be the same at all coffee shops in the area. In the real world, one coffee shop might sell coffee for $0.99 per cup, another for $1.10, while a third charges $1.25. Does this observation conflict with our basic model?

One response is that each coffee shop faces a *separate* demand curve for its coffee. So the equilibrium price at one shop may differ from the equilibrium price at another, depending on such factors as their relative labor costs, the quality of their coffee, or the ambiance of each shop. But even if market conditions are similar for different coffee shops, we may still observe some variation in prices.

precise: describes something that is exact (though it may be unrealistic)

accurate: describes something that is correct (even if only in a general way)

The model presented here is **precise** because it describes outcomes exactly, such as our equilibrium price being exactly $1.10 per cup. The advantage of precision is that we have eliminated uncertainty. Another example of precision is making an economic prediction that the unemployment rate at the end of next year will be exactly 6.0 percent. However, when we are being precise we run the risk of being inaccurate. Our unemployment rate prediction will likely turn out to be wrong. A prediction that stands a better chance of being **accurate** is saying that the unemployment rate will be between 5 percent and 7 percent. An accurate prediction is one that is correct, even if only in a general way.

Often there is a tradeoff between accuracy and precision. Rather than saying that the equilibrium coffee price is precisely $1.10 per cup, it may be more accurate to say that the equilibrium price is between $1.00 and $1.20 per cup. The distinction between precision and accuracy is one that we face frequently. The statement "He is middle-aged" is untrue of a 20-year-old and a 70-year-old and perhaps clearly true of a 45-year-old. But middle age does not begin abruptly at 40 or 43, nor does it end abruptly some years later. Rather, it is a more or less appropriate description of people at varying ages. "He is middle-aged" may be perfectly accurate, without being precise.

Ideally, we would like our economic analyses to be characterized by both accuracy and precision—but sometimes we have to choose between these qualities. How should we decide which to choose?

Precision often has the virtue of simplicity. For example, it is easier to contemplate a single point than it is to deal with ranges of various possibilities. Precision and simplicity together are qualities that are often helpful—sometimes essential—to translate economic concepts into readily understood mathematical representations and graphs.

In contrast, accuracy is especially important when we are attempting to understand the real world. We keep the theory "in our head" to help us understand economic activity, but what we actually observe is often more messy and complicated than a simple graph could represent, as our discussion of electronics and plane tickets suggested.

If we mistakenly confuse precision with accuracy, then we might be misled into thinking that an explanation expressed in precise mathematical or graphical terms is somehow more rigorous or useful than one that takes into account particulars of history, institutions, or business strategy. This is not the case. Therefore, it is important not to put too much confidence in the apparent precision of supply and demand graphs. Supply and demand analysis is a useful, precisely formulated, conceptual tool that helps gain an abstract understanding of a complex world. It does not—nor should it be expected to—also give us an accurate and complete description of any particular real-world market.

Discussion Questions

1. In Chapter 1 we discussed the three basic economic questions: *What* should be produced, and *what* should be maintained? *How* should production and maintenance be accomplished? *For whom* should economic activity be undertaken? Discuss how the workings of markets provide some answers to these questions.

2. Explain which of the three situations—shortage, scarcity, or inadequacy—is illustrated by each of the following, and why.
   a. You go to a store to buy a certain computer game and find that it is sold out.
   b. Jasmine cannot afford to go to a doctor.
   c. Rafe can think of dozens of music CDs he would like to buy, but he also would like to buy a lot of new clothing.

REVIEW QUESTIONS

1. Define and sketch a supply curve.
2. Illustrate on a graph:
   (a) a decrease in quantity supplied; and
   (b) a decrease in supply.
3. Name six nonprice determinants of supply for a product sold by firms.
4. Define and sketch a demand curve.
5. Illustrate on a graph:
   (a) a decrease in quantity demanded; and
   (b) a decrease in demand.

6. Name five nonprice determinants of demand for a product purchased by households.
7. Draw a graph illustrating surplus, shortage, and equilibrium.
8. Explain the difference between market value and social value.
9. Name three ways in which supply can be inadequate.
10. Explain the difference between precision and accuracy.

EXERCISES

1. Explain in words why the supply curve slopes upward.
2. Explain in worlds why the demand curve slopes downward.
3. Suppose that the supply and demand schedules for a local electric utility are as follows:

Price	17	16	15	14	13	12	11
Quantity supplied	9	7	5	3	1	–	–
Quantity demanded	3	4	5	6	7	8	9

The price is in cents per kilowatt hour (kWh), and the quantity is millions of kilowatt hours. The utility does not operate at prices less than 13 cents per kWh.

   a. Using graph paper and a ruler, or a computer spreadsheet or presentation program, carefully graph and label the supply curve for electricity.
   b. On the same graph, draw and label the demand curve for electricity.
   c. What is the equilibrium price of electricity? The equilibrium quantity? Label this point on your graph.
   d. At a price of 17 cents per kWh, what is the quantity supplied? What is the quantity demanded? What is the relationship between quantity supplied and quantity demanded? What term do economists use to describe this situation?
   e. At a price of 14 cents per kWh, what is the relationship between quantity supplied and quantity demanded? What term do economists use to describe this situation?
   f. Sometimes cities experience "blackouts," in which the demands on the utility are so high relative to its capacity to produce electricity that the system shuts down, leaving everyone in the dark. Using the analysis that you have just completed, describe an *economic* factor that could make blackouts more likely to occur.

4. Continuing on from the previous problem, suppose that new innovations in energy efficiency reduce people's need for electricity. The supply side of the market does not change, but at each price buyers now demand 3 million kilowatt hours fewer than before. For example, at a price of 11 cents per kWh, buyers now demand only 6 kWh instead of 9 kWh.

   a. On a new graph, draw supply and demand curves corresponding to prices of 16 cents per kWh or less, after the innovations in efficiency. Also, for reference, mark the old equilibrium point from the previous exercise, labeling it E_1.
   b. If the price were to remain at the old equilibrium level (determined in part (c) above), what sort of situation would result?
   c. What is the new equilibrium price? The new equilibrium quantity? Give this point on your graph the label E_2.
   d. Has there been a change in demand? Has a change in the price (relative to the original situation) led to a change in the quantity demanded?
   e. Has there been a change in supply? Has a change in the price (relative to the original situation) led to a change in the quantity supplied?

5. Using your understanding of the nonprice determinants of supply and of demand, analyze each of the following market cases. Draw a graph showing what happens in each situation, indicate what happens to equilibrium price and quantity, and explain why, following this example: Market for gasoline: A hurricane hits the Gulf of Mexico, destroying many refineries that produce gasoline from crude oil.

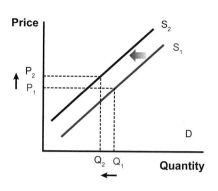

S shifts back; *P* rises; *Q* falls; the hurricane reduces the number of producers.

a. Market for bananas: New health reports indicate that people can gain important health benefits from eating bananas.

b. Market for shoes: A new technology for shoe making means that shoes can be made at a lower cost per pair.

c. Market for Internet design services: Several thousand new graduates of design schools enter the market, ready to supply their services.

d. Market for expensive meals: A booming economy raises the incomes of many households.

e. Market for grapes *from California:* A freeze in Chile, usually a major world provider of fresh fruit, raises the price of Chilean grapes.

f. Market for salsa dance lessons: The only nightclub featuring salsa music triples its entrance fee.

g. Market for bottled water: A rumor circulates that the price of bottled water is about to triple. (Think only about the demand side.)

h. Market for Internet design services: Several thousand new graduates of design schools enter the market, ready to supply their services, *at the same time* that many firms want to create new Web sites.

i. Market for bananas: New health reports indicate that people can gain important health benefits from eating bananas, while *at the same time* an infestation of insects reduces the banana harvest in several areas.

6. At a price of $5 per bag, William is willing to supply 3 bags of oranges, Marguerite 2 bags, and Felipe 5 bags. At a price of $7 per bag, William is willing to supply 5 bags, Marguerite 4 bags, and Felipe 7 bags. Graph and carefully label the individual supply curves, and then graph the market supply curve for oranges (at these two prices).

7. At a price of $8 per ticket, Shalimar goes to 2 movies per month, Wen goes to 1 movie per month, and Adam goes to 3 movies per month. At a price of $10 per ticket, Shalimar goes to 1 movie, Wen goes to 0 movies, and Adam goes to 2 movies. Graph and carefully label the individual demand curves, and then graph the market demand curve for movie tickets (at these two prices).

8. Suppose that a newspaper report indicates that the price of wheat has fallen. For each of the following events, draw a supply-and-demand graph showing the event's effect on the market for wheat. Then state whether the event could explain the observed fall in the price of wheat.

a. A drought has hit wheat-growing areas.

b. The price of rice has risen, so consumers look for alternatives.

c. As a consequence of increasing health concerns, tobacco farmers have begun to plant other crops.

9. Match each concept in Column A with an example in Column B.

Column A	Column B
a. Substitute goods	1. Price and quantity along the supply curve
b. A nonprice determinant of demand	2. Tea and coffee
c. A nonprice determinant of supply	3. A change in technology
d. Mark-up pricing	4. Hunger
e. Positive relationship	5. Shoes and shoelaces
f. Negative relationship	6. Consumer income
g. Inadequacy	7. Price and quantity along the demand curve
h. Complementary goods	8. Setting price equal to cost plus 20 percent

NOTE

1. See Gary E. McIlvain, Melody P. Noland, and Robert Bickel, "Caffeine Consumption Patterns and Beliefs of College Freshman," *American Journal of Health Education* 42(4) (2011): 235–244.

4 Elasticity

In 2012 the Massachusetts Bay Transportation Authority (MBTA), which operates buses, subways, and commuter trains in the Boston area, raised its fares in order to address major budget deficits. Based on what we learned in Chapter 3, we would expect overall ridership to decline when fares are raised (a decrease in the quantity demanded). So we have two market forces affecting the MBTA's revenues, working in opposite directions:

- The fare increase would bring the MBTA more revenue for each ride taken.
- The fare increase would reduce the number of rides taken.

Whether the MBTA's total revenue increases as a result of the fare increase depends on how responsive riders are to price changes. In order to plan properly, the MBTA needed to estimate how much the quantity demanded would decline with an increase in fare prices. If ridership decreases only a little, then total revenue would probably increase. However, if the fare increase causes ridership to decline significantly, then perhaps revenues would actually decrease.

This is one example in which economists, businesses, or policymakers require information about the responsiveness of the quantity demanded, or the quantity supplied, to price changes. For example, a restaurant may wish to know how its customers will respond to higher prices. A state government may need to estimate how its revenues will change if it increases taxes on cigarettes or another product. Agencies that monitor traffic patterns may want to know how much vehicle travel will respond to changes in gas prices.

elasticity: a measure of the responsiveness of an economic actor to changes in market factors, including price and income

In this chapter, we introduce the concept of **elasticity**. Elasticity measures the responsiveness of economic actors to changes in market factors, including price and income. The most common kinds of elasticity are those related to changes in the quantity demanded or quantity supplied with changes in price (i.e., movement along a demand or supply curve). But we can also measure elasticity with respect to changes in income or other nonprice determinants (i.e., shifts in demand or supply).

1. THE PRICE ELASTICITY OF DEMAND

price elasticity of demand: the responsiveness of the quantity demanded to a change in price

When the MBTA raised its prices in July 2012, by an average of 23 percent, do you think ridership declined a little or a lot? It depends on the **price elasticity of demand** (often just called the "elasticity of demand"), which is the responsiveness of the quantity demanded to a change in price. Elasticity of demand is the particular elasticity most studied by economists. Businesses can use information on the elasticity of demand for their products to set prices. Governments can use elasticity of demand estimates to determine how much revenue they will raise with a tax on a particular product.

1.1 PRICE-INELASTIC DEMAND

price-inelastic demand: a relationship between price and quantity demanded characterized by relatively weak responses of buyers to price changes

Demand for a good is **price inelastic** if the effect of a price change on the quantity demanded is fairly small. Demand might be price inelastic for three main reasons:

1. There are very few good, close substitutes for the good or service.
2. The good or service is something that people need, rather than just want.
3. The cost of the good or service is a very small part of a buyer's budget.

For example, gasoline has no good, close substitutes for powering nonelectric motor vehicles. When gas prices rise, most drivers still need to use their vehicles to get to work, run errands, and so on. So gasoline is an example of a good that is price inelastic because of the lack of any good substitutes and because people believe that they need it. Other examples of goods that tend to be price inelastic for these reasons include water for basic needs, essential health care, and electricity.

Some goods are price inelastic because expenditures on them represent such a small portion of people's incomes that most consumers are not affected much by a change in prices. Consider that a 50 percent increase in the price of dental floss is not likely to reduce the quantity demanded significantly.

1.2 PRICE-ELASTIC DEMAND

price-elastic demand: a relationship between price and quantity demanded characterized by relatively strong responses of buyers to price changes

Conversely, demand for a good is **price elastic** if the effect of a price change on the quantity demanded is fairly large. Demand may be price elastic for three main reasons:

1. The good has a number of good, close substitutes.
2. The good is merely wanted, rather than needed.
3. The cost of the good makes up a large part of the budget of the buyer.

An example of a good that is likely to be price elastic is orange juice. This product is not necessary for most people, and various substitutes exist, such as apple juice or other fruit juices. Although gasoline is a price-inelastic good, the elasticity of demand for a particular brand of gasoline is likely to be very elastic. Gasoline may not have readily available substitutes, but the gasoline from Exxon-Mobil or BP does. For another example of elastic demand, see Box 4.1.

To the extent that a good is merely wanted (e.g., ice cream), rather than needed (e.g., essential medicines), demand for it will tend to be more elastic. Studies typically find that demand for airline travel is more elastic for people going on vacation than for business travelers. Demand also tends to be more price elastic when the good makes up a large part of the budget of the buyer, because then the buyer will be more motivated to seek out substitutes when prices increase.

1.3 MEASURING PRICE ELASTICITY

To obtain useful economic forecasts, we need to be more precise than simply stating that quantity demand changes "a little" or "a lot" in response to a given price change. The elasticity of demand is mathematically calculated as:

$$Price\ elasticity\ of\ demand = \left| \frac{\%\ change\ in\ quantity\ demanded}{\%\ change\ in\ price} \right|$$

where the vertical bars indicate absolute value. As we discussed in Chapter 3, price and the quantity demanded normally change in opposite directions (an inverse relationship), so the

BOX 4.1   GYM MEMBERSHIPS AND ELASTICITY

The city of New York operates dozens of recreation centers, which offer facilities such as indoor pools, weight rooms, basketball courts, and dance centers. These centers offer a low-cost alternative to expensive private gyms.

In an effort to raise revenue, in 2011 the city doubled its recreation center adult membership fees, to $150 per year for centers with pools and $100 per year for those without pools. The Parks Department projected that the fee increase would result in a 5 percent drop in memberships, but a $4 million increase in revenues. In other words, their analysis concluded that demand for the recreation centers was rather inelastic.

Instead, the fee change resulted in a 45 percent drop in membership, and a $200,000 decline in revenues! The demand for the city's recreation centers turned out to be much more elastic than the city anticipated. In January 2013 the Parks Department Commissioner, Veronica M. White, acknowledged that the plan to increase revenues had backfired.

One change that she suggested was to make memberships available to those age 18–24 for only $25 per year, the same rate charged to seniors. Memberships for those under age 18 are free, so those turning 18 had to suddenly pay at least $100 per year. Membership among this age group dropped by the highest percentage after the fee change, by 55 percent. The Parks Department hopes that the new lower membership fees will encourage young adults to exercise, as 52 percent of young adult males and 31 percent of young adult females in New York City are overweight or obese.

Many of the clientele of the recreation centers are low-income individuals. Thus the fee increase posed a particular hardship for them. Holly Leicht, executive director of New Yorkers for Parks, a nonprofit advocacy group, noted, "Thirty percent of Bronx residents alone are living at or below the poverty rate of $23,021 per year for a family of four. For these families, an extra $50 or $75 is often prohibitive."

Source: Lisa W. Foderaro, "Public Recreation Centers Looking to Stem Exodus," *New York Times*, February 15, 2013.

---

fraction inside the vertical bars tends to be a negative number. For example, if price increases (a positive sign in the denominator of the fraction), we would expect the quantity demanded to decrease (a negative sign in the numerator of the fraction). So after dividing, we would end up with a negative number. Taking the absolute value turns the negative number into a positive number.

The reason we take the absolute value is so that when we talk about a "large" responsiveness to price, we can represent this using a "larger" number. If we did not take the absolute value, we would have to talk about –2 being "bigger" than –1, which would be confusing.*

An example illustrates how we calculate the price elasticity of demand for a particular good. Suppose that executives at Braeburn Publishing are trying to decide what price to charge for a new book of poetry. Although the firm competes with many other firms in the market for books in general, it has sole rights to sell this particular book, so it has some power over the price that it sets. In order to see how responsive demand for the new poetry book is to variations in price, Braeburn decides to test-market it in three locations that are very similar in terms of consumer preferences and incomes but are far enough apart geographically so that the company can set a different price in each location. Table 4.1 and Figure 4.1 show the data the marketing department has collected on prices and the quantity sold during the month of the test. As in this example, real empirical data on prices and quantities are generally limited to specific points along a demand curve without knowing data points for the entire demand curve. For simplicity, we have assumed that the demand curve is a straight line between the three known data points.

---

*If you look at economic studies that estimate the price elasticity of demand, sometimes the elasticity estimates are presented as negative numbers (i.e., they do not take the absolute value). Remember that price and quantity demanded almost always change in the opposite direction. So you can safely make this assumption, unless information is presented to the contrary.

Table 4.1   **Relationship Between Price and Quantity Demanded for Braeburn's Poetry Book**

Book price	Quantity of books sold
$12	720
$10	800
$5	1,000

Figure 4.1   **Demand Curve for Braeburn's Poetry Book**

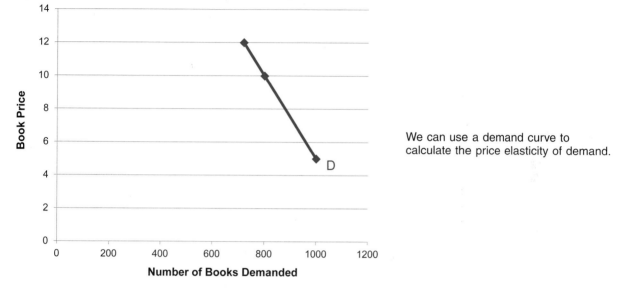

We can use a demand curve to calculate the price elasticity of demand.

We can now calculate the price elasticity of demand for Braeburn's poetry book. We work our way "up" the demand curve starting at the lowest price, $5. To calculate the percentage change in a variable, we define one number as the starting, or "base," value and the other as the ending, or new, value. So, working up the demand curve, $5 would be our base value and $10 would be our new value. A percentage change is calculated as:

$$Percent\ change = \left[\frac{New\ value - Base\ value}{Base\ value}\right] \times 100$$

So, going from a base of $5 to a new value of $10, the percentage change is:

$$
\begin{aligned}
Percentage\ change\ in\ price &= [(\$10 - \$5)/\$5] \times 100 \\
&= [\$5/\$5 \times 100] \\
&= 1 \times 100 \\
&= 100\%
\end{aligned}
$$

For the percentage change in quantity demanded, our base is 1,000 and our new value is 800. So the percentage change is:

$$
\begin{aligned}
Percentage\ change\ in\ quantity &= [(800 - 1,000)/1,000\ ] \times 100 \\
&= [-200/1,000\ ] \times 100 \\
&= -0.2 \times 100 \\
&= -20\%
\end{aligned}
$$

We can then calculate the elasticity of demand as the absolute value of the percentage change in quantity demanded divided by the percentage change in price, or:

$$Elasticity = |-20\%/100\%|$$
$$= |-0.2|$$
$$= 0.2$$

price-inelastic demand (technical definition): the percentage change in the quantity demanded is smaller than the percentage change in price. The elasticity value is less than 1.

In this example, notice that the percentage change in the quantity demanded is less than the percentage change in price. Whenever this is the case, the elasticity value will be less than 1. This is the **technical definition of price-inelastic demand**.

The **technical definition of price-elastic demand** is that the percentage change in the quantity demanded is larger than the percentage change in price. With price-elastic demand, the elasticity value will be more than 1.

1.4 TWO EXTREME CASES

Perfectly Inelastic Demand

price-elastic demand (technical definition): the percentage change in the quantity demanded is larger than the percentage change in price. The elasticity value is more than 1.

perfectly inelastic demand: the quantity demanded does not change at all when price changes. The elasticity value is 0.

Perfectly inelastic demand means that quantity demanded does not respond at all to price changes. Suppose that you are on medication, and you must take exactly three pills a day to survive. Would a 10 percent increase in the price of the medication change the quantity that you demand? Chances are your demand would be perfectly inelastic in the range of that price change, because you unquestionably need the medicine.

Think about what a demand curve would look like for a good with perfectly inelastic demand. For any price level (i.e., any point on the vertical axis), the quantity demanded would be unchanged. Thus a perfectly inelastic demand curve would be a vertical line at the quantity demanded, as shown in Figure 4.2. As the quantity demanded is constant (i.e., percentage change is 0), the elasticity value for a good with a perfectly inelastic demand would be 0.

For a good with perfectly inelastic demand, such as lifesaving drugs and basic foodstuffs, profit incentives may be at odds with social well-being. Because a seller of such a good could raise prices without reducing the quantity demanded, by continually raising prices, up to the absolute maximum that people could afford, the seller would maximize profits.

For this reason, in markets for certain kinds of health-care commodities or basic foodstuffs, governments sometimes regulate prices to give the seller a fair return but not an excessive

Figure 4.2   **Perfectly Inelastic Demand and Perfectly Elastic Demand**

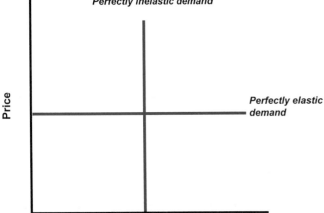

When the quantity demanded is constant regardless of price, demand is perfectly inelastic. When even a small increase in price will reduce the quantity demanded to zero, demand is perfectly elastic.

one while ensuring that many people will get what they need. Controversies have recently arisen in the United States over whether prices for pharmaceuticals and hospital stays are reasonable or are out of line with actual production costs and human needs.

Sometimes, sellers themselves are guided by notions of what is a "fair" price. Economists have noticed that, for example, few stores raise the price of umbrellas during rainstorms. The stores could almost certainly get away with charging higher prices to people whose only alternative is to get soaking wet. However, the sellers also know that if they want repeat business from their customers, they should not ruin their reputation for fair dealing by engaging in such price gouging.

Perfectly Elastic Demand

perfectly elastic demand: any change in price leads to an infinite change in quantity demanded. The elasticity value is infinity.

Perfectly elastic demand, by contrast, means that any price change, no matter how small, leads to an "infinite" change in quantity demanded. This occurs when there is a "going price" for a particular good or service and any attempt to charge above that price will eliminate all demand for it. One case in which demand tends to be very elastic in the real world is in the market for general-skilled labor, when general-skilled workers are plentiful. Employers are the buyers, or demanders, in this case. If all you had to offer on the labor market were general skills, such as flipping burgers or sweeping floors, then you and all workers similar to you would be the sellers, or suppliers. Chances are that you would face a demand curve for your labor that would be horizontal at the going wage. Competing against many other sellers, all with the same basic skills, you would have very little or no ability to affect the wage that you would get in the market.

A perfectly elastic demand curve would be horizontal at the "going price," as shown in Figure 4.2. Almost any quantity can be sold at the going price, but charging even slightly above this price will reduce demand to 0. Because even a slight change in price will result in an "infinite" change in quantity demanded, the elasticity value for a good with a perfectly elastic demand is essentially infinite.

In reality, examples of perfectly elastic or perfectly inelastic demand curves are rare. However, actual demand curves may come close to these two extremes, at least for some portion of the demand curve.

1.5 DEMAND CURVES AND ELASTICITY

The Shape of a Demand Curve and Elasticity

Let's take another look at Figure 4.1. We have already calculated the elasticity of the demand curve when the price increased from \$5 to \$10, which was 0.2. Given that the demand "curve" is a straight line, you might think that the elasticity would also be 0.2 if the price increased further from \$10 to \$12. Let's see if this is true, inserting the appropriate values from Table 4.1.

$$Elasticity = \left| \frac{[(720 - 800)\,/\,800] \times 100}{[(12 - 10)\,/\,10] \times 100} \right|$$

$$= \left| \frac{0.1 \times 100}{0.2 \times 100} \right|$$

$$= 0.5$$

The elasticity value within this range of the demand curve is higher (more elastic) than it was previously. This result will be true for any straight-line, or linear, demand curve: As we

Figure 4.3   **Elasticity Varies Along a Straight-Line Demand Curve**

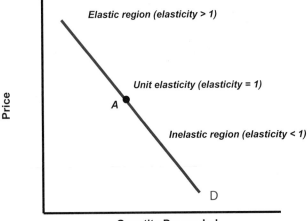

Above point A demand is elastic but
below point A demand is inelastic.

**unit-elastic de-
mand:** the percent-
age change in the
quantity demanded is
exactly equal to the
percentage change in
price. The elasticity
value is 1.

move "up" the demand curve (to the left), the elasticity value will increase. Often a linear demand curve will have both an elastic region (with an elasticity value greater than 1) and an inelastic region (with an elasticity value less than 1).*

This is illustrated in Figure 4.3. Note that at some point along this linear demand curve, the elasticity value is exactly 1. Economists call this **unit-elastic demand,** when the percentage change in the quantity demanded is exactly equal to the percentage change in price. This is shown as point A on the demand curve. (Note that the point of unit elasticity does not necessarily occur in the "middle" of a linear demand curve.)

Elasticity and the Direction of the Price Change

Next, let's consider another question: Does the direction of the price change matter when calculating elasticity?

Referring again to our data in Table 4.1, let's calculate elasticity with price decreasing from $10 to $5, instead of increasing from $5 to $10. Inserting the appropriate values, we get:

$$Elasticity = \left| \frac{[(1000 - 800) / 800] \times 100}{[(5 - 10) / 10] \times 100} \right|$$

$$= \left| \frac{0.25 \times 100}{0.5 \times 100} \right|$$

$$= 0.5$$

So while the elasticity value was 0.2 when price increased from $5 to $10, it is 0.5 when price decreases from $10 to $5, even though we are moving along the same exact segment of the demand curve! So when we quote an elasticity value for a particular good or service, do we also need to indicate whether this elasticity applies to a price increase or a price decrease?

Fortunately, this problem can be avoided. As explained in Box 4.2, we can use the "midpoint" formula to obtain the same elasticity value regardless of whether the price increases or decreases along the same segment of a linear demand curve.

---

*Economists often work with "constant-elasticity" demand curves, where the elasticity value is the same at any point along the demand curve. Constant-elasticity demand curves are actual curves, not straight lines, that bow in toward the origin. Constant-elasticity demand curves tend to be more realistic representations of demand for many goods and services.

BOX 4.2   THE MIDPOINT ELASTICITY FORMULA

The reason that the direction a price change matters when we calculate an elasticity value is that the denominators change when we calculate the percentage change in each variable. The denominator used to calculate the percentage change is the "base" value. But by changing the direction of the change, the base value can be the higher or the lower number. So the key to obtaining the same elasticity value regardless of the direction of the price change is to obtain the same denominators when calculating the percentage changes. We can do this by using the "midpoint formula."

Consider our example of price changing from $5 to $10 (or vice versa). The percentage change is either 50 percent or 100 percent depending on the direction of the change. To use the midpoint formula, instead of using the base value as the denominator when calculating the percentage change, we use the midpoint, or average, of the two values:

$$Midpoint = (new\ number + base\ number)/2$$

So for the price change between $5 and $10, in either direction, the base value for the denominator when calculating the percentage change in price is now 7.5. For the quantity change, the midpoint between 800 and 1,000 is 900. Thus the elasticity value for a price increase from $5 to $10 using the midpoint formula would be:

$$Elasticity = |[(-200/900) \times 100]/[(5/7.5) \times 100]|$$
$$= |-22.22/66.67|$$
$$= 0.3333$$

You can test yourself by proving that you get the same elasticity value if the price decreases from $10 to $5. Note that the elasticity value here, 0.3333, is between our two previous elasticity estimates (0.2 and 0.5) based on prices of $5 and $10. However, realize that the elasticity obtained using the midpoint formula is *not* the midpoint of the two elasticity values using the conventional approach.

Elasticity and Slope

You may recall from a math class that the equation for a straight line is:

$$y = b + m\,x$$

where m is the slope of the line and b is the intercept term. The slope defines the numerical change in the y value every time the x value increases by 1.

Some students mistakenly think that elasticity is the same thing as the slope of a linear demand curve. But note that the slope of the line in Figure 4.3 does not change. As we have already seen, the elasticity value differs as we move along a linear demand curve.

Although a "steeper" slope generally suggests a less elastic demand curve than a "flatter" curve, we can make any demand curve look flatter or steeper depending on how we draw (i.e., scale) the two axes. Compare Figure 4.4 to Figure 4.1. At first glance, the demand curve in Figure 4.4 appears flatter than the curve in Figure 4.1, suggesting that it is a more elastic demand curve. But the underlying data are exactly the same in the two figures—the x-axis in Figure 4.4 has merely been adjusted to start at a quantity of 700 rather than 0, making the curve appear flatter. Thus we cannot determine elasticity, even approximately, simply by looking at a demand curve without making the necessary calculations.

1.6 ELASTICITY AND REVENUES

A common application of elasticity estimates is predicting how a company's revenues will change in response to a price change. A business, such as Braeburn Publishing, can use an elasticity estimate to determine what price it should charge to maximize its revenues. Recall the example from the beginning of the chapter regarding the MBTA's raising fares to eliminate a budget deficit. If the MBTA had a reliable estimate of the elasticity of demand for public transportation, it could calculate how much revenues would be expected to change with different fare levels. Other government agencies can rely on elasticity estimates to determine how different tax rates will affect revenues.

Figure 4.4 **Changing the Scale of Braeburn's Demand Curve**

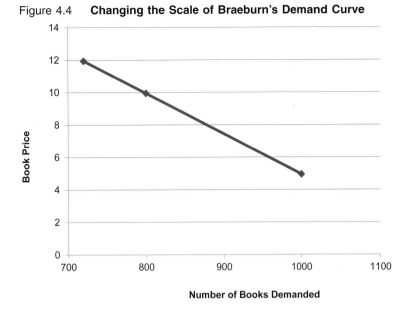

We cannot make conclusions about elasticity simply by looking at a demand curve. By changing the scale of the axes we can make a demand curve "look" more or less elastic.

The revenues that a business (or government agency) will receive from selling a good or service at a specific price is simply that price multiplied by the quantity sold:

Revenues = Price × Quantity Sold

So in the case of Braeburn, the revenue that it obtains from selling 1,000 books at a price of $5 per book is:

Revenue = $5 × 1,000 = $5,000

We can also represent revenues graphically based on a demand curve. First, recall that the area of a rectangle is its height multiplied by its length. Thus the revenue obtained at any point on a demand curve can be shown as a rectangle equal to its height (price) multiplied by its length (quantity sold). This is illustrated in Figure 4.5, which is the same demand curve presented in Figure 4.1. At a price of $5, book revenues are equal to area A plus area B, which is $5,000.

Figure 4.5 **Braeburn's Book Revenues**

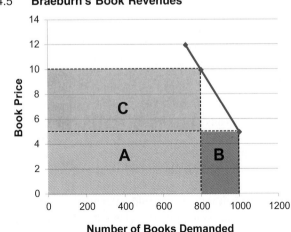

Braeburn's book revenues equal areas A+B at a price of $5 per book. Revenues equal areas A+C at a price of $10 per book.

Now suppose that price is increased to $10—will revenues increase or decrease? We can see in Figure 4.5 that if the price is $10, revenues will be equal to area A plus area C. So increasing the price from $5 to $10, Braeburn loses area B in revenues but gains area C (Braeburn obtains area A at either price). From looking at the figure, it seems apparent that area C is greater than area B. So we can conclude that Braeburn's revenues will increase as a result of a price increase. We can confirm this by calculating revenues at a price of $10 as $8,000 ($10 × 800 books).

What does this have to do with elasticity? When we calculated the elasticity of demand moving from a price of $5 to a price of $10, we found that demand was price inelastic (with a value of 0.2). Whenever demand is price inelastic, increasing price will have a relatively small effect on quantity demanded. Thus a business will be able to sell almost the same quantity but at a higher price, earning higher revenues. In other words, whenever demand is price inelastic, increasing the price will increase revenues. Conversely, with inelastic demand, decreasing price will decrease revenues.

But if demand is price elastic, then increasing price will lead to a relatively large decrease in the quantity demanded. A business will receive more revenue per unit sold, but the quantity sold will decrease substantially, earning lower overall revenues. So whenever demand is price elastic, increasing prices will lower revenues. Decreasing prices will increase revenues if demand is price elastic.

If the elasticity value for a good or service is 1, then the percentage changes in price and quantity demanded are the same magnitude (but in opposite directions). For example, doubling price would reduce the quantity demanded by half. Selling twice as many of something at half the price will result in the same exact revenue. So if the elasticity value for a good or service is 1, changing the price will have no effect on revenues.

The effects of price changes on revenues for different elasticities are summarized in Table 4.2. As mentioned previously, a demand curve may be elastic for one range of prices but inelastic over a different range. Thus revenue changes may vary considerably as one moves along a demand curve.

Table 4.2 **Effects of Price Changes on Revenues**

Elasticity value (e)	Elasticity description	Effect of a price increase on revenues	Effect of a price decrease on revenues
$e = 0$	Perfectly inelastic	Increase	Decrease
$0 < e < 1$	Inelastic	Increase	Decrease
$e = 1$	Unit elastic	No change	No change
$1 < e < \infty$	Elastic	Decrease	Increase
∞	Perfectly elastic	Revenues fall to zero	Decrease

1.7 PRICE ELASTICITY OF DEMAND IN THE REAL WORLD

Economists have estimated the elasticity of demand for many goods and services. In order to estimate an elasticity, one needs information on the quantity demanded at different prices. In some cases, variations in prices commonly occur over time. Gasoline is a good example of a product whose price fluctuates. In other cases, price variations may occur across geographic regions. For example, different electric utilities charge different electricity rates.

However, estimating elasticity is not as simple as tracking how the quantity sold responds to price variations. Remember that elasticity measures movement along a demand curve as price changes, ceteris paribus. Thus an accurate measurement of elasticity requires that none of the nonprice determinants of demand have caused the demand curve to shift and that the supply curve has not shifted either. Although economists cannot prevent these changes from occurring, they can use statistical techniques to attempt to isolate the effects of price changes on the quantity demanded.

We normally cannot speak of "the" elasticity of demand for a particular good. Different economists may obtain different elasticity values for the same product because of variations in the statistical techniques that they use or the region studied. For example, the elasticity of demand for cigarettes has been found to vary between developed and developing countries. As we discuss further later in the chapter, elasticity can change depending on the time allowed for consumers to adjust their behavior. See Box 4.3 for more on how the elasticity for a product can vary.

For these reasons, many economic analyses present a range of elasticity values for a particular good. Thus the effect of a price change on revenues will commonly be difficult to predict accurately, but we hope that the actual result will fall within our forecasted range. This is another illustration of the tradeoff between precision and accuracy, as discussed in Chapter 3.

Table 4.3 presents the range of elasticity values found for some products. In air travel, for example, we see that demand is inelastic for first-class travelers, who might either be on business trips or wealthy enough to disregard some price changes, but that demand is elastic for pleasure travelers, who might decide to take a road trip instead for vacation if air fares rise significantly. Note also that elasticity tends to be higher in developing countries, where lower incomes tend to make people more sensitive to price changes.

Table 4.3   **Some Estimated Price Elasticities of Demand**

Good or service	Price elasticity of demand	
	Low range	*High range*
Cigarettes	0.4 (developed countries)	0.8 (developing countries)
Gasoline	0.1 (short term)	0.3 (long term)
Residential water	0.1 (lower estimates)	0.7 (higher estimates)
Air travel	0.3 (first-class travelers)	1.4 (pleasure travelers)
Soft drinks	0.8 (soft drinks in general)	4.4 (specific drink brands)
Eggs	0.1 (United States)	0.6 (South Africa)
Rice	0.3 (United States)	0.8 (China)

BOX 4.3   THE SHIFTING DEMAND ELASTICITY FOR GASOLINE

Gasoline is perhaps the good whose demand elasticity has been most studied by economists. Numerous estimates of the demand elasticity for gasoline have been published going back to the 1960s. Because so much data are available, economists have been able to explore whether the demand elasticity for gasoline has changed over time.

A 2008 paper compared gasoline demand in the United States in the late 1970s with data from 2001–6. The results indicated that the elasticity value had decreased significantly over time, from about 0.30 in the 1970s to only 0.05 in the 2000s.

What may be responsible for such a large decrease in the demand elasticity for gasoline? The authors propose several explanations, including:

- American drivers have become more dependent on their vehicles over time. In particular, an increase in suburban development has increased the travel distances between where people live and where they work and shop. Thus alternatives such as walking and biking are less viable now than in the past.
- As incomes have increased over time, gasoline purchases comprise a smaller share of overall expenses. Thus consumers may be less responsive to increases in gas prices.
- Vehicles have become more fuel efficient over time. Consumers with relatively fuel efficient vehicles may be less responsive to gas price increases.

The authors conclude that attempts to reduce gas consumption significantly by increasing gas taxes are likely to be ineffective. Instead, they suggest that higher fuel-economy standards for new vehicles are likely to be both more effective and more politically acceptable.

Source: Jonathan E. Hughes, Christopher R. Knittel, and Daniel Sperling, "Evidence of a Shift in the Short-Run Price Elasticity of Gasoline Demand," *Energy Journal* 29(1) (2008): 113–134.

Going back to our MBTA example, what did it estimate for the elasticity of demand for public transportation? The MBTA obtained elasticity estimates based on analysis of the impacts of previous fare increases. It estimated separate elasticity values for different types of public transportation, such as buses, subways, and commuter trains. Moreover, it differentiated between riders who purchase monthly passes and those who pay for each ride.

As one example, the MBTA estimated that the elasticity of demand for commuter rail passengers with monthly passes was about 0.1 but for "single-fare" riders of the commuter trains it was 0.35. In either case, demand is inelastic, meaning that MBTA revenues would increase with a fare increase. But why would demand be relatively more inelastic for those with monthly passes? A likely explanation is that those with monthly passes use the commuter trains for daily transportation to their workplace. Although car travel is a potential alternative, the cost of parking and the hassle of traffic jams may make the commuter rail a better choice, even with a modest fare increase. Alternatively, single-fare riders may only take the commuter train occasionally, for work or pleasure, and might have viable transportation alternatives or decide just to stay home.

The MBTA also estimated that demand would be less elastic for students than nonstudents. Again, this seems a reasonable result, given that students are less likely to have their own vehicles as a transportation alternative. The MBTA decided on an average fare increase of 23 percent in July 2012. According to its analysis, it expected that overall ridership would decline by about 5.5 percent. Because public transportation demand is inelastic, revenues were expected to increase.

How accurate was the MBTA's prediction? It turned out that in the immediate months after the fare increase, overall ridership actually increased slightly! Does this result refute the basic inverse relationship between price and quantity demanded? Not necessarily. Remember, elasticity only estimates movement along a demand curve. The increase in ridership after the fare increase may have been the result of an increase in demand (i.e., a shift in the demand curve), which more than offset a decrease in the quantity demanded as a result of the fare increase. The increase in demand may have been due to improving economic conditions, an increase in gas prices, the weather, or some other factor. It may also suggest that the actual elasticity of demand is almost perfectly inelastic. This example demonstrates that economic forecasting is not an exact science and that human behavior is difficult to predict. (See Box 4.1 for another example of the problem with economic predictions.)

Discussion Questions

1. Consider the goods and services for which estimated elasticity values are given in Table 4.3. Can you think of some reasons why demand for cigarettes, eggs, and rice is inelastic? Can you think of an explanation for the two different elasticity values for soft drinks?
2. Suppose that when Winged Demons Athletic Shoes offers a 15 percent discount on its latest model of shoe, it finds that it sells 20 percent more of them. Calculate the price elasticity of demand for these shoes. Describe whether demand is price elastic or price inelastic, and describe what happens to the company's revenues after it offers the discount.

2. THE PRICE ELASTICITY OF SUPPLY

price elasticity of supply: a measure of the responsiveness of quantity supplied to changes in price

Just as movements along a demand curve can be described by elasticity, so can movements along a supply curve, which reflect the **price elasticity of supply**. The price elasticity of supply measures the responsiveness of quantity supplied to changes in price.

Suppose, for example, that a manufacturing company is having trouble getting adequate supplies of a needed component that is an input to its production process. Only a limited number of companies have the equipment to make this particular component, and those companies are not willing to produce more of it at the going price. The company's buyer might consider offering the suppliers a higher price. By how much will the buyer need to sweeten his firm's offer to induce suppliers to supply the quantity of components that the company needs? What the company's buyer needs to know is the responsiveness of quantity supplied to price.

If the suppliers will significantly increase the quantity that they sell with a modest increase in price, then we would say the supply curve is price elastic. Meanwhile, if it takes a considerably higher price to induce suppliers to increase quantity, then we would say the supply curve is price inelastic.

The company's dilemma is illustrated in Figure 4.6. It is initially able to purchase a quantity of Q_0 of the components at a price of P_0. Then suppose that it wishes to increase the quantity it purchases to Q_1. If supply is relatively elastic (represented by the supply curve S_e), it can induce suppliers to increase supply to Q_1 with a price of only P_e. However, if supply is relatively inelastic (such as supply curve S_i), it will need to pay a higher price, say P_i. Obviously, the company needing the components will hope that the supply curve is relatively elastic, such as S_e, which means that it will have to pay less to obtain Q_1. Note that the known starting point, at a price of P_0 and a quantity supplied of Q_0, lies on both supply curves. The elasticity of supply determines how the curves diverge from the known starting point.

Figure 4.6   **The Price Elasticity of Supply**

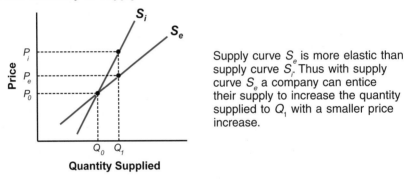

Supply curve S_e is more elastic than supply curve S_i. Thus with supply curve S_e a company can entice their supply to increase the quantity supplied to Q_1 with a smaller price increase.

As in the equation for the price elasticity of demand, the price elasticity of supply is calculated as:

Elasticity = % change in quantity supplied / % change in price

Given that supply curves normally slope upward, price and quantity supplied change in the same direction and thus taking the absolute value is not required. If the price elasticity of supply is greater than 1, we would say the supply curve is price elastic. If the price elasticity of supply is less than 1, we would say the supply curve is price inelastic. A price elasticity of supply equal to 1 is "unit elastic."

A perfectly inelastic supply curve is vertical and indicates that supply is completely fixed. The supply of authentic 1940 Chevrolets, for example, can no longer be increased, no matter what the price. A perfectly elastic supply curve is horizontal, indicating that buyers can buy all they want at the going price. As individual consumers, for example, each of us makes up such a small part of the total market for things like supermarket groceries and mass-produced clothing that such a horizontal curve is a reasonable representation of what we face. We generally pay the same price, no matter how many units we buy of a good.

Hundreds of economic studies have estimated the elasticity of demand, but relatively few estimate the elasticity of supply. Several studies have estimated the elasticity of supply for housing, primarily in the United States. The results indicate that the supply of housing is normally, but not always, price elastic. Estimates of the elasticity of supply for housing range from below 1.0 (inelastic) to as much as 30 or higher.[1] The elasticity of supply for labor, however, is generally found to be price inelastic. The U.S. Congressional Budget Office uses a value of 0.40 for the elasticity of supply for labor in its analyses.[2]

Discussion Questions

1. Suppose that a government alternative-energy program is having difficulty hiring enough engineers to work on a project, and so it raises the wage that it offers to pay by 15 percent. Who are the buyers in this case? Who are the sellers? What does the wage represent, in terms of a supply-and-demand framework? If the program finds that employment applications then increase by 30 percent, what can you conclude about the price elasticity of supply of engineering labor?

2. Economists draw supply curves as upward sloping. But sometimes, as consumers, we notice that the price per unit goes down if we buy more of something, not up. For example, a liter bottle of Pepsi costs less per ounce than a can of Pepsi, warehouse stores sell breakfast cereal in "jumbo size" for a low per-unit price, and clothing stores offer "buy one, get one free." Why might sellers offer such prices?

3. INCOME ELASTICITY OF DEMAND

income elasticity of demand: a measure of the responsiveness of demand to changes in income, holding price constant

The final kind of elasticity that we consider in this chapter is the **income elasticity of demand**. This measures how much the quantity demanded changes when income changes, but holding price constant. Recall from Chapter 3 that income is a nonprice determinant of demand that shifts the entire demand curve.

Figure 4.7 illustrates the concept of income elasticity. Suppose that D_0 represents an initial demand curve. At a price of P_0, the quantity demanded is Q_0. Now suppose that consumer incomes increase. At higher incomes, demand will normally increase (i.e., shift to the right). Income elasticity indicates how much demand shifts. If demand for the good is relatively income inelastic, then demand might only shift slightly, say to D_i. At D_i and with price constant at P_0, the quantity demanded increases to Q_i. The demand curve D_e represents a relatively elastic response, with the quantity demanded increasing to Q_e.

Figure 4.7   **Income Elasticity of Demand**

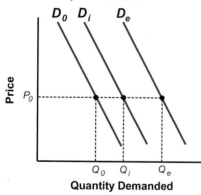

An increase in income shifts the demand curve outward (to the right). The greater the income elasticity of demand, the greater the shift.

As in the equations for price elasticity, income elasticity is calculated as:

normal goods: goods for which demand increases when incomes rise and decreases when incomes fall

income elasticity of demand = % change in quantity demanded / % change in income

For most goods, when income increases, demand also increases. Thus income elasticity is positive. Goods for which demand rises when a household's income rises are called **normal goods**. As people can afford more, they tend to buy more.

inferior goods: goods for which demand decreases when incomes rise and increases when incomes fall

However, demand for some goods may fall when incomes rise; these goods are called **inferior goods**. Individuals and families tend to buy less of goods like ramen noodles or second-hand clothes as incomes rise. For an inferior good, the income elasticity of demand is negative.

When income elasticity is positive but less than 1, demand is called income inelastic. Spending rises with income, but less than proportionately. For example, when income rises by 10 percent, spending on a particular good may rise by only 5 percent. When the income elasticity is positive and greater than 1, a good is called income elastic. In this case, expenditures on that good will take up a greater share of total spending by the buyer. For example, income may rise by 10 percent, but spending on the good rises by 20 percent. (If some goods are income elastic, then other goods must be income inelastic—or a buyer would end up exceeding his or her budget!)

Income-elastic goods are referred to as "luxuries," because the rich spend proportionately more on them than do the poor. By the same token, goods for which demand is inelastic are sometimes called "necessities." These labels, however, are only economists' shorthand for specifying ranges of income elasticity and have nothing to do with human well-being. For example, studies of consumer demand usually find cigarettes to be, by this definition, "necessities" because poorer people (who are more likely to smoke) spend a greater proportion of their income on them.

Households are not the only economic actors that have to work within a budget. Divisions of businesses, branches of government, and other organizations also find that the budgets for their operations may vary. Thus we can also speak of income elasticity for these economic actors. Businesses that make high profits often spend more on holiday parties and other perks. Offices with tight budgets may spend more on low-grade copier paper, an inferior good. As discussed in Chapter 3, income changes—or, more generally, changes in any overall ability to pay—shift the demand curve, changing the quantity demanded at any price.

Discussion Questions

1. Suppose that your income increases. Which goods and services would you buy more of (i.e., normal goods)? Which goods and services would you buy less of (i.e., inferior goods)?
2. Which goods might be normal goods at some income levels but inferior goods at other income levels? (Hint: You might think of a household that is desperately poor, then becomes moderately poor, and eventually becomes middle income.)

4. INCOME AND SUBSTITUTION EFFECTS OF A PRICE CHANGE

Returning to the impact of price changes on the quantity demanded, we can think further about the motivations of consumers. It makes intuitive sense that consumers will buy more of a good when prices fall and less of it when prices rise. But we can define two underlying reasons for these responses.

First, a change in the price of a particular good or service changes how consumers evaluate that good or service relative to other goods and services. Specifically, if the price of something falls, it becomes relatively more attractive to consumers. If the price rises, it becomes relatively less attractive. For example, suppose that the price of apples and oranges start out at $1.00 and $1.50 per pound, respectively. Now suppose the price of oranges rises to $2.00 per pound while the price of the apples remains at $1.00. The oranges are now twice as expensive as apples, instead of 1.5 times as expensive. Oranges have become relatively more expensive, and apples relatively cheaper.

substitution effect of a price change: the tendency of a price increase for a particular good to reduce the quantity demanded of that good, as buyers turn to relatively cheaper substitutes

Economists refer to changes in consumer behavior as a result of changes in relative prices the **substitution effect of a price change**. When one good becomes more expensive relative to others, people will reduce the quantity demanded of that good and turn toward the relatively cheaper substitutes. If you think that apples and oranges are good substitutes for each other, then the rise in the relative price of oranges will tend to make you buy fewer oranges and more apples. If the price of natural gas water heating rises relative to the price of solar water heating, one can expect any household or organization that uses hot water to lean more toward solar than before, when the time comes to replace its system.

Note that a substitution effect occurs only when relative prices change. For example, if the price of apples rose to $2.00 per pound at the same time that the price of oranges rose to $3.00 per pound, then their relative prices would remain unchanged (oranges are still 1.5 times more expensive than apples). In this case, there is no substitution effect.

income effect of a price change: the tendency of a price increase to reduce the quantity demanded of normal goods (and to increase the quantity demanded of any inferior goods)

In addition to a substitution effect, economists also speak of the **income effect of a price change**. The income effect arises because an increase in the price of any good that a buyer purchases reduces her or his overall purchasing power (given a set income or budget). For example, suppose that you could buy 12 apples and 5 oranges at their initial prices, but then the price of oranges rise. Given your limited income, you can no longer afford 12 apples and 5 oranges. In other words, the effect of the rise in the price of oranges is essentially the same as a decrease in your income. Any price rise for a good that you usually purchase makes you, in a sense, poorer. Similar to a decrease in income, the income effect indicates that people will respond to a price increase by reducing the quantity of normal goods that they buy (and increase the quantity demanded of any inferior goods).

Because you are now poorer, your response to the price increase will depend, in part, on which goods are normal and which (if any) are inferior, as defined earlier in the chapter. If both apples and oranges are normal goods, you, now being poorer, will tend to buy less of each. If, however, apples are inferior goods to you, which you buy only because you cannot afford more oranges, you will tend to buy even more apples (but fewer oranges) when you are made poorer by a rise in orange prices. (What if, instead, oranges were the inferior good?)

When the price of a good or service changes, the income and substitution effects act together:

- If the good is a normal good and its price rises, both the income effect and the substitution effect will tend to reduce the quantity demanded of the good. The quantity demanded falls with a price rise, both because the buyer is poorer and because other goods now look relatively more attractive.
- If the good is inferior and its price rises, the income effect will encourage greater expenditures, at the same time that the substitution effect pushes toward lower expenditures. In general, though, we expect that the substitution effect will be stronger than the income effect in the case of inferior goods, so the demand curve will still be downward-sloping.

The exception, where a price rise for an inferior good leads to such a large income effect that quantity demanded increases, is called the case of a "Giffen good." It is rare in practice, especially in industrialized countries. In very poor countries, however, it is sometimes the case that the poorest of the poor spend a large proportion of their income on a basic foodstuff, such as low-quality rice or starchy root vegetables, and tiny amounts of income on more expensive vegetables and protein-rich foods. If the price of the basic foodstuff rises, survival may demand that they stop purchasing the more expensive foods entirely and make up for these lost calories by buying more of the basic foodstuff. In terms of market analysis, the demand curve for the basic foodstuff will slope upward (and the price elasticity will be positive, even before taking the absolute value). In terms of well-being, of course, the situation represents a human disaster; the starchy food will not supply the vitamins or protein needed for healthy functioning and development.

Discussion Questions

1. Which of the following might be inferior goods? Could they be normal goods at some portion of the income scale and inferior goods at others?
   a. A community college education
   b. Cigarettes
   c. BMW cars
   d. Supermarket food
   e. Restaurant food

2. Suppose that the prices of all goods and services available to a particular buyer go up by 20 percent, all at the same time, while the buyer's income (or budget) remains unchanged. What is the effect on the buyer's purchase of normal goods? Of inferior goods? Is there a substitution effect?

5. SHORT-RUN VERSUS LONG-RUN ELASTICITY

short-run elasticity: a measure of the relatively immediate responsiveness to a price change

So far, our analysis has essentially assumed that adjustment from one equilibrium point to another equilibrium point happens without any lapse of time. In the real world, the time taken for adjustments is important. For example, we noted how the price elasticity of demand for a good depends on the availability of substitute goods. If substitutes are readily available, demand for the good in question will tend to be more price elastic than it would be if substitutes were hard to get. But what if substitutes are hard to get right away but easier to get over time?

long-run elasticity: a measure of the response to a price change after economic actors have had time to make adjustments

It is possible for a good to be highly price inelastic in the short run but more price elastic as people can make adjustments over time. We can distinguish **short-run elasticity**, which measures relatively immediate responses to a price change, from **long-run elasticity**, which measures how much quantity responds after economic actors have had some time to adjust.

Gasoline is a good example for which the passage of time is important in determining the elasticity of demand, as we saw in Table 4.3. In the short run, when gas prices increase, consumers are mostly unable to reduce the amount of gas that they use for commuting and shopping. But over time they may be able to purchase a more fuel-efficient vehicle, rely more on public transportation, consider carpooling, and even move closer to where they work. We see in Table 4.3 that the long-run elasticity of demand for gas is still inelastic at 0.3, but it is more elastic than the short-run elasticity of 0.1.*

Discussion Questions

1. Maria rents on a month-to-month basis an apartment that she can barely afford, in a market where apartments are hard to find. Her landlord announces that she is doubling the rent, effective immediately. What is likely to be Maria's short-run response (say, over the next few days or weeks)? What might be her likely long-run response (over the next few months)?

2. Suppose that new technological breakthroughs make solar water heaters extremely cheap to run, compared with water heaters that use fossil fuels, and only moderately expensive to install. Illustrate on a graph what you might expect the short-run and long-run demand adjustments to this price drop to be. What sorts of factors affect how long, in real time, it might take for the "long-run" situation to occur?

REVIEW QUESTIONS

1. List three reasons why the demand for a good or service may be elastic. List three reasons why the demand for a good may be inelastic.

2. What is the formula for the price elasticity of demand?

3. What is the "technical definition" of a price-elastic demand? What is the technical definition of a price-inelastic demand?

4. What does a perfectly inelastic demand curve look like? What does a perfectly elastic demand curve look like?

5. How does elasticity change along a linear demand curve?

6. Is elasticity the same thing as the slope of a curve?

---

* The difference between the short run and the long run, as specific periods, is rather vague. In the case of gasoline demand, the short run might be only a few months. A period of a year or more would probably be considered the long run.

7. What is the relationship between elasticity and how a firm's revenues change as it changes its prices?

8. How can we represent revenues on a graph?

9. Describe quantity and revenue responses to price changes when the price elasticity of demand takes on the following values: (a) 0, (b) between 0 and 1, (c) 1, (d) greater than 1.

10. What are examples of goods that are price elastic? What are some examples of price inelastic goods?

11. Sketch, on a single graph, a relatively price-elastic supply curve and a relatively price-inelastic supply curve. (Make sure that they go through the same point.)

12. What is the equation for calculating the price elasticity of supply?

13. What is the income elasticity of demand?

14. Give one example of a normal good and one example of an inferior good.

15. Can you illustrate the income elasticity of demand using a single demand curve? Why or why not?

16. Explain how a price change has both "income effects" and "substitution effects" on buyer behavior.

17. Explain why the long-run elasticity of demand for a good may differ from the short-run elasticity.

EXERCISES

1. For each of the following items, discuss whether you think the demand that the seller faces will be price inelastic or price elastic, and explain why.
   a. A new CD by an extremely popular recording artist
   b. One share of stock, when there are millions of shares for that company outstanding
   c. Bottled drinking water, at a town in the desert
   d. Your used textbooks, at the end of the term

2. Calculate the price elasticity of demand for the following cases:
   a. When price rises by 5 percent, quantity demanded drops by 10 percent.
   b. When price rises by 10 percent, quantity demanded drops by 2 percent.
   c. When price rises by 0.05 percent, quantity demanded drops by 99 percent. (Which extreme case is this approaching? Note that the price rise is a fraction of 1 percent, not 5 percent.)
   d. When price rises by 99 percent, quantity demanded drops by 0.05 percent. (Which extreme case is this approaching?)
   e. When price falls by 10 percent, quantity demanded rises by 2 percent.

3. Calculate the percentage change in revenue that would result from each of the actions in Exercise 2 above. Assume that the initial price in all cases is $100 per unit, and the initial quantity demanded is 1,000 units.

4. Braeburn Publishing decides to try to cut its costs of printing books by cutting the price that it offers to companies that supply it with paper.
   a. Suppose that the supply is perfectly price inelastic (at least in the short run), because Braeburn buys the entire output of the Morales Paper Company. Because it has no other customers (for now), Morales has no choice but to sell to Braeburn. Illustrate on a graph what will happen to the quantity that Braeburn buys, the price that it pays, and the amount that it will spend on paper.
   b. Suppose, instead, that the supply of paper is very (but not perfectly) price elastic, because all the companies that sell paper to Braeburn can easily sell their paper elsewhere. Illustrate on a graph what will happen to the quantity that Braeburn will be able to buy, the price that it will pay, and the amount that it will spend on paper, if it follows through with its plan to offer a lower price.

5. Use the formulas for elasticity to answer the following questions.
   a. When Mariba's income rises by 10 percent, her expenditures on carrots rise 12 percent. What is Mariba's income elasticity of demand for carrots? Are carrots, for her, a normal or an inferior good?
   b. Suppose that the price elasticity of demand for milk is 0.6. If a grocer raises the price of milk by 15 percent, by what percentage will milk sales decrease as a result of the price increase? Will the grocer's revenue from milk sales go up or down?
   c. Suppose that the price elasticity of supply for paper is 1.5. You notice that the quantity of paper supplied decreases by 6 percent as the result of a change in the price of paper. Determine by what percentage the price of paper must have declined.

6. Clark Marketing Services has found, through market tests, that the demand for Sonya's Peanuts has

a price elasticity of 0.5 and an income elasticity of 1.8. You, an economist employed by Sonya's Peanuts, have been asked by the executives of the company to explain what this means for its pricing policy and choice of sales outlets. Company executives have been thinking of lowering the firm's prices and concentrating on selling to discount stores. What do you advise? Explain in a paragraph.

7. Many environmentalists think that an increase in the price of petroleum products to consumers would be a good thing. Many policymakers believe that an increase in the price of higher education (say, through increased tuitions), however, would be a bad thing. Discuss why these beliefs might be held, using the concepts of "externalities" (discussion in Chapter 1) and "substitution effects of a price change."

8. Look at the estimated price elasticity of demand for cigarettes in Table 4.3. If the government raises taxes on cigarettes, the price to consumers goes up. The extra revenue collected from the higher price goes to the government. Describe in a few sentences the effectiveness of taxing cigarettes as (a) part of a campaign to stop people from smoking and (b) a way of raising revenue.

9. Match each concept in Column A with the corresponding fact or example in Column B:

	Column A	Column B
a.	Price-inelastic demand	1. Income elasticity of 1.4.
b.	Inferior good	2. A 12% rise in price is associated with a 12% fall in quantity demanded.
c.	Income effect of a price change	3. Dining out more often because your landlord reduced your rent.
d.	Perfectly price elastic supply	4. Expenditures on a good increase when your income rises.
e.	Unit price elasticity of demand	5. Any rise in price will cause quantity demanded to fall to zero.
f.	Perfectly in-elastic supply	6. Buying fewer muffins, and more donuts, because the relative price of muffins has risen.
g.	Normal good	7. Revenues rise as a seller increases her price.
h.	Perfectly elastic demand	8. What you face when buying milk at the grocery store.
i.	Substitution effect	9. The acres of land in downtown Chicago.
j.	Income-elastic demand	10. People spend less on this as they get richer.

NOTES

1. See Sock-Yong Phang, Kyung-Hwan Kim, and Susan Wachter, "Supply Elasticity of Housing," in *International Encyclopedia of Housing and Home* (Oxford: Elsevier Science, 2012).

2. Felix Reichling and Charles Whalen, "Review of Estimates of the Frisch Elasticity of Labor Supply," Congressional Budget Office Working Paper 2012-13, Washington, DC, October 2012.

5 Welfare Analysis

Adam Smith's *An Inquiry into the Nature and Causes of the Wealth of Nations,* published in 1776, laid down the theoretical framework for modern capitalist economies. In perhaps the most famous passage from the book, Smith asserted that a seller interested only in maximizing his own gain would be

> led by an invisible hand to promote an end which was no part of his intention. . . . By pursuing his own interest he frequently promotes that of the society more effectually than when he really intends to promote it.

Thus Smith suggests that an economic system based on markets can effectively promote the general welfare of society. In the eighteenth century, this was a new, even radical, idea. Until Smith's time, societies tended to be authoritarian and hierarchical. For the average person, individual freedoms were few and opportunities for economic advancement were virtually nonexistent. Many thinkers worried that if people were free to pursue their own self-interest, then the rigid organization of society might break down, leading to a chaotic situation in which nothing would get done. But Smith detailed how the self-regulating features of markets could not only impose order on society but even potentially create the best outcome for society as a whole.

But what do we mean by the "best" outcome? And how can we measure the general welfare of a society in a meaningful way? In this chapter, we extend our understanding of markets to consider their implications for social welfare. We see that under certain conditions and assumptions, markets do, indeed, produce an outcome for society that may be considered "best." But in the real world, these conditions and assumptions rarely apply, and a more accurate assessment of markets requires us to consider the benefits of markets in a broader social and environmental context.

1. Welfare Economics

welfare economics: the branch of microeconomics that seeks to estimate the social welfare of different scenarios in order to determine how to maximize net social benefits

In Chapter 1, we stated that a central objective of economics is enhancing the well-being of society. **Welfare economics** is a branch of microeconomics that seeks to estimate the social welfare of different scenarios in order to determine ways to maximize net social benefits. Welfare economics can be studied from both a theoretical perspective and a quantitative applied perspective.

As a theoretical approach, welfare economics provides insights into situations in which markets produce desirable outcomes as well as other situations in which markets either require policy interventions or are ineffective at meeting our final goals. As a quantitative approach, welfare economics seeks to measure social costs and benefits numerically so that different policy scenarios can be compared. Ideally, we can then choose the policy that produces the greatest social welfare.

Welfare economics offers an appealing feature—the possibility of measuring the quantitative costs and benefits of different policy scenarios. If this can be done reliably, it should then be possible to simply choose the option that results in the greatest social welfare, where **social welfare** is defined as total benefits minus total costs, or total net benefits.

social welfare: total benefits to society minus total costs, or total net benefits

Some economists use such terms as "social welfare" and "social well-being" interchangeably. However, the two concepts have a subtle, but critical, distinction. As defined above, social welfare is something that can potentially be measured quantitatively, although this approach has numerous limitations. Well-being, which we regard as the final goal of economics, is a broader concept that cannot be measured in quantitative terms. Well-being includes such objectives as fairness, participation, and social relations (recall Table 1.1 in Chapter 1). A particular outcome may maximize social welfare in a quantitative sense but not necessarily be the best outcome from the perspective of social well-being.

The goal of maximizing social welfare is sometimes viewed as a positive framework, which does not require normative judgments. In particular, it may seem that simply adding up all benefits and costs and choosing the option that yields the greatest net benefits avoids the influence of value judgments. But explicit and implicit value judgments are almost always involved in stating that a particular policy is "best." For example, in a highly unequal society, would it be better to add $20 billion to the income of those who are already rich or $10 billion to the income of those who are currently poor? The former option offers the greatest net benefits in monetary terms, but the latter might be considered preferable on social and ethical grounds.

Welfare economics considers the costs and benefits of three basic economic actors:

1. consumers
2. producers
3. the rest of society (including, for this discussion, future generations and the ecological context)

Consumers obtain benefits when they can voluntarily purchase a desired product at an acceptable price. Producers obtain benefits when they profitably sell products. Often a market transaction results in costs or benefits to those not directly involved in the transaction, that is, the "rest of society." For example, the production of paper can generate pollution that is harmful to the health of local residents. Such impacts on people not involved in the transaction were identified as externalities in Chapter 1, also sometimes called **third-party effects.** In this chapter, we focus mainly on the costs and benefits to consumers and producers. However, we should be aware that any analysis that focuses exclusively on the consumers and producers involved in a market is likely to be incomplete. In Chapter 12, we study impacts on the "rest of society" in more detail, with a particular focus on environmental impacts.

third-party effects: impacts of an economic transaction on those not involved in the transaction, such as the health effects of pollution

We next turn to how to estimate market benefits to consumers. Then we consider market benefits to producers. Section 4 combines our results to determine the overall social welfare arising from market transactions, both in equilibrium and in cases of surplus or shortage. The final section makes some initial policy inferences based on welfare analysis.

Discussion Questions

1. Do you believe, in principle, that the costs and benefits of various policies can be quantified in monetary terms? Do you believe that some impacts cannot be fundamentally measured in dollars? How would you suggest that we evaluate these impacts?
2. Think of a government policy that is currently being debated in the news. Describe how you would evaluate the costs and benefits of this policy differently if you were concerned primarily about social welfare or social well-being.

2. CONSUMER SURPLUS

In order to understand what our market model tells us about benefits to sellers and buyers, we need to reconsider supply and demand curves. In this section, we take a closer look at demand curves, and in the next section we apply a similar approach to supply curves. The analysis requires some detailed thinking, but after you grasp the concepts in this chapter, you will have a solid foundation for much of microeconomic analysis.

2.1 QUANTIFYING CONSUMER BENEFITS

We will see in Chapters 7 and 8 that consumer decision-making is a complex process—one that appears reasonably rational in some cases but quite irrational in others. For now, we assume that consumers make rational choices that effectively move them toward their final goals.

Every time you contemplate buying something, you have to make a decision about whether you should part with a particular amount of money in exchange for a certain good or service. For example, say that you are considering whether you should spend $1.10 for a cup of coffee. You must decide whether the cup of coffee is worth $1.10 to you. If you decide to buy the coffee, then presumably the loss of $1.10 is more than offset by the amount of welfare that you get by consuming the coffee. Economists use various terms to describe the benefits that people get from their purchases, including utility, welfare, and well-being. As discussed above, we use the term "welfare" here to represent a concept that can be quantitatively measured, as opposed to well-being that cannot be reduced to a single number.

The benefits that people gain from their purchases are mainly "psychic" benefits—they are somehow happier as a result of their purchases. So how can we take this vague notion of a psychic benefit and measure it quantitatively? And in what units should it be measured?

As you might guess, economists tend to prefer to measure this benefit in monetary terms, in dollars in the case of the United States. This allows us to compare these benefits directly with the cost of a product. So, if a cup of coffee costs $1.10, and you decide to purchase it, then those psychic benefits must in some sense exceed $1.10. A rational consumer who buys a cup of coffee is willing to part with $1.10 for it, while a rational consumer who does not buy the coffee does not believe that it is worth $1.10.

But obviously some consumers realize more personal benefits from the same cup of coffee. In other words, the welfare that someone gets from a cup of coffee can vary considerably from one consumer to another. Some people's "happiness" might increase only a little, while others may obtain a big increase in their happiness from the coffee. According to welfare economics, these differences in consumer preferences are expressed in differences in their willingness to pay for something.

maximum willingness to pay (WTP): the maximum amount that a rational consumer will pay for a particular product. In welfare economics, consumers' maximum WTP represents the total benefits that they expect to obtain from a product, expressed in monetary terms.

The key to measuring consumer benefits using welfare analysis is to identify consumers' **maximum willingness to pay (WTP)** for something. Welfare economics assumes that consumers' maximum WTP represents the total benefits that they expect to obtain from a product, expressed in monetary terms. A rational consumer is someone who buys a product as long as the actual price is not greater than her maximum WTP for it. Imagine that the price of coffee increases from $1.10 per cup to, say, $1.40. Some people who were willing to buy coffee at $1.10 would not be willing to pay $1.40. Theoretically, every consumer has a maximum amount that he is willing to pay for a particular product, given the fact that he has alternative choices, for example, purchasing another product or just saving his money.

Suppose that a particular consumer, Luis, is willing to pay a maximum of $1.40 for a cup of coffee, and not a penny more. If the price of coffee is $1.40, then Luis would view trading $1.40 for the coffee as essentially an equal trade—he gives up $1.40 and obtains an equivalent value in welfare from the coffee.

Now suppose that a different consumer, Madeleine, is willing to pay a maximum of $1.75 for the same cup of coffee. Thus $1.75 represents the welfare that she would get if she buys the same cup of coffee. Given that Madeleine has to pay only $1.40 for it, she is willing to

consumer surplus:
the net benefits obtained from a purchase, equal to the difference between a consumer's maximum willingness to pay and the price

buy the coffee. In fact, she is getting a bargain in a sense because she can buy the coffee for $0.35 less than the maximum amount she is willing to pay. Welfare economics defines the difference between a consumer's maximum WTP and the price one must actually pay as the net welfare benefit from the purchase, referred to as **consumer surplus**. Consumer surplus represents the "extra benefits" received from buying something above what is paid for it.

So, in Madeleine's case, she obtains a consumer surplus of $0.35 from buying a cup of coffee, calculated as her maximum WTP of $1.75 minus the price of $1.40:

$$Consumer\ surplus = \$1.75\ (maximum\ WTP) - \$1.40\ (price) = \$0.35$$

Suppose that a third consumer, Emma, is willing to pay a maximum of $2.00 for the same cup of coffee. Note that this may reflect either Emma's greater appreciation for coffee or her higher disposable income, a point to which we return later. Emma's consumer surplus would be $0.60. Finally, suppose that a fourth potential consumer, Tom, is willing to pay a maximum of only $1.00 for a cup of coffee. Because the market price is $1.40, Tom would choose not to buy the coffee, assuming rational behavior. Of course, anyone who is not willing to pay the going price will not receive any consumer surplus.

2.2 CONSUMER SURPLUS AND DEMAND CURVES

Of course consumers are rarely required to think about the exact maximum amount that they would be willing to pay for something. In the real world, consumers are normally presented with a price, and either they buy the product or they don't. So, at first glance, it seems that estimating consumer surplus quantitatively is not a realistic option.

But if we think about a demand curve in more detail, we see that it actually provides us with the information that we need to estimate consumer surplus, not only for an individual but for the entire market. Let's go back to our demand curve for coffee. Figure 5.1 repeats Figure 3.4. We know that at a price of $1.40 per cup, 600 cups of coffee will be demanded per week, as shown at Point A in Figure 5.1.

Next, imagine that we look at a demand curve with a magnifying glass, zooming in on a single point like Point A. This is shown in Figure 5.2.* Note that the *y*-axis now covers

Figure 5.1   **Demand Curve for Cups of Coffee**

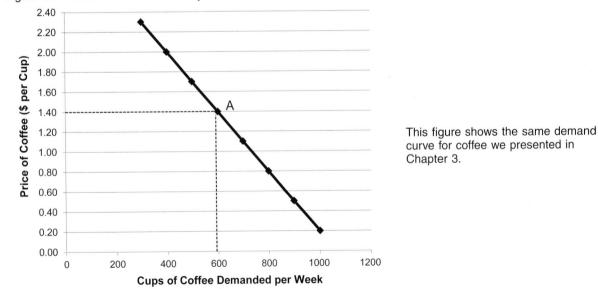

This figure shows the same demand curve for coffee we presented in Chapter 3.

---

*The "magnified" demand curve in Figure 5.2 is not actually the same as the one in Figure 5.1; in Figure 5.2 we use a different slope, in order to focus on a price change that causes the quantity demanded to decrease by 1.

Figure 5.2   **Detailed Demand Curve for Coffee**

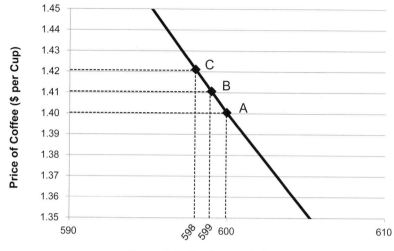

By "zooming in" on the demand curve we can associate marginal price changes with marginal changes in the quantity demanded.

only the range between $1.35 and $1.45, and the *x*-axis covers only the range between 590 and 610 cups of coffee. Point A shows that once again at a price of $1.40, exactly 600 cups of coffee are demanded per week. Now suppose that the price of coffee were increased slightly, by only a penny, from $1.40 to $1.41 per cup. We see in Figure 5.2 that the quantity demanded decreased from 600 to 599 cups per week, as shown by Point B. In other words, one person in our market was willing to pay $1.40 for a cup of coffee, but not $1.41. That one person is the reason that the quantity demanded decreases by 1 when the price rises from $1.40 to $1.41.

Going back to the idea of consumer surplus, Point A represents the maximum willingness to pay ($1.40) of that one person. So we can actually determine the consumer surplus for this person by comparing this point on the demand curve to the price. If the price of coffee were, say, $1.10, then we can conclude that this person's consumer surplus would be $0.30.

If price rises by another penny, from $1.41 to $1.42, then the quantity demanded decreases by 1 again, from 599 to 598 cups (Point C). This is because one other person was willing to pay $1.41, but not $1.42. Again, we can calculate the consumer surplus for the person represented by Point B (the point at which this person is still willing to buy coffee) as the difference between his maximum WTP ($1.41) and price. So if the price of coffee were $1.10, the person at Point B would receive a consumer surplus of $0.31.

The point of this detailed look at a demand curve is to emphasize that a demand curve is not really a smooth line, but a collection of points that represent the decisions of many individuals. Every time the quantity demanded decreases by 1, it is because the price has increased sufficiently for one person to switch from being willing to pay for the product to being not willing to pay.

marginal change: a change of one unit (either an increase or a decrease)

Much economic analysis involves considering **marginal changes**, which means very small changes, either an increase or a decrease; often this is modeled as a change of one unit, as when (above) we add *one* penny to a price, or subtract *one* customer from a large number. We go into this important topic in more detail in relation to production decisions (Chapters 15 and 16).

marginal benefit (for consumers): the benefit of consuming one additional unit of something

In the case that we have been discussing, for each one unit increase in quantity, the corresponding point on the demand curve represents the maximum WTP of the individual (or other economic actor) now willing to buy the product. Another way to understand this is that the points on a demand curve indicate the **marginal benefits**, measured in monetary

marginal benefits curve: a curve showing the additional benefit from each unit consumed. Another name for a demand curve, as applied to welfare economics.

units, of each additional unit of the product to those demanding them. We can say that a demand curve is actually a **marginal benefits curve**, because it tells us the benefits of each additional unit to consumers.

Note that there is a difference between the benefit of consuming a product, which is defined as the maximum WTP, and the **net benefits**, which are the benefits minus any costs. Consumer surplus is a measure of *net* benefits because the price of the product is subtracted from the maximum WTP.

Going back to our demand curve, we can show consumer surplus for any individual by subtracting his maximum WTP (his point along the demand curve) from the price. This is shown in Figure 5.3. Here Luis's maximum WTP is at Point A; he is willing to pay a maximum of $1.40 for a cup of coffee. This is the vertical distance between his point on the demand curve and the *x*-axis. If the price of coffee is $1.10, then the difference ($0.30) is his consumer surplus. This is the net benefit that he obtains from buying a cup of coffee.

Figure 5.3   **Consumer Surplus and a Demand Curve**

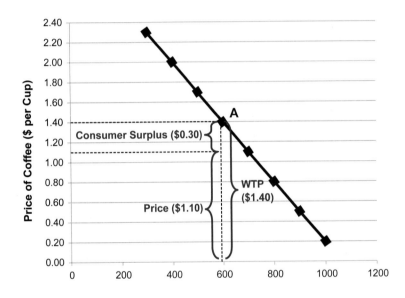

Consumer surplus is the difference between price and someone's maximum willingness to pay (i.e., the demand curve).

2.3 CONSUMER SURPLUS IN AN ENTIRE MARKET

net benefits: benefits minus any costs. Consumer surplus is a measure of net benefits because it is equal to the difference between the maximum willingness to pay and price.

aggregate (or market) benefits: the benefits to all consumers in a market

Now we are ready to take the final step in our analysis of consumer benefits. We have just seen that a demand curve tells us the marginal benefits of each additional unit of a product to consumers. But what really interests us is the benefits of a product to the entire market. Welfare economics assumes that the **aggregate (or market) benefits**, or the benefits to all consumers, is simply the sum of the benefits to each individual consumer. For example, if the entire coffee market consisted of just Luis, Madeleine, and Emma, market benefits would be the sum of the benefits of these three consumers.

The same logic applies to consumer surplus. Aggregate consumer surplus, or aggregate net benefits, is simply the sum of the consumer surpluses for all individuals who buy a product.

Although an individual's maximum WTP is shown by a single point on the demand curve, aggregate benefits can be represented by areas under a demand curve.* So, the area under a demand curve represents the total WTP for all consumers, or the aggregate benefits for all

---

*If you have studied calculus, you can use integration to determine areas under demand (and supply) curves. This is done in more advanced economics courses.

consumers. The consumer surplus for all consumers in a market is the difference between their aggregate benefits and the aggregate costs that they must pay.

We can illustrate these concepts in another graph, as shown in Figure 5.4. This is the same demand curve for coffee, but in this case extended all the way back to the y-axis. The price of coffee is $1.10 per cup, and at this price the quantity demanded is 700 cups per week. The amount that consumers must pay for these 700 cups of coffee is the gray rectangle equal to the price multiplied by the quantity sold. This is also the revenue that coffee sellers receive.

market consumer surplus: the difference between aggregate costs and aggregate benefits, or net benefits obtained by all consumers in a market. On a supply-and-demand graph, it is equal to the area under a demand curve but above the price.

Aggregate benefits are the area under the demand curve, up to the quantity actually sold (700 cups). Of course, no benefits are obtained for cups of coffee that are not sold. The **market consumer surplus** is the difference between aggregate costs and aggregate benefits—the blue-shaded triangle in the graph. In other words, market consumer surplus is the area under the demand curve but above the price. According to welfare economics, this area represents the net benefits consumers receive from a market. Thus we can now use a supply-and-demand graph to estimate the quantitative welfare benefits that accrue to consumers—measured as the area below the demand curve but above price. This approach allows us to convert the aggregate psychic benefits of consumers, a rather vague concept, into something we can actually measure. We now turn our attention to the benefits of producers.

Figure 5.4   **Market Consumer Surplus**

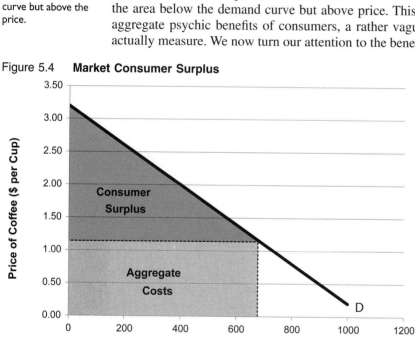

Market consumer surplus is the area below the demand curve but above the price.

Discussion Questions

1. Think about a good or service that you have purchased recently. Try to estimate the maximum amount that you would have been willing to pay for it. What factors influenced your WTP decision? How do you think your willingness to pay might differ from that of other consumers?

2. Do you think that the concept of consumer surplus is an effective tool for converting "psychic" benefits to a monetary value? Do you have any reservations about the concept?

3. PRODUCER SURPLUS

Now that we understand welfare analysis from the perspective of consumers, we can apply much of the same logic to producers. In particular, we will take a closer look at supply curves to determine how we can use them to understand the benefits producers receive from markets.

3.1 QUANTIFYING PRODUCER BENEFITS

producer surplus:
the net benefits that
producers receive
from selling products,
equal to the differ-
ence between the
selling price and the
marginal costs

marginal cost: the
cost of producing
one additional unit of
something

Whereas the benefits to consumers were defined somewhat vaguely as "psychic" benefits, the benefits that producers receive from markets are much more concrete. So, while consumers seek something vague like happiness or well-being, economists assume that producers seek profits. This makes our analysis of producer benefits relatively straightforward. Rather than needing to convert consumer psychic benefits to monetary units based on their WTP, profits are already measured in dollars.

Welfare economics uses the term **producer surplus** to indicate the benefits that accrue to producers from selling products. For the purpose of our analysis, we essentially assume that producer surplus and profits are the same thing.* The producer surplus for any unit of a product is the difference between its selling price and the cost of producing that particular unit, that is, its **marginal cost**. (We examine the concept of marginal cost more closely in Chapter 15.)

Are sellers really interested only in profits? We consider this issue later in the book. For now, we can note that sellers are also people who seek to enhance their well-being. Making a healthy profit is, of course, a component of their well-being, but they may have other motivations and goals as well. But producer surplus considers only sellers' financial benefits. Again, we must realize that welfare, as defined in economics, is different from well-being.

3.2 PRODUCER SURPLUS AND SUPPLY CURVES

In order to estimate producer surplus, we need information on sellers' production costs. You might think that we need to come up with some new curves to illustrate production costs, but that is not necessary. In fact, a supply curve is actually a marginal cost curve. In order to understand why, we need to reconsider how a supply curve relates to the decisions of individual suppliers.

We start with our supply curve from Chapter 3, shown here as Figure 5.5. We can see, for example, that at a price of $1.00 per cup, 600 cups of coffee are supplied. But at that price, why are exactly 600 cups of coffee supplied, and not 601 or more?

Welfare economics assumes that sellers will offer a given unit of a product for sale *only* if they can make a profit on that unit. In other words, if the price they can receive by selling

Figure 5.5   **Supply Curve for Cups of Coffee**

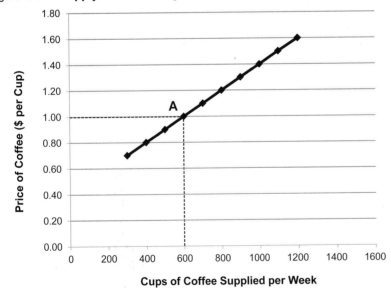

This figure shows the same supply curve for coffee we presented in Chapter 3.

---

*Technically speaking, this is not quite true. From a marginal perspective, producer surplus is the difference between the price of a product and its marginal cost. Some of this surplus, however, may be used to pay fixed expenses and thus not represent profit to the producer.

is higher than their production costs, they will produce that unit and offer it for sale. If the price is less than their production costs, they will not produce it.

Just as we did with a demand curve, we can zoom in on a supply curve to understand why exactly 600 cups of coffee are offered for sale at a price of $1.00 per cup. We do this with Figure 5.6. The graph shows us that in order for more than 600 cups of coffee to be offered for sale, the price must rise from $1.00 per cup to $1.01 per cup.* So assuming that sellers will offer a product only if they can make a profit on it and will not offer a product if they cannot make a profit on it, we can make the following statements:

- The seller *does* make a profit on the 600th cup of coffee when price is $1.00, because it *is* offered for sale (Point A).
- The seller *does not* make a profit on the 601st cup of coffee when price is $1.00, because it *is not* offered for sale.
- If the price rises to $1.01, then the 601st cup of coffee then becomes profitable and is offered for sale (Point B).

Now ask yourself: How much does it cost the seller to produce the 601st cup of coffee? Realizing that it is not profitable at a price of $1.00, but is profitable at a price of $1.01, we can conclude that the production cost must be more than $1.00 but less than $1.01. In other words, the marginal cost of producing the 601st cup of coffee is slightly more than $1.00.** Looking at Figure 5.6, that is exactly what the supply curve indicates—moving from 600 cups (Point A) to 601 cups (Point B) of coffee, the corresponding price is between $1.00 and $1.01. The supply curve is telling us the marginal cost of producing coffee.

At a price of $1.01, the seller offers 601 cups of coffee, but not 602. Again, it would take a further price increase, from $1.01 to $1.02, to induce the seller to offer the 602nd cup of coffee (Point C). So we conclude that the marginal cost of supplying the 602nd cup is between $1.01 and $1.02. Again, this is exactly what the supply curve indicates.

Now that we know that the supply curve tells us the marginal cost of producing each unit, all we need to do to obtain producer surplus is to compare the supply curve to the price. If the

Figure 5.6   Detailed Supply Curve for Coffee

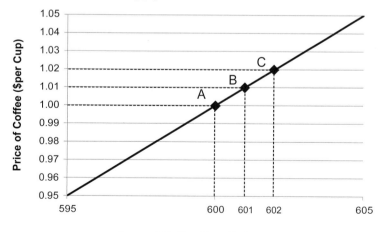

By zooming in on the supply curve we can associate marginal price changes with marginal changes in the quantity supplied.

Cups of Coffee Supplied per Week

---

*We have again adjusted the slope of the curve in order to focus on a change in quantity of one.

**Note that there may be points where the marginal production cost exactly equals the price. Thus the producer would not increase profits by offering the unit for sale but would not lose money either. In this case, we would say that the producer is indifferent between selling and not selling the unit.

price of coffee is $1.40, then the producer surplus on the 600th cup of coffee is the difference between the production cost and the price, as shown in Figure 5.7. So the seller obtains a producer surplus, or profit, of $0.30 on the 600th cup of coffee.

Figure 5.7   **Producer Surplus and a Supply Curve**

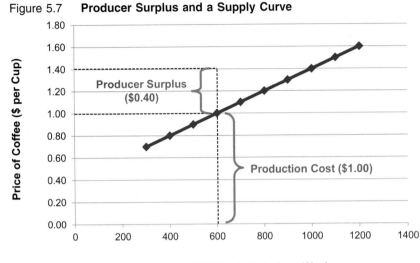

Producer surplus is the difference between price and the production cost (i.e., the supply curve).

3.3 PRODUCER SURPLUS IN AN ENTIRE MARKET

The final step in our analysis of producer benefits is to determine the producer surplus for the entire market. As with market consumer surplus, we need to extend our analysis from points *along the supply curve* to *areas above the supply curve*. Note that we are focused on the area *above* the supply curve because the supply curve represents the marginal costs to producers. It is only the revenue above costs that represents producer surplus, or profits.

market producer surplus: the net benefit (profits) obtained by all producers in a market. On a supply-and-demand graph, it is the area below price but above the supply curve.

Figure 5.8 shows the same supply curve shown above but now extended back to the *y*-axis. Given that the supply curve represents the marginal production costs, the aggregate production cost for the entire market is the area under the supply curve, up to the quantity that is produced. So if the price of coffee is $1.10 and a quantity of 700 cups is offered for sale at this price, the aggregate production cost equals the gray-shaded area under the supply curve. The difference between price and the supply curve, for each unit produced, is producer surplus. Thus **market producer surplus** is the blue-shaded area below price but above the supply curve. This is the net benefit obtained by all producers in the market.

Figure 5.8   **Market Producer Surplus**

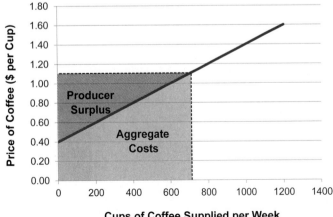

Market producer surplus is the area above the supply curve but below the price.

Discussion Questions

1. Do you think that the concept of producer surplus accurately represents the benefits that producers obtain from selling goods and services? Do you have any reservations about the concept?
2. Have you ever operated a business, even a small one, such as a lemonade stand when you were younger? If so, what factors motivated you to start a business? Do you think that your profits (producer surplus) overstated or understated your benefits? Does your answer have any implications for welfare analysis?

4. SOCIAL EFFICIENCY

social efficiency (in welfare economics): an allocation of resources that maximizes the net benefits to society

Recall that in Chapter 1 we defined efficiency as the use of resources in a way that does not create waste. In welfare economics, efficiency is defined more precisely. Specifically, **social efficiency (in welfare economics)** means an allocation of resources that maximizes the net benefits to society.

This is normally what modern economists mean when they say that a certain result is "best" or "optimal." But we must emphasize that this definition of optimality is a normative one, and it does not mean the same thing as maximizing well-being. A result may be "socially efficient" but fail to address final goals such as fairness, justice, or environmental sustainability.

Even with such caveats in mind, our study of social efficiency is worthwhile because it helps us understand when markets work well and when markets fail to produce efficient results. We reach two conclusions in this section:

1. Under certain conditions, a private market in equilibrium results in the socially efficient outcome.
2. When these conditions are not met, private markets fail to produce the socially efficient outcome. When this occurs, market interventions may be justified in order to increase social efficiency.

Current economic debates are often centered around whether private markets produce socially efficient outcomes. Conservative economists tend to believe that private markets, without regulations, produce efficient outcomes. Liberal economists are more likely to believe that market outcomes can be improved with some regulations, either because regulation will increase social efficiency or to achieve final goals other than efficiency.

Whether a market outcome enhances overall well-being is a normative question, dependent on one's final goals and, especially, on the question of whose welfare is given more weight and how the weighting is done. For example, if the weighting is purely according to willingness to pay, then more weight is given to the desires, happiness, or well-being of those with more money. Whether a market outcome is socially efficient is mostly a positive question, estimated by calculating the size of the consumer and producer surpluses. Even then, however, normative value judgments may be involved.

Later chapters explore in more detail under what conditions markets fail to produce socially efficient outcomes. For example, Chapter 9 focuses on market outcomes and inefficiencies in the labor market. Chapter 12 considers the effects of pollution and other negative externalities. Chapter 17 looks at how concentration of power in a small number of producers can be inefficient.

However, before we can analyze situations in which markets fail to produce efficient outcomes, we must first understand how markets can lead to social efficiency. To do this, we can combine our knowledge of consumer and producer surplus to determine the net benefits of a market to those involved in it. At this point, we are considering market benefits *only to the market participants*. As mentioned earlier, the impacts of markets on the "rest of society" are also relevant to social welfare. So the analysis below is an incomplete, preliminary analysis. We extend our model to consider impacts on the rest of society in Chapter 12.

Figure 5.9   **Social Welfare at Market Equilibrium**

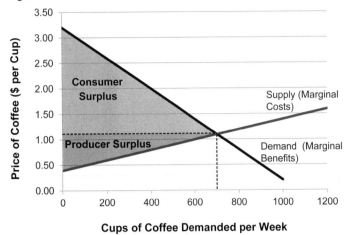

Net welfare benefits are the sum of consumer and producer surplus.

4.1 MARKET EQUILIBRIUM AND SOCIAL EFFICIENCY

Figure 5.9 shows the consumer and producer surplus of a market in equilibrium. This is the same equilibrium outcome that we obtained in Chapter 3, with a coffee price of $1.10 per cup and 700 cups sold per week. Consumer surplus is the area below the demand curve but above the price. Producer surplus is the area below the price but above the supply curve. The net benefits to the market participants (buyers and sellers) are simply the sum of consumer and producer surplus.

In this example, consumer surplus is larger than producer surplus. This is a result of the relative elasticity of the two curves. You can easily imagine situations in which the majority of the market benefits accrue to producers rather than consumers. An important point is that social welfare considers only the aggregate benefits in the market, *not the distribution of benefits.* So whether the majority of benefits accrue to buyers or sellers, social efficiency seeks only to maximize total benefits. Of course, this ignores the final goal of fairness. Again, social efficiency is not a final goal and is not the same thing as well-being.

Another way to visualize the net benefits in a market is to recall that a demand curve can be considered a marginal benefits curve, and a supply curve can be considered a marginal cost curve. The difference between these two curves at any point represents the gap between the maximum willingness to pay of consumers and the production costs of suppliers. Although some of this difference is "captured" by producers as profits, the rest is consumer surplus. As long as the demand curve is higher than the supply curve, society receives net benefits by producing that unit of a product. However, if the supply curve is higher than the demand curve, then marginal costs exceed marginal benefits, and society would actually be worse off if that unit were produced. So, as long as the demand curve is higher than the supply curve, it makes sense (from the perspective of social welfare) for society to produce each unit, to the point where marginal benefits equal marginal costs. Note in Figure 5.9 that this is true up to the equilibrium quantity of 700 cups of coffee. However, when the supply curve is higher than the demand curve, marginal costs exceed marginal benefits and society should not produce these units. Any production above 700 cups of coffee would decrease social welfare. Thus the market equilibrium is the outcome that maximizes social welfare.

We now test this result by considering what happens when the market is not allowed to reach equilibrium—when a regulation is enacted that sets a price different from the equilibrium price.

4.2 PRICE CEILINGS

Sometimes, governments intervene in markets to set price limits, either above or below the market equilibrium price. Somewhat confusingly, a price set *below* the market price is called

Figure 5.10   **A Price Ceiling**

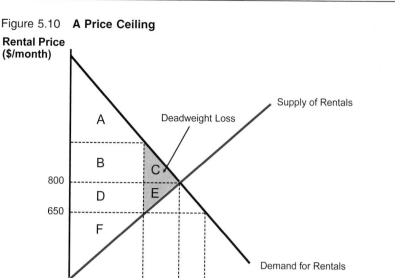

Rental Price ($/month)

A

Deadweight Loss

B

C

800

D

E

650

F

Supply of Rentals

A price ceiling sets a maximum
allowable price, which creates a
deadweight loss.

Demand for Rentals

7   10   12

Quantity (Number of Rentals, Thousands)

price ceiling: a regulation that specifies a maximum price for a particular product

a **price ceiling,** or price control (it is a "ceiling" because it establishes a maximum allowable price).

Price ceilings are usually set with a goal of helping certain groups of consumers by keeping prices low. A classic example is rent control, which specifies maximum prices for rental units. A welfare analysis of a rent control is shown in Figure 5.10.

In the absence of rent control, the market equilibrium rent would be $800 per month and the quantity of rental units would be 10,000 apartments. Consumer surplus to renters would be areas (A + B + C) and producer surplus to landlords would be areas (D + E + F). Total social welfare would be the sum of these two areas. This graph also portrays a situation in which rent control limits the amount of rent that a landlord can charge, to no more than $650 per month. At this price, we have a shortage—the quantity demanded (12,000) exceeds the quantity supplied (7,000). Without regulation, market forces would push prices up and eliminate the shortage, but this cannot happen with rent control.

In the case of a price ceiling, the quantity is determined *only by the supply curve* (because producers will react to the price set by the government in deciding how much to supply). So, the market quantity at a rent control price of $650/month is 7,000 rental units. Note that this leaves many potential renters unable to find a rental unit at a price of $650/month (5,000 in this example).

The intention of rent control is normally to help renters. Their consumer surplus would still be the area above the price and below the demand curve up to the quantity sold. At a quantity supplied of 7,000, this is equal to areas (A + B + D). Because consumer surplus was areas (A + B + C) before rent control, renters have lost area C and gained area D. The question of whether consumer surplus has increased thus depends on the relative sizes of areas C and D. The way the graph is drawn, it appears that consumer surplus has indeed increased, since D is larger than C. But this may not always be the case. You can try to draw a different graph such that consumer surplus would decrease as a result of a price ceiling.

We can be more definitive with the change in producer surplus. Producer surplus with rent control is only area F, which is clearly smaller than areas (D + E + F). Producers have lost (D +E). Of this amount, D has been gained by consumers, so we can say that it has been *transferred* from producers to consumers.

Note than in addition to this transfer from producers to consumers, two areas, C and E, have been lost completely. This loss, which benefits no one, decreases total social welfare. Before

deadweight loss:
a reduction in social
welfare as a result of
a market regulation

rent control, total social welfare was (A + B + C + D + E + F). With rent control, it is areas (A + B + D + F). Economists call the net loss of (C + E) a **deadweight loss**, a reduction in social welfare as a result of a market regulation. This seems to indicate that from the point of view of total social welfare, rent control is a bad policy, implying a loss of economic efficiency. In more commonsense terms, the reason for the deadweight loss is that at the enforced lower price, less housing is available overall.

But this conclusion can be controversial. Sometimes, for example, in wartime or during other emergencies, many people favor price controls on essential goods. Many apartments in New York City and other cities in New York State are subject to rent control, and, of course, it is very popular with tenants who benefit from it, so it has proved politically resilient. Can this be justified economically? Many economists would say no, for the reasons discussed above. But note that the conclusions above are affected by the elasticity of the supply and demand curves. In particular, if supply is inelastic, the deadweight loss will be small (visualize this, or draw another set of inelastic supply and demand curves to see how areas C and E shrink).

The deadweight loss may be small in the case of apartments in New York City, where there is little room for new construction (i.e., an inelastic supply curve). In addition, not all apartments are covered by rent control, so, where possible, new, uncontrolled apartment buildings can be developed. To those who sympathize with the original goal of rent control—to help renters and keep at least some apartments affordable—the benefits to renters justify the relatively small efficiency loss.

But in other cases, especially where elasticity of supply is high, price controls can be disastrous. One example was in Zimbabwe, where extensive price controls were imposed in 2007 with the goal of keeping prices for food and other essential goods low. As our example leads us to expect, the result of enforced low prices was to destroy the incentive for farmers and other suppliers to produce, leading to severe shortages. So, the poor people whom the policy was supposed to help were instead hurt by unavailability of food and other basic goods, while farmers and other merchants were forced into bankruptcy. The price controls had to be abandoned after they forced the economy into virtual collapse.

4.3 Price Floors

price floor: a regulation that specifies a minimum price for a particular product

Governments also sometimes intervene in markets with the opposite goal—to keep prices from falling. A price set above the market price is called a **price floor** or price support (because it establishes a minimum allowable price).

Why would governments want to keep prices at higher levels? The obvious reason is to aid producers. In the agricultural sector, price supports are common. Governments commonly specify minimum prices for agricultural products such as grain or milk. Of course, this also pushes up prices to consumers. The goal is to help farmers, who often have considerable political influence.

The economic effect is the opposite of a price ceiling. Rather than creating a shortage, price floors create a *surplus,* as producers increase their output to take advantage of profitable higher prices, but the same higher prices cause consumers to cut back their purchases. In general, the government will have to buy up the surplus in order to maintain the price floor. From an economic point of view, this is clearly inefficient, because it encourages excess production and involves both higher prices to consumers and large government expenditures. A more efficient approach would be to give direct aid to farmers if this is considered necessary but to leave market prices alone.

Another classic example of a price floor is the minimum wage. Most governments have minimum wage laws specifying that hourly wages must be at least a given level. The United States has a federal minimum wage of $7.25 per hour (as of 2013), although about 20 states have set higher minimum wage rates. Most other developed countries have higher minimum wage rates. For example, the minimum wage is equivalent to about $10/hour in Canada, about $13/hour in France, and $16/hour in Australia.

Figure 5.11 **A Price Floor**

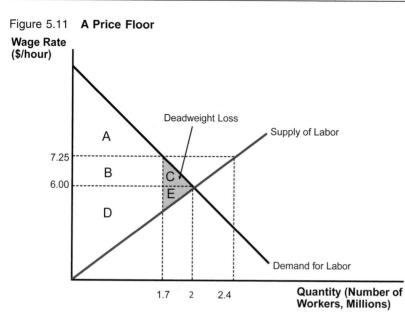

A price floor sets a minimum allowable price, which creates a deadweight loss.

The impact of a minimum wage is illustrated in Figure 5.11, which illustrates a hypothetical labor market for unskilled workers such as cashiers or manual laborers. In this case, the demand curve represents the willingness to pay of employers for workers. The "sellers" are potential workers willing to supply their labor in exchange for pay. (We discuss labor markets in more detail in Chapter 9.)

If the labor market were allowed to reach equilibrium, the market-clearing wage rate would be $6.00 per hour and employment would be 2 million workers. But the minimum wage of $7.25/hour prevents market forces from pushing the wage rate any lower than $7.25/hour. The minimum wage is called a price floor because it prevents the wage rate from moving lower. Note that if the minimum wage were set below the equilibrium wage, say at $5.00/hour, it would have no effect on the market price.

At $7.25/hour, the graph tells us that the supply of labor is 2.4 million workers and the demand for labor is 1.7 million workers. Although an equilibrium quantity is determined by the interaction of supply and demand, in the case of a price floor, the market quantity is determined *only by the demand curve*. In other words, the situation of surplus (excess supply) cannot be eliminated with a price decline, so demand limits the amount that is sold. Thus the presence of the minimum wage, relative to the equilibrium outcome, reduces employment from 2 million to 1.7 million. (Again, these are only hypothetical numbers.)

What does this price floor mean in terms of social welfare? Presumably, a minimum wage law is intended to benefit workers, rather than employers. In a labor market, producer surplus represents the social welfare benefits to workers—they are the suppliers. Remember that producer surplus is the area above the supply curve and below the price, up to the quantity sold. We see in Figure 5.11 that if the market were allowed to reach equilibrium (a wage rate of $6.00/hour), consumer surplus would be areas (A + B + C) and producer surplus would be areas (D + E). Total social welfare would be the sum of both surpluses, or (A + B + C + D + E).

But with the minimum wage set at $7.25 producer surplus becomes areas (B + D). Without the minimum wage, producer surplus was (D + E). The way the graph is drawn, it appears that producer surplus has increased (i.e., area B, which has been gained, is larger than area E, which has been lost). However, this is not necessarily always the case. To test this, try to draw a market in which a price floor decreases producer surplus. (Hint: Make the price floor even further above the equilibrium price.)

We also need to see what has happened to consumer surplus (keeping in mind that in this story the "consumers" are employers). Recall that consumer surplus is the area above price but below the demand curve, up to the quantity sold. So, with the minimum wage in place, consumer surplus is only area A, instead of (A + B + C). We can definitively conclude that consumer surplus has decreased, by the area (B + C). This is *always* the case with a price floor.

Returning to Figure 5.11, we see that total social welfare with the minimum wage is the sum of areas (A + B + D); it has decreased by areas (C + E). Area C used to be part of consumer surplus, and area E used to be part of producer surplus. Also note that area B represents a transfer of benefits, from consumers (employers) to producers (workers). As in the rent control example above, there is a deadweight loss of areas (C + E), representing a loss of economic efficiency.

So on the basis of economic efficiency, a price floor such as a minimum wage law seems to be a bad idea. In theory, at least, it reduces both social welfare and employment. Although workers who have jobs earn higher wages, the theory predicts that more workers will be unable to find jobs.

But as we discussed earlier, economic efficiency is just one of many societal goals. Figure 5.11 shows that the minimum wage law did benefit workers (i.e., producer surplus has increased). If we believe that employers are exploiting low-wage workers, then perhaps the loss in economic efficiency could be justified on the basis of social justice. For example, we might conclude that benefits to the workers whose salary rises to at least a "living wage" are so significant that they outweigh the other losses, in profits and in number of jobs.

Another important question in weighing the merits of minimum wage laws is how much they actually do reduce employment. It is an empirical question whether raising the minimum wage increases unemployment by a significant amount. If demand for labor is relatively inelastic, the effect on unemployment will be relatively small. Indeed, empirical research has found that in some cases there is no detectable effect of increased unemployment as a result of a higher minimum wage! (See Box 5.1 for details on this surprising result.)

Given these findings, you might wonder why the empirical reality does not necessarily support the predictions of the theory. This example reminds us that it is important to both learn the theory and, at the same time, to be cautious in its application. The minimum wage example raises important issues of social justice; it also emphasizes the fact that wages are in many ways not standard prices. Markets for labor, as discussed further in Chapter 9, make it clear that economics is a social science—about people—and the behaviors of people cannot be predicted with mathematical precision.

Discussion Questions

1. Think of another real-world example of a price floor or a price ceiling, not discussed in the text. Based on what you read in this section, as well as your own views, do you think that price regulation is a "good" policy?
2. Do you think that social efficiency is an appropriate tool for analyzing the net impact of different policies? Can you think of some policy situations in which social efficiency is a sufficient measure for determining which policies should be enacted? Can you think of other policy situations in which social efficiency would be an inappropriate goal of policy decisions?

5. POLICY INFERENCES FROM WELFARE ANALYSIS

A simple conclusion from basic welfare analysis is that private unregulated markets, bringing together self-interested consumers and producers, can produce an outcome that is the "best" overall for society, where best is defined as maximizing economic efficiency (i.e., social welfare). But as we have already seen, this simple conclusion often needs to be qualified or questioned in terms of real-world effects. Bearing this in mind, we now look at some of the policy implications of welfare analysis.

Box 5.1 The Debate over the Impact of Minimum Wage Laws

The model presented in this chapter illustrates that a minimum wage, a type of price floor, will reduce employment. The only question, it seems, is how much.

In the most referenced research on the topic, two economists, David Card and Alan Krueger, took advantage of a real-world experiment to try to answer this question. In 1992 the minimum wage in New Jersey was raised from $4.25 to $5.05 per hour. In the neighboring state of Pennsylvania, the minimum wage remained at $4.25/hour. Card and Krueger then collected employment data from fast-food restaurants, which paid many workers the minimum wage, in New Jersey and eastern Pennsylvania. According to economic theory, fast-food restaurant employment should have decreased in New Jersey relative to Pennsylvania.

Instead, Card and Krueger found that employment at fast-food restaurants in New Jersey actually *increased*—the opposite of what the theory predicted! This result initiated a lively debate among economists, with some arguing that it was simply impossible based on the market model. Research subsequent to Card and Krueger's 1994 paper has produced mixed results. Some studies have identified a negative employ-

ment impact from minimum wage laws, while others have found no discernible impacts. A 2006 article in *The Economist* notes: "Today's consensus, insofar as there is one, seems to be that raising minimum wages has minor negative effects at worst." However, the article does note that raising the minimum wage is not a very effective tool for reducing poverty. For example, many people paid the minimum wage are teenage workers who are not from poor families. The article suggests that tax credits paid to low-income workers, such as the Earned Income Tax Credit in the United States, are more effective at reducing poverty.

There may also be a difference between the United States and Europe. In the United States, the minimum wage may be fairly close to the equilibrium wage, and thus its impact on employment is relatively small. In Europe, minimum wages are much higher and consequently are more likely to be a significant cause of unemployment among low-skilled workers.

Sources: David Card and Alan B. Krueger, "Minimum Wages and Employment: A Case Study of the Fast-Food Industry in New Jersey and Pennsylvania," *American Economic Review* 84(4) (1994): 774–793; "The Minimum Wage: A Blunt Instrument," *Economist*, October 26, 2006.

5.1 Laissez-Faire Economics

laissez-faire: the view that government intervention in markets should be limited to what is absolutely necessary. The term is French and means "leave alone."

The type of analysis presented in this chapter is the reason that some economists are supportive of a **laissez-faire** (pronounced lays-say fair) approach to regulation. We saw above that government intervention in markets, such as price floors and price ceilings, generally decreases social welfare, defined strictly in terms of economic efficiency. In this analysis, total benefits are maximized *only when the market is allowed to reach equilibrium.* Laissez-faire advocates thus believe that government intervention in markets should be limited only to what is absolutely necessary to ensure that markets function smoothly. For example, proponents of laissez-faire recognize that regulations are needed to protect private property rights.

But defining the "best" outcome for society as maximizing economic efficiency obviously implies that economic efficiency is a paramount goal. As we saw in Chapter 1, numerous other social goals, such as fairness and ecological sustainability, may be as important, or more important, than efficiency.

One justification often given for a focus on efficiency is that it is considered an objective way to assess policy options. Maximizing efficiency is concerned only with increasing overall social benefits, not the allocation of those benefits. So, by looking only at total benefits, in principle we avoid making subjective judgments about who receives those benefits.

As in our discussion of positive and normative statements in Chapter 1, we need to look further to understand any subjective inferences from this viewpoint. In particular, an emphasis on efficiency implicitly views the current distribution of economic resources as acceptable. In order to understand this, we need to expand our notion of efficiency. Although we have been discussing efficiency as it applies in a single market, we can also define efficiency as maximizing social benefits across the totality of markets.

Consider that markets allocate resources across different markets based on consumers' willingness to pay. In one sense, markets are democratic in the sense that everyone is free to participate in them and can thus make their preferences known. But unlike in the democratic principle of "one person, one vote," markets operate according to a "one dollar, one vote" principle. In other words, those with more economic resources have a greater say in determining what a society produces. So whether a society allocates resources at the margin to luxury cars or school lunches depends to some extent on the relative willingness to pay for each.* If the demand by wealthy consumers for luxury cars exceeds the demand by other consumers for school lunches, then that society's production will shift toward producing more luxury cars and fewer school lunches.

So, while at first glance it seems that a focus on efficiency avoids having to make subjective assessments, we see that efficiency cannot be separated from questions about fairness. Whether the existing distribution of wealth and income in the United States is fair is a question that we consider in more detail in Chapter 10.

5.2 MARKET FAILURE

Can we conclude from welfare analysis that unregulated markets are always efficient and that the only justification for government intervention is to further other social goals such as justice or ecological sustainability? No, because economists also recognize situations in which unregulated markets *are not efficient*. In these cases, government intervention may be justified solely to increase economic efficiency.

market failure: situations in which unregulated markets fail to produce the socially efficient outcome

Situations in which unregulated markets fail to maximize social efficiency are referred to as **market failure**. In response to market failure, we may be able to design policies that "correct" the market failure—an intervention that then allows the outcome to be socially efficient.

We consider several instances of market failure in later chapters. These examples include:

- In Chapter 8 we look at how consumer behavior can lead to inefficient market outcomes. These outcomes may be due to irrational consumer behavior, as discussed in Chapter 7, arising from either decision-making limitations or external factors that lead consumers to make inefficient choices, such as advertising.
- In Chapter 9 we look at labor markets, which may also be subject to market failure. For example, employers may have significantly more power than workers, or institutional arrangements may prevent an efficient outcome.
- Situations in which there are significant impacts on "the rest of society" (including the natural environment, and people of the future). Costs and benefits to "the rest of society" should be included in a complete welfare analysis of any market. In Chapter 12, we consider the importance of these impacts, particularly with regard to environmental policy.
- Not all products can be efficiently allocated using private markets. In extreme cases, no private market will arise at all, as no potential for profits exists. The provision of some goods and services directly by public sphere entities is addressed in Chapter 13.
- In Chapters 16 and 17, we consider different market structures based on the degree of producer competition. We see that insufficient competition is another common example of market failure.

Going beyond the theoretical model presented in this chapter, to a more real-world perspective on economics in these future chapters, we see that unregulated efficient markets are more the exception rather than the rule. Yet this does not mean that government intervention is always justified in situations of market failure. We must consider the details of individual markets to determine whether intervention is justified. If an intervention is justified, we must

---

*The allocation will also depend on the cost of production. For example, even if the willingness to pay for luxury cars exceeds the willingness to pay for school lunches, if producers cannot make equal or greater profits selling luxury cars, they will not have an incentive to produce them.

decide what type is appropriate—a tax, a subsidy, or some other regulation. We must also decide the magnitude of the intervention. For example, if we institute a tax on gasoline to correct for a market failure, should it be 10 cents a gallon, $1.00 per gallon, or more?

We also have to be clear whether the justification for intervention is based on increasing efficiency or achieving another goal. In some cases, increased efficiency may be possible while also making progress on other social goals. In other cases, we must assess whether we should place a higher priority on economic efficiency or on another objective.

Discussion Questions

1. Do you think that the current level of government regulation is too high or too low? Do you generally support a laissez-faire approach to regulation or more active regulation? Does your answer change depending on the policy issue under consideration?
2. Considering everything that we have covered so far in the book, have you changed your mind about any policy issues in your country? What lessons from the book do you find particularly relevant to current policy debates?

REVIEW QUESTIONS

1. What is the difference between social welfare and well-being?
2. Define consumer surplus.
3. What do different points on a demand curve represent?
4. What is a marginal change?
5. What is another name for a demand curve, in reference to welfare analysis?
6. What does each point on a demand curve represent?
7. How is consumer surplus for an individual consumer represented in a supply-and-demand graph?
8. How is market consumer surplus represented in a supply-and-demand graph?
9. Define producer surplus.
10. What is another name for a supply curve, in reference to welfare analysis?
11. What does each point on a supply curve represent?
12. How is producer surplus for an individual transaction represented in a supply-and-demand graph?
13. How is market producer surplus represented in a supply-and-demand graph?
14. What is social efficiency? What are some limitations of this concept?
15. Why is a market equilibrium socially efficient?
16. What is a price ceiling? How can it be represented in a supply-and-demand graph?
17. What limits the quantity sold with a price ceiling: supply or demand?
18. How does a price ceiling affect consumer and producer surplus?
19. What is a deadweight loss? How is it represented in a supply-and-demand graph?
20. What is a price floor? How can it be represented in a supply-and-demand graph?
21. What limits the quantity sold with a price floor: supply or demand?
22. How does a price floor affect consumer and producer surplus?
23. What is the laissez-faire approach to government regulation?
24. What is market failure?

EXERCISES

1. Consider the following demand schedule for umbrellas at a local store:

Price	Quantity demanded per day
$20	0
$18	5
$16	10
$14	15
$12	20
$10	25

a. Draw the demand curve for umbrellas. Be sure to label the axes.
b. Suppose the price of umbrellas is $14. Indicate the area of market consumer surplus in your graph. Also indicate the area that represents the total amount that consumers spend on umbrellas.
c. Next, assume that Rebecca is willing to pay a maximum of $18 for an umbrella. What is Rebecca's consumer surplus if she purchases an

umbrella? Show her consumer surplus on your graph.

d. Another consumer, Andy, is willing to pay a maximum of $10 for an umbrella. What is his consumer surplus in this market?

e. If the demand schedule above represents demand on a normal summer day, what would you expect to happen to market consumer surplus if the forecast is for a heavy rainfall? Assume that the store does not raise its price. Draw a graph to support your answer.

2. Suppose the maximum willingness to pay for a new iPhone by the different consumers in a market is given in the table below.

Consumer	Maximum Willingness to Pay
#1	$550
#2	$530
#3	$490
#4	$440
#5	$420
#6	$370
#7	$350
#8	$310

a. If the price of iPhones is $420, how many iPhones will be sold?

b. What is the total consumer surplus in the market?

c. Suppose the price of iPhones decreases to $390. Now how many iPhones will be sold? What is the new consumer surplus?

3. Consider the following supply schedule for apartments in a local market.

Rent (per month)	Quantity of apartments supplied
$800	100
$700	80
$600	60
$500	40
$400	20
$300	0

a. Draw the supply curve for apartments. Be sure to label the axes.

b. Suppose the going rental price for apartments is $550 per month. How many apartments will be supplied? (Assume the supply curve is a straight line between the points in the table above.)

c. Indicate the area of market producer surplus in your graph. Also indicate the area that represents the total cost of supplying apartments.

d. Next, assume that a particular landlord is willing to supply an apartment only if the rental price is at least $450 per month. What is her producer surplus in this market? Use a graph to support your answer.

e. Suppose that the price for condominiums in the area increases. This creates an incentive for apartment owners to sell their apartments as condominiums, thus removing them from the rental market. What would you expect to happen to producer surplus in the apartment market as a result of this change? Draw a graph to support your answer.

3. Suppose that the market equilibrium price for a basic medical check-up is $50, in a market in which there is no health insurance. To encourage more people to get a check-up, the local government mandates that the price of a check-up cannot be more than $40.

a. Is this a price floor or a price ceiling?

b. Draw a graph to illustrate the implementation of this government policy.

c. What happens to the number of check-ups in this market? Show this in your graph.

d. What happens to consumer surplus in this market? What happens to producer surplus? Show these changes on your graph.

e. Was the government's policy successful? What has happened to social welfare? Show this in your graph.

f. Can you think of a different policy that would likely be more successful at encouraging more people to obtain check-ups?

g. Is this a typical market? Is there any reason to suppose that producers of health care would respond differently to price regulation than, say, producers of umbrellas? What does the producer's responsiveness have to do with the cost of providing health care? What other factors might be involved?

4. Consider the market for wheat. Suppose that the demand for wheat decreases because of dietary concerns.

a. How does the decrease in the demand for wheat affect total net social welfare in the wheat market? Use a graph to support your answer, and indicate the area that represents the change in social welfare.

b. Can we clearly say what happens to producer surplus as a result of the decrease in demand? Use a graph to support your answer.

5. Consider the market for electricity. Suppose that the price of producing energy decreases due to lower fuel costs.

   a. How does the decrease in electricity production costs affect total net social welfare? Use a graph to support your answer and indicate the area that represents the change in social welfare.

   b. Can we clearly say what happens to consumer surplus as a result of the decrease in energy production costs? Use a graph to support your answer.

6. Match each concept in Column A with an example in Column B:

Column A	Column B
a. Consumer surplus	1. Profits
b. The government mandates that the price of milk must be at least $3 per gallon.	2. A price ceiling
c. Marginal change	3. An increase in demand of one unit
d. Producer surplus	4. A loss in social welfare that occurs when a market is not in equilibrium
e. Deadweight loss	5. Part of the psychic benefits of buying something
f. The government mandates that the price of gas can be no higher than $4 per gallon.	6. A school of economics that opposes government regulation
g. Laissez-faire economics	7. A price floor

6 International Trade and Trade Policy

What does the United States export more of than anything else on the global market? The answer might surprise you (hint: think food). And which country purchases more U.S. exports—China or Mexico? In fact, the United States exports twice as much to Mexico as to China in terms of value. Are there similar surprises to be found when we look at Japan, for example, or Brazil? More generally, what factors determine which goods a country produces for trade with other countries? Classical economists Adam Smith and David Ricardo noticed that countries will tend to produce an abundance of goods that they are especially good at producing and trade their surplus for other goods that they are not as skilled at producing. Smith and Ricardo also believed that such trades would always benefit both countries. Yet, as we see, the world has grown increasingly complex over the past two centuries, and, despite obvious advantages to free trade, there are also reasons for caution. This chapter considers some of these issues and discusses ways in which national governments have addressed them.

1. Trade, Specialization, and Productivity

As we saw earlier, Adam Smith is generally credited with the idea that leaving decisions of production and distribution to a market system is superior to having the government impose its will. Many recognize this as the meaning of "laissez-faire" as discussed in Chapter 5. Here we look at what it is about free markets that, in theory, produces desirable outcomes in terms of trade, both within and between countries.

In *An Inquiry into the Nature and Causes of the Wealth of Nations* (1776), Smith made a connection between specialization and efficiency. We have seen that one way to define "efficiency" is to say that efficient production allows us to obtain the maximum product from a given amount of resources, *or* conversely to require the least possible resources to produce a given amount of a product. This is a fundamental economic goal because it has very important consequences for the well-being of individuals, groups, and countries. What Smith argued was that specialization (he called it "division of labor") would make people more efficient, because focusing our time on one task (or a few tasks) instead of many would make us learn it more quickly and become better at it.

Smith then noted that the *extent* of the specialization achieved in a society would be governed by the extent or size of the market. If, for example, the market for shoes were tiny, it would make no sense for you to devote all your time to shoe production, as you would not make enough money in such a small market to support yourself. If, however, the market were large, specialization would make sense—and the larger the market, the more that you would want to specialize. Nobody speaks more eloquently on this subject than Smith himself:

> As it is the power of exchanging that gives occasion to the division of labour, so the extent of this division must always be limited by the extent of that power, or, in other words, by the

extent of the market. When the market is very small, no person can have any encouragement to dedicate himself entirely to one employment, for want of the power to exchange all that surplus part of the produce of his own labor, which is over and above his own consumption, for such parts of the produce of other men's labour as he has occasion for.[1]

Taking this logic to its extreme, economic productivity in all areas would be maximized if all markets were extended around the world. It is for this reason that Smith advocated not only a system of free markets for a specific economy but also free and unfettered trade among countries. Although the same logic applied at any scale of participation—that is, the logic of mutual gains for both parties—it seemed perfectly reasonable that under globalized markets *more would be gained* because of the maximized productive efficiency that results from maximum specialization.

In Smith's view, specialization at the national level would lead each country to become so efficient in the production of some things that it would enjoy an "absolute advantage" over other countries in their production. Other countries would enjoy such an advantage in the production of other goods, and because each country would produce far more than it needed because of its remarkable productivity, there would be ample opportunity for mutually beneficial trade between countries.

As we mentioned in the last chapter, Smith's book was considered revolutionary. He was writing at a time when the so-called mercantilist philosophy prevailed—a philosophy that supported strong involvement by the state in economic affairs and was highly skeptical of free trade. Even today, more than two centuries later, debate over the benefits and drawbacks of free trade continues. But the influence of Smith's book is indisputable; today, his pronouncements in favor of free trade are about as far as one could imagine from "revolutionary," having been widely accepted by many economists and policymakers.

Discussion Questions

1. Does it make sense that the larger or more extended a market is, the greater would be the incentive to specialize in supplying that market? What if everyone decided to specialize in shoemaking because the shoe market went global? What would Adam Smith say?
2. Do you currently "specialize" in something? If not, what do you plan to do after college? Do you hope to develop knowledge or expertise in only one area or more than one? Why?

2. GAINS FROM TRADE

Economists and policymakers have argued for centuries about whether it is better for a country to engage in free trade with other countries or to place some limits on such trade. Adam Smith presented the argument for free trade in general terms, as we have discussed. Many who argue for "**free trade**"—exchange in international markets that is not regulated or restricted by government actions—often appeal more specifically to David Ricardo's 1817 book *On the Principles of Political Economy and Taxation* to demonstrate that a country that engages in trade can reap significant welfare gains. In this section, we present Ricardo's basic model, along with other arguments in favor of free trade.

free trade: exchange in international markets that is not regulated or restricted by government actions

2.1 THE THEORY OF COMPARATIVE ADVANTAGE

In Chapter 1, we discussed the production-possibilities frontier (PPF), which illustrates how a society might make tradeoffs between the production of two different goods, reaching higher output levels when it uses its resources efficiently. We showed how some points, which represent combinations of the two outputs (guns and butter), would be unattainable. But to take our analysis only that far, it turns out, would be misleading.

Points outside a societal PPF represent unattainable levels of *production* for the society on its own. However, they may not reflect unattainable levels of *consumption*. The key to this apparent magic trick is in the benefits that can arise from a system of exchange. Economists call these benefits the "gains from trade," and they are actually *efficiency* gains. People also often point to other important advantages derived from a system of exchange, as well as to important disadvantages, and we elaborate on these as the chapter progresses.

Ricardo's model relies on a trade example with two goods—wine and cloth—and two countries—Portugal and England. Although here we give a simple numerical version of his story, using PPFs, the point is more general. The principles might be applied to any pair of economic actors—for example, housemates, companies, governments—that produce and exchange goods or services at any level of organization—local, regional, national, or global.

Returning to Ricardo's story, suppose that, given its resources or productive factors, Portugal can produce a maximum of 200 bottles of wine if it devotes all its resources to wine production or 100 units of cloth (a unit of cloth is a "bolt") if it devotes all of its resources to cloth production. In Figure 6.1 we have assumed constant opportunity costs, so the PPF is just a straight line.* Meanwhile, England can produce a maximum of 200 bottles of wine or 400 bolts of cloth, as illustrated in Figure 6.2.

Figure 6.1   **Portugal's Production-Possibilities Frontier**

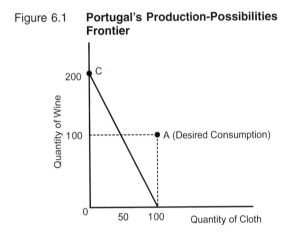

Figure 6.2   **England's Production-Possibilities Frontier**

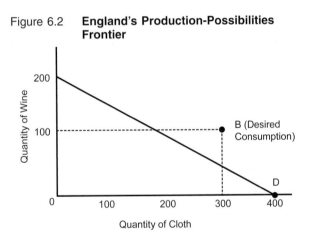

Portugal can produce 200 units of wine if it specializes in wine, or 100 units of cloth, if it specializes in cloth. Or it can produce any combination on the line between these two points. However it would like to consume a larger bundle—represented by point A.

England can produce 200 units of wine if it specializes in wine, or 400 units of cloth, if it specializes in cloth. Or it can produce any combination on the line between these two points. However it would like to consume a larger bundle—represented by point B.

Suppose that the Portuguese would like to be able to consume 100 bottles of wine and 100 bolts of cloth, as represented by point A, and the English would like to be able to consume 100 bottles of wine and 300 bolts of cloth, represented by point B. As we can see, if each relies only on its own production possibilities, points A and B are unachievable.

But suppose that Portugal produced only wine and England produced only cloth. This production combination is illustrated in the "Production" section of Table 6.1 and by points C and D in Figures 6.1 and 6.2. Total production would be 200 bottles of wine and 400 bolts of cloth.

---

*This means that, contrary to our earlier guns vs. butter example, Portugal does *not* give up more and more of, say, wine as it increasingly specializes in the production of cloth. Here we are simplifying in order to more easily illustrate the advantage of trade.

Table 6.1 **Production, Exchange, and Consumption of Wine and Cloth**

	Country	Wine	Cloth
Production:	Portugal	200	0
	England	0	400
Total production		*200*	*400*
Exchange:	Portugal	sell 100	buy 100
	England	buy 100	sell 100
Consumption:	Portugal	100	100
	England	100	300
Total consumption		*200*	*400*

Further, suppose that Portugal and England were to agree to *exchange* 100 bottles of Portuguese wine for 100 bolts of English cloth, as listed in the "Exchange" section of Table 6.1. Now Portugal and England could each *consume* the quantities listed in the "Consumption" section of Table 6.1. Note that their total consumption does *not* exceed the total amount produced of each good. Yet Portugal would consume at point A and England at point B—the desired points that they could not each reach on their own!

The "magic" behind this result is that Portugal and England differ in their opportunity costs of production. For every bolt of cloth that Portugal produces, it forgoes production of 2 bottles of wine. You can see this by examining the slope of the PPF in Figure 6.1. Comparing the two endpoints, moving from left to right, we can see that a fall (or negative "rise") of 200 bottles of wine is accompanied by a "run" of +100 bolts of cloth. Because the curve is straight, the slope is therefore –200/100 = –2 throughout. At any point, then, reducing wine production by 2 bottles (i.e., a fall or "negative rise" of 2) is needed to increase cloth production by 1 bolt (that is, to create a "run" of 1 unit to the right). However, for every bolt of cloth that England produces, it forgoes production of only half a bottle of wine (check this yourself using Figure 6.2). We say that England has a **comparative advantage** in cloth production, because cloth costs less in terms of the other good (wine) in England than in Portugal. In other words, England has a lower opportunity cost associated with its cloth production.

comparative advantage: the ability to produce some good or service at a lower opportunity cost than other producers

The above example is undoubtedly a product of the geographical reality in Ricardo's time. England had energy resources (coal) that made it relatively good at industrial production such as spinning and weaving and a relatively cool and cloudy climate that was not suitable for growing grapes. Portugal, by contrast, enjoyed a comparative advantage in production of wine, owing to its relatively warm and sunny climate—good for growing grapes—but lacked the necessary energy sources to produce cloth as efficiently as England. In our example, an additional bottle of wine comes at the cost of half a bolt of cloth when produced in Portugal but requires giving up 2 bolts of cloth when produced in England, as noted in Table 6.2.

Put simply, the principle of comparative advantage says that one should *specialize* in what one does best. This means that even if it turned out that one of the countries was more efficient at producing *both* goods, it would still pay for that country to specialize. Indeed, it is on this

Table 6.2 **Opportunity Cost and Comparative Advantage**

Country	Opportunity cost of 1 unit of cloth	Opportunity cost of 1 unit of wine
Portugal	2 units of wine	½ unit of cloth
England	½ unit of wine	2 units of cloth

point especially that Ricardo goes further than Smith. While Smith had earlier expounded on the benefits of trade, in his view the benefits existed only if each country possessed an *absolute* advantage in the production of at least one good. To Smith, if a country did not produce at least one good more efficiently than its trading partner, the latter would have no incentive to engage in trade with it.

Ricardo recognized that even in such a circumstance both countries gain. He would say that a country has a comparative advantage in the good that it produces *less relatively inefficiently*. Both countries gain by having the economically "stronger" country produce only what it produces *most* efficiently and then trading. Regarding our example above, Ricardo would have said that even if England produced wine *and* cloth more efficiently (i.e., using fewer resources per unit), it would still face a higher opportunity cost than Portugal for the good that it was *relatively* less efficient at producing—so there would still exist mutual gains from trade. Only if both countries faced exactly the *same* opportunity costs (an exceedingly rare phenomenon in the real world) would there be no possible gains from trade.

The source of comparative advantage in the above example is climate and other resource endowments, which differed between England and Portugal. It is not hard, by extension, to understand why, for example, bananas are currently exported by Ecuador, while Sweden finds it advantageous to import bananas rather than grow them in greenhouses. But comparative advantage can also be created by human action. Countries can become more efficient at producing particular goods by investing in the physical capital needed to produce them. Sometimes, technological advances or changes in the social organization of work can change the pattern of comparative advantage, and the evolution of comparative advantage over time may thus be unpredictable.

Ricardo's example concerned trade between countries, but the principle of comparative advantage has also been used to show how other economic actors can reap gains from trade. Organizations seek gains from trade when they specialize in a particular area—say, production of training workshops—while contracting with other companies to provide support services—say, transportation or advertising design. You may reap gains from trade in your household if, instead of splitting all chores 50–50, you put the person who is relatively more "efficient" (i.e., better) at shopping in charge of shopping and the person who is relatively efficient at cleaning in charge of cleaning.

The mere fact that some companies, or some people, *could* be self-sufficient in producing everything that they need does not mean that they *should* provide everything for themselves. The story of specialization and gains from trade is a powerful one.

labor-intensive production: production using methods that involve a high ratio of labor to capital

capital-intensive production: production using methods that involve a high ratio of capital to labor

factor-price equalization: the theory that trade should eventually lead to returns to factors of production that are equal across countries

Economists often make a distinction between countries that are thought to be more suited for **labor-intensive production** processes, such as stitching clothing or making handicrafts, and others that specialize in relatively **capital-intensive production**, such as the manufacture of airplanes or automobiles. The fact that the United States has more manufactured capital per worker than does Bangladesh, for example, is considered an explanation for Bangladeshi exports of clothing. Bangladesh presumably has a comparative advantage in relatively labor-intensive industries. Clothing production, meanwhile, has nearly disappeared from the United States.

The economic theory of **factor-price equalization** predicts that free trade should tend to equalize the returns to capital (profits) and labor (wages) across countries. For example, to the extent that the United States is rich in capital and relatively lacking in labor power, in the absence of trade, returns to capital are theorized to be relatively low and returns to labor relatively high. The logic of this is that a scarce factor commands a higher return—higher demand for a factor, relative to available supplies, increases the price that must be paid for it. Because factor endowments in Bangladesh are the opposite, capital investments there would be expected to receive high returns in the absence of trade, while workers receive low wages compared to those in the United States.

After the two countries start to trade, however, the demand for capital in the United States should rise (because the country now has a larger market for selling its capital-intensive goods), increasing the return on investments there. The demand for labor, however, will fall, because the United States will now be importing labor-intensive goods from Bangladesh. Meanwhile, the demand for labor in Bangladesh should rise (because it now exports labor-intensive goods), putting upward pressure on wages in that country, while returns to capital there fall. According to this theory, in a (hypothetical) world of perfectly free trade, we would expect wages to converge eventually, so that workers in the United States and Bangladesh would be paid about the same. Returns to capital investments would also be equalized.

Of course, in the real world wages are much higher in the United States than in Bangladesh—about 30 times higher. The theory of factor-price equalization merely states that wages should *eventually* converge, yet it says nothing about how long this process may take.

We find evidence of factor-price equalization in other cases, such as economic growth in Asia over the past 50 years. It is hard to remember now that Japan (in the 1950s) and then South Korea were the first two Asian countries that "bootstrapped" their economic growth by depending heavily on the export of very cheap goods made with very cheap labor. We could use factor-price equalization to explain how wages in those countries have risen to the levels of other industrialized countries—although it is evident that this did not just happen automatically but was urged in the right direction by a combination of factors, including government policies of industrial support and strong support for economic equality. It is now possible to see substantially rising wages in China. Will the same happen in Bangladesh, for example? The theory of factor-price equalization does not say what institutions or policies are necessary for this to happen.

The theory of factor-price equalization also disregards the possibility that, instead of an international equalization of wages, higher unemployment would result. This has, in fact, been a far more common outcome in countries like the United States; internationally as well as locally, wages seem to rise with some ease, while being "sticky" downward (as we will discuss in Chapter 9). More often than not, rich country labor markets "adjust" by seeing capital move overseas to take advantage of lower wages in other countries. The result is that wages remain relatively high in the United States, but some people lose their jobs.

Another reason that the theory can mislead is that investments in *human* capital—health, skills, and education—blur the distinction between "labor" and "capital." Some studies suggest that the comparative advantage of the United States is now tilted toward goods that require production by an *educated and skilled* workforce and away from production that involves lower-skilled work or heavy machinery. When production is intensive in *human* capital, the earlier two-way classification is harder to apply. Meanwhile, studies of factor prices are mixed in their support of the theory of factor-price equalization. Ongoing changes in technology, skills, and the composition of production, as well as deliberate government policies that limit and shift patterns of trade, make it difficult to test the theory.

2.2 OTHER BENEFITS OF FREE TRADE

Specialization and trade can lead to improvements in economic efficiency, as the story of comparative advantage points out. Trade allowed Portugal and England to organize their use of resources more efficiently for producing wine and cloth. The result was a more highly valued combination of outputs than the countries could have achieved through self-sufficiency. Yet many also point to additional advantages of systems based on exchange.

Exchange relations, for example, give economic actors (whether countries, businesses, or workers) clear incentives to be productive: Because these relations are *quid pro quo,* in order to get something, you must have something to give! Unless you happen to be sitting on a pile of wealth, it means that you have to do or make something that other people value before you can participate in exchange. If you see something that you want, and exchange is the only way to get it, exchange relations provide a strong extrinsic motivation to participate in productive activities.

In particular, *decentralized* exchange through markets is thought to have advantages, in terms of incentives, that lead to efficiency even in the case of changing conditions. In decentralized market exchange, individual actors make agreements to trade at a particular moment in time or for some span of time specified by a contract. When that particular trade is completed, each partner can choose to try to continue this trading relationship or can look for new ones.

Suppose that after trading with England for some time, Portugal discovered that it could get more cloth (or other valuable goods) by growing table grapes for Germany than by producing wine for England. In a system of decentralized, or "free market," unregulated exchange, it could freely move resources into producing the more highly valued product. A system of market exchange gives producers incentives to produce the goods that command the highest market value. Such an incentive therefore has the potential to encourage competition and innovation, to the ultimate benefit of all consumers.

Another desirable consequence of free trade or exchange is technical. A production process is characterized by "economies of scale" (we'll discuss this topic in more detail in Chapter 15) if the cost per unit of production falls as the volume of production rises. With trade, the volume of a country's production of a good can be substantially higher than its internal (domestic) market can use, increasing the opportunity for economies of scale to be realized. A larger market means that goods can be produced more cheaply, a fact related to Smith's earlier point about specialization.

In addition to the incentive to generate greater value and economies of scale, many economists also believe that exchange is a morally praiseworthy form of distribution because of its *noncoercive* nature. People enter into exchanges *voluntarily*. As we noted in Chapter 1, freedom is among the final goals that you might hope for in an economic system. Presumably, if what you are offered in exchange does not meet your idea of what you think your item is worth, you can refuse to make the trade.

Finally, some argue that exchange relations encourage economic actors to think in terms of their common interests. Rather than each actor watching out for just him- or herself or close kin, exchange relations bind actors together in a sort of cooperative venture. Classical economists like Ricardo and Smith often argued along these lines. Indeed, writers of that era often waxed eloquent on the moral and community-building advantages that they saw in a system of exchange. A seventeenth-century business textbook, for example, claimed that

> [Divine Providence] has not willed for everything that is needed for life to be found in the same spot. It has dispersed its gifts so that men [*sic*] would trade together and so that the mutual need which they have to help one another would establish ties of friendship among them. This continuous exchange of all the comforts of life constitutes commerce and this commerce makes for all the gentleness of life. [2]

If England and Portugal came to rely on each other for trade, such thinking goes, they might think twice about engaging in a war with each other. Citizens of any city, such writers argued, would likewise be motivated to act more respectfully to each other when they shared commercial interests.

You can find real-world cases in which this appears to be true. For example, after World War II the United States acted beneficently toward the devastated countries of Europe. It gave them significant aid for rebuilding their industries and infrastructure though a program called the Marshall Plan. Why? The actual name of the act that created the Marshall Plan was "The Economic Cooperation Act of 1948." U.S. policymakers realized that their own economy would not prosper unless the economies of its major trading partners prospered as well.

In contemporary times, as well, some invoke the image of a market-based "global village," in which countries, linked by economic interdependence, also enter into harmonious mutual understanding and cultural exchange. Advocates of free trade argue that increased globalization of economic activity, free of barriers set up by governments, will lead to greater good for all.

Discussion Questions

1. Suppose that in a one-hour period, you can buy six bags of groceries *or* clean three rooms. Your housemate, however, is slower moving and can buy only three bags of groceries or clean only one room in an hour. You clearly have an absolute advantage in production of both these services. Does this mean you should do all the work?

2. Ricardo's model discusses benefits to countries at an aggregate level. But what if you were a Portuguese cloth maker or an English winemaker? Might you have a different view about the benefits of trade? Which factors might influence what you think about your country's trade policies?

3. DRAWBACKS OF FREE TRADE

David Ricardo's simple example of two countries and two goods neglects some political, social, and environmental issues that can sometimes offset "gains from trade" or eliminate them altogether. Because rational thinking about the role that societies should allow exchange to have as a mode of distribution requires weighing both benefits and costs, we must also examine the drawbacks of organizing distribution by exchange. The potential disadvantages of exchange as a form of distribution, and of the specialization that often accompanies exchange, include increased vulnerability, becoming locked into disadvantageous production patterns, abuse of power, and the destruction of community.

3.1 VULNERABILITY

One obvious potential problem with specialization and exchange is that each party becomes more vulnerable to the actions of its trading partners. Supplies of the things that you need, and markets for what you sell, could deteriorate or be cut off at any time. This is as true for individuals and businesses as for countries. If you let your housemate specialize in shopping and cooking, for example, you may find yourself hungry if the exchange relationship suddenly breaks down. Businesses may find themselves unable to obtain needed inputs when the source of the inputs is not under their direct control. If Portugal and England were to go to war, to continue the earlier example, or if Portugal were to find a better buyer, England might temporarily find itself with an excess of cloth and no wine to drink.

For many nonessential goods for which substitutes exist, the issue of vulnerability may seem relatively unimportant. But vulnerability is a more serious issue at the national or international level when the goods in question are resources such as oil, minerals, food, or water, the lack of which would seriously weaken an economy or country. In the United States, for example, some of the same people who argue for "free trade" in most goods also argue for increased development of domestic energy resources, on grounds that excessive reliance on petroleum imports decreases economic self-sufficiency and military preparedness.

Vulnerability is also a serious issue for countries that rely heavily on sales of a single, or a few, export goods for much of their national income. In Ethiopia, for example, producing coffee for export is currently the vastly dominant source of cash income for about one-quarter of the population. When the price of the export commodity is high in international markets, such national economies do well. When prices weaken—or plummet, as coffee prices did in 1989—economies dependent on single exports are subjected to major crises that are beyond their control.

Besides making an economy vulnerable to the whims of its trading partners, widespread monoculture (growing of a single kind of crop) carries other risks as well. It can make agricultural economies more susceptible to crises arising from events such as drought, an agricultural pest, or disease. In a more diversified economy, some sectors and crops may do well while others are hard hit; in a very specialized agricultural economy, the entire economy may spin into crisis from one adverse event.

Thus, although the "gains from trade" argument appears logically correct, the benefits of specialization and trade must be weighed against its costs. When *diversification* increases national security, economic stability, or ecological diversity, then a decision *not* to rely on trade for certain things may be better than pure specialization.

3.2 LOCK-IN

Some production processes are characterized by increasing returns: The more of something that you do, the more efficient you become. In dynamic economic systems, patterns of comparative advantage can change over time as a consequence of learning by doing.

To draw a personal analogy, during your early years of school, it may have seemed more efficient for you, when you were first doing simple arithmetic problems, to use a calculator. Chances are that your teachers told you that you could not use a calculator, however. They demanded that you not use the easy (and, in the short run, more efficient) method and, instead, build up a base of cognitive skills (for greater long-run efficiency). They did not want you to become locked into an arithmetic "production technology" that was dependent on the presence of a calculator.

Similarly, an important question for a company deciding which lines of business to enter, or for a country trying to build a healthy national economy, is whether it should engage in some kinds of production that may seem inefficient now but have the potential to improve with time and growth. Should a country, for example, stay locked into its current pattern of comparative advantage—for example, by importing cars and not even thinking of building a domestic auto industry? Or should it, at least temporarily, restrict automobile imports (as Japan did), while developing its own auto industry past the start-up stage?

The critical issue here is that people, companies, or countries should not become "locked in" to specializing in what they do well today if doing so prevents them from developing their future potential in other, more rewarding, pursuits. If, in other words, workers stood to eventually gain from producing cars and electronics instead of bananas and coffee, specializing and getting "locked into" banana and coffee production would likely be harmful to future development prospects.

3.3 COERCION AND POWER DIFFERENTIALS

Our simple story of England and Portugal also ignored the real-world political context of exchange relations. Some element of voluntariness is always present in exchange, but real-world exchange relations are also heavily influenced by the relative power of the parties involved.

For example, we described England and Portugal as exchanging 100 bottles of wine for 100 bolts of cloth—a 1:1 ratio. But what if England were more powerful and could demand different terms, more in its own favor? England might have such a power advantage if it were the only seller of cloth or the only buyer of wine, or through its military might, or through controlling important financial institutions or access to technology.

Whatever the source of its power, suppose England were to demand that Portugal give it 100 bottles of wine in exchange for only 60 bolts of cloth instead of 100. Under such a deal, production, exchange, and consumption would be as described in Table 6.3. England would end up consuming more, and Portugal consuming less, than in the consumption outcome described earlier.

Table 6.3   **A Different Outcome of Exchange and Consumption**

	Country	Wine	Cloth
Production:	Portugal	200	0
	England	0	400
Total production		*200*	*400*
Exchange:	Portugal	sell 100	buy 60
	England	buy 100	sell 60
Consumption:	Portugal	100	60
	England	100	340
Total consumption		*200*	*400*

Would Portugal *voluntarily* accept such an exchange? Looking back at Figure 6.1, you can see that a consumption pattern of 100 bottles of wine and 60 bolts of cloth is still outside of Portugal's own PPF. Thus Portugal might, indeed, still find it advantageous to trade rather than go it alone. (Note that if England offered only 50 bolts of cloth or less, Portugal would not want to trade, because it could do at least as well on its own.)

England does not need to coerce Portugal directly into trading: Portugal's trade is still voluntary. But if England had more power than Portugal, it could force Portugal to accept terms of trade that favor England. In fact, it was England's superior military power that led to the opening of Portuguese cloth markets to English manufactures (see Box 6.1). If, instead, Portugal had been the country with more power, it might have been able to enforce terms of trade that were more in its own favor (say, 100 bottles of wine for 150, rather than 100, bolts of cloth). Similarly, if you and your housemate engage in specialization and exchange of your services, a variety of equitable and inequitable distributions of tasks are possible, based on your relative bargaining power. Just because an exchange is *voluntary* does not mean that it is fair or that differences in power are irrelevant.

Similar struggles for power go on *within* countries that are considering engaging in world trade. Countries in the real world are not simple, unitary decision makers but, rather, are made up of a diversity of citizens, workers, companies, and so on. Although importing wine may be to the advantage of England as a whole, in the sense shown in our graphs and charts, it could be disastrous for *part* of England—namely England's previous wine producers, who would lose their livelihood.

BOX 6.1   ENGLAND, PORTUGAL, AND THE TREATY OF METHUEN

When Ricardo wrote about trade between England and Portugal in 1817, it was indeed true that England exported cloth to Portugal in return for wine. But this was not pure "free trade," and it had not come about simply due to the impersonal forces of economic efficiency and comparative advantage.

Before the Treaty of Methuen in 1703, Portugal had severely restricted the importation of cloth from abroad, and England had imported wine primarily from France. But England lost much of its access to French wine during the War of the Spanish Succession (1701–1714). Portugal, meanwhile, was pressured to join a military alliance with England by displays of England's superior naval power. The 1703 treaty cementing their alliance also contained economic terms: Portugal would admit English cloth without charging any tariffs at all, while England would reduce its tariffs on Portuguese wine to two-thirds of what it collected on French wine. Some commentators argue that this was a crucial—and negative—turning point for the development of Portuguese manufacturing.

A concern for human well-being, rather than just for efficiency per se, demands that such distributional considerations be taken into account. When increased trade threatens a major industry, the negative effects on certain people and regions can be deep and prolonged. This happened in Detroit, formerly a bustling industrial city, which became economically depressed—part of the U.S. "rust belt"—as auto manufacturing gradually moved overseas. In parts of Africa during the late twentieth century, increases in export agriculture, run largely by men, caused hardships for those engaged in subsistence agriculture, primarily women and children. It may be that efficiency gains for the country as a whole outweigh local losses. But the local losses, and the costs of redistribution policies designed to alleviate hardship and move people to new occupations, must be properly weighed when the benefits and costs of exchange relationships are considered.

3.4 OTHER SOCIAL AND POLITICAL IMPACTS

Is it appropriate to establish trade in anything? There is reasonable resistance to the idea of "commodifying" certain things that society does not generally treat as commodities. Most agree, for example, that kidneys, votes, and babies should never be a part of exchange relations. Treating such things as though they were on a par with shoelaces or cars is thought to destroy the bonds of respect necessary for social life. Potentially life-saving kidney operations, for example, might become available based on ability to pay rather than medical urgency.

Current tensions between government and corporate interests are another area for controversy. In Ricardo's time, it was natural to think about international trade in terms of the actions and policies of countries such as England and Portugal, but in the twenty-first century, discussing trade in terms of multinational corporations such as Microsoft and Daimler-Benz might be at least as appropriate. Corporations have grown ever larger and have become able to move their financial capital and their physical production facilities across international boundaries with increasing ease.

This leads to a dilemma for governments. Traditionally, democratic governments have been able to enact policies perceived to be in the public interest, even though they were not always in the interest of business. Minimum standards for pay and safety on the job, for example, or environmental standards and taxation to support public projects, are widely considered necessary for a healthy, just society. Yet members of the business sphere often oppose such policies because they generally increase costs and decrease profits.

race to the bottom: a situation in which countries or regions compete in providing low-cost business environments, resulting in deterioration in labor, environmental, or safety standards

Because capital is increasingly mobile, businesses exclusively concerned with profits are able to move their operations to countries with lower labor and environmental standards and taxes. Countries or states that want to hold onto their business base may therefore find themselves drawn into a "**race to the bottom**," in which they compete to attract businesses on the basis of their *lack* of attention to social and environmental concerns. This is a serious concern for cities and states, as well as for countries; some regions, in their eagerness to compete for businesses that will bring jobs, have offered to soften environmental regulations, while providing other incentives—tax holidays, building infrastructure, and so on—that have, in some cases ended up costing the region hundreds of thousands of dollars per job created. For an example of this from the United States, see Box 6.2.

Powerful corporations can also attempt to influence international organizations and agreements directly. These issues began to receive more public attention in the United States after the 1999 "anti-globalization" demonstrations at the Seattle meetings of the World Trade Organization. The ability of people to make democratic decisions about the direction of their society is threatened when the power of democratic governments is overshadowed by the power of nondemocratic economic interests.

These political and social impacts need to be considered as we evaluate the impacts of trade. They do not necessarily invalidate the basic message of Ricardo regarding the great benefits to be gained from freer trade. But they must at least be considered as economists and policymakers try to formulate appropriate trade policies.

BOX 6.2 THE HIGH COST OF COMPETING FOR JOBS

Politicians commonly talk about the need to "create jobs," but often the competition among different regions for jobs can come at a high cost to taxpayers. In the United States, individual states often find themselves courting companies to locate a new production facility or other large employment center in their state. The winning state in such competitions is normally the one that offers the largest financial incentive to the company.

One notable example of this competition for jobs occurred in the 1990s, as the states of North Carolina, South Carolina, and Alabama vied to become the location of the first Mercedes-Benz factory in the United States. As each state sweetened its offer, Mercedes eventually requested that the winning state pay some of the workers' wages. The apparent frontrunner, North Carolina, balked at this request, which allowed Alabama to win the competition for the factory. Alabama additionally agreed to purchase the land for the factory for $30 million, with public funds, and lease it to Mercedes for only $100. On top of that the state provided tax breaks valued at about $300 million. Ultimately, it is estimated that the cost to taxpayers for each job created was between $153,000 and $220,000.

Some economists believe Alabama's offer was economically irrational. Joel Kotkin, an economic analyst who has followed various competitions among states for corporate investment, said "They went crazy. This is lunatic stuff." Noting Alabama's need for improved education, he added, "The question is, what have you taken out of your economy in order to do this? Most studies show it doesn't work. You're essentially giving away three-quarters of what you're going to gain."

Now that the factory is operating, employing about 3,000 workers, it is unclear whether Alabama's investment has paid off. According to economic analysis by Mercedes, the factory has added $1.3 billion annually to the state's economy. But academic economists remain divided.

Annette Watters, assistant director for the Center for Business & Economic Research at University of Alabama, has noted, "Some of the benefits are so difficult to measure. There are still strongly held opinions in the academic community that it's good and that it's bad."

Sources: Donald W. Nauss, "Bids by States to Lure Businesses Likely to Escalate," *Los Angeles Times*, October 1, 1993; Adam M. Zaretsky, "Are States Giving Away the Store? Attracting Jobs Can Be a Costly Adventure," *The Regional Economist*, Federal Reserve Bank of St. Louis, January 1994; "Ten Years after Mercedes, Alabama Town Still Pans for Gold," *Savannah Morning News*, October 9, 2002.

Discussion Questions

1. Think of a recent situation in which you bought something that you could, if you had wanted to, have produced for yourself (a restaurant meal that you could have cooked, a bus ride when you could have walked, or the like). Do any of the advantages or disadvantages of exchange discussed up to now apply to your case?
2. What do you suppose Smith or Ricardo would have had to say about the disadvantages of free trade discussed in this chapter? Do you agree with them? Why or why not?

4. GLOBALIZATION AND POLICY

globalization: the extension of free trade and communications across the entire world, leading to a great increase in the volume of traded goods and services, and in expanded interconnections among different regions

As the global scope and volume of trade has increased, we need to consider the realities of globalization rather than simply of trade between two countries such as England and Portugal. **Globalization** involves increasing trade and communications among all parts of the world, leading to a great increase in the volume of traded goods and services. These interconnections turn up in a large variety of ways, including:

- a global audience for music, films, fashion, and other aspects of culture;
- expanded communications through the Internet, regardless of distance;
- exchanges of scientific, medical, and technical knowledge;
- inspiration regarding the possibility of freedom from hunger and want and from repressive government;
- shared images of a "good life," often based on images of material affluence associated with the West; and

• trade relationships that allow those who have money to purchase goods and services from virtually anywhere in the world—and that attract poor people into jobs producing for global consumers.

Although many of these developments are conducive to increased well-being overall, globalization can also accentuate some of the problems with free trade discussed above. Trade does create winners and losers; how is one to determine the relative importance of each group—for example, consumers, workers, citizens, children, and businesspeople? Are the wishes of consumers for lower prices as important as workers' fears of losing their jobs to foreign competition? Chapter 5, on welfare analysis, supplied some tools for measuring gains and losses in social welfare, but, as emphasized there, those tools depended entirely on market valuations. Thus, for example, if the workers' wages are low to begin with, their loss will not be counted as heavily in a standard welfare analysis as it would be if the "social loss" came out to a larger dollar figure.

In addition to economic threats, globalization is sometimes also criticized for its political and cultural effects, as people feel as if they are losing control over their local customs and livelihoods in a globalized world. This has often led to some degree of popular and government resistance to free trade and globalization.

4.1 TRADE PROTECTIONISM

protectionism: the use of government policies to restrict trade with other countries and protect domestic industries from foreign competition

Exchange, as we have noted, has the potential to produce mutually beneficial outcomes for the parties involved, whether countries, companies, or family members. Yet we have also considered some reasons to be wary of too much reliance on exchange. National governments have always been aware of these problems and have historically tried, through a variety of policy tools, to control the degree to which their markets were "free." The use of such policies is often referred to as **protectionism**.

tariffs: taxes (or duties) charged by national governments to the importers of goods from other countries

One example of protectionism, probably the most commonly used throughout history, is a **tariff** (sometimes called a "duty"). Tariffs are taxes charged by national governments to importers of merchandise from other countries. They often reduce trade to some degree, because the tariff raises the price of the good sold in the importing country, thereby reducing the import quantity demanded. The tariff can also have the effect of raising the price of domestically produced goods that compete with the imported good. Tariffs therefore tend to benefit domestic producers while raising prices to consumers. They also provide the government with often critically important tax revenue; indeed, this has often been the primary motivation for tariffs through history. Finally, tariffs sometimes even force foreign producers to lower their prices in order to remain competitive with domestic producers who do not pay the tariff.

trade quota: a nationally imposed restriction on the quantity of a particular good that can be imported from another country

Another example of protectionism is a **trade quota**, which is a limit on the quantity of a good that can be imported from another country. By restricting supply, a quota generally has the effect of increasing the price of the good. Like a tariff, it helps domestic producers by shielding them from lower-price competition, and it hurts consumers by making them pay a higher price. Unlike tariffs, quotas generally do not provide monetary benefit to the government, except when the quotas are sold or auctioned to the importers (this may be done out in the open or "unofficially"). The effect on the exporting foreign country is, however, more ambiguous than with a tariff. On the one hand, the quota may hurt foreign producers because it limits how much of a particular good they can export. On the other hand, they may obtain some benefit from extra revenues from the artificially higher price. Which effect prevails depends on, among other things, the elasticity of demand (discussed in Chapter 4) for the imported good.

trade-related subsidy: payments given to producers to encourage more production, either for export or as a substitute for imports

Imposing either tariffs or quotas or both has historically been the most frequently method of engaging in protectionism. But a few others, while less direct, have gained in importance in recent decades. One of these is the **trade-related subsidy**, which, unlike a tariff or quota, may be used to either expand or contract trade (and therefore cannot always precisely be regarded as

import substitution: a policy undertaken by governments seeking to reduce reliance on imports and encourage domestic industry. These often include the use of industry subsidies as well as protectionist policies.

administrative obstacles: use of environmental, health, or safety regulations to prevent imports from other countries under the pretext of upholding higher standards

"protectionist"). Trade expansion is facilitated through subsidies to exporters, since such payments reduce their production costs and therefore help exporters price their goods more competitively in foreign markets. Such payments can also be granted to domestic producers to encourage the production of certain goods for domestic markets, with a goal of reducing the quantity of imports. This is achieved to the extent that the demand for imports can be diverted to the domestic product (which is nothing more than a substitute for the imported product). Such subsidies fall into the more general policy of **import substitution**, which refers to government promotion of greater economic independence by decreasing the country's dependence on imports.

A final category of protectionism is subtle and often not easy to detect. It is when countries use **administrative obstacles** such as regulations relating to the environment, consumer protection, and labor standards to block importation of goods from foreign countries. They are difficult to detect because most of the time the pretext seems legitimate—and often it *is*. But in some cases it is clear that the standard being upheld is nothing more than a form of protectionism. In 1984, for example, the European Union (EU) struck down the German "beer purity" law—in effect for more than 300 years—a law that required all beer sold in Germany to use only a select few ingredients. The EU overturned the law because it found that it was motivated less by true concerns about "purity" than by the desire to keep beer imports out of the country. Another more amusing example occurred in the 1980s when Japan sought to ban imports of European ski equipment on grounds that Japanese snow was "unique" and that only Japanese-manufactured equipment was suitable for skiing on it.

Countries do not necessarily choose sets of policies that consistently lead toward "openness" or consistently toward "closedness." Often there is a mix—policies are chosen for a wide variety of reasons and can even work at cross-purposes. Nor do countries choose their policies in a vacuum. Policymakers need to take into account the reactions of foreign governments to their policies. Increasingly, they also need to pay attention to whether their policies are in compliance with international agreements.

4.2 INTERNATIONAL TRADE AGREEMENTS

Many countries remained quite closed to trade up through the early decades of the twentieth century, charging high tariffs or imposing strict quotas on imported goods. It was only after World War II that this began to change. Despite Smith and Ricardo's famous pronouncements in favor of free trade, throughout history countries have seldom reduced their barriers to trade unilaterally. But starting in the 1940s, many countries became more interested in negotiating mutual reductions in tariffs and quotas.

Some trade agreements are "bilateral," meaning that two countries negotiate directly with each other. Other agreements are "multilateral," involving a group of countries. In 1948, 23 countries joined the General Agreement on Tariffs and Trade (GATT), which sought to set out rules for trade and enhance negotiations. The GATT has sponsored eight subsequent negotiation "trade rounds," some of which led to significant reductions in average tariff rates among participating countries over the next several decades.

World Trade Organization (WTO): an international organization that provides a forum for trade negotiations, creates rules to govern trade, and investigates and makes judgment on trade disputes

In 1995, the Uruguay Round of GATT trade negotiations led to the creation of a new forum for multilateral negotiations, the **World Trade Organization (WTO)**. As of 2013, the WTO has 159 member countries. In addition to being a forum for trade negotiations, the WTO attempts to set out rules about trade and is charged with investigating and making rulings on trade disputes between member countries. Many believe that its rulings are not without bias, because the WTO tends to rule in favor of the party in the dispute that is upholding free trade principles. In 2009, for example, the United States appealed to the WTO over dozens of subsidies that China was granting to its apparel, agriculture, and electronics industries. Anticipating the WTO's unfavorable ruling, China voluntarily ended the subsidies.

Some critics argue that, because of its bias toward free trade, the WTO's scope is too narrow. Yet in its assiduous pursuit of universal free trade, the WTO is also seeking to ensure that global trade is "fair." In other words, to the extent that it can create a world free of trade restrictions, the WTO is "leveling the playing field." The goal is for no country to be able to display favoritism toward or discriminate against others by subjecting them to different tariff levels or quota restrictions.

Can the WTO so easily impose its will on other countries? Well, not exactly; it technically has no sovereignty over countries that wish to ignore its rulings. Yet the loser in a dispute almost always has strong reasons for abiding by the WTO's decision. For one thing, the WTO considers it fair for the injured country to retaliate against its adversary if the latter ignores the judgment. So a country that wishes to breach WTO regulations must seriously consider the possibility of a trade war, in which each country keeps retaliating against the protectionist acts of the others, leading to escalating losses for both countries.

What if a country enjoys disproportionate economic power and therefore has little reason to fear retaliation? One might, for example, believe that the United States has the ability to impose tariffs on all (or at least most) imports from, say, Mozambique with impunity, because any attempted retaliation would likely just shift U.S. demand from Mozambique's markets to those of its neighbors. Yet the United States also must be concerned with its international image. As a leading global advocate of free trade, it would probably suffer diminished goodwill from its allies if it were seen to be flouting WTO rulings simply because it could. Consequently, trade dispute rulings from the WTO are almost always binding.

In addition to being members of the WTO, many countries have also entered into regional trade agreements with their neighbors. Leading examples of such attempts to integrate trade within a geographic area include the European Union (EU), formed in 1992, which now counts 27 countries as members; the North American Free Trade Agreement (NAFTA), entered into in 1994 by the United States, Canada, and Mexico; and Mercosur (Southern Cone Common Market) in South America, established in 1991, which now has five full members and five associate members. Although each of these regional agreements is unique regarding its specific policies, they all share a general commitment to reducing trade barriers such as tariffs or quotas.

There is some debate over whether such regional integration promotes "free trade" or retards it, because it promotes both trade *expansion* (within the region) and trade *diversion* (away from trade with other regions). To some degree, regional trade agreements have the same objective as the WTO—to lower tariffs and other barriers to trade. At the same time, these regional agreements can implicitly promote trade discrimination against countries outside the membership in any particular trade agreement.

4.3 WHY COUNTRIES FOLLOW PROTECTIONIST POLICIES

One very important reason that many policymakers have, historically, restricted trade is that they believe it is necessary to "protect" domestic industries and jobs from foreign competition. The United States, for example, still engages in protection of a variety of industries including Southern cotton, Northwestern timber, and Midwestern sugar beets. Without government protection, these industries would lose market share to lower-cost foreign producers. Such adjustment to global competition can be very painful. When U.S. automakers began to lose out to foreign competition, for example, a swath of the Midwest became so economically depressed that it became known as the "rust belt."

Sometimes protectionism is called a "beggar-thy-neighbor" approach, because each country is, in effect, trying to gain at the expense of other countries. Each country wants to *raise* its own production levels while simultaneously *reducing* the access of foreign producers to its market. Even after decades of trade negotiations—and encouragement by economists to "liberalize" their trade regimes—many countries continue to employ protectionist policies, at least of a modest, piecemeal sort. Although simple economic theory ignores the power differentials between countries and assumes that labor and capital resources can immediately and smoothly adjust to new patterns of commerce, in real life things can be quite different. Trade relations continue to be an arena in which countries try to exert dominance over one another. Policymakers continue to be concerned about the job losses and industrial dislocations that global competition can cause. Policies to ease unemployment may help, but there is no sign that—at least in democratic countries—policymakers will completely abandon protectionist tendencies any time soon.

A particular weakness of Ricardo's two-country, two-good model is that, like many economic models, it is a "static" model that does not take into account the passage of time. Patterns of comparative advantage can, after all, change. Should a country simply follow whatever comparative advantage it happens to have at a given time, or should it explore policies that might *change* its comparative advantage? If the country could end up better off in the long run by deliberately changing its mix of productive capabilities, it might achieve "dynamic efficiency" overall—that is, efficiency-based welfare gains over a sustained period of years—even if "static efficiency" is sacrificed over the short run.

In fact, many countries that have achieved high rates of industrialization—including the United States, the United Kingdom, Japan, and South Korea—did so by erecting substantial tariff barriers. If these countries had maintained their natural comparative advantages as they had existed in the past, the United States might still be known mostly for its production of wheat and raw cotton and the UK for its wool, while South Korea and Japan would still import all their cars. Policies that excluded foreign imports of manufactured textiles or automotive parts helped these countries to shift their economies away from less-processed goods toward a more industrial economic base. Now they all compete in global markets for sophisticated manufactured goods.

infant industry:
an industry that is relatively new to its region or country, and thus may be protected from international competition by tariffs and other trade barriers until it can better compete on world markets

The **infant industry** argument claims that sometimes governments should "protect" domestic industries from foreign competition until they become better able to compete on world markets. Usually, the government subsidizes the industry or places tariffs or quotas on imports of the good. Many industrializing countries have engaged in such import substitution policies in attempts to diversify their (earlier, often agriculture- or mining-based) economies. Sometimes, an entire package of industry-promoting policies is referred to as "industrial policy," and the goal is stated as the creation of a superior "*dynamic* comparative advantage."

The downside of deliberate, comparative-advantage-shifting industrial policy is that current potential "gains from trade" are sacrificed. The upside is that, over the long run, the country might be able to increase its national productivity and competitiveness and thus avoid getting locked into a disadvantageous pattern of production and trade.

Whether the gains from protectionist policies outweigh their costs is a matter of dispute. Many analysts point to long-term government protection of persistently high-cost production in India and some countries in Latin America as evidence that, once started, infant-industry policies tend to serve political special interests, rather than the interests of rational economic development. However, many economic historians point out that, into the early twentieth century, industries in France, Germany, the UK, and the United States all developed by erecting stiff tariff protection. These early industrializing countries bought raw materials from colonized or previously colonized areas, while refusing, as also noted earlier, to open their markets to imports of many manufactured goods. Japan, Taiwan, and South Korea are more recent examples of countries in which some varieties of protectionist policies were important in the history of their industrial development.

But even an advanced industrialized economy can become too specialized, which can sometimes lead to an unhealthy dependence on other countries for important goods like food and energy. Japan, for example, at the forefront when it comes to electronics and other manufactured goods, is heavily dependent on food imports, which could make the country vulnerable in the event of a war or other disruption in trade. Japan has long used quotas and tariffs to limit rice imports, providing protection for its domestic rice producers. Energy security is another important concern. In recent years, the United States has been pushing, through the use of generous subsidies to domestic producers, to develop alternatives to petroleum—most notably natural gas, with the attendant controversy over the manner in which it is extracted. Developers of renewable energy like solar and wind power have also been receiving subsidies, albeit at a smaller scale. The goal of U.S policymakers is reduce dependence on petroleum imports from other countries.

Another important reason that some countries engage in protectionism is perceived lack of "fairness" by trading partners. Companies that are not required by their governments to abide by certain labor, safety, or environmental laws or regulations receive an indirect subsidy in that they face lower production costs, ceteris paribus, than foreign competitors. So we can say, for example, that clothing made in countries that are hostile to labor unions are likely to be priced more competitively than clothing made in countries where workers enjoy more rights and benefits (which tend to be more costly to employers). It is a "fairness" issue in that countries that observe higher standards believe themselves to be unjustly penalized.

One way in which countries can try to avoid such a "race to the bottom" is to ban both the domestic manufacture and importation of goods that are considered hazardous to consumers, have been made under labor standards considered inhumane, or were made using production processes that cause serious damage to the environment. In this way, at least the domestic market is reserved for producers who follow higher standards. The setting of standards may also encourage potential trading partners to raise their environmental, labor, or safety standards, so that their goods can be admitted.

At the same time, setting standards may provoke strong resistance. For example, in 1994, the United States sought to ban tuna imports from Mexico, an act generally prohibited by the GATT. Its claim was based on its higher environmental standards: The United States accused Mexico of using nets that tended to inadvertently catch and drown dolphins—nets that were also much cheaper to use than "dolphin-friendly" nets. Mexico appealed to the GATT, which ruled in its favor and required the United States to lift the ban. Since then, numerous other instances of protectionism have occurred on the basis of asymmetric (unequal) standards for, among other things, labor, the environment, safety, and health.

Another justification for protectionism, mentioned earlier, is the need for government revenue. This has without a doubt been one of the greatest motivators for such policies over the years, specifically in the case of tariffs. Until 1913, for example, the United States had no income tax, and the federal government relied heavily on tariffs to run its operations. Of course, this is no longer the case, as the U.S. federal government today obtains a tiny fraction of its revenue from import tariffs. Yet in many poor countries, it is, even today, very difficult to collect taxes on income and property. People may be spread over wide areas, and much of the economy may not be monetized. Because tariffs are taxes on monetized transactions at harbor facilities or airports, they are, as a rule, relatively easy to collect. Tariffs can therefore be an important source of revenue for health, education, defense, and other government activities.

4.4 WHEN IS LIMITING TRADE "UNFAIR"?

When should a restriction on trade be considered legitimate, and when should it not be? This complicated question is a topic of vigorous, ongoing debate. Most countries staunchly defend their right to restrict trade for purposes such as military security or consumer safety, so international trade agreements tend to stop short of banning all restrictions.

But beyond agreement on a few principles, debates become heated. Consider three examples.

GMO Products. The EU has banned the importation of products containing genetically modified organisms (GMO), on grounds that they present a threat to public health and the environment. The United States and other grain-producing countries have contested this at the WTO, arguing that GMO products are safe and the real reason for the ban is that the EU simply wants to protect its farmers. The WTO ultimately ruled that the ban was illegal, a ruling entirely consistent with its pro–free trade bias. But the ruling has only intensified the debate.

Dumping. The United States has accused China of subsidizing the production of many of its products and **dumping** them on the U.S. market. "Dumping," the selling of products

dumping: selling products at prices that are below the cost of production on foreign markets at prices that are unfairly low (that is, below the cost of production), is forbidden in international agreements. The United States argues that it has the right to retaliate by levying quotas and tariffs on Chinese goods. But China, of course, can argue that it simply is blessed with a low-cost production environment and that the United States is engaging in protectionism.

Labor Standards. In some extreme cases, such as the use of slave labor, restrictions on trade are usually considered permissible. But should countries be allowed to use trade restrictions to punish unfair labor practices? Some poorer countries have accused richer countries of imposing unreasonably high labor standards. Under the pretext of trying to protect global workers, they say, the richer countries are just trying to protect their workers from fair competition. But the lack of such standards can have disastrous consequences, for example, the death of hundreds of workers in Bangladesh in factory fires and building collapses (see Box 6.3).

Questions of what will be ruled "fair" or "unfair" by the WTO—and whether such rulings can be enforced—often come down to questions of political economy. Large, powerful countries and corporations use the WTO negotiations and dispute resolution mechanisms as ways to advance their own interests. Smaller and less powerful groups have a more difficult time having their voices heard. Many labor, environmental, and social justice groups, for example, charge that the WTO primarily serves the interests of powerful multinational corporations. They worry that WTO negotiations have served to speed up the "race to the bottom" and have reduced national sovereignty. Observers concerned about economic development believe that WTO rules disadvantage countries that are still relatively poor, by forbidding the use of the sorts of industrial policies that helped other countries achieve economic growth at an earlier time. In other words, in its zeal to support the elimination or reduction of trade restrictions, the WTO appears to be forgetting the economic path that today's wealthier countries followed during their own rise.

In 2001, the WTO officially launched the Doha Round of negotiations (also officially called the Doha Development Agenda), which was, in its official statements, intended to take into account the needs and interests of poorer countries. Now, even a dozen years later, the Doha Round remains at an impasse. Many poorer countries pushed for richer countries to reduce their tariffs and subsidies, particularly on agricultural goods. At the same time, top priorities for richer countries included persuading poorer countries to open their service sector

---

BOX 6.3 LABOR STANDARDS, TRAGEDY, AND REFORM IN BANGLADESH

The Rana Plaza complex was built on swampy ground outside Dhaka, Bangladesh. Code violations included the building of several illegal floors. The building's collapse on April 24, 2013, ranked among the world's worst industrial accidents, killing more than a thousand garment workers. A fire at another garment factory in Bangladesh the previous year killed 112 people.

Low wages in Bangladesh, along with tax concessions offered by Western countries, have helped turn the country's garment sector into its largest employment generator. Annual exports from the sector are worth $21 billion, with 60 percent of these exports going to Europe. After the recent industrial accidents, the European Union, which gives preferential access to the Bangladeshi garment industry, threatened punitive measures if worker safety standards were not improved.

In July 2013, Bangladesh approved a new labor law to boost worker rights, including the freedom to form trade unions. The legislation puts in place provisions including a central fund to improve living standards of workers, a requirement for 5 percent of annual profits to be deposited in employee welfare funds, and an assurance that union members will not be transferred to another factory of the same owner after labor unrest.

The legislation is seen as a crucial step toward curbing rising cases of exploitation in a country with 4 million garment factory workers. But activists said it failed to address several concerns and blamed the government for enacting the law in a hurry to please foreigners.

Source: Nandita Bose, "Stronger Labour Law in Bangladesh after Garment Factory Collapse," Reuters, July 15, 2013.

(including banking and airline transportation) to foreign companies and to abide by stricter rules on intellectual property (e.g., to stop making less expensive versions of patented drugs). Because the wealthier countries showed little willingness to reduce protection of their domestic agricultural industries, Doha Round talks were suspended in July 2006. Negotiations again broke down in 2008, and since then no notable progress has been made to restart them.

Discussion Questions

1. What international trade issues have been in the news recently? What views are presented by different interest groups in trade debates? Are there any issues that particularly affect your community?

2. Debates between advocates of "free trade" and advocates of "protectionism" have gone on for hundreds of years. How aware are you of current debates, which are now often framed in terms of pro- and anti-"globalization"? Do you have more sympathy for one side than for the other? What do you think you need to know more about—in terms of theories or real-world facts—to be able to decide with confidence whether increased world trade, in a specific situation, is a good idea?

5. CONCLUSION

We have seen that the observations made by Adam Smith and David Ricardo in support of free trade have an almost unassailable logic based on economic efficiency. And one could argue that their logic has been borne out in practice, because much of what they observed two centuries ago has since played out at a much greater scale. Yet if there is a lesson in our experience with trade, it is that theory often does not account for what practice later reveals.

The world was a much simpler place during the time of Smith and Ricardo. Large multinational corporations did not yet exist for the most part, and businesses could not readily pick up and migrate to another country if they found conditions more favorable there. Indeed, in those days such actions might even have been considered treasonous. The simple comparative advantage model discussed earlier was more suited to the relatively simple world that existed during that time. The far greater complexity in today's world is much more difficult—if not impossible—to capture in a simplified model.

This is a good time to remind ourselves once again that models best serve us as simplifications of reality that grant us some basic insight into the functioning of real-world systems. The original insights about the advantages of free trade—that is, that it can be of substantial benefit to both parties to an exchange—appear no more contestable today than during Smith and Ricardo's time. Yet beyond this important insight, numerous complicating factors should cause us to be cautious in interpreting the model.

Here we briefly list and review three such factors, though the list is far from exhaustive. First, as noted above, the logic of unfettered free trade does not account for the fact that today capital can easily migrate across borders. What this means is that countries do not have to conform to mutually beneficial exchange. Recalling an earlier example, let us assume that the United States has a comparative *dis*advantage in clothing production compared to Bangladesh. Instead of trading with Bangladesh, U.S companies today can move there and hire local workers—at a relatively low wage—to produce clothes for global markets. Easy capital mobility could, in such cases, reduce opportunities for mutually beneficial trade.

Second, in Smith and Ricardo's time, the economic landscape consisted of only about a dozen economic powers at a more or less similar level of development. The "playing field" was, in other words, more or less level. Today, because former colonies have achieved political independence over the past 50 to 60 years, the world is far more imbalanced. One danger facing poor countries today is that they will follow the "logic" of comparative advantage and continue to specialize in simple primary goods that offer them scant hope of someday becoming stronger, more diversified economies.

Third, there is the role of the WTO. It might appear that Smith and Ricardo would have supported an agency empowered to promote global free trade. Yet because inequality between countries is so much greater today than it was then, it seems increasingly doubtful, the WTO's mission notwithstanding, that today's brand of "free trade"—meaning a wholesale dismantling of protectionist policies—is always mutually beneficial. It is indeed quite possible that by making it more difficult for developing countries to actively nurture their fledgling industries, some WTO policies may worsen inequality around the world. This is especially true because more powerful countries can often win exceptions to the rule for their products in certain areas, notably agriculture.

Perhaps the greatest controversy exists over asymmetric "standards"—whether motivated by labor, environmental, safety, or other concerns. There is no question that rigid adherence to, say, labor standards might result in trade restrictions against countries that do not place a high priority on workers' rights. For this reason alone, the WTO is likely to disallow their use as a basis for blocking trade, except in extreme cases such as child or slave labor. Yet such a case vividly illustrates how in some cases the "gains from trade" might mask social or environmental losses resulting from the "race to the bottom" that the WTO's pro-trade policies might foster.

The question arises as to how to balance the "gains" to importers and consumers against the potential losses to workers, domestic industry, and the environment. And, again, although economics can provide some concepts and methods to use in reaching for answers, important decisions in these areas often require ethical judgments that go beyond the discipline of economics.

REVIEW QUESTIONS

1. How does specialization lead to greater productivity?
2. Explain how more extensive markets tend to produce a higher degree of specialization.
3. Was Adam Smith a revolutionary? Explain.
4. Describe the Ricardian model of trade.
5. What is meant by the "principle of comparative advantage"?
6. On what does a country's comparative advantage depend?
7. What does it mean to say that a particular country is labor intensive (or capital intensive)?
8. What is the theory of "factor-price equalization"?
9. How does free trade produce an incentive to work hard?
10. What are some other advantages of free trade?
11. Explain how the concepts of vulnerability and "lock-in" are related. How do they weaken the case for free trade?
12. What is "protectionism," and why do countries often engage in it?
13. List and describe four types of protectionist policies.
14. What is import substitution?
15. What are some international organizations and agreements that involve trade relations?
16. What does the World Trade Organization do?
17. What is the "infant industry" argument?
18. How does the notion of "dynamic comparative advantage" explain some countries' adoption of "infant industry" policies?
19. How can international openness cause a "race to the bottom"?
20. Give some examples of recent controversies in trade policy.

EXERCISES

1. Hereland and Thereland are two small countries. Each currently produces both milk and corn, and they do not trade. If Hereland puts all its resources into milk, it can produce 2 tanker truckloads, while if it puts all its resources in corn production, it can produce 8 tons. Thereland can produce either 2 loads of milk or 2 tons of corn. (Both can also produce any combination on a straight line in between.)
   a. Draw and label production-possibilities frontiers for Hereland and Thereland.

b. Suppose that Hereland's citizens would like 1 truckload of milk and 6 tons of corn. Can Hereland produce this?

c. Suppose that Thereland's citizens would like 1 load of milk and 2 tons of corn. Can Thereland produce this?

d. What is the slope of Hereland's PPF? Fill in the blank: "For each truckload of milk that Hereland makes, it must give up making ___ tons of corn."

e. What is the slope of Thereland's PPF? Fill in the blank: "For each truckload of milk that Thereland makes, it must give up making ___ tons of corn."

f. Which country has a comparative advantage in producing milk?

g. Create a table similar to Table 6.1, showing how Hereland and Thereland could enter into a trading relationship in order to meet their citizens' consumption desires as described in (b) and (c).

h. Suppose that you are an analyst working for the government of Hereland. Write a few sentences, based on the above analysis, advising your boss about whether to undertake trade negotiations with Thereland.

i. Would your advice change if you knew that unemployment in Hereland is high and that retraining corn farmers to be dairy farmers, or vice versa, is very difficult to do?

j. Would your advice change if Thereland insisted in trade negotiations that 1 truckload of milk be exchanged for exactly 4 tons of corn?

2. Continuing the Ricardian story from Section 2.1 of this chapter, suppose that England were, after a while, to put a tariff on imports of Portuguese wine. Since we only have wine and cloth in this story, we will have to (somewhat unrealistically) express this tax in terms of units of goods rather than units of currency. Say that England demands that Portugal "pay a tariff of 40 units of cloth" if it wants to sell 100 units of wine. Or, in other words, England now says that it will give Portugal only *60 units of cloth* instead of 100, in exchange for 100 units of wine.

a. With production unchanged, what would exchange and consumption be like under these modified terms of trade? (Create a table like Table 6.1.)

b. Does England benefit from instituting this tariff?

c. Would Portugal voluntarily agree to continue trading, with these changed terms of trade? (Assume that Portugal has no power to change the terms of trade—it can only accept England's deal or go back to consuming within its own PPF.)

d. If trade is voluntary, does that mean it is *fair*? Discuss.

3. Match each concept in Column A with a definition or example in Column B.

Column A	Column B
a. Tariff	1. Economic weakness resulting from too much import dependence
b. Import substitution	2. When a region competes by providing a low-cost business environment, resulting in deterioration of labor, environmental, or safety standards
c. Vulnerability	3. An organization charged with facilitating international trade
d. Race to the bottom	4. Getting trapped into the long-term production of primary goods for export
e. Dumping	5. The theory that trade should eventually lead to returns to factors of production that are equal across countries
f. Quota	6. A tax levied on an internationally traded item
g. Dynamic comparative advantage	7. Changes in the opportunity cost of production over time
h. WTO	8. The use of environmental, health, or safety regulations to prevent imports from other countries under the pretext of upholding higher standards
i. Factor-price equalization	9. The deliberate promotion of domestic goods production to reduce reliance on imports
j. Comparative advantage	10. An industry that needs protection until it is able to compete
k. Lock-in	11. Selling goods abroad at a price that is below the cost of production
l. Administrative obstacles	12. Putting a quantity limit on imports or exports
m. Infant industry	13. Putting a tariff on orange juice imports to help Florida orange growers
n. Protectionism	14. A country is relatively more efficient in the production of some good(s)

APPENDIX: A FORMAL THEORY OF GAINS FROM TRADE

Here we explore in more detail the "gains from trade" example given in the text. There, for simplicity, we explored a case in which both countries completely specialize, because their level of desired total consumption just happens to match each country's total production level with complete specialization. Graphing a *joint* PPF for the two countries enables us to relax this assumption, while also exploring more fully the concepts of opportunity costs and comparative advantage.

Recall that in this example, Portugal can produce a maximum of either 200 bottles of wine or 100 bolts of cloth. Portugal's PPF was shown in Figure 6.1. Examining its slope more closely reveals that, moving left to right starting at the (0, 200) point, a fall (or negative "rise") of 200 bottles of wine is accompanied by a "run" of +100 bolts of cloth. Because the curve is straight, the slope is therefore –2 throughout. At any point, then, reducing wine production by 2 bottles (i.e., a negative "rise" of 2) is needed to increase cloth production by 1 bolt (i.e., to create a "run" of 1 unit to the right).

England can produce a maximum of 200 bottles of wine or 400 bolts of cloth, as was shown in Figure 6.2. The slope of its production possibilities frontier is –0.5 (= –200/400). For each additional bolt of cloth, England gives up producing half a bottle of wine.

In Figure 6.3, we create a *joint* PPF for the two countries. Suppose that they both start out producing only wine. Adding Portugal's 200 bottles to England's 200 bottles, we find that jointly they can produce 400 bottles if they produce no cloth, as shown at the point (0, 400). Now suppose that they would like to consume *some* cloth, and they make a joint decision about where it should be produced. They see that if Portugal produces the first bolt of cloth, it will cost them 2 bottles of wine. If England produces the first bolt of cloth, it will cost them only half a bottle of wine. Clearly, England should produce it. This kind of reasoning will tell England to produce not only the first bolt of cloth but also every succeeding bolt of cloth, as long as possible. Portugal will keep producing only wine, at its maximum level of 200 bottles.

The possibility of exploiting England's relatively low-cost cloth production runs out when these two countries reach point A. At point A, England produces the maximum amount of cloth it can—400 bolts—and Portugal still produces only wine (200 bottles). This was the point used as an example in the text, for simplicity. Now if they want to continue to have even more cloth (and less wine), Portugal will have to produce it. Each extra bolt of cloth will now cost 2 bottles of wine, up to the point (500, 0), where they both produce only cloth.

Figure 6.3   **Joint Production Possibilities Frontier for England and Portugal**

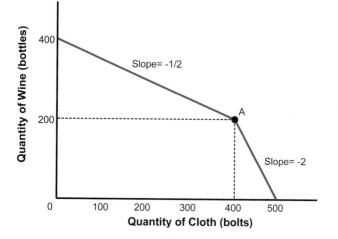

By specializing efficiently, England and Portugal together can produce these combinations of wine and cloth.

What if, instead, the countries were to follow their comparative *dis*advantages, having Portugal change to cloth production first, and England only after Portugal was producing at capacity? Figure 6.4 contrasts the efficient PPF with this case. With inefficient full specialization represented by the point where Portugal produces 100 bolts of cloth and England produces 200 bottles of wine, the PPF bends *inward*. The bold line is the efficient production possibilities frontier, and the lighter line reflects the most inefficient production choices. As you can see, following the rule of comparative *advantage* leads to a much larger PPF than doing the reverse! A similarly inefficient result would follow if you were better at cleaning, and your housemate at shopping, but you tended to shop and your housemate tended to clean.

Figure 6.4   **Efficient and Inefficient Joint Production Possibilities Frontier**

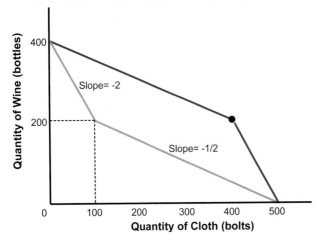

If England and Portugal specialized in an inefficient way, the joint production possibilities frontier would bow in rather than out.

Along with the concept of comparative advantage, economists also discuss the concept of absolute advantage. A producer has an absolute advantage when, using the same amount of some resource as another producer, it can produce more. Usually, labor hours are the resource considered. For example, suppose that in a one-hour period you can buy enough groceries for six days *or* clean three rooms. Your housemate, by contrast, moves more slowly and can buy enough groceries for only three days, or clean only one room, in an hour. You clearly have an absolute advantage in production of both these services. Does this mean you should do all the work?* (See whether you can figure out the answer before looking at the footnote.)

NOTES

1. Adam Smith, *An Inquiry into the Nature and Causes of the Wealth of Nations* (London: Methuen, 1930), pp. 6, 7.

2. Jacques Savary, *Le parfait négociant* (Paris, 1675), quoted in Albert O. Hirschman, *The Passions and the Interests* (Princeton: Princeton University Press, 1997), pp. 59–60.

---

*No. Comparative, not absolute, advantage should guide the assignment of tasks. Although you have an *absolute* advantage over your housemate in both activities, your housemate has a *comparative* advantage in shopping. That is, to get enough groceries for six days would "cost" only two rooms' worth of cleaning if your housemate does it (taking two hours). But if you shop for six days' worth of food, the opportunity cost is more—the three rooms you could have cleaned. Therefore, on efficiency grounds at least, your housemate should shop and you should clean. (You can also come to the same result by examining your own comparative advantage—in cleaning.)

PART

III

Economics and Society

7 Economic Behavior and Rationality

In Chapter 1, we defined economic actors, or economic agents, as people or organizations engaged in any of the four essential economic activities: production, distribution, consumption, and resource maintenance. Economic actors can be individuals, small groups (such as a family or a group of roommates), or large organizations such as a government agency or a multinational corporation. Economics is about how these actors behave and interact as they engage in economic activities. In this chapter we explore the behavior of individual economic actors—people. We look at contemporary research on this topic, and, where it seems relevant, compare this with older approaches.

1. Economic Understandings of Human Motivations

Economics is a *social* science—it is about people and about how we organize ourselves to meet our needs and enhance our well-being. Ultimately, all economic behavior is human behavior. Sometimes institutional forces appear to take over (witness the tendency of some bureaucracies to expand over time), but if you look closely at all economic outcomes, you will find that they are ultimately determined by human decisions or behavior. Thus economists have traditionally used, as a starting point, some kind of statement about the motivations behind economic actions.

1.1 Classical Economic Views of Human Nature

In Chapter 5, we mentioned Adam Smith's concept of the invisible hand, according to which people acting in their own self-interest would, through markets, promote the general welfare of society. The concept of the invisible hand has become very famous, but it is often taken out of context to mean that if people *only* behave with self-interest, they will do what is best for the entire society.

This interpretation would have astonished Smith, who, before writing *An Inquiry into the Nature and Causes of the Wealth of Nations,* had written another long book, *The Theory of Moral Sentiments,* in which he examined with care how people are motivated. His emphasis there is on the desire of people to have self-respect and the respect of others. He assumes that such respect depends on people acting honorably, justly, and with concern and empathy for others in their community. Smith recognizes that selfish desires play a large role but believes that they will be held in check both by the "moral sentiments" (the universal desire for self-respect and the respect of others) and also by the fortunate accident by which "in many cases" (not all!) selfish acts can "promote the public interest."[1]

Thus Smith's vision of human nature and human motivation was one in which individual self-interest was mixed with more social motives. Rather than starting with Robinson Crusoe, who lived alone on an island, he perceived that the behavior of any one person always had to be understood within that person's social context.

Smith was followed by other economists, such as the trade theorist David Ricardo and the philosopher/economist John Stuart Mill. They held similarly complex views of human nature and motivations. In 1890 Alfred Marshall tried to codify these ideas in a very influential text called *Principles of Economics,* which was published in eight editions, the last published in 1920. Marshall viewed the motives of human actors in an optimistic light—including those of economists, whom he assumed were motivated by a desire to improve the human condition. He specifically focused on the reduction of poverty so as to allow people to develop their higher moral and intellectual faculties, rather than being condemned to lives of desperate effort for simple survival.

1.2 THE NEOCLASSICAL MODEL

neoclassical model: a model that portrays the economy as a collection of profit-maximizing firms and utility-maximizing households interacting through perfectly competitive markets

In the twentieth century, the approach that came to dominate economics was known as the **neoclassical model**. This approach took a narrower view of human motivations. The basic neoclassical or traditional model builds a simplified story about economic life by assuming that there are only two main types of economic actors and by making simplifying assumptions about how these two types of actors behave and interact. The two basic sets of actors in this model are firms, which are assumed to maximize their profits from producing and selling goods and services, and households, which are assumed to maximize their utility (or satisfaction) from consuming goods and services. The two kinds of agents are assumed to interact in perfectly competitive markets (the subject of Chapter 16). Given some additional assumptions, explored later in this book, the model can be elegantly expressed in figures, equations, and graphs.

Some benefits can be gained from looking at economic behavior in this way. The assumptions reduce the actual (very complicated) economy to something that is much more limited but also easier to analyze. The traditional model is particularly well suited for analyzing the determination of prices, the volume of trade, and efficiency issues in certain cases.

The neoclassical model was introduced to generations of students in 1948 with the publication of Paul Samuelson's textbook *Economics: An Introductory Analysis*, which went on to become the best-selling economics text ever. Samuelson's text promoted the idea that economics should be "value free" (i.e., it should be developed without reference to any human goals or values) and that it should be largely or purely deductive, meaning that it should derive conclusions from the simple assumptions stated above, about the motivations of market actors.

rationality axiom: the statement that "rational economic man maximizes his utility (or self-interest)"

In addition to the claim of being value free, through the second half of the twentieth century, many economists used another belief to assert that their discipline was more scientific than other social sciences. They claimed that the entire system of economic theory is so purely deductive that everything in it can be deduced from one essential axiom.* This, the **rationality axiom**, states that "rational economic man maximizes his utility." (Some economists substitute for "utility" another term such as "self-interest," or "well-being.") This statement has often been interpreted to mean that pursuit of self-interest is the *only* thing that is done by rational economic actors—and that anything else is *irrational.*

The statement that the subject of economics is "completely axiomatized" (i.e., everything in it can be deduced from this single basic axiom) has come under considerable criticism. To discuss that in depth, however, would be to get into issues of methodology that are beyond the scope of an introductory textbook. Instead of addressing these arcane matters, we describe some real-world tests that have been applied in recent years to a model of human behavior that states that all that economics needs to know about human behavior is that people are rational and self-interested. We return to the issue of selfishness in Section 3 of this chapter. Section 2 first focuses on the assumption that people are rational in those portions of human

---

*An axiom is a statement that is considered to be self-evident, without need of proof.

behavior that are related to the economic activities of production, distribution, consumption, and resource maintenance.

Discussion Questions

1. Do you agree with the assumption of the neoclassical model that human behavior is rational and self-interested? Can you think of some examples of economic behavior that might contradict these assumptions?
2. Do you believe economics should strive, as much as possible, to be value free? What do you think are the advantages and disadvantages of this approach?

2. ECONOMIC BEHAVIOR

Recent economic theory has explored views of human nature and decision-making that go beyond the simple axioms of the basic neoclassical model. In this chapter, we examine other models of economic behavior that consider people's (1) choice of goals, (2) the actions they take to achieve these goals, and (3) the limitations and influences that affect their choices and actions.

As we learned in Chapter 2, any model highlights some aspects of reality while ignoring others. In this case, we employ the term "model" to mean a description of human behavior that emphasizes what is most important to understand about how people act most of the time when engaging in economic activities. Such a model obviously cannot explain all human actions, but it should be sufficient to provide a general outline of what to expect. We work our way gradually toward such a descriptive model.

2.1 BEHAVIORAL ECONOMICS

behavioral economics: a subfield of microeconomics that studies how individuals and organizations make economic decisions

In the past few decades, the neoclassical view of human behavior has been challenged by a strong alternative called **behavioral economics,** which studies how individuals and organizations make economic decisions. Studies in this area suggest that a more sophisticated model of human motivations is required to explain behaviors such as those that lead to stock market swings, the ways that people react to good and bad fortune, and why people often seem to act against their own self-interest.[2]

Rather than making assumptions about human behavior, behavioral economics relies heavily on scientific experiments to determine how people behave in different situations. Consider the insights from one such experiment, which concerns a three-hour seminar class that has a short break in the middle, when the professor offers the students a snack. Every week, the professor provides the students with a list of possible snacks, and the students vote on which snack they want. Only the snack with the most votes is then provided. The results of this experiment show that every week students tend to pick the same snack—the one that is their favorite.

With a different group of students, who are also taking a three-hour seminar class with a break, the students are instead asked in advance which snacks they will prefer for the next three weeks. In this case, students tend to vote for variety, thinking that they will not want the same snack every week. But this is precisely what students actually do want when they get to vote every week! When planning ahead, students think they will want variety, but when the time comes to consume a snack students tend to stick with their favorite each time. Similar experiments have shown that people who go grocery shopping infrequently also tend to think that they will want variety, but in reality they tend to want their favorite foods more often.

Another illustration of behavior that does not fit older, rigid definitions of rationality concerns the way that we process information. Perhaps the most famous contemporary behavioral economist is not an economist by training. Despite being educated as a psychologist, Daniel Kahneman won the 2002 Nobel Memorial Prize in economic science. Kahneman's

availability heuristic: placing undue importance on particular information because it is readily available or vivid

research has found that people tend to give undue weight to information that is easily available or vivid, something he called the **availability heuristic**. ("Heuristic" means a method for solving problems.) For example, suppose that college students are deciding which courses to take next semester, and they see a summary of evaluations from hundreds of other students indicating that a certain course is very good. Then suppose that they watch a video interview of just one student, who gives a negative review of the course. Even when students were told in advance that such a negative review was atypical, they tended to be more influenced by the vivid negative review than the summary of hundreds of evaluations, even though such behavior seems irrational.

framing: changing the way a particular decision is presented to people in order to influence their behavior

Kahneman has also shown that the way a decision is presented to people can significantly influence their choices, an effect he referred to as **framing**. For example, consider a gas station that advertises a special 5-cent-per-gallon discount for paying cash. Meanwhile, another station with the same prices indicates that they charge a 5-cent-per-gallon surcharge to customers who pay by credit card. Although the prices end up exactly the same, experiments suggest that consumers respond more favorably to the station that advertises the apparent discount. For one of Kahneman's famous experiments on the importance of framing, see Box 7.1.

A common area of seemingly irrational economic behavior is personal finance. Some companies offer their employees the option of matching contributions to their retirement plans; for each $1 the employee voluntarily contributes to his or her retirement plan, the employer matches it with an additional contribution. For example, with a 50 percent matching program, for each $1 an employee contributes, the employer contributes 50 cents. This amounts to an instant 50 percent rate of return on the employee's investment.

Although most financial advisers suggest taking advantage of matching contributions, many employees do not enroll in such programs, voluntarily forgoing the opportunity to garner thousands of additional dollars for retirement. This is not necessarily irrational, as some employees may have pressing current economic needs. However, one research study

---

Box 7.1   The Effect of Framing on Decisions

Suppose that you are presented with the following question:

> Imagine you are a physician working in an Asian village, and 600 people have come down with a life-threatening disease. Two possible treatments exist. If you choose treatment A, you will save exactly 200 people. If you choose treatment B, there is a one-third chance that you will save all 600 people, and a two-thirds chance you will save no one. Which treatment do you choose, A or B?

Kahneman and Tversky found that the majority of respondents (72 percent) chose treatment A, which saves exactly 200 people. Now consider the following scenario:

> You are a physician working in an Asian village, and 600 people have come down with a life-threatening disease. Two possible treatments exist. If you choose treatment C, exactly 400 people will die. If you choose treatment D, there is a one-third chance that no one will die, and a two-thirds

chance that everyone will die. Which treatment do you choose, C or D?

In this case, they found that the majority of respondents (78 percent) chose treatment D, which offers a one-third chance that no one will die. But if you compare the two questions carefully, you will notice that they are exactly the same! Treatments A and C are identical, and so are treatments B and D. The only thing that changes are the way the options are presented, or framed, to respondents.

According to Tversky and Kahneman people evaluate gains and losses differently. Thus while treatments A and C are quantitatively identical, treatment A is framed as a gain (i.e., you save 200 people) while treatment C is framed as a loss (i.e., 400 people die). It seems people are more likely to take risks when it comes to losses than gains. In other words, people prefer a "sure thing" when it comes to a potential gain but are willing to take a chance if it involves avoiding a loss.

Source: Amos Tversky and Daniel Kahneman, "The Framing of Decisions and the Psychology of Choice," *Science* 211(4481) (1981): 453–458.

looked at what happened when a large company changed its policy from a matching program that required employees to sign up for it (an "opt in" program) to a similar program in which employees were automatically enrolled but could opt out if they wanted to.[3] Under the new (opt-out) program, 86 percent of employees stayed in the program. For comparable employees prior to the change, the participation rate was only 37 percent. The economic advantages were the same in either case, and the huge difference in participation rates is difficult to justify on the basis of the paperwork needed to sign up for the program. Again, the results demonstrate that framing can have a significant influence on people's choices.

anchoring effect: overreliance on a piece of information that may or may not be relevant as a reference point when making a decision

An effect similar to framing is known as **anchoring**, in which people rely on a piece of information that is not necessarily relevant as a reference point in making a decision. In one powerful example, graduate students at the MIT Sloan School of Management were first asked to write down the last two digits of their Social Security numbers.[4] They were then asked whether they would pay this amount, in dollars, for various products, including a fancy bottle of wine and a cordless keyboard. Assuming rational behavior, the last digits of one's Social Security number should have no relation to one's willingness to pay for a product. However, the subjects with the highest Social Security numbers indicated a willingness to pay about 300 percent more than those with the lowest numbers; apparently they used their Social Security numbers as an "anchor" in evaluating the worth of the products.

In a real-world example of anchoring, a high-end kitchen equipment catalog featured a particular bread maker for $279. Sometime later, the company began offering a "deluxe" model for $429. Although they did not sell too many of the deluxe model, sales of the $279 model almost doubled because now it seemed like a relative bargain.

2.2 THE ROLE OF TIME IN ECONOMIC DECISIONS

The retirement program example cited above suggests that in making their decisions people might not appropriately weigh the future. In other words, people seem to place undue emphasis on gains or benefits received today without considering the implications of their decisions for the future. Further evidence of this is the large number of people who have acquired significant high-interest credit card debt; indeed, about 6 percent of Americans are considered "compulsive shoppers," who seek instant gratification with little concern for often very troublesome consequences of running up a great deal of debt.[5] But you do not need to be a compulsive shopper to fall short of the ideal "rational consumer" who knows and weighs all the relevant costs and benefits.

time discount rate: an economic concept describing the relative weighting of present benefits or costs compared to future benefits or costs

You may know someone who does not pay much attention to the future consequences of his or her actions. Economists would say that this person has a very high **time discount rate**, meaning that in his or her mind, future events are very much discounted or diminished when weighed against the pleasures of today. (The technical meaning of "discount rate" is discussed in Chapter 12.)

On the other hand you might also know people who seem to have the attitude "I've got to work hard and prepare now; enjoying myself will have to wait for later." Economists would say that people like this have low time discount rates if by their current work they are gaining benefits for tomorrow. The later benefits loom large (i.e., are *not* "discounted") in their decisions.

Time discount rates are important in all sorts of situations. Economists usually assume that people who invest in a college education have a relatively low time discount rate, because they are willing to forgo current income or relaxation to study for some expected future gain. (Of course, this is not true for individuals who enjoy college or regard it as more appealing than the prospects for postcollege experience.)

Company leaders with high time discount rates may concentrate on making this quarter's financial statement look good, whereas those with more concern about the future will look toward longer-term goals. In deciding on environmental regulations, people who work at government agencies are forced to make decisions about how much weight to give the well-being of future generations. The lower their discount rate, the more important safeguarding the well-being of future generations appears.

2.3 THE ROLE OF EMOTIONS IN ECONOMIC DECISIONS

The potential conflict between our reasoning and our emotions has long been studied by philosophers and writers. The conventional view is that emotions get in the way of good decision making, as they tend to interfere with logical reasoning. The American author Marya Mannes once wrote: "The sign of an intelligent people is their ability to control their emotions by the application of reason." This implies that excessive reliance on emotions to make economic decisions could result in irrational behavior.

But again, research from behavioral economics suggests a more nuanced reality. It does not seem to be true that decisions based on logical reasoning are always "better" than those based on emotion or intuition. Instead, studies suggest that reasoning is most effective when used for making relatively simple economic decisions, but for more complex decisions we can become overwhelmed by too much information.

The 2010 book *Predictably Irrational*, by the psychologist Dan Ariely, describes how people consistently tend to procrastinate, overpay in certain situations, and fail to understand the role of emotions in our decision making. The book also reveals that we often place an above-market value on what we possess because we are "irrationally" attached to our possessions and that we use price as a "signal" in selecting among medicines, to the point that the placebo effect is stronger for more expensive drugs.

Research by Ap Dijksterhuis, a psychologist in the Netherlands, has shed some valuable insight on the limits of reasoned decision making. In one experiment, he and his colleagues surveyed shoppers about their purchases as they were leaving stores, asking them how much they had thought about items before buying them. A few weeks later, they asked these same consumers how satisfied they were with their purchases. For relatively simple products, like small kitchen tools or clothing accessories, those who thought more about their purchases tended to be more satisfied, as we might suspect. But for complex products, such as furniture, those people who deliberated the most tended to be *less* satisfied with their purchases. Dijksterhuis and his colleagues conclude:

> Contrary to conventional wisdom, it is not always advantageous to engage in thorough conscious deliberation before choosing. On the basis of recent insights into the characteristics of conscious and unconscious thought, we [find] that purchases of complex products were viewed more favorably when decisions had been made in the absence of attentive deliberation.[6]

Even for relatively simple decisions, there is such a thing as "thinking too much." Another experiment with college students involved their tasting five brands of strawberry jam.[7] In one case, students simply ranked the jams from best to worst. The student rankings were highly correlated with the results of independent testing by *Consumer Reports,* suggesting that the students' rankings were reasonable. But in another case students were asked to fill out a written questionnaire explaining their preferences. As a result of the additional deliberation, students' rankings were no longer significantly correlated with the *Consumer Report* rankings. The researcher concluded:

> This experiment illuminates the danger of always relying on the rational brain. There is such a thing as too much analysis. When you overthink at the wrong moment, you cut yourself off from the wisdom of your emotions, which are much better at assessing actual preferences. You lose the ability to know what you really want.[8]

Discussion Questions

1. Why do you think economists are so interested in questions of how decisions are made?
2. Discuss how one or more conclusions reached by behavioral economists helps you to understand an experience that you have had.

3. ECONOMIC RATIONALITY

"Rationality" has become a loaded word in economics, bringing with it the baggage of earlier models that did not anticipate the findings of behavioral economics or take into account other everyday observations. In this section we formulate an alternative view of human behavior that is more realistic.

3.1 CHOOSING GOALS AND TRYING TO ACHIEVE THEM

Economists generally proceed from a belief that people should be free to choose their own goals, even if their chosen goals differ from those of most others. However, what can be considered a rational goal has limits, especially considering that people usually have more than one final goal. Some goals that people pursue may be unachievable. People may also choose reasonable goals, but engage in irrational behavior that leads them *away from* their achievement rather than toward it. A reasonable definition of rational behavior includes (1) selecting goals that are consistent with present and future well-being, and (2) pursuing the goals in a manner that can reasonably be assumed to lead to their achievement.

3.2 THE ROLE OF CONSTRAINTS AND INFORMATION

It is important to note that economic decisions are always made subject to constraints, including limits on income and other resources and on physical or intellectual capacities. A universal constraint is time. Every day you face the choice of how to allocate 24 hours among competing activities such as sleeping, studying, going to class, eating, and entertainment. You cannot decide to allocate 10 hours each day to sleeping, 5 hours to studying, and 10 hours to hanging out with friends because you do not have 25 hours available. To put this in terms that we introduced in Chapter 1, your "production possibilities frontier" has only 24 hours per day.

Another important factor in an economic model of rationality is *information*. In assessing their options, economic actors make use of their existing knowledge but often need to collect additional information. Consider the decision to purchase a new automobile. Numerous factors go into such a decision. Should you buy a new car or a used one? What is the relative importance of fuel economy, safety, and luxury features? What about resale value and maintenance costs? Making a rational decision requires that you obtain information on these various factors.

optimizing behavior: behavior that achieves an optimal (best possible) outcome

The neoclassical approach tends to assume that rational behavior is **optimizing behavior**, based on the further assumption that rational economic actors have "perfect information." A slightly more modest version says that people will collect information until the perceived costs of acquiring additional information exceed the perceived benefits. However, there is no way of guaranteeing either that people can know enough to make that "cost/benefit" calculation (i.e., to make an informed decision about when to stop gathering information) or that, when they do stop gathering information, they will know enough to make an optimal or even a good choice.*

One challenge to the traditional assumption of rationality comes from Herbert Simon, another psychologist who received a Nobel Memorial Prize in economic science (in 1978). Considering the matter of whether it is indeed possible for people to identify the optimal

---

*The uses of cost-benefit analysis, and some issues with this approach, are examined in Chapter 12.

satisfice: to choose an outcome that would be satisfactory and then seek an option that at least reaches that standard

point at which one should cease gathering additional information, Simon logically showed that, in fact, one first needs to have complete knowledge of all choices in order to identify that optimal point! Moreover, determining what additional information might be out there and then gathering it can be very costly in time, effort, and money. Accordingly, Simon maintained, people rarely optimize. Instead they do what he called **satisficing**; they choose an outcome that would be satisfactory and then seek an option that at least reaches that standard.

Given constraints of time and so forth, satisficing seems to be a reasonable behavior. If an individual finds that the "satisfactory" level was set too low, a search for options that meet that level will result in a solution more quickly than expected or perhaps even multiple solutions. In this case, the level may then be adjusted to a higher standard. Conversely, if the level is set too high, a long search will yield nothing, and the "satisficer" may lower his or her expectations for the outcome.

meliorating: starting from the present level of well-being and continuously attempting to do better

path dependence: situations in which what is possible, or what is chosen, in the present depends on what has happened in the past

bounded rationality: the hypothesis that people make choices among a somewhat arbitrary subset of all possible options due to limits on information, time, or cognitive abilities

Another deviation from rational behavior as traditionally defined has been called **meliorating**—defined as starting from the present level of well-being and then taking any opportunity to do better. A simple example is a line fisherman who has found a whole school of haddock but wants to keep only one for his supper. When he catches the second fish, he compares it to the first one, keeps the larger, and releases the other. Each subsequent catch is compared to the one held in the bottom of the boat. At the end of the day, the fish that he takes home will be the largest of all those caught.

One result of using melioration as the real-world substitute for theoretical optimization is its implication that *history matters:* People view each successive choice in relation to their previous experience. It is commonly observed, for example, that people are reluctant to accept a situation that they perceive as inferior to previous situations. This psychological **path dependence**—the idea that where you are going depends on where you have been—is relevant to feelings about rising prices and even more so to attitudes about declining wages.

Satisficing and meliorating may both be included under the term **bounded rationality**. The general idea is that, instead of considering all possible options, people limit their attention to some more-or-less arbitrarily defined subset of the universe of possibilities. With satisficing or meliorating behavior, people may not choose the "best" choices available to them, but they at least make decisions that move them toward their goals.

3.3 THE ROLE OF INFLUENCE

The discussion above cautions that in modeling human behavior, it is necessary to recognize that there is no known decision rule within human capabilities that guarantees an entirely satisfactory conclusion, let alone the "best of all possible" conclusions.

A very important aspect of decision making relates to the outside influences on us. In the discussion of behavioral economics, we saw examples of ways that others can affect our decisions by setting a "frame" or providing extra emphasis on one conclusion at the expense of others. Available information is, of course, a critical feature, and actors other than the decision maker may have a strong influence on which information is available. The literature in behavioral economics provides a wide array of other ways that decision making can be distorted by influences not related to the goals of the particular actor.

These realities have long been well known to politicians and advertisers, who, since the early part of the twentieth century, have often based their successes on assuming *irrational* consumers and voters. For example, food companies are well known to cater to the innate physical preference for sugar, fat, and salt. These three elements are crucial for health when eaten in appropriate amounts, but they were rarely available in sufficient quantity during most of human evolution. We are all therefore born with some degree of craving for these substances; learning is required to recognize when we have had "enough." Makers of potato chips and other sweet, salty, fatty, prepared foods would prefer that this learning *not* take place. And just as corporations gravitate toward behavior that fattens profits, even if their products do more harm than good, politicians also often find it hard to resist the easy appeal to emotions of greed, even fear, rather than offering sound information on which voters can make good decisions.

As we go through this book, applying microeconomic principles to different issues, we continue to explore whether economic actors are making rational decisions and whether there are policies that could encourage decisions that enhance both individual well-being and the well-being of society.

3.4 SELF-INTEREST, ALTRUISM, AND THE COMMON GOOD

We have referred to the neoclassical model of economic behavior that is deduced from the axiom: "Rational economic man acts so as to maximize his utility." This could be—and often has been—interpreted by teachers, students, and practitioners of economics to mean: "Rational people try to get what they want." That in turn was often understood as saying, "Rational people are only self-interested—*any non-self-interested acts are irrational.*"

Many students found this approach so unappealing that they dropped economics as their major, while others who stayed with these courses more or less bought in to the lesson that "Only self-interested behavior is rational." This probably explains a good deal of why economics students (and economics faculty) have frequently been shown, in tests, to be less altruistic than others (see Box 7.2).

altruistic behavior: actions focused on the well-being of others, with no thought about oneself

The opposite of pure self-interest is **altruism**, which means a concern for the well-being of others, with no thought about oneself. Although it would be excessively idealistic to assume that altruism is the prime mover in human behavior, it is reasonable to assert that some elements of altruism enter into most people's decision making—contrary to the simple neoclassical model of "rational" selfishness.

BOX 7.2   ECONOMICS AND SELFISHNESS

Are people who have studied economics more likely than other individuals to behave selfishly? For more than 30 years, various research studies have explored this question. In one example, economics students expressed a lower willingness than other students to contribute money to pay for public goods. The same was found of economics faculty, though their average pay was higher than that of the faculty in the other disciplines to which they were compared.

Another study found that economics students offered less to others in the Ultimatum Game (see Box 7.3 for a description of the Ultimatum Game). Although most studies have found that economics students tend to be relatively more selfish, one study found that students in upper-level economics classes were more likely than students in other upper-level classes to return a lost envelope containing cash. According to the authors of one research study, "We . . . found evidence that the giving behavior of students who became economics majors was driven by nature, not nurture: Taking economics classes did not have a significant negative effect on later giving by economics majors."

The same study did find, however, that taking economics classes did reduce the generosity of students who did not go on to become economics majors. These non-majors may have experienced a "loss of innocence" as a result of being exposed to economic theories such as efficiency and profit maximization. The authors conclude:

> Our research suggests that economics education could do a better job of providing balance. Learning about the shortcomings as well as the successes of free markets is at the heart of any good economics education, and students—especially those who are not destined to major in the field—deserve to hear both sides of the story.

Source: Yoram Bauman and Elaina Rose, "Selection or Indoctrination: Why Do Economics Students Donate Less Than the Rest?" *Journal of Economic Behavior and Organization* 79(3) (August 2011): 318–327; Yoram Bauman, "The Dismal Education," *New York Times*, December 16, 2011.

the common good:
the general well-being
of society, including
one's own well-being

Especially relevant to economics is the fact that much economic behavior may be motivated by a desire to advance **the common good**—the general good of society, of which one's own interests are only a part. Striving to advance the common good means seeing your own well-being as connected to the larger well-being of society. That is, people are often willing to participate in the creation of social benefits as long as they feel that others are also contributing.

Economists are increasingly realizing that a well-functioning economy cannot rely only on self-interest. Without such values as honesty, for example, even the simplest transaction would require elaborate safeguards or policing. Imagine if you were afraid to put down your money before having in your hands the merchandise that you wished to purchase—and the merchant was afraid that as soon as you had what you wanted, you would run out of the store without paying. Such a situation would require police in every store—but what if the police themselves operated with no ethic of honesty? Without ethical values that promote trust, inefficiencies would overwhelm any economic system.

If all those in business cheated whenever they thought they could get away with it, business would grind to a halt. If everyone in the government worked only for bribes, meaningful governance would disappear. In addition, people have to work together to overcome problems from externalities. And it is hard to imagine how the human race could survive if altruism was not common enough that people would be willing to make sacrifices of time, convenience, and resources to meet the needs of those who cannot take care of themselves, such as children or sick people.

Fortunately, recent experiments on human behavior demonstrate that people really *do* pay attention to social norms, and they are willing to reward those who follow these norms and to punish people who violate them, even when this has a cost in terms of their narrow self-interest. (See Box 7.3.)

3.5 THE MODEL OF ECONOMIC BEHAVIOR IN CONTEXTUAL ECONOMICS

Many real-world problems would be difficult, if not impossible, to solve in the absence of a reasonable number of people willing to work for the common good. These people are often especially concentrated in the public purpose sphere, while individual altruism is most often evident in the core sphere of the economy. Does that mean that business is the sphere that operates only on self-interest? From about 1970 to the end of the twentieth century, economists, especially from

---

BOX 7.3   THE ULTIMATUM GAME

A famous behavioral economics experiment is known as the "Ultimatum Game." In this game, two people (who are in situations in which they cannot communicate with each other) are told that they will be given a sum of money, say $20, to share. The first person gets to propose a way of splitting the sum. This person may offer to give $10 to the second person or only $8 or $1 and plan to keep the rest. The second person cannot offer any input to this decision but can only decide whether to accept the offer or reject it. If the second person rejects the offer, both people will walk away empty-handed. If the offer is accepted, they get the money and split it as the first person indicated.

If the two individuals act only from narrow financial self-interest, then the first person should offer the second person the smallest possible amount—say $1—in order to keep the most for himself or herself. The second person should accept this offer because, from the point of view of pure financial self-interest, $1 is better than nothing.

In fact, researchers find that deals that vary too far from a 50–50 split tend to be rejected. People would rather walk away with nothing than be treated in a way that they perceive as unfair. Also, whether out of a sense of fairness or a fear of rejection, individuals who propose a split often offer something close to 50–50. In the context of social relations, even the most selfish person will gain by serving the common good and thus walking away with somewhere around $10, rather than just looking at his or her own potential personal gain and quite possibly ending up with nothing.

what was known as the "Chicago School," pressed this case. Even early in this period concern arose that individuals who acted solely to achieve their *personal* goals could not be counted on to operate a business in ways that would be good for the business itself. This concern resulted in various efforts to reward business leaders for the success of their business.

These efforts had the unintended consequences of escalating compensation of top management in the United States to levels that were many times greater than anything that had previously been considered normal (or were normal in other countries). They also resulted in an increasingly short-term vision on the part of business leaders, whose compensation was set up to provide large rewards for quick profits. Large-scale frauds, Ponzi schemes, tax evasion, and environmental and human costs that businesses externalized during this period have made it increasingly evident that society cannot afford to encourage a definition of economic activity in which normal human motivations are stripped down to selfish pursuit of personal gain.

Modern research in behavioral economics suggests that the neoclassical rationality axiom does not stand up to tests of logic, experience, or the needs of society. (And some feminist economists have pointed out that the reference to "rational economic *man*" may be related to this one-dimensional view of human nature.)[9] With that said, the following statements concerning motivations and behavior may provide a better grounding for economic theory.

- We start with a definition of rationality that includes
  1. *choosing goals* such that (a) when the actor achieves the goals, she or he will be glad to have done so; or (b) the pursuit of the goal itself contributes to well-being; and
  2. *pursuing those goals* in a manner that the actor expects will lead toward their achievement.
- This definition does not insist that the goals be either entirely *self-interested* or entirely *altruistic*. Rather, based on common experience and observation, it appears that most people operate with some mixture of these kinds of goals.
- Our model then posits that *most adults attempt to act rationally*. However, sometimes lack of information, the influence of conflicting emotions, or influence from others who are pursuing different goals may cause rational actors to choose goals that are not consistent with well-being or to do things that lead away from their goals.

Although, compared to the rationality axiom, these statements are obviously much more inclusive, and closer to reality, they are also much looser and cannot be used in the same, deterministic manner. For example, because they do not claim that people optimize or maximize, they provide less opportunity for developing mathematical models based on simple axioms about behavior. Nor is there any claim that these statements are all that the economist needs to know about human behavior. Explanations or predictions of economic phenomena sometimes require individual judgment, experience, or inputs from other social sciences. Thus they do not conform to the ideal of "scientific" social science pursued by neoclassical economists.

However, many people have come to believe that neoclassical economics, which achieved many fruitful insights in its early decades, has explored all the territory that it initially opened up and has contributed less and less value as time has gone on. Moreover, its narrow view of human nature and lack of contextual awareness are criticized for leading to some of today's problems. Neoclassical economists almost uniformly failed to see the growth of the financial and real estate bubbles that led to the Great Recession, beginning in 2007. More broadly, some people believe the emphasis on selfishness has been used to justify a "culture of greed" (see Chapter 8), the dramatic increase in income and wealth inequality in recent decades (see Chapter 10), and ever greater concentration of economic and political power in ever larger corporations (see Chapter 17).

Once again, we face tradeoffs. If we are to develop economic theories equipped to deal with the critical issues of the twenty-first century, we probably need to give up a degree of tidiness, amenability to mathematical modeling techniques, and the appearance of completely value-free objectivity. As you proceed through this book, you will be the judge of how well the view of human nature developed in this chapter supports a useful approach to understanding the economy.

Discussion Questions

1. Under what circumstances can you imagine making poor decisions because of lack of information? Which economic actors might affect your decision making, and how?

2. Is "satisficing" always a rational way of behaving? What about "meliorating"? For example, recall the example of the fisherman who compares each fish that he catches to the one in the boat, keeping the larger one and throwing the others back into the water. What might be wrong with an attempt to perform the same exercise with choosing friends, instead of fish? Have you ever heard of anyone who selected a spouse in this manner?

REVIEW QUESTIONS

1. What is the invisible hand?
2. What is the neoclassical model?
3. What is the rationality axiom?
4. How does "framing" affect decision making?
5. What is the anchoring effect?
6. What is the effect of time discounting?
7. Do people typically engage in optimizing behavior?

8. Explain the concept of bounded rationality.
9. Why is self-interest not sufficient as a social organizing principle?
10. Discuss various ways of defining rationality. Which do you think is best as a basis for economic theory?

EXERCISES

1. Which of the following is consistent with the view of human behavior as purely self-interested? Which may indicate broader motivations?
   a. Michael sells his car on eBay.
   b. Jane joins a community clean-up group.
   c. Ramon studies to become a doctor.
   d. Joe buys a birthday present for his daughter.
   e. Susan buys a new pair of shoes for herself.

2. Consider the process of applying to college and choosing a college to attend if admitted. Would you say that this process involves:
   a. Optimizing behavior
   b. Satisficing behavior
   c. Meliorating behavior
   d. Path dependence
   e. Bounded rationality
   Could it involve a combination of them? Could this differ from person to person?

3. How does time discounting affect your own decision making? Do you do things today with a view toward future benefits, or do you look mainly for short-term satisfaction? Does your time discount rate differ in different areas of your life?

4. Consider a rational, profit-maximizing business firm. What motivations might the firm have that are not directly related to making a profit? For example, what if the firm made a donation to a community organization or voluntarily cleaned up

pollution resulting from its production process? Why might it do this? How about if it offered employees a good health-care plan or subsidized day care? Are these actions all ultimately directed at making more profit, or could there be something else involved?

5. Match each concept in Column A with an example in Column B.

Column A	Column B
a. Self-interest	1. Finding a restaurant that is close by and has food that is "good enough"
b. Altruism	2. The study of how economic actors make decisions
c. Satisficing	3. You buy a $500 watch because it seems inexpensive compared to a $1,000 watch
d. Path dependence	4. Looking for a job that's better than your current job
e. Meliorating	5. Volunteering at a homeless shelter
f. Anchoring	6. Choosing a college because your older brother or sister went there
g. Behavioral economics	7. How households act in the neoclassical model

NOTES

1. A. Smith, *Correspondence of Adam Smith (Glasgow Edition of the Works and Correspondence of Adam Smith)* (Oxford: Oxford University Press, 1982), vol. 2a, p. 456.

2. Material from this section is drawn from Barry Schwartz, *The Paradox of Choice* (New York: HarperCollins, 2005).

3. Brigitte C. Madrian and Dennis F. Shea, "The Power of Suggestion: Inertia in 401(k) Participation and Savings Behavior," *Quarterly Journal of Economics* 16(4) (November 2001): 1149–1187.

4. Example from Dan Ariely, *Predictably Irrational: The Hidden Forces That Shape Our Decisions* (New York: Harper Perennial, 2010).

5. Lorrin M. Korna et al., "Estimated Prevalence of Compulsive Buying Behavior in the United States," *American Journal of Psychiatry* 163 (2006): 1806–1812.

6. Ap Dijksterhuis, Maarten W. Bos, Loran F. Nordgren, and Rick B. van Baaren, "On Making the Right Choice: The Deliberation-Without-Attention Effect," *Science* 311(5763) (February 17, 2006): 1005.

7. Example from Jonah Lehrer, *How We Decide* (Boston: Mariner/Houghton-Mifflin, 2009).

8. Ibid., pp. 142–143.

9. See Marianne A. Ferber and Julie A. Nelson, ed., *Beyond Economic Man: Feminist Theory and Economics* (Chicago: University of Chicago Press, 1993).

8 Consumption and the Consumer Society

We have defined the economic activity of consumption as the process by which goods and services are put to final use by people. But this rather dry, academic definition fails to capture the multifaceted role of consumerism in our lives. As one researcher put it:

> For a start, it is immediately clear that consumption goes way beyond just satisfying physical or physiological needs for food, shelter, and so on. Material goods are deeply implicated in individuals' psychological and social lives. People create and maintain identities using material things. . . . The "evocative power" of material things facilitates a range of complex, deeply ingrained "social conversations" about status, identity, social cohesion, and the pursuit of personal and cultural meaning.[1]

Until recently, most economists paid little attention to the motivations behind consumer behavior. As we discussed in Chapter 7, economic theory in the twentieth century simply assumed that the vast majority of people act rationally to maximize their utility. But as suggested in the quotation above, perhaps no other economic activity is shaped by its social context more than consumption. Our consumption behavior conveys a message to ourselves and others about who we are and how we fit in with, or separate ourselves from, other people.

Modern consumption must also be placed in a historical context. When can we say that "consumer society" originated? Furthermore, is consumerism as experienced in the United States and other countries something that is ingrained in us by evolution, or is it something that has been created by marketing and other social and political forces?

Finally, it is impossible to present a comprehensive analysis of consumption without considering its environmental context. Specifically, ecological research suggests that consumption levels in the United States and many other developed countries have reached unsustainable levels. According to one recent analysis, if everyone in the world had the same living standard as the average American, we would need at least four earths to supply enough resources and process all the waste.[2] So any serious discussion of sustainability must consider the future of consumption patterns throughout the world.

1. Economic Theory and Consumption

1.1 Consumer Sovereignty

Before focusing on the historical, social, and environmental contexts of consumption, we present the economic theory on the topic. Adam Smith once said, "Consumption is the sole end and purpose of all production and the welfare of the producer ought to be attended to, only so far as it may be necessary for promoting that of the consumer."[3]

consumer sovereignty: the idea that consumers' needs and wants determine the shape of all economic activities

The belief that satisfaction of consumers' needs and wants is the ultimate economic goal and that the economy is fundamentally ruled by consumer desires is called **consumer sovereignty**.

Consumer sovereignty suggests that all economic production and distribution are ultimately driven by the preferences of consumers. For example, consider the fact that sales of sport utility vehicles (SUVs) in the United States approximately doubled during the 1990s, while sales of cars decreased. The theory of consumer sovereignty would suggest that the primary reason for the growth of SUV sales is that consumers began to prefer larger vehicles over cars. Referring to Chapter 3, we would say that a change in consumers' tastes and preferences increased the demand for SUVs and decreased the demand for cars. The idea that the shift in demand was driven primarily by automakers' marketing efforts to sell large vehicles with higher profit margins would not be consistent with consumer sovereignty.

The notion of consumer sovereignty has both positive and normative components. From a positive perspective, we can consider whether consumers really do "drive the economy." In Chapter 7, we briefly mentioned the possibility that consumers can be swayed by advertising. We consider the impact of advertising in more detail in this chapter.

living standard (or lifestyle) goals: goals related to satisfying basic needs and getting pleasure through the use of goods and services

Consumer sovereignty can also be viewed from a normative perspective. *Should* people's preferences, as consumers, drive all decisions about economic production, distribution, and resource maintenance? People are more than just consumers. Consumption activities most directly address **living standard (or lifestyle) goals**, which have to do with satisfying basic needs and getting pleasure through the use of goods and services.

But people are often interested in other goals, such as self-realization, fairness, freedom, participation, social relations, and ecological balance. To some extent, these goals may be attained through consumption, but often they conflict with their goals as consumers. People also often obtain intrinsic satisfaction from working and producing. For many people, work defines a significant part of their role in society. Work can create and maintain relationships. It can be a basis for self-respect and a significant part of what gives life purpose and meaning.

If the economy is to promote well-being, all these goals must be taken into account. An economy that made people moderately happy as consumers but absolutely miserable as workers, citizens, or community members could hardly be considered a rousing success. We evaluate the relationship between consumption and well-being further toward the end of this chapter. But now we turn to the formal economic theory on consumption.

1.2 THE BUDGET LINE

The choices that we make as consumers illustrate yet another example of economic tradeoffs. In this case, consumers are constrained in their spending by the amount of their total budget. We can represent this in a simple model in which consumers have only two goods from which to choose. In Figure 8.1 we present a **budget line**, which shows the combinations of two goods that a consumer can purchase. In this example, our consumer—let's call him Quong—has a budget of $8. The two goods that are available for him to purchase are chocolate bars and bags of nuts. The price of chocolate bars is $1 each, and nuts sell for $2 per bag.

budget line: a line showing the possible combinations of two goods that a consumer can purchase

If Quong spends his $8 only on chocolate, he can buy 8 bars, as indicated by the point where the budget line touches the vertical axis. If he buys only nuts, he can buy 4 bags, as indicated by the (4, 0) point on the horizontal axis. He can also buy any combination in between. For example, the point (2, 4), which indicates 2 bags of nuts and 4 chocolate bars, is also achievable. This is because (2 × $2) + (4 × $1) = $8. (We draw the budget line as continuous to reflect the more general case that might apply when there are many more alternatives, although here we assume that Quong buys only whole bars and whole bags, not fractions of them.)

A budget line is similar to the concept of a production possibilities frontier, which we discussed in Chapter 1. A budget line defines the choices that are *possible* for Quong. Points

Figure 8.1   The Budget Line

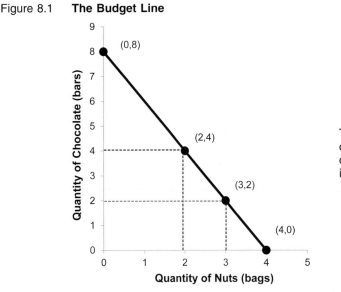

The budget line shows the combination of goods that a consumer can buy with a given income.

above and to the right of the budget line are not affordable. Points below and to the left of the budget line are affordable but do not use up the total budget. In this simple model, economists assume that people always want *more* of at least one of the goods in question. Consuming below the budget line would hence be inefficient; funds that could be used to satisfy Quong's desires are being left unused. Therefore, economists assume that consumers will choose to consume at a point *on* the budget line.

The position of the budget line depends on the size of the total budget (income) and on the prices of the two goods. For example, if Quong has $10 to spend, instead of $8, the line would shift outward in a parallel manner, as shown in Figure 8.2. He could now consume more nuts, or more chocolate, or a more generous combination of both.

If (starting at the original income of $8) the price of nuts dropped to $1 per bag, the budget line would rotate out, as shown in Figure 8.3. Now, if Quong bought only nuts, he could buy

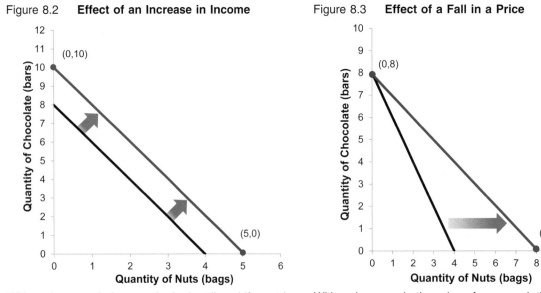

Figure 8.2   Effect of an Increase in Income

With an increase in income the budget line shifts out in a parallel manner. The consumer can now buy more of either good, or more of both goods.

Figure 8.3   Effect of a Fall in a Price

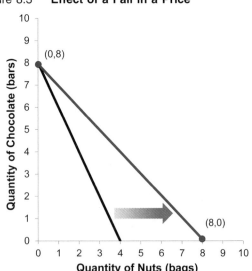

With a decrease in the price of one good, the budget line rotates out to indicate that the consumer can afford more of that good (or of both goods).

8 bags instead of 4. With the price of chocolate unchanged, however, he still could not buy more than 8 chocolate bars.

A budget line tells us what combinations of purchases are possible, but it does not tell us how the consumer will decide *which* combination to consume. To get to this, we must add the theory of utility.

1.3 CONSUMER UTILITY

utility: the pleasure or satisfaction received from goods, services, or experiences

Economists have traditionally defined consumers' "problem" as how to maximize **utility** given their income constraints. Utility is a somewhat vague concept, similar to the idea of welfare defined in Chapter 5. However, although economists attempt to measure welfare quantitatively, utility is generally recognized as something that cannot be measured quantitatively and cannot be aggregated across individuals.* We define utility as the pleasure or satisfaction that individuals receive from goods, services, or experiences. Furthermore, we assume that individuals make consumer decisions to increase their utility. But as discussed in Chapter 7, we recognize that consumers often do not always make the best decisions, because they sometimes act irrationally or are unduly influenced by certain information (or misinformation). We discuss the implications of this further in the next section.

Economists have developed a model of utility that, like many economic models, is an abstraction from reality that is useful for illustrating a particular concept. So despite the fact that we just said that utility cannot be measured quantitatively in the real world, for the purposes of our model we assume that we actually can measure utility in some imaginary units of "satisfaction." Thus Table 8.1 presents the total utility that Quong obtains from purchasing different quantities of chocolate bars in a given period, say a day.

Table 8.1 **Quong's Utility from Chocolate Bars**

Quantity of chocolate bars	Total utility	Marginal utility
0	0	—
1	10	10
2	18	8
3	24	6
4	28	4
5	30	2
6	29	-1

utility function (or total utility curve): a curve showing the relation of utility levels to consumption levels

diminishing marginal utility: the tendency for additional units of consumption to add less to utility than did previous units of consumption

We can then plot Quong's total utility from consuming chocolate bars in Figure 8.4. This relationship between utility and the quantity of something consumed is called a **utility function**, or a **total utility curve**.

Quong's utility curve levels off as his consumption of chocolate bars increases. This is generally expected—that successive units of something consumed provide less utility than the previous unit. In other words, consumers' utility functions generally display **diminishing marginal utility**. This is shown in Table 8.1. We see that Quong obtains 10 units of "satisfaction" from consuming his first chocolate bar. While his utility increases from 10 to 18 units by consuming his second chocolate bar, his marginal utility is only 8 units. Consuming his third chocolate bar, he obtains a marginal utility of 6 units. This is shown in Figure 8.4, where his utility is shown as increasing from 18 to 24 units. Eventually, Quong's consumption of chocolate becomes much less pleasurable, and when he consumes his sixth chocolate bar, his utility actually starts to decline. Assuming that Quong is rational, he would never consume more than five chocolate bars in a day.

---

*Some economists in the 1800s, such as William Stanley Jevons (1835–1882) actually did believe that utility was something that could eventually be measured numerically.

Figure 8.4   **Quong's Utility Function for Chocolate Bars**

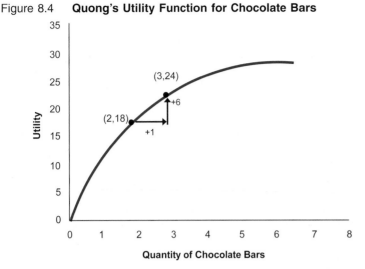

Utility rises steeply for the first few chocolate bars and then more slowly as Quong gets sated.

Now we can apply the concept of utility to the budget line that Quong faces. Realize that Quong will also have a utility function for bags of nuts, which will display a similar pattern of diminishing marginal utility. Let's assume that his first bag of nuts provides him with 20 units of utility, his second bag with 15 units, and each successive bag with less units of utility. How can Quong allocate his limited budget to provide him with the highest amount of total utility?

We provide a formal model of utility maximization in the appendix to this chapter, but we can easily see how Quong might approach his problem in a purely rational manner using marginal thinking. Suppose that Quong is thinking about how he will spend his first $2. With $2 he can buy either two chocolate bars or one bag of nuts. If he buys two chocolate bars, he will obtain 18 total units of utility, as shown in Table 8.1. If he buys one bag of nuts instead, he will obtain 20 units of utility. Thus Quong will receive greater utility by spending his first $2 on a bag of nuts.

What about his next $2? If he spends this on his *second bag of nuts,* he obtains an additional 15 units of utility. But if he instead purchases his *first two chocolate bars,* he will obtain 18 units of utility. So, by spending his next $2 on chocolate bars, he increases his utility by a greater amount. After spending $4 Quong has purchased one bag of nuts and two chocolate bars, thus obtaining a total utility of 38 units. Quong can continue to apply marginal thinking to maximize his utility until he has eventually spent his entire budget. The basic decision rule to maximize utility is to allocate each additional dollar on the good or service that provides the greatest marginal utility for that dollar.* Again, see the appendix for a formal presentation of utility maximization.

1.4 LIMITATIONS OF THE STANDARD CONSUMER MODEL

We suspect that you have never thought about how to spend your money in a manner similar to Quong's marginal analysis of chocolate and nuts. It is less important that people behave exactly as a model suggests than it is to consider whether people generally act *as if* they are always trying to increase their utility as much as possible. There are several reasons to be skeptical about this. First, the utility model assumes that people are rational, but as we saw in Chapter 7, this is not always the case. The model also assumes that all the benefits from consumption can be identified, compared, and added up.

---

*As most goods and services are not available in $1 increments, such as bags of nuts, consumers will not always be able to allocate every single dollar in a way that maximizes utility.

While comparing the utility from chocolate and nuts may be relatively easy to imagine, consumers' decisions become much more complicated when they are faced with a wide variety of options.

Economists have traditionally assumed that having more options from which to choose can only benefit consumers, but recent research demonstrates that there is a cost in trying to process additional information. In fact, having too many choices can actually "overload" our ability to evaluate different options. Consider a famous example demonstrating the effect of having too much choice.[4] In one experiment, researchers at a supermarket in California set up a display table with six different flavors of jam. Shoppers could taste any (or all) of the six flavors and receive a discount coupon to purchase any flavor. About 30 percent of those who tried one or more jams ended up buying some.

The researchers then repeated this experiment but, instead, offered 24 flavors of jam for tasting. In this case, *only 3 percent* of those who tasted a jam went on to buy some. In theory, it would seem that more choice would increase the chances of finding a jam that one really liked and would be willing to buy. But, instead, the additional choices decreased one's motivation to make a decision to buy a jam. A 2010 article from *The Economist* addressed this topic:

> As options multiply, there may be a point at which the effort required to obtain enough information to be able to distinguish sensibly between alternatives outweighs the benefit to the consumer of the extra choice. "At this point," writes Barry Schwartz in *The Paradox of Choice*, "choice no longer liberates, but debilitates. It might even be said to tyrannise." In other words, as Mr. Schwartz puts it, "the fact that *some* choice is good doesn't necessarily mean that *more* choice is better."
>
> Daniel McFadden, an economist at the University of California, Berkeley, says that consumers find too many options troubling because of the "risk of misperception and miscalculation, of misunderstanding the available alternatives, of misreading one's own tastes, of yielding to a moment's whim and regretting it afterwards," combined with "the stress of information acquisition."[5]

Another important point is that when consumers make a decision to purchase a good or service, they are essentially making a prediction about the utility that the purchase will bring them. Daniel Kahneman, whom we encountered in Chapter 7, distinguishes between *predicted* utility and *remembered* utility. Predicted utility is the utility that you expect to obtain from a purchase (or other experience), whereas remembered utility is the utility that you actually recall after you have made a purchase. In other words, Kahneman considers whether people actually receive the benefits they expect in advance of their purchases. According to the standard consumer model with rational decision makers, these two utilities should match relatively closely.

Once again research from behavioral economics suggests that people's predictions can often turn out to be incorrect. In one well-known experiment, young professors were asked to predict the effect of their tenure decision on their long-term happiness. Although being granted tenure essentially ensures a professor lifetime employment, being denied tenure means he or she must find a new job. Most young professors predict that being denied tenure will have a long-term negative impact on their happiness. Yet surveys of professors who actually have and have not been granted tenure indicate that there is no significant long-term effect of tenure decision on happiness levels. A similar experiment showed that college students overpredicted the negative effects of a romantic breakup.[6]

These findings have implications for welfare analysis, as discussed in Chapter 5. Realize that a demand curve is an expression of predicted utility. Welfare analysis measures consumer surplus based on demand curves, thus implicitly assuming that predicted utility matches well with remembered utility. But if predicted and remembered utility differs, any welfare implications based on demand curves will be an inaccurate estimate of the utility that people actually receive from their purchases.

We must also recognize the potential for consumers to be swayed by advertising and other influences into making poor consumer decisions, as we discussed in Chapter 7. Advertising expenditures in the United States totaled about $250 billion in 2012, equivalent to close to 2 percent of the entire national economy, or about $800 per person.[7] Of course, the purpose of advertising is not necessarily to assist consumers to make the best choices. We further discuss the impact of advertising later in this chapter.

Discussion Questions

1. Budget lines can be used to analyze various kinds of tradeoffs. Suppose that you have a total "time budget" for recreation of 2 hours. Think of two activities you might like to do for recreation, and draw a budget line diagram illustrating the recreational opportunities open to you. What if you had a time budget of three hours instead?
2. Explain in words why the total utility curve has the shape that it does in Figure 8.4.

2. CONSUMPTION IN HISTORICAL AND INTERNATIONAL CONTEXT

Perhaps the greatest limitation of the standard consumer model is that it does not really tell us anything interesting about *why* consumers make particular choices. For example, why might Quong purchase so many chocolate bars that it has a negative impact on his health? Can someone who smokes cigarettes truly be acting in a utility-maximizing manner? Why do people acquire huge credit card debts by making seemingly frivolous purchases? Why would someone spend $60,000 or more on a new car when a car costing much less may be perfectly adequate for all practical purposes?

consumer society: a society in which a large part of people's sense of identity and meaning is found through the purchase and use of consumer goods and services

To answer such questions, we must recognize the historical and social nature of consumption. We are so immersed in a culture of consumption that we can be said to be living in a **consumer society**, a society in which a large part of people's sense of identity and meaning is achieved through the purchase and use of consumer goods and services. Viewing consumption through the lens of a consumer society is quite different from looking at consumption from the standard economic model of consumer behavior.

We first consider the historical evolution of consumer society, along with the institutions that allowed consumer society to flourish. Then we take a brief look at consumer society around the world today.

2.1 A BRIEF HISTORY OF CONSUMER SOCIETY

consumerism: having one's sense of identity and meaning defined largely through the purchase and use of consumer goods and services

When can we say that consumer society originated? Historians have placed the birth of the consumer society variously from the sixteenth century to the mid-1900s.[8] To some extent, the answer depends on whether we consider **consumerism**, understood as having one's sense of identity and meaning defined largely through the purchase and use of consumer goods and services, as an innate human characteristic. In other words, does consumerism come naturally to humans or is it an acquired trait?

Of course, for thousands of years a small elite class has existed that enjoyed higher consumption standards and habitually bought luxury goods and services. One story of the birth of consumer society says that it is human nature to want to acquire more goods, so all that is needed for the birth of consumer society is for a significant portion of the population to have more money than is necessary for basic survival. However, this explanation is incorrect or at least a vast oversimplification.

Before the eighteenth century, families and communities that acquired more than enough to meet basic needs did not automatically respond by becoming consumers. Religious value systems generally taught material restraint. Patterns of dress and household display were dictated by tradition, depending on the class to which one belonged, with little change over time. Unlike the norm in modern times, in the past emphasis was more often placed on community spending, such as for a new church, as opposed to private spending.

The historical consensus is that the consumer society as a mass phenomenon originated in the eighteenth century in Western Europe. Although it is no coincidence that this time and location coincides with the birth of the Industrial Revolution, consumer society was not solely the result of greater prosperity. The Industrial Revolution clearly transformed production. It is less obvious, but equally true, that it transformed consumption, as much through the social changes it produced as through the economic changes.

> The arrival of consumerism in Western Europe involved truly revolutionary change in the way goods were sold, in the array of goods available and cherished, and in the goals people defined for their daily lives. This last—the redefinition of needs and aspirations—is the core feature of consumerism.[9]

The large-scale emigration of people from the agricultural countryside to cities in search of work brought significant social disruption. Instead of finding personal and social meaning in tradition and community, people sought new ways to define themselves, often through consumer goods. Also, shopkeepers for the first time began to create window displays, engage in newspaper advertising, and use other methods to attract customers. Furthermore, the breakdown of strict class lines meant that common people had the freedom to express themselves in new ways, including displays of wealth that would have been discouraged, or even illegal, in the past.

Yet although consumerism took root in the eighteenth century, it took some time before it fully blossomed. At the dawn of industrialization, it was not at all clear that workers would or could become consumers. Early British industrialists complained that their employees would work only until they had earned their traditional weekly income and then stop until the next week. Leisure, it appeared, was more valuable to the workers than increased income. This attitude, widespread in preindustrial societies, was incompatible with mass production and mass consumption. It could be changed in either of two ways.

At first, employers responded by lowering wages and imposing strict discipline on workers to force them to work longer hours. Early textile mills frequently employed women, teenagers, and even children, because they were easier to control and could be paid less than adult male workers. As a consequence of such draconian strategies of labor discipline, living and working conditions for the first few generations of factory workers were worse than in the generations before industrialization.

Over time, however, agitation by organized workers, political reformers, and civic and humanitarian groups created pressure for better wages, hours, and working conditions, while rising productivity and profits made it possible for business to respond to this pressure. A second response to the preindustrial work ethic gradually evolved: As workers came to see themselves as consumers, they would no longer choose to stop work early and enjoy more leisure; rather, they preferred to work full-time, or even overtime, in order to earn and spend more. In the United States, the "worker as consumer" view was fully entrenched by the 1920s, when the labor movement stopped advocating a shorter workweek and instead focused on better wages and working conditions.

Other historical developments were important to the spread of consumer society. One was the invention of the department store, in the mid-nineteenth century in England. Department stores quickly spread to other European countries and the United States. Featuring lavish displays, department stores presented shoppers with the opportunity to purchase an entirely new lifestyle, all under one roof. Department stores introduced the idea of shopping as "spectacle," with entertainment, elaborate interiors, seasonal displays, and parades.[10]

The department store was a permanent fair, a dream world, a spectacle of excessive proportions. Going to the store became an event and an adventure. One came less to purchase a particular article than to simply visit, to browse, to see what was new, to try on new fashions and even new identities.[11]

Modern shopping malls originated in the United States in the early twentieth century. Suburbanization in the United States in the mid-twentieth century was supported by the construction of large shopping malls far from city centers but easily accessible by automobile. By the 1980s and 1990s enormous shopping malls, such as the Mall of America in Minnesota, were being constructed with entertainment options including indoor roller coasters and aquariums.

Another institution created to support the consumer society was expanded consumer credit, particularly the invention of credit cards in the 1940s. In 2012, nearly three-fourths of U.S. households had at least one credit card. Although some cardholders use them only for convenience, paying off their balances in full each month, about half of cardholders use them as a form of borrowing by carrying unpaid balances, on which they pay interest, with annualized rates that can exceed 30 percent.

Figure 8.5 illustrates the growth of revolving debt in the United States over the past several decades, adjusted for inflation.* We see that revolving debt, which consists almost entirely of credit card debt, increased by a factor of 100 from 1968 until about 2007, when the Great Recession caused households to reduce their debt, as spending declined and credit became less available. In early 2013, total outstanding credit card debt in the United States was about $830 billion, equivalent to more than $7,000 per household. However, given that about half of households do not carry an unpaid monthly balance on their credit cards, those households that do carry a balance had an average credit card debt of around $15,000.

2.2 LIMITS TO MODERN CONSUMERISM

Can we say, at the start of the twenty-first century, that consumerism has become a global phenomenon? It is true that people all over the world are increasingly exposed to similar

Figure 8.5　**Revolving Debt in the United States, 1968–2012, Adjusted for Inflation**

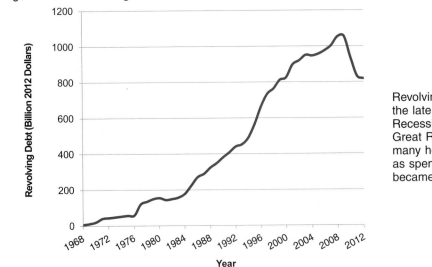

Revolving debt rose steeply from the late 1960s up until the Great Recession starting in 2007. The Great Recession resulted in many households reducing debt as spending declined and credit became less available.

*Revolving debt allows consumers to borrow money against a line of credit, without the requirement that the amount borrowed be fully paid off each month. Thus the balance from one or more months can carry over, or "revolve," to the next month. The vast majority of revolving debt is credit card debt.

commercial messages and images of "the good life," but consumer society is not yet universal for two main reasons. First, about 2.4 billion people around the world (about one-third of humanity) live in absolute poverty, defined by the World Bank as living on less than $2 per day. Obviously, consumerism is not an option for the global poor. Second, in numerous places around the world cultural and religious values exist that seek to restrain, or even reject, the consumer society. We first discuss global poverty and then turn to a brief discussion of nonconsumer values.

Insufficient Consumption: Poverty

absolute depriva-tion: severe deprivation of basic human needs

One-third of the global population lives in extreme poverty, or **absolute deprivation**. What constitutes absolute deprivation? The United Nations has defined it as "a condition characterized by severe deprivation of basic human needs, including food, safe drinking water, sanitation facilities, health, shelter, education and information. It depends not only on income but also on access to services."

The poorest of developing countries, particularly in sub-Saharan Africa and Southern Asia, are simply too poor to lift their entire populations out of absolute deprivation. Increasingly, however, the more economically successful developing countries in Asia and Latin America have sufficient resources to provide everyone with basic necessities; the fact that absolute deprivation still exists for the poor in these countries reflects inequality in the distribution of income. Absolute deprivation may also vary with factors such as race and ethnicity and even within a household on the basis of age or gender.

Because insufficient consumption is not simply a matter of having a low household income, even in regions that could be generally characterized as middle or high income, examples of absolute deprivation can still be found. Some people—particularly young children and the ill and handicapped—have dependency needs for care that may be unmet. Even people with a fairly high household income may sometimes, then, find themselves lacking basic necessities. Advocates for the elderly, the sick, and children, for example, often claim that the United States has an inadequate system of care.

relative depriva-tion: the feeling of lack that comes from comparing oneself with someone who has more

Absolute deprivation is only one type of insufficiency. Modern communication technology means that nearly everyone has some exposure to the "lifestyles of the rich and famous." The result is the creation of widespread feelings of **relative deprivation**, that is, the sense that one's own condition is inadequate because it is inferior to someone else's circumstances. The richest man in a small village may be quite content with traditional clothing and diet, an outdoor latrine, and water drawn from a communal well, so long as that way of life is consistent with honor and self-respect. However, after he begins to compare his circumstances with those in the city, he may begin to feel that they are less than they should be.

The government-defined poverty level in the United States was $23,550 for a family of four in 2013. This income would be at or above the national average in many countries; in most developing countries, a family income of $23,550 would be considered wealthy. It may be possible to buy the bare physical necessities of life for this sum, even in the United States—at least in areas of the country with low housing costs. Yet it is likely that most of the Americans who fall below the poverty level (15 percent of the population in 2011) do not feel able to enjoy a "normal" American lifestyle. They clearly do not have the resources to buy the kinds of homes, cars, clothing, and other consumer goods commonly shown on American television. They may need to rely on inadequate public transportation and wait in long lines for health care. People with sufficient physical means of survival may still feel ashamed, belittled, and socially unaccepted if they have much less than everyone around them. The 22 percent of U.S. children who live in poverty do not start out on an "even playing field" with nonpoor children, in terms of nutrition, health care, and other requirements. The fact that people who cannot afford to consume at "normal" societal consumption levels feel relative deprivation suggests that poverty, even relative poverty, is not conducive to promoting well-being and self-respect.

Nonconsumerist Values

The spread of consumerism has met considerable resistance in some societies, usually because it conflicts with existing values, either religious or secular. For example, the Muslim concept of *riba* prohibits charging interest on loans. Buddhism teaches a "middle path" that emphasizes material simplicity, nonviolence, and inner peace. Various passages of the New Testament of the Bible emphasize the spiritual dangers of wealth, such as the saying that it is easier for a camel to pass through the eye of a needle than for a rich man to enter heaven.

Traditional cultural values in some countries have restrained the spread of consumerism. In some countries, consumerism is associated with foreign, typically American, values.

> Consumption expansion thus tends to lead to some level of global homogenization of culture among consumers, an effect that gives rise to negative responses to globalization. As consumer goods are always also cultural goods, expansion of consumption of imported products and services often gives rise to an exaggerated sense of "panic," of cultural "invasion" which, supposedly, if left unchecked will result in the demise of the local culture.[12]

Social norms and government policies in various European countries aim to promote nonconsumerist values. For example, many retail stores in France, Italy, and other European countries are normally closed at lunchtime and on Sundays. European policies on vacation time, parental leave, and flexible working hours emphasize a work–life balance.

Even in the United States, the spread of consumerism has not been an even, uninterrupted process. The history of consumer society in the United States reveals periodic movements against consumerism. The Quakers in the eighteenth century, the Transcendentalists of the mid-nineteenth century (most famously, Henry David Thoreau), the Progressives at the turn of the twentieth century, and the hippies of the 1960s all espoused a simpler, less materialistic life philosophy.[13] More recently, starting in the 1980s the idea of voluntary simplicity, which we discuss further later in the chapter, has attracted a following among Americans motivated by objectives such as reducing environmental impacts, focusing more on family and social connections, healthy living, and stress reduction.

Discussion Questions

1. Considering what you know about the societies in which your grandparents or great-grandparents grew up, would you say that they lived in a "consumer society"? How do you think their views on consumerism as young adults might have differed from those of you and your friends?
2. What do you know about views on consumerism in other countries, either from what you have read or what you have observed from traveling? Which societies, if any, do you find too focused on consumerism? Which societies, if any, do you think have appropriate views on consumerism?

3. CONSUMPTION IN A SOCIAL CONTEXT

As mentioned at the beginning of this chapter, in modern consumer societies, consumption is as much a social activity as an economic activity. Consumption is tied closely to personal identity, and it has become a means of communicating social messages. An increasing range of social interactions are influenced by consumer values.

Consumption pervades our everyday lives and structures our everyday practices. The values, meanings, and costs of what we consume have become an increasingly important part of our social and personal experiences. . . . [Consumption] has entered into the . . . fabric of modern life. All forms of social life—from education to sexual relations to political campaigns—are now seen as consumer relations.[14]

3.1 SOCIAL COMPARISONS

As social beings, we compare ourselves to other people. Our income and consumption levels are some of the most important ways in which we evaluate ourselves relative to others. As discussed above, whether people consider themselves poor often depends on the condition of those around them.

You have probably heard of the saying "Keeping up with the Joneses." This saying refers to the motivation to maintain a material lifestyle that is comparable to those around us. A **reference group** is a group of people who influence the behavior of a consumer because the consumer compares himself or herself with that group. Most people have various reference groups, traditionally including our neighbors, our coworkers, and other members of our family. We also are influenced as consumers by **aspirational groups**, groups to which a consumer *wishes* he or she could belong. People often buy, dress, and behave like the group—corporate executives, rock stars, athletes, or whoever—with whom they would like to identify.

reference group: the group to which an individual compares himself or herself

aspirational group: the group to which an individual aspires to belong

Economist Juliet Schor argues that the nature of social comparisons related to consumption has changed in the past few decades. She suggests that in the 1950s and 1960s the idea of "Keeping up with the Joneses" emphasized comparisons between individuals or families with similar incomes and backgrounds. Because prosperity was broadly shared in the postwar decades, people did not want to feel left out as new consumer goods and living standards emerged. More recently, however, she has observed a different approach to consumption comparisons.

> Beginning in the 1980s, those conditions changed, and what I have termed the new consumerism emerged. The new consumerism is more upscale in the sense that there is more aggressive, rather than defensive, consumption positioning. The new consumerism is more anonymous and is less socially benign than the old regime of keeping up with the Joneses. In part, this is because reference groups have become vertically elongated. People are now more likely to compare themselves with, or aspire to the lifestyle of, those far above them in the economic hierarchy.[15]

Schor presents the results of a survey to support this view, which indicates that 85 percent of respondents aspire to become someone who "really made it" or is at least "doing very well." But the survey results also show that only 18 percent of Americans are members of these groups based on income.[16] If 85 percent of people aspire to be in the top 18 percent, obviously most will end up disappointed.

Changes in economic inequality, which we discuss further in Chapter 10, are also relevant to her hypothesis. During the 1950s and 1960s, economic inequality in the United States was decreasing—that is, the gap between different levels of the income hierarchy was generally shrinking. However, beginning in the 1970s economic inequality began to increase, thus making it difficult to maintain even the existing distance between an individual and his or her aspirational group.

Media representations of wealthy lifestyles also became more common. In the 1950s and 1960s, most television shows depicted middle-class lifestyles. But starting in the 1980s, television shows as well as advertisements increasingly depicted upper-class lifestyles. Exposure to media representations of wealth influences people's values and spending patterns. Schor's own research indicates that the more television a person watches, the more he or she is likely to spend, holding constant other variables such as income. Higher rates of television watching have also been associated with having materialistic values.[17] Other research has found that heavy television watchers are likely to overstate the percentage of the population that owns luxury items, such as convertibles and hot tubs, or that have maids or servants.[18]

Schor's conclusion is that identifying with unrealistic aspirational groups leads many people to consume well above their means, acquiring large debts and suffering frustration as they attempt to join those groups through their consumption patterns but fail to achieve the income to sustain them. As people tend to evaluate themselves relative to reference and aspirational groups, with increasing inequality some may feel as if they are falling behind even if their incomes are actually increasing.

> The more our consumer satisfaction is tied to social comparisons—whether upscaling, just keeping up, or not falling too far behind—the less we achieve when consumption grows, because the people we compare ourselves to are also experiencing rising consumption. . . . The problem is not just that more consumption doesn't yield more satisfaction, but that it always has a cost. The extra hours we have to work to earn the money cut into personal and family time. *Whatever* we consume has an ecological impact. . . . We find ourselves skimping on invisibles such as insurance, college funds, and retirement savings as the visible commodities somehow become indispensable. . . . We are impoverishing ourselves in pursuit of a consumption goal that is inherently unattainable. In the words of one focus-group participant, we "just don't know when to stop and draw the line."

3.2 ADVERTISING

Although advertising has existed as a specialized profession for only about a century, it has become a force that rivals education and religion in shaping public values and aspirations. We already saw that advertising spending in the United States totals about $800 per person annually. According to various estimates, arrived at before the widespread use of the Internet, Americans are exposed to between 200 and 3,000 commercial messages per day.

About one-third of global advertising spending takes place in the United States (see Figure 8.6). Japan is the world's second-largest advertising market, followed by China. Advertising is

Figure 8.6 **Global Advertising Expenditures, by Country/Region, 2011**

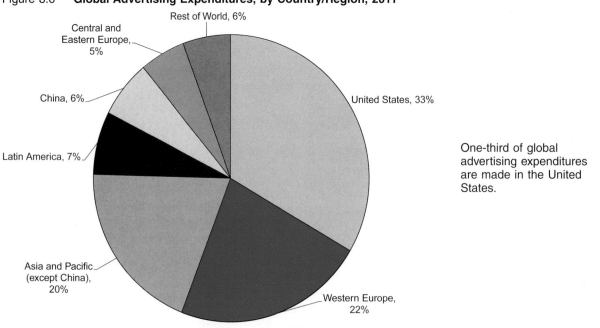

One-third of global advertising expenditures are made in the United States.

Source: Advertising Age, December 5, 2011.

increasing most rapidly in China and other emerging markets. Per-capita advertising spending in China increased from just 9 cents in 1986 to $22 in 2011.

Advertising is often justified by economists as a source of information about products and services available in the marketplace. Although it certainly plays that role, it also does much more. Advertising appeals to many different values, emotional as well as practical needs and a range of desires and fantasies. The multitude of advertisements that we encounter carry their own separate messages; yet on a deeper level, they all share a common, powerful cultural message.

> What the vast amount of advertising really sells is consumer culture itself. Even if advertising fails to sell a particular product, the advertisements still sell the meanings and values of a consumer culture. As Christopher Lasch writes, "The importance of advertising is not that it invariably succeeds in its immediate purpose, . . . but simply that it surrounds people with images of the good life in which happiness depends on consumption. The ubiquity of such images leaves little space for competing conceptions of the good life."[19]

According to one estimate, the typical American will spend about three years of his or her life watching television ads.[20] We have already mentioned how watching television can influence people's spending behavior and values. Other research details how television, and advertising in particular, is associated with obesity, attention deficit disorder, heart disease, and other negative consequences. Furthermore, advertising commonly portrays unrealistic body images, traditionally for women but more recently for men as well. (See Box 8.1 for more on the effects of advertising on girls and women.)

Box 8.1   Women and Advertising

A 2007 report by the American Psychological Association concluded that advertising and other media images encourage girls to focus on physical appearance and sexuality, with harmful results for their emotional and physical well-being. The research project reviewed data from numerous media sources, including television, music videos and lyrics, movies, magazines, and video games. The report found that 85 percent of the sexualized images of children were of girls.

The lead author of the report, Dr. Eileen L. Zurbriggen, said, "The consequences of the sexualization of girls in media today are very real and are likely to be a negative influence on girls' healthy development. We have ample evidence to conclude that sexualization has negative effects in a variety of domains, including cognitive functioning, physical and mental health, and healthy sexual development."

Three of the most common mental health problems associated with exposure to sexualized images and unrealistic body ideals are eating disorders, low self-esteem, and depression. It is estimated that 8 million Americans suffer from an eating disorder—7 million of them women. About 20 percent of anorexics will eventually die from the disorder. According to a 2012 article, most female models would be considered anorexic according to their body mass index. Twenty years ago the average model weighed 8 percent less than the average woman; now it is 23 percent less.

Jean Kilbourne, an author and filmmaker who holds a Ph.D. in education, has been lobbying for advertising reforms since the 1960s. She has produced four documentaries on the negative effects of advertising on women, most recently in 2010, under the title *Killing Us Softly*. Kilbourne notes that virtually all photos of models in advertisements have been touched up, eliminating wrinkles, blemishes, extra weight, and even skin pores. She believes that we need to change the environment of advertising through public policy. Dr. Zurbriggen concludes, "As a society, we need to replace all of these sexualized images with ones showing girls in positive settings—ones that show the uniqueness and competence of girls."

Sources: Jean Kilbourne Web site, www.jeankilbourne.com; Edward Lovett, "Most Models Meet Criteria for Anorexia, Size 6 Is Plus Size: Magazine," ABC News, January 12, 2012; "Sexualization of Girls Is Linked to Common Mental Health Problems in Girls and Women," *Science Daily*, February 20, 2007; South Carolina Department of Mental Health, Eating Disorder Statistics, www.state.sc.us/dmh/anorexia/statistics.htm.

3.3 PRIVATE VERSUS PUBLIC CONSUMPTION

The growth of consumerism has altered the balance between private and public consumption. Public infrastructure has been shaped by the drive to sell and consume new products and the availability of public and private options, in turn, shapes individual consumer choices.

In the early 1930s, for example, many major U.S. cities—including Los Angeles—had extensive, relatively efficient, and nonpolluting electric streetcar systems. Then, in 1936, a group of companies involved in bus and diesel gasoline production, led by General Motors, formed a group called the National City Lines (NCL). They bought up electric streetcar systems in 45 cities and dismantled them, replacing them with bus systems that also tended to promote automobile dependency. U.S. government support for highway construction in the 1950s further hastened the decline of rail transportation, made possible the spread of suburbs far removed from workplaces, and encouraged the purchase of automobiles.

Many of the choices that you have, as an individual, depend on decisions made for you by businesses and governments. Los Angeles would look much different today—more like the older sections of many East Coast and European cities—if it had been built up around streetcar lines rather than cars and buses. Even today one can see tradeoffs between public (or publicly accessible) infrastructure and private consumption. As more people carry cell phones and bottled water, pay telephones and drinking fountains come to be less well maintained in some cities, leading more people to need to carry cell phones and bottled water.

Discussion Questions

1. What are your reference groups? Describe why you consider these your reference groups. What are your aspirational groups? Why do you aspire to be a member of these groups?
2. Think about at least one fashion item you own, such as an item of clothing, jewelry, or accessory, that you think says a lot about who you are. What do you think it says about you? Do you think others interpret the item in the same way that you do? How much do you think that you were influenced by advertising or other media in your views about the item?

4. CONSUMPTION IN AN ENVIRONMENTAL CONTEXT

The production process that creates every consumer product requires natural resources and generates some waste and pollution. However, we are normally only vaguely aware of the ecological impact of the processes that supply us with consumer goods.

> The problem is that we do not often see the true ugliness of the consumer economy and so are not compelled to do much about it. The distance between shopping malls and their associated mines, wells, corporate farms, factories, toxic dumps, and landfills, sometimes half a world away, dampens our perceptions that something is fundamentally wrong.[21]

Most of us are unaware that, for example, it requires about 600 gallons of water to make a quarter-pound hamburger or that making a computer chip generates 4,500 times its weight in waste.[22] (For another example of the ecological impacts of consumption, see Box 8.2.)

4.1 THE LINK BETWEEN CONSUMPTION AND THE ENVIRONMENT

In quantifying the ecological impacts of consumerism, most people focus on the amount of "trash" generated by households and businesses. In 2011, the U.S. economy generated about 250 million tons of municipal solid waste, which consisted mostly of paper, food waste, and yard waste.[23] Although the total amount of municipal solid waste generated has increased

BOX 8.2   THE ENVIRONMENTAL STORY OF A T-SHIRT

T-shirts, along with jeans, are perhaps the most ubiquitous articles of clothing on college campuses. What is the environmental impact of each of these t-shirts?

Consider a t-shirt constructed of a cotton/polyester blend, weighing about four ounces. Polyester is made from petroleum—a few tablespoons are required to make a t-shirt. During the extraction and refining of the petroleum, one-fourth of the polyester's weight is released in air pollution, including nitrogen oxides, particulates, carbon monoxide, and heavy metals. About *10 times* the polyester's weight is released in carbon dioxide, contributing to global climate change.

Cotton grown with nonorganic methods relies heavily on chemical inputs. Cotton accounts for 10 percent of the world's use of pesticides. A typical cotton crop requires six applications of pesticides, commonly organophosphates that can damage the central nervous system. Cotton is also one of the most intensely irrigated crops in the world.

T-shirt fabric is bleached and dyed with chemicals including chlorine, chromium, and formaldehyde. Cotton resists coloring, so about one-third of the dye may be carried off in the waste stream. Most t-shirts are manufactured in Asia and then shipped by boat to their destination, with further transportation by train and truck. Each transportation step involves the release of additional air pollution and carbon dioxide.

Despite the impacts of t-shirt production and distribution, most of the environmental impact associated with t-shirts occurs *after purchase*. Washing and drying a t-shirt 10 times requires about as much energy as was needed to manufacture the shirt. Laundering will also generate more solid waste than the production of the shirt, mainly from sewage sludge and detergent packaging.

How can one reduce the environmental impacts of t-shirts? One obvious step is to avoid buying too many shirts in the first place. Buy shirts made of organic cotton or recycled polyester or consider buying used clothing. Wash clothes only when they need washing, not necessarily every time you wear something. Make sure that you wash only full loads of laundry and wash using cold water whenever possible. Finally, avoid using a clothes dryer—clothes dry naturally for free by hanging on a clothesline or a drying rack.

Source: John C. Ryan and Alan Thein Durning, *Stuff: The Secret Lives of Everyday Things* (Seattle: Northwest Environment Watch, 1997).

---

in recent decades (an increase of nearly 200 percent since 1960), the portion recycled has increased from around 6 percent in the 1960s to about one-third today.

But most of the waste generation in a consumer society occurs during the extraction, processing, or manufacturing stages—these impacts are normally hidden from consumers. According to data from 2000, the U.S. economy required about 30 billion tons of material inputs, which is equivalent to more than *100 tons per person.*[24] The vast majority of this material is discarded as mining waste, crop residue, logging waste, chemical runoff, and other waste prior to the consumption stage.

ecological footprint: an estimate of how much land area a human society requires to provide all that the society takes from nature and to absorb its waste and pollution

Perhaps the most comprehensive attempt to quantify the overall ecological impact of consumption is the **ecological footprint** measure. This approach estimates how much land area a human society requires to provide all that it takes from nature and to absorb its waste and pollution. Although the details of the ecological footprint calculations are subject to debate, it does provide a useful way to compare the overall ecological impact of consumption in different countries.

We see in Figure 8.7 that the ecological footprint per capita varies significantly across countries. The United States has one of the highest per-capita ecological footprints (the per-capita footprints of some oil-producing countries are higher). The average European has a footprint about half the U.S. level, while the typical Chinese has a footprint one-quarter the U.S. level.

Perhaps the most significant implication of the ecological footprint research is that the world is now in a situation of "overshoot"—our global use of resources and generation of waste exceeds the global capacity to supply resources and assimilate waste, by about 50 percent according to recent estimates. The situation is much worse when we consider whether everyone in the world can consume at a level equivalent to the typical American. In that case, we would require four to five earths to provide the needed resources and assimilate the waste.

Figure 8.7   **Ecological Footprint per Capita, Select Countries, 2007**

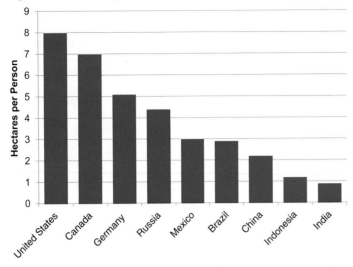

The ecological impacts of consumption are relatively high in the United States, with a per-capita impact about twice as high as most European countries and four times as high as China.

Source: Global Footprint Network, www.footprintnetwork.org/en/index.php/GFN/page/footprint_for_nations/

4.2 GREEN CONSUMERISM

green consumerism: making consumption decisions at least partly on the basis of environmental criteria

Green consumerism means making consumption decisions at least partly on the basis of environmental criteria. Clearly, green consumerism is increasing: More people are recycling, using reusable shopping bags and water containers, buying hybrid cars, and so on. Yet some people see green consumerism as an oxymoron—that the culture of consumerism is simply incompatible with environmental sustainability.

Whether green consumerism is an oxymoron depends on exactly how we define it. Green consumerism comes in two basic types:

1. "shallow" green consumerism: consumers seek to purchase "ecofriendly" alternatives but do not necessarily change their overall level of consumption
2. "deep" green consumerism: consumers seek to purchase ecofriendly alternatives but also, more importantly, seek to reduce their overall level of consumption

Someone who adheres to shallow green consumerism might buy a hybrid car instead of a car with a gasoline engine or a shirt made with organic cotton instead of cotton grown with the use of chemical pesticides. But those who practice deep green consumerism would, when feasible, take public transportation instead of buying a car and question whether they really need another shirt. In other words, in shallow green consumerism the emphasis is on substitution while in deep green consumerism the emphasis is on a reduction in consumption. Note that people who buy so-called ecofriendly products such that their overall consumption increases, or as status symbols, could hardly be said to be practicing green consumerism.

ecolabeling: product labels that provide information about environmental impacts, or indicate certification

Ecolabeling helps consumers make environmentally conscious decisions. An ecolabel can provide summary information about environmental impacts. For example, stickers on new cars in the United States rate the vehicle's smog emissions, on a scale from one to ten. More commonly, ecolabels are placed on products that meet certain certification standards. One example is the U.S. Environmental Protection Agency's Energy Star program, which certifies products that are highly energy efficient. The Forest Stewardship Council, headquartered in Germany, certifies wood products that meet certain sustainability standards.

In addition to environmental awareness by consumers, many businesses are seeking to reduce the environmental impacts of their production processes. Of course, some of the motivation may be to increase profits or improve public relations, but companies are also becoming more transparent about their environmental impacts. The Global Reporting Initiative (GRI) is a nonprofit organization that promotes a standardized approach to environmental impact reporting. In 2011 more than 2,300 companies used the GRI methodology, including Coca-Cola, Walmart, Apple, UPS, and Verizon.

Discussion Questions

1. Think about one product you have purchased recently that is not mentioned in the text. Try to list the environmental impacts of this product, considering the production, consumption, and eventual disposal of it. What steps do you think could be taken to reduce the environmental impacts associated with this product?

2. Do you think that green consumerism is an oxymoron? Do you think that your own consumer behaviors are environmentally sustainable? Why or why not?

5. CONSUMPTION AND WELL-BEING

If the goal of economics is to enhance well-being, as we discussed in Chapter 1, then we need to ask whether current levels of consumerism are compatible with well-being goals. If not, then what should we do about it?

5.1 DOES MONEY BUY HAPPINESS?

subjective well-being (SWB): a measure of welfare based on survey questions asking people about their own degree of life satisfaction

Earlier in the chapter, we mentioned that utility is a somewhat vague concept, one that cannot be easily measured quantitatively. But a large volume of scientific research in the past few decades suggests that we actually can obtain meaningful data on well-being rather simply—just by asking people about their well-being. Data on **subjective well-being (SWB)** can provide insight into social welfare levels and the factors that influence well-being.

Collecting data on SWB involves surveying individuals and asking them a question such as: "All things considered, how satisfied are you with your life as a whole these days?" Respondents then answer based on a scale, say, from 1 (dissatisfied) to 10 (satisfied). How much credence can we give to the answers to such questions?

> Research has shown that it is possible to collect meaningful and reliable data on subjective as well as objective well-being. Quantitative measures of [SWB] hold the promise of delivering not just a good measure of quality of life per se, but also a better understanding of its determinants, reaching beyond people's income and material conditions. Despite the persistence of many unresolved issues, these subjective measures provide important information about quality of life.[25]

One of most interesting questions that SWB research can address is the relationship between income level and life satisfaction. We can ask whether the higher-income individuals in a society tend to have higher average SWB. A 2010 paper, based on the results of more than 400,000 surveys conducted in the United States, found that higher income does tend to be associated with higher SWB, but at a decreasing rate.[26] This finding is consistent with the concept of diminishing marginal utility; additional income does increase utility, but each additional dollar tends to result in smaller utility gains. It is also consistent with the idea that people evaluate themselves relative to others.

The paper went on to measure well-being in a different way, referred to as "emotional well-being," which asks people to describe the positive and negative emotions that they feel on a daily basis. In this case, higher income was associated with more positive, and fewer negative, emotions, again at a decreasing rate, *but only up to a point*. At an income level of around $75,000, further increases in income did not improve emotional well-being. The authors conclude that "high income buys life satisfaction but not happiness, and that low income is associated both with low life evaluation and low emotional well-being."

Other research has explored how people's values and goals affect their well-being. Psychologist Tim Kasser and his colleagues have studied the mental and physical consequences of holding materialistic values. They have used surveys to determine how strongly oriented different people are toward financial and material goals, by asking whether it is important that, for example, they "be financially successful," "have a lot of expensive possessions," and "keep up with fashions in hair and clothing." Respondents were also asked about their SWB, as well as questions about how often they experience negative mental and physical symptoms such as depression, anxiety, headaches, and stomachaches. Based on results for both college students and older adults, their results were clear:

> [Those] who focused on money, image, and fame reported less self-actualization and vitality, and more depression than those less concerned with these values. What is more, they also reported experiences of physical symptoms. . . . This was really one of the first indicators, to us, of the pervasive negative correlates of materialistic values—not only is people's psychological well-being worse when they focus on money, but so is their physical health.[27]

Additional research by Kasser and others finds that people who hold materialistic values tend to be less happy with their family and friends, have less fun, are more likely to abuse drugs and alcohol, and to display antisocial symptoms such as paranoia and narcissism.

For some individuals, consumerism itself can be addictive. According to a 2006 paper, about 6 percent of Americans are considered compulsive shoppers.[28] This is similar to the percentage of Americans considered alcoholics. People are classified as compulsive shoppers based on their answers to questions about whether they went on shopping binges, bought things without realizing why, had financial problems as a result of their spending, or frequently bought things to improve their mood. Compulsive shoppers were just as likely to be men as women, but they tended to be younger than average and have a lower income than the average. Compulsive shoppers are more likely to experience depression and anxiety, suffer from eating disorders, and have financial problems.

5.2 AFFLUENZA AND VOLUNTARY SIMPLICITY

Economists have traditionally assumed that more income and more goods are always better, holding all else constant. But we can never hold all else constant. One of the main lessons of economics is that we should always weigh the marginal benefits of something against its marginal costs. In the case of consumerism, these costs include less time for leisure, friends, and family, greater environmental impacts, and negative psychological and physical effects. In short, there can be such a thing as too much consumption—when the marginal benefits of additional consumption are exceeded by the associated marginal costs.

As we have seen, people tend to evaluate themselves relative to other people. The situation of rising consumption levels has been compared to one in which one row of a crowd of spectators stands up in order to see a show better. Then, the row behind them has to stand up, just in order to see as well as before. The same with the row behind them, and so on. Eventually, everyone is uncomfortable standing up, and no one is really seeing any better. Everyone would be better off just sitting down.

Economist Robert Frank discussed this problem in his 1999 book *Luxury Fever.* He suggests that the lavish spending of the superrich, whose incomes have increased dramatically in recent decades, creates pressure on the merely rich to ratchet up their spending as well. This pressure then eventually trickles down to middle- and even low-income individuals. Again, we must consider the cost of this competitive spending.

Even among those who can easily afford today's luxury offerings, there has been a price to pay. All of us—rich and poor alike, but especially the rich—are spending more time at the office and taking shorter vacations; we are spending less time with our families and friends; and we have less time for sleep, exercise, travel, reading, and other activities that help maintain body and soul. . . . At a time when our spending on luxury goods is growing four times as fast as overall spending, our highways, bridges, water supply systems, and other parts of our public infrastructure are deteriorating, placing lives in danger.[29]

Two public television specials, as well as a book,[30] refer to the problem of "affluenza"—a "disease" with symptoms of "overload, debt, anxiety and waste resulting from the dogged pursuit of more." The use of reference groups creates a paradox in consumption: We can apparently never have enough to be satisfied, because (unless we are Bill Gates) there is always someone who has more than we do.

Some people see the solution to affluenza as rejecting consumerism as a primary goal in life. The term **voluntary simplicity** refers to a conscious decision to live with a limited or reduced level of consumption, in order to increase one's quality of life.

voluntary simplicity: a conscious decision to live with limited or reduced level of consumption, in order to increase one's quality of life

> [W]e can describe voluntary simplicity as a manner of living that is outwardly more simple and inwardly more rich. . . . Simplicity in this sense is not simple. To maintain a skillful balance between the inner and outer aspects of our lives is an enormously challenging and continuously changing process. The objective is not dogmatically to live with less, but is a more demanding intention of living with balance in order to find a life of greater purpose, fulfillment, and satisfaction.[31]

The motivations for voluntary simplicity vary, including environmental concerns, a desire to have more free time to travel or raise a family, and to focus on nonconsumer goals. Voluntary simplicity does not necessarily mean rejecting progress, living in the country, or a life of poverty. Some people ascribing to voluntary simplicity have left high-paying jobs after many years, while others are young people content to live on less.

Perhaps the unifying theme for those practicing voluntary simplicity is that they seek to determine what is "enough"—a point beyond which further accumulation of consumer goods is either not worth the personal, ecological, and social costs, or simply not desirable. Unlike traditional economics, which has assumed that people always want more goods and services,* voluntary simplicity sees these as only intermediate goals toward more meaningful final goals. (For more on voluntary simplicity, see Box 8.3.)

5.3 CONSUMPTION AND PUBLIC POLICY

It is unrealistic to expect that a majority of people in rich countries will become adherents of voluntary simplicity. If we accept that overconsumption is problematic, for reasons of ecological impacts, social cohesion, or personal well-being, then we must consider whether government regulations are needed to curb consumerism.

Of course, some people will argue that government intrusion into personal consumption decisions is unwarranted. But current government regulations already influence consumer decisions, for instance, high taxes on products such as tobacco and alcohol and limits on advertising. Rather than dictating consumer behaviors, thoughtful regulations can encourage people to make choices that better align with social and personal well-being. A 2009 book titled *Nudge* proposes that changing the "choice architecture"—how choices are presented to people—can have a dramatic influence on people's behavior.[32] Often this relates to changing

---

*Economists use the term "nonsatiation" to describe the tendency to always want more.

Box 8.3 VOLUNTARY SIMPLICITY

Greg Foyster had a good job in advertising, creating television commercials and print ads in Australia. But in 2012 he and his partner Sophie Chishkovsky decided to give up their consumer lifestyles and bicycle along the coast of Australia, interviewing people who have decided to embrace voluntary simplicity and eventually write a book about their experience.

Voluntary simplicity is a growing movement in Australia, with a popular Web site (www.aussieslivingsimply.com.au) and a regular column on the topic in the *Australian Women's Weekly*. Foyster explains,

> The overall idea is that you should step out of the consumer economy that we're all plugged into and start doing things for yourself because that is how you'll find happiness. The best way to think of it is as an exchange. In our society people trade their time for money, and then they spend that money on consumer items. . . . It's really about stepping back and deciding what's important to you in your life.

Foyster found that his career in advertising conflicted with his personal sense of ethics. His "eureka" moment came during an advertising awards event when he saw colleagues being praised for their efforts to sell people products they didn't need or even want. He realized that most of the world's environmental problems stem from overconsumption, not overpopulation. He was so overwhelmed that he left the event and sobbed. He says,

> When I worked in advertising, I had a decent income, I had a prestigious job, and I was miserable. I chose to leave the industry because it wasn't making me happy; it wasn't my purpose in life. And now I have a much lower income; I work as a freelance writer, which isn't the most prestigious job. But I am so much more happy because I know what is important to me and I'm doing what I love and I have everything I need.

Source: Michael Short, "Seeking a Simple Life," *The Age* (Australia), July 9, 2012.

the default option for a particular choice. For example, employees' retirement savings increase significantly when they are automatically enrolled in a 401(k) savings program, with the option of dropping out if they so choose (an opt-out program), as opposed to a policy that requires them to sign up for the savings program (an opt-in program). People are still entirely free to decide whether to participate in the savings program, but the opt-out option results in more savings for retirement.

Flexible Work Hours

One specific policy to reduce the pressure toward consumerism is to allow for more flexibility in working hours. Current employment norms, particularly in the United States, create a strong incentive for full-time employment, if available. Employees typically have the option of seeking either a full-time job, with decent pay and fringe benefits, or a part-time job with lower hourly pay and perhaps no benefits at all. Thus even those who would prefer to work less than full time and make a somewhat lower salary may feel the imperative to seek full-time employment. With a full-time job, working longer hours with higher stress, one may be more likely to engage in "retail therapy" as compensation.

Europe is leading the way in instituting policies that allow flexible working arrangements. Legislation in Germany and the Netherlands gives workers the right to reduce their work hours, with a comparable reduction in pay.[33] An employer can only refuse such requests if it can demonstrate that the reduction will impose serious hardship on the firm. A Dutch law also prohibits discrimination between full-time and part-time employees regarding hourly pay, benefits, and advancement opportunities. Some government policies encourage part-time employment particularly for parents, such as a Swedish law that gives parents the right to work three-quarter time until their children are eight years old. Norwegian parents also have the right to work part-time or combine periods of work with periods of parental leave.

Such policies encourage "time affluence" instead of material affluence. Economist Juliet Schor also argues that policies to allow for shorter work hours are one of the most effective ways to address environmental problems such as climate change.[34] Those who voluntarily decide to work shorter hours will be likely to consume less and thus have a smaller ecological footprint.

Advertising Regulations

A second policy approach is to focus on the regulation of advertising. Government regulations in most countries already restrict the content and types of ads that are allowed, such as the prohibition of cigarette advertising on television and sporting events. Additional regulations could expand truth-in-advertising laws, ensuring that all claims made in ads are valid. For example, laws in the United States already restrict what foods can be labeled "low fat" or "organic."

Children are particularly susceptible to advertising, as they generally cannot differentiate between entertainment and an ad intended to influence consumers. Again, European regulations are leading the way. Sweden and Norway have banned all advertising targeted at children under 12 years old. Regulations in Germany and Belgium prohibit commercials during children's TV shows.

Another option is to change the tax regulations regarding advertising expenditures. In the United States, companies are generally able to fully deduct all advertising costs. Restricting the amount of this tax deduction (or eliminating the deduction entirely) would create an incentive for companies to reduce their advertising.

Consumption Taxation

Economics tells us that one of the ways to reduce the extent of any activity is to tax it. One option is to impose luxury taxes on specific goods that are seen as representing conspicuous consumption—consumption primarily for the display of high economic status. For example, from 1992 to 2002 the United States imposed luxury taxes on new automobiles that cost more than $30,000. Australia still collects a luxury tax on new vehicles that sell for more than about $60,000.

Rather than classifying particular goods and services as luxuries, some economists prefer broader tax reforms. In *Luxury Fever,* Robert Frank proposes replacing the current emphasis in the United States on taxing income with taxes on consumption. Under his proposal, the tax on a household would be determined by the amount it spends each year. Rather than saving receipts, taxpayers would calculate their annual spending simply as the difference between total income and savings. A certain amount of spending would be exempt from taxation so that low-income households would be exempt from the tax—Frank suggests $30,000 per family. Beyond that, consumption would be taxed at successively higher rates. For example, while the first $30,000 of spending would be nontaxable, he suggests that the next $40,000 of spending be taxed at a 20 percent rate. Then the next $10,000 of spending might be taxed at a 22 percent rate. In his example, consumption tax rates on spending above $500,000 rise to 70 percent.* He argues that such high tax rates on conspicuous consumption are necessary:

> If a progressive consumption tax is to curb the waste that springs from excessive spending on conspicuous consumption, its rates at the highest levels must be sufficiently steep to provide meaningful incentives for the people atop the consumption pyramid. For unless their spending changes, the spending of those just below them is unlikely to change either, and so on all the way down.[35]

Frank notes that both conservatives and liberals have expressed support for a shift from taxation of income to taxation of consumption, although they disagree on the details.

*A progressive tax imposes higher tax rates with higher income levels. We discuss progressive taxation in more detail in Chapter 11.

Exempting all savings from taxation would increase savings rates, which he suggests is reason enough for the shift. But the main objective would be to reduce the pressures toward consumerism and promote true well-being.

> We currently waste literally trillions of dollars each year as a result of wasteful consumption patterns. Much of this waste can be curbed by the adoption of a steeply progressive consumption tax. Taking this step would greatly enhance every citizen's opportunity to pursue independent visions of the good life.[36]

Discussion Questions

1. In what ways do you think money can buy happiness? In what ways can having a lot of money decrease one's happiness? How does money enter into your own conception of what happiness means?
2. Do you believe that the government has a right to influence or otherwise interfere in consumer decisions? What additional policies, if any, do you think are needed regarding consumer behaviors?

REVIEW QUESTIONS

1. What is consumer sovereignty?
2. What is a budget line? How can we show one on a graph?
3. How does a budget line change when one's income changes?
4. How does a budget line change when the price of one of the items changes?
5. What is a utility function? How can we represent one on a graph?
6. What is diminishing marginal utility? What does it imply about the shape of a utility function?
7. What are some of the limitations of the standard consumer model?
8. What is the consumer society?
9. What were some of the key developments in the history of the consumer society?
10. What is the difference between absolute and relative deprivation?
11. What are reference and aspirational groups?
12. About how much is spent annually on advertising in the United States, on a per-person basis?
13. What is the ecological footprint approach to quantifying environmental impacts? What are some of the findings of ecological footprint research?
14. What is green consumerism? What is the difference between "deep" and "shallow" green consumerism?
15. What is subjective well-being?
16. What are the results of research on the relationship between subjective well-being and happiness?
17. What are the results of research on the relationship between materialistic values and well-being?
18. About what percentage of Americans are considered compulsive shoppers?
19. What is voluntary simplicity?
20. What policies might reduce levels of consumerism?

EXERCISES

1. Monifa plans to spend her income on concert tickets and movie tickets. Suppose that she has an income of $100. The price of a concert ticket is $20, and the price of a movie ticket is $10.
   a. Draw, and carefully label, a budget line diagram illustrating the consumption combinations that she can afford.
   b. Can she afford 6 movie tickets and 1 concert ticket? Label this point on your graph.
   c. Can she afford 2 movie tickets and 6 concert tickets? Label this point on your graph.
   d. Can she afford 4 movie tickets and 3 concert tickets? Label this point on your graph.
   e. Which of the combinations mentioned just uses up all her income?
2. Continuing from the previous exercise, suppose that Monifa's income rises to $120. Add her new budget line to the previous graph.
3. Next, suppose that Monifa's income stays at $100, but the price of concert tickets drops from $20 to $12.50 each.
   a. Draw and carefully label both her original and her new budget lines.

b. Can she afford 2 movie tickets and 6 concert tickets after the price drop?

4. Suppose that Antonio's total utility from different quantities of snacks per day is given by the table below.

Quantity of snacks per day	Total utility	Marginal utility
0	0	
1	20	
2	40	
3	60	
4	75	
5	85	
6	90	
7	85	
8	75	

a. Draw and label Antonio's utility function for snacks.

b. Fill in the last column of the table above, calculating Antonio's marginal utility from snacks.

c. Does Antonio always display diminishing marginal utility in his satisfaction from snacks?

d. Assuming Antonio is rational, what is the maximum number of snacks that he could choose to consume per day?

5. Various U.S. government agencies, among them the Food and Drug Administration (FDA) and the Environmental Protection Agency (EPA), include "consumer protection" as one of their goals. The FDA, for example, decides whether drugs that pharmaceutical companies want to sell are safe and effective, and the EPA decides whether particular pesticides are safe for consumer use. Some people believe that such government oversight unnecessarily interferes with companies' freedom to sell their goods and with consumers' freedom to buy what they want. Indicate how you think each of the following individuals would evaluate consumer protection policies, in general.

a. Someone who believes strongly in consumer sovereignty

b. Someone who believes strongly that consumers make rational choices

c. Someone who believes that consumers sometimes have less than perfect information about what they are buying

d. One who believes that consumers can be overly influenced by marketing campaigns

6. Match each concept in Column A with an example in Column B.

Column A	Column B
a. Diminishing marginal utility	1. Janet hopes to become a CEO someday
b. Reference group	2. You decide that you have enough clothing and do not need any more
c. Aspirational group	3. Your income increases
d. Absolute deprivation	4. You feel poor because you cannot afford the same designer clothing as your classmates
e. Relative deprivation	5. The price of one good that you purchase increases
f. Deep green consumerism	6. You start getting bored after watching your third TV show in a row
g. Shallow green consumerism	7. You buy clothing made with organic cotton instead of cotton produced with pesticides
h. Your budget line rotates	8. You compare your car to those of your neighbors
i. Your budget line shifts	9. You cannot afford basic medical care

APPENDIX: A FORMAL THEORY OF CONSUMER BEHAVIOR

A1. THE ASSUMPTIONS

This appendix presents in more detail the standard economic model of consumer behavior. In this model, the consumer is seeking to maximize his or her utility. The consumer is assumed to be well informed and rational and to consider only his or her own preferences, budget, and prices in making a consumption decision. For simplicity, we assume there are only two goods, good X and good Y.

A2. THE BUDGET LINE AND ITS SLOPE

The combinations of X and Y that are available to the household are shown by a budget line, like that in Figure 8.8. The budget line arises because the sum of the consumer's expenditures must add up to—not exceed—the consumer's income. Mathematically:

$$P_x x + P_y y = Income$$

where x and y denote the quantities purchased of each good, and P_x and P_y are their respective prices. This equation can be rearranged, algebraically, into slope-intercept form (i.e., $y = a + bx$, where the intercept a gives the value of y when x equals 0, and b is the slope of the line). This yields:

$$y = \frac{Income}{P_y} - \frac{P_x}{P_y} x$$

For example, in Figure 8.8, income could be $40, the price of X could be $10, and the price of Y could be $5. The budget line crosses the y-axis at $40/5 = 8$ units of Y and has a slope of $-10/5 = -2$. In general, we note that the budget line has a slope equal to $-P_x / P_y$.

Figure 8.8   **The Budget Line and Its Slope**

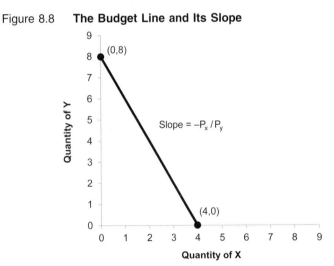

The slope of the consumer's budget line is $-P_x / P_y$.

A3. INDIFFERENCE CURVES

indifference curve: a curve consisting of points representing combinations of various quantities of two goods, such that every such combination gives the consumer the same level of utility

The consumer's preferences concerning the two goods can be illustrated on the same graph by using the concept of **indifference curves** pioneered by the economist Paul Samuelson.

Indifference curves show combinations of the two goods with which the consumer would be equally satisfied (i.e., has the same utility). Indifference curves are generally thought to have the bowed-in-toward-the-origin shape shown in Figure 8.9. This shape arises because we assume that the consumer experiences diminishing marginal utility for both X and Y.

Suppose the consumer starts out at point A, with a large amount of Y (7 units) but relatively little of X (only 1 unit). At point A, the consumer has a fairly low marginal utility of Y, because she is already consuming a lot of it, and a fairly high marginal utility of X, because she has only a little of it. (Refer to the shape of Figure 8.4 if necessary. Utility flattens out if you have a lot of a good and rises steeply if you have little.) She will be willing to give up some of the Y—marginal units from which she is getting relatively little utility, anyway—to get more of

X, a good that still has fairly high marginal utility. If she is just willing to give up 3 units of good Y to get 1 additional unit of good X, then she is indifferent between point A and point B. The slope of the indifference curve can be mathematically shown to be equal to $-MU_x/MU_y$, where MU_x is the marginal utility of X and MU_y is the marginal utility of Y. As we see on the graph, the slope of the indifference curve between point A and point B is -3 (rise/run on a straight line between the points $= -3/1$). The ratio of marginal utilities, MU_x/MU_y is called the **marginal rate of substitution**, which tells how much of one good the consumer is willing to give up to get more of the other.

marginal rate of substitution: how much of one good the consumer is willing to give up to get more of another

However, at point B, the consumer's marginal utility from good Y will have risen from what it was at point A, because she is consuming less of it. Meanwhile, her marginal utility from X will have fallen, because she is consuming more of it. She will be more reluctant to give up more units of Y in exchange for further units of X. Likewise, because she is now consuming more X, she is less eager to get more of it than she was before. This means that if she is presented with further opportunities to trade, she will demand *more X* to compensate her for giving up any more Y. If forced to give up 2 more units of Y, Figure 8.9 shows that she will now require 3 more units of X to keep her just as happy. The slope of the indifference curve between point B and point C is $-2/3$, and the marginal rate of substitution is now 2/3. Indifference curves tend to be steep at low levels of consumption of X and then flatten out as you move to the right, as a consequence of diminishing marginal utility. Thus we have a falling marginal rate of substitution.

Figure 8.9   **An Indifference Curve**

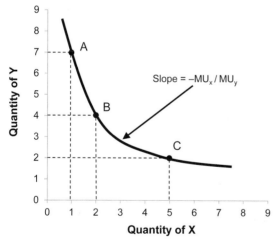

An indifference curve shows all combinations of goods that give the consumer the same level of utility. Its slope is $-MU_x/MU_y$.

A4. UTILITY MAXIMIZATION

Different levels of utility are represented by different indifference curves. Because the standard economic view assumes that consumers always want more of at least one good (and usually of both goods), this "more is better" assumption means that utility rises as you move upward and to the right on the graph. Figure 8.10 shows three examples of indifference curves, corresponding to three different levels of utility.

The consumer's problem, then, is to get to the highest level of utility possible, given her budget. This problem and its solution are illustrated in Figure 8.11. The consumer can afford many points on the lowest indifference curve—much of the curve lies below and to the left of the budget line. If she chose to consume at point C, she would use up all her budget. But this is not the best that she can do. Points A and B would both give her more utility than point C, and point D would give her even more. Points B and D are unobtainable, however, because they are above the budget line.

Figure 8.10   **Different Levels of Utility**

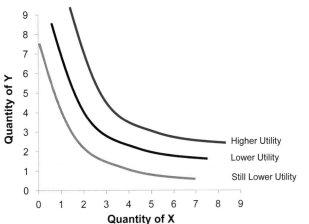

Moving above and to the right, indifference curves represent higher levels of utility.

Figure 8.11   **Utility Maximization**

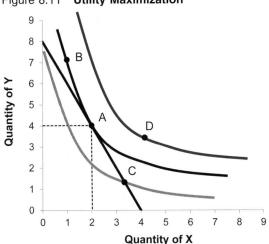

The consumer's utility is maximized by choosing a consumption point on the highest achievable indifference curve. This happens at point A.

The best the consumer can do is get onto the indifference curve that just touches his budget line, at point A, purchasing 4 units of Y and 2 units of X. At point A, the two curves just touch and have the same slope. That is:

$$-\frac{MU_x}{MU_y} = -\frac{P_x}{P_y}$$

which can be algebraically rearranged into:

$$\frac{MU_x}{P_x} = \frac{MU_y}{P_y}$$

This equation states that the consumer will maximize her utility when the marginal utility per dollar spent on X is equal to the marginal utility per dollar spent on Y. If this were not true, and the last dollar spent on good X produced more utility than the last dollar spent on good Y, the consumer could increase her utility by switching a dollar from Y to X. She can continue to increase her utility in this manner until the last dollar spent on each good provides similar marginal utility.

If we add a third good, Z, or as many as we want, the rule remains the same. To maximize utility, a consumer should equate the marginal utility per dollar spent for all goods, or:

$$\frac{MU_x}{P_x} = \frac{MU_y}{P_y} = \frac{MU_z}{P_z} = \dots$$

A5. RESPONSE TO VARIATIONS IN PRICE

We can also use a utility theory graph to theorize about consumer response to a price change. For example, Figure 8.12 shows what might happen if the price of X drops from $10 to $5 (with income held constant at $40). Now the budget line is higher at all points, except where it meets the y-axis. The consumer is thus able to afford more of the goods than before and to reach a higher indifference curve. The consumer portrayed in Figure 8.12 will now choose to consume at point B.

Given the assumptions of this model, it is clear that the consumer has higher utility after the fall in price. Generally, it will be true that consumers will buy more of a good when its price falls. In Figure 8.12, we see that point B is farther to the right than point A.

This is one of the rationales for the downward-sloping demand curve discussed in Chapter 3 on supply and demand. By no means, however, is it the only explanation. First, downward-sloping demand curves may be a useful tool for analyzing the behavior of many other kinds of buyers, such as businesses, nonprofits, and governments. The foregoing is not an explanation for their behavior. Second, the tool of utility theory is not necessary for deriving demand curves. In a 1962 article, economist Gary Becker showed that market purchases of a good will tend to rise when prices fall, even if consumers act only impulsively or out of habit.

What happens to the level of purchases of good Y when the price of good X falls? This is hard to predict without knowing more about the particular goods. This question was discussed under the topics of "substitutes" and "complements" in Chapter 3.

Figure 8.12 **Response to a Change in Price**

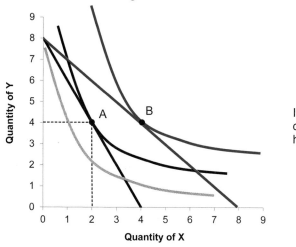

If the price of good X falls, the consumer will be able to reach a higher utility level.

NOTES

1. Tim Jackson, "The Challenge of Sustainable Lifestyles," in *State of the World 2008* (Washington, D.C., Worldwatch Institute, 2008), p. 49.

2. Living Planet Report 2012, WWF, Global Footprint Network, and Zoological Society of London, 2012.

3. Adam Smith, *An Inquiry into the Nature and Causes of the Wealth of Nations* (London: Methuen, 1930), p. 625.

4. Sheena S. Iyengar and Mark R. Lepper, "When Choice Is Demotivating: Can One Desire Too Much of a Good Thing?" *Journal of Personality and Social Psychology* 79(6) (2000): 995–1006.

5. "The Tyranny of Choice: You Choose," *Economist,* December 16, 2010.

6. Daniel T. Gilbert, Elizabth C. Pinel, Timothy D. Wilson, Stephen J. Blumberg, and Thalia T. Wheatley, "Immune Neglect: A Source of Durability Bias in Affective Forecasting," *Journal of Personality and Social Psychology* 75(3) (1998): 617–638.

7. Bradley Johnson, "Big U.S. Advertisers Boost 2012 Spending by Slim 2.8 Percent with a Lift from Tech," *Advertising Age,* June 23, 2013, http://adage.com/article/news/big-u-s-advertisers-boost-2012-spending-slim-2-8/242761/.

8. Material from this section is drawn primarily from Peter N. Stearns, *Consumerism in World History: The Global Transformation of Desire* (New York: Routledge, 2006).

9. Ibid., p. 25.

10. George Ritzer, *Enchanting a Disenchanted World: Revolutionizing the Means of Consumption* (Thousand Oaks, CA: Pine Forge Press, 1999).

11. Douglas J. Goodman and Mirelle Cohen, *Consumer Culture* (Santa Barbara, CA: ABC-CLIO, 2004), p. 17.

12. Ibid., p. 68.

13. See David E. Shi, *The Simple Life: Plain Living and High Thinking in American Culture* (Athens, GA: University of Georgia Press, 2007).

14. Goodman and Cohen, *Consumer Culture,* pp. 1–4.

15. Juliet Schor, "What's Wrong with Consumer Society?" in *Consuming Desires: Consumption, Culture, and the Pursuit of Happiness,* ed. Roger Rosenblatt (Washington, DC: Island Press, 1999), p. 43.

16. Juliet B. Schor, *The Overspent American* (New York: Harper Perennial, 1998).

17. See, for example, L.J. Shrum, James E. Burroughs, and Aric Rindfleisch, "Television's Cultivation of Material Values," *Journal of Consumer Research* 32 (2005): 473–479.

18. Thomas C. O'Guinn and L. J. Shrum, "The Role of Television in the Construction of Consumer Reality," *Journal of Consumer Research* 23(4) (1997): 278–294.

19. Goodman and Cohen, *Consumer Culture,* pp. 39–40.

20. Debra J. Holt, Pauline M. Ippolito, Debra M. Desrochers, and Christopher R. Kelle, "Children's Exposure to TV Advertising in 1977 and 2004," Federal Trade Commission, Washington, DC, 2007.

21. David Orr, "The Ecology of Giving and Consuming," in *Consuming Desires,* pp. 145–146.

22. John C. Ryan, and Alan Thein Durning, *Stuff: The Secret Lives of Everyday Things* (Seattle: Northwest Environment Watch, 1997).

23. U.S. Environmental Protection Agency, "Municipal Solid Waste Generation, Recycling, and Disposal in the United States: Facts and Figures for 2011," EPA530-F-13–001, Washington, DC, 2013.

24. Donald Rogich, Amy Cassara, Iddo Wernick, and Marta Miranda, "Material Flows in the United States," World Resources Institute, Washington, DC, 2008.

25. Joseph Stiglitz, Amartya Sen, and Jean-Paul Fitoussi. "Report by the Commission on the Measurement of Economic Performance and Social Progress," www.stiglitz-sen-fitoussi.fr/documents/rapport_anglais.pdf, p. 16.

26. Daniel Kahneman and Angus Deaton, "High Income Improves Evaluation of Life but Not Emotional Well-Being," *Proceedings of the National Academy of Sciences* 107(38) (2010): 16489–16493.

27. Tim Kasser, *The High Price of Materialism* (Cambridge, MA: MIT Press, 2002).

28. Lorrin M. Koran, Ronald J. Faber, Elias Aboujaoude, Michael D. Large, and Richard T. Serpe, "Estimated Prevalence of Compulsive Buying Behavior in the United States," *American Journal of Psychiatry* 163 (2006): 1806–1812.

29. Robert H. Frank, *Luxury Fever: Why Money Fails to Satisfy in an Era of Excess* (New York: Free Press, 1999).

30. John de Graaf, David Wann, and Thomas H. Naylor, *Affluenza: The All-Consuming Epidemic* (San Francisco: Berrett-Koehler, 2005).

31. Duane Elgin, "Voluntary Simplicity and the New Global Challenge," in *The Consumer Society Reader,* ed. Juliet Schor and Douglas B. Holt (New York: New Press, 2000).

32. Richard H. Thaler and Cass R. Sunstein, *Nudge: Improving Decisions About Health, Wealth, and Happiness* (New York: Penguin Books, 2009).

33. See Anders Hayden, "Europe's Work-Time Alternatives," in *Take Back Your Time: Fighting Overwork and Time Poverty in America,* ed. John de Graaf (San Francisco: Berrett-Koehler, 2003).

34. See Juliet B. Schor, *Plentitude: The New Economics of True Wealth* (New York: Penguin Press, 2010).

35. Frank, *Luxury Fever,* p. 216.

36. Ibid., p. 224.

9 Markets for Labor

When you next look for a job—during the summer, perhaps during the school year, or after you graduate from college—what characteristics will you be seeking in your job? Some possibilities include: good pay, opportunities for advancement, opportunities for learning, doing a variety of interesting activities, a feeling that you are contributing something of value, and a comfortable and congenial work environment.

And what will you want to avoid? Studies of human happiness find that one of the leading causes of dissatisfaction in modern life is a long commute. Other things that are generally not preferred include work that is dangerous, dirty, or physically uncomfortable, mindlessly repetitive, or exhausting. Low pay is generally a disincentive, as is a lack of benefits such as health care and paid vacations.

Traditionally, economics has been most concerned with understanding the compensation attached to different jobs. We will see that some of the other characteristics of work just mentioned may have some impact on compensation—and are of importance in their own right as well.

1. Labor in the Traditional Neoclassical Model

"The labor market" is a familiar phrase, but markets for labor are different from other markets in many ways. For a start, consider what is sold in a labor market. It is not human beings; slavery, one of the worst practices in human history, is illegal everywhere in the world (although it still exists, even in developed countries). Rather, what is sold in labor markets is what is sometimes called "labor power"—that is, what a given person is able and willing to do in a given amount of time. An employer who hires a certain amount of labor power (X number of people working for Y hours) expects that it will produce a certain level of output. But it is not the actual output that is being purchased in this market—it is the contribution that employees make toward the production of output. This makes labor markets somewhat more abstract than markets for the things that labor can directly produce, such as sweaters, jet planes, or a sales pitch over the telephone.

We examine some unique characteristics of labor markets and some of the factors that determine the level of earnings for different kinds of jobs. However, we start with a familiar supply-and-demand picture as a point of reference. The very simple neoclassical model that we discussed in Chapter 7, for the most part, treats the demand for and supply of labor very much like other things that are bought and sold on markets. Labor, in this model, is demanded by profit-maximizing firms and is supplied by utility-maximizing households. The stylized utility-maximizing consumers who were described in Chapter 8 are now simply dressed in overalls or suits and sent into the workplace, with the single goal of earning the money that will allow them to be consumers.

On the side of the demander—the firm—this model assumes a number of characteristics that are not usually found in the real world: for example, that all firms are powerless entities forced by competition to maximize profits and minimize costs; that productivity can be easily measured; and that historical and social contexts can be ignored. (Markets with powerless firms are described in Chapter 16; more realistic markets are described in Chapter 17.)

The traditional model, which we quickly survey, describes how these sets of actors make decisions about *how much* labor will be supplied and purchased, and at *what price (wage)*.

1.1 LABOR DEMAND

On the demand side of the labor market, consider a firm seeking to hire a specific type of labor. What should guide the firm's decisions about how much labor to hire? From the viewpoint of a profit-maximizing firm, an additional person-hour of labor will be desirable if it increases profits, but not otherwise. Hiring an additional person-hour does two contradictory things to the firm's profit position:

• Costs are raised by the amount of the additional wages paid.
• Revenue is increased by the value of the increase in output produced by the additional hour of work.

Clearly, as long as the firm gets *more* additional revenue than it has to pay out in additional wages, it should keep hiring workers. But if it is getting *less* in additional revenue than it is paying out in additional wages, it should reduce the number of workers that it hires. The profit-maximizing decision rule for the firm can thus be expressed as:

$$MRP_L = MFC_L$$

marginal revenue product of labor (MRP_L): the amount that a unit of additional labor contributes to the revenues of the firm

marginal factor cost of labor (MFC_L): the amount that a unit of additional labor adds to the firm's wage costs

where MRP_L is the **marginal revenue product of labor,** or the amount that an additional unit of labor contributes to revenues, and MFC_L is the **marginal factor cost of labor,** or the amount that the additional unit of labor adds to the firm's wage costs.*

In other words, the firm should hire additional units of labor until the marginal benefits just equal the marginal costs. We will see very similar reasoning in Chapter 16, concerning a firm's decision about how much to produce—for exactly the same reasons. A formal derivation of this rule is described in the appendix to this chapter.

If the firm buys labor services in a competitive market, MFC_L will simply be the competitively determined market wage, and the rule will simplify to:

$$MRP_L = Wage$$

The traditional neoclassical model offers an elegant solution for this simplified case. It gives a formalized statement of the intuitive sense that workers should be rewarded in relation to their contribution to the organization. However, actual measurement of productivity is difficult. Moreover, the market valuation of a production process—its direct outputs and its side effects—can differ from social valuations because of externalities and distributional issues. Hence, you must be careful about inferring that, in the real world, any observed wage accurately represents the worker's contribution to society's well-being.

1.2 LABOR SUPPLY

The traditional model of consumer behavior presented in Chapter 8, in which consumers seek to maximize their utility, can be extended to decisions about labor supply. Specifically, we can consider how much time an individual is willing to work, given different wage levels.

---

*Note that hiring an additional unit of labor may increase other costs, such as energy and supplies. These costs would be subtracted from the MRP_L to determine the net increase in revenues associated with an additional unit of labor.

In this model, the potential labor market participant is assumed to have perfect information and to be free to vary his or her hours of paid work. However, the labor market model differs from the model of consumer choice in that here the "budget line" is defined according to the number of *hours* that the individual has available to "spend" on activities, rather than according to the amount of money that he or she has to spend on goods.

The model imagines essentially three kinds of activities:

• paid work
• unpaid work
• leisure

Hours "spent" on paid labor result in wages, which in turn give opportunities for consumption. Hours spent on other activities yield utility either directly (as in the case of leisure) or indirectly through unpaid production. (In this model, paid work is generally assumed to yield no direct utility.) According to the model, the potential labor market participant will choose the level of labor market participation that maximizes his or her utility.

Two forces govern the supply of factors of production: the total quantity available at any point in time and the willingness of their owners to actually supply them. Labor is fundamentally "owned" by the individual, who may be thought of as renting out his or her services when working for pay. In many cases, actual decisions about supplying paid labor are made not by individuals but jointly with other household members, as part of a general plan for family support and investments for the future. Continuing with the simple model, however, for now we discuss paid labor supply as though an individual person is making the decision. Also, because this chapter discusses labor *markets,* we focus on labor that is performed in exchange for a wage or salary.

The Opportunity Cost of Paid Employment

In general, the willingness of an individual to supply work may be analyzed in terms of the wages and other benefits that he or she can get, compared to the benefits to him or her of not supplying it or supplying it elsewhere. An individual weighing these decisions is assessing the opportunity cost of labor supply. This idea may be applied broadly; the "costs" and the "benefits" of supplying labor may be seen in terms of money but also reflect any other gains or losses that are valued by the individual.

Most of the alternatives facing an able-bodied adult who is considering going out to work for a wage or salary fall under the following headings:

• *Household production:* A paid job may reduce the time that can be spent in productive but unpaid work at home—raising children, caring for elderly or sick relatives, cooking, keeping house, gardening, and the like.
• *Education:* As an alternative to seeking paid work immediately, individuals may decide to stay in school or return to school—either to prepare for better-paid future employment or simply to enjoy the process of education or the life of a student.
• *Self-employment:* People can work for themselves in household enterprises, making crafts, providing personal services (such as day care or yard work), writing, painting, or starting another home-based business. (The income of self-employed proprietors tends to be a mix of returns to labor, returns to capital, and profits. In this chapter, we do not discuss the nature of their labor compensation because we are focusing only on people who work *for wages or salaries.*)
• *Leisure:* Work cuts into the time available for playing music, fishing, camping, reading novels, playing or watching sports, hanging out with friends, playing computer games, traveling, and other pleasurable activities.

To the extent that you value any of these pursuits and reduce the hours you devote to them when you take a paid job, that job has a "cost." The cost is the lost opportunity for other activities. In addition to the opportunity costs associated with your time, you may incur direct monetary costs when taking a paid job, such as the costs of work-related clothing and transportation. You may incur increased monetary expenditures for things that otherwise might have been home-produced (using your time resources), such as child care and meal preparation.

The Benefits of Paid Employment

At the same time, of course, paid jobs have many benefits. Most obvious is the fact that they are *paid*. In a contemporary industrialized economy, households need some money income to survive and to participate in society. Even if paid work is unpleasant, boring, stressful, or even demeaning, wages and salaries are strong extrinsic motivators that encourage individuals to supply their labor.

In addition, however, paid work itself has great intrinsic significance in most people's lives. Evidence from state lotteries in the past few decades, for example, illustrates this point. In a number of cases, winners of large lottery prizes have decided *not* to quit their jobs entirely, even when they could easily have done so. They usually cite their friendships on the job and the sense of identity that they have found in their work as reasons for continuing at least some of their usual work activities. For billions of people, the nature of the work experience is a decisive part of the quality of life: The work process determines whether a major part of life will be boring or interesting, lonely or companionable, comfortable or filled with bodily discomfort, tranquil or full of anxiety, stunts personal growth or offers opportunities to develop mental or physical capacities.

Household production and self-employment can also supply many of the same intrinsic rewards, though often with less companionship and social interaction. Sometimes, people who only work at unpaid household production activities feel marginalized due to a social perception that only work for wages or salaries is "real work." Again, we focus on paid work in this chapter, but we recognize that many people provide valuable contributions to society without being paid.

1.3 THE INDIVIDUAL PAID LABOR SUPPLY CURVE

We look at the decision of an individual to supply various amounts of hours over a week or year, assuming, for the moment, that the worker can find part-time, full-time, or overtime paid jobs that satisfy his or her desires. For now, we also abstract from a worker's choices among different kinds of paid jobs, focusing only on the decision about how much time to put into paid work. As in many other supply curve thought experiments, we abstract from all considerations *other than* the relationship between price and quantity. In this case, we look only at the effect of different wage levels on the individual's willingness to supply labor to the market.

In Figure 9.1 we show an upward-sloping supply curve like those presented for markets for coffee in Chapter 3. The "wage," which we use as a shorthand term for the price paid for an hour of labor, is on the vertical axis. In practice, many blue-collar and service jobs pay an hourly *wage,* whereas professional and managerial jobs tend to pay a weekly or monthly *salary* independent of how many hours they actually work. Jobs may also pay in the form of tips, bonuses, or stock options, and they may provide fringe benefits such as health insurance. For our simple supply-and-demand analysis, we include all these in the concept of a "wage." The quantity of labor, which might be thought of as the number of hours that the individual works in a week or a year, is on the horizontal axis.

Does this "usual" curve apply to labor? Following one line of reasoning, we can see that in many cases it does. From the perspective of an individual, the upward-sloping supply curve reflects the *substitution effect* of changes in prices: Individuals decide whether to substitute the benefits of paid work for the benefits of other activities. When offered a very low wage,

Figure 9.1   **Upward-Sloping Labor Supply Curve**

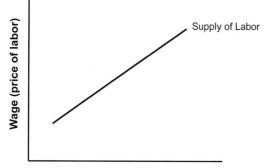

Like other supply curves we have discussed, the labor market supply curve may be expected to be upward-sloping.

an individual may be reluctant to join the labor market, or to supply many hours of work, because he or she may get more benefits from self-employment or other activities. The higher the market wage rate, the more attractive it is to engage in additional paid labor instead of unpaid household work, education, self-employment, or leisure.*

However, one of the important reasons that an individual works is to earn an income, which in turn is used to buy goods and services that he or she can then enjoy. As the wage gets higher and higher, will the person *always* want to work more and more? Probably not. Economists explain this in terms of the fact that leisure (and perhaps other unpaid activities) are usually "normal goods," in the sense explained in Chapter 4. As people earn higher incomes, they may also want more time to enjoy the fruits of their labor. The rising wage also has an *income effect:* The higher the market wage, the more leisure (and other unpaid activities) that people might want to "buy." Because "buying" leisure means reducing work hours, the paid labor supply curve will be *downward*-sloping if the income effect is dominant.

backward-bending individual paid labor supply curve: a pattern that arises because, beyond some level of wages, income effects may outweigh substitution effects in determining individuals' decisions about how much to work

People may have a target level of income in mind, beyond which they have less need for additional money. As we saw in Chapter 8, workers early in the industrial era often had such income targets. Increases in wages above the traditional level led individuals to take longer weekends and offer fewer hours of work the next week. Today such extreme cases of income "targeting" are rare, but there still is a tendency for some people to reduce their hours of work as their income rises. In such a case, the substitution effect may dominate at low wage levels, but the income effect dominates at high wage levels. The result is a **backward-bending individual paid labor supply curve,** as shown in Figure 9.2.

Figure 9.2   **Backward-Bending Individual Labor Supply Curve**

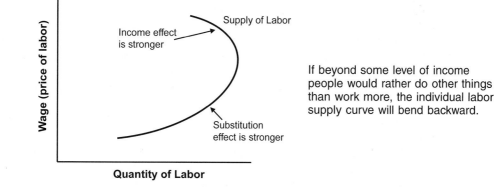

If beyond some level of income people would rather do other things than work more, the individual labor supply curve will bend backward.

*We are assuming that the potential worker can enjoy at least a minimal standard of living from activities other than market work when the wage is too low to make market work attractive. In situations of dire poverty, however, this may not be the case, and people may need to work two or three jobs at very low wages just to get by.

The presence of the income effect makes individual paid labor supply different from the usual supply curves of businesses or other economic actors. As businesses or nonprofits rarely have a target level of revenues, they will display no income effect. Usually, even if high revenues allow some employees to enjoy more leisure (e.g., the founder might cut back on his or her work hours), the organization as a whole will expand its operations, perhaps by hiring more people.

1.4 HOW THE STANDARD MODEL EXPLAINS VARIATIONS IN WAGES

Among the things that economists are especially eager to understand about labor markets are the reasons for differences in wages. Why do star basketball players make so much more than aerospace engineers, who earn so much more than preschool teachers? In addition, within the same job definition it is possible to find workers who receive very different compensation, even though they seem to have equivalent qualifications. Are such patterns of wage differentials determined solely by the logic of markets? If not, what other forces affect them?

Some economists stress productivity differences as nearly the sole source of wage variation over the long run. This emphasis requires a number of assumptions: that people behave in a rational, purely self-interested way, that market forces are strong, and that markets are fully competitive. A high wage, in this view, is merely a sign that an individual is making a highly valued contribution.

The demand for labor—the employers' willingness to pay for different types of labor services—is related to just *how productive* workers are. Employers generally are not willing to pay their workers more than the value that each one contributes to what the employer finally sells—what we have called marginal revenue product of labor. Employers who can get away with paying workers less than their MRP_L are motivated to do so in order to minimize costs and therefore to maximize profits. Theoretically, this should not be possible, if the labor market is truly competitive. In that case, workers who do not receive a "fair" wage in one place (a wage equal to their MRP_L) can find another employer who will offer the wage that actually represents the worker's contribution to the value of output.

Human Capital

In the standard model, the main reason for variations in labor productivity and, hence, in wages is human capital. This consists of people's knowledge and skills. It is affected by:

- formal education and job-related training
- informal education and job-related experience
- innate talents
- the physical and mental health of the worker*

Obviously, different kinds of jobs require different kinds of human capital. Different levels of human capital often result from different levels of investment, in terms of education and training. The wages for skilled occupations, such as aerospace engineers (e.g., compared to farm manual laborers), reflect in part the fact that aerospace engineers have normally engaged in formal training to acquire skills and credentials, whereas farm laborers largely use more common skills that, it is assumed, most people possess.

We can see the impact of education levels in Figure 9.3, which shows median earnings by education level in the United States. Those with a master's degree earn about 22 percent more than those with just a bachelor's degree, and those with a bachelor's degree earn 63 percent more than those with just a high school diploma.

---

*The last determinant of human capital is sometimes overlooked; however, malnourishment and mental or physical ill-health can seriously affect a worker's energy, motivation, and general capacity to use her or his knowledge and skills.

Figure 9.3 **Median Weekly Earnings of U.S. Workers, by Educational Attainment, 2012**

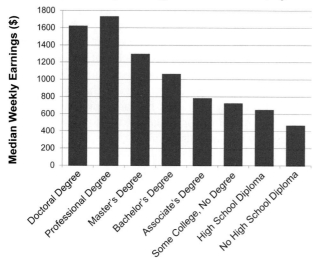

Median earnings tend to rise with higher levels of educational attainment.

Source: U.S. Bureau of Labor Statistics, "Employment Projections," www.bls.gov/emp/ep_chart_001.htm, May 22, 2013.

The income benefits associated with education have increased in recent decades. For example, between 1975 and 1999 the ratio of average earnings of those with advanced degrees to those with a high school diploma increased from 1.8 to 2.6. According to analysis by the U.S. Census Bureau, the increase in the economic benefits of education

> may be explained by both the supply of labor and the demand for skilled workers. In the 1970s, the premiums paid to college graduates dropped because of an increase in their numbers, which kept the relative earnings range among the educational attainment levels rather narrow. Recently, however, technological changes favoring more skilled (and educated) workers have tended to increase earnings among working adults with higher educational attainment, while, simultaneously, the decline of labor unions and a decline in the minimum wage in constant dollars have contributed to a relative drop in the wages of less educated workers.[1]

general human capital: knowledge and skills that workers can take with them as they move from one employer to another

In addition to formal education, human capital may also be accumulated through on-the-job training. For example, a more experienced farm laborer can do some of the work faster, or to a higher standard, and might therefore be paid more than a new hire. Human capital acquired on the job may be either general or employer-specific. **General human capital** consists of the knowledge and skills that workers can take with them if they leave one organization and go to work for another. **Employer-specific human capital** consists of knowledge and skills that are valued only by a particular employer. For example, many farming and engineering skills may be general, but knowledge about a specific piece of land or crop, or a specific engineering project, may be useless away from a particular employer.

employer-specific human capital: knowledge and skills that have been gained on a particular job and are useful only as long as a worker remains with the same employer

How do employers judge the human capital embodied in a prospective worker? Ideally, before offering a wage, they should be able to assess which skills the worker possesses and how much these skills will contribute to productivity. Because this assessment is often difficult to make, employers may use credentials, such as educational degrees or training certificates, as proxies for observed skills. A firm that is seeking to employ an aerospace engineer would look for someone with the appropriate degree. A college degree is a common **screening method** that employers use to limit their job search to specific candidates. Other screening methods used by employers include requirements that applicants have a minimum number of years of work experience, or certification that they have been trained to do specific tasks.

screening methods: approaches used by employers to limit their job search to specific candidates

signaling theory: a theory of the value of an education that suggests that an educational credential *signals* to an employer that a potential worker has desired character traits and work habits

In a subtler, but also common, example, firms may require credentials such as a college degree, or even a graduate degree, not because they are convinced that the undergraduate or graduate education has directly provided essential knowledge or skills but because the possession of the degree *signals* that the person is a certain kind of worker. Educational credentials such as these are used by employers as reassurance that the applicant possesses desirable characteristics such as self-discipline, patience, and the ability to work under pressure. The **signaling theory** of the value of education suggests that the value of a college education may be not so much in the way it creates human capital as in how it solves information problems for employers, revealing, or signaling, what type of worker a person already was before starting college (or became during college).

Other Factors Affecting Productivity

A worker's productivity may also depend on several factors that are at least somewhat under the control of the employer. These include:

- *The level of effort with which workers work:* The workers' level of effort on a job includes the pace at which they work, as well as how careful they are to do the job right. The level of work effort depends on employer management practices, such as rewards and punishments, but it may also depend on historical, cultural, personal, or other circumstances beyond the manager's control.
- *The efficiency with which workers apply their skills:* Management is also an important contributor to worker efficiency; a good manager can put each worker in the job that best suits his or her abilities, can see to it that work groups are organized in more rather than less efficient ways, and can try to organize an optimal interaction of workers with the technology available to them.
- *The quantity and characteristics of the resources available to each worker:* In the simplest terms, those who work with more, newer, and better technology and equipment, energy resources and materials, are more productive. A lack of the appropriate quantity or quality of resources can make even the most skilled and motivated worker unproductive.

Discussion Questions

1. Think of a job that you have held. Describe how your productivity on the job was affected by:
   a. your skills
   b. the organization of the workplace (whether it encouraged efficiency)
   c. your level of effort (and what it was about the job that encouraged this specific level of effort)
   d. the resources you had available to work with
2. In any production process, when one factor limits what can be produced and other factors are in abundant supply, that one factor is called the *limiting factor.* Continue to reflect on the job that you considered in Question 1. Which contributor to productivity would you identify as the "limiting factor" in that case? What change would have been most effective in bringing about increased productivity?

2. LABOR SUPPLY AND DEMAND AT THE MARKET LEVEL

labor force participation rate: the percentage of the adult, noninstitutionalized population that is either working at a paid job or seeking paid work

In order to think about labor markets in terms of supply and demand, we need to consider how labor supply at the individual level translates into labor supply at the market level. We start with a bit of history.

Since the early twentieth century, industrialized countries have shown a striking trend toward an increase in the (paid) **labor force participation rate** (defined as the percentage of the adult, noninstitutionalized population that is either working at a paid job or seeking paid work). In most countries, this increase has been accounted for entirely by the increasing labor force participation of women. The increase in women's participation in the labor force has been partially offset by a small decline in men's participation; most of the change for men has resulted from decisions to stay in school longer or to retire earlier.

If we think about these social trends in "opportunity cost" terms, we can see that they involve changing perceptions of the costs and benefits of entering the paid labor market. The cost of this choice has declined as improved technologies for the home and the increased availability of substitute services (such as child care and prepared meals) have reduced the number of hours of household work strictly necessary to maintain a household. The benefits have risen in societies where activism and changes in social norms and laws have opened a greater variety of paid occupations to women. The perceived benefits have also risen to the extent that increased consumerism (discussed in Chapter 8) has encouraged people to focus more on making money at the expense of time for household production or leisure.

2.1 MARKET LABOR SUPPLY

The supply of labor to a particular market, such as the national market for aerospace engineers or the market for restaurant wait staff in Chicago, can be thought of as the horizontal sum of the supply curves of those individuals who could participate in the market. Although the supply curves of some individuals might bend backward, the supply curve for a particular market can generally be assumed to have the usual upward slope shown in Figure 9.1. This is because employers can obtain a larger quantity of labor in two ways. The first is by persuading workers already in the market to supply more hours, in which case income effects could become important. The second way, however, is to attract more workers to enter the particular market, either by drawing them away from other jobs or by drawing them into the paid labor force from other activities. For most of these workers, we can assume that this substitution effect dominates, and so the aggregate supply curve will slope upward.

Market labor supply is relatively wage elastic if a variation in the wage brings a large change in the quantity of labor supplied. This could occur if the (upward-sloping sections of) individual worker's supply curves are elastic. It also occurs when a rise in the wage readily draws more workers into the particular market. Markets for types of labor that use general or more easily acquired skills generally tend to have relatively elastic supply curves. If the wage for local restaurant wait staff rises, for example, people may leave jobs as salesclerks and delivery truck drivers in order to offer their services to restaurants. If the wages paid by restaurants fall, wait staff may fairly readily look for jobs as salesclerks and drivers.

Market labor supply is relatively wage inelastic, however, if a variation in the wage brings little change in the quantity of labor supplied. At the extreme, the supply of labor might be "fixed" for some occupations, at least in the short run. For example, there are only so many aerospace engineers in the United States at any point in time. (What slope would the supply curve have?) Raising the wage might draw a few engineers out of retirement or self-employment, but it cannot instantly produce a large quantity of new engineers, because obtaining the skills necessary for this job requires many years of education. A drop in the wage, similarly, might not much decrease the quantity of labor supplied in the short run, because the engineers' specialized skills are not valued nearly as much in other markets. Changes in the quantity supplied will occur only over the long run, as high wages attract more students to train for the job or low wages cause more engineers to become dissatisfied and retrain for something else. The United States has also used immigration policies to increase the quantity of labor supplied in certain high-skilled areas where there are labor shortages. (For a real-world example of a labor shortage, see Box 9.1.)

So far, we have discussed the responsiveness of quantity to price *along* a supply curve. Market labor supply curves can also *shift,* in response to nonprice factors, just like the shifts in other supply curves that we studied in Chapter 3. For the economy as a whole, for example,

BOX 9.1　A SHORTAGE OF DOCTORS

Nevada is experiencing a shortage of doctors. According to a 2013 study by John Packham, a health policy researcher at the University of Nevada, the state has one of the lowest numbers of primary care physicians per capita in the United States. Packham also notes a shortage of orthopedic and general surgeons, which will become more critical as the state's population ages. The impacts of the doctor shortage include longer wait times to get an appointment, higher costs, and lower-quality health care.

Many other regions of the United States are also experiencing a shortage of doctors, with this problem forecast to increase. According to the Association of American Medical Colleges, in 2015 the doctor shortage will reach 30,000. By the mid-2020s, the shortage will approach 70,000. One reason for this is that doctors have migrated to specialized, high-paying fields such as dermatology and cardiology, instead of primary care and general surgery. Also, the demand for health care has increased due to an ageing population. Expanded health-care coverage under the Affordable Care Act (i.e., Obamacare) will also increase the demand for doctors.

On the supply side, the number of doctors is relatively fixed in the short term. It commonly takes about 10 to 15 years from the time an undergraduate student decides to pursue a career as a doctor to the time he or she can actually start practicing. Thus the labor market for doctors is an example of a market that can persist in a condition of disequilibrium for many years.

In Nevada it is particularly difficult to attract doctors to rural areas, particularly those with high minority populations. Trudy Larson, director of community health sciences at the University of Nevada, Reno, says, "There are plenty of students who apply to medical school, but we need to diversify the physician workforce. We need to provide an outreach for people who are interested in health care [so they can] know the pathway."

Source: Editorial Board, "Nevada Must Get Creative Solutions for Doctor Shortage," *Reno Gazette-Journal*, August 3, 2013.

---

labor supply curves tend to shift outward over time because of population growth. Changes in laws and norms and in household technology caused the supply curve to shift outward in many areas when women joined men seeking employment in many high-skill markets such as law and medicine.

Changes in one labor market may also have repercussions in other markets. For example, a rise in the wages of salesclerks (a movement *along* the supply curve for salesclerks) might decrease the supply of wait staff (that is, *shift* the supply curve for wait staff back), as people exit the wait staff market in order to take advantage of the higher wages now being offered for salesclerks.

2.2 MARKET LABOR DEMAND

For the most part, the demanders of labor (i.e., potential employers) are organizations, including businesses, nonprofits, and governments. A very small fraction of employers are households or individuals, who may directly employ people for tasks such as in-home child care and domestic service.

The demand curve for paid labor—whether for an individual organization or for an entire market—can generally be thought of as downward sloping, like the demand curves we examined in previous chapters. The reason for the downward slope is as follows. When wages are high, employers have incentives to economize on the use of labor. They may cut back on their activities or try to substitute other inputs (e.g., another type of labor, machinery, or computerization) for the type of labor whose wage is high. But when wages are low, employers may be able to expand their productive activities or substitute relatively cheap labor for other inputs.

Labor demand will tend to be relatively wage elastic if there are good substitute inputs available and if the wage bill is a large proportion of total production costs (so that the employers are motivated to seek out substitutes). Labor demand will tend to be relatively inelastic if no good substitute inputs are available and the wage bill is a small proportion of total costs.

The labor demand curve may shift if there is a change in the demand for the good or service that it is used to produce, if technological developments alter the production process, if the number of employers changes, or if the price or availability of other inputs changes. For example, when an organization experiences a fall in demand for its products, its labor demand curve will shift back as well.

2.3 MARKET ADJUSTMENT

Still using the same simplifying assumptions as in Chapter 3 about how markets work, we can examine how market forces might influence wage rates and the quantity of labor employed.

For example, let Figure 9.4 depict a stylized market for e-commerce Web site designers. In the late 1990s, e-commerce was booming, and demand for the services of such designers was high, as depicted by demand curve D_1. The short-run supply curve was fairly inelastic, because the job required a certain amount of specialized education and talent. Stories in the newspapers at the time touted the fat salaries being offered to talented, self-taught computer experts just out of high school and told of people being aggressively recruited by businesses, with large signing bonuses.

In 2000, however, many investors decided that e-commerce was not going to be the money maker that they had expected, and investment funds for e-commerce dried up considerably. Many firms went out of business, and others laid off many of their employees. The market for Web site designers went from boom to bust. We can think of this as the demand curve shifting to D_2.

Comparing equilibrium E_1 to equilibrium E_2, we can see that the model predicts that the number of Web site designers will fall and that the wage will fall as well. In fact, many Web site designers became unemployed and had to search for other types of jobs, while signing bonuses and premium wage offers became a thing of the past. Students who had been training to enter the field found that they had to make other plans.

Labor market adjustment takes time—the movement from E_1 to E_2 is not instantaneous. It takes time for workers to change their career plans and for employers to adjust wages and salaries, which may be set by labor contracts. Given that labor market conditions are constantly changing, it may be unclear whether a particular labor market is in equilibrium. Much of the recent labor economics research has focused on the persistence of "friction" in labor markets, which slows the transition of workers from one job to another. In particular, unemployed workers may spend considerable time searching for a job that meets their specific requirements.

Figure 9.4   The Market for Website Designers

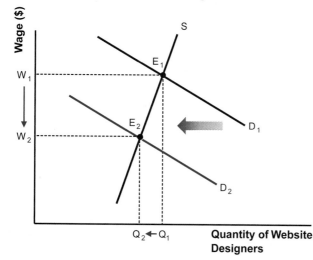

A drop in the demand for website designers leads to lower employment and a fall in wages.

The existence of labor market friction means that a significant number of jobs are commonly available, even when unemployment is high. For example, in June 2013 unemployment was 7.6 percent, and 11.8 million people were unemployed, but there were also 3.9 million job openings. Discussion of labor conditions at a national level is an important topic in macroeconomics.

Discussion Questions

1. Suppose that your college or university substantially raises the wages that it offers to pay students who tend computer laboratories, monitoring the equipment and answering questions. What do you think would happen to the quantity of labor supplied? Why? Where would the extra labor hours come from? Do you think the supply of this kind of labor is elastic or inelastic? Why?

2. Opticians fit people who have poor eyesight with glasses or contact lenses, prescribed by an optometrist. Beginning in the 1990s, technological developments in laser eye surgery made surgery an increasingly popular way of correcting bad eyesight. What effect do you think this development had on the market for opticians? Draw a graph, carefully showing whether the shift is in demand or supply and showing the resulting predicted changes in the quantity of labor demanded and in the wage.

3. CHANGES IN JOBS AND IN THE LABOR FORCE

For the remainder of this chapter, we move away from the idealized world of perfect competition and equilibrium markets, to paint a more realistic portrait of paid work in the United States. We start with a reminder that what we see today is not exactly the way that things were in the past—and is not necessarily the way that things will be in the future, either. In 1933, when unemployment was widespread because of the Great Depression, the U.S. Senate voted overwhelmingly to establish a 30-hour workweek. The House of Representatives voted down this measure, but in 1938 the Fair Labor Standards Act became law, establishing the 40-hour workweek as the legal norm. By the 1960s U.S. workers were regarded with envy in much of the rest of the world, as having legal protection for relatively less time spent in paid work. This is no longer the case. What happened?

3.1 EMPLOYMENT FLEXIBILITY

For most of the twentieth century, Americans generally thought of "a job" (or at least a good job) as something that you typically did Monday through Friday, 40 hours a week, for a wage or salary and benefits (such as health insurance and pension plans). People often expected to stay in the same job for years or even decades. In recent years, however, it has become popular to talk about how employment is becoming more "flexible." But the term "flexibility" has two very different meanings, depending on whether it is considered from the point of view of the worker or the employer.

One meaning of "flexible" work is that it is more suited to workers' varying needs. Some workers—especially professional and managerial workers—now enjoy "flextime" or the ability to set their daily starting and ending times. Job sharing and part-time work allow employment to be more easily combined with family care, studying, or leisure pursuits. However, many jobs remain inflexible and are not "family friendly." The United States is practically alone among industrialized countries in lacking a federal law that mandates paid parental leave for new parents. According to a 2013 book that studied nearly 200 countries, 180 of those mandated paid leave to new mothers, and 81 require paid leave to fathers.[2] In the United States, a two-parent family is entitled to 24 weeks of parental leave but without pay. In most other industrialized countries, families receive 52 or more weeks of parental leave (as much as 318 weeks in France!), with 22 weeks of that with full-time pay.[3] The effects of insufficient parental leave fall disproportionately on women:

In the absence of paid parental leave policies, traditional gender roles that involve women as "caregivers" and men as "providers," and the typically lower earnings of mothers (relative to fathers) in the labor market, create strong incentives for women to reduce their employment and take on a large majority of child care responsibilities. The most obvious problems associated with such outcomes are that women bear a disproportionate burden of child care responsibilities and pay both a short- and a long-term penalty in the labor market.[4]

"Flexibility" can refer to people's ability to change jobs when they want to or retrain for new careers. However, the term "flexibility" has also been used to refer to policies that make things easier for employers—and often make life more difficult from a worker's perspective. Many employers would like to have complete discretion over setting their workers' hours and pay, to offer few or no benefits, and to be able to terminate employees quickly and without fuss. Increasingly, some firms have hired "independent contractors," "consultants," or part-time workers to avoid having to extend the benefits that they provide to their regular full-time employees. More people now work nonstandard workweeks, regardless of whether they want to, in an economy that is increasingly "24/7."

To some extent, "flexibility" from the employee's perspective is also in the interest of employers. Workers who are better rested and less stressed about their families, thanks to accommodating schedules and expectations, can be more productive. And to some extent, "flexibility" from the employer's perspective is also in the workers' interest. An overly rigid labor market, in which workers are too expensive and difficult to fire, could cause employers to try to minimize the number of workers that they hire, thus reducing the number of jobs. From a well-being perspective, the question is how to achieve a good balance in this aspect of work organization.

3.2 WORK HOURS

Another important labor issue is weekly work hours and the availability of paid time off for vacations and illness. Although some workers may wish to work long hours for financial or personal reasons, recent surveys suggest that one-third to half of American workers would prefer to work shorter hours with an equivalent reduction in pay.[5]

The average number of hours worked each week by employed Americans has stayed relatively constant since the mid-1970s, at around 39 hours. The percentage of workers working long hours (49 or more hours) generally increased from the 1970s to the 1990s, but has generally declined since then (to about 16 percent of workers in 2010).

International comparisons generally look at average annual work hours, instead of weekly work hours, to account for differences in vacation time. Average annual work hours among employed Americans have stayed relatively constant since the 1980s at around 1,800 hours.[6] This differs from the situation in most other industrialized countries, where average work hours have declined in recent decades. For example, over the period 1980 to 2006 average annual work hours declined by 18 percent in Germany, 15 percent in France, and 7 percent in the United Kingdom.

Figure 9.5 shows the average annual work hours in several OECD countries in 2012. The average work year in the United States was 1,790 hours, compared to 1,728 in Australia, 1,654 in the United Kingdom, and 1,479 in France. We used to think of hard-working Asian populations as suffering much longer work hours than Americans, and, of course, this is still true for the poorer countries in Asia. However as of 2000 Japan, a former leader in long hours, had reduced its annual work hours to below the U.S. level. The difference of 400 hours per year between American and German workers is the equivalent of having American workers put in an additional 10 full-time weeks per year!

Movements in Europe toward shorter standard working hours have often been motivated by stronger labor unions and by macroeconomic considerations, with the goal of reducing

Figure 9.5   **Average Annual Hours Worked, Select OECD Countries, 2012**

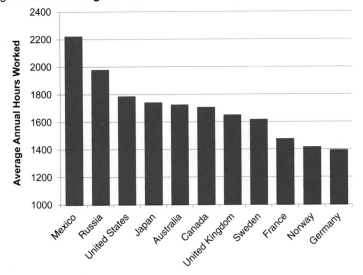

Average annual hours worked varies significantly across countries.

Source: OECD Employment Outlook 2013, Statistical Annex, Table K.

unemployment. Other goals are to encourage strong families and to reduce consumption for ecological reasons. Most European countries have legal limits on the number of hours per week an employee is allowed to work, and paid vacation time of at least one month per year is standard—even for workers who are just starting. European employers are also normally required to provide several holidays, with pay. The United States is the only industrialized country that does not require employers to provide any paid vacation days or holidays.[7]

3.3 IMMIGRATION AND LABOR MARKETS

One of the most controversial topics in discussions of labor markets and wages is the impact of immigration, particularly the immigration of workers seeking low-wage jobs. According to the traditional neoclassical labor model, an influx of unskilled workers willing to work for relatively low wages will clearly drive down equilibrium wages in markets for unskilled labor and displace some domestic workers. But as in any economic analysis, we must consider all the costs and benefits of immigration to determine its overall impact on society.

Economists generally agree that immigration, both legal and illegal, does decrease the wages of unskilled workers, mainly those without a high school diploma. But they disagree on the magnitude of this impact. According to one study, between 1980 and 2000 immigration to the United States reduced the wages of men without a high school diploma by 7 percent. However, another study found that the wage reduction was only about 1 percent, and decreased over time as education levels increased.[8]

Other research has estimated the impact of immigration to the United States differently, depending on whether workers were born in the United States.[9] The results indicate that due to immigration from 1994 to 2007 wages fell for foreign-born workers in the United States by about 5 percent but slightly *increased* for U.S.-born workers, by 0.4 percent. These findings suggest that new immigrants compete for jobs mostly with previous immigrants, rather than taking jobs away from U.S.-born workers. Meanwhile, U.S.-born workers may benefit as new immigrants increase the demand for goods and services.

Despite common media representations to the contrary, a National Research Council study found that U.S. immigrants collectively pay more in taxes than they consume in public services and benefits. According to economist Michael Clemens, the net effect on American society of immigration is "definitely positive." He notes that immigration led to a massively more prosperous economy. Everyone across the board is way, way better off now. The whole economy is the richest and most powerful in the world, and of all time, and that's the effect that quadrupling our population, largely through immigration, had.[10]

Discussion Questions

1. What evidence have you seen—in your own family, or through the media—of increasing "flexibility" in labor markets? Do you think that these changes have been beneficial, harmful, or both?
2. Do you think that all employees should receive paid vacation? What are the advantages and disadvantages of mandated vacation time?

4. ALTERNATIVE EXPLANATIONS FOR VARIATIONS IN WAGES

The standard model of labor markets assumes that they operate in such a way that everyone is paid exactly the amount of his or her contribution to revenues. We saw that discussions of wages in this model focus on human capital, but with some allowance for the idea (emphasized especially in business schools) that the employer also has some responsibility for getting the best out of the workers. They may do so by providing appropriate management, a motivating and efficient work environment, and complementary factors of production that will maximize the workers' productivity.

The idea of the employer's responsibility complicates the simple story because it blurs the question of which factors should receive which part of the compensation. If a new manager can get increased productivity out of the same group of workers, should the increased revenue that results all be assigned to the manager? Should it be shared with the workers?

Consider another scenario, in which one group of workers is provided with new equipment that makes them more productive, while another group stays at a lower level of productivity, using the older equipment. What should be done with the increased revenue resulting from the more productive work group? Some of it, clearly, can be used to pay for the equipment (maybe repaying a loan that was taken out to purchase it), but after that cost has been covered, then should it go to the workers in that group? Or should it be shared among both groups, on the grounds that they are all putting in the same amount of time and effort? Or should it go to the manager who had the idea to introduce the new equipment? As we continue to look at variations in wages, we see that issues of fairness and justice frequently combine with the economic issues.

4.1 COMPENSATING WAGE DIFFERENTIALS

Early economic thinkers put forth the idea that extra pay is required to attract workers to take jobs that are especially unappealing, compared to other work that is available for people at the same skill level. Apart from the wage, what would make one job either less or more appealing than another? A short list would probably include:

- *Working conditions.* These include physical discomfort or danger, stress, whether the job is interesting, how the worker is treated, degree of autonomy, flexibility of hours.
- *Nonwage benefits.* Some firms provide nonwage benefits such as more vacation time, educational benefits for the worker's children, meals at company cafeterias, and subsidized housing.
- *Opportunities for advancement* either within the firm or by moving to a new firm.
- *Social contribution.* Many workers will ask not only whether the job is good for themselves but also whether it contributes to society and is consistent with their beliefs.
- *Job security.* Because there are costs to being unemployed or searching for work, the likelihood that a job will continue is an important characteristic.

compensating wage differentials: the theory that, all else being equal, workers will demand higher wages for jobs with unappealing characteristics, and be willing to accept lower wages for jobs with better characteristics

It is possible to find some real-world examples in which people demand, and get, a higher wage to take on jobs with less appealing characteristics. For example, because most people prefer to work days, night-shift work generally pays slightly more than day-shift work, even though the skills needed and the tasks accomplished are identical. In some cases, people accept a lower-than-necessary wage to perform an especially appealing job. The example that professors usually give is the job of being a professor: For those who like the intellectual life, it may be a very rewarding job, even though the pay is often below what professors believe that they could earn elsewhere. The idea that workers will demand higher wages for jobs with unappealing characteristics, and be willing to accept lower wages for jobs with better characteristics, is known as the theory of **compensating wage differentials**.

At the same time, you have probably noticed that many of the least attractive jobs in a society—such as garbage collection, agricultural work, and boring and repetitive work in clothing manufacture or meat processing—are found at the lowest end of the pay scale. This is partly because they require relatively little in the way of formal qualifications. To the extent that this is true, the low wages do not violate the theory of compensating wage differentials; this theory compares only jobs of equal skill. But even within the class of jobs that require few qualifications, some unpleasant jobs pay particularly badly, and one tends to find that the workers here belong to particular groups—usually minority or female, nonunionized, and often immigrants.

For the theory of compensating differentials to operate in reality, it is necessary for workers to have good information about job conditions and risks and to be able to move freely to alternative jobs for which they are qualified. It turns out that, especially when unemployment is high, the effect of compensating differentials within jobs in the same skill class can be swamped by other factors, such as bargaining power or discrimination.

4.2 SOCIAL NORMS, BARGAINING POWER, AND LABOR UNIONS

In any society it is usually possible to find a set of norms about how much most types of jobs *should* be paid. A norm is an expectation, usually based to some degree on experience, but sometimes lagging, as when, for example, employers find that they can get a certain type of work done more cheaply by machines than by people. According to the standard labor model, we would expect that the wage rate would fall to a level that allows people to be competitive with cheaper machines. In fact, employers are usually slow to offer lower wages, and people will resist taking the offers if made, because each side is aware that this would be contrary to existing norms.

monopsony: a situation in which there is only one buyer but many sellers. This situation occurs in a labor market in which there are many potential workers but only one employer.

In addition to norms, an essential aspect of any labor market is the bargaining power on each side. One obvious situation that allows a firm to bargain down wages, below what is the norm in other places, is if it is the only employer to whom a certain group of workers can look for work. This is called a condition of **monopsony**—with only one buyer but many sellers. In the 1900s, for example, some manufacturing companies (including Hershey's for chocolate and Pullman for railway cars) set up "company towns" in which they were the sole major employer. Remote mining towns and logging camps are other examples. In such cases, employers have more discretion in setting wages than if workers could easily choose between working for them and working for other employers. The workers may have to accept the company's demands as the price of keeping their jobs—unless they have the ability and the determination to leave the area.

In other situations, workers have market power in the sale of their services. This can happen if they have unique talents. It can also happen if a strong union represents all the workers in a particular occupation or region, so employers have to bargain with one organization representing a number of sellers. Then employers may have to accept union demands as the price of remaining in business; the only limit is that if wages exceed a certain level, an employer may find it more profitable to close its local operation and reopen in a region where labor is cheaper.

bilateral monopoly: the situation in which there is only one buyer confronting only one seller

oligopsony: the case of a relatively small number of buyers

labor unions: legally recognized organizations that collectively bargain for their members (workers) regarding wages, benefits, and working conditions

These examples—a single employer, on the one hand, and a single "star" or union federation, on the other—represent the extremes of concentration of power in the labor market. If a single employer (buyer) faces a single seller, the case can be described as a **bilateral monopoly**. In this case, results will be determined by bargaining, rather than by any kind of auction procedure. The outcome depends on the strength, cleverness, and perhaps political power of the parties and on the skills of professional mediators and litigators.

More common in labor markets are cases of **oligopsony**, in which there are a relatively small number of buyers. For example, in the U.S. music-recording industry, oligopsonistic record label *buyers* of music face uniquely talented but as yet unorganized *sellers* of musical work.

Labor unions are legally recognized organizations that collectively bargain for their members regarding wages, benefits, and working conditions. Unions first appeared in the mid-nineteenth century, but they were not legally recognized in the United States until 1935. As seen in Figure 9.6, membership in labor unions in the United States increased until the mid-1950s, when about one-quarter of the labor force was unionized. Since then, membership in unions has gradually but steadily declined. In 2012, only about 11 percent of workers in the United States belonged to a union. Labor union membership is much higher in the public sector than the private sector. About 36 percent of public sector employees belong to a union, but only 7 percent of private sector workers.

One of the reasons for the decline in union membership in recent decades has been an anti-union regulatory environment. Perhaps most famously, in 1981 President Ronald Reagan responded to an illegal strike by air traffic controllers, who were federal employees, by giving them 48 hours to return to work or face termination. More recently, since 2011 states such as Wisconsin and Indiana have passed new laws limiting the power of labor unions. Another reason for the decline of labor unions has been a shift in employment from traditional unionized occupations such as manufacturing to service occupations in which it is more difficult to unionize, such as retail and restaurant workers.

Union membership rates are higher in most other industrialized countries. For example, union membership is 18 percent in Australia, 26 percent in the United Kingdom, 29 percent

Figure 9.6   **Union Membership in the United States, 1940–2012**

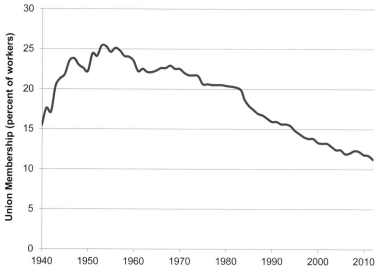

Union membership reached a peak of around 25 percent of the labor force in the 1950s, but has declined since then to only 11 percent in 2012.

Source: U.S. Bureau of Labor Statistics, Union Membership Data from the National Directory Series and Union Affiliation Data from the Current Population Survey.

in Canada, 55 percent in Norway, and 70 percent in Finland.[11] However, in most countries union membership rates have been declining in recent years.

Labor unions have generally been effective at providing good-paying jobs for their members. According to the U.S. Bureau of Labor Statistics, the average weekly earnings of unionized workers in 2012 were $943 per week, compared to average earnings of $742 for non-union workers. Union workers are also more likely to have employer-provided benefits such as health insurance and paid vacations.

Some economists see the decline in labor union membership as a positive development, arguing that unions had pushed wages to above-market levels.[12] This argument concludes that while unions were probably necessary to counter the excessive power of corporations in the first half of the twentieth century, they had become a source of market inefficiency by the end of the century.

Other economists see labor unions as a necessary way for workers to bargain on an equal footing with management. The decline of unions is widely considered to be a contributing factor in the rise of economic inequality in the United States, which we discuss in more detail in Chapter 10. Also, the benefits of unions may extend beyond those who actually belong to them.

> [Unions] affect nonunion pay and practices [by instituting] norms and practices that have become more widespread throughout the economy, thereby improving pay and working conditions for the entire workforce. . . . Many fringe benefits, such as pensions and health insurance, were first provided in the union sector and then became more commonplace. Union grievance procedures, which provide due process in the workplace, have been adapted to many nonunion workplaces. . . . [Unions] remain a source of innovation in work practices (e.g., training and worker participation) and in benefits (e.g., child care, work-time flexibility, and sick leave).[13]

4.3 EFFICIENCY WAGES AND EMPLOYEE MORALE

efficiency wage theory: the theory that an employer can motivate workers to put forth more effort by paying them somewhat more than they could get elsewhere

Economists have theorized that employers may sometimes pay wages somewhat above the market-determined level as a way of motivating and retaining workers. **Efficiency wage theory** proposes that workers will work harder and "smarter" when they know that their present employer is paying them more than they could receive elsewhere. Because these wages are above the market-clearing level, there is likely to be a queue of potential workers who would like to get the relatively high wages. This fact adds to employee motivation, because they understand that if they were to shirk and be fired there would be plenty of applicants for their position.

In a perfectly competitive labor market, the workers, knowing they could get a job elsewhere at the same wage, would be fairly indifferent about whether their current employer wants to keep them on. If an employer pays more than the going wage, however, the employee has an incentive to try to hold on to their particular job. He or she may be motivated by the fear of losing the current "good" job and having to take one that pays less. The extra effort may also be motivated by a sense of gratitude, or identification with the firm, because we tend to like people who treat us well. Thus it is theorized that efficiency wages can be profit maximizing: The cost to the firm of the extra wages may be more than made up for by the superior work effort and loyalty that they elicit. (See Box 9.2 for more on the potential benefits of efficiency wages.)

employee morale: the attitude of workers toward their work and their employer

Researchers have found that **employee morale**—the attitude of workers toward their work (and toward their employer)—can be very important in explaining productivity variations among workers who have the same skills and are using identical equipment. Morale is a subtle thing that can be analyzed in relation to many factors, including particular personalities, work organization and management, traditions within a firm or a culture, and relative pay.

BOX 9.2 GOOD JOBS ARE GOOD FOR BUSINESS

According to research by Zeynep Ton at Massachusetts Institute of Technology (MIT), providing employees with "good" jobs and paying efficiency wages can frequently be good for business, too. She notes that this idea runs counter to prevailing notions of cost minimization.

The conventional wisdom is that many companies have no choice but to offer "bad" jobs—especially retailers whose business models entail competition by offering low prices. If retailers invest more in employees, customers will have to pay more, so the assumption goes.

She studied several businesses that provide their employees with good jobs, including Trader Joe's and Costco. Trader Joe's starting salary of around $40,000 per year is about twice what many of its competitors offer. Costco's wages are about 40 percent higher than those of their main competitor, Walmart's Sam's Clubs. Both Trader Joe's and Costco also offer good opportunities for advancement. Turnover at these companies is low, and employee morale is relatively high. They are both also known for high-quality customer service.

Ton finds that, rather than hurting these firms' profits, they actually financially outperform their competitors. For example, annual revenues per square foot are $986 at Costco, but only $588 at Sam's Club. Sales rates at Trader Joe's are about three times that of a typical U.S. supermarket. She notes that companies offering well-paying jobs also institute policies that promote worker efficiency, including training workers for a variety of tasks and allowing them to make relatively small decisions on their own. Ton concludes:

> Today many retail managers believe that there is a tradeoff between investing in employees and offering the lowest prices. That is false. Retailers that persist in believing in it forgo the opportunity to improve their own performance and contribute the kind of jobs the U.S. economy urgently needs. When backed up with a specific set of operating practices, investing in employees can boost customer experience and decrease costs. Companies can compete successfully on the basis of low prices and simultaneously keep their customers and employees happy.

Source: Zeynep Ton, "Why Good Jobs Are Good for Retailers," *Harvard Business Review* (January–February 2012): 124–131.

In some cases, employers try to increase good feelings through direct means, such as by hosting parties, giving nonmonetary honors to let employees know that they are appreciated, or having "team-building" activities designed to increase cooperation among coworkers and identification with the organization.

A key factor in morale is perceived equity: whether the workers feel that they are being treated fairly by management, especially compared to expectations raised by history and by the wider culture. For example, people have expectations about the relative wages of different jobs. If the wage for one job goes up, there is strong psychological pressure for the wages of what are seen as related jobs (whether they are paid more, less, or the same) to rise enough to keep the wages in about the same relation.

4.4 DUAL LABOR MARKETS

dual labor markets: a situation in which *primary* workers enjoy high wages, opportunities for advancement, and job security, while *secondary* workers are hired with low wages, no opportunities for advancement, and no job security

The theory of **dual labor markets** also presents a different picture from the standard labor model, based on the idea that there can be different segments within a labor market. Although not all economists agree with the theory, it is useful for explaining some real-world labor outcomes.

The theory describes labor markets in which the "primary" portion of a workforce is motivated by high wages, opportunities for advancement, job security, and perhaps other favorable working conditions. Employment in the "secondary" workforce, by contrast, is more closely driven by market conditions. These workers receive generally lower wages, have minimal opportunities for advancement (even if they increase their human capital), and have low job security. Obviously, many workers in the secondary sector would prefer to work in primary sector jobs. Secondary sector workers could be assumed to be willing to accept something less than the normal wages in primary sector jobs; yet those employers do not jump on the chance to lower their wage bill.

Such labor market segmentation may take place across firms. A primary sector of large, established firms (or entrenched government agencies), which use some of their surplus revenues to pay high wages, may exist side by side with a secondary sector of smaller organizations that are more subject to competitive pressures.

Dual labor markets may also exist within a single organization. For example, a firm may employ regular workers with health and retirement benefits and, alongside them, hire temporary workers on short contracts with no benefits. In many colleges and universities, tenured faculty constitute the "primary" workforce. Then lecturers, adjuncts, and research associates, who constitute a secondary workforce, are hired as the need arises—and let go when the need falls. Such a structure allows an employer to keep a loyal core of employees *and* to avoid making new long-term commitments in times of temporary high demand. But for an individual worker, moving from the secondary to the primary labor force may be difficult indeed. Workers in the secondary sector have fewer opportunities to build up human capital and may quickly develop an "unstable"-looking work history.

An extreme type of dual labor market is what some economists call a "winner-take-all" market, such as the ones for star athletes, famous actors, and top managers. In such markets, the rewards for being in first place are vastly greater than the rewards for being a step down, even if the actual difference in talents and skills between the top tier and the next is negligible. Welfare analysis applied to such markets would find significant inefficiency. Very few people can actually get into the top tier in, for example, Olympic sports or an acting career; yet the rewards for winning are so appealing that many individuals devote huge amounts of time and effort to trying to "reach for the gold." Except in cases in which the effort to "be the best" is rewarding in itself, those who unsuccessfully devote their lives to the effort would probably have happier, more productive lives working toward different goals.

4.5 DISCRIMINATION

labor market discrimination: a condition that exists when, among similarly qualified people, some are treated disadvantageously in employment on the basis of race, gender, age, sexual preference, physical appearance, or disability

Not all social norms and customs that influence the labor market can be considered benign. **Labor market discrimination** exists when, among similarly qualified people, some are treated disadvantageously in employment on the basis of race, gender, age, sexual preference, physical appearance, or disability. Workers who belong to disfavored groups may be paid less for the same work, may be denied promotions, or may simply be excluded from higher-paying and higher-status occupations.

Historically, much labor market discrimination, particularly against African Americans and other minorities, was based on racist beliefs that certain groups were innately inferior. Some discrimination against women was similarly based on sexist notions of inferiority. However, sexual discrimination was also historically rooted in social norms that reserved better-paying jobs for men (who were assumed to be supporting families), while making women (who were assumed to have husbands to rely on) solely responsible for providing unpaid household labor and family care.

Discriminatory attitudes may be held by employers, who discriminate on the basis of their own biases, expectations, and beliefs. They may also be held by customers or coworkers. This case poses a dilemma for employers, even if they themselves are not prejudiced. For example, suppose that a law firm hires a skilled minority lawyer, but clients feel more confident being represented by European-American lawyers. The firm may find that the new lawyer attracts little business to the firm. A construction firm that hires a female forklift driver or a preschool that hires a male teacher may find that the morale of its other workers sinks, as the workers react badly to seeing someone of the "wrong" sex in "their" jobs. More insidiously, discriminatory attitudes can become self-fulfilling prophecies: Even though the minority lawyer, the female construction worker, and the male preschool teacher are all fully qualified in a technical sense, their contribution to the firm can be low, and perhaps even negative, if social norms create an environment in which their skills go unused or work group cooperation is jeopardized. Employers concerned with immediate productivity may therefore fail to hire disfavored groups, even if they themselves do not harbor discriminatory beliefs about racial differences or gender roles. Such discrimination can be eliminated only by socially coordinated—and even courageous—action.

In Figure 9.7 we compare median weekly earnings in the United States of full-time, year-round workers in various groups, using government data from 2013. *Median* earnings are at a level where half the people in the group make more and half less. We see that median earnings vary significantly by both race and gender. The median earnings of black male workers were about 77 percent of the earnings of their white male counterparts, and the median earnings of Hispanic male workers were only 67 percent of white male earnings. Disparities among female workers of different races also exist, although the differences are somewhat less pronounced. White female workers only earn 82 percent of the earnings of their white male counterparts. Sexual disparities are also evident among male and female workers of other races.

We must realize that the data in Figure 9.7 are not necessarily evidence of wage discrimination. Some variations in wages may be due to other factors such as differences in experience, education, and occupational choice (although some of these differences may also be a result of discrimination). For example, we saw earlier in the chapter that educational attainment can have a significant impact on earnings. Education levels vary by race. About 30 percent of white individuals have a bachelor's degree or higher, but only 20 percent of black and 14 percent of Hispanic individuals have at least a bachelor's degree.[14] So differences in education levels may explain the variation in wages by race, rather than discrimination. But again, differences in educational attainment may be a result of past, and current, discrimination.

Educational attainment does not vary significantly by gender in the United States. So the differences in earnings between male and female workers in Figure 9.7 cannot be attributed to differences in education. Part of the explanation for women's lower earnings is that women have traditionally had less work experience than men, on average. Men as a group have tended to work more continuously at their jobs, whereas, given social norms and, sometimes, individual preferences or requirements concerning family responsibilities, many mothers participate in the labor market less than full time when their children are young. To the extent that time on the job can contribute to productivity, this could explain some of the difference.

occupational segregation: the tendency of men and women to be employed in different occupations

Another important factor in explaining earnings differences by gender is **occupational segregation**—the tendency of men and women to be found in different kinds of jobs. For example, in the United States, jobs like bookkeeper, dental hygienist, child-care worker,

Figure 9.7   **Median Weekly Earnings, Select Groups of U.S. Workers Age 25–54, 2013**

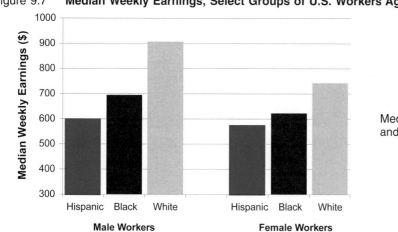

Median earnings vary based on race and gender.

Source: U.S. Bureau of Labor Statistics, "Usual Weekly Earnings of Wage and Salary Workers," *Economic News Release,* July 18, 2013.

registered nurse, and teacher of young children are held overwhelmingly by women. Meanwhile, men notably dominate in occupations such as construction, metal working, truck driving, and engineering. Occupational segregation could be a result of differences in preferences, or it could also reflect discrimination. For example, existing stereotypes may lead more women to become nurses while doctors are more likely to be men.

Statistical studies suggest that about a third of the differences between men's and women's pay in the United States can be associated with differences in occupational choice. Various reasons have been offered to explain why the sorts of jobs women tend to work at pay less on average. One explanation is that, because women were historically "crowded" into a narrow range of occupations, the supply curve in these job markets was artificially shifted outward, thus lowering the wage. Some have suggested that the average difficulty level of the job or the skill required might be less for "female" jobs. Others argue that differences in preferences between male and female workers could lead women to trade high wages for other beneficial job characteristics (such as flexibility in working hours). And still others argue that entrenched wage norms systematically devalue certain kinds of work (e.g., work involving emotional empathy or work with children).

Even after accounting for differences in education, experience, *and* type of job, however, over a third of the difference between men's and women's earnings in the United States remains unexplained. That is, even comparing men and women with equal qualifications who hold the same jobs, differences in pay remain. In the United States, discrimination by sex and race in hiring and wages was made illegal by Title VII of the Civil Rights Act of 1964. (This act also covered discrimination by "color," religion, and national origin. Later acts have addressed discrimination according to age and disability, and various states and localities have passed laws concerning employment treatment on the basis of sexual preference.) Enforcement, however, has proved difficult. Evidence suggests that bias, both blatant and subtle, still plays a significant role. (See Box 9.3 for more on labor discrimination.)

BOX 9.3   LABOR DISCRIMINATION BY FEDEX

In March 2012 the delivery company FedEx reached a settlement with the U.S. Department of Labor over allegations that the company discriminated against more than 20,000 job seekers. As part of the settlement, FedEx agreed to pay $3 million in back wages and offer jobs to about 2,000 rejected applicants as new openings become available. The company also agreed to revise its hiring practices to avoid future discrimination.

The allegations were brought against FedEx by the Labor Department's Office of Federal Contract Compliance Programs. The office said it found evidence of discrimination in hiring on the basis of sex, race, and national origin based on a regular audit of hiring practices. Such audits are conducted for all companies that contract with the federal government for services and goods.

Of the rejected applicants, 61 percent were female and 52 percent African American—percentages that were disproportionate to the number of applicants. As one example of discrimination, it was found that women were automatically excluded from certain positions that required the lifting of heavy objects. Hiring rates for Hispanics and Native Americans were also significantly lower than hiring rates for whites.

Labor Secretary Hilda L. Solis commented on the settlement: "When you do business with the government, we expect you to do the right thing. That includes giving all Americans an equal shot at a good job. It's about more than just the law—diversity is smart for business."

Source: Steven Greenhouse, "FedEx Agrees to Pay $3 Million to Settle Bias Case," *New York Times,* March 21, 2012.

Discussion Questions

1. "Economists assume that people just want to make as much money as possible." Is this statement correct or incorrect? Of the nonwage working conditions listed in the text, which ones are most important to you as you think about your future career?

2. Think about your current job or the last job that you held. Would you say that it is in a "primary" or "secondary" labor market? To what extent do you think that the factors discussed above—human capital, market power, compensating wage differentials, or discrimination—explain the wage and working conditions you experience(d)?

5. WAGES AND ECONOMIC POWER

In Section 4, we considered various explanations for why wages vary among different groups of employees. In this final section, we look at changes in overall wages over time, based on data for the United States. In order to understand how wages have changed over time, it is necessary to address the topic of economic power. In particular, how much of total revenues must firms pay their workers versus how much do they allocate in other ways, including to profits and taxes?

5.1 WAGE TRENDS

Figure 9.8 repeats a graph that we presented in Chapter 0, showing the time trend for real (inflation-adjusted) median weekly wages and corporate profits in the United States from 1980 to 2012. After adjusting for inflation, median weekly wages in 2012 were nearly the same level they were in 1980. Meanwhile, corporate profits, also adjusted for inflation, nearly tripled.

Historical data indicate that American workers fared much better earlier in the twentieth century. According to the U.S. Census Bureau, real average annual earnings increased by a factor of about four between 1900 and 1970.[15] During the 1970s real earnings essentially stopped increasing. *Household* income continued to increase slightly beyond the 1970s, only because more people per household entered the labor force.

Figure 9.8 suggests that corporations have effectively been able to dramatically increase their profits in the past few decades without having to pay their workers higher wages and salaries. Meanwhile, the incomes of management executives, particularly those at the very top, have soared. As we also discuss in Chapter 10, the pay of chief executive officers (CEOs) of large U.S. corporations in 1965 was 20 times the pay of an average worker. But in 2012, CEO pay stood at 273 times the pay of an average worker!

Are CEOs really worth so much more today than they were 50 years ago? It would require the use of very questionable assumptions to make the case that either the supply of CEOs has greatly diminished or the demand for them has greatly increased, relative to the supply and demand for

Figure 9.8   **Real Median Weekly Wages Versus Real Corporate Profits, United States, 1980–2012**

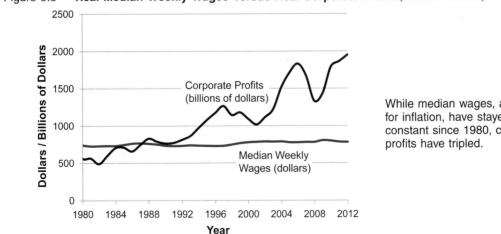

While median wages, adjusted for inflation, have stayed virtually constant since 1980, corporate profits have tripled.

Sources: U.S. Bureau of Economic Analysis, National Income and Product Accounts Tables; U.S. Bureau of Labor Statistics, Weekly and Hourly Earnings Data from the Current Population Survey.

workers. However, American culture has evolved along with the rise in executive pay so that the lack of protest has suggested that people accepted these relative valuations for different kinds of work, at least until the emergence of the Occupy Wall Street movement in 2011.

These trends indicate a shift in economic power, away from workers and toward corporate profits and executive compensation. American workers have lost economic power as a result of various factors, including globalization, technological change, and the decline of labor unions (which we also discuss further in Chapter 10). (For a real-world illustration of the relative fortunes of workers, CEOs, and corporations, see Box 9.4.)

Box 9.4 Wage Cuts and Record Profits

Caterpillar, maker of bulldozers, backhoes, and other construction machinery, is widely seen as one of the most aggressive companies in seeking steep concessions from employees during labor negotiations. In 2012 the company pressed its long-term workers to accept a six-year wage freeze, while also instituting a two-tier wage system, so that new hires are put on a significantly lower wage scale than those who had been there longer. Wages for those employed at Caterpillar for at least seven years average $26 per hour. However, new employees are typically given an initial wage of only $13 per hour.

The company has stated that such concessions are necessary so that they can remain competitive. Rusty L. Dunn, a Caterpillar spokesman, said the company's stance is that wages should reflect market conditions, and that such adjustments would help Caterpillar "keep competitive when times are bad." But Caterpillar reported profits in 2012 of $5.7 billion. If Caterpillar's 2012 profits had been divided among all employee salaries, each worker would have earned an *additional* $45,000. If even a third of the profit had gone to additional employee salaries, they could each have received an additional $15,000 that year.

Meanwhile the compensation of Caterpillar's CEO, Douglas Oberhelman, increased by 113 percent between 2010 and 2012; his total compensation in 2012 was $22.4 million. Only $6 million of this was in direct salary, with the rest in stock options and other incentives. (A large part of the compensation of top management in large modern corporations comes in the form of gifts of stock and/or stock options. The latter are often, in effect, permissions to buy the company's stock at a relatively low price, and sell it at a higher price.)

Timothy O'Brien, president of an Illinois union that represents Caterpillar workers, notes, "A company that earned [record profits in 2011 and 2012] should be willing to help the workers who made those profits for them. Caterpillar believes in helping the very rich, but what they're doing would help eliminate the middle class."

Sources: Steven. Greenhouse, "At Caterpillar, A Test Case for U.S. Unions; Despite a Record Profit, Heavy Machinery Giant Is in Cost-Cutting Vanguard," *International Herald Tribune*, July 24, 2012; "Compensation for Cat's Oberhelman Jumps 60%," *Chicago Tribune*, April 11, 2012; Executive Profile, Caterpillar, Inc., Bloomberg Businessweek, 2013.

5.2 An Alternative Framework: Worker Cooperatives

Much of the discussion in this chapter has assumed a working arrangement in which the goals of the "employee" do not necessarily align with those of the "employer." For example, we discussed how the relative bargaining power of employees and employers can influence wages and how "flexibility" can mean very different things to employees and employers. A typical for-profit corporation is owned by those who hold shares of the company's stock, in proportion to the amount of stock that they own. Top executives answer directly to shareholders and manage subordinate workers with the goal of maximizing profits. From the perspective of shareholders and top executives, maintaining (or increasing) worker productivity while lowering wage costs is desirable, as it leads to higher profits. From the perspective of workers, however, increases in wages are seen as desirable, and workers may have little concern for the profitability of the company.

worker cooperatives: a labor arrangement in which the owners of an enterprise are the workers themselves

Worker cooperatives, an alternative labor framework, seek to reduce or eliminate the potential for labor conflicts by specifying that the owners of the enterprise are the workers themselves. Worker cooperatives are sometimes viewed as a "third way" of labor organization, in contrast to standard for-profit companies and government-run enterprises. The organizational structure of worker cooperatives can vary, but in a typical cooperative every worker is also an owner. Worker cooperatives normally do seek to make a profit, and any profits are distributed among the worker-owners (in addition to receiving wages or a salary). Some workers may hold more ownership shares than others and thus receive a greater share of profits, say perhaps because of seniority, but in many cooperatives all workers have equal ownership shares. Important decisions are generally voted upon by all worker-owners, including decisions about wages, working hours, and benefits. Despite any differences in ownership shares, decisions are typically made on a "one person, one vote" basis.

Worker cooperatives arose as an alternative labor framework during the Industrial Revolution. Cooperatives are found throughout the world, the most famous being the Mondragón Cooperative Corporation in the Basque region of Spain, founded in 1956. Mondragón, which consists of more than 250 separate cooperatives with a total of about 85,000 worker-owners, is the seventh-largest company in Spain. Some of the differences between Mondragón and a typical capitalist company were described as follows:

> One of the co-operatively and democratically adopted rules governing [Mondragón] limits top-paid worker-members to earning *6.5 times* the lowest-paid workers. Nothing more dramatically demonstrates the differences distinguishing this from the capitalist alternative organization of enterprises. . . . [I]ts pay equity rules can and do contribute to a larger society with far greater income and wealth equality than is typical in societies that have chosen capitalist organizations of enterprises. Over 43 percent of members are women, whose equal powers with male members likewise influence gender relations in society different from capitalist enterprises.[16]

Italy has about 8,000 worker cooperatives, and France has nearly 2,000. In India, the India Coffee House is a cooperative restaurant chain with nearly 400 locations. In the United States, the U.S. Federation of Worker Cooperatives, whose membership comprises more than 100 cooperatives, works to promote cooperative formation, advocacy, and development. One example of a successful worker cooperative in the United States is Evergreen Cooperatives in Cleveland, OH, based in a low-income neighborhood and providing living wage jobs. The cooperative's main business is an environmentally conscious laundry facility that provides service to local hospitals.

Based solely on economic performance, such as worker productivity, the scientific evidence suggests that worker cooperatives can perform at least as well as traditional capitalist companies.[17] According to a 2011 paper that studied Mondragón, cooperative member-owners tend to be better paid than their peers in comparable firms, with greater opportunities for involvement and training. Although the cooperative labor framework is a "viable and possibly even superior alternative" to the traditional capitalist firm, it is not a "universal panacea" either. For example, job satisfaction was lower in cooperatives than in traditional firms, perhaps a reflection of higher worker expectations. Obviously, estimating the overall impact of worker cooperatives on well-being requires a multifaceted analysis in which all factors cannot be easily quantified.

5.3 HOW ARE REVENUES ALLOCATED?

Workers are one group that lays a claim on the revenues of firms, while their executives are another claimant. We now briefly consider other groups that also expect to share in the revenues of corporations and how allocations among these groups affect wages.

Government

The claims that governments make on businesses most often come in the form of taxes, though they may also at times levy fines on firms that are found to be disobeying a law. This money allows governments to supply much of the institutional and physical infrastructure necessary to operate businesses and to try to keep their activities somewhat in line with the social good. Businesses generally dislike paying taxes and complying with regulations and reporting requirements. However, without tax revenue governments cannot maintain services on which businesses depend, such as emergency call centers, firefighters, and police. Businesses as well as citizens depend on these services, as well as on roads, communications infrastructure, and the legal and other infrastructure that supports commerce. Moreover, all of society depends on government to monitor and regulate businesses to ensure safety in food, pharmaceuticals, and other products as well as a degree of honesty in claims made about the goods and services that they provide.

Suppliers of Physical Capital

Suppliers of physical capital include individuals or firms that supply both natural resources and manufactured capital. The price at which natural resources are sold depends to some extent on the cost of extraction, but also on economic power. For example, owners of oil wells have sometimes colluded to hold the selling price of this valuable commodity well above the cost of extraction and transportation. Owners of mines that produce gems or precious metals similarly have a long tradition of "fixing" prices, in part by strictly controlling the amount that is produced in a given time frame.

In other cases, scarcity is a critical factor in the price of the resource, as may be seen in the case of renewable resources such as some wood species or nonrenewable ones such as bauxite, oil, or copper. Some analysts predict that increasing scarcity of certain important natural resources will drive up the cost of production of many goods. This prediction, if true, is especially important in relation to wages; the same wage will be able to purchase less of the products that have become more expensive. On the other hand, "technological optimists" predict that human ingenuity will stay ahead of this trend, so that the prices of most natural resources will not affect the relative prices of wages and goods.

Prices of manufactured capital are more likely to be set according to our familiar supply-and-demand models. Their supply curve reflects the costs of producing the equipment (including what the producers had to pay for the natural resources used in their intermediate products). This interacts with the quantities demanded and the prices offered in the market.

Suppliers of Financial Capital

From the point of view of the firm, these can be divided into those whose claim can be considered part of "the necessary cost of doing business" and those that are the "residual claimants." When a firm takes out a loan, the payments of interest and principal are considered part of the necessary cost of doing business. They are taken out of revenues, along with taxes and the cost of purchasing inputs (including labor services), *before* anything remains that can be called a profit.

Investors, as distinct from lenders, are generally considered residual claimants; their return comes out of profits—what is left over after the firm has covered all necessary costs to sustain its activity. There is no clear law that states who else is a residual claimant, but top management often receive part of the profits, in one form or another.

A Useful Image

To summarize, the necessary costs of doing business include payments to factors of production (labor, financial capital, and material inputs) as well as taxes. The commonest uses for corporate profits include paying dividends to shareholders, investing in buildings and equipment, purchasing other companies, and buying stock shares from shareholders, to be held by the company. (The last of these actions increases the company's power when it is confronted by proposals from outside shareholders, on subjects such as environmental protection, employee rights, or obligations of the board of directors.)

One image that you can take away from this discussion is of a very fancy kind of sprinkler hose, which is filled by the revenues generated by the sale of a firm's products. As you look along the hose, you can see places where it sprinkles out appropriate payments for the necessary inputs to production—wages, salaries, payments for physical inputs, and taxes or fees. Finally, you come to the end of the hose; what is left—whether it be a trickle or a fountain—is considered profit.

The salient word in the preceding paragraph is "appropriate"—what is the appropriate amount of revenue to allocate to each factor of production? The analysis in the first half of this chapter gives us the simple, neoclassical answer: Every factor should be compensated according to its marginal revenue product—the amount contributed to the market value of the product by the last unit of that factor. And the assumption of perfect competition (which we discuss in more detail in Chapter 16) further insists that firms must set wages exactly equal to MRP_L, just as the returns to capital must be set exactly equal to the marginal revenue product of capital.

Box 9.4 suggests that diverting all or part of the company's profits could have prevented the wage freeze at Caterpillar, or even significantly increased worker compensation. Is this realistic? It is, in principle, possible. For comparison, consider for a moment another factor of production: raw materials. Supposing that the cost of some critical raw material were to rise, so that at least in the short run, before it could find any alternative, Caterpillar would be forced to pay a great deal more for these materials. This would be expected to cut immediately into profits. For a comparable thought-experiment, imagine that a very strong union is formed, and it is joined by all of the types of workers that Caterpillar requires. Imagine, additionally, that this union is able to make a credible threat of a strike, unless Caterpillar raises workers' salaries by an amount that cuts its profits by a third. Again, in the short run, the necessary cost of doing business would rise. Unless the firm decided to simply shut down, it would have a smaller profit left over at the end of its metaphorical sprinkler hose.

The second of these imaginary scenarios is not about to happen for at least two reasons: Unions have greatly dwindled in the United States, to the point that it is hardly imaginable that they would have this kind of power; and globalization allows even a maker of heavy, expensive-to-transport machinery to threaten to move to another country where labor is cheaper. The world has shifted in such a way that it is hard for workers to make credible threats and relatively easy for employers to do so. The relative loss of worker power is one of the explanations for the growing inequality that we discuss in Chapter 10.

Discussion Questions

1. Do you think that the relative wages of average workers and top executives reflect their respective marginal revenue product? Do you think that the relative wages of average workers and top executives should be regulated by the government? What, if any, specific regulations do you propose?
2. Do you believe that worker cooperatives can become a widespread alternative to traditional firms? Do you know of any worker cooperatives in your area?

REVIEW QUESTIONS

1. In the traditional neoclassical model, how does a firm decide on the quantity of labor to hire?
2. What are some of the opportunity costs of paid employment?
3. Why might the individual labor supply curve bend backward?
4. How is human capital important in explaining wage variations?
5. What is signaling theory in relation to labor markets?
6. In what types of labor markets might labor supply be relatively wage elastic? In what types of markets

might labor supply be relatively wage inelastic?
7. In what types of labor markets might labor demand be relatively wage elastic? In what types of markets might labor demand be relatively wage inelastic?
8. How can we use a supply-and-demand graph to illustrate the operation of a labor market?
9. What is employment flexibility from the perspective of workers? From the perspective of employers?
10. How have annual work hours changed in recent decades in the United States and other industrialized countries?
11. What are compensating wage differentials?

12. What is monopsony?
13. What is oligopsony?
14. What is efficiency wage theory?
15. What are dual labor markets?
16. How can we identify labor discrimination?
17. What is occupational segregation?
18. What has been the trend in median wages in the United States in the past few decades? How does this compare with the trend in corporate profits?
19. What are worker cooperatives, and how do they differ from traditional firms in terms of labor organization?
20. In addition to workers and management executives, who are some other claimants on business revenues?

EXERCISES

1. Reviewing Chapters 3 and 4 if necessary, illustrate on a labor market graph the following examples that were described in the text.
   a. A relatively elastic supply curve for wait staff.
   b. A virtually "fixed" supply of aerospace engineers, in the short run.
   c. The effect on the supply of lawyers of the reduction of barriers to women's participation in the practice of the law.
   d. The effect on the market for wait staff of a rise in the wage of salesclerks.
2. Draw labor market graphs illustrating the following examples that were mentioned in the text.
   a. A labor demand curve, when very good substitutes for labor in the production process exist.
   b. The effect of a drop in demand for the organization's product.
   c. The effect of a rise in the price of other inputs that have been used as substitutes for labor.
3. Suppose that you observe that the wages for accountants in your town have gone up and that the number of accountants employed has also gone up. Which one of the following conditions could explain this? Illustrate your answer with a graph and explain in a brief paragraph.
   a. Businesses are failing, reducing the need for accountants.
   b. Many accountants are leaving the field in order to train to become financial analysts instead.
   c. A rash of business scandals has increased the demand for auditing services performed by accountants.
   d. The local university has just graduated an unusually large group of accountants.
4. The U.S. Bureau of Labor Statistics keeps track of the average wages and number of workers involved in various occupations over time and also makes projections about what jobs may show the most growth in the future. Using data available at the bureau's Web site, www.bls.gov, try to look up information on an occupation that interests you. How does it pay, compared to other jobs? Is demand projected to rise in the future?
5. Match each concept in Column A with an example in Column B.

Column A	Column B
a. An alternative to wage employment	1. "Insurance adjustor" jobs are traditionally given to men while "insurance representative" jobs go to women
b. The income effect on individual labor supply	2. Isabella cuts back her hours at her job after she gets a raise
c. A cause of a shift in the demand for professors	3. Many professors reach retirement age
d. A cause of a shift in the supply of professors	4. Acme Corp. hires only college graduates for sales jobs, but doesn't care about their majors
e. Using education as a "signal"	5. Acme Corp. pays above prevailing market wages to motivate and retain its employees
f. Labor market monopoly	6. Westinghouse is the major employer in the county
g. Labor market monopsony	7. Marshall is the only person who knows how to run his company's antiquated database
h. Compensating wage differential	8. Household production
i. Occupational segregation	9. Resident assistants get a rent-free apartment but little pay
j. Efficiency wages	10. A rising college-student-age population

NOTES

1. Jennifer Cheeseman Day and Eric C. Newburger, "The Big Payoff: Educational Attainment and Synthetic Estimates of Work-Life Earnings," U.S. Census Bureau, Current Population Reports, P23–210, 2002.

2. Jody Heymann, *Children's Chances: How Countries Can Move from Surviving to Thriving* (Cambridge: Harvard University Press, 2013).

3. Rebecca Ray, Janet C. Gornick, and John Schmitt, "Parental Leave Policies in 21 Countries," Center for Economic and Policy Research, Washington, DC, 2009.

4. Ibid., pp. 1–2.

5. Lonnie Golden and Tesfayi Gebreselassie, "Overemployment Mismatches: The Preference for Fewer Work Hours," *BLS Monthly Labor Review* (April 2007): 18–27.

6. Susan E. Fleck, "International Comparisons of Hours Worked: An Assessment of the Statistics," *BLS Monthly Labor Review* (May 2009): 3–31.

7. Rebecca Ray, Milla Sanes, and John Schmitt, "No-Vacation Nation Revisited," Center for Economic and Policy Research, Washington, DC, 2013.

8. Nell Henderson, "Effect of Immigration on Jobs, Wages Is Difficult for Economists to Nail Down," *Washington Post,* April 15, 2006.

9. Heidi Shierholz, "Immigration and Wages: Methodological Advancements Confirm Modest Gains for Native Workers," Economic Policy Institute, EPI Briefing Paper 255, Washington, DC, 2010.

10. Dylan Matthews,"Immigration's Effect on Wages: 'Definitely Positive, Without Any Doubt Whatsoever,'" *Washington Post,* April 17, 2013.

11. OECD Employment Database, "Trends in Union Density, 1960–2011," http://stats.oecd.org/Index.aspx?DataSetCode=UN_DEN.

12. See, for example, Michael Watchner, "The Rise and Decline of Unions," *Washington Post,* July 18, 2007.

13. Lawrence Mishel, "Unions, Inequality, and Faltering Middle-Class Wages," Economic Policy Institute, Policy Brief 342, Washington, DC, 2012.

14. Educational attainment data from the *Statistical Abstract of the United States 2012,* table 231.

15. U.S. Census Bureau, *Bicentennial Edition: Historical Statistics of the United States, Colonial Times to 1970,* Series D 722–727, 1976; U.S. Census Bureau, *Statistical Abstract of the United States 1982–1983,* table 667, 1982.

16. Richard Wolff, "Yes, There Is an Alternative to Capitalism: Mondragon Shows the Way," *The Guardian,* June 24, 2012.

17. Chris Doucouliagos, "Worker Participation and Productivity in Labor-Managed and Participatory Capitalist Firms: A Meta-Analysis," *Industrial and Labor Relations Review* 49(1) (1995): 58–77.

APPENDIX: A FORMAL MODEL OF A FIRM'S HIRING DECISION

marginal physical product of labor (MPP_L): the amount that a unit of additional labor contributes to the physical product of a firm

Suppose that a firm produces disposable razors. Holding all other inputs fixed, the relationship between the number of workers (the "quantity of labor") hired and the number of razors that can be produced in a day is given in the first two columns of the table on the following page. From these first two columns, the **marginal physical product** of each additional worker (**of labor**) (MPP_L) can be computed. For example, one worker can produce 5 razors, but adding an additional worker makes possible the production of 12 razors, so the *marginal* physical product of the second worker is 7 razors. Note that the marginal physical product of labor first rises and then falls.

We further assume that the firm sells razors in a competitive market and that the price received per razor is constant at $3. Hence the marginal revenue product of labor (MRP_L), the monetary value of the additional physical production, is always just $3 \times MPP_L$. We assume that the firm buys labor in a perfectly competitive labor market, at a constant wage of $12. Hence the marginal factor cost of labor (MFC_L) is constant at $12.

Quantity of labor	Quantity of razors	MPP_L	MRP_L	MFC_L
1	5	5	15	12
2	12	7	21	12
3	18	6	18	12
4	23	5	15	12
5	27	4	12	12
6	30	3	9	12
7	32	2	6	12
8	33	1	3	12

The MRP_L and MFC_L curves are graphed in Figure 9.9. The MRP_L curve has an initial hump, because the MPP_L initially increases and then declines. For all workers up to the fifth worker, hiring the additional worker adds more to revenues than to costs. The profit-maximizing firm should stop hiring workers when $MRP_L = MFC_L$, at an employment level of five workers.

Figure 9.9   **Marginal Revenue Product of Labor and Marginal Factor Cost of Labor**

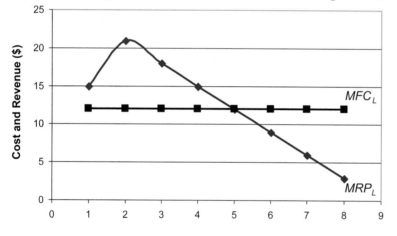

The optimal amount of labor for a firm to hire occurs where the marginal revenue product equals the marginal factor cost.

PART

IV

**Essential Topics for
Contemporary Economics**

10 Economic and Social Inequality

Which do you think is a more important dimension of human well-being: the quantity of goods and services that an economy produces or the ultimate distribution of those goods and services within society? Many economists believe that only the first is a meaningful goal—the second should just take care of itself through market allocation. Or if markets result in an unacceptable distribution, some economists suggest that politicians can always step in and make whatever redistributions are necessary. But what are the consequences of a distribution of income and assets that is highly unequal? How does economic policy relate to inequality? Because of growing inequality, both in the United States and abroad, it is an issue to which many more economists than in the past have been paying attention.

1. Defining and Measuring Inequality

We can think of social equality as a "goal" in economics, just as efficiency is an important goal. But there is an important difference. Few would argue that we could be "too" efficient. As long as efficiency is carefully defined and is not pursued in ways that are destructive to other goals, the more efficient we are, the better. The same does not hold for equality. Whether we are talking about income, opportunities, or education, it is possible to be "too equal." Few desire a society in which everyone earns the same exact income or where everyone is a carpenter or a Ph.D. Our goal should be to strive to be a society that is neither "too equal" nor "too unequal."

How do we know whether we are successful? This is a more complex issue than dealing with efficiency because, as we will see, it is impossible to prescribe a degree of inequality that works ideally for everyone. Compounding the problem is that inequality, unlike efficiency, presents a problem that has both an ethical *and* an economic dimension.

1.1 Inequality of What?

When the subject of inequality is raised, most people think of income or wealth inequality. Because this is an economics textbook, we also emphasize these, especially inequality of income. But it is important to recognize that inequality is a broader concept that extends beyond the realm of money.

Let us consider a few examples. Public health is an area in which vast inequality exists. Preventable or treatable diseases in numerous tropical countries (such as malaria, measles, and tuberculosis) cause average life expectancy to be significantly shorter than in the United States or in other rich countries. There is also significant health inequality within many countries. Increasingly, access to adequate medical care can make a difference in terms of whether one can obtain effective treatment for a particular ailment. This is generally not much of a problem in advanced industrialized countries that have a "single payer" system, but in countries that lack universal health insurance one's health condition can be dictated by whether one can reliably see a doctor, which often depends on whether one has adequate insurance coverage.

There is also a considerable imbalance in education, both nationally and internationally. The majority of adults in the United States lack a college education, which today is regarded as almost indispensable to economic success (as we saw last chapter). However, most Americans do have a high school degree. Although this is true in other rich countries, it is not the case in most others. Primary and secondary education are not a priority in many parts of the world, where poverty and hunger are widespread—not to mention violence or civil war, as well as gender discrimination, which makes it especially hard for girls to go to school in some countries. Even where families want to send their children to school, national governments often lack the funds to support basic education. Without a proper education, many millions are inadequately prepared for competing in today's global economy.

Related to both health and education is what Nobel laureate Amartya Sen has famously referred to as "capabilities." By his reckoning, money is only one dimension—albeit an important one—of an individual's "capability" to function in his or her economic environment. To Sen, what matters most is that people possess the necessary tools—for example, money, health, education, friends, social connections—to provide them with realistic economic *choices.* As Sen has pointed out, there is considerable inequality of capabilities in the world, not just in the poor countries.

Inequality is also manifest in certain environmental outcomes. Proponents of "environmental justice," generally studying the United States, point out that polluting industries and toxic waste disposal sites tend to be located disproportionately near poor and minority communities. This effect is even more pronounced in countries like Ecuador and Brazil. Tribal residents in Ecuador confront widespread pollution from petroleum extraction in the remote areas where they live as well as extensive harm to their local habitat. Native Brazilians suffer from the environmental toxicity of the gold-mining process as well as from the alteration of their landscape resulting from deforestation. These effects are generally associated with inequality—not of income but of land ownership or property rights. People who reside in these areas often lack the legal power to keep the miners or timber companies out.

One also sees considerable inequality when confronting the issue of climate change. Countries with sizable portions of land near sea level—for example, Egypt and Bangladesh—are likely to be affected by climate change in the coming decades more adversely than, say, the mountain kingdom of Bhutan. Some of the most northern countries, like Canada and Russia, may actually benefit, at least in the short term, from climate change, in that warmer global temperatures would lengthen the agricultural season and potentially allow these countries to produce crops that they formerly could not. In addition to these specific effects, however, a critical fact about climate change, as well as other environmental damage, is that the rich can protect themselves much better than the poor can.

1.2 MEASURING INEQUALITY

To illustrate one approach for measuring inequality, we begin by looking at the distribution of household income in the United States in 2011 (Table 10.1). The data are arranged in order of income, and the share of the total income "pie" that accrues to each twentieth percentile (or quintile) is in the second column. To understand what this table means, imagine dividing up U.S. households into five equal-sized groups, with the poorest households all in one group, the next-poorest in the next group, and so on. The last group contains the richest quintile among all households. The poorest quintile, with household incomes below $20,262, received only 3.2 percent of all the household income in the country. The richest quintile, those with incomes of $101,582 or more, received 51.5 percent—in other words, more than half—of all the income received in the United States.

Table 10.1   **Distribution of U.S. Household Income in 2011**

Group of households	Share of aggregate income (%)	Income range
Poorest fifth	3.2	Below $20,262
Second fifth	8.4	$20,262 – $38,519
Middle fifth	14.3	$38,520 – $62,433
Fourth fifth	23.0	$62,434 – $101,581
Richest fifth	51.1	Above $101,582
Richest 5%	22.3	Above $176,000

Source: U.S. Census Bureau, Table A-2 of "Income, Poverty, and Health Insurance Coverage in the United States," 2011.

Suppose that we further separate the richest group into two groups: those with income of less than $176,000 and those with income higher than this. The group with household income above $176,000 constitutes the richest 5 percent, or one-twentieth, of the population. As we can see, this richest 5 percent earned 22.3 percent of national income, close to the amount earned by all of those in the fourth quintile. (See also figures illustrating similar points in Chapter 0.)

Based on these data, we can now construct many different measures of inequality. For instance, we could calculate the ratio of the income share of the richest fifth to that of the poorest fifth of the population; in this case, we obtain 51.1/3.2 = 16.0—that is, a household in the richest quintile has about 16 times the income, on average, of a household in the poorest quintile. We can then see how this ratio has changed over time to track changes in inequality. For example, in 1979 this ratio was only about 7, indicating an increase in inequality between the richest and poorest fifth of the population.

Lorenz curve: a line used to portray an income distribution, drawn on a graph with percentiles of households on the horizontal axis and the cumulative percentage of income on the vertical axis

However, a simple ratio is somewhat arbitrary, focusing on some parts of the income distribution while ignoring others. Economists frequently prefer to use a more comprehensive measure that reflects the shape of the entire income distribution. This measure first involves creating a graph of the income distribution, referred to as a **Lorenz curve**—named after Max Lorenz, the statistician who first developed the technique. A Lorenz curve for household income in the United States is shown in Figure 10.1. In this graph, the horizontal axis represents households, lined up from left to right in order of increasing income. The vertical axis measures the *cumulative* percentage of all income received by households up to a given income level.

Figure 10.1   **Lorenz Curve for the United States**

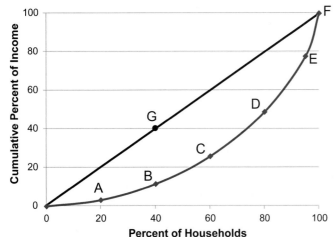

A Lorenz curve shows the cumulative amount of all income obtained by different percentiles of households, ordered from those with the lowest incomes to those with the highest incomes.

Source: U.S. Census Bureau, Historical Income Tables, Households, Table H-2.

We use the data in Table 10.1 to draw the Lorenz curve in Figure 10.1. Point A represents the fact that the poorest 20 percent of households received 3.2 percent of all income. To obtain Point B, we need to calculate the cumulative percent of income received by the bottom 40 percent of households. So we add the income received by the bottom 20 percent to the income received by the next 20 percent. Thus the cumulative percent of income received by the bottom 40 percent is 3.2 + 8.4 = 11.6 percent of total income. For point C, we need to calculate the cumulative percent of income received by the bottom 60 percent of households, which is 3.2 + 8.4 + 14.3 = 25.9 percent of total income. Similarly, point D shows that the income share of the bottom 80 percent is 48.9 percent of all income. Finally, point E shows that the bottom 95 percent received 77.7 percent of all income (everyone except the top 5 percent). The Lorenz curve must start at the origin, at the lower left corner of the graph (because 0 percent of households have 0 percent of the total income) and must end at point F in the upper right corner (because 100 percent of households must have 100 percent of the total income).

The Lorenz curve provides information about the degree of income inequality in a country. Note that the 45-degree line in Figure 10.1 represents a situation of absolute equality. If every household had the same exact income, then, for example, the "bottom" 40 percent of households would receive 40 percent of all income. This is shown by point G in Figure 10.1. Imagine the other extreme—a situation in which one household received all the income in a country. In this case, the Lorenz curve would be a flat line along the horizontal axis at a value of zero until the very end, where it would suddenly shoot up to 100 percent of income (at point F).

Of course these two extremes do not occur in reality, but they indicate that the closer a country's Lorenz curve is to the 45-degree line, the more equal its income distribution. This is illustrated in Figure 10.2, which shows the Lorenz curve for three countries: Sweden, the United States, and Bolivia. Income is distributed relatively equally in Sweden; its Lorenz curve is closer to the 45-degree line of absolute equality than the U.S. Lorenz curve. Bolivia is an example of a country which has greater income inequality than the U.S.; its Lorenz curve bows further from the line of absolute equality.

The more the Lorenz curve bows away from the line of absolute equality, the greater is the extent of inequality in the income distribution. This observation led a statistician by the name of Corrado Gini to introduce a numerical measure of inequality that came to be known

Figure 10.2   **Lorenz Curves for Sweden, the United States, and Bolivia**

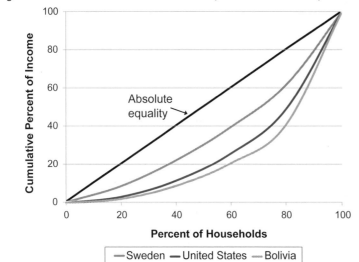

The closer the Lorenz curve is to the line of absolute equality, the lower the degree of economic inequality.

Sources: Statistics Sweden, online database, Disposable Income in Deciles 2011–2014; U.S. Census Bureau, Historical Income Tables, Households, Table H-2; World Bank, World Development Indicators database.

Figure 10.3 **The Gini Coefficient: A/(A+B)**

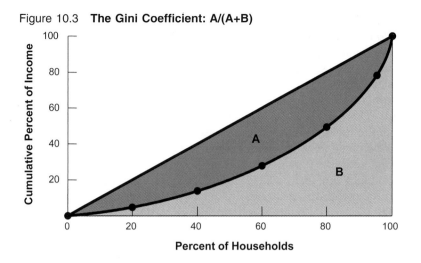

The larger area A is, the greater the deviation from absolute equality, and thus the higher the Gini coefficient.

Gini ratio (or Gini coefficient): a measure of inequality, based on the Lorenz curve, that goes from 0 (absolute equality) up to 1 (absolute inequality). Greater inequality shows up as a larger area between the Lorenz curve and the diagonal line of absolute equality.

as the **Gini ratio** (or "Gini coefficient"), which is defined as the ratio of the area between the Lorenz curve and the diagonal line of equality to the total area under the diagonal line.

Referring to areas A and B in Figure 10.3, the Gini ratio is A/(A+B). Clearly, the Gini ratio can vary from 0 for absolute equality (since in such a case area A would equal zero as the Lorenz curve overlaps the line of absolute equality) to 1 for absolute inequality (where area B would equal zero). According to U.S. Census Bureau calculations, the Gini ratio for U.S. household income in 2011 was 0.477. We will present international comparisons of inequality, along with data trends, later in the chapter.

You might be wondering about some details of the measure of income we are using. Higher-income people, after all, pay more taxes, so they really do not have control over all the money income that they have been counted as receiving. Meanwhile, poor people may qualify for noncash programs such as food stamps, or for subsidized housing and medical care, and arguably the value of these programs should be included as part of income.

On the basis of considerations like these, the U.S. Census Bureau has experimented with at least 15 different definitions of income. One definition, for example, is meant to approximate what the distribution of income would be if—hypothetically—the impact of government activity were excluded. For this definition, the Census Bureau starts with the measure of pretax money income that we have been working with until now and subtracts government cash transfers (such as welfare payments). Then it adds the value of health insurance fringe benefits paid by businesses for their (often middle-class or higher) employees and the value of net capital gains (usually earned by the relatively wealthy). Under this definition, the Gini ratio, not surprisingly, rises, showing greater inequality. The share of the bottom fifth drops considerably, while the share of the top fifth rises.

Adjusting that measure of income for the effects of the tax system causes some change at the top, but little at the bottom. When the Census Bureau further adds in the effects of both cash government transfer programs and noncash programs (such as food stamps, Medicare, and Medicaid), the distribution becomes somewhat less unequal. Government tax and transfer policies—and especially the transfer side—have significant effects on the U.S. household income distribution. Even with the most thorough accounting for aid to low-income households from transfer payments, however, the income of the top fifth of the population is still roughly ten times that of the bottom fifth.

How much importance should we place on income inequality and the Gini index? Many important goods and services are, after all, obtained without the use of cash income. Many families prefer to produce at least some services (such as child care and cooking) for themselves. In addition, many of the things that we enjoy—such as pleasant parks, safe roads, or clean air—add to our well-being without requiring payments out of our cash income (although some of these things are financed through taxes). If we were to look at the distribution of *well-being* rather than just the distribution of income, we would need to take account of these nonincome sources of important goods and services. Some of these goods may contribute to lessening inequality—for example, everyone, rich or poor, can enjoy a public park or use a public library. Evidence suggests, however, that at least in some cases the distribution of such nonpurchased goods may accentuate, rather than lessen, measures of inequality. For example, as noted earlier, proponents of "environmental justice" point out that polluting industries and toxic waste disposal sites tend to be located disproportionately near poor and minority communities. Moreover, considerable evidence indicates that families that are money-poor are also time-poor; they cannot devote the time that they would wish to child care and cooking, often being forced to use the television as the babysitter and to depend on fast foods for meals—with serious known health consequences.

Gini coefficients may also be calculated for the distribution of wealth rather than income. This distribution, which depends on what people own in assets, tends to be much more unequal than income distribution. Most people own relatively little wealth, relying mainly on labor income and perhaps government or family transfers to support their expenditures. It is even possible to have *negative* net wealth. This happens when the value of a person's debts (e.g., for a car, house, or credit cards) is higher than the value of her assets. For people in the middle class, the equity that they have in their house is often their most significant asset. By contrast, those who *do* own substantial wealth are generally in a position to put much of it into assets that increase in value over time or yield a flow of income and dividends—which can in turn be invested in the acquisition of still more assets.

capital gains: increase in the value of an asset at the time it is sold compared to the price at which it was originally purchased by the same owner

The distribution of wealth is, however, less frequently and less systematically recorded than the distribution of income—in part because wealth can be hard to measure. Much wealth is held in the form of unrealized **capital gains**. A household realizes—turns into actual dollars—capital gains if it sells an appreciated asset, such as shares in a company, land, or antiques, for more than the price at which it purchased the asset. An asset can appreciate in value for a long time before it is actually sold. No one, however, will know exactly how much such an asset has really gained or lost in value until the owner actually *does* sell it, thus "realizing" the capital gain. Another reason that it is harder to get information on wealth is that although the government requires people to report their annual *income* from wages and many investments for tax purposes, it does not require everyone to regularly and comprehensively report their asset holdings. Finally, wealth consists not only of financial assets but also commodities, paintings, real estate, and the like. Such disparate forms of wealth make estimating aggregate wealth statistics reliably much more cumbersome.

These caveats notwithstanding, estimates of the U.S. Gini ratio for the distribution of wealth are in the neighborhood of 0.8, and those for most other countries are also considerably higher than the corresponding income Gini ratios. Should we be concerned about such a global concentration of wealth?

To be sure, ownership of wealth is usually a very good thing, because it can help households maintain their accustomed consumption patterns, if income temporarily becomes low. But contemplating such vast wealth inequality brings us back to the question of opportunity. Are there sufficient compensatory assets available to those with little or even negative wealth? It is critically important not to ignore wealth inequality because it bears heavily on the much more advertised income inequality. And the effect is cumulative: To the extent that income is unequally distributed, it will further concentrate wealth.

Perhaps most important, great wealth confers its owners with both economic and political power. When the ownership of wealth is highly uneven, the power to direct the operations of businesses and to influence government policy through campaign contributions and the like may become concentrated in the hands of relatively few. We return to this point below.

Discussion Questions

1. What is the difference between inequality of incomes and inequality of "capabilities"? How are the two related? Which one do you think deserves more attention from policymakers?
2. What do you think is the minimal amount of annual income that an individual, or a small family, would need to live in *your* community? (Think about the rent or mortgage on a one- or two-bedroom residence, etc.) What does this probably mean about where the average level of income in your community fits into the U.S. income distribution shown in Table 10.1?

2. DATA AND TRENDS

We now have a quantitative method to use for comparing inequality, both across different populations and over time. Yet it is important to fully understand that, although Gini coefficients help us measure the extent of inequality that exists, they do *not* help us decide whether the inequality is acceptable or excessive. This will always be a judgment call, and different people will render different judgments.

2.1 INEQUALITY IN THE UNITED STATES

No one disputes that income inequality in the United States has generally increased in recent decades. We can see this in Figure 10.4, which shows the Gini coefficient in the U.S. from 1967 to 2010, based on data from the U.S. Census Bureau. The Gini coefficient reached a record low of 0.386 in 1968. After that, the Gini coefficient increased in 31 of the next 42 years. In 2010 the Gini coefficient reached a record high of 0.469.

While comparable government data are not available for the years prior to 1968, academic researchers have estimated longer trends in income inequality by focusing on the share of total income going to the top income groups. Figure 10.5 shows the income share of the top 10 percent and the top 1 percent from 1917 to 2012. After the Great Depression, the share of income going to the top income groups generally declined, suggesting that income inequality was decreasing. The share of income going to the top 10 percent remained low at around 32 percent from 1950 until the early 1970s. The share of income going to the top 1 percent reached a low of less than 8 percent in the

Figure 10.4 **Gini Coefficient in the United States, 1967–2010**

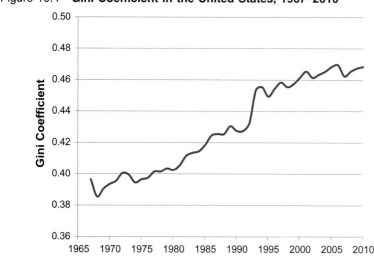

Since the late 1960s income inequality in the United States has tended to increase.

Source: U.S. Census Bureau, Historical Income Tables, Households, Table H-2.

Figure 10.5   **Income Share of the Top 10 Percent and Top 1 Percent in the United States, 1917–2012**

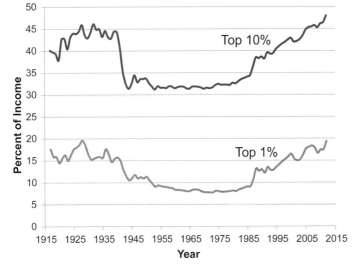

The share of income going the highest income groups generally decreased from the Great Depression until the early 1970s. Since then, the share of income going to the top groups has increased, reaching levels even higher than those prior to the Great Depression.

Source: Emmanuel Saez, income inequality database updated to 2012, University of California, Berkeley, http://elsa.berkeley.edu/~saez/.

early 1970s. Since the early 1970s, the income share going to these top groups has increased, surpassing the high levels that occurred prior to the Great Depression.

As mentioned earlier, inequality of wealth tends to be even higher than inequality of income. This is illustrated in Figure 10.6, which shows the distribution of wealth in the United States in 2009. We see that the top 1 percent own more than a third of all wealth in the U.S., and the top fifth (the 80th percentile and above) own 87 percent of wealth. Collectively, the bottom 80 percent own only 13 percent of all wealth. Analysis of wealth data suggests that wealth inequality has also increased in recent decades. For more on wealth inequality, see Box 10.1.

We can look at inequality from several other perspectives. For example, inequality is clearly evident across race in the United States, as shown in Table 10.2 (p. 228). Asian households have the highest median annual income, about $69,000, while black households have the lowest at only $33,000. Married couples, with the potential for two adult workers, have higher incomes than households with just one adult male or female. Among households with just

Figure 10.6   **The Distribution of Wealth in the United States, 2009**

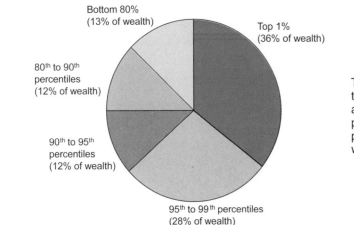

The top 1 percent owns over one-third of wealth in the United States and the top 20 percent own 87 percent of wealth. The bottom 80 percent own only 13 percent of wealth.

Source: Sylvia A. Allegretto, "The State of Working America's Wealth, 2011," Economic Policy Institute, EPI Briefing Paper #292, March 23, 2011.

BOX 10.1 WEALTH INEQUALITY IN THE UNITED STATES

Figure 10.6 presented data on the actual distribution of wealth in the United States. However, political debates about inequality are often based upon perceptions rather than facts. In a 2011 paper, researchers Michael Norton and Dan Ariely surveyed people regarding their perceptions of wealth inequality in the U.S. Specifically, respondents were asked to estimate what percentage of total wealth was owned by each wealth quintile. Further, they also asked people to construct their ideal distribution of wealth, again assigning a percentage of total wealth to each quintile.

The results are presented in Figure 10.7, along with the actual distribution of wealth in the U.S. We see, for example, that the top quintile actually own 84 percent of all wealth in the U.S. according to the paper. (Note that the "actual" distribution of wealth in Figure 10.7 differs from the distribution given in Figure 10.6—the two figures rely upon different data sources and apply to different years.) However, respondents estimated that the top quintile only owned 59 percent of all wealth. But most respondents thought that this estimated concentration of wealth was excessive. On average, their ideal wealth distribution allocated only 32 percent of all wealth to the top quintile.

Looking at the other end of the wealth spectrum, the bottom quintile actually owns only 0.1 percent of wealth in the U.S. Respondents estimated that the bottom quintile owns about 3 percent of wealth. According to their ideal distribution, the bottom quintile should own about 11 percent of all wealth.

The results clearly illustrate the difference between reality, perceptions, and subjective preferences. Norton and Ariely draw two primary messages from the results:

First, a large nationally representative sample of Americans seems to prefer to live in a country more like Sweden than like the United States. Americans also construct ideal distributions that are far more equal than they estimated the United States to be—estimates which themselves were far more equal than the actual level of inequality. Second, there was much more consensus than disagreement across groups from different sides of the political spectrum about this desire for a more equal distribution of wealth, suggesting that Americans may possess a commonly held "normative" standard for the distribution of wealth despite the many disagreements about policies that affect that distribution, such as taxation and welfare.

Source: Michael I. Norton and Dan Ariely, "Building a Better America—One Wealth Quintile at a Time," *Perspectives on Psychological Science* 6(1) (2011): 9–12.

Figure 10.7 **Actual, Estimated, and Ideal Distribution of Wealth in the United States**

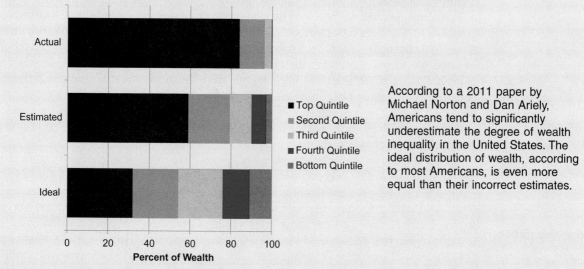

According to a 2011 paper by Michael Norton and Dan Ariely, Americans tend to significantly underestimate the degree of wealth inequality in the United States. The ideal distribution of wealth, according to most Americans, is even more equal than their incorrect estimates.

Source: Michael I. Norton and Dan Ariely, "Building a Better America—One Wealth Quintile at a Time," *Perspectives on Psychological Science* 6(1) (2011): 9–12.

Table 10.2   **Median Household Income in the United States by Select Characteristics, 2012**

Group	Median Household Income
All households	$51,017
Households by Race	
Asian	$68,636
Black	$33,321
Hispanic	$39,005
White	$53,706
By Type of Household	
Married Couples	$75,694
Female householder, no husband	$34,002
Male householder, no wife	$48,634
By Age of Householder	
Age 15 – 24	$30,604
Age 25 – 34	$51,381
Age 35 – 44	$63,629
Age 45 – 54	$66,411
Age 55 – 64	$58,626
Age 65 and older	$33,848
By Residence Area	
Metropolitan area	$52,988
Outside of metropolitan area	$41,198

Source: Carmen DeNavas-Walt, Bernadette D. Proctor, and Jessica C. Smith, "Income, Poverty, and Health Insurance Coverage in the United States: 2012," U.S. Census Bureau, Current Population Report P60-245, September 2013.

one adult, male households have higher incomes than female households. Median incomes increase with age up until age 55, and then decline as people retire. Finally, households in metropolitan areas have higher incomes than those outside of metropolitan areas.

Economic inequalities based on race, age, and other demographic factors are even more pronounced when we consider household wealth. Table 10.3 presents data on the median value of household assets for different types of households. While white households' incomes are 61 percent higher than the incomes of black households, the assets of white households are more than 17 times higher than those of black households! Hispanic households also have little in assets. We see that education has a significant impact on household assets. For example, those with a college degree have about three times the household wealth as those with a high school diploma. The median value of household assets also tends to rise with age.

Some inequality is to be expected in any society given that people's incomes and assets tend to increase as they become older and more established in their careers. So at any point in time in a country, we are likely to have younger people with relatively low incomes and few assets, middle-aged people with higher incomes and more assets, and retirees who tend to have relatively low incomes but relatively high assets. Thus we have people moving from lower income groups to higher income groups, and vice versa. This possibility of people or households to change their economic status, for better or worse, is called **economic mobility**. For a given level of economic inequality, we may be more tolerant if economic mobility is higher because it implies that people have the opportunity to improve their economic condition.

A common way to measure economic mobility is to track the frequency with which individuals or households move into different income groups. A study by economists at Harvard University

economic mobility: the potential for an individual or household to change its economic conditions (for better or worse) over time

Table 10.3 **Median Value of Household Assets in the United States by Select Characteristics, 2011**

Group	Median Household Assets
All households	$68,828
By Race of Householder	
White	$110,500
Asian	$89,339
Hispanic	$7,683
Black	$6,314
By Type of Household	
Married Couples	$139,032
Female householder, no husband	$22,184
Male householder, no wife	$27,310
By Age of Householder	
Less than 35 years	$6,676
Age 35–44	$35,000
Age 45–54	$84,542
Age 55–64	$143,964
Age 65 and over	$170,516
By Education Level of Householder	
No high school diploma	$9,800
High school diploma	$43,945
Some college, no degree	$49,082
Associate's degree	$56,512
Bachelor's degree	$147,148
Graduate or professional degree	$240,750

Source: U.S. Census Bureau, Survey of Income and Program Participation, 2008 Panel, Wave 10, Table 1, Release date March 21, 2013.

and the University of California at Berkeley found that, overall, the chance that a child in the United States from the bottom fifth (with household income below $25,000) could get into the top fifth by age 30 was about 8 percent.[1] They found that economic mobility in the U.S. varied considerably across metropolitan areas. The chances of moving from the lower fifth to the highest were as high as 11 percent in Salt Lake City and San Francisco, and as low as 4 percent in Atlanta and 5 percent in Detroit.

2.2 Cross-Country Comparisons

The Gini ratio for the United States is higher than that of all other major industrialized countries, signifying that the country has a higher degree of income inequality. Recall our international comparison of economic inequality in Chapter 0. Figure 10.8 repeats the figure presented in Chapter 0, showing the range in income inequality across different countries. Sweden, with a Gini ratio of 0.23, has the lowest degree of income inequality of any country. While many of the countries with the lowest income inequality are also high-income countries, inequality is also low in Hungary, Belarus, Ethiopia, and Pakistan, among others.

Patterns across geographic regions are fairly consistent. Latin American countries, for example, tend to have relatively high degrees of inequality. In addition to Brazil and Mexico, Guatemala has a Gini coefficient of 0.55, Honduras 0.58, and Haiti and Colombia 0.59. Asian countries, in contrast, appear, by this measure, to be more economically equal. Most countries in the Asian continent have Gini coefficients between 0.3 and 0.4. Sub-Saharan Africa appears to have the greatest variability, ranging from 0.30 (Ethiopia) to 0.63 (South Africa and Lesotho).

Figure 10.8   **Income Gini Coefficients for Select Countries**

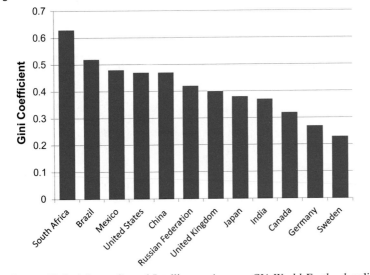

Country-level Gini coefficients range from a low of 0.23 (Sweden) to a high of 0.63 (South Africa). Among developed nations, the United States has the most inequality.

Source: United States Central Intelligence Agency, *CIA World Factbook* online database.

In the related area of mobility, a variety of studies have shown that economic mobility in the United States is lower than in a number of other rich countries, including Japan, Canada, Australia, France, Germany, and the Nordic countries.[2] A 2008 paper surveyed international research on economic mobility, looking specifically at how children's incomes fare relative to their parents' incomes. The results indicated that:

> a growing number of economic studies have found that the United States stands out as having less, not more, inter-generational mobility than do Canada and several European countries. American children are more likely than other children to end up in the same place on the income distribution as their parents. Moreover, there is emerging evidence that mobility is particularly low for Americans born into families at the bottom of the earnings or income distribution.[3]

We have seen that from around 1930 until the late 1960s inequality diminished in the United States. The relatively recent intensification of inequality is not limited to the United States. According to a recent OECD study, income inequality has been increasing over the past few decades in most, if not all, rich countries. Inequality may not be automatically self-perpetuating, but there is some evidence of a consistent pattern of increased inequality in rich countries. To what can this be attributed? The next section explores some possible causes and consequences.

Discussion Questions

1. Were your parents better off economically than their parents? Do you believe that you will be better off than your parents? Do you think that this is true of most of your friends?
2. Do you think the fact that the United States is more unequal than other rich countries is an advantage or disadvantage? Why?

3. CAUSES AND CONSEQUENCES OF INEQUALITY

The question of why inequality has been increasing in the United States and many other countries is a source of much debate. We now consider several of the explanations proposed by economists, recognizing that rising inequality is something that cannot be attributed to a single cause. We then turn to a discussion of the consequences of a high degree of inequality in a society.

3.1 CAUSES

One point on which economists appear to agree is that some of the increase in inequality is due to changing demographics. As people worldwide live longer on average, the proportion of the population that is elderly increases. This trend, coupled with an increase in the rate of single parenthood, has tended to drive down incomes at the low end. People too old to work and people in single-parent households (where paid work and caring activities compete for a limited resource—the adult's time) often lack economic resources. About 23 percent of U.S. children live in poor families. (A household is defined as poor if its income falls below a poverty threshold based on its family size. In 2013, the poverty threshold for a family of four was $23,550.) Meanwhile, the increasing number of women entering the labor force has helped boost the income of married-couple households at the top of the income range.

labor income: payment to workers, including wages, salaries, and fringe benefits

capital income: rents, profits, and interest

rent: payments for the direct or indirect use of any capital assets

Another factor that helps explain growing inequality is that the wage "share" of the income "pie" has diminished over time. Wages and salaries make up the majority of **labor income**, which includes the implicit value of fringe benefits. **Capital income** includes rents, profits, and interest. "**Rent**," as economists use the term, refers not just to rent for housing but to payments for the use of any capital asset, such as machinery or an e-mail list. (See Box 10.2 on "rent-seeking.") In general, higher-income households receive a larger portion of their total income from capital income.

The shrinking of wages as a share of total income over time suggests that inequality is intensifying because it means that the 60 or 70 percent of the population with the lowest incomes are falling behind, relative to those who count on profits and rent—as interest payments and dividends—as major sources of income. Generally, a declining wage share over time suggests that wage growth, if present, is not keeping up with overall economic growth. This has, in fact, been the case over the past four decades or so, and is partially responsible for rising inequality. Since 1970, the share of total income that comes from wages in the United States has fallen from about 72 percent to less than 64 percent.

Similar trends have been observed in most of the other rich countries. The critical question is *why* this has been happening, and on this there is no universal agreement. In what follows, we look at some of the more likely causes.

The first likely factor in increased inequality is globalization and the growth in trade that it produces. Because markets are increasingly interconnected, domestic producers of certain goods encounter greater competition from imports from other countries. In many instances,

---

BOX 10.2 RENT SEEKING AND INEQUALITY

"Rent seeking" refers to the act of expending time or other resources in the hope of obtaining value that already exists somewhere else instead of using those resources to produce new economic value. In other words, a rent seeker will try to provoke redistribution of existing wealth in his or her favor instead of generating new wealth.

One example of rent seeking is when lobbyists try to convince government officials to adopt policies favorable to their interests, at the expense of other economic actors. This is considered rent seeking because, even though such lobbying can produce benefits for the lobbyists' employers, it does not generate new economic value. One could even make the case that it subtracts from value creation in an "opportunity cost" sense: by diverting potentially useful or productive resources for the purpose of some zero-sum gain.

The effect of rent seeking can be to exacerbate inequality, because those who are already rich and powerful are most effective at directing government support and subsidies to themselves. The economist Mancur Olson has proposed a depressing scenario in which countries tend to grow less competitive and efficient over time, as organized interest and lobby groups gain in importance, and are increasingly able to influence government.

Clearly, the motivation of groups such as the Occupy Wall Street movement and other critics of inequality and the dominance of the top "1 percent," is based on a perception that much of the wealth of those at the very top is based on rent-seeking activities rather than genuine economic productivity.

the price of such imports is significantly lower than that for the domestically produced good, compelling the producer either to lower prices (and therefore wages, too) or simply leave the business. Competition from imports has indeed eliminated many industrial jobs—in textiles and automobiles, for example—that formerly fell in the middle of the U.S. wage distribution. The replacement of such jobs by lower-income service and retail jobs has probably contributed to the increase in inequality, although economists generally do not consider it a major factor, as it may explain only 10 percent of the increase.

It is worth noting that, while job opportunities and wages in certain sectors are decreasing in countries like the United States, they are increasing in many poor countries that previously lacked opportunities to produce for a global market. In this sense, freer trade may *reduce* inequality *across* countries.

The second, perhaps more important, factor has been the advent of rapid technological change. New technologies related to computers and biotechnology have become more important, increasing the income of skilled workers who understand and use the new techniques and equipment, while leaving behind the less-skilled workers who remain in low-technology occupations. The income of the skilled workers has risen relative to those of the less skilled simply because their skills are relatively scarce. Recalling our discussion of the labor market in Chapter 9, labor resembles other commodities in the sense that the more scarce it is (i.e., there is less supply), the higher its "price." The less-skilled workers are, in contrast, relatively abundant, depressing their average wage or "price."

Technological change has also, especially in the long run, led machines to replace human workers for certain types of jobs (especially in services), making workers at the "low-skill" end of the spectrum especially abundant. It has contributed substantially to what we defined in Chapter 9 as labor market segmentation, which is a polarization of the labor market into groups of "high-skill" jobs at one end and many more "low-skill" jobs at the other end. A defining feature of a segmented labor market is its inflexibility; it is extremely difficult, if not impossible, to move from one segment to the other.

The third likely cause of rising income inequality is the progressive weakening of labor unions, especially in the United States. Government policy has become decidedly less supportive of unions and low-wage workers, and the rate of participation in them has declined markedly, as discussed in Chapter 9. Recall that labor union membership in the United States declined from a peak of around 25 percent in the 1950s to only about 11 percent today.

The final reason proposed to explain rising inequality is that policies have been instituted that, intentionally or unintentionally, have led to higher inequality. There have, for example, been a series of tax cuts—starting in the 1980s under President Ronald Reagan, but continuing during George W. Bush's presidency—that primarily reduced the tax burden on the wealthiest groups. (The Bush tax cuts were partially reversed by the Obama administration in January 2013.) The primary consequence for the distribution of income has been this: For the past few decades, rather than providing tax revenue to the government, the richest households have increasingly been *lending it money at interest* through government bonds (the loans were necessary as a result of the shortfall in tax revenue), thus allowing the wealthy continued access to their capital. Economists such as Paul Krugman maintain that tax policy over the past four decades has indeed increased income inequality by enabling far greater access to capital for the wealthiest Americans than for lower-income ones.

Another policy change has been reduction in welfare expenditures, starting in the 1990s, with the phasing out of programs such as Aid for Families with Dependent Children (AFDC). The federal minimum wage ($7.25 as of 2013) has fallen significantly behind inflation, lowering the purchasing power of the lowest-income workers. In addition to directly reducing such subsidies to the poor, the diminished generosity of the welfare state also adversely affects workers' bargaining power, hence their wage. With less government benefits on which to rely, employees threatened with unemployment are more likely to accept a wage cut. Researchers have found a direct relationship between a reduction of the welfare state in the European

Union—where, because of its greater initial size, cuts have been more dramatic—and the increase in inequality that has resulted in most EU countries.

As noted earlier, many of these policy changes have a political as well as economic component. A major problem associated with increased inequality is that those who gain a greater share of total wealth are able to translate it into greater political power. This plays out through the U.S. system of campaign finance, in which candidates for political office can accept disproportionate donations from wealthy individuals or large corporations with an interest in, say, keeping taxes low for the rich or minimizing regulations on the financial sector. Well-endowed individuals or companies may also hire representatives (or lobbyists) to seek private interviews with influential politicians, in hopes of ensuring favorable legislation. This is another example of "rent-seeking" activity that does not produce any economic value but, rather, redistributes it, accentuating other trends towards greater income inequality.

3.2 CONSEQUENCES

Recall from Chapter 8 that consumers' marginal utility of successive units of a good tends to decrease. Economic evidence suggests the same is true of income. For example, an additional $1,000 in income when one is making $20,000 per year tends to provide greater marginal utility than when one is making $50,000 per year. While some economists avoid making interpersonal comparisons of utility, a reasonable implication of this principle is that overall welfare may be lower in a society with a high degree of inequality as opposed to a society with a low degree of inequality, assuming the same amount of total income. So from a social welfare perspective too much inequality may be economically inefficient as well as unfair.

Many researchers have studied the relationship between economic status and other measures of well-being. Intuitively, it seems reasonable that those with low incomes and little assets tend to have reduced access to quality education, adequate health care, and other resources. And the facts do support this view, see Box 10.3.

BOX 10.3 INEQUALITY IN THE UNITED STATES

While most attention regarding inequality in the United States has focused on income, inequality is evident in many other ways. Despite being one of the richest countries in the world, the United States has the highest level of infant and maternal mortality among developed nations. Life expectancy in the U.S. is one of the lowest among developed nations. Richer households in the U.S. generally have access to adequate, if not excellent, health care. Thus the main reason that the U.S. ranks so poorly according to these measures is that those at the bottom fare so poorly.

The same is true with education. Richer households can afford to send their children to high-quality schools, while most students from disadvantaged families attend school with lower-quality resources. Consider that the gap between American students at the top and those at the middle, according to standardized tests, is equivalent to the gap between the average scores of the U.S. and Azerbaijan.

While inequality in the U.S. has been increasing for decades, so far the policy response has been negligible. Proposals by President Barack Obama to reduce inequality include raising the minimum wage, improving infrastructure, and universal preschool for 4-year-olds. However, in a highly partisan environment, such proposals seem unlikely to meet approval in Congress.

You would think Americans must be tiring of their lack of progress. The disposable income of families in the middle of the income distribution shrank by 4 percent between 2000 and 2010, according to data compiled by the O.E.C.D. In Australia, by contrast, it increased 40 percent. Middle-income Germans, Dutch, French, Danes, Norwegians and even Mexicans gained more ground.

And indeed Americans are tiring of it. Over half—52 percent—say that the government should redistribute wealth by taxing the rich more, according to a Gallup poll in April, the highest share since Gallup first asked the question in 1998.

Source: Eduardo Porter, "Inequality in America: The Data Is Sobering," *New York Times*, August 1, 2013.

But going even further, we consider whether a high degree of inequality imposes broad costs on society—impacts that not only affect the poor, but all members of society. One of the most studied issues is the relationship between inequality and health. Imagine two countries with the exact same average income levels. However, one of these countries has a high degree of economic inequality, while the other has low inequality. Are health outcomes better in the country with lower inequality?

In their 2009 book *The Spirit Level*, Richard Wilkinson and Kate Pickett (both epidemiologists) argue that higher inequality, ceteris paribus, is indeed associated with reduced health. They reason that economic and social inequality creates stress and anxiety, which increases one's susceptibility to disease and also leads to destructive behaviors like substance abuse. They support their position by presenting data showing that rich countries with greater inequality tend to have lower life expectancy, higher rates of infant mortality, and higher rates of mental illness. In addition to the relationship between inequality and health, Wilkinson and Pickett also find that higher inequality is associated with various social problems, including homicide rates, teenage pregnancy, and school dropout rates.

The findings of Wilkinson and Pickett that many social problems are a result of inequality are controversial. For example, a 2010 article in the *Wall Street Journal* criticized *The Spirit Level* for presenting selective data.[4] Also, a 2003 journal article by health economist Angus Deaton concluded that "it is not true that income inequality itself is a major determinant of public health."[5]

There seems to be greater acceptance among economists that excessive inequality can lead to reduced economic growth. One reason is that economic reforms may be more difficult to institute in unequal countries with concentrated political power. Also, if economic mobility is low, those at the bottom have little incentive to invest in their own productivity, and thus overall growth suffers. A 2011 study published by the International Monetary Fund found that greater equality is associated with longer periods of sustained economic growth.[6] The paper concludes that "attention to inequality can bring significant longer-run benefits for growth."

In the 2001 book *Bowling Alone: The Collapse and Revival of American Community*, Robert Putnam argues that an inverse link exists between income inequality and social cohesion. He notes that greater equality causes people to trust one another more, and trust is a cornerstone of social welfare. Putnam has traced the relationship through the twentieth century and found that during periods when the United States had a more equal income distribution (such as the 1950s), there was much more community engagement in general, and that there has been much less over the past few decades as inequality has become more pronounced.

Finally, inequality tends to perpetuate itself. We often prefer to believe that success in our society is based on individual merit, but in fact the family situation in which we start out tends to matter a great deal. Economic mobility is more difficult in a more unequal society because the change in income needed to move to a higher income quintile becomes larger. Again, this maintains existing concentrations of political power, which reduces the possibility for broad-based economic and social reforms. Policies tend to be instituted which benefit a powerful minority, while the preferences of the majority are not heard.

Discussion Questions

1. If you could change a single one of the "causes" of inequality described above, on which would you choose to focus? Why?

2. People are often ashamed of coming from a relatively poor family, even if it is poor only relative to its immediate neighbors (and might appear wealthy to someone in another community, or another country). Why do you suppose this is? Do you think this psychological factor is relevant to the perpetuation of inequality in society?

4. RESPONDING TO INEQUALITY

As we mentioned at the beginning of the chapter, there is no consensus regarding the "right" amount of inequality in a society. So before we consider what policies might be instituted to respond to inequality, we first consider various philosophical perspectives on the topic of inequality.

4.1 PHILOSOPHICAL PERSPECTIVES ON INEQUALITY

Unlike the goal of efficiency, which has a specific technical meaning that we have discussed in earlier chapters, there is no single standard of equity or fairness. Yet to many people, there is something disturbing about the current degree of income and wealth inequality in the United States. What are some standards that can be used to judge the kind and degree of equity in a society?

Several philosophical standards of equity have been suggested; we will focus on five standards here:

1. Equality of outcomes
2. Equality of opportunities
3. Equal rewards for equal contributions
4. Equal rights
5. The basic needs approach

Equality of outcomes is an easily stated—but rarely adopted—standard of equity which says that everyone should achieve the same level of well-being. The idea of everyone being equally happy has a certain appeal, but no country has ever tried to translate this into practice by precisely equalizing economic outcomes such as wealth or income. In all existing economies, at least some degree of inequality of outcomes is thought to serve as an important incentive for people to develop skills, to work, and to innovate.

Although complete equality is not a feasible goal, governments frequently seek to reduce the *inequality* of outcomes, and this has historically been done through redistribution. The most common example is the practice of taxing those who earn high incomes and redistributing some of the tax revenue to the most needy groups. The effectiveness of such a policy in reducing inequality has, however, varied considerably over time and across regions.

Equality of opportunity is another popular standard of equity, based on the thinking of, among others, the philosopher John Rawls. According to this principle, all individuals should have the same opportunity to create a life and a livelihood for themselves that will allow them to acquire the things that they value. After they have been given the same opportunities, people who are ambitious and want to work hard to acquire wealth should be able to do so. People who choose not to take as much advantage of these opportunities can accept a lesser economic standing. This standard has the appeal of rewarding effort, while putting everyone on a presumed "level playing field."

Unfortunately, this is much simpler and appealing in theory than it is in practice. Although a society can try to *approach* this standard through programs like public education and antidiscrimination laws, it is a hard standard to apply in any precise sense. If opportunity is to be equal in each generation, then no material wealth should be passed along by inheritance. It is not equitable for some children to be able to start out in safe neighborhoods with parents who encourage them, while others grow up surrounded by crime or indifference. Thus creating equal opportunity for the next generation would mean great changes in this one.

And what does it mean to create "equality of opportunity" if some people are naturally endowed with greater intelligence or talents than others? Should a society allow those endowed with more talent to realize more economic gain for less work effort? The essential point is that when we speak of equality of opportunity, what we really mean is equality of the "wherewithal to conduct a prosperous, happy, and meaningful life," and this "wherewithal" really comes down to *assets,* whether financial, social, mental, physical, or other (recalling Amartya Sen's concept, mentioned above, of "capabilities"). It is an essential point because, as we see, income inequality stems from asset inequality. If we address the latter, we go a long way toward correcting the former. This is not an easy thing to do because, while relatively few would object to a philosophy based on "equality of opportunity," many more would strongly oppose "equality of total assets."

The "equal rewards for equal contributions" principle is similar to the "equality of opportunity" concept, but it is more of an exchange-based standard that tends to conform to traditional economic logic. According to this standard, those who contribute the most to an economy should be entitled to receive the most in return. Discrimination should not be allowed among individuals who do the same work, according to this principle, but market outcomes, even fairly unequal ones, are acceptable, whether they are due to differences in work effort or innate talents. In support of this view, there is a long-standing belief that people are entitled both to the products of their labor and to the fruits of their property (where property is viewed as the product of past labor).

The fourth perspective on equality focuses on equal rights as opposed to a focus on income or wealth. Societies often specify certain rights to which each individual should have an equal claim (e.g., liberty, the pursuit of happiness). As another example, modern democracy usually assumes the principle of "one person, one vote." This means that all eligible citizens have an equal right to cast a ballot and be fairly represented in the electoral system. Sen has suggested a rather direct link between democracy and economic outcomes. He points out that famines in which thousands or even millions of people die of hunger tend to occur in dictatorial states—even, sometimes, in the face of plentiful food supplies—and have not arisen in democratic ones, where those in power are accountable to the people.

A rights-based interpretation of equality assumes that equal rights are more fundamental to well-being than a particular level of material goods. There is no universal agreement, however, on just what these rights should include or on how they should be related to economic issues. Among the things that have been thought to belong to everyone by right, in some (but not all) countries, are free education, free health care, and easy access to resources for family planning.

Finally, attention to the least fortunate presents a different interpretation of equity. Sometimes referred to as the "basic needs" approach, it also echoes positions traditionally taken by many religions. According to this principle, the success of a society should be judged not by its members' average, or total, well-being (if such a thing could be calculated) but, rather, by its treatment of those who are worst off. While some philosophers such as Rawls support this perspective, others are critical of it because it places disproportionate attention on the poorest groups. Focusing exclusively on the poorest groups ignores the fairness (or lack thereof) of the distribution over the middle and upper-income ranges.

Which definition of equity should an economist use? There is no simple answer; different people have strongly held political and ethical preferences for one or another concept of equity. It should be clear from our description that in particular situations, different concepts might have conflicting implications.

Yet few if any advocate either extreme inequality or complete equality. For many economists the question is *how much* inequality is tolerable, or desirable, and what policies are appropriate to achieve this desirable level. We turn to policies that can affect the degree of inequality in a society.

4.2 TAX AND WAGE POLICIES

One way of reversing the trend toward greater inequality is through the tax system. By shifting more of the overall tax burden to high-income households, after-tax income inequality can be reduced. As we will see in more detail in Chapter 11, federal income tax rates on the highest-income households in the United States have changed significantly over time, from above 90 percent in the 1950s to as low as 28 percent in the 1980s. The maximum federal income tax rate is currently 39.6 percent. However, the tax rate that wealthy people actually pay is often considerably less than this due to tax provisions that allow them to claim many deductions, such as the mortgage interest on a second home. Also, income from investments, such as stocks and mutual funds, are taxed at a lower rate—a maximum of 20 percent.

Tax rates on those at the highest income levels have tended to decrease in recent decades. For example, a 2007 paper found that the top 0.01 percent in the U.S. paid over 70 percent of their income in federal taxes in 1960, but only about 30 percent in 2005.[7] Some politicians have suggested reversing this trend by increasing tax rates at the top of the income spectrum, not necessarily to the levels of the 1950s but to ensure that wealthy households are not able to lower their taxes excessively through deductions. Specifically, in 2012 President Barack Obama proposed the "Buffet Rule," named for billionaire investor Warren Buffet, who in 2011 publicly stated that it was unfair that wealthy people like himself were able to pay a lower overall tax rate than many middle-class people. President Obama's proposal was that households making more than $1 million per year should have to pay at least 30 percent of their total income in taxes regardless of how many deductions they could claim. This proposal, however, was unable to pass the U.S. Congress.

Another approach for reducing inequality is to increase the federal minimum wage, which is now $7.25 per hour. Although the federal minimum wage has been increased at times over the years, it has not kept up with inflation. If the minimum wage in the late 1960s is adjusted for inflation, in current dollars it comes to approximately $10 per hour. Many believe that the current $7.25 minimum is insufficient even to provide for the basic necessities of a family. In several U.S. states, "living wage" campaigns have advocated passing legislation at the state level that requires a minimum wage higher than the federal standard. About 20 states have a higher minimum wage than $7.25, the highest minimum wage being $9.19 in Washington state.

4.3 SPENDING PRIORITIES

Another area where reforms have the potential to redress inequality is government spending. There is little question that government spending priorities have long been skewed in a way that does not favor a more equitable distribution of income. Two important examples are military spending and debt financing.

Defense expenditures have been estimated to be between one-fourth and one-third of the total federal budget. Critics suggest that this level of this expense is a relic of the cold war and that we could easily do with less. Because the military accounts for a sizable share of the budget, even a modest cutback would make a considerable amount of funds available in other areas that could increase economic opportunities for low-income households, such as better access to education and health care.

Debt financing is another way that the federal budget effectively helps transfer income from the poor and middle classes to the wealthy. In recent years, between 6 percent and 12 percent of the federal budget is devoted to paying interest on existing debt. (Recently it is on the low end, because of historically low interest rates). Because it is overwhelmingly the wealthy who own government bonds, they are the ones who receive these flows from the government. To the extent that the government is able to reduce its relative debt burden—raising taxes would be an effective way of doing this—doing so would contribute to reducing income inequality.

As for areas in which the government could spend more to address inequality, education stands out. As we saw in Chapter 9 and earlier this chapter, education levels are highly correlated with economic outcomes. According to the U.S. Department of Education, educational inequalities are increasing—meaning that the gap in education access and affordability between high and low income households is increasing.[8] Under President Barack Obama, Pell grants to college students based on economic need have increased, but the Department of Education notes that the benefits of more Pell grant money are likely to be more than offset by tuition increases. Policy recommendations of the Department of Education include further increasing need-based financial assistance, expanding loan forgiveness for student debt, and promoting the ability of students to transfer from 2-year to 4-year colleges.

4.4 CONCLUDING THOUGHTS

It is increasingly evident that income and wealth in the United States are increasingly concentrated. As noted earlier, as wealth becomes concentrated in fewer hands, it also becomes more of a challenge to pursue countervailing reforms. Nonetheless, both economic theory and practical policy analysis suggest that policy reform can make a difference in reducing inequality.

In the aftermath of the Great Recession of 2007–9, much more attention has been focused on inequality, in the United States and in other countries. It is possible that this will lead to policy changes such as those discussed above. The high degree of inequality in the years leading up to the Great Depression (recall Figure 10.5) helped usher in the New Deal policies of the 1930s. Now that inequality has returned to, and even exceeded, the levels that existed prior to the Great Depression, many concerned citizens feel the time has finally come to address the issue. Thus the economic analysis both of inequality, and of policies to respond to inequality, is likely to be of great relevance in the immediate future.

Discussion Questions

1. Do you generally believe that raising taxes on the rich is an appropriate approach for reducing economic inequality? What level of taxation on the rich do you think is fair? (Note that we will also consider this topic in the next chapter.)
2. Do you think the spending priorities of the government should be changed in order to reduce economic inequality? Beyond the suggestions in the text, can you think of any other ways that government spending priorities could be changed?

REVIEW QUESTIONS

1. About what share of aggregate income does each quintile of households receive in the United States?
2. How is a Lorenz curve constructed? What does it measure?
3. What is the Gini ratio? What does a higher value of the ratio signify?
4. What effect do taxes and transfer payments have on the distribution of U.S. household income?
5. What tends to be more unequal—the distribution of income or wealth?
6. How has income inequality in the United States changed in recent decades?
7. How does income and wealth vary by race?
8. What is economic mobility?
9. How does economic inequality in the United States compare to other countries?
10. What are some of the causes of growing inequality in the United States?
11. What are some of the consequences of inequality?
12. Describe the five different philosophical perspectives on inequality.
13. How can tax and wage policies be used to reduce inequality?
14. How are government spending priorities related to inequality?

EXERCISES

1. Statistics from the government of Thailand describe the household income distribution in that country, for 2000, as follows:

Group of households	Share of aggregate income (%)
Poorest fifth	5.5
Second fifth	8.8
Middle fifth	13.2
Fourth fifth	21.5
Richest fifth	51.0

Source: National Statistics Office Thailand, "Household Socio-Economic Survey," table 6, http://web.nso.go.th/eng/en/stat/socio/soctab6.htm.

a. Create a carefully labeled Lorenz curve describing this distribution. (Be precise about the labels on the vertical axis.)
b. Compare this distribution to the distribution in the United States. Would you expect the Gini ratio for Thailand to be much higher or lower or about the same? Why?

2. How does inequality vary across countries? Choose two countries not mentioned in the text, and write a paragraph comparing their performance on the Gini ratio and according to income share by quintile. Which country seems to have a more unequal distribution of income? For data, consult the World Bank's *World Development Indicators* online database or the CIA's *World Factbook*, also available online. Note which data source you used.

3. Match each concept in Column A with a definition or example in Column B.

Column A	Column B
a. Economic mobility	1. A very unequal income distribution
b. Equality of outcomes	2. Wages, salaries, and fringe benefits
c. Capital gain	3. Focuses on the well-being of the least fortunate
d. Quintile	4. Rents, profit, and interest
e. Labor income	5. A very equal income distribution
f. A Gini ratio close to 1	6. A group containing 20 percent of the total
g. Equality of opportunities	7. Changes in one's economic status over time
h. A Gini ratio close to 0	8. An increase in the value of an asset at the time of sale
i. Capital income	9. Everyone has the same income level
j. Basic needs approach	10. Everyone has access to the same quality of education

NOTES

1. Raj Chetty, Nathaniel Hendren, Patrick Kline, and Emmanuel Saez, "The Economic Impacts of Tax Expenditures: Evidence of Spatial Variation across the U.S.," Harvard University, Department of Economics, 2013, http://scholar.harvard.edu/hendren/publications/economic-impacts-tax-expenditures-evidence-spatial-variation-across-us/.

2. For example, Marcus Jäntti et al., "American Exceptionalism in a New Light: A Comparison of Intergenerational Earnings Mobility in Nordic Countries, the United Kingdom, and the United States," IZA Discussion Paper 1938, Bonn, Germany January 2006; Linda Levine, "The U.S. Income Distribution and Mobility: Trends and International Comparisons," Congressional Research Service, Washington, DC, November 29, 2012.

3. Julia B. Isaacs, "International Comparisons of Economic Mobility," The Brookings Institution, Washington, D.C., www.brookings.edu/~/media/research/files/reports/2008/2/economic%20mobility%20sawhill/02_economic_mobility_sawhill_ch3.pdf.

4. Nima Sanandaji, Tino Sanandaji, Arvid Malm, and Christopher Snowdon, "Un-Level Ground," *Wall Street Journal*, July 9, 2010.

5. Angus Deaton, "Health, Inequality, and Economic Development," *Journal of Economic Literature* 41(1) (2003):113-158.

6. Andrew G. Berg and Jonathan D. Ostry, "Inequality and Unsustainable Growth: Two Sides of the Same Coin?" International Monetary Fund, IMF Staff Discussion Note SDN/11/08, April 8, 2011.

7. Thomas Piketty and Emmanuel Saez, "How Progressive Is the U.S. Federal Tax System? A Historical and International Perspective," *Journal of Economic Perspectives* 21(1) (2007): 3–24.

8. United States Department of Education, "The Rising Price of Inequality," Advisory Committee on Student Financial Assistance, Washington, D.C., June 2010.

11 Taxes and Tax Policy

Albert Einstein reportedly once said: "The hardest thing in the world to understand is income taxes." It is true that taxes can be complicated. The United States federal tax code is more than 70,000 pages long. Browsing the tax code's table of contents offers a glimpse into the vast complexity of federal taxation. Entire sections of the tax code apply specifically to the taxation of vaccines (Sec. 4131–4132), shipowners' mutual protection and indemnity associations (Sec. 526), specially sweetened natural wines (Sec. 5385), and health benefits for certain miners (Sec. 9711–9712).

Fortunately, one need not comprehend the imposing complexity of tax laws to understand the crucial role of taxes in modern societies. Taxation is an important topic for students of economics. Tax policies have important economic consequences, both for a national economy and for particular groups within the economy. Tax policies are often designed with the intention of stimulating economic growth—although economists differ significantly about which policies are most effective at fostering growth. Taxes can create incentives promoting desirable behavior and disincentives for unwanted behavior. Taxation provides a means to redistribute economic resources toward those with low income or special needs. Taxes provide the revenue needed for important public services such as social security, health care, national defense, and education.

Taxation is as much a political issue as an economic issue. Political leaders have used tax policy to promote their agendas by initiating various tax reforms: decreasing (or increasing) tax rates, changing the definition of taxable income, creating new taxes on specific products, and so forth. Of course, no one particularly wants to pay taxes. Specific groups, such as small business owners, farmers, or retired individuals, exert significant political effort to reduce their share of the tax burden. Tax codes are packed with rules that benefit a certain group of taxpayers while inevitably shifting more of the burden to others.

In this chapter, we take a look at taxes and tax policy. First, we consider taxes from a theoretical perspective based on the economic models already discussed. Second, we summarize the different types of taxes, with an emphasis on the United States. Third, we present an international comparison of tax policies. Finally, we address current tax debates, including the distribution of the tax burden.

1. Economic Theory and Taxes

1.1 Taxes in the Supply-and-Demand Model

excise tax: a per-unit tax on a good or service

The supply-and-demand model we presented in Chapter 3 can be used to gain insights into the effects of taxation on consumers and producers. To incorporate taxes into our model, we consider a per-unit tax on a product or service, referred to as an **excise tax**. Let's suppose that an excise tax is imposed on cups of coffee—$0.30 per cup. In this section, we use our model to answer the following two questions:

1. How will the tax affect the price of cups of coffee?
2. How will the tax affect the quantity of coffee sold?

Common sense provides part of the answer to these questions. It seems reasonable to expect that taxing a product will increase its price. It also seems reasonable that the tax will reduce the quantity of coffee sold, given that the quantity demanded will decrease if the price rises.

But our model helps us to answer questions that we might not be able to answer with common sense alone. In particular, how much will the price of coffee increase as a result of the tax? You might think that a tax of $0.30 per cup should increase the equilibrium price by $0.30 per cup. In other words, the tax would be "passed on" to the consumer. Our model determines whether this logic is correct.

To determine how to incorporate an excise tax into our supply-and-demand model, we can recall our discussion of marginal costs and marginal benefits from Chapter 5. We stated then that a supply curve is a marginal cost curve and a demand curve is a marginal benefit curve. A tax is essentially an additional cost. We assume for simplicity that the $0.30 excise tax is paid by coffee suppliers directly to the government. So, in addition to the production cost of actually making a cup of coffee, the coffee supplier must pay the government $0.30 per cup. Effectively, the tax increases the marginal cost of supplying coffee.

We express an increase in the marginal cost of supplying coffee due to a tax just as we express an increase in input prices—the supply curve shifts upward.* The upward shift would be exactly equal to the amount of the tax. In other words, the marginal supply cost of each cup of coffee increases by $0.30 as a result of the tax.

This is shown in Figure 11.1, which presents our market for cups of coffee. The supply curve without any tax is $Supply_0$, with equilibrium at E_0—a price of $1.10 per cup and a quantity sold of 700 cups per week. Instituting the excise tax raises the supply curve upward by $0.30 per cup to $Supply_{Tax}$. Note that $Supply_{Tax}$ is parallel to $Supply_0$ because the cost of supplying each cup of coffee has increased by the same amount of $0.30.

Suppliers will seek to recoup the cost of the tax by raising their prices. You might think that they will increase their price by $0.30, to $1.40. But notice that at a price of $1.40 (the dashed blue line in Figure 11.1) the quantity supplied exceeds the quantity demanded—a situation of surplus. As we discussed in Chapter 3, this creates a downward pressure on prices.

The new equilibrium with the tax occurs at E_{Tax}, at a price of $1.33 per cup and a quantity sold of 625 cups per week. As we expected, the price has risen and the quantity sold has decreased. However, the price has not risen by the amount of the tax. The $0.30 per cup tax led to a $0.23 increase in the price. Most of the cost has been passed on to consumers, but the suppliers also bear some burden of the tax.

How much of the tax burden is borne by consumers and producers depends on the elasticity of demand. In Figure 11.2 we see the impact of a tax when demand is highly inelastic, such as the demand for gasoline or cigarettes. Before the tax, the supply curve is $Supply_0$, and the equilibrium price is P_0 and quantity is Q_0. The tax shifts the supply curve upward to $Supply_{Tax}$, and the equilibrium price rises to P_{Tax} and quantity falls to Q_{Tax}. The vertical distance between P_{Tax} and P_1 is the amount of the tax—the distance between the two supply curves. In this case, we see that the price has risen by nearly as much of the tax. Thus when demand is inelastic, most of the tax is passed on to consumers. An inelastic demand curve implies that consumers' quantity demanded will change little when prices rise.

---

*We could also visualize the supply curve shifting "back" instead of "up." But in the case of a tax, it is easier to think of the curve shifting upward—an increase in the marginal cost of supply.

Figure 11.1   **The Impact of a Tax on the Market for Cups of Coffee**

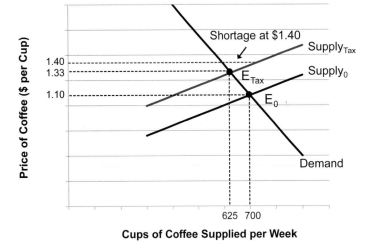

An excise tax on a product results in a higher price and a lower quantity sold.

Cups of Coffee Supplied per Week

Figure 11.2   **The Impact of an Excise Tax with an Inelastic Demand Curve**

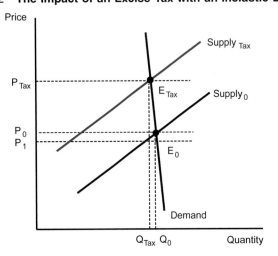

When demand is highly inelastic, most of the burden of an excise tax will fall on consumers. In other words, producers will be able to pass on most of the cost of the tax by raising price.

At the extreme, if demand is perfectly inelastic, the demand curve is a vertical line and the quantity demanded does not change when prices rise. With a perfectly inelastic demand curve, the price rises by the exact amount of the tax and the full burden of the tax is borne by consumers.

However, if demand is highly elastic most of the burden of the tax is borne by producers. This is shown in Figure 11.3. Again, the supply curve before a tax is $Supply_0$, with an equilibrium price of P_0 and quantity of Q_0. The supply curve with the tax is $Supply_{Tax}$. We see that as producers raise their prices, the quantity demanded falls significantly, from Q_0 to Q_{Tax}. Recall that an elastic demand curve means that consumers have many alternatives or consider the good nonessential. Producers are able to raise prices only slightly, to P_{Tax}, which is much less than the per-unit tax, which is again the vertical distance between P_{Tax} and P_1.

The elasticity of supply also affects the distribution of the tax burden. It is a little more difficult to see why this is so, but in general if supply is very elastic, more of the tax burden is passed on to consumers. This might be true, for example, in a very competitive industry in which it is not possible for producers to accept a lower price without going out of business. If supply is very inelastic, by contrast, suppliers can accept a price reduction without affecting the quantity supplied by much. (Try varying the elasticity of supply in a graph like Figure 11.3 to see this effect.)

Figure 11.3   **The Impact of an Excise Tax with an Elastic Demand Curve**

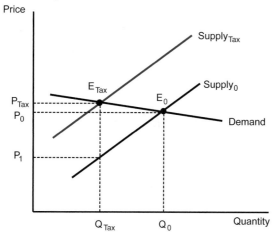

When demand is highly elastic, most of the burden of an excise tax will fall on producers. Price will rise slightly, but the quantity sold will decline significantly.

1.2 TAX REVENUES

We now consider using our supply-and-demand model to explore how much revenue is generated from a tax. The tax revenue from a per-unit tax is simply:

$$Tax\ revenue = Per\text{-}unit\ tax * Quantity$$

So if the tax on cups of coffee is $0.30 per cup and 625 cups of coffee are sold per week, then the tax revenue collected by the government each week is:

$$Tax\ revenue = \$0.30 * 625 = \$187.50$$

We can represent this tax revenue in Figure 11.4, which again shows our market for coffee with a tax of $0.30 per cup. The vertical distance between the two supply curves is $0.30, as shown in the graph. So the shaded rectangle, with a height of $0.30 and a length of 625 cups, represents our tax revenue of $187.50 per week. Being able to represent tax revenues on our supply-and-demand graph is important as in the next section we analyze the welfare effects of a tax.

Figure 11.4   **Tax Revenues from a Tax on Cups of Coffee**

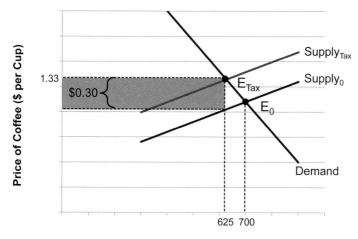

We can represent the revenue from an excise tax as the shaded area in the graph.

Cups of Coffee Supplied per Week

But first consider a government's decision about which goods and services to tax. Products are taxed for two basic reasons:

1. to discourage purchases of that product
2. to generate revenue

Any tax creates a disincentive, so consumers will reduce their purchases and seek alternatives. Comparing Figures 11.2 and 11.3 we see that the disincentive effect of a tax is greatest when the demand curve is highly elastic. However, the products that society generally wants to discourage people from buying, such as cigarettes and alcohol, tend to have inelastic demand curves. As shown in Figure 11.2, a tax on a good with inelastic demand will only reduce the quantity sold a little bit. So, in order for a tax to significantly reduce the quantity sold when demand is inelastic, the tax must be substantial.

The elasticity of demand also has implications for tax revenues. If the demand curve is elastic, an excise tax significantly reduces the quantity demanded (see Figure 11.3), and the government does not collect that much tax revenue. But if the demand curve is inelastic, the tax does not reduce the quantity demanded much (see Figure 11.2), and the government collects significant revenues.

It is no surprise that excise taxes tend to be imposed on products with inelastic demand curves, such as gasoline, cigarettes, and alcohol. This suggests that the primary motivation for taxes on these products is revenue generation rather than encouraging behavioral changes. But recall that demand for these products tends to be more elastic in the long run. So we would expect tax revenues to decline gradually over time, ceteris paribus, as people have more time to adjust their behavior.

We can summarize the impact of an excise tax on products with elastic and inelastic demand curves in Table 11.1.*

Table 11.1   **Summary of Excise Tax Impacts for Products with Elastic and Inelastic Demand Curves**

	Inelastic demand	Elastic demand
Change in price	Large, nearly equal to the per-unit tax	Small, much less than the per-unit tax
Change in quantity sold	Relatively small	Relatively large
Tax revenues	Relatively large	Relatively small
Tax burden	Primarily borne by consumers	Primarily borne by producers

1.3 WELFARE ANALYSIS OF TAXATION

We can now apply welfare analysis, as presented in Chapter 5, to the issue of taxation. We consider what happens to consumer and producer surplus when an excise tax is applied to a product. Again, we can rely on common sense to predict what the welfare effects will be. Consumers generally do not like taxes on the products that they purchase, so we might expect that consumer surplus will decline when a product is taxed. Producers also do not favor taxes on the products that they sell, so it seems reasonable to expect producer surplus to decline.

Recall from Chapter 5 we mentioned that welfare analysis should also consider the impacts of a market on "the rest of society," meaning those not directly involved in a market transaction. Taxes represent revenue to a government entity, but these revenues can be used for any beneficial social use—building schools or roads, providing health care, protecting

---

*As noted, the elasticity of supply also affects distribution of the tax burden, but in general this effect is less important, so we concentrate here on demand elasticity.

the environment, scientific research, or any other use. Although the ultimate benefit of tax revenues depends on their particular use, in this chapter our analysis only goes as far as the tax collection. In other words, if a government collects $5 million in taxes, that revenue represents a potential $5 million benefit to society. If the government uses these tax dollars wisely, say, investing in education or infrastructure, $5 million may generate more than $5 million in long-run benefits. Of course, if the government squanders its tax revenues, less than $5 million in social benefits may result.

Figure 11.5 shows the welfare effects of an excise tax on a product. Before the tax, we again have the supply curve $Supply_0$, with an equilibrium price of P_0 and quantity of Q_0. The welfare of the market without a tax is:

$$Consumer\ Surplus = A + B + E + H$$
$$Producer\ Surplus = C + D + F + G + I$$

There is no tax revenue, so total social welfare is simply the sum of consumer and producer surplus.

Instituting a tax shifts the supply curve to $Supply_{Tax}$, with a new equilibrium at E_{Tax}. With price rising to P_{Tax}, consumer surplus is only area A. Thus we can conclude that consumer surplus has decreased, as we expected.

Figuring out the producer surplus is a little tricky. First, realize that producers receive total revenues of price times quantity, or $(P_{Tax} * Q_{Tax})$. In Figure 11.5, total revenues are:

$$Total\ Producer\ Revenues = B + C + D + E + F + G + J$$

Producers have two costs: the cost of production and the tax. The cost of production is the area under their marginal cost curve, $Supply_0$, which is area J. The tax is:

$$Tax\ Revenues = B + C + E + F$$

When we subtract production costs and the tax paid from total revenues, we are left with producer surplus:

$$Producer\ Surplus = (B + C + D + E + F + G + J) - J - (B + C + E + F)$$
$$= D + G$$

Figure 11.5 **Welfare Analysis of an Excise Tax**

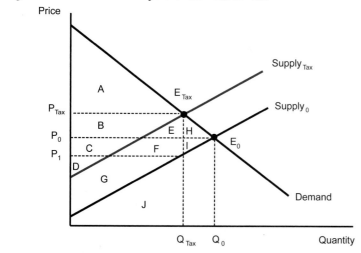

An excise tax in a market results in a deadweight loss equal to areas H and I.

Note that producer surplus has also decreased. Total social welfare with the tax is the sum of consumer and producer surplus, plus the tax revenues:

$$Social\ Welfare = A + (D + G) + (B + C + E + F)$$

How does this compare to social welfare before the tax? Before the tax, social welfare also included area (H + I). So even accounting for the benefits of the tax revenues, the tax has resulted in a deadweight loss, similar to the price controls that we discussed in Chapter 5. We can conclude that imposing a tax on a product:

- reduces consumer surplus
- reduces producer surplus
- provides social benefits in the form of tax revenues
- creates a deadweight loss

Based on this analysis, it may seem that taxing is always a bad idea. But as usual, we need to consider a broader context in order to determine whether a particular tax is justified. The potentially valid reasons for taxing include:

1. Governments obviously cannot rely on voluntary donations, thus *something* must be taxed in any society.
2. As mentioned earlier, a tax may be justified on the basis that it creates a disincentive for something. As we saw in Chapter 7, consumer behavior is not always rational and a tax can be used to encourage people to make better decisions.
3. The tax revenues may be spent wisely such that the net increase in social benefits exceeds the deadweight loss.
4. A tax may be justified on the basis of equity, in order to reduce inequality. This is generally not true of excise taxes, but may apply to other taxes, such as the income tax, which falls more heavily on higher-income individuals and families.

An excise tax is just one type of tax. In most countries, the majority of tax revenues come from other taxes, such as taxes on income or property. We now turn to a summary of the tax system of the United States. Later, we compare the U.S. tax system to that of other countries.

Discussion Questions

1. What recent news stories have you heard about taxes? How does the material in the previous section relate to these stories?
2. What goods and services do you think should be subjected to excise taxes? How would these taxes affect different groups of people?

2. THE STRUCTURE OF TAXATION IN THE UNITED STATES

2.1 TAX PROGRESSIVITY

progressive tax:
a tax in which the percentage of one's income that is paid in taxes tends to increase with increasing income levels

Before we discuss the different types of taxes in the United States, we need to first define the concept of tax progressivity. By a **progressive tax**, we mean that the percentage of income an individual (or household) pays in taxes tends to increase with increasing income. Not only do those with higher incomes pay more in total taxes, but they pay a higher *rate* of taxes. For example, a person making $100,000 a year might pay 25 percent of his or her income in taxes ($25,000 in taxes), while someone with an income of $30,000 might pay a tax rate of only 10 percent ($3,000 in taxes). So the higher-income person pays a higher tax rate, and thus this tax is progressive.

regressive tax: a tax in which the percentage of one's income paid in taxes tends to decrease with increasing income levels

proportional tax: a tax in which all taxpayers pay the same tax rate, regardless of income

A tax can also be regressive or proportional. A **regressive tax** is one in which the proportion of income paid in taxes tends to decrease as one's income increases. A **proportional tax** means that everyone pays the same tax rate regardless of income. Most countries' overall tax system, including that of the United States, includes a mix of progressive and regressive taxes, as different taxes are designed with different purposes.

The overall tax system of the United States and most other countries is progressive. A progressive tax system is used for many reasons, including:

1. A progressive tax embodies the concept that those with high incomes should pay more of their income in taxes because of their greater ability to pay without a harmful sacrifice. By paying a tax, any household must forgo an equivalent amount of spending on goods, services, or investments. For a high-income household, these forgone opportunities might include a second home, an expensive vehicle, or a purchase of corporate stock. A low-income household, by comparison, might have to forgo basic medical care, postsecondary education, or vehicle safety repairs.

2. A progressive tax system can be used to address economic inequality in a society. If the benefits of programs funded by taxation primarily benefit low-income households while high-income households pay the majority of taxes, then a tax system effectively operates as a means to reduce inequality.

3. There is also an economic argument for a progressive tax system—it can yield a given level of public revenue with the least macroeconomic impact. To see why, consider how households with different levels of income respond to a $1,000 tax cut. A low-income household tends to spend the entire amount quickly on needed goods and services—injecting $1,000 of increased demand into the economy. By comparison, a high-income household might only spend a fraction of the tax cut on goods and services, choosing to save or invest a portion of the money. The money that a high-income household saves or invests does not add to the overall level of effective demand in an economy.* In economic terms, we say that the **marginal propensity to consume** (the tendency to spend, rather than save, an additional dollar of income) tends to decrease as income increases. Collecting proportionately more taxes from high-income households thus has less effect on total effective demand in the economy.

marginal propensity to consume: the tendency to spend, rather than save, an additional dollar of income

Despite these arguments for a progressive tax, it is possible for a tax system to become too progressive. Extremely high tax rates on income create a disincentive for individuals to expend economically productive effort. Very high taxes might limit the risks taken by entrepreneurs, stifling innovation and technological advance. The desire to "soak the rich" through an extremely progressive tax system might be viewed as unfair and economically unwise and can promote "tax flight," in which wealthy individuals relocate in order to avoid high tax rates. We consider these issues in more detail later in the chapter. But next we turn to a discussion of the U.S. tax system.

2.2 Federal Income Taxes

The federal income tax is the most visible, complicated, and debated tax in the United States. The federal income tax was established with the ratification of the Sixteenth Amendment to the U.S. Constitution in 1913. It is levied on wages and salaries as well as income from many other sources, including interest, dividends, capital gains, self-employment income, alimony, and prizes. To understand the basic workings of federal income taxes, fortunately you need to comprehend only two major issues:

---

*Money saved or invested can, however, provide the financial capital necessary to increase the productive capacity of the economy. "Supply-side" economics stresses the importance of investment by the wealthy as critical to macroeconomic growth.

1. Not all income is not taxable—there are important differences between "total income" and "taxable income."
2. There is also an important difference between the "effective tax rate" and the "marginal tax rate."

total income: the sum of income that an individual or couple receives from all sources

Total income is simply the sum of income that an individual or couple receives from all sources.* For most people, the largest portion of total income comes from wages or salaries. Many people also receive investment income from interest, capital gains, and dividends. Self-employment income is also included in total income, along with other types of income such as alimony, farm income, and winnings from gambling.

The amount of federal taxes that a person owes is not calculated based on total income. Instead, after total income is calculated, tax filers are allowed to subtract some expenses as nontaxable. Each filer receives an exemption as well as various deductions. For example, in 2013 a single filer with no children was allowed to deduct the first $10,000 of income as nontaxable.** Other expenses that can be deducted include individual retirement account (IRA) contributions, allowable moving expenses (e.g., for a job), student loan interest, and certain tuition expenses.

taxable income: the portion of one's income that is subject to taxation after deductions and exemptions

Taxable income is the income that is subject to taxation, after all deductions and exemptions. However, the amount of tax owed is not simply a multiple of taxable income and a single tax rate. The federal income tax system in the United States uses increasing **marginal tax rates** (the tax rate applicable to an additional dollar of income). This means that different tax rates apply to different portions of a person's income. The marginal tax rates in effect for 2013 are listed in Table 11.2. For a single filer, the first $8,925 of taxable income is taxed at a rate of 10 percent. Taxable income above $8,925 but less than $36,250 is taxed at a rate of 15 percent, and so on up to a maximum marginal tax rate of 39.6 percent. The income levels that are taxed at each rate are higher for married filers, filing jointly.

marginal tax rate: the tax rate applicable to an additional dollar of income

The way that one's income tax bill is determined is best illustrated with an example. Suppose that we want to calculate the taxes owed by a single person (let's call her Susan) with no children and a total income of $49,000. As mentioned above, in 2013 she would be allowed to claim the first $10,000 of income as nontaxable. Assume that Susan contributed $2,000 to an IRA, so this contribution can also be deducted from her total income. Thus her taxable income would be $37,000, as shown in Table 11.3. On the first $8,925 of taxable income, she owes 10 percent in taxes, or $892.50. The tax rate on her taxable income above $8,925 but below $36,250 is 15 percent, for a tax of (($36,250 − $8,925) × 0.15), or $4,098.75. Finally, her tax rate is 25 percent for her taxable income above $36,250, for a tax of (($37,000 − $36,250) × 0.25), or $187.50. So, we see in Table 11.3 that her total federal income tax bill is $5,178.75.

Table 11.2 **U.S. Federal Marginal Tax Rates, 2013**

Marginal tax rate	Income range for single filers	Income range for married couples
10%	Up to $8,925	Up to $12,750
15%	$8,925 to $36,250	$12,750 to $48,600
25%	$36,250 to $87,850	$48,600 to $125,450
28%	$87,850 to $183,250	$125,450 to $203,150
33%	$183,250 to $398,350	$203,150 to $398,350
35%	$398,350 to $400,00	$398,350 to $425,000
39.6%	Above $400,000	Above $425,000

*Married couples have the option of filing their federal taxes either jointly or separately.

**Couples, and those with children, can deduct higher amounts of income as nontaxable. Filers have the option of "itemizing" their deductions rather than taking the "standard" deduction, depending on which deduction is larger. Deductions that can be itemized include mortgage interest, state and local taxes, major health-care expenses, real estate taxes, and gifts to charity.

Table 11.3 **Susan's Federal Income Tax Calculations**

Variable	Amount	Taxes owed
Total income	$49,000	
Nontaxable deduction	–$10,000	
Retirement contribution	–$2,000	
Taxable income	$37,000	
Income taxed at 10% rate	$8,925	$892.50
Income taxed at 15% rate	$27,325	$4,098.75
Income taxed at 25% rate	$750	$187.50
Total income tax owed		$5,178.75

effective tax rate: one's taxes expressed as a percentage of total income

Note that Susan paid a maximum *marginal* tax rate of 25 percent but *only* on her last $750 of income. Someone's **effective tax rate** is their total taxes divided by total income, expressed as a percentage. Thus Susan's effective tax rate is:

$$\frac{\$5,178.75}{\$49,000} = 0.1057 \times 100 = 10.57 \; percent$$

As we see later in the chapter, which tax rate is most relevant—marginal or effective—depends on the policy situation. But the distinction can help us dispel one common myth about federal income taxes. Many people mistakenly worry that if they move into a higher tax bracket, their remaining income after taxes will decline. But if one moves, for example, from the 15 percent tax bracket to the 25 percent tax bracket, it is only the *additional* income that is taxed at 25 percent, not total income. Thus if Susan had recently received a raise of $750 that increased her total income to $49,000, she paid $187.50 in taxes on her additional income, but all her other income was taxed at the same rates as before her raise. The only way one's total after-tax income could decline with an increase in income would be if the marginal tax rate exceeded 100 percent.*

2.3 FEDERAL SOCIAL INSURANCE TAXES

social insurance taxes: taxes used to fund social insurance programs such as Social Security, Medicare, and Medicaid

Taxes for federal social insurance programs, including Social Security, Medicaid, and Medicare, are collected in addition to federal income taxes. **Social insurance taxes** are levied on salaries and wages, as well as income from self-employment. For those employed by others, these taxes are generally withheld directly from their pay—that is, deducted from their pay before they receive it. These deductions commonly appear as FICA taxes—a reference to the Federal Insurance Contributions Act.

Federal social insurance taxes are actually two separate taxes. The first is a tax of 12.4 percent of pay, which is used primarily to fund Social Security. Half this tax is deducted from an employee's pay, and the employer is responsible for matching this contribution. The other is a tax of 2.9 percent for Medicare and Medicaid, for which the employee and employer again each pay half. Thus social insurance taxes normally amount to a 7.65 percent deduction from an employee's pay (6.2 percent + 1.45 percent). Self-employed individuals are responsible for paying the entire share, 15.3 percent, themselves.

These two taxes have a very important difference. The Social Security tax is due *only* on the first $113,700 of income, as of 2013. On income above $113,700, *no* additional Social

---

*Some low-income workers in the United States are subjected to marginal income tax rates that approach and even exceed 100 percent. Low-income workers are eligible for the Earned Income Tax Credit (EITC), which provides a tax rebate as an incentive to work, but the EITC is phased out as income increases. At some income levels, increases in income can be fully offset by a reduction in the EITC rebate.

Security tax is paid. In other words, the maximum Social Security tax that could be deducted from total pay in 2013 was $7,049.40 ($113,700 × 0.062). The Medicare tax, however, is paid on *all* wages and salaries. Thus, the Medicare tax is truly a proportional tax while the Social Security tax is a proportional tax on the first $113,700 of income but then becomes a regressive tax when we consider income above this limit.

Consider the impact of social insurance taxes on two individuals, Susan with her $49,000 annual salary and Leah, who makes $300,000. Susan would pay a social insurance tax of 7.65 percent on all her income, or $3,748.50. Leah would pay the maximum Social Security contribution of $7,049.40 plus $4,350 for Medicare/Medicaid (1.45 percent of $300,000) for a total social insurance tax bill of $11,399.40. This works out to an effective tax rate of 3.8 percent, or less than half the tax rate paid by Susan. Thus we see that overall social insurance taxes are regressive, with higher-income individuals paying a significantly lower effective rate.

2.4 Federal Corporate Taxes

Corporations must file federal tax forms that are in many ways similar to the forms that individuals complete. Corporate taxable income is defined as total revenue minus the cost of goods sold, wages and salaries, depreciation, repairs, interest paid, and other deductions. Thus corporations, like individuals, can take advantage of many deductions to reduce their taxable income. In fact, a corporation may have so many deductions that it actually ends up paying no tax at all or even receives a rebate check from the federal government.

Corporate tax rates, like personal income tax rates, are progressive and calculated on a marginal basis. In 2013, the lowest corporate tax rate, applied to profits of less than $50,000, was 15 percent. The highest marginal corporate tax rate, applied to profits of between $100,000 and $335,000, was 39 percent.* As for individuals, the effective tax rate that corporations pay is lower than their marginal tax rate. For more on federal corporate taxes, see Box 11.1.

2.5 Other Federal Taxes

The U.S. federal government collects excise taxes on numerous commodities and services, including tires, telephone services, air travel, transportation fuels, alcohol, tobacco, and firearms. Consumers may be unaware that they are paying federal excise taxes, as the tax amounts are normally incorporated into the prices of products. For example, the federal excise tax on gasoline is about 18 cents per gallon.

estate taxes: taxes on the transfers of large estates to beneficiaries

The final federal taxes that we consider are federal estate and gift taxes. The **estate tax** is applied to transfers of large estates to beneficiaries. Like the federal income tax, the estate tax has an exemption amount that is not taxed—in 2013 it was $5.25 million. Only estates valued above the exemption amount are subject to the estate tax, and the tax applies only to the value of the estate above the exemption. The maximum marginal tax rate on estates in 2013 was 40 percent.

gift taxes: taxes on the transfer of large gifts to beneficiaries

The transfer of large gifts is also subject to federal taxation. The estate tax and **gift tax** (taxes on the transfer of large gifts to beneficiaries) are complementary because the gift tax essentially prevents people from giving away their estate to beneficiaries tax-free while they are still alive. In 2013, gifts under $11,000 per year per recipient were excluded from taxation. Like federal income tax rates, the gift tax rates are marginal and progressive, with a maximum tax rate of 40 percent.

The estate and gift taxes are the most progressive element of federal taxation. The estate tax is paid exclusively by those with considerable assets. Moreover, the majority of estate taxes are paid by a very small number of wealthy taxpayers. According to the Tax Policy Center, in 2011 the richest 0.1 percent of those subject to the estate tax paid 51 percent of the total estate tax revenue.[1]

---

*For the highest profit bracket—profits above $18,333,333—the marginal rate was 35 percent.

BOX 11.1 CORPORATE TAXES: THE USE AND MISUSE OF INFORMATION

You may have heard politicians and media commentators mention that the United States has the highest corporate taxes in the world, normally when arguing in favor of lower tax rates. For example, a 2012 article noted:

> Our high corporate tax rate has long made the United States an uncompetitive place for new investment. . . . The U.S. rate [of 39 percent] is well above the 25 percent average of other developed nations in the Organization for Economic Cooperation and Development (OECD). In fact, the U.S. rate is almost 15 percentage points higher than the OECD average. (Dubay 2012)

Looking only at top marginal rates, it is true that the United States does have the highest corporate tax rate among OECD member countries. But as we discussed in Chapter 1, this is an example of a positive statement with normative policy implications that needs to be scrutinized in order to get a more complete picture. In particular, the article mentions nothing about effective tax rates, which as we saw with federal income taxes, can differ significantly from marginal tax rates.

A different 2012 article presents a more balanced approach, indicating that the top marginal rate

> only tells part of the story. Loopholes and other special treatment for different kinds of businesses mean that businesses pay an effective rate of only 29.2 percent of their income, which puts the United States below the average of 31.9 percent among

other major economies, according to analysis by the Treasury Department. (Isidore 2012)

Providing yet another way of viewing corporate taxes in an international perspective, the same article mentions that

> the Organization for Economic Cooperation and Development, the multinational group that tracks global economic growth, estimates the United States collects less corporate tax relative to the overall economy than almost any other country in the world. Some economists argue that tax collection relative to gross domestic product is the more relevant measure. That's because different accounting rules around the world mean what's counted as income in one country isn't counted in another, making comparisons of tax rates misleading.

So depending on one's perspective, the United States either has the highest corporate taxes in the world or one of the lowest! Marginal tax rates are relevant when making decisions about *additional* income. But effective tax rates are generally more relevant when a company decides where to locate in the first place. As with many economic policy applications, what information we focus on depends on the details of the situation.

Sources: Curtis Dubay, "No Fooling: U.S. Now Has Highest Corporate Tax Rate in the World," *The Foundry*, Heritage Foundation, March 30, 2012; Chris Isidore, "U.S. Corporate Tax Rate: No. 1 in the World," CNN Money, March 27, 2012.

2.6 STATE AND LOCAL TAXES

Like the federal government, state and local governments rely on several different tax mechanisms, including income taxes, excise taxes, and corporate taxes. Thus much of the above discussion applies to the tax structures in place in most states. However, some important differences deserve mention.

First, nearly all states (45 as of 2013) have instituted some type of general sales tax. State sales tax rates range from 2.9 percent (Colorado) to 7.25 percent (California). A few states reduce the tax rate on certain goods considered necessities, such as food and prescription drugs. For example, the general sales tax in Illinois is 6.25 percent, but most food and drug sales are taxed at only 1 percent. Many states with sales taxes exempt some necessities from taxation entirely. In most states, municipal localities can charge an additional sales tax. Although local sales taxes are generally lower than state sales taxes, there are exceptions. In New York the state sales tax is 4 percent, but local sales taxes are often higher than 4 percent. The combined state and local sales tax can be higher than 11 percent in Arizona, Arkansas, and Illinois.

Unlike income taxes, sales taxes tend to be quite regressive. The reason is that low-income households tend to spend a larger share of their income on taxable items than do high-income households. Consider gasoline—a product that tends to comprise a smaller share of total expenditures as income rises. An increase in state taxes on gasoline affects low-income households more than high-income households, measured as a percentage of income. Some states, such as Idaho and Kansas, offer low-income households a tax credit to compensate for the regressive nature of state sales taxes.

Forty-one states levy an income tax.* Most of these states have several progressive tax brackets (as many as 12 rates), like the federal income tax. However, state income taxes tend to be less progressive than the federal income tax. Six states have only one income tax rate, meaning that their income tax approaches a proportional tax. Several additional states approach a proportional tax because the top rate applies at a low income or the rates are relatively constant. For example, North Carolina's tax rates only range from 6.0 percent to 7.75 percent.

Another important distinction between the federal system of taxation and the taxes levied at state and local levels is the use of property taxes. Property taxes tend to be the largest revenue source for state and local governments. The primary property tax levied in the United States is a tax on real estate, including land, private residences, and commercial properties. Generally, the tax is calculated as a proportion of the value of the property, although the formulas used by localities differ significantly.

Property taxes tend to be regressive, although less regressive than excise and sales taxes. The reason is that high-income households tend to have a lower proportion of their assets subjected to property taxes. Although renters do not pay property taxes directly, economic analysis indicates that the costs of property taxes are largely passed on to renters as part of their rent, as we discuss later in the chapter.

Discussion Questions

1. Do you think it is necessary for the United States to have so many different types of taxes? What would you change about the structure of taxation in the United States?
2. Compare the tax policies of the area in which you live to a neighboring state or country? What factors do you think explain the differences in tax policies?

3. TAX ANALYSIS AND POLICY ISSUES

3.1 TAX DATA FOR THE UNITED STATES

One of the main debates about tax policy in the United States, which we discuss later in this section, concerns the overall level of taxation. Although tax receipts have grown dramatically in recent decades, to provide the proper context, economists normally measure taxes as a percentage of GDP. Figure 11.6 presents data on overall U.S. tax receipts, as a percentage of GDP, from 1950 to 2012.

We see that the overall level of taxation tended to rise from 1950 to 2000, from about 23 percent to 34 percent. Although critics of "big government" often focus on the growth of the federal government, most of the growth in total tax receipts was due to an increase in state and local taxation from 1950 to the early 1970s. Federal tax revenues have remained at about the same level over most of this period and have declined as a percentage of GDP since 2000.

Note that the fluctuations in total tax receipts closely follow the fluctuations in federal tax receipts. The reason for this is that state and local tax revenues remain relatively constant whether the economy is expanding or in a recession. State and local governments rely heavily on property and sales taxes, which fluctuate relatively less than income and corporate taxes as economic activity varies.

We see in Figure 11.6 that federal tax receipts did increase during the 1990s. Although federal income tax *rates* increased slightly in the early 1990s, the primary reason that federal tax *receipts* grew was an economic expansion that raised incomes. As incomes rise, people

---

*Two additional states, Tennessee and New Hampshire, levy no state income tax but do tax dividends and interest.

Figure 11.6 **Tax Receipts in the United States, as a Percent of GDP, 1950–2012**

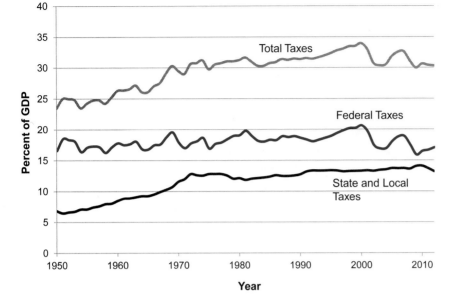

Total tax receipts in the U.S. as a share of GDP have generally increased since the 1950s, but have declined in recent years.

Source: U.S. Bureau of Economic Analysis, online database.

tend to move into higher marginal tax brackets, and thus their effective tax rate increases. In addition, corporate profits rose during this period. Another reason that federal tax receipts rose was an increase in capital gains taxes, which are paid on the profitable sale of investments such as stocks and mutual funds.

When the economy fell into a recession in 2001, federal tax receipts declined along with falling income and profits. In addition, significant tax cuts were implemented under the George W. Bush administration. As the economy recovered in the mid-2000s, federal tax receipts began to rise. But with the Great Recession (2007–9), federal tax receipts declined further and then began to rise starting in 2010.

As we discuss later, some of the variations in tax receipts are related to tax policy changes. But we can draw three important lessons from Figure 11.6—lessons that are not necessarily consistent with discussions of tax issues in the media:

1. The primary reason that tax receipts have fluctuated in the past couple of decades is due not to major changes in tax policy but to macroeconomic fluctuations.
2. Federal tax receipts are relatively low by historical standards. In fact, in 2009 federal tax receipts reached their lowest level, as a percentage of GDP, since before 1950.
3. Total tax receipts, as of 2012, are also relatively low, considering the period since 1970. Total tax receipts as a percentage of GDP were at the same level in 2012 as in the early 1970s and early 1980s.

3.2 INTERNATIONAL DATA ON TAXES

In addition to looking at historical data, we can also gain some context for tax policy discussions by comparing the United States to other countries. Figure 11.7 shows the overall rate of taxation in various member countries of the Organisation for Economic Co-operation and Development (OECD).* We see that the overall rate of taxation in the United States is relatively low—with a rate similar to that in Turkey but lower than that in all other industrialized countries.

---

*The OECD's mission is "to promote policies that will improve the economic and social well-being of people around the world." It has 34 member countries, most of them advanced industrialized countries with high income.

Figure 11.7   **International Comparisons of Overall Tax Receipts, 2011**

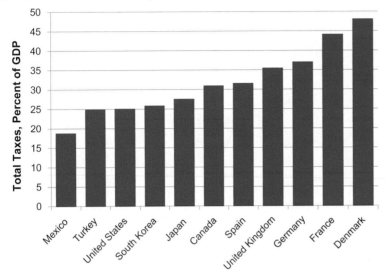

The United States has a relatively low overall rate of taxation compared to other industrialized countries.

Source: Organisation for Economic Co-operation and Development, online tax statistics database.

In addition to the overall level of taxation, another difference in tax policy across countries is the relative reliance upon different types of taxes. For example, the United States tends to rely on individual income taxes more than most countries do. Income taxes comprised 33 percent of all tax revenue in the United States in 2010, compared to an OECD average of 24 percent. Several other types of taxes are relied on more in other countries than in the United States. For more on these other types of taxes, see Box 11.2.

3.3 CURRENT TAX POLICY ISSUES

Taxation and Economic Growth

Although this book is concerned primarily with microeconomics, any discussion of tax policy should consider the debate over the relationship between taxation and macroeconomic growth. In addition to raising revenues, taxes generally create a disincentive to engage in certain activities. For example, high taxes on investment are expected to reduce overall investment.

supply-side economics: the macroeconomic theory that low marginal tax rates lead to higher rates of economic growth by encouraging entrepreneurship and investment

One theory is that a high overall rate of taxation creates a disincentive for people to work hard and invest, because they will keep less of their money after taxes. This theory implies that rates of macroeconomic growth will be higher when tax rates are low. Many proponents of this theory focus in particular on the marginal tax rates of high-income earners. According to **supply-side economics**, low marginal tax rates encourage entrepreneurs and investors to increase their economic efforts, leading to more employment and, ultimately, benefits that "trickle down" to workers and the broader economy.

Does the evidence support the view that taxes represent a drag on economic growth? We can analyze the relationship between economic growth and taxes by comparing data across countries and by looking at data over time within a single country. When we analyze a broad range of developing and developed countries, the evidence does not support the view that low taxes lead to high growth rates.

If you look at the relationship between the tax ratio and the level of prosperity, measured by GDP per capita, there is no supportive evidence for the claim that low taxes guarantee

BOX 11.2   INTERNATIONAL TAX ALTERNATIVES

Several tax types are heavily used in other countries but are relatively insignificant in the United States. Some of these tax types are central to different tax policy reforms proposed in the United States. We summarize five tax types here:

- *National sales tax:* This would function similar to a state sales tax—as an addition to the retail price of certain products. A national sales tax would clearly be simpler and cheaper to administer than the current U.S. federal income tax. It would also encourage savings because, under most proposals, income that is not spent on taxable goods and services is not taxed. However, a national sales tax has two significant disadvantages. First, it would create a strong incentive for the emergence of black market exchanges to evade the tax. Second, it can be highly regressive. A national sales tax could be made less regressive, or even progressive, by providing rebates for low-income households. Eligible households could complete a form at the end of the year to determine their rebate amount.
- *National consumption tax:* This is slightly different from a national sales tax. A household would pay the tax at the end of the year, or through estimated monthly payments, based on the value of its annual consumption of goods and services. Rather than having a household keep track of everything purchased, consumption can be calculated as total income less money not spent on goods and services (i.e., invested or saved). Again, a consumption tax would promote savings by exempting it from taxation. A consumption tax could also be designed to

be progressive by taxing different levels of consumption at different marginal rates.
- *Value-added tax:* Most developed countries levy some form of value-added tax (VAT). A VAT is levied at each stage in the production process of a product, collected from manufacturers according to the value added at each stage. Thus the tax is not added to the retail price but incorporated into the price of the product, similar to the way excise taxes become embedded in the price of products.
- *Wealth taxes:* Although the U.S. tax system includes local property taxes and estate taxes, it does not have a tax on holdings of other assets such as corporate stocks, bonds, and personal property. Several European countries, including Sweden, Spain, and Switzerland, have instituted an annual wealth tax. A wealth tax could be very progressive by applying only to very high wealth levels.
- *Environmental taxes:* Such a tax is levied on goods and services in proportion to their environmental impact. One example is a carbon tax, which taxes products based on the carbon emissions attributable to their production or consumption. The rationale of environmental taxation is that it encourages the use and development of goods and services with reduced environmental impacts. Like other taxes on goods and services, environmental taxes can be regressive—suggesting that environmental taxes need to be combined with other progressive taxes or rebates for low-income households. Among developed countries, the United States collects the smallest share of tax revenues from environmental taxes, both as a share of GDP and as a share of total tax revenues.

prosperity. In fact, if you just plot out the points, you will find a clear, positive correlation between high tax rates and prosperity, and that is because developed countries are the ones with the high tax ratios . . . that evidence [does not] necessarily mean that high taxes (and high government spending) cause prosperity, but it is a troubling fact that the people who say low taxes are the key to prosperity must confront.[2]

If we look instead at a smaller group of countries, some studies have found that low tax levels are associated with higher growth rates. For example, a 2010 study found that OECD member countries with higher tax levels as a percentage of GDP had lower rates of economic growth from 1991 to 2006, but that the net effect was "very small."[3] Another study that looked at tax levels across different U.S. states found that property and sales taxes did have a negative effect on economic growth rates but that income taxes did not.[4]

Data over time within a single country do not offer support for supply-side economics. As shown in Figure 11.8, the top marginal federal income tax rate in the United States has varied considerably over time, from above 90 percent to as low as 28 percent. Figure 11.8 also shows the average annual rate of economic growth in each decade since 1950. We see that the periods with the highest average growth rates, the 1950s and 1960s, were associated with the highest marginal tax rates. When the top marginal rate fell significantly in the 1980s, growth rates stayed about the same as they were in the 1970s. The top rate increased in the early 1990s, without a noticeable effect on average growth rates. It fell in the early 2000s, but that decade experienced the lowest overall growth rates.

Figure 11.8 **The Top Marginal Federal Tax Rate and Average Economic Growth, 1950–2010**
(Average Economic Growth Shown by Decade as a Percentage)

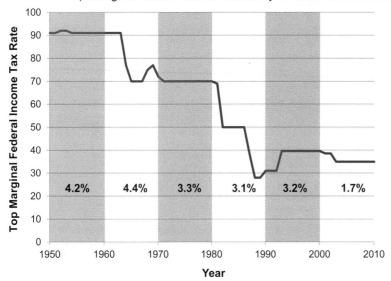

The graph indicates that lowering the top marginal federal income tax rate does not seem to be correlated with higher economic growth.

Source: Sarah Anderson, "Full Testimony to the Senate Budget Committee on Inequality, Mobility, and Opportunity," Institute for Policy Studies, February 8, 2012.

The Distribution of Taxes

An often-quoted fact is that nearly half of Americans do not pay any federal income tax. Some people conclude that this implies that nearly half of Americans are not paying *any* taxes and thus are a drain on government resources who are not paying their fair share. But this represents an incomplete picture of who pays taxes. Of course, we have learned that the federal income tax is just one of the many taxes paid by Americans. In order to analyze the distribution of the tax burden accurately, we need to consider all taxes, not just focus on one specific tax.

Another important point is that we need to understand the difference between who actually pays a tax and who feels the burden of the tax. Let's take the Social Security tax as an example. On paper, both an employee and an employer pay half the tax. But are employers able to essentially pass on the burden of their share of the tax to employees by offering them lower wages? Another example is property taxes paid by landlords. Do landlords bear the burden of these taxes or are they able to pass them on to renters by charging higher rents than they would otherwise?

tax incidence analysis: the study of who bears the ultimate burden of a tax

Economists rely upon **tax incidence analysis** to determine who bears the ultimate burden of a tax. Tax incidence analysis is:

the study of who bears the economic burden of a tax. More generally, it is the positive analysis of the impact of taxes on the distribution of welfare within a society. It begins with the very basic insight that the person who has the legal obligation to make a tax payment may not be the person whose welfare is reduced by the existence of the tax.[5]

Tax incidence analysis has produced some generally accepted conclusions regarding the burden of different taxes.

- Social insurance taxes, even though they are split evenly on paper, are borne almost entirely by employees. The reason is that an employer will pay a worker only the value of his or her marginal contribution to profits (recall our discussion from Chapter 9). As an employer's share of social insurance taxes reduces their profits, employers will accordingly reduce the amount of pay offered to employees.
- The burden of corporate taxes ultimately falls on real people. The general consensus is that the burden of corporate taxes falls primarily on owners of capital investments such as stocks and mutual funds.
- Excise taxes, though paid by manufacturers and retailers, are actually mostly paid by consumers based on their consumption patterns. In other words, businesses are generally able to pass on excise taxes to consumers. The reason is that most excises taxes are placed on goods with relatively inelastic demand curves.
- Property taxes paid by landlords are passed on to renters.

Based on research using tax incidence analysis, we can gain a complete picture of how taxes are distributed within a society. Table 11.4 provides an estimate of the U.S. tax burden in 2013 at different income levels.

We see that the overall U.S. tax system is progressive—meaning that tax rates tend to increase with increases in income. But, far from paying nothing in taxes, even those in the lowest income group pay nearly 20 percent of their income in taxes (even if they do not pay federal income tax) when we consider all taxes. Those in the middle-income group pay about 27 percent of their total income in taxes. After the middle-income group, average tax rates continue to rise, though rather modestly, especially for the top 20 percent.

Table 11.4 **The Distribution of Taxes in the United States, 2013**

Income group	Average income	Average total tax rate	Share of all taxes	Share of all income
Lowest 20%	$13,500	18.8%	2.1%	3.3%
Second 20%	$27,200	22.5%	5.1%	6.9%
Middle 20%	$43,600	26.6%	9.9%	11.2%
Fourth 20%	$71,600	29.8%	18.2%	18.4%
Next 10%	$109,000	31.4%	14.6%	14.0%
Next 5%	$154,000	32.0%	10.7%	10.1%
Next 4%	$268,000	32.2%	15.3%	14.3%
Top 1%	$1,462,000	33.0%	24.0%	21.9%

Source: Citizens for Tax Justice, "New Tax Laws in Effect in 2013 Have Modest Progressive Impact," April 2, 2013.

It is true that high-income earners bear a large share of the tax burden, but this must be assessed relative to their income. For example, those in the top 1 percent pay 24 percent of all taxes, but they also receive about 22 percent of all income. Combined, the top 20 percent pay 65 percent of all taxes and receive about 60 percent of all income. These figures indicate that the overall tax system is slightly, but not heavily, progressive.

Whether the current progressivity of the overall tax system in the United States is appropriate is, of course, a normative issue. According to a 2012 survey, 58 percent of Americans think that the "rich" pay too little in taxes, 26 percent say that the rich pay their fair share, and only 8 percent say that the rich pay too much.[6] Changes in tax policies can be used to change the overall progressivity of the tax system. Most tax policy debates emphasize the federal income tax. But considering that nearly half of Americans do not pay federal income taxes, reducing those rates would benefit only the richer half. Similarly, raising federal income tax rates tends to affect higher-income taxpayers. Again, we should assess any change in tax policy by considering its impact on the overall progressivity of taxes, rather than focusing on a single tax.

Discussion Questions

1. Do you think the current tax system in the United States is too progressive, about right, or not progressive enough? How much do you think different income groups should pay in taxes?
2. Suppose that a relative of yours is complaining that taxes are always going up on average people while the rich can always avoid taxes because of exemptions, deductions, and other loopholes. How would you respond to him or her based on what you learned in this chapter?

REVIEW QUESTIONS

1. How is an excise tax represented in a supply-and-demand graph?
2. How does the elasticity of demand affect a price increase as a result of an excise tax?
3. What are the two motivations for taxing a product?
4. How are tax revenues represented in a supply-and-demand graph?
5. How does the elasticity of demand affect the amount of tax revenues from an excise tax? How does it affect the distribution of the tax burden?
6. How does an excise tax affect the amount of consumer and producer surplus in a market?
7. How does an excise tax affect overall social welfare?
8. What are the four justifications for taxation?
9. What is a progressive tax? A regressive tax? A proportional tax?
10. What are three reasons in support of progressive taxation?

11. What is the difference between total income and taxable income, with respect to federal income taxes?
12. How do marginal tax rates work in calculating one's income taxes?
13. How is an effective tax rate calculated?
14. What are federal social insurance taxes?
15. How have tax revenues changed in the United States over time?
16. How do overall tax rates in the United States compare with those in other countries?
17. What is supply-side economics?
18. What does the research on the relationship between taxes and economic growth indicate?
19. What is tax incidence analysis? What are some of the findings of this research?
20. How progressive is the overall tax system in the United States?

EXERCISES

1. Suppose that your town decides to impose a tax on 2-liter bottles of soda to encourage healthier dietary habits. Before the tax, the supply and demand schedules for bottles of soda are given in the table below.

Price per bottle	Quantity supplied per month	Quantity demanded per month
$1.00	16,000	20,000
$1.10	17,000	19,000
$1.20	18,000	18,000
$1.30	19,000	17,000
$1.40	20,000	16,000
$1.50	21,000	15,000

a. Draw a supply-and-demand graph illustrating the market before the tax. What is the equilibrium price and quantity for bottles of soda?
b. The town then imposes a tax of $0.20 per bottle. Illustrate this on your graph. What is the new equilibrium price and quantity for bottles of soda?
c. How much in taxes will the local government collect?

2. For each of the taxes below, indicate whether you think the tax burden will be borne primarily by consumers or producers. Also, how successful do you think each tax will be in raising revenues?
   a. A city tax on the use of paper bags in supermarkets. Consumers have the option of asking for plastic bags or bringing their own bags.
   b. An increase in the national gasoline tax.

c. A tax on paper copies of textbooks when online versions of the books are available. Discuss why students' preferences (i.e., whether they are willing to use online texts) are important in determining the effect of the tax.

3. Suppose that gasoline is not currently taxed in the country of Autopia, and the price of gasoline is $3.00 a gallon. In order to alleviate problems with air pollution and traffic, the government of Autopia decides to institute a $0.50 a gallon tax on gasoline. After the tax, the price of gasoline rises to $3.45 a gallon.

a. Assuming no other significant changes in the gasoline market, what can we conclude about the elasticity of demand for gasoline in Autopia?

b. Draw a supply-and-demand graph illustrating the effects of the gasoline tax. Assume that the supply of gasoline is not particularly elastic or inelastic.

c. Who has borne most of the burden of this tax, consumers or producers?

d. Do you think that the tax will be effective in reducing Autopia's problems with air pollution and traffic? Why or why not? Support your answer with reference to your graph.

4. Consider the following table, which shows the total amount of taxes paid at different total income levels in a society. For each income level, calculate the effective tax rate. Is this tax system progressive or regressive? Explain.

Total income	Total taxes paid
$200,000	$50,000
$100,000	$22,000
$80,000	$16,000
$50,000	$8,000
$40,000	$4,000
$20,000	$1,000

5. Suppose that Shafik is a single person in the United States with a total income of $52,000. He is allowed to claim $10,000 of his income as nontaxable. He also contributes $1,000 to his retirement account. Based on the data in Table 11.2, how much would Shafik owe in federal income taxes?

6. As mentioned in the text, social insurance taxes in the United States are currently split equally between employers and employees. If Congress were considering a law in which employers would pay the entire amount for social insurance taxes, in order to reduce the burden on employees, would you support such a law? If the law passed, would you expect average wages to increase, decrease, or stay the same?

7. Match each concept in Column A with an example in Column B.

Column A	Column B
a. An example of a progressive tax	1. The tax burden falls primarily on producers
b. An example of a regressive tax	2. A tax on each unit of a product
c. A proportional tax	3. Total taxes divided by total income
d. An excise tax	4. Estate taxes
e. Inelastic demand	5. The study of how tax burdens are distributed
f. Elastic demand	6. Social insurance taxes
g. Effective tax rate	7. The tax burden falls primarily on consumers
h. Supply-side economics	8. A tax that is the same rate regardless of income levels
i. Tax incidence analysis	9. The theory that economic growth depends on low marginal tax rates

NOTES

1. Tax Policy Center, "The Tax Policy Briefing Book." www.taxpolicycenter.org/briefing-book/TPC_briefingbook_full.pdf. 2012.

2. "The Truth About Taxes and Economic Growth: Interview with Joel Slemrod," *Challenge* 46(1) (2003): 5–11.

3. Keshab Bhattarai, "Taxes, Public Spending and Economic Growth in OECD Countries," *Problems and Perspectives in Management* 8(1) (2010): 11–30.

4. Andrew Ojede and Steven Yamarik, "Tax Policy and State Economic Growth: The Long-Run and Short-Run of It," *Economics Letters* 116(2) (2012): 161–165.

5. Gilbert Metcalf and Don Fullerton, "The Distribution of Tax Burdens: An Introduction," National Bureau of Economic Research Working Paper 8978, Cambridge, MA, 2002, p. 1.

6. Kim Parker, "Yes, the Rich Are Different," Pew Research, Social and Demographic Trends, August 27, 2012.

12 The Economics of the Environment

A 2012 opinion poll asked Americans which should be given the higher priority: economic growth or protecting the environment.[1] By 49 percent to 41 percent, more people thought that economic growth was the higher priority. This result is a reversal of similar polls conducted between 1985 and 2007, in which large majorities were more concerned about protecting the environment. The way that this survey was formulated reflects a common perspective that a tradeoff frequently exists between economic goals and environmental goals. For example, we often hear from politicians and media pundits that environmental regulations lead to job losses and hamper economic growth. But is this perspective factually accurate?

Environmental issues are certainly not separate from economics. Deteriorating environmental conditions can create serious health problems as well as reduce the quantity and quality of natural resources that contribute to productivity and other important aspects of quality of life. Climate change is an example of environmental deterioration that is also imposing costs on people in many countries. Although no individual weather event can be linked conclusively to global climate change, more "extreme weather events" are likely to result from a global buildup of carbon dioxide (CO_2) and other greenhouse gases that contribute to planetary warming.

Because improvements in environmental quality enhance most people's well-being, economists would not be expected to oppose protecting the environment. In fact, economics has subdisciplines known as environmental economics, natural resource economics, and ecological economics. The Nobel prize–winning economist Paul Krugman has written that:

> my unscientific impression is that economists are on average more pro-environment than other people of similar incomes and backgrounds. Why? Because standard economic theory automatically predisposes those who believe in it to favor strong environmental protection.[2]

In this chapter and Chapter 13, we summarize how to use insights from economics to better manage our shared environment. Among other things, we find that environmental concerns often present a valid justification for government intervention in markets. Recall from our study of welfare analysis in Chapter 5 that government intervention is often expected to decrease economic efficiency. In this chapter, we see important examples of where, even by the most standard definitions of efficiency, this is not always the case. When economic production and consumption cause negative environmental impacts, government intervention can actually *increase* economic efficiency.

We also discuss the environmental policy tools that economists have developed to address environmental problems, and the ways in which economists express the value of the environment in monetary terms. By the end of the next chapter, we will have developed the rationale behind the following quotation:

> If you want to fight for the environment, don't hug a tree, hug an economist. Hug the economist who tells you that fossil fuels are not only the third most heavily subsidized economic sector after road transportation and agriculture but that they also promote vast inefficiencies. Hug the economist who tells you that the most efficient investment of a dollar is not in fossil fuels but in renewable energy sources that not only provide new jobs but cost less over time. Hug the economist who tells you that the price system matters; it's potentially the most potent tool of all for creating social change.[3]

1. THE THEORY OF EXTERNALITIES

In Chapter 1 we introduced the concept of externalities. Recall that externalities are side effects, positive or negative, of an economic transaction that affect those not directly involved in the transaction. Pollution is the classic example of a negative externality. When a consumer buys a product, such as a t-shirt, he or she rarely considers the negative environmental impacts associated with its production. T-shirt producers generally do not consider these environmental impacts either. But these impacts clearly do occur, and society as a whole suffers some damages from them.

1.1 NEGATIVE EXTERNALITIES IN THE SUPPLY-AND-DEMAND MODEL

We can analyze externalities using our standard supply-and-demand graph. As discussed in Chapter 5, a demand curve represents the marginal benefits to consumers while a supply curve represents the marginal costs to producers. How can we incorporate the concept of externalities into this framework?

Remember that our welfare analysis in Chapter 5 excluded "the rest of society." We considered only the welfare of consumers and producers in the market. But a complete welfare analysis of a market must consider the impacts to all of society, even those outside the particular market. The key point to understand if we are to incorporate negative externalities into our supply-and-demand graph is that *negative externalities represent an additional cost of production,* over and above actual production costs. The producers do not pay this cost, but the rest of society does. So if we want to determine the total cost of providing a good or service, we must add the externality costs to the regular production costs.

Therefore, we can incorporate it into our supply-and-demand model by *adding it to the supply curve.* We do this in Figure 12.1, which represents a market for t-shirts. The normal supply curve represents the private marginal costs of producing t-shirts—the actual manufacturing costs. But to obtain the marginal cost of providing t-shirts from the broader social perspective, we need to add the negative externality costs. The externalities associated with producing t-shirts include the pesticides used to grow the cotton, the chemicals used to dye the shirts, the fuels burned to transport the shirts to stores, and other costs.

Supply–and-demand curves are expressed in monetary units. So in order to incorporate externalities into this model, they also need to be measured in dollars. Assume for now that the negative externalities associated with the production of each t-shirt total $3.00 in damages. We consider the issue of how these damages are actually measured later in the chapter.

The social marginal cost curve in Figure 12.1 equals the private production costs plus the $3.00 externality cost. But for the market participants—the consumers and producers—the externalities costs are irrelevant. The equilibrium outcome will be determined through the normal interaction of demand and (private) supply. Thus market equilibrium is at point E_M, at a price of $8.00 per shirt and a quantity of 25,000 shirts.

Our welfare analysis from Chapter 5 found E_M to be the economically efficient outcome. But now we consider the impact of the negative externalities. The vertical distance between

Figure 12.1   **The Negative Externalities of T-Shirt Production**

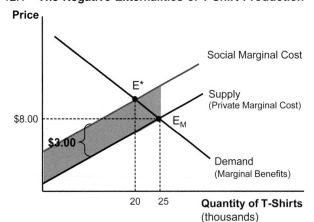

A negative externality can be represented in a supply-and-demand graph as an additional marginal cost. The socially efficient level of production occurs at E^*, but the unregulated market outcome is E_M.

the two marginal cost curves represents the $3.00 externality damage per shirt. This damage occurs for every shirt up to the quantity sold of 25,000. Thus the total externality damage is the shaded area in Figure 12.1. With 25,000 shirts and damage of $3.00 per shirt, the externality damage thus totals $75,000.

1.2 INTERNALIZING NEGATIVE EXTERNALITIES

In a market without externalities, we learned in Chapter 5 that the market outcome was economically efficient. Any government intervention, such as price floors or price ceilings, reduced total welfare. But when we introduce negative externalities, is the market outcome still efficient?

We can answer this question by looking at Figure 12.1. The marginal benefits of t-shirts exceed the social marginal costs up to point E^*, at 20,000 t-shirts. So up to 20,000 t-shirts, net social benefits are positive, and even with the externality damage, it makes sense to produce each of these t-shirts.

But notice that, beyond point E^*, the social marginal costs exceed the marginal benefits. For every t-shirt above 20,000, society is actually becoming worse off when we consider the externality damage as well as the production costs. Thus the market equilibrium quantity of 25,000 is too high. The economically efficient outcome is E^*, at 20,000 shirts. The market outcome is inefficient.

Pigovian tax: a tax levied on a product to reduce or eliminate the negative externality associated with its production

Given that the unregulated market outcome is inefficient when externalities are present, can economic efficiency be increased through government intervention? The most common policy response to a market with externalities is to tax the product. When a product causes a negative externality, a tax that is levied specifically to lower or eliminate that externality is called a **Pigovian tax**, after British economist Arthur Pigou, who proposed the idea in the 1920s.

internalizing negative externalities: bringing external costs into the market (for example, by instituting a Pigovian tax at a level equal to the externality damage), thus making market participants pay the true social cost of their actions

A Pigovian tax operates in the same way as an excise tax. As you will remember from Chapter 11, instituting a tax increases production costs, effectively shifting the supply curve upward. By setting the Pigovian tax at the "right" level, we obtain a new supply curve, $Supply_{Tax}$, illustrated in Figure 12.2. Note that this supply curve is the same as the social marginal cost curve from Figure 12.1. With this tax in place, the new market outcome will be E_{Tax}, which is the efficient outcome, corresponding to E^* in Figure 12.1.

We say that the Pigovian tax has "**internalized the negative externality**" because the external costs of $3.00 per t-shirt are now integrated into the market. Setting the tax equal to the externality damage, $3.00 per shirt, now means that the market participants pay the true social cost of producing t-shirts. Note that the price of t-shirts has increased from $8 to $10. So some of the burden of the tax has been passed on to consumers as higher prices, but

Figure 12.2 **Internalizing a Negative Externality with a Pigovian Tax**

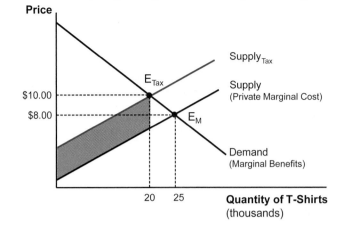

A Pigovian tax reduces the magnitude of a negative externality. If set at the correct level, the tax results in the socially efficient level of production.

producers also bear some of the tax burden in terms of lower profits (again, similar to our discussion of taxes from last chapter).

A detailed welfare analysis of a Pigovian tax with a negative externality is presented in the appendix to this chapter. That analysis proves that total social welfare increases when the negative externality is internalized. So unlike our welfare analysis of a tax in Chapter 11, in the case of a negative externality a Pigovian tax is economically efficient and increases social welfare.

Even with a Pigovian tax, we still have some externality damage, represented by the shaded area in Figure 12.2. Externality damages are still $3.00 per shirt, but the quantity sold is now only 20,000 shirts, for a total damage of $60,000. But note that the revenue from the tax is also $60,000 (a $3.00 tax per shirt, collected on 20,000 shirts). Thus the government collects exactly enough in tax revenue to compensate society for the damage done by producing t-shirts! If conditions change in such a way that the same kind of pollution caused greater harm—suppose, for example, that more people develop allergic reactions to the chemicals used to dye the shirts—then it would be appropriate to raise the tax accordingly.

Although the use of a Pigovian tax corrects the inefficiency caused by the negative externality, it does not provide a mechanism for compensating those who continue to suffer pollution damage. Nor does it indicate how the government revenues from the tax should be used. Some economists suggest that the tax revenues should be used simply to lower other taxes (discussed further below). It is also possible to use the revenues for direct compensation of those affected or environmental improvement. Given that environmental taxes tend to be regressive (because, e.g., purchases of t-shirts would be a higher proportion of income for a poor person than for a rich one), it may make sense to devote at least part of the revenues to rebates to compensate lower-income people for the impact of the tax.

1.3 POSITIVE EXTERNALITIES

Externalities can also be positive, meaning that an economic transaction positively affects those outside the market. One example is a homeowner who installs solar panels on his or her house. Society as a whole benefits because the solar panels reduce the need for generating electricity from fossil fuels, thus improving air quality and reducing other ecological damages.

We present a basic analysis of a positive externality in Figure 12.3. The normal demand curve represents the marginal benefits of the product, solar panels in this example, to consumers—or the "private" marginal benefits. The market equilibrium is E_M, which is the normal intersection of supply and demand. The market price of solar panels would be P_M and the quantity sold would be Q_M.

Figure 12.3 **Analysis of a Positive Externality**

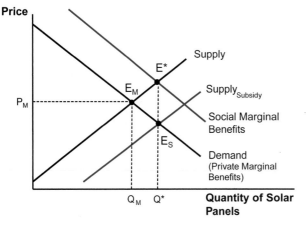

A positive externality can be represented in a supply-and-demand graph as an additional marginal benefit. A subsidy can be used to obtain the socially efficient level of production, at Q^*.

We can incorporate a positive externality into our supply-and-demand model by realizing that a positive externality is *an additional benefit obtained by society,* over and above the private benefits of consumers. Thus we can add the positive externality benefits to the demand curve to obtain the social marginal benefits of the product. This is shown in Figure 12.3. Note that for every solar panel between Q_M and Q^*, the social marginal benefits exceed the marginal costs (i.e., the supply curve). The economically efficient level of solar panel production is E^*, not E_M. The unregulated market produces too few solar panels, from the broader perspective of social welfare.

In the case of a positive externality, a common policy recommendation is to subsidize the product to encourage greater production. A **subsidy** is a per-unit payment to producers to offset, and thus lower, their production costs. This effectively encourages greater production. We model a subsidy by shifting the supply curve downward. With the subsidy in place, the new supply curve is *Supply*$_{Subsidy}$, and the new equilibrium point is E_S. The resulting level of solar panels sales, Q^*, is the "right" level from the broader social perspective.

subsidy: a per-unit payment to producers to lower production costs and encourage greater production

The complete welfare analysis of a positive externality is slightly complex, so we do not present it here. But the conclusion of a formal welfare analysis is that a subsidy in the case of a product with a positive externality increases overall social welfare. As in the case of a negative externality, the unregulated market is inefficient and government intervention is necessary to obtain the efficient outcome.

1.4 POLICY IMPLICATIONS OF EXTERNALITIES

The existence of externalities presents one of the strongest justifications for government intervention in markets. Externalities are an example of market failure, as discussed in Chapter 5. When externalities exist, the unregulated market does not produce the socially efficient outcome.

Our analysis of externalities has profound policy implications, particularly for negative environmental externalities. Virtually every product produced in modern markets results in *some* pollution and polluting waste. Given that a Pigovian tax increases economic efficiency, is it then reasonable to ask whether we should tax *every* product based on its environmental impacts?

Few economists would support trying to place an environmental tax on every product. The first reason is that we must consider the administrative costs of collecting Pigovian taxes. For some products with relatively minor environmental impacts, the social benefits probably are not worth the administrative costs. Second, the task of estimating the environmental damage of every product, in dollars, is clearly excessive. Again, for many products the cost of obtaining a monetary estimate probably is not worth the effort.

upstream taxes:
taxes instituted as
close as possible in a
production process to
the extraction of raw
materials

But some economists have suggested a broad system of **upstream taxes** on the most environmentally damaging products, particularly on fossil fuels (coal, oil, and natural gas) and important minerals. An upstream tax is placed as close as possible to the point where raw materials are extracted. In the case of coal, for example, an upstream tax might be instituted on each ton of coal extracted from coal mines. In addition to administrative simplicity, another advantage of upstream taxes is that the environmental damages of final consumer products do not need to be estimated. Instead, after we have estimated the damages associated with coal extraction and burning, the costs of the upstream tax would carry through numerous production processes and eventually increase the price of goods and services that are dependent on coal as an input, such as electricity.

Although various countries have some negative externality taxes, such as excise taxes on gasoline, no country has such a broad system of upstream Pigovian taxes. Figure 12.4 shows the magnitude of environmental taxation, as a percentage of total tax revenues, in various developed countries. Few countries collect more than 10 percent of their total tax revenue from environmental taxes. Among developed countries, the United States collects the lowest percentage.

**revenue-neutral
(taxes):** offsetting
any tax increases with
decreases in other
taxes such that overall
tax collections remain
constant

The main barrier to increasing environmental taxes is that few politicians are willing to support higher taxes. However, environmental taxes can be **revenue-neutral** if any tax increases are offset by lowering other taxes so that the total taxes on an average household remain unchanged. Given that environmental taxes tend to be regressive, revenue neutrality could be achieved by reducing a regressive tax, such as social insurance taxes. In addition to economic efficiency, a broad shift away from taxes on income and toward taxes on negative externalities also provides people with more options to reduce their tax burden.

If environmental taxes constituted a large portion of someone's total tax burden, he or she could reduce this burden by using more efficient vehicles and appliances, relying more on public transportation, reducing energy use, and numerous other options. Of course, that is not always easy to do; one example is someone whose job requires a long commute in a location in which public transportation is not available. In such a case, it becomes necessary

Figure 12.4   **Environmental Taxes in Select Developed Countries, as a Percent of Total Tax Revenue, 2010**

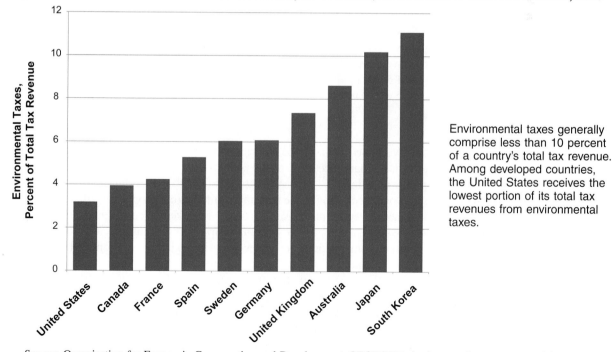

Environmental taxes generally comprise less than 10 percent of a country's total tax revenue. Among developed countries, the United States receives the lowest portion of its total tax revenues from environmental taxes.

Source: Organisation for Economic Co-operation and Development, OECD/EEA database on instruments used for environmental policy and natural resources management. Updated April 13, 2012.

for government involvement to go beyond taxes and subsidies, to take into account the social infrastructure and institutions that will allow people—especially those whose financial resources limit their individual options—to respond without undue pain to the signals given by a market that has been shifted toward greater environmental responsibility.

Despite the economic logic supporting taxes on negative externalities, many environmentally damaging activities, including fossil-fuel production, mining minerals, and harvesting timber, are actually subsidized instead of taxed (see Box 12.1). Obviously, this results in pollution levels that are not optimal. From an economic point of view, these subsidies are perverse—that is, they encourage exactly those activities that we should be seeking to discourage.

Box 12.1   FOSSIL-FUEL SUBSIDIES

According to analysis by Bloomberg New Energy Finance, global subsidies for fossil fuels are about twelve times higher than those allocated for renewable energy. In 2009 global subsidies for renewable energy totaled $43 million to $46 billion, mainly in the form of tax credits and price guarantees. Meanwhile, the International Energy Agency estimated that governments spent about $550 billion to subsidize fossil fuels.

The Group of 20, a group of major countries including the United States, China, Germany, and Russia, have agreed to phase out fossil-fuel subsidies over "the medium term," but progress has been slow and no specific target date has been set. Meanwhile, many countries are ramping up their commitment to renewable energy. The most expensive renewable energy subsidy in 2009 was about $10 billion for Germany's feed-in tariff, a policy that guarantees long-term prices for suppliers of renewable energy. Other feed-in tariffs in Europe totaled another $10 billion.

The United States spent more than any other country in renewable-energy subsidies in 2009, around $18 billion. China provided about $2 billion, although this figure is likely too low as it does not include the value of low-interest loans offered for renewable energy projects by state-owned banks.

Source: Alex Morales, "Fossil Fuel Subsidies Are Twelve Times Renewables Support," Bloomberg, July 29, 2010.

2. VALUING THE ENVIRONMENT

In order to set a Pigovian tax at the correct level, we need to estimate the negative externality damage in monetary terms. Environmental damage includes such diverse effects as reduced air and water quality, biodiversity loss, human health impacts, and lost recreation opportunities. Economists have developed various techniques to estimate environmental values. We summarize some of these methods below, but first we address the conceptual approach to measuring the value of the environment.

2.1 TOTAL ECONOMIC VALUE

willingness-to-pay (WTP) principle: the economic value of something, such as an environmental benefit, is equal to the maximum amount people are willing to pay for it

In a broad sense, everyone "values" the environment. All life depends on various natural systems, including those that process waste and provide energy. But to an economist, the term "value" has a specific meaning. The **willingness-to-pay (WTP) principle** states that something has economic value only according to the maximum amount that people are willing to pay for it. Note that this principle represents an extension of the market concept of marginal benefits. As discussed in Chapter 3, a demand curve is made up of points that indicate the maximum willingness-to-pay of consumers for a good or service. Although most environmental attributes are not traded in markets, people may still place significant value on them.

The aggregate social value of something is the sum of each individual's WTP. Although each individual's preferences count in this framework, it is also important to recognize that the ability to pay varies across individuals. Thus instead of a "one person, one vote" approach, the WTP principle translates to "one dollar, one vote."

Another implication of this approach is that if no one is willing to pay to preserve something, then it does not have economic value. So the economic value of an endangered insect species in a remote forest, which has no obvious human uses, may well be zero. However, some economists believe that nature has certain inherent rights apart from any human economic values. In particular, even if the WTP to preserve a species is zero, the species could still be said to have **intrinsic value,** or value in a broader ecological or ethical sense, and thus have a right to exist.* Intrinsic value is especially difficult to express in monetary terms.

People's willingness to pay for environmental attributes may derive from a variety of motivations. Potential reasons for valuing the environment include:

intrinsic value: the value of something in an ecological or ethical sense, apart from any economic value based on willingness to pay

1. *Profit-making enterprises:* activities such as harvesting timber, fishing, grazing, and agriculture depend on natural systems.
2. *Recreation:* natural sites provide places for outdoor recreation, including camping, hiking, fishing, hunting, and viewing wildlife.
3. **Ecosystem services**: tangible benefits obtained freely from nature, simply as a result of natural processes. Ecosystem services include nutrient recycling, flood protection from wetlands and vegetation, waste assimilation, carbon storage in trees and other plants, water purification, and pollination by bees.
4. **Nonuse benefits**: nontangible welfare benefits that we obtain from nature. Nonuse benefits include the psychological benefits that people gain just from knowing that natural places exist, even if they will never visit them. The value that people gain from knowing that ecosystems will be available to future generations is another type of nonuse benefit.

ecosystem services: tangible benefits that humans obtain from natural processes, such as nutrient recycling, flood control, and pollination

nonuse benefits: nontangible welfare benefits that people derive from ecosystems without physical interaction (i.e., psychological benefits)

total economic value: the sum of all the benefits for which people are willing to pay, with respect to an ecosystem or natural place

The **total economic value** of a natural system is the sum of all the benefits for which people are willing to pay. Thus the total economic value of, for eample, a national forest is the sum of any profits obtained from harvesting timber, the WTP of all those who engage in recreation in the forest, the value of the ecosystem services such as soil erosion prevention and carbon storage, and the nonuse benefits that people obtain from knowing that the forest exists. It is important to realize that in calculating total economic value, priority is not given to any particular use of the forest. When uses are incompatible, such as deciding whether a particular tract of forest should be clear cut or preserved for recreation and wildlife habitat, economic analysis can help to determine which use provides the highest overall economic value to society.

2.2 NONMARKET VALUATION METHODOLOGIES

We have already seen how we can determine the economic benefits of a market good or service—it is equal to the sum of consumer and producer surplus. But many of the benefits that we obtain from the environment are not traded in markets. If we are to estimate total economic value, we need techniques to estimate such values as recreation benefits, ecosystem services, and nonuse values. These techniques are referred to as **nonmarket valuation,** because they produce benefit estimates for goods and services that are not directly traded in markets.

nonmarket valuation techniques: economic valuation methods that obtain estimates for goods and services not directly traded in markets

Nonmarket valuation techniques come in four main types:

1. the cost of illness method
2. replacement cost methods
3. revealed preference methods
4. stated preference methods

We summarize each of these methods, including the advantages and disadvantages of each.

---

*There is a disciplinary distinction between economists who study environmental issues. Traditional environmental economics generally recognizes only values backed by WTP. The notion that nature has certain inherent rights is a principle of ecological economics, a more recent subdiscipline that emphasizes the need to preserve ecosystem functions.

Cost of Illness Method

cost of illness method: a nonmarket valuation technique that estimates the direct and indirect costs associated with illnesses with environmental causes

The **cost of illness method** is used to estimate the damage of reductions in environmental quality that have human health consequences. Conversely, it can be used to estimate the benefits of improvements in environmental quality (i.e., the avoided damages). This method estimates the direct and indirect costs related to illnesses with environmental causes. The direct costs include medical costs such as office visits and medication paid by individuals and insurers and lost wages due to illness. Indirect costs can include decreases in human capital (e.g., if a child misses a significant number of school days due to illness), welfare losses from pain and suffering, and decreases in economic productivity due to work absences.

lower-bound estimate: an estimate that represents the minimum potential value of something. The actual value is thus greater than or equal to the lower-bound estimate.

The cost of illness method generally provides us with only a **lower-bound estimate** of the WTP to avoid illnesses. The true WTP could be higher because the actual expenses may not capture the full losses to individuals from illness. But even a lower-bound estimate could provide policy guidance. For example, in 2007 the cost of asthma in the United States was estimated to be $56 billion, based on direct medical costs and productivity losses from missed days of school and work.[4] The costs for a typical affected worker totaled about $3,500. These estimates provide a starting point for determining whether efforts to reduce asthma cases are economically efficient.

Replacement Cost Methods

replacement cost methods: nonmarket valuation techniques that estimate the value of ecosystem services based on the cost of actions that provide substitute services

Replacement cost methods can be used to estimate the value of ecosystem services. These approaches consider the costs of human actions that substitute for lost ecosystem services. For example, a community could construct a water treatment plant to make up for the lost water purification benefits from a forest habitat. The natural pollination of plants by bees could, to some extent, be done by hand or machine. If we can estimate the costs of these substitute actions, in terms of construction and labor costs, these can be considered an approximation of society's WTP for these ecosystem services.

revealed preference methods: valuation techniques that infer the value of nonmarket goods and services based on people's decisions in related markets

Although replacement cost methods are often used to estimate ecosystem service values, they are not necessarily measures of WTP. Suppose that a community could construct a water treatment plant for $50 million to offset the water purification services of a nearby forest. This estimate does not tell us whether the community would actually be willing to pay the $50 million should the forest be damaged. Actual WTP could be more or less than $50 million and is fundamentally unrelated to the cost of the water purification plant. So, in this sense, replacement cost estimates should be used with caution. However, if we know that the community would be willing to pay $50 million for a water treatment plant if the ecosystem services of the forest are lost, then we could conclude that $50 million represents a lower bound of the value of the water purification benefits of the forest.

Revealed Preference Methods

travel cost models: a revealed preference method used to obtain estimates of the recreation benefits of natural sites based on variations in the travel costs paid by visitors from different regions

Although markets do not exist for many environmental goods and services, we can sometimes infer the values that people place on them through their behavior in other markets. **Revealed preference methods** are techniques that obtain nonmarket values based on people's decisions in related markets. Economists generally prefer deriving nonmarket values based on actual market behavior. Thus revealed preference methods are generally considered the most valid approach to nonmarket valuation. However, the environmental benefits for which revealed preference methods can be used to provide nonmarket values are limited.

One common type of revealed preference method is represented by **travel cost models**. These models are used to estimate the economic benefits that people obtain by engaging in recreation at natural sites such as national parks or lakes. Even if the recreation site does not charge an entry fee, all visitors must pay a "price" equal to their costs to travel to the site, such as gas, plane tickets, accommodations, and even the time required to travel to the site. As visitors to a recreation site from different regions effectively pay a different price, economists can use this information to derive a demand curve for the site using statistical models, and thus estimate consumer surplus. Travel cost models are most applicable for recreation sites that attract visitors from distant places, in order to provide enough variation in travel costs to estimate a demand curve.

Numerous travel cost models have estimated the recreational benefits of natural sites. For example, a 2010 study of recreational visitors to the Murray River in Australia found that the average visitor received a consumer surplus of US$155 per day.[5] Travel cost models have been used to explore how changes in the fish catch rate affect the consumer surplus of anglers visiting sites in Wisconsin[6] and how a drought affects the benefits of visitors to reservoirs in California.[7]

defensive expenditures approach: a nonmarket valuation technique that obtains benefit estimates based on the cost of actions that people take to avoid environmental harm

Another type of revealed preference method is the **defensive expenditures approach.** This approach is applicable in situations where people are able to take actions to reduce their exposure to environmental harm. For example, people with concerns about their drinking water quality may choose to purchase bottled water or install a water filtration system. These expenditures may reflect their WTP for water quality. For example, a 2006 study in Brazil found that households were paying US$16–$19 per month on defensive expenditures to improve drinking water quality.[8]

A limitation of the defensive expenditures approach is that people may be taking defensive actions for a variety of reasons, some unrelated to environmental quality. For example, other reasons for buying bottled water may include convenience or status. Thus attributing the entire cost of bottled water as a measure of concern about drinking water quality would not be appropriate in such cases. It also suffers from the inherent problem of any market valuation: The preferences of the rich weigh much more heavily than the preferences of the poor. Plenty of people around the world who are actually suffering from the health effects of impure water may not be able to afford to buy bottled water; thus their abstract WTP is made invisible by inability to pay.

In addition to the serious problem of unequal ability to pay, the approaches just described— the defensive expenditures approach and travel cost models—cannot be used to obtain benefit estimates for ecosystem services and nonuse values. Thus in order to obtain estimates of total economic value for many environmental goods and services, we need a technique that can provide us some estimate of these values.

Stated Preference Methods

stated preference methods: nonmarket valuation techniques that directly ask survey respondents about their preferences in a hypothetical scenario

The final nonmarket valuation technique that we consider is the most used, as well as the most controversial. **Stated preference methods** directly obtain information on people's preferences in a hypothetical scenario simply by asking them. The most common stated preference method is **contingent valuation**, in which survey respondents are asked questions about their WTP for a specific hypothetical outcome.

contingent valuation: a stated preference method where survey respondents are asked about their willingness to pay for a hypothetical outcome

The main advantage of contingent valuation is that surveys can be designed to ask respondents about *any* type of environmental benefit. For example, a 2012 study found that households in Spain were willing to pay an average of $22 per year for a hypothetical reduction in highway noise and air pollution.[9] A 2011 paper determined that the WTP for preserving marine biodiversity in the Azores Islands was $121 to $837 (as a one-time payment).[10]

Although hundreds of contingent valuation studies have been conducted in the past several decades, the validity of the results remains highly controversial. Given that respondents' preferences are based on a hypothetical scenario, and they do not actually have to pay anything, some economists consider the results flawed because of various biases. For example, a respondent who generally favors biodiversity preservation may have an incentive to overstate his or her actual WTP in order to influence the policy process. Some respondents may not accurately consider their income limitations when stating WTP values; this gets around the "ability to pay" problem, but does not produce the kind of WTP estimates that many economists seek as "realistic."

Yet contingent valuation remains the only way to estimate some environmental benefits, particularly nonuse values. So, the debate over the method often centers on whether some estimate is better than no estimate. The debate over contingent valuation occurs mostly among academics, but the issue became relevant to businesses and policymakers in the wake of the 1989 *Exxon Valdez* oil spill in Alaska. The lawsuit against Exxon sought compensation for billions of dollars in lost nonuse values, as a result of the damage done to a relatively pristine marine environment. The federal government convened a panel of top economists, including two Nobel Prize winners, to review the contingent valuation method. Their report concluded that contingent valuation studies "can produce estimates reliable enough to be the starting point of a judicial process," but it also recognized the method's "likely tendency to exaggerate willingness to pay" and provided a list of demanding guidelines for future studies.[11]

> **contingent ranking:** a stated preference method in which respondents are asked to rank various hypothetical scenarios

Some of the problems associated with contingent valuation can be avoided by using **contingent ranking**, another stated preference method. In contingent ranking, respondents are asked to rank various hypothetical scenarios according to their preferences. Thus there is no potential for respondents to exaggerate their WTP.

2.3 COST-BENEFIT ANALYSIS

> **cost-benefit analysis:** a technique to analyze a policy or project proposal in which all costs and benefits are converted to monetary estimates, if possible, to determine the net social value

The nonmarket valuation methods discussed above can be used to estimate the negative externalities associated with various goods and services. These methods can also be used to determine whether a particular policy or public project should be undertaken. For example, consider a proposal to build a large dam or a new law to increase air quality standards. One of the approaches used to evaluate these proposals is to ask whether its economic benefits exceed its costs. **Cost-benefit analysis** (CBA) seeks to convert all costs and benefits to a common metric.

In theory, measuring all impacts in dollars (or another monetary unit) produces a "bottom-line" result (i.e., a single number) so that we can choose which alternative results in the highest net social value. In practice, however, CBA is often incomplete, with some impacts unable to be estimated in monetary terms. The results may be dependent on specific assumptions. Sometimes, one side of the analysis—the costs or the benefits—are more fully fleshed out than the other, making it difficult to arrive at an objective recommendation.

The basic steps of a CBA are relatively straightforward:

1. List all costs and benefits of the project or policy proposal. Typically, this involves developing several scenarios.
2. Convert all costs and benefits to monetary values. Some values can be obtained based on market analysis, while other values will require nonmarket valuation.
3. Add up all the costs and benefits to determine the net benefits of each scenario. Sometimes, the results are expressed as a ratio (i.e., benefits divided by costs).
4. Choose the scenario that is the most economically efficient.

The most appealing feature of CBA may be its seeming objectivity. It also presents a way to argue for environmental protection in economic terms, rather than on ethical or ecological terms. Many CBAs have shown that the WTP for environmental protection can be quite high.

Of course, all the problems with the nonmarket valuation techniques discussed above can complicate CBA. Two additional issues often arise in environmental CBAs: how to value costs and benefits that occur in the future, and how to value human lives.

Discounting the Future

Many environmental policies involve paying costs in the short term, while the benefits will be obtained further in the future. For example, installing pollution control equipment has an upfront cost, while the health benefits of reduced cancer rates will only be realized decades in the future. Thus we need a way to compare impacts that occur at different times.

There is a natural human tendency to focus on the present more than the future. Most people would prefer to receive a benefit now over a similar benefit in the future. There may also be practical reasons to prefer monetary benefits now, if they can be invested to provide increased returns in the future. Economists incorporate this concept into CBA through **discounting**. Discounting effectively reduces the weight placed on any cost or benefit that occurs in the future. The further in the future the cost or benefit occurs, the less weight is given to that impact. In order to compare an impact that occurs in the present to an impact that occurs in the future, the future impact must be converted to an equivalent **present value** using the following formula:

$$PV(X_n) = X_n / (1 + r)^n$$

where X_n is the monetary value of the cost or benefit, n is the number of years in the future the impact occurs, and r is the **discount rate**—the annual percentage rate by which future impacts are reduced, expressed as a proportion. For example, if the discount rate was 3 percent, r would be 0.03.

A simple example illustrates how discounting works. Suppose that we are analyzing a proposal to improve air quality. Assume that the cost of this proposal, including the installation of new pollution control equipment, is $10 million, to be paid right now. The benefits of cleaner air are estimated at $20 million, but these benefits will occur 25 years in the future.* Should we approve this law?

In order to obtain the present value of the $20 million benefit, we need to choose a discount rate. Suppose that we apply a discount rate of 5 percent. The present value of the benefits would be:

$$PV = \$20 \text{ million} / (1.05)^{25} = \$5,906,055$$

As the present value of the $20 million benefit in 25 years is only about $6 million, it does not make economic sense to pay $10 million now to obtain this benefit. But suppose instead that we apply a discount rate of 2 percent. In this case, the present value of the benefits is:

$$PV = \$20 \text{ million} / (1.02)^{25} = \$12,190,617$$

In this case, the net benefits of the proposal are positive (i.e., the present value of the benefits exceeds the costs by about $2 million). At the lower discount rate, the proposal makes economic sense. This example illustrates the importance of the choice of a discount rate. We will see that this is particularly true in Chapter 13, when we discuss analyses of global climate change.

One approach for choosing a discount rate is to set it equal to the rate of return on low-risk investments such as government bonds. The rationale for this is that any funds used for a beneficial public project could otherwise be invested to provide society with greater resources in the future. In early 2013, the nominal rate of return on a 30-year U.S. Treasury bond was 3 percent.[12] However, this rate has varied considerably over time. Thus some economists question whether we should base the valuation of long-term environmental impacts on an interest rate that is subject to changeable financial market conditions.

Other approaches to choosing a discount rate consider the ethical dimension of valuing future impacts. In some sense, a positive discount rate implies that future generations count less than the current generation. Although nearly all economists believe in the principle of

discounting: an approach in which costs and benefits that occur in the future are assigned less weight (i.e., discounted) relative to current costs and benefits

present value: the current value of a future cost or benefit, obtained by discounting

discount rate: the annual percentage rate at which future costs and benefits are discounted relative to current costs and benefits

---

*In reality, the benefits would occur over the course of several years in the future. Here, for the sake of simplicity, we assume that all the benefits occur in a single year, 25 years from now.

discounting, economists who are more concerned about long-term environmental damages tend to prefer lower discount rates.*

Valuing Human Lives

Another controversial aspect of CBA is analyzing policies that affect human mortality rates. The benefits of many environmental policies, such as those addressing air and water quality, are often expressed in terms of the number of avoided deaths. In a CBA framework, we seek to convert all benefits to monetary values to make them directly comparable to the costs. Suppose that we are analyzing a policy that will improve air quality at a cost of $500 million to society, but reduce the number of deaths associated with air pollution by 50. Is such a policy "worth it" to society?

value of a statistical life (VSL): society's willingness to pay to avoid one death, based on the valuation of relatively small changes in mortality risks

Although economists are not in the business of placing a value on the life of any particular person, their goal is to estimate how people value relatively minor changes in mortality risk and use this information to infer the **value of a statistical life (VSL)**. A VSL estimate, in theory, indicates how much society is willing to pay to reduce the number of deaths from environmental pollution by one, without any reference to whose death will be avoided.

An example illustrates how a VSL is estimated. Let's assume that we conduct a contingent valuation survey to ask people how much they would be willing to pay to improve air quality such that the number of deaths from air pollution would decline by 50. Each respondent's risk of dying from air pollution would decline slightly as a result of the policy. Suppose that the survey results indicate that the average household is willing to pay $10 per year for this policy. If society comprises 100 million households, then the total WTP for the policy would be:

$$100 \text{ } million * \$10 = \$1 \text{ } billion$$

Because this is the aggregate WTP to reduce deaths by 50, the VSL would be:

$$\$1 \text{ } billion / 50 = \$20 \text{ } million$$

Some people object to valuing human lives on ethical grounds. Others counter that we must explicitly or implicitly analyze the tradeoffs between public expenditures and health benefits, and the VSL methodology provides a transparent approach. Major environmental policy proposals in the United States must be reviewed using CBA, and thus government agencies must often apply a VSL. The VSLs used by government agencies have varied but generally increased over time, from around $2 million in the 1980s to nearly $10 million more recently. In other words, regulations that can reduce environmental deaths at a cost of less than $10 million per avoided death would be considered economically efficient. (For more on the economic, and political, debate about the VSL in the United States, see Box 12.2.)

Other Difficulties with Cost Benefit Analysis

Most environmental cost-benefit analyses are further complicated by several other issues. These include:

1. analysis of uncertainty
2. missing monetary values
3. sensitivity to assumptions

Consider a proposal to build a large dam for flood protection. The benefits of flood protection depend somewhat on future climate conditions, which are difficult to predict with

---

*A 0 percent discount rate implies that any impact that occurs in the future, even those in the distant future, count the same as a current impact. Economists have tended to justify some discounting on the assumption that future generations will have higher incomes and better technology and will thus be better equipped to deal with problems created in the present. However, some economists note that environmental damages and resource constraints could lead to lower standards of living in the future.

BOX 12.2 THE POLITICS OF VALUING LIFE

The valuation of human lives is not merely an economic issue but a political one, as demonstrated by changes in the VSLs used by U.S. federal agencies in recent years. During the administration of George W. Bush, the VSL used by the Environmental Protection Agency (EPA) was as low as $6.8 million. But in 2010, the EPA increased its VSL to $9.1 million in a cost-benefit analysis of air pollution standards. Under the administration of Barack Obama, the Food and Drug Administration also increased its VSL, from $5 million in 2008 to $7.9 million in 2010. Based on higher VSLs, the Transportation Department now requires stronger car roofs—a regulation that was rejected under the Bush administration as too expensive.

Under the Obama administration, federal regulators are also considering adjusting the VSL based on the type of risk. For example, the EPA is considering the application of a "cancer differential" that would increase the VSL for cancer risks, based on surveys that show that people are willing to pay more to avoid cancer, as opposed to other health risks. The Department of Homeland Security has suggested that the willingness to pay to avoid terrorism deaths is about double that of other risks.

Manufacturers and power companies have traditionally advocated the use of cost-benefit analysis for environmental policies, essentially forcing regulators to prove the economic efficiency of environmental improvements. But the recent VSL increases have led them to reconsider their approach. For example, the U.S. Chamber of Commerce (a group that represents businesses) is now lobbying for Congress to have greater oversight of federal regulators. On the other hand, environmental groups, which remain critical of the VSL methodology, have praised the Obama administration for increasing these values.

Source: Binyamin Appelbaum, "As U.S. Agencies Put More Value on a Life, Businesses Fret," *New York Times,* February 16, 2011.

---

precautionary principle: the notion that policies should err on the side of caution when there is a low-probability risk of a catastrophic outcome

a high degree of certainty. There may also be a small chance that the dam will fail, perhaps causing catastrophic damage. Another example is analyzing the risk of a major oil spill, which requires one to estimate the probability that such a spill will occur. Incorporating such uncertainty into a CBA is possible if we have some idea of the probability of various outcomes, but some risks are fundamentally difficult to predict. In these cases, some economists advocate the **precautionary principle**: that policies should err on the side of caution when there is a low-probability risk of a catastrophic outcome.

In almost any real-world environmental CBA, we will be unable to estimate all impacts in monetary terms. For example, how can we estimate the benefits of a recreation site that is not yet available? We may be able to "transfer" an estimate from an existing similar recreation site, but we cannot be sure that the transferred estimate is valid for the new site. Also, government agencies frequently do not have the resources to fund original studies to estimate all needed values. We may be able to make an educated guess about certain missing values, but this obviously reduces the objectivity of a CBA.

Finally, the recommendations of many CBAs are highly dependent on various assumptions. As we saw earlier, the choice of a discount rate may determine whether a particular policy is recommended. Other assumptions may relate to how risk is analyzed or how contingent valuation results are interpreted. Ideally, a CBA should consider a broad range of assumptions. Of course, if different assumptions produce different results, then we must make a subjective decision about which result we should rely upon. These considerations suggest that CBA is often not as objective as it may seem at first.

3. ENVIRONMENTAL POLICIES IN PRACTICE

3.1 POLICY OPTIONS

A Pigovian tax is just one type of environmental policy. Policymakers generally have other policy options, and which one is appropriate depends on the particular context. The four basic environmental policy options are:

1. pollution standards
2. technology-based regulation
3. Pigovian (or pollution) taxes
4. tradable pollution permits

Pollution Standards

pollution standards: policies that control pollution by setting allowable pollution standards or controlling the uses of a product or process

Pollution standards control environmental impacts by setting allowable pollution levels or controlling the uses of a product or process. Many people are faced with such standards at an automobile inspection. Cars must meet certain standards for tailpipe emissions; if your car fails to meet them, you must correct the problem before you can receive an inspection sticker.

The clear advantage of standards is that they can specify a definite result. This is particularly important in the case of substances that pose a clear hazard to public health. By imposing a uniform rule on all producers, we can be sure that no factory or product will produce hazardous levels of pollutants. In extreme cases, a regulation can simply ban a particular pollutant, as has been the case with DDT (a toxic pesticide) in most countries.

However, requiring all firms or products to meet the same standard is normally not cost effective. The overall use of society's resources is reduced if firms that can reduce pollution at low marginal costs reduce pollution more than firms that have high marginal reduction costs. Thus requiring all firms to reduce pollution by the same amount or to meet the same standards is not the least-cost way to achieve a given level of pollution reduction. Another problem with standards is that after firms meet the standard, they have little incentive to reduce pollution further.

Technology-Based Regulation

A second approach to environmental regulation is requiring firms or products to incorporate a particular pollution-control technology. For example, in 1975 the United States required that all new automobiles include a catalytic converter to reduce tailpipe emissions. Although auto manufacturers are free to design their own catalytic converters, each must meet certain emissions specifications.

Perhaps the main advantage of technology-based regulation is that enforcement and monitoring costs are relatively low. Unlike a pollution standard, which requires that firms' pollution levels be monitored to ensure compliance, a technology-based approach might require only an occasional check to ensure that the equipment is installed and functioning properly.

Technology-based approaches are also unlikely to be cost effective, however, because they do not provide firms with the flexibility to pursue a wide range of options. Like meeting pollution standards, the cost of implementing specific technologies varies among firms. Technology-based approaches may, however, offer a cost advantage due to standardization. If all firms must adopt a specific technology, then widespread production of that technology may drive down its production cost down over time.

Pigovian (or Pollution) Taxes

market-based approaches (to pollution regulation): policies that create an economic incentive for firms to reduce pollution without mandating that firms take any specific actions

Pollution taxes, along with tradable pollution permits, are considered **market-based approaches** to pollution regulation because they send information to polluters about the costs of pollution without mandating that firms take specific actions. Individual firms are not required to reduce pollution under a market-based approach, but the regulation creates a strong incentive for action.

As we saw earlier in the chapter, a pollution tax reflects the principle of internalizing externalities. If producers must bear the costs associated with pollution by paying a tax, they will find it in their interest to reduce pollution so long as the marginal costs of reducing pollution are lower than the tax.

Figure 12.5   **A Firm's Response to a Pollution Tax**

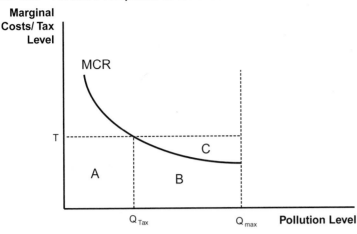

When faced with a pollution tax, a firm will reduce its pollution level as long as the marginal cost of reducing pollution is lower than the tax.

Figure 12.5 illustrates how an individual firm will respond in the presence of a pollution tax. Q_{max} is the level of pollution emitted without any regulation. The MCR curve shows the marginal cost of pollution reduction for the firm. If a pollution tax of T is imposed, the firm will be motivated to reduce pollution to level Q_{Tax}, at a total cost of B, equal to the area under its MCR curve between Q_{Tax} and Q_{max}. If the firm maintained pollution at Q_{max} it would have to pay a tax of (B + C) on these units of pollution. Thus the firm saves area C by reducing pollution to Q_{Tax}.

After reducing pollution to Q_{Tax}, the firm will still need to pay a tax on its remaining units of pollution, equal to area A. The total cost to the firm from the pollution tax is the sum of its pollution reduction costs and tax payments, or areas (A + B). This is smaller than areas (A + B + C), which is what it would have to pay in taxes if it undertook no pollution reduction. The firm's response to the tax is cost effective, as any other level of pollution different from Q_{Tax} would impose higher costs.

All other firms in the industry will determine how much to reduce their pollution based on their own MCR curve. Assuming that each firm is acting in a cost-effective manner, the total cost of pollution reduction is minimized. Firms that can reduce pollution at low cost will reduce pollution more than firms that face a higher cost. This is the main advantage of market-based approaches to pollution regulation—they achieve a given level of pollution reduction at the lowest overall cost. In other words, they are more economically efficient than pollution standards or technology-based approaches.

Tradable Pollution Permits

Economic efficiency in pollution control is clearly an advantage. One disadvantage of pollution taxes, however, is that it is very difficult to predict the total amount of pollution reduction a given tax will achieve. It depends on the shape of each firm's MCR curve, which is usually not known to policymakers.

tradable pollution permits: a system of pollution regulation in which a government allocates permits that are required in order to produce pollution. After they are allocated, these permits may be traded among firms or other interested parties.

An alternative is to set up a system of **tradable pollution permits**. The total number of permits issued equals the desired target level of pollution. These permits can then be allocated freely to existing firms or sold at auction. After they are allocated, they are fully tradable, or transferable, among firms or other interested parties. Firms can choose for themselves whether to reduce pollution or to purchase permits for the pollution that they produce—but the total volume of pollution produced by all firms cannot exceed a maximum amount equal to the total number of permits.

Firms with higher MCR curves will generally seek to purchase permits so that they do not have to pay high pollution reduction costs. Firms that can reduce pollution at a lower cost may be willing to sell permits, as long as they can receive more money for the permits than it would cost them to reduce pollution. Under this system, private groups interested in reducing pollution could purchase permits and simply not use them to emit pollution, thus reducing total emissions below the original target level. Pollution permits are normally valid only for a specific period. After this period expires, the government can issue fewer permits, resulting in lower overall pollution levels in the future.

A detailed analysis of tradable permits, which we do not present here, demonstrates that a given level of pollution reduction is achieved at the same total cost as levying a tax. Thus whether one prefers pollution taxes or tradable permits depends on factors other than pollution reduction costs (however, the administrative costs of the approaches may differ). Taxes are generally easier to understand and implement. But taxes are politically unpopular, and firms may prefer to use a permit system if they believe that they can successfully lobby in order to obtain permits for free.

The main difference between the two approaches is where the uncertainty lies. Using pollution taxes, firms have certainty about the cost of emissions, which makes it easier for them to make decisions about long-term investments. But the resulting level of total pollution with a tax is unknown in advance. If pollution levels turn out to be higher than expected, then the government might have to take the unpopular step of raising taxes further.

Under a permit system, the level of pollution is known because the government sets the number of available permits. But the price of permits is unknown, and permit prices can vary significantly over time. This has been the case with the European permit system for carbon emissions. The price of permits initially rose to around €30/ton in 2006, shortly after the system was instituted. But then prices plummeted to €0.10/ton in 2007, when it became evident that too many permits had been allocated. After some changes to the system, prices rose to exceed €20/ton in 2008 but then fell again to less than €3/ton in 2013. Such price volatility makes it difficult for firms to decide whether they should make investments in technologies to reduce emissions.

3.2 DESIGN AND PERFORMANCE OF ENVIRONMENTAL POLICIES

Summary of Major Environmental Policies

Early pollution regulations enacted in the 1960s and 1970s relied primarily on standards and technology-based approaches. For example, the Clean Air Act, enacted by Congress in 1970, set maximum allowable levels of emissions for several key pollutants. The Clean Air Act specifies that pollution standards are to be set based on the best scientific evidence to protect human health with an "adequate margin of safety" and adjusted over time as new evidence becomes available. The Act specifically rules out CBA as a factor in setting standards.

The Clean Air Act has been very successful at reducing pollution levels in the United States. The aggregate concentration of the six major air pollutants* has declined 68 percent between 1970 and 2011.[13] The decline in lead pollution has been particularly dramatic—lead concentrations have declined 97 percent over this period, primarily as a result of banning lead in gasoline. A comprehensive CBA of the Clean Air Act found that in 2010 the annual compliance costs of the Act were $53 billion but estimates of the benefits ranged from $160 billion to $3.8 *trillion*.[14] In other words, for every dollar spent to meet the requirements of the Clean Air Act, society receives between $3 to $72 in economic benefits.

Technology-based approaches are often used to regulate other air pollutants as well as surface water quality. The Clean Water Act of 1972, for example, requires the U.S. Environmental Protection Agency to specify the "best available technology" for various

---

*The six major, or criteria, pollutants are particulate matter, ground-level ozone, carbon monoxide, sulfur oxides, nitrogen oxides, and lead.

types of facilities. The Act initially focused on reducing surface water pollution from clearly-identified sources, such as industrial plants. More recently, legislation has shifted toward the reduction of water pollution from stormwater and agricultural runoff.

As discussed above, the extent of environmental taxation varies across countries. One indication of this is the difference in national gas taxes. Gas prices vary across countries, even though the wholesale price of gasoline on the global market is fairly even around the world. The main reason for varying gasoline prices to consumers in different countries is that the level of taxation differs, sometimes significantly. In the United States, federal gasoline taxes are 18 cents per gallon, combined with state and local taxes that range from 8 to 51 cents per gallon, for a total average tax of 49 cents per gallon. In European countries, gasoline taxes are typically about 10 times higher, equivalent to around $4 or $5 per gallon. At the same time, some countries actually subsidize gasoline prices. In 2010 the cheapest gasoline prices were found in Venezuela ($0.09/gallon), Iran ($0.37/gallon), and Saudi Arabia ($0.61/gallon).

We can see the effect of differences in gas taxes in Figure 12.6, which shows gasoline prices in various countries plotted against average annual consumption per person. We observe a general inverse relationship, similar to a demand curve—higher gasoline prices tend to be associated with lower consumption. The relationship shown here, however, is not exactly the same as a demand curve. As we are looking at data from different countries, the assumption of "other things equal," which is needed to construct a demand curve, does not hold. Differences in consumption may be partly a function of differences in factors other than prices, such as income levels. For example, while Saudi Arabia has very low gasoline prices, income levels are only about half those in the United States. Other reasons that gasoline consumption is so high in the United States may be that people need to drive longer distances for work (especially in the Western United States) and that public transportation options are less prevalent than in European countries. But the overall negative relationship suggests that higher gasoline taxes can be effective at reducing gasoline consumption, and thus emissions of various air pollutants.

The first major attempt to use a tradable pollution system to control pollution was the U.S. program to regulate sulfur dioxide, enacted with the 1990 Amendments to the Clean Air Act. The goal of the program was to reduce sulfur dioxide emissions to 50 percent of 1980 levels by 2010. The program is widely considered a success, with a decline in emissions of 83 percent by 2010 and costs significantly lower than expected. (For more on this program, see Box 12.3.)

Figure 12.6   Gasoline Prices and Consumption, Select Countries, 2010

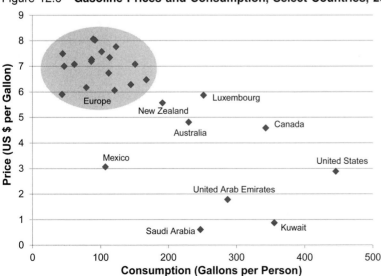

Higher gas prices, typically as a result of higher gas taxes, generally result in lower average consumption.

Sources: GIZ, *International Fuel Prices 2010/2011,* 7th ed. Federal Ministry for Economic Cooperation and Development (Germany), 2011; U.S. Energy Information Administration online database.

BOX 12.3   SULFUR DIOXIDE EMISSIONS TRADING

The 1990 Clean Air Act Amendments in the United States created a national program to allow trading and banking of sulfur dioxide (SO_2) emissions, the primary cause of acid rain. The program applies to more than 2,000 large electricity plants, which must hold permits in order to emit SO_2. Most permits are freely allocated to plants based on their capacity to generate electricity. About 3 percent of the permits are auctioned off every year. Permits may then be traded, normally with brokers facilitating trades. Although most trades occur between two electricity-generating plants, some permits are purchased by environmental groups or individuals (and even economics classes!) and then "retired" to reduce the overall quantity of SO_2 emissions.

Economic theory suggests that a system of tradable permits can reduce pollution at a lower overall cost than a uniform standard. Dallas Burtraw, an economist with Resources for the Future, notes that the "SO_2 allowance market presents the first real test of economists' advice, and therefore merits careful evaluation." After about twenty years in operation, how has the program performed?

To evaluate the policy, the effects of emissions trading must be isolated from other factors. Even without a trading system, declining prices for low-sulfur coal in the 1990s, along with technological advances, would have reduced the cost of lowering emissions. Economic simulation models comparing the SO_2 program to an emissions standard suggest that the cost savings from trading were about 50 percent. The savings are even greater than in a technology-based approach.

The emissions targets of the SO_2 program have been met at a lower cost than originally anticipated. Acidification problems in the Northeastern states, widespread in the past, have declined. However, aquatic systems in the Southeastern states are expected to continue to decline without further emissions reductions. And although the program has been effective, analysis of the marginal benefits and marginal costs of emissions suggests that further emissions reductions would produce even larger net benefits.

Burtraw, along with colleague Sarah Jo Szambelan, concludes that the SO_2 market has

> been liquid and active, and according to most observers [has] worked well in achieving the emissions caps at less cost than would have been achieved with traditional approaches to regulation. There is evidence that both process and patentable types of innovation are attributable to the [SO_2 program]. At the same time, there is evidence that some cost savings have been not been realized. Moreover, despite substantial emissions reductions, ultimate environmental goals have not been achieved.

Sources: Dallas Burtraw, "Innovation Under the Tradable Sulfur Dioxide Emission Permits Program in the U.S. Electricity Sector," Resources for the Future Discussion Paper 00-38, Washington, DC, 2000; Dallas Burtraw and Sarah Jo Szambelan, "U.S. Emissions Trading Markets for SO_2 and NO_x," Resources for the Future Discussion Paper 09-40, Washington, DC, 2009.

The other major attempt at emissions trading has been the European Union's carbon trading system, enacted in 2005. The initial phase covered major facilities such as electricity plants, cement plants, and paper mills. In 2012 the program was extended to cover airline transportation. As mentioned earlier, the main problem with the program has been price volatility, generally attributed to an over-allocation of permits during the initial phases. In the current phase (2013–20) the European Union is moving toward setting an overall EU emission limit rather than individual national limits.

The Economic Impact of Environmental Regulation

Finally, we briefly consider the economic impact of environmental regulations. Environmental laws are often accused of slowing economic growth and causing job losses. However, most of the evidence suggests that the notion of a tradeoff between environmental quality and economic vitality is a myth. For example, a 2008 analysis of the U.S. economy found that

> contrary to conventional wisdom, [environmental protection (EP)], economic growth, and jobs creation are complementary and compatible: Investments in EP create jobs and displace jobs, but the net effect on employment is positive.[15]

A 2007 study in the United Kingdom also studied the effect of environmental regulation on employment. The results found that regulations had a slightly negative impact on employment, although the results were not statistically significant. They concluded that their analysis found "no evidence of a trade-off between jobs and the environment."[16]

Under various executive orders in the United States, starting with Ronald Reagan and more recently by Barack Obama, all major federal regulations, including environmental laws, must be reviewed using CBA. This process is designed to screen out inefficient policy proposals. A 2011 study by the U.S. Office of Management and Budget found that the aggregate cost of all federal environmental regulations enacted from 2000 to 2010 was $24 billion to $29 billion, but benefits were estimated to be $82 billion to $550 billion.[17] During this period, environmental laws were responsible for about 60 percent to 85 percent of the benefits of all federal regulations.

Analysis by the United Nations concludes that a significant increase in global investment in renewable energy and energy efficiency—an amount equal to 2 percent of global GDP—would result in higher rates of long-term economic growth than a "business-as-usual" scenario.[18] The report finds that "green" investments benefit the world's poorest in particular. The poor disproportionately depend on natural resources for their livelihood. So investment in natural capital, including water resources, sustainable agriculture, and forests, increases incomes while also improving the natural environment. Investment in natural capital also fosters ecotourism, which offers another way to increase incomes in developing countries.

We have seen in this chapter that a strong *economic* case can be made for protecting the natural environment. Given existing market failures, especially those arising from externalities, government intervention is not only justified; it is necessary to achieve an efficient outcome. Nature has significant economic value, and techniques have been devised to measure these values. Despite common perceptions, environmental regulations are generally effective and do not harm economic vitality. Economic research suggests that we need more, not less, environmental regulation.

In Chapter 13, we turn to additional theoretical insights from economics on environmental management. We also focus on the issue of global climate change, one of the major challenges of the twenty-first century.

REVIEW QUESTIONS

1. How are negative externalities represented in a supply-and-demand graph?
2. What is a Pigovian tax? How is it represented in a supply-and-demand graph?
3. How are positive externalities represented in a supply-and-demand graph?
4. How does a subsidy result in the efficient quantity in a market with a positive externality?
5. What is an upstream tax? What is a revenue-neutral tax?
6. What is the willingness-to-pay principle?
7. What is intrinsic value?
8. What are ecosystem services?
9. What are nonuse benefits? What is total economic value?
10. What is nonmarket valuation? What are the four main nonmarket valuation techniques?
11. What is the cost of illness method? Why is it considered a lower-bound estimate?
12. What are replacement cost methods?
13. What are revealed preference methods? What are stated preference methods?
14. What is cost-benefit analysis?
15. What is discounting? How do we calculate a present value using discounting?
16. How can human lives be valued?
17. What is the precautionary principle?
18. What are the four main approaches for regulating pollution levels?
19. Demonstrate how a firm would respond to a pollution tax, using a graph.
20. How does a system of tradable pollution permits operate?

EXERCISES

1. Suppose that a friend of yours states: "The optimal pollution level is clearly zero. Any level of pollution is obviously undesirable." How would you respond to your friend? Use a graph to support your answer.

2. Burning gasoline generates negative externalities. Assume the current tax on gas in the country of Optiland fully internalizes these externalities. But suppose that gas prices in Optiland have risen lately due to increased demand. A politician gives a speech in which he says that the best response to rising gas prices is to eliminate the gas tax temporarily. Do you agree with his position? Use a graph to support your answer.

3. The supply and demand schedules for gasoline in the country of Drivia are given in the table below. Initially, there are no taxes on gasoline. Assume that the externality damage from consuming gasoline in Drivia is 60 cents per gallon.

Price per gallon	Quantity supplied (gallons per day)	Quantity demanded (gallons per day)
$3.00	60,000	90,000
$3.20	70,000	85,000
$3.40	80,000	80,000
$3.60	90,000	75,000
$3.80	100,000	70,000
$4.00	110,000	65,000
$4.20	120,000	60,000

a. Draw a supply-and-demand graph for gasoline in Drivia. What are the equilibrium price and quantity?

b. Illustrate the externality damage in your graph. How much is externality damage (in dollars per day)?

c. What is the optimal Pigovian tax on gas in Drivia?

d. If Drivia instituted an optimal Pigovian tax on gasoline, what would the new equilibrium price and quantity be? Create a new graph illustrating the impacts of the tax.

e. How much would Drivia collect in taxes with an optimal Pigovian tax? Illustrate this on your graph.

4. Suppose that the World Bank is considering funding a dam project in the developing country of Hydroland which will generate hydroelectricity and reduce flooding. The reservoir will be used for recreation but will require relocation of several villages. You have been hired by the Bank to determine the economic costs and benefits of the dam. Develop a list of potential costs and benefits. Be sure to include at least two potential ecosystem service impacts and one nonuse cost or benefit. For each of these impacts, what nonmarket valuation techniques do you think are appropriate for estimating the economic value?

5. Suppose that the government of Aqualand is considering a new law that would improve drinking water quality. The cost of complying with the new regulation is $100 million. The benefits of improved drinking water are estimated to be $250 million, but these benefits will occur 25 years from now.

a. At a discount rate of 5 percent, do you recommend that Aqualand institute this new regulation?

b. Would your recommendation change if the discount rate were 3 percent?

6. For each of the four main approaches for regulating pollution, list at least one advantage and one disadvantage of the approach.

7. Match each concept in Column A with an example in Column B.

Column A	Column B
a. A negative externality	1. A policy to increase production when a good generates a positive externality
b. A Pigovian tax	2. Represented by the difference between the private marginal benefits and the social marginal benefits
c. A positive externality	3. A tax on raw materials
d. A subsidy	4. Converting future costs and benefits to present value
e. An upstream tax	5. Represented by the difference between the private marginal costs and the social marginal costs
f. An ecosystem service benefit	6. Using the costs of building a water treatment plant to estimate the value of natural water purification
g. A nonuse benefit	7. Using surveys to elicit willingness to pay information
h. Replacement cost method	8. Internalizes a negative externality
i. Revealed preference method	9. Flood protection from a wetlands
j. Contingent valuation	10. Estimating the recreation benefits of a lake using data on visitation patterns
k. Discounting	11. The value of just knowing a national park exists

APPENDIX: FORMAL ANALYSIS OF NEGATIVE EXTERNALITIES

In this Appendix, we present a more formal analysis of negative externalities. The objective is to demonstrate that internalizing a negative externality using a Pigovian tax clearly makes society "better off," based on an application of welfare analysis. Prior to the imposition of any tax on a product that generates a negative externality, social welfare includes three components:

1. consumer surplus
2. producer surplus
3. externality damages

Consumer and producer surplus are both positive contributions to social welfare, while the externality damages decrease welfare.

We refer to Figure 12.7 to determine each of these three effects. Figure 12.7 is essentially the same as Figure 12.1, with the addition of labels for various areas. You might also note that Figure 12.7 is very similar to Figure 11.5, which presented the welfare analysis of a tax. As some of the same concepts we learned in Chapter 11 are applicable here, the labels for various areas are the same in both figures.

Without any regulation, the market equilibrium is E_M. Consumer surplus is the area above price but below the demand curve:

$$Consumer\ Surplus = A + B + E + H$$

Producer surplus at the market equilibrium Q_M is the area below price but above the supply curve:

$$Producer\ Surplus = C + D + F + G + I$$

As in Figure 12.1, the externality damages are represented by the shaded area between the private marginal costs and the social marginal costs, equal to:

$$Externality = E + F + G + H + I + K$$

Figure 12.7 **Welfare Analysis of a Negative Externality, without a Pigovian Tax**

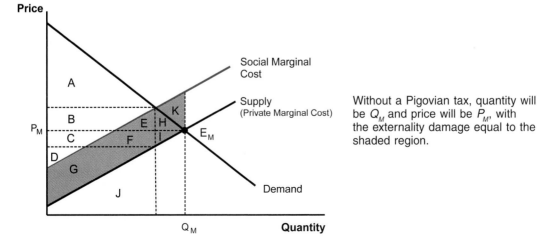

Without a Pigovian tax, quantity will be Q_M and price will be P_M, with the externality damage equal to the shaded region.

Because the externality represents a cost, to determine the net social welfare we need to subtract these costs from the market benefits. Thus the net social welfare of the unregulated market is:

$$Net\ Benefits = (A + B + E + H) + (C + D + F + G + I) - (E + F + G + H + I + K)$$

Canceling out the positive and negative terms, we are left with:

$$Net\ Benefits = A + B + C + D - K$$

Now, we impose a Pigovian tax that fully internalizes the externality. This is shown in Figure 12.8, which is similar to Figure 12.2. We again need to determine the areas that represent consumer surplus, producer surplus, and the externality damage. But we also need to consider that tax revenues represent a benefit to society, as we did in Chapter 11.

With the Pigovian tax, the new equilibrium is E_{Tax}, with a higher price of P_{Tax} and a lower quantity of Q_{Tax}. At the higher price, consumer surplus is:

$$CS = A$$

As in Chapter 11, we can figure out producer surplus by first realizing that total revenues equal price times quantity, or $(P_{Tax} * Q_{Tax})$. In Figure 12A.2, total revenues are:

$$Total\ Producer\ Revenues = B + C + D + E + F + G + J$$

Producers have two costs: the cost of production and the tax. The cost of production is the area under their marginal cost curve, which is area J. The tax per unit is equal to the difference between P_{Tax} and P_0, which must be paid for every unit produced. Total taxes paid equal the shaded area in Figure 12.8, or*

$$Taxes = E + F + G$$

Figure 12.8   **Welfare Analysis of a Negative Externality, with a Pigovian Tax**

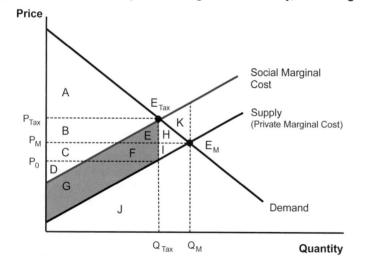

With a Pigovian tax, quantity falls to Q_{Tax} and price rises to P_{Tax}, with the externality damage reduced to the shaded region.

---

*Note that in Figure 11.5 tax revenues equaled area $(B + C + E + F)$. However, this is exactly the same as area $(E + F + G)$. We represent tax revenues differently here because we wish to demonstrate that the tax revenues are equal to the externality damages.

When we subtract production costs and the tax paid from total revenues, we are left with producer surplus:

$$Producer\ Surplus = (B + C + D + E + F + G + J) - J - (E + F + G)$$
$$= B + C + D$$

Note that both consumer and producer surplus have decreased as a result of the Pigovian tax. If both consumer and producer surplus have gone down, how can it be that the tax increases social welfare? First, we need to account for the reduced pollution. With quantity reduced to Q_{Tax}, the total externality damage is now the shaded area in Figure 12A.2:

$$Externality = E + F + G$$

The externality damage associated with production between Q_{Tax} and Q_M, or area $(H + I + K)$, has been avoided. Note that the tax revenues exactly equal the externality damages—both are equal to $(E + F + G)$.

Considering all welfare impacts, net social benefits are now:

$$Net\ Benefits = (A) + (B + C + D) + (E + F + G) - (E + F + G)$$

Canceling out the positive and negative terms we get:

$$Net\ Benefits = A + B + C + D$$

How does this compare to net benefits before the tax? Recall that benefits were $(A + B + C + D - K)$. So benefits have increased by area K as a result of the tax. Another way of looking at this is that we have avoided the negative impacts of "too much" production, represented by area K, which shows the excess of marginal costs (including external costs) over marginal benefits. The level of production that maximizes social welfare is Q_{Tax}.

Unlike our welfare analysis in Chapters 5 and 11, in the case of negative externality the unregulated market is inefficient. Market intervention, in the form of a Pigovian tax, increases social welfare.

NOTES

1. Dennis Jacobe, "Americans Still Prioritize Economic Growth Over Environment," Gallup Economy, March 29, 2012.

2. Paul Krugman, "Earth in the Balance Sheet: Economists Go for the Green," *Slate,* April 18, 1997.

3. Bill Moyers, Keynote address to the Environmental Grantmakers Association, Brainerd, Minnesota, October 16, 2001.

4. Sarah Beth L. Barnett and Tursynbek A. Nurmagambetov, "Costs of Asthma in the United States, 2002–2007," *Journal of Allergy and Clinical Immunology* 127(1) (2011): 142–152.

5. John Rolfe and Brenda Dyack, "Testing for Convergent Validity between Travel Cost and Contingent Valuation Estimates of Recreation Values in the Coorong, Australia," *Australian Journal of Agricultural and Resource Economics* 54 (2010): 583–599.

6. Jennifer Murdock, "Handling Unobserved Site Characteristics in Random Utility Models of Recreation Demand," *Journal of Environmental Economics and Management* 51(1) (2006): 1–25.

7. Frank Ward, Brian Roach, and Jim Henderson, "The Economic Value of Water in Recreation: Evidence from the California Drought," *Water Resources Research* 32(4) (1996): 1075–1081.

8. Marcia A. Rosado, Maria A. Cunha-e-Sa, Maria M. Dulca-Soares, and Luis C. Nunes, "Combining Averting Behavior and Contingent Valuation Data: An Application to Drinking Water Treatment in Brazil," *Environment and Development Economics* 11(6) (2006): 729–746.

9. Fernando Lera-Lopez, Javier Faulin, and Mercedes Sanchez, "Determinants of the Willingness-to-Pay for Reducing the Environmental Impacts of Road Transportation," *Transportation Research: Part D: Transport and Environment* 17(3) (2012): 215–220.

10. Adriana Ressurreição, James Gibbons, Tomaz Ponce Dentinho, Michel Kaiser, Ricardo S. Santos, and Gareth Edwards-Jones, "Economic Valuation of Species Loss in the Open Sea," *Ecological Economics* 70(4) (2011): 729–739.

11. Kenneth Arrow, Robert Solow, Paul R. Portney, Edward E. Leamer, Roy Radner, and Howard Schuman, "Report of the NOAA Panel on Contingent Valuation," *Federal Register* 58(10) (1993): 4601–4614.

12. U.S. Office of Management and Budget, "Memorandum for the Heads of Departments and Agencies," OMB Circular No. A-94, January 24, 2013.

13. http://epa.gov/airtrends/images/comparison70.jpg.

14. U.S. Environmental Protection Agency, "Benefits and Costs of the Clean Air Act, Second Prospective Study—1990 to 2020," 2011.

15. Roger H. Bezdek, Robert M. Wendling, and Paula DiPerna, "Environmental Protection, the Economy, and Jobs: National and Regional Analyses," *Journal of Environmental Management* 86 (2008): 63–79.

16. Matthew A. Cole and Rob J. Elliott, "Do Environmental Regulations Cost Jobs? An Industry-Level Analysis of the UK," *Journal of Economic Analysis and Policy: Topics in Economic Analysis and Policy* 7(1) (2007): 1–25.

17. U.S. Office of Management and Budget, "Draft 2011 Report to Congress on the Benefits and Costs of Federal Regulations and Unfunded Mandates on State, Local, and Tribal Entities," Washington, DC, 2011.

18. United Nations Environment Programme, "Towards a Green Economy: Pathways to Sustainable Development and Poverty Eradication, A Synthesis for Policymakers," 2011.

13 Common Property Resources and Public Goods

The theory of negative externalities, presented in Chapter 12, provides us with one important way of thinking about environmental issues. In that approach, we start with the market equilibrium and examine ways of modifying it to take into account environmental costs and benefits. But what if there is no market equilibrium, or even no market? This might be the case when social or environmental resources are not owned or ownership rights are not clear. In other cases, there may be a market equilibrium, but one that is highly distorted by failure to reflect crucial costs or benefits of the resource in question. Some important examples are:

- The oceans, which generally are not subject to private property rights and for the most part are not controlled by individual countries, except in coastal zones. The world's oceans contain some of the most important planetary ecosystems. Healthy fisheries are a critical source of food for the world's population, supplying an important source of protein for many lower-income people.
- Many forested areas and wetlands are not privately owned. They may be considered national assets or may be managed by local communities, but in many cases there may be no clear management rules.
- The earth's atmosphere is crucial to all of us but is owned by nobody. Atmospheric functions include the carbon cycle that supports both plant and animal life, climate stabilization, and parts of the water cycle—all crucial to planetary ecology. The issue of climate change has become particularly important in recent years, and is one that we will focus on later in this chapter.
- At the national level, public parks, public beaches, river and lake fisheries, and many recreational areas are important aspects of social and economic life for which there is generally no established market.
- A slightly different kind of example is public airwaves, which are often available for use by private companies under rules set by government.

This chapter provides further insights into economic policies concerning issues such as the public airwaves, ocean fisheries, and climate change as well as other policy issues in related areas. We consider several new instances of market failure—where private markets fail to maximize social welfare. In each of these cases, we also suggest policy responses that can increase the well-being of society.

1. Goods Other Than Private Goods

In the previous chapters, we discussed economic activities related to **private goods**. A private good can be defined as having two distinguishing characteristics:

private good: a good that is excludable and rival

excludable good: a good whose consumption by others can be prevented by its owner(s)

rival good: a good that can only be consumed by only one person at a time

public good: a good that is nonexcludable and nonrival

nonexcludable good: a good whose benefits are freely available to all users

nonrival good: a good that can be consumed by more than one person at a time. The marginal cost of providing a nonrival good to an additional person is zero.

common property resource: a resource that is nonexcludable and rival

artificially scarce good: a good that is excludable but nonrival

congestion: the point at which the demand for a nonrival good results in a diminished benefit to each user, and thus it becomes rival

1. A private good is **excludable**. This means that owners of the good can prevent others from consuming it or enjoying its benefits. For example, the textbooks that you own are excludable goods because, if you wish, you can prevent anyone else from using them. Generally, purchasing a private good establishes an owner's legal right to exclude others from accessing the good.
2. A private good is **rival**. This means that a unit of the good can be consumed by only one person at a time. So, if you are wearing a shirt, no one else can wear that shirt at the same time.

It will help us understand the concept of a private good if we contrast it with three other types of goods.

First, we can define a **public good** as one that is **nonexcludable** and **nonrival**. This means that no one can be excluded from consuming it because they did not pay for it and that more than one person at a time can enjoy its benefits. An important economic result is that, because many people can simultaneously enjoy a nonrival good at the same time, the marginal cost of providing it to one more person is zero.

A common example of a public good is national defense—everyone in a country can simultaneously enjoy its benefits, and none can be excluded. Another example is a national park, because it is freely available to everyone, and many people can enjoy it at the same time.*

Some people mistakenly consider any good "owned" or managed by a government a public good. But a natural reserve managed by an environmental group may also meet the qualifications of a public good, while some public resources may be managed by governments as private goods. An example would be a plot of public grazing land that is leased exclusively to the highest-bidding rancher.

Some goods, known as **common property resources,** are nonexcludable but rival. In other words, common property resources can be freely consumed or enjoyed by anyone, but their use by one person diminishes their availability to others. A classic example of a common property resource is the stock of fish in an open ocean fishery. Anyone with a boat can catch as much fish as he or she is able to. However, a fish caught by one fisher is not available to be caught by anyone else.

The concepts of common property resource and public good may overlap. We mentioned above that a national park can be considered a public good. But if the park becomes so crowded that the benefits of each visitor start to decline, then we can say that the park no longer meets the strict definition of a nonrival good. In general, the availability or quality of a common property resource eventually declines when demands on it increase. But a public good remains available in undiminished quality despite increasing demands.

Finally, we have **artificially scarce goods,** which are excludable but nonrival.** In other words, artificially scarce goods can be simultaneously consumed by many people at a time, but those who do not pay can be excluded from enjoying the good. An example of an artificially scarce good is a toll road. Those who do not pay the toll can be excluded from using the road, but (at least up to a point) many people can simultaneously use the road.

So we can classify different goods into four basic categories as shown in Table 13.1, with examples for each type of good. These categories are not absolutely distinct; particular goods often display characteristics along a spectrum from rival to nonrival and from excludable to nonexcludable. Many goods are subject to **congestion**, meaning that they are nonrival if relatively few people use them at once, but when demand reaches a certain level each user's benefit begins to decrease due to crowding or scarcity. For example, a health club is

---

*Some national parks do charge a small entry fee, but these fees rarely present a significant barrier for visitors. So, for practical purposes they are available for everyone's enjoyment.

**Artificially scarce goods are also called club goods.

Table 13.1 **Classification of Different Types of Goods**

	Excludable	Nonexcludable
Rival	**Private goods** t-shirts, groceries, cars, cell phones, haircuts	**Common property resources** ocean fisheries, groundwater, a community basketball court
Nonrival	**Artificially scarce goods** cable television, health clubs, toll roads	**Public goods** national defense, free radio, public education, national parks

a nonrival good if only a few people are using it. But if the club becomes too crowded, it becomes more like a rival good.

Private goods are most often distributed through markets. This is also the case with artificially scarce goods—those who do not pay can be excluded from obtaining the good's benefits, so suppliers can charge a price to those who wish to consume or enjoy the good. But some artificially scarce goods, such as toll roads, are provided by governments without necessarily yielding a profit.

Common property resources and public goods tend to be supplied or managed by governments. But other organizations can also provide goods or services that benefit everyone, such as land conservation by environmental groups. Also, some resources may not be managed at all, such as a river with unregulated water withdrawals.

We have seen in other chapters that markets that provide private goods can suffer from market failure. For the other three types of goods in Table 13.1, distribution via private markets *almost always results in market failure*. In other words, private markets are generally inefficient in the provision of artificially scarce goods, common property resources, and public goods. Thus market intervention is generally justified for these goods solely on the basis of economic efficiency. Intervention may also be justified on the basis of equity and other final goals. We now turn to the economic theory and policy implications for each of these three types of goods.

Discussion Questions

1. In addition to the examples listed in Table 13.1, try to think of other instances of artificially scarce goods, common property resources, and public goods. Discuss how these goods are supplied—whether through markets, through government provision, or through other approaches.
2. Do you think that the current balance in your society among the four different types of goods is appropriate? Should policies be enacted to shift production so that, in general, society has more public goods and common property resources? Or should more goods be made available instead through private markets? Can you think of specific policies that could achieve the kinds of shifts that you would favor?

2. ARTIFICIALLY SCARCE GOODS

In a market for a private good, the efficient level of provision occurs when the marginal benefits just equal the marginal costs, assuming no other market failures. But for an artificially scarce good, the marginal cost of providing it is zero, at least within a specific quantity range. For example, for homes equipped with cable television, the cost to the provider of sending the broadcast signal to one more household is essentially zero. Note that this does not mean that total production costs are zero. The start-up cost of a cable television company is quite high. Instead, what distinguishes an artificially scarce good from a private good is that its *marginal* supply costs are zero.

Figure 13.1   **The Market for an Artificially Scarce Good** (Cable Television)

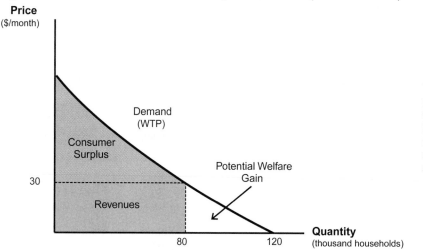

The socially efficient level of provision is to supply cable television to 120,000 households, but at the market price of $30/month, only 80,000 households are willing to pay for a subscription.

Figure 13.1 illustrates the market for an artificially scarce good, cable television. The demand curve shows the maximum willingness to pay for different households in the region. Assume the cable television company charges $30 per month for a basic cable subscription. At this price, 80,000 households sign up for the service, as shown in the graph. The revenues of the cable company are $2.4 million per month ($30 × 80,000 households). The consumer surplus in the market is represented by the shaded region above the price but below the demand curve.

But you might note that something is missing from Figure 13.1—*there is no supply curve!* As the supply curve represents the marginal costs of providing the good, for an artificially scarce good, there is no supply curve. Or more precisely, the supply curve is a horizontal line at a price of zero.

So if we apply our rule that social welfare is maximized when the marginal benefits are equal to the marginal costs, then the efficient quantity of cable television is to provide it to all 120,000 households that are willing to pay something for it. Note that if the cable company provided services at no cost to the 40,000 additional households that value it (but are not willing to pay $30/month), then total social welfare would increase by the triangle on the right-hand side of the graph.

Of course, the cable company will not do this. Profit-making companies are rarely inclined to provide their goods and services for free. Note that the company could theoretically attract additional customers by charging them a monthly fee of less than $30/month. However, this requires that the company engage in **price discrimination**—a seller's charging different prices to different buyers, depending on their ability and willingness to pay. So, while it would keep charging $30/month to most of its customers, the company might charge $10/month to other customers who have a lower willingness-to-pay. As the marginal cost of providing cable services is zero, the company's profits would increase nonetheless and those additional customers would obtain some consumer surplus.

price discrimination: a seller's charging different prices to different buyers, depending on their ability and willingness to pay

This outcome is unlikely, because price discrimination is often illegal, and even where it is legal it is difficult to implement. One common exception is college tuition. Students from households that are unable to pay the full tuition commonly receive financial aid, so these students can obtain the same education at a lower cost. (Note that this is not a case in which the marginal cost of supply is zero—the reason for price discrimination in education is a matter of society's ethical standards more than profit-maximizing.)

The cable TV company in Figure 13.1 will seek to set its price to maximize its profits, based on the elasticity of demand. However, this price will not result in a level of provision that maximizes social welfare. For this reason, government intervention sometimes occurs in markets for artificially scarce goods, which are often supplied by monopolies. Government regulation could require, for example, that a lower price be set or that special rates be made available to lower-income consumers. We discuss markets with monopoly suppliers and the role of government regulation in more detail in Chapter 17.

Discussion Questions

1. Do you think that price discrimination should be illegal? Does it make economic sense for everyone to pay the same price for something? Do you think that it is fair for everyone to pay the same price for something?
2. Do you think that the profits of a company that provides cable television should be regulated by the government? Is competition in the cable industry sufficient to keep prices reasonable? How is technology changing the nature of competition for video programming?

3. COMMON PROPERTY RESOURCES

A common property resource is available to essentially anyone, but it cannot be used or enjoyed by multiple people at the same time, at least with the same level of quality. Overuse is often a problem with a common property resource, as when too many people fish the same fishery, want to play ball games in the same recreation area, or withdraw groundwater from the same aquifer. We can use tools of economic analysis to examine how this problems arises and what policy solutions may be available.

3.1 MODELING A COMMON PROPERTY RESOURCE

One way to model a common property resource is to realize that every user of the resource essentially imposes a cost on other users. In the example of a fishery, if the number of fishing trips is relatively low, adding one more trip is unlikely to affect the catch of other fishers. But above a critical level, each additional fishing trip begins to harm the overall health of the fishery and thus reduce the catch of everyone in the fishery. Each individual fisher will consider only whether he or she is making a profit. So, the fact that others' profits have declined will not be taken into account by additional fishers. This is similar to the idea of a negative externality, but in this case market participants are harming other market participants.

Figure 13.2 models a fishery as an example of a common property resource. The horizontal axis indicates the number of fishing trips taken in the fishery. Assume that it costs $15,000 to operate a fishing trip, considering labor costs, boat payments, fuel, and other costs. This is the private cost of each fishing trip, as shown by the PC line in the graph. Note that the cost to operate a fishing trip is constant, regardless of the number of trips taken.

Next, we need to consider the revenue obtained from each fishing trip. Obviously, this depends on the number of fish caught. For the first few trips, we assume that each fishing trip yields $25,000 in revenues per trip (see curve RT in the graph). When we subtract operating costs, each fishing trip results in $10,000 in profits.

Initially, plenty of fish are available for all fishers, so each additional trip does not affect the catch of anyone else. Until T_0, each fisher is able to obtain revenues of $25,000 per trip. But after the number of trips exceeds T_0, the revenue per trip begins to decline. The fishery is becoming crowded, and because more fishers are competing for limited fish stocks, it becomes more difficult to catch fish. Each fishing trip will still result in a profit but, instead of making a $10,000 profit, each trip will result in a lower profit.

Each fisher will obviously be disappointed to have lower profits. But as long as profits are still positive (RT > PC), there is an incentive for more fishers to take trips to the area. In fact, as fishers begin to realize declining catches, they may be motivated to increase their fishing efforts further in order to catch fish while they still have the opportunity.

Figure 13.2   **Common Property Model of a Fishery**

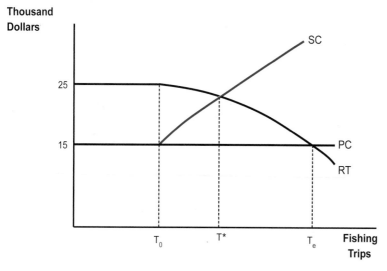

The unregulated outcome will result in T_e fishing trips. But above T_0 trips, each additional trip imposes a cost on other fishers. The socially efficient level of fishing trips is T^*.

We can model the cost that additional fishers impose on others much as we modeled a negative externality. It represents an additional cost above the private cost of operating a boat trip. Above T_0, each additional trip imposes a social cost as shown by curve SC, equal to the reduction in the profits of *all other fishers*. In other words, SC represents the total social cost of operating a boat trip above T_0, considering the out-of-pocket costs of $10,000 plus the external cost equal to the reduction in others' profits.

The socially efficient level of fishing trips is equal to T^*. This is the level at which the profits from a new fishing trip are just enough to compensate the loss of others' profits.

But in an unregulated fishery, there is no reason for fishers to stop at T^*. So long as individual fishers can make profit, the number of fishing trips will continue to increase until we reach T_e. At this point, profit for each fishing boat falls to 0. There will then be no further incentive for additional fishing trips. But at such a high level of fishing effort, the health of the fishery may begin to decline. Over time, the stock of fish may become so depleted that the fishery crashes, leading to the collapse of the local fishing industry.

3.2 POLICIES FOR COMMON PROPERTY RESOURCE MANAGEMENT

One solution to the problem of the overuse of a common property resource is much like the implementation of a Pigovian tax. We could charge a fee for each fishing trip equal to the external cost imposed on others. If fishers had to pay this fee in addition to their out-of-pocket costs of $15,000, we could adjust the fee until we reached the efficient level of fishing trips, T^*.

individual transferable quota (ITQ): tradable rights to access or harvest a common property resource, such as the right to harvest a particular quantity of fish

Another solution is to institute **individual transferable quotas (ITQs)**. These operate much like tradable pollution permits, discussed in Chapter 12. With this approach, an organization managing the resource (such as a government agency) sets the total allowable fishing level, such as the number of fishing trips or the total harvest per season. This level of effort is set low enough to maintain the ecological integrity of the resource. The ITQs can be distributed for free or auctioned off to the highest bidders. If they are auctioned, the proceeds can be used by the government to maintain the quality of the resource or as compensation for those who are forced out of the industry. Holders of ITQs may then use them to fish or offer them for sale to interested parties. The price of an ITQ is not set by the government but allowed to vary depending on supply and demand. ITQ programs for ocean fisheries have been established in several countries, including Australia, Canada, Iceland, and the United States. (For a real-world example of ITQs, see Box 13.1.)

BOX 13.1   FISHERIES MANAGEMENT IN PRACTICE: INDIVIDUAL TRANSFERABLE QUOTAS

One real-world example of regulating a fishery through individual transferable quotas is the Long Island clam fishery. This example shows that the details of the quota system can significantly influence the efficiency of the industry.

The New York Department of Environmental Conservation allocates only 22 clam permits, which limit the total annual harvest to 300,000 bushels (about 13,600 bushels per permit). Based on 2011 clam prices, the gross revenue potential of each permit was about $135,000.

However, clam fishers claimed that after deducting operating costs, a single permit was insufficient to make a living. The permits are transferrable, meaning that a single fisher could purchase multiple permits. But the permit system initially required each permit to be associated with one boat. If you purchased a second permit then you would have to also operate a second boat, effectively doubling your operating costs. This requirement meant that efficiency gains from applying multiple permits to the same boat could not be realized.

In 2011 the state changed the law to allow "cooperative harvesting"—meaning that a fisher could buy additional permits without having to operate more boats. Given that the total quota allocation remained at 300,000 bushels, the law change shouldn't affect the health of the fishery, but it offers the potential to increase the economic efficiency of the industry.

Source: "Ensure that Permits Protect Long Island's Surf Clam Fishery," *Newsday* (New York), July 6, 2012, p. A28.

Although ITQs or other regulations of a common property resource may not be popular with those who are used to accessing the resource for free, these policies are required to prevent the unsustainable use of the resource.

tragedy of the commons: a situation in which an unregulated common property resource is seriously degraded due to overuse

The overuse of a common property resource has famously been described as the "**tragedy of the commons**" (see Box 13.2), and it also can be viewed as a type of negative externality. Each user of the resource imposes a negative cost on others, yet makes decisions based solely on his or her own profits. Just as in our externality analysis, the unregulated market outcome with a common property resource will be inefficient.

Discussion Questions

1. Suppose that you and three roommates are living in an apartment or dorm suite with a common area for living, dining, and cooking. Do you think that a "tragedy of the commons" outcome is a likely result without some rules regarding cleaning? What rules would you propose instituting?

2. Suppose that a small fishing community in a developing country has been operating successfully for centuries without any regulations. Each fishing family owns a boat and makes a small profit. However, suppose that climate change reduces the health of the fish stock, and the community is forced to reduce its overall fishing activities. Should the community institute an auction system to allocate fishing rights or begin charging a license fee? Can you think of a fair way to reduce the community's fishing activities?

4. PUBLIC GOODS

Public goods are at the opposite end of the spectrum from private goods. Public goods are both nonexcludable and nonrival. We saw examples of market failure with artificially scarce goods and common property resources. As you might expect, private markets fail to provide the efficient level of public goods. In fact, even though many people value the benefits of public goods, private markets often fail to provide any public goods at all.

In private market goods, the ability to charge a price acts as a way to exclude nonbuyers and thus make a profit. Anyone can enjoy the benefits of a public good without paying, and each additional user does not affect the amount or quality of the good available to others. Consider national defense as an example of a public good. Could we rely on a megacorporation

BOX 13.2   THE "TRAGEDY OF THE COMMONS" DEBATE

The term "tragedy of the commons" comes from an influential paper written by ecologist Garrett Hardin in 1968. Discussing the degradation of common grazing properties in England, Hardin wrote:

Picture a pasture open to all. It is to be expected that each herdsman will try to keep as many cattle as possible on the commons. Such an arrangement may work reasonably satisfactorily for centuries because tribal wars, poaching, and disease keep the numbers of both man and beast well below the carrying capacity of the land. Finally, however, comes the day of reckoning, that is, the day when the long-desired goal of social stability becomes a reality. At this point, the inherent logic of the commons remorselessly generates tragedy.

As a rational being, each herdsman seeks to maximize his gain. Explicitly or implicitly, more or less consciously, he asks, "What is the utility to me of adding one more animal to my herd?" This utility has one negative and one positive.component.

1. The positive component is a function of the increment of one animal. Since the herdsman receives all the proceeds from the sale of the additional animal, the positive utility is nearly +1.
2. The negative component is a function of the additional overgrazing created by one more animal. Since, however, the effects of overgrazing are shared by all the herdsmen, the negative utility for any particular decision-making herdsman is only a fraction of [the shared negatives].

Adding together the component partial utilities, the rational herdsman concludes that the only sensible course for him to pursue is to add another animal to his herd. And another; and another. . . . But this is the conclusion reached by each and every rational herdsman sharing a commons. Therein is the tragedy. Each man is locked into a system that compels him to increase his herd without limit—in a world that is limited. (Hardin, 1968, p. 1244)

The "tragedy of the commons" essentially describes the fate of an "open-access resource"—one to which everyone has access without limitation or regulation. But there has often been confusion between the concepts of common property and open access. Common property resources are not necessarily open-access resources; their use may be regulated, for example, by customs and traditional rules.

The story told by Hardin was significantly modified by the political scientist Elinor Ostrom, who won the Nobel Memorial Prize in economic science for work "showing how common resources—forests, fisheries, oil fields or grazing lands—can be managed successfully by the people who use them, rather than by governments or private companies." Ostrom's point was that it was not just "tribal wars, poaching, and disease" that kept the system in balance. Instead, many societies have worked out institutional arrangements that operate with the same result as government regulations but that depend on social norms and customs instead of laws. In many parts of the world, such systems have endured for generations, sometimes centuries.

It is often the encroachment of market institutions on situations in which community management of common property has been successful that leads to degradation. As Hardin pointed out, when a common property resource exists within a market context, without any regulation by institutions of government or of society, there is an incentive at the individual level to keep using the resource as long as profits can be made. But each individual fails to consider the cost he or she imposes on other users, and the likely outcome is the destruction of the resource. Thus in the case of an open-access resource, the unregulated market outcome is both inefficient and ecologically unsustainable.

Sources: Garrett Hardin, "The Tragedy of the Commons," *Science* 162 (3859): 1243-1248, 1968; Elinor Ostrom, *Governing the Commons: The Evolution of Institutions for Collective Action* (Cambridge, UK: Cambridge University Press, 1990).

to provide national defense in a market setting? Obviously not. No individual would have an incentive to pay because he or she could receive essentially the same level of benefits without paying. Thus the "equilibrium" quantity of public goods in a market setting is normally zero, as no company would want to produce something for which no one is willing to pay. Clearly, this is an example of market failure.

Perhaps, we could rely on donations to supply public goods. This is done with some public goods, such as public radio and public television. Also, some environmental groups conserve habitats that, while privately owned, can be considered public goods because they are open for

free riders: those who obtain the benefits of a public good without paying anything for it

public enjoyment. Donations, however, generally are not sufficient for an efficient provision of public goods. Because public goods are nonexclusive, each person can receive the benefits of public goods regardless of whether he or she pays. So although some people may be willing to donate money to public radio, many others simply listen to it without paying anything. Those who do not pay are called **free riders**.

It is obvious that a voluntary donation system would not work for the provision of many public goods, including national defense. Although we cannot rely on private markets or voluntary donations to supply public goods, their adequate supply is of crucial interest to the entire society. In democracies, decisions regarding the provision of public goods are commonly decided in the political arena. This is generally true of national defense. A political decision must be made, taking into account that some citizens may favor more defense spending and others less. After the decision is made, we all pay a share of the cost through taxes.

Similarly, decisions on the provision of environmental public goods may be made through the political system. Congress, for example, must decide on funding for the national park system. Will more land be acquired for parks? Might some existing park areas be sold or leased for development? In making decisions like this, we need some indication of the level of citizen demand for public goods. What insights can we gain from economic theory?

Recall that in Chapter 3 we referred to a demand curve as both a marginal benefit curve and a willingness-to-pay curve. A consumer is willing to pay, say, as much as $30 for a t-shirt because that is his or her perceived benefit from owning the shirt. But in the case of a public good, the marginal benefits that someone obtains from a public good are *not* the same as his or her willingness to pay for it. In particular, the person's willingness to pay is likely to be significantly lower than his or her marginal benefits.

A simple example illustrates this point. Consider a society with just two individuals: Doug and Sasha. Both individuals value forest preservation—a public good. Figure 13.3 shows the marginal benefits that each person receives from the preservation of forest land. As in a regular demand curve, the marginal benefits of each acre preserved decline with more preservation. We see that Doug receives greater marginal benefits than Sasha does. This may be because Doug obtains more recreational use of forests, or it may simply reflect different preferences.

The social marginal benefits from preserved forest land are obtained by the vertical addition of the two marginal benefit curves. In the top graph in Figure 13.3, we see that Doug receives a marginal benefit of $5 for an additional acre of forest preservation if 10 acres are already preserved. Sasha receives a marginal benefit of only $2. The social, or aggregate, benefits of an additional acre of preserved forest are $7, as shown in the bottom graph. The "social benefits" graph represents the addition of the marginal benefits to both Doug and Sasha. In this case, the aggregate curve is kinked (i.e., not straight) because to the right of the kink Sasha's marginal benefits are zero, and the curve showing the value of preserving additional acres reflects only Doug's marginal benefits.

Suppose for simplicity that forest preservation costs society a constant $7/acre for administrative and management costs. This is shown in the bottom graph in Figure 13.3. In this example, the optimal level of forest preservation is 10 acres—the point where the marginal social benefits just equal the marginal costs.

But we have not addressed the question of how much Doug and Sasha are actually willing to pay for forest preservation. In the case of a public good, a person's marginal benefit curve is not the same as his or her willingness-to-pay curve. For example, although Doug receives a marginal benefit of $5 for an acre of forest preservation, he has an incentive to be a free rider and he may be willing to pay only $3 or even nothing at all.

The problem is that we do not have a market in which people accurately indicate their preferences for public goods. Perhaps we could conduct a survey to collect information on how much people value certain public goods, but sometimes people do not provide accurate responses (recall our discussion of contingent valuation surveys in Chapter 12). Ultimately,

Figure 13.3   **The Benefits of Public Goods**

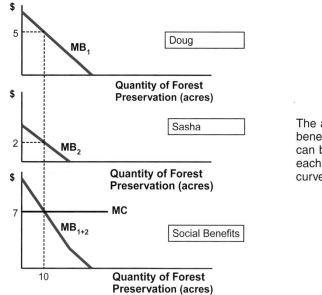

The aggregate social marginal benefits of supplying public goods can be obtained by vertically adding each individual's marginal benefit curve.

decisions regarding public goods require some kind of social deliberation. One option is to rely on elected officials to make public goods decisions for their constituents. Another is to rely on a democratic process such as direct voting or local town meetings.

Suppose that we correctly determine that the appropriate level of forest preservation in Figure 13.3 is 10 acres. At a marginal cost of $7/acre, we need to raise $70 in revenues to pay for preservation. We could tax Doug and Sasha $35 each to cover these costs. Doug receives at least $5 in benefits for every acre preserved, or a total of at least $50 in benefits, so he may not object to the $35 tax. However, Sasha receives significantly lower benefits, and she may view the tax as excessive.

Now, let us extend our two-person example to the entire population of the United States—about 115 million households. If preferences in the general population are similar to Doug and Sasha's, we will need to raise $35 multiplied by 115 million, or about $4 billion, for forest preservation in order to reflect its true social benefits. This could be done with a tax of $35 per household. But, of course, marginal benefits vary across households. It is clearly impractical to assess the actual marginal benefit of each household. A society-wide decision must be made.

After this decision has been made, some people might think that they have to pay too much and others that the allocation of money for forest preservation is inadequate. But assessing a broad tax is essential for achieving the goal of forest preservation. Debates regarding efficiency and fairness in the case of public goods are thus inevitably both political and economic in nature.

Discussion Questions

1. Some people have suggested that certain public lands would be managed more efficiently if they were auctioned off to the highest bidders. In theory, the highest bidder would put the land to its highest-valued use. Employing a market valuation, that use might be logging or developing the land for vacation homes. Such an auction would provide the government with revenue, which could be used for socially beneficial purposes or for lowering taxes. Do you think that some public lands should be sold to private interests?

2. Consider the provision levels of the following public goods in society: national defense, public education, environmental quality, and highways. Do you think that the current

"supply" of each of these goods is too high, too low, or about right? What factors do you think determine the amount of resources that are allocated toward each of these goods? Do policies need to be changed to adjust the allocation?

5. CLIMATE CHANGE

climate change: long-term changes in global climate, including warmer temperatures, changing precipitation patterns, more extreme weather events, and rising sea levels

Global warming, sometimes more accurately described as **climate change**, has become a major issue in recent decades. The vast majority of scientists concur that global climate change is largely caused by human activity, in particular, the emission of atmospheric pollutants.* See Box 13.3 for more on the scientific opinion on climate change.

According to the National Oceanic and Atmospheric Administration (NOAA), a U.S. government agency, 2012 was the tenth-warmest year on record. More importantly, it marked the thirty-sixth consecutive year of above-average global temperatures.**

Climate change has significant economic costs. According to NOAA's National Climate Data Center, 11 severe weather events in 2012 in the United States cost the country $110 billion. The two costliest events that year were Hurricane Sandy ($65 billion) and the yearlong drought across the country ($30 billion).[1]

Numerous projections conclude that these impacts will become more severe over time unless significant steps are taken. In 2013 the managing director of the International Monetary

---

BOX 13.3   THE SCIENTIFIC CONSENSUS ON CLIMATE CHANGE

Although few dispute the finding that the world is becoming warmer, media reports commonly refer to the debate over the causes of this warming as ongoing. The global climate has varied considerably over time due to natural factors. Some people think the current warming represents just another natural variation, while others attribute the warming primarily to human factors, mainly the burning of fossil fuels. What is the unbiased scientific opinion on the causes of climate change?

Several articles have been published based on surveys of either the scientific literature on climate change or climate scientists themselves. In a 2004 paper published in the highly respected journal *Science*, the abstracts of 928 articles on the topic of climate change were reviewed. Of these, 75 percent agreed with the "consensus position" that humans are causing climate change, and 25 percent dealt with methods or past climate change and thus took no position on current warming. But the author writes, "Remarkably, none of the papers disagreed with the consensus position."

In a 2013 study climate researchers were directly asked whether their research supported or refuted the view that humans are affecting the climate. Of those who expressed an opinion, 97 percent supported the consensus position. The paper concludes that the

"number of papers rejecting [the view that humans are impacting the climate] is a minuscule proportion of the published research." The results of a larger survey of earth scientists, published in 2009, concluded:

> It seems that the debate on the authenticity of global warming and the role played by human activity is largely nonexistent among those who understand the nuances and scientific basis of long-term climate processes. The challenge, rather, appears to be how to effectively communicate this fact to policy makers and to a public that continues to mistakenly perceive debate among scientists.

Sources: William R.L. Anderegg, James W. Prall, Jacob Harold, and Stephen H. Schneider, "Expert Credibility in Climate Change," *Proceedings of the National Academies of Science* 107(27) (2010): 12107–12109; J. Cook, D. Nuccitelli, S.A. Green, M. Richardson, B. Winkler, R. Painting, R. Way, P. Jacobs, and A. Skuc, "Quantifying the Consensus on Anthropogenic Global Warming the Scientific Literature," *Environmental Research Letters* 8(2) (2013): 1–7; Peter T. Doran and Maggie Kendall Zimmerman, "Examining the Scientific Consensus on Climate Change," *EOS* 90(3) (2009): 22–23; Naomi Oreskes, "Beyond the Ivory Tower: The Scientific Consensus on Climate Change," *Science* 306 (5702) (2004): 1686.

---

*We use the term "climate change" instead of "global warming" because, in addition to warmer average temperatures, this hugely complex system change has numerous other effects—sometimes even including colder than normal temperatures in certain locations.

**Relative to the twentieth-century average of 57 degrees Fahrenheit (about 13.9 degrees Celsius).

Fund, Christine Lagarde, called climate change "the greatest economic challenge of the twenty-first century." She went on to say:

> Make no mistake: without concerted action, the very future of our planet is in peril. So we need growth, but we also need green growth that respects environmental sustainability. Good ecology is good economics.[2]

A well-known 2006 report on climate change sponsored by the British government concluded:

> Climate change presents a unique challenge for economics: it is the greatest and widest-ranging market failure ever seen. . . . Our actions over the coming few decades could create risks of major disruption to economic and social activity, later in this century and in the next, on a scale similar to those associated with the great wars and the economic depression of the first half of the twentieth century.[3]

Many of the principles discussed in this chapter and Chapter 12 are applicable to solving the challenge of climate change. But an adequate response to climate change is not simply a matter of instituting economic policies. It will also involve questions about fairness concerning rich and poor countries as well as different groups within countries. Other relevant issues concern how to act under uncertainty and how to define well-being, both now and in the future.

5.1 CLIMATE CHANGE DATA AND PROJECTIONS

greenhouse gases: gases such as carbon dioxide and methane whose atmospheric concentrations influence global climate by trapping solar radiation

Humans can influence the global climate by the emissions of various **greenhouse gases**. These gases act much like the glass in a greenhouse—allowing solar radiation to penetrate but then trapping it and increasing temperatures. Although various greenhouse gases exist naturally in the earth's atmosphere and make life possible on earth, human activities have increased the concentration of many of these gases and introduced greenhouse gases into the atmosphere that do not occur naturally. The most relevant greenhouse gas emitted by humans is carbon dioxide (CO_2), which is formed when fossil fuels (coal, oil, and natural gas) are burned. Other important greenhouse gases include methane, nitrous oxide, and chlorofluorocarbons (CFCs).*

As shown in Figure 13.4, global emissions of CO_2 have increased significantly over the past couple of decades and are projected to increase a further 30 percent between 2015 and 2035. We see that virtually all the increase in emissions in the coming decades will be a result of higher emissions in developing countries (i.e., those that are not members of the OECD). Most of the carbon emitted from human activities to date, however, has come from developed countries.

Further, CO_2 emissions *per capita* are much higher in developed countries and will continue to be so for the foreseeable future. For example, annual emissions per capita are currently about 18 tons in the United States, 9 tons in Germany, 7 tons in China, 1.4 tons in India, and 0.3 tons in Kenya. This disparity in emissions per capita roughly reflects the global disparity in income. Any climate proposal that seeks broad international participation will need to allow the world's poorest to increase their material living standards. Thus simply requiring all countries, say, to reduce emissions by 50 percent would reinforce current inequality.

CO_2 and other greenhouse gas emissions remain in the atmosphere for a long time, decades or even centuries. This means that even if we reduce annual emissions by 50 percent or more, total concentrations will continue to rise. The atmosphere can be viewed as a bathtub with a

---

*CFCs have also been implicated in depletion of the ozone layer, a critical layer of the atmosphere. It is important to note that degradation of the ozone layer, while serious, is an issue almost entirely unrelated to global climate change.

Figure 13.4   **Past and Projected Global Emissions of Carbon Dioxide, 1990–2035**

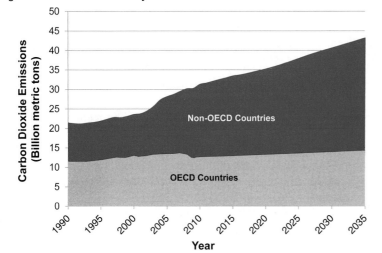

Global emissions of carbon dioxide are projected to increase 30 percent between 2015 and 2035, with most of the increase a result of higher emissions in developing countries.

Source: United States Energy Information Administration database.
Note: OECD is the Organisation for Economic Co-Operation and Development, comprised mostly of developed nations.

very, very slow leak. As long as we keep adding more water (i.e., greenhouse gases) beyond a slight trickle to the bathtub, its level will continue to rise.

As atmospheric concentrations of greenhouse gases increase, the world is expected to become warmer, on average. Not all regions will warm equally, and some regions may actually become cooler. Warmer average temperatures increase evaporation, which in turn leads to more frequent precipitation, but again all regions will not be affected equally. In general, areas that are already wet will become wetter and dry areas will become drier. Climate change is also expected to result in more frequent and more intense tropical storms. The melting of polar ice caps and glaciers will contribute to rising sea levels. Sea levels are also rising because the volume of ocean water expands when it is heated.

Global average temperatures have already increased by about 1 degree Celsius (1.8 degrees Fahrenheit) over the past several decades. At a 2009 international meeting on climate change in Copenhagen, Denmark, more than 130 countries agreed that it was necessary to limit the eventual warming to no more than 2 degrees Celsius, based on the scientific consensus that warming above this level is likely to cause dangerous impacts.

Climate scientists have developed complex models to predict how much average temperatures will increase as CO_2 concentrations increase. Because predicting long-term climate trends involves considerable uncertainty, these models have produced a range of potential outcomes. Adding to the uncertainty in models is the extent to which warming will be influenced by the policy decisions made in the next couple of decades.

The Intergovernmental Panel on Climate Change (IPCC) was established in 1988 by the United Nations Environment Programme (UNEP) and the World Meteorological Organization (WMO) under the United Nations to assess the science of climate change. A 2007 IPCC report estimated that temperatures will rise between 1.1 and 6.4 degrees Celsius in the twenty-first century, with the most likely range between 1.8 and 4.0 degrees.[4] A 2009 analysis by researchers at MIT, however, predicted that, without significant policy changes, warming would be much greater—in the range of 3.5 to 7.4 degrees Celsius.[5] Warming above 5 degrees is considered particularly dangerous, as 5 degrees represents the difference in global average temperatures between now and the last ice age. Such a large temperature change in a short period (although in the opposite directions) would cause significant ecological impacts, such as the extinction of as much as 50 percent of the earth's species according to one estimate.

5.2 ECONOMIC ANALYSIS OF CLIMATE CHANGE

Strong policy action to reduce emissions of greenhouse gases could avoid the most damaging effects of climate change. Scientists at the IPCC estimate that, rather than increasing as projected in Figure 13.4, global CO_2 emissions must be reduced 50–80 percent by 2050. Of course, most countries are highly dependent on fossil fuels as an energy source. Transitioning to a low-carbon economy will require investment in energy efficiency and renewable energy technologies.

Various economic studies have analyzed climate change using the techniques of cost-benefit analysis, which was discussed in Chapter 12. Cost-benefit analysis of climate change is particularly difficult for two main reasons: the high degree of uncertainty about future impacts and the long period of the analysis. Most of the costs of responding to climate change are borne in the short term, while most of the benefits (in terms of avoided damages) occur in the long term. Thus the choice of a discount rate is critical.

Virtually all economists agree that carbon emissions represent a negative externality and that a market-based policy such as a Pigovian tax or a tradable permit system should internalize this externality. However, there is a lively debate among economists about how aggressive such policies should be. Until recently, most economic studies of climate change suggested a relatively modest carbon tax, perhaps around $20–$40 per ton of carbon emitted (a $30 per ton tax on carbon would increase the price of gasoline by about 8 cents per gallon).

The economic debate over climate change changed significantly in 2006 when Nicholas Stern, a former chief economist at the World Bank, released a 700-page report, sponsored by the British government, titled *The Economics of Climate Change: The Stern Review*. Publication of the "Stern Review" generated significant media attention and has intensified the debate over climate change in policy and academic circles. Unlike previous studies, the Executive Summary of the "Stern Review" strongly recommends immediate and substantial policy action:

> The scientific evidence is now overwhelming: climate change is a serious global threat, and it demands an urgent global response. This Review has assessed a wide range of evidence on the impacts of climate change and on the economic costs, and has used a number of different techniques to assess costs and risks. From all these perspectives, the evidence gathered by the Review leads to a simple conclusion: the benefits of strong and early action far outweigh the economic costs of not acting.

The "Stern Review" estimated that if humanity continues "business as usual," the costs of climate change in the twenty-first century would reach at least 5 percent of global GDP and could be as high as 20 percent. It also suggested the need for a much higher carbon tax—over $300 per ton of carbon.

What accounts for the difference between the "Stern Review" and most earlier analyses? The primary difference was that Stern applied a lower discount rate, 1.4 percent, compared to 4–5 percent in most other studies. Stern argued that his discount rate reflected the view that each generation should have approximately the same inherent value. Stern's analysis also incorporated the precautionary principle (discussed in Chapter 12), in that he placed greater weight on the possibility of catastrophic damages.

5.3 CLIMATE CHANGE POLICY

Because climate change can be considered a very large environmental externality associated with carbon emissions, economic theory suggests a carbon tax as an economic policy response. Alternatively, a tradable permit system (also known as cap-and-trade) could be applied to carbon emissions.

As discussed in Chapter 12, a tax offers price certainty, while a tradable permit system offers emissions certainty. If you take the perspective that price certainty is important because it allows for better long-term planning, then a carbon tax is preferable. If you believe that the relevant policy goal is to reduce carbon emissions by a specified amount with certainty, then a cap-and-trade approach is preferable, although it may lead to some price volatility.

Both approaches have been used. Carbon taxes have been instituted in several countries, including a nationwide tax on coal in India (about $1/ton, enacted in 2010), a tax on new vehicles based on their carbon emissions in South Africa (also enacted in 2010), a carbon tax on fuels in Costa Rica (enacted in 1997), and local carbon taxes in the Canadian provinces of Quebec, British Columbia, and Alberta that apply to large carbon emitters and motor fuels.

The European Union instituted a cap-and-trade system for carbon emissions in 2005. The system covers more than 11,000 facilities that collectively are responsible for nearly half the EU's carbon emissions. In 2012 the system was expanded to cover the aviation sector, including incoming flights from outside the EU. The state of California instituted a cap-and-trade system in 2013 for electrical utilities and large industrial facilities, with a goal of an annual decline in carbon emissions of 3 percent.

global public good: a public good available to the entire population of the planet

Regardless of which policy approach is taken, it must ultimately be applied at the international level. Each individual country has very little incentive for reducing its emissions if other countries do not agree to similar reductions. Action to reduce climate change can be regarded as a public good that also generates a positive externality. As we have noted, in the case of public goods, the problem of free riders means that they will not be provided effectively without collective action. In the case of stabilizing the health of a **global public good** such as the climate, international agreement is required.

The most comprehensive international agreement on climate change was the Kyoto Protocol, which was drafted in 1997. Under that treaty, industrialized countries agreed to emission reduction targets by 2012 compared to their baseline emissions, normally set to 1990 levels. For example, the United States agreed to a 7 percent reduction, France to an 8 percent reduction, and Japan to a 6 percent reduction. Developing countries such as China and India were not bound to emissions targets under the treaty (an omission that drew objections from the United States and some other countries).

By 2012, 191 countries had signed and ratified the Kyoto Protocol. The United States was the only country that signed the treaty but never ratified it. In 2001, the George W. Bush administration rejected the Kyoto Protocol, arguing that negotiations had failed and that a new approach was necessary. Despite the U.S. withdrawal, the Kyoto Protocol entered into force in early 2005 after Russia ratified the treaty in November 2004.

Countries that have met their targets under the Kyoto Protocol include France, Germany, Russia, and the United Kingdom. Countries that have apparently failed to meet their targets include Canada, Australia, Spain, and Sweden. The overall Kyoto program target of a 5 percent reduction in industrialized country emissions was likely to be met based on preliminary data, but only because of very large reductions in Russia due largely to its economic collapse after the demise of the Soviet Union in 1991 rather than any deliberate policy.

Countries that failed to meet their targets are supposed to make up for it in the future, but attempts to create a successor to the Kyoto Protocol have so far been unsuccessful. Perhaps, the most contentious point of disagreement is still whether developing countries should be bound by mandatory cuts in emissions. Although some countries, particularly the United States, argue that all participants must agree to reductions in order to address the problem, developing countries contend that mandatory cuts would limit their economic development and reinforce existing global inequities.

A more radical approach, which treats the entire atmosphere as a common property resource, is described in Box 13.4. Although such a solution is politically highly unlikely, it indicates that the application of standard economic principles to dealing with common property resources and public goods could respond effectively to the problem of climate change as well as promote greater global equity.

BOX 13.4   AN EARTH ATMOSPHERIC TRUST

The global atmosphere is a common property resource with respect to carbon emissions. For the most part, anyone can emit carbon into the atmosphere without cost. The apparent outcome is the largest example of the tragedy of the commons that the world has ever seen.

A common property resource is essentially equally "owned" by all with access to it. As a global resource, the atmosphere can be viewed as something to which all people on earth have an equal right. This principle forms the basis for perhaps the most innovative and comprehensive policy approach to reducing carbon emissions, called an Earth Atmospheric Trust.

The program would establish a global cap-and-trade system for carbon emissions. The cap would be established to prevent damaging climate change, based on the best available scientific evidence. All permits would be auctioned off to the highest bidders, such as electricity plants, industrial facilities, and transportation companies. The cost of permits would ultimately be reflected as higher prices to consumers.

A global auction system would yield significant revenues, about $1 trillion–$4 trillion annually depending on the price of permits. Some of this money (the Earth Atmospheric Trust) would be used to invest in low-carbon technologies, fund adaption measures, and restore ecological damage. The remainder, perhaps half or more, would be distributed to all people on earth as an equal per-capita annual payment. This reflects the concept of equal "ownership" of the atmosphere, such that everyone is equally compensated for the damage done to the resource.

Of course, the logistics of distributing an annual payment to all people on the planet are currently daunting, but the principle is supported by standard economic theory. The annual payment would amount to about $300 per person per year. In rich countries, the payment would partially, but not totally, offset higher prices for goods such as electricity and gasoline. In poor countries, the payment would reflect a substantial increase in annual incomes. Consider that about a billion people currently live on $1 or less per day. Thus in addition to limiting carbon emissions, the Trust would significantly reduce abject poverty in the world.

Source: Peter Barnes, Robert Costanza, Paul Hawken, David Orr, Elinor Ostrom, Alvaro Umana, and Oran Young, "Creating an Earth Atmospheric Trust," *Science* 319 (2008): 724.

Discussion Questions

1. How serious a problem do you think climate change is? Compare your judgment of this based on news reports and the economic studies that have tried to evaluate the costs and benefits of climate change. How effective do you think economic analysis has been in approaching the problem?
2. Which policies do you think are most likely to be effective in responding to climate change? Given the political resistance to taxes, what do you think would be the best strategy for achieving reduction of greenhouse gas emissions?

REVIEW QUESTIONS

1. What are the two characteristics of private goods? Provide some examples.
2. What are the two characteristics of public goods? Provide some examples.
3. What are the two characteristics of common property goods? Provide some examples.
4. What are the two characteristics of artificially scarce goods? Provide some examples.
5. How do economists define congestion?
6. What is the supply curve for an artificially scarce good?
7. Why does the private provision of an artificially scarce good result in economic inefficiency?

8. What is price discrimination?
9. How can we model the market for a common property resource?
10. How can we determine the utilization or harvest for a common property resource without any regulation?
11. How do we determine the efficient outcome for a common property resource?
12. What policies can be implemented in the case of a common property resource?
13. What is the tragedy of the commons?
14. What is the likely equilibrium outcome for a public good in a private market?

15. Can voluntary donations result in the efficient provision of public goods?
16. What are free riders?
17. How can we model the demand for a public good in a simple society with two individuals?
18. Why do someone's marginal benefits differ from his willingness to pay in the case of a public good?
19. What policies are needed to provide for the efficient provision of public goods?

20. What is climate change?
21. What are the projections for future greenhouse gas emissions, considering both developed and developing countries?
22. What do most economic analyses of climate change conclude? What are some major differences?
23. What are some economic policies to address climate change?

EXERCISES

1. For each of the following examples, discuss whether it is a private good, a public good, a common property resource, or an artificially scarce good. Note that some examples may be considered more than one type of good.
   a. Seats in a movie theater
   b. Traffic lights
   c. A lake on private land
   d. A lake on public land
   e. Cars owned by a car rental company
   f. The water in a currently pure river, which can be used for drinking water as well as waste disposal
   g. A hospital that provides free health care to low-income households

2. An underground aquifer in a developing country is available to all farms in a small community. Assume that it costs 50 pesos per day to operate a pump that can extract groundwater from the aquifer. The value that a farm can obtain by using or selling the water depends on how many farms extract water, as given in the table below.

Number of farms extracting water	Revenue per day per farm (pesos)	Profit per day per farm (pesos)	Total profit (pesos)
1	100		
2	100		
3	100		
4	90		
5	80		
6	65		
7	55		
8	40		
9	20		

   a. Assuming that there is no regulation of the aquifer, how many farms will extract ground-

water? Assume that as long as each farm is making a profit, there is an incentive for more farms to extract water. Fill in the third column of the table to help you answer this question.
   b. Is this unregulated outcome economically efficient? Explain.
   c. What would be the economically efficient level of groundwater extraction (number of farms extracting water)? Hint: calculate total profit by multiplying number of farms by profit per farm and see where total profit reaches a maximum. At this point, the extra profit made by adding one more farm is just balanced by the losses to other farms.

3. The marginal benefits of wildlife habitat preservation in a society with just two individuals, Katya and Miguel, are given in the table below.

Acres of wildlife habitat	Katya's marginal benefits (dollars)	Miguel's marginal benefits (dollars)
1	50	30
2	40	25
3	30	20
4	20	15
5	10	10
6	0	5

   a. Draw a graph showing the social marginal benefits of wildlife preservation.
   b. Suppose that wildlife preservation costs $40 per acre. How many acres of wildlife habitat should be preserved in this society?
   c. What policy would you propose to achieve the efficient provision of wildlife habitat?
   d. Which individual do you think would be less willing to support your policy proposal? Explain.

4. Match each concept in Column A with an example in Column B.

Column A	Column B
a. A private good	1. A policy solution to the tragedy of the commons
b. A free rider	2. National defense
c. Price discrimination	3. The primary factor on which some economists disagree regarding climate policy
d. A public good	4. Your shoes
e. An artificially scarce good	5. Someone who listens to public radio without contributing to it
f. Individual transferable quotas	6. Charging airline passengers different fares
g. The discount rate	7. The wifi signal at a hotel that charges for Internet access

Notes

1. NOAA press release, "2012 Was the Tenth Warmest Year on Record," June 13, 2013.

2. Jeremy Hance, "Head of IMF: Climate Change Is the 'Greatest Economic Challenge of the Twenty-First Century,'" REGATTA, United Nations Environment Programme, February 6, 2013.

3. Nicholas Stern, *The Economics of Climate Change: The Stern Review* (Cambridge: Cambridge University Press, 2007).

4. Intergovernmental Panel on Climate Change, *Climate Change 2007: The Physical Science Basis* (Cambridge: Cambridge University Press, 2007).

5. David Chandler, "Climate Change Odds Much Worse Than Thought," *MIT News,* May 19, 2009.

PART

V

Resources, Production, and Market Organization

14 Capital Stocks and Resource Maintenance

Economics is about how people manage their resources. All economic actors—businesses, governments, nonprofit organizations, and each of us as individuals—have to make decisions every day about how to use (or not use) our resources. In managing your financial resources, you choose how to allocate your money between food, entertainment, books, and many other things. Companies decide how to use their workers and physical resources to produce efficiently. Governments must allocate tax revenues among many competing needs. As a society, we are faced with choices about how to use our natural resources and how much to save for the future.

In this final section of the book, we focus on how we manage our resources and use them to produce goods and services, generally for sale in markets. We saw in Chapter 1 that production decisions always involve tradeoffs—recall our discussion of the production-possibilities frontier. Producing more of one thing requires us to give up something in return. We can also think of tradeoffs over time. Using up a critical natural resource now may increase current production, but lead to reduced opportunities in the future. Thus the activity of resource maintenance goes hand-in-hand with production decisions.

In this chapter, we focus on the different types of resources available to society, from manufacturing equipment to credit worthiness, from oil reserves to human knowledge. We see how we can track the availability of resources over time. The importance of each type of resource is discussed. We end with a discussion about the sustainable management of resources.

1. CAPITAL STOCKS

As you have probably learned by now, sometimes economists speak a slightly different language from most people. Let's consider how most people define the following words:

- *Capital:* This commonly refers to something to do with finance, such as "capital markets" or "venture capital."
- *Stocks:* This commonly refers to ownership shares in companies, which are traded in "stock markets."
- *Investment:* This commonly refers to activity such as buying stocks or "investing" in a retirement account.

capital: any resource that is valued for its potential economic contributions

To an economist, these terms mean slightly different things. The economist's definition of **capital** includes not only financial resources, but any resource that is valued for its potential economic contributions. Money is one type of capital, but other types of capital include a factory, a highway, a natural gas field, or a farm. Capital does not even need to be something physical. The knowledge that you are gaining from your education is a form of capital. So, too, are systems of laws and customs that facilitate economic activities. Below we will define the main different types of capital.

stock: the quantity of something at a particular point in time

To an economist, a **stock** refers to the quantity of something at a particular point in time. For example, the amount of water currently in a bathtub is a stock, as is the amount of money in your checking account on January 1. The number of hairs on your head right now is a stock. In this chapter, we often focus on the stock of a particular capital resource, such as the stock of oil reserves or the stock of a species of fish in a lake. Stocks of capital may increase or decrease as a consequence of natural forces, as in the case of a natural forest, or they may be deliberately managed by humans to provide the inputs for production.

investment: any activity intended to increase the quantity or quality of a resource over time

Finally, economists view **investment** as any activity intended to increase the quantity or quality of a resource over time. In other words, investment is designed to result in the growth of capital stocks. An employee who puts funds into her individual retirement account (IRA) is investing in the stock of financial assets that she will draw on in the future. So is the business that trains its workers, the subsistence farmer who sets aside seeds for his next planting season, and the community that works to clean up its air and water. The economic activity of resource maintenance can be viewed as investment, leading to greater production possibilities in the future.

1.1 STOCKS VERSUS FLOWS

flow: something whose quantity is measured over a period of time

Capital stocks can increase over time, with proper investment, or decrease if they are simply used up. While the stock of something is measured at a single point in time, a **flow** is measured *over a period of time.* An obvious example is the amount of water flowing into a bathtub. We could speak of the amount of water flowing into the tub per minute, per hour, or another time interval. The flow of new tools into a warehouse, and the flow of tools out of it as they are sold, can be measured over the day or week. The number of haircuts that you had in the previous year is a flow of services. (Note that it is impossible to keep a stock of haircuts in a warehouse. Flows can be of either goods or services, but stocks can only be goods.)

stock-flow diagram: a diagram that shows how a stock changes over time, as flows add to it or subtract from it

Flows can either add to capital stocks or decrease them. Figure 14.1 presents a **stock-flow diagram,** which shows how flows change the level of a stock over time, by either adding to it or subtracting from it. Some of the stocks in Figure 14.1 carry over, meaning that they are still there in the next period. In this figure, the new stock is larger than the initial stock, because the additions are greater than the subtractions (represented by the thickness of arrows).

Figure 14.2 provides a specific example of a stock-flow diagram using a bank account as an example. Suppose that you start the month with exactly $1,400 in your checking account. This is your initial stock. During the month, the flows into your checking account include $700 from your job, $50 from someone who owed you money, and $5 in interest on the account, for a total of $755. Note that this is a flow that represents an addition to your stock over time.

Figure 14.1 **A Stock-Flow Diagram**

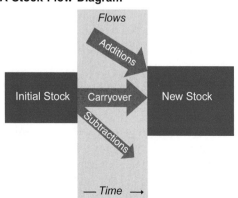

A stock-flow diagram shows how flows change the quantity of a stock over time. In this case, additions exceed subtractions, so the stock increases over time.

Figure 14.2 **A Stock-Flow Diagram for a Checking Account**

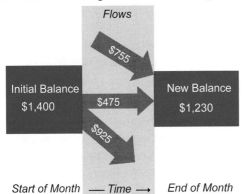

In this example, flows out of the checking account exceed the flows into the account, so the checking account balance declines over time.

The flows out of your account over the month include $600 for rent and $325 in other expenses, for a total of $925. Thus your new bank account balance at the end of the month (i.e., your stock of money on that day) is $1,230. Your balance has declined over the month because the flows out of your account were greater than the flows into it.

1.2 THE FIVE TYPES OF CAPITAL

Capital can be classified into five basic categories:

1. natural capital
2. manufactured (or produced) capital
3. human capital
4. social capital
5. financial capital

natural capital: physical assets provided by nature

manufactured (or produced) capital: all physical assets that have been made by humans using natural capital

human capital: people's capacity for engaging in productive activities

social capital: the stock of relationships, including trust and shared values, that facilitates economic activities

financial capital: funds of purchasing power available to purchase goods and services or facilitate economic activity

physical capital: resources that are tangible (i.e., can be touched or seen)

Natural capital consists of physical assets provided by nature, such as land that is suitable for agriculture or other human uses, sources of fresh water, and stocks of minerals and fossil fuels (such as crude oil or coal) that are still in the ground. **Manufactured capital** is physical assets that are produced by humans using natural capital. These include such things as buildings, machinery, stocks of refined oil, and inventories of produced goods that are waiting to be sold.

Human capital is the capacity of people to engage in productive activities. Specifically, it includes the knowledge and skills that each person can bring to his or her work as well as the physical and mental health that allows people to make use of their knowledge and skills. **Social capital** is the stock of relationships among people that facilitates economic activities, including shared norms, values, and trust. For example, when you buy something on eBay, you trust that the seller will actually send you the item that you purchased after you pay for it, based on a mutual understanding of how an eBay transaction works.

Financial capital consists of resources that can be used to purchase goods and services. Money, either cash or bank accounts, is probably the most common form of financial capital, but it can also include assets such as stocks and bonds and one's ability to borrow in the form of loans or credit cards. Although financial capital does not directly produce anything, it contributes to production by making it possible for people to produce goods and services in advance of getting paid for them.

Capital can be classified as being either in physical or intangible forms (some capital can be both). Capital takes the form of **physical capital** when it can be touched or seen. Natural capital is primarily physical in form. Anything that we produce or use in the physical world either comes directly from a natural capital stock—as a fruit is picked from a wild tree—or has been transformed from its original, natural form. Even such human inventions as plastics, microchips, and advanced medicines are all made out of something physical that was at one time a part of the stock of natural capital.

intangible capital: resources that cannot be seen or touched

Intangible capital, which cannot be seen or touched, is less visible but no less important. Some human capital, such as knowledge about economics or biophysics or Chinese art, is a purely intangible type of capital. Social capital is also commonly intangible, such as the trust between a buyer and seller. But many forms of physical capital can also be viewed as a representation of intangible capital. A DVD, for example, is a physical object, but its true value lies in the information and entertainment that it can provide. Even a machine can be viewed as not only a hunk of physical metal but also the embodiment of intangible knowledge and software. Paper money is more than just physical paper because it also represents intangible, socially created trust that it can be used in payment.

Discussion Questions

1. Linda thinks that a rich person is someone who earns a lot of money. Meng thinks that a rich person is someone who has a big house and owns lots of stocks and bonds. How would the distinction between stocks and flows lend clarity to their discussion?
2. Think of a common activity that you enjoy. For example, perhaps you like to get together with friends and listen to music while making popcorn in the microwave. List the stocks of natural, manufactured, human, financial, and social capital on which you draw when engaging in this activity.

2. NATURAL CAPITAL

Natural capital forms the basis for all life on earth. Yet it is less obvious that natural capital is crucial to all economic activity. Sometimes, it is easy to forget that everything we see around us—computers, books, cars, buildings—can all be traced back to a natural capital origin. As human economic activity has increased, our demands on natural capital have also increased. Whether natural resources will be sufficient to meet human demands in the future has become a question of considerable debate. Moreover, some forms of natural capital are becoming degraded or fundamentally changed due to human activities, such as the changes in the global climate that we discussed in Chapter 13.

2.1 RENEWABLE AND NONRENEWABLE NATURAL CAPITAL

renewable resource: a resource that regenerates through short-term natural processes

Different kinds of natural capital can be classified according to whether they are renewable. A **renewable resource** regenerates through biological or other short-term processes, which may be helped by human activity. The quantity and quality of its stock depend simultaneously on the rate at which the stock regenerates or renews and on the rate at which it is harvested or polluted. A healthy forest will go on indefinitely producing trees that may be harvested, yielding a flow of lumber that will be used up in production processes such as papermaking. (For more on the management of renewable natural capital stocks, see Box 14.1.)

nonrenewable resource: a resource that can only diminish over human time scales

Other kinds of natural capital are **nonrenewable resources**. Their supply is fixed, although new discoveries can increase the stock that is known to be available. For example, there is a finite amount of oil reserves, and a finite amount of each kind of mineral, available on earth. Although these resources were created over a very long period spanning millions of years, they are considered nonrenewable on a human time scale. Nonrenewable resources do not have self-regenerating flows, and the stock can only diminish over time as a result of human use or natural deterioration, as illustrated in Figure 14.3.

How much of its stock of natural resources a society chooses to use as inputs into current production, rather than to preserve for the future, is clearly a very important economic question. In addition to any carryover, the initial stock of a renewable resource is able

BOX 14.1 RENEWABLE RESOURCE MANAGEMENT: FISHERY STOCKS

Since 1971 the Food and Agriculture Organization (FAO) of the United Nations (UN) has published reports on the status of the world's ocean fisheries. The FAO classifies fishery stocks into three categories, based on the relationship between actual harvest levels and the "maximum sustainable yield," which is the harvest level that equals the rate of natural regeneration of the stock. The three FAO fishery stock categories are:

1. *Non–fully exploited:* stocks with harvest levels below the maximum sustainable yield; harvest levels can be potentially increased without harming the fishing stock
2. *Fully exploited:* stocks with harvest levels at or near the maximum sustainable yield; harvest levels cannot be increased any further without harming the fishing stock
3. *Overexploited:* stocks with harvest levels already above the maximum sustainable yield; harvest levels need to be reduced in order to preserve the health of the fishing stock

According to the FAO, in 2009 57 percent of the world's fishery stocks were considered fully exploited, a percentage that has not significantly changed since the 1970s. About 30 percent of fishery stocks in 2009 were classified as overexploited, compared to only about 10 percent in the 1970s. Meanwhile, the percentage of stocks classified as non–fully exploited decreased from about 40 percent in the 1970s to only 13 percent in 2009.

These results suggest that about 87 percent of the world's fishery stocks are already being fished at or above their natural limits. For the 13 percent of stocks that are not being fully exploited, the FAO notes that these stocks generally have a low production potential and that the "potential for increase in catch may be generally limited." The FAO also mentions that the increase in overfished stocks is a cause for concern. It indicates that, at the global level, the UN targets for rebuilding the overfished stocks and implementing an ecosystem approach are not being met.

The FAO concludes that careful fisheries management is needed to restore overexploited stocks to ecological health and to ensure that fully exploited stocks are not overfished.

Source: Food and Agriculture Organization of the United Nations, "Review of the State of the World Marine Fishery Resources," FAO Fisheries and Aquaculture Technical Paper 569, Rome, 2011.

Figure 14.3 **Depletion of Nonrenewable Natural Capital Over Time**

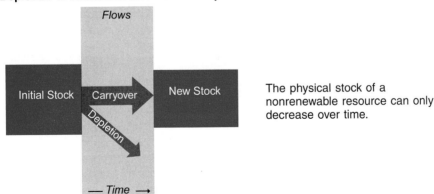

The physical stock of a nonrenewable resource can only decrease over time.

to regenerate and thus contribute to greater stocks in the future, as illustrated in Figure 14.4. But natural inputs that are renewable—such as lumber from forests and fish from the seas—can be exhausted if so much of them are destroyed or extracted that they can no longer renew themselves.

In addition, nature's ability to absorb pollution and break down waste is limited, and there are tipping points beyond which degraded natural capital may be dramatically altered in some essential respect. As we saw with climate change, dramatic ecological change may occur over the next several decades, including the extinction of numerous species. It is very difficult to predict whether ecosystems will be sustainable in the face of such dramatic changes. Rising

Figure 14.4 **Stock Changes for a Renewable Natural Resource**

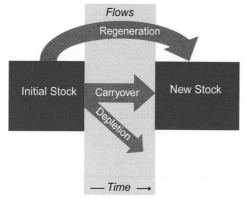

The stock of a renewable resource can remain stable, or even increase, over time due to natural regeneration. But if managed poorly or exploited, the stock of a renewable resource can also decrease over time.

sea levels could cause the flooding of many low-lying areas; New Orleans and southern Florida, in the United States, and Bangladesh are examples, but many cities worldwide are in low-lying areas close to oceans. Some island countries are already losing significant land mass. Resource maintenance for natural capital means tracking the size, quality, and changes in natural resources and making wise decisions about their management.

2.2 NATURAL CAPITAL AND SUSTAINABILITY

substitutability: the possibility of using one resource instead of another

Production and consumption levels in modern societies, particularly in industrialized countries, may be leading to the depletion of important natural capital stocks. Thus it becomes important to determine the extent of possible **substitutability** of resources. That is, the depletion of any one resource (e.g., fossil fuels) is a less serious problem for future generations if other resources (such as nuclear or solar energy) can be cheaply and safely substituted for it. The extent of substitutability that can be achieved depends both on the characteristics of the resources and on the speed of technological advance.

sustainable socio-economic system: one that maintains its resources such that at least the same level of social well-being can be maintained over time

A **sustainable socioeconomic system** is one that maintains its resources such that at least the same level of social well-being can be maintained over time. For renewable resources, this generally means that rates of depletion and use do not exceed natural regeneration rates. Ecological impacts are kept safely below critical levels to ensure ecosystem stability. For nonrenewable resources, depletion rates are kept to a minimum and adequate investment is made to develop renewable substitutes. It is important to identify critical natural resources, for which substitution may be difficult if not impossible.

Discussion Questions

1. Give three examples of renewable natural capital. Give three examples of nonrenewable natural capital. (Do not duplicate examples given in the text.)
2. Do you think that a cheap and safe substitute for the use of fossil fuels in cars will ever be found? Discuss. (Note that the electricity for electric cars is currently generated primarily by fossil fuels.)

3. MANUFACTURED CAPITAL

The stock of manufactured capital is the stock of physical things produced by human beings, which in turn are used to produce other goods. In modern societies, manufactured capital includes such things as roads, factories, communication systems, buildings, machinery, and computers. The major form of manufactured capital is fixed manufactured capital. Inventories are another form of manufactured capital. We turn now to a discussion of these two types of manufactured capital.

3.1 FIXED MANUFACTURED CAPITAL

fixed manufactured capital: manufactured goods that yield a flow of productive services over an extended period

Most of what we consider manufactured capital is in the form of **fixed manufactured capital**, which is designed to supply a flow of productive services over an extended period. When economists speak of "capital" as an input to production, what they usually mean is that *stocks of manufactured capital,* such as tools, machines, buildings, and infrastructure, yield *flows of services,* such as making it possible to dig or drill more rapidly, expediting communications and transportation or giving shelter. The fixed manufactured capital stocks themselves are not used up during the production process (aside from normal wear and tear), nor do they become part of the product itself.

If you find the distinction between stocks and flows confusing, consider the example of a tax accountant renting an office from a real estate firm. The stock of manufactured capital here—the physical office itself—belongs to the real estate firm, but the service arising from the use of the office space is an input flow into the production of services to the tax account's clients. Similarly, when truckers drive along a highway, they are using the services of the government-provided physical road. The actual physical office and the road are not in themselves inputs into production—they do not get used up or converted into something else on the way to creating new goods and services. Only the *flow of services* yielded by these capital goods can properly be referred to as inputs.

The stock of fixed manufactured capital is increased when people decide to make physical investments—that is, to build or improve productive assets. Although fixed manufactured capital is not directly used up in the process of production, physical assets commonly lose their usefulness over time, as computers become obsolete, roads develop potholes, and equipment breaks. Commonly, these losses are referred to as **depreciation** of the manufactured capital stock. Resource maintenance activities for fixed manufactured capital include all the checking, cleaning, protection, and repair activities needed to keep buildings, machines, and other manufactured capital in good working order.

depreciation: decrease in the usefulness of a stock of capital due to wear and tear or obsolescence

A society's stock of manufactured capital is dependent upon its technology. For example, a plow pulled by an ox and a modern tractor are both manufactured capital, but they incorporate very different technologies. In a way, manufactured capital can be viewed as an embodied form of human capital, representing accumulated human knowledge and innovation. Thus investment in human capital tends to yield benefits in terms of improved manufactured capital stocks.

3.2 INVENTORIES

inventories: stocks of raw materials or manufactured goods being stored until they can be used or sold

A smaller amount of manufactured capital exists in the form of **inventories**. Inventories are stocks of raw materials or produced goods that are not currently being used or sold but are expected to be used or sold in the foreseeable future.

Like other forms of capital, inventories contribute to production. For example, you cannot start baking bread until you have accumulated a stock of flour, nor can you provide retail services selling shoes until you have an inventory of shoes. Also like other forms of capital, inventories are valuable assets. If you were to sell your shoe store, the value of your stock of salable shoes would be figured into the sale price of the business. But unlike fixed manufactured capital, inventories are generally meant to be used up relatively quickly or to become part of another product, rather than to provide a flow of services over an extended period.

Recall the definition of a stock as something measured at a point in time. Imagine that at one single moment we could freeze all useful manufactured goods where they are—including those in warehouses and on shelves—and make a long list. Everything on the list that is not fixed manufactured capital would be counted, *at that moment,* as inventory manufactured capital. (If we unfreeze those goods, however, we see that inventories are constantly being added to and drawn down, as stocks of materials are used up and goods are sold.)

3.3 MANUFACTURED CAPITAL IN THE CORE AND PUBLIC PURPOSE SPHERES

When we think of manufactured capital as the stock of physical assets that provide inputs to productive activities, it is important to remember that productive activities take place in all spheres. Sometimes, economists discuss manufactured capital largely in terms of business investment, ignoring the manufactured capital stocks that have accumulated in the core and public purpose spheres. For example, economists have traditionally viewed a stove purchased by a restaurant as an investment in manufactured capital. But exactly the same stove purchased by a household would normally be classified as "consumption" rather than a productive investment (unless the household used the stove to cook meals for sale).

To account fully for the productive capacity of an economy, some economists suggest that manufactured capital should be accounted for in similar ways, no matter who holds it. Production by households, neighborhoods, nonprofits, and governments depends on stocks of manufactured capital, just as much as production by businesses does.

Discussion Questions

1. Come up with one new example of each of the following: fixed manufactured capital, inventory, investment, depreciation.
2. In the early twentieth century, photos or drawings of big factories with tall stacks belching smoke were popularly used to represent the productivity of the contemporary economy. What images come to mind now, when you think of economic activity in the early twenty-first century?

4. HUMAN CAPITAL

Human bodies are amazing machines that have evolved to survive in a wide variety of conditions, from arctic cold to tropical heat. We are extremely adept at endurance activities. For example, over long distances human runners can outpace almost any other animal, including dogs, horses, and cheetahs.* But the most remarkable evolutionary achievement of humans is our large and complex brain. No one can claim to have yet explored the full potential for human creativity and innovation.

Our human capital includes both our physical capacity for exertion and our mental capacity for productive application of our knowledge and skills. Such individual productive capabilities must be created and enhanced through nurturance, nutrition, education, training, and other aspects of life experience.

The raw quantity of human capital in an economy might be crudely measured in terms of the number of people in its population who are of normal working age. To attempt to measure its quality, measures of health status or of years of schooling achieved might also be considered. As with the various kinds of physical capital, we can think of human capital as a stock of capabilities, which can yield a flow of services. Economists often view "labor" as the flow of effort, skill, and knowledge that humans directly provide as inputs into productive activities. Because it is a flow, labor is usually measured over a period of time, such as by the number of person-hours of work of a particular skill that has been used in the course of a week or month.

4.1 PHYSICAL HUMAN CAPITAL

Human capital can take physical and intangible forms. In physical form, humans operate much like a manufactured machine—requiring energy inputs to produce physical work. Manual

---

*Since 1980 an annual "horse versus human" marathon race has been held in Wales, UK. Although a horse with a rider is normally the winner, a couple of times the winner was human.

labor, for example, taps human physical energy, just as another productive process might tap a stock of fossil fuel. Thus the term "human capital" is based on an analogy between a human being and a manufactured machine. Although some people find this analogy offensive, others find it a useful way of analyzing an important input to production—as long as it does not lead to treating human beings as though they really were machines!

Health, strength, and fitness are important forms of physical human capital. In circumstances of deprivation, in which some workers perform below their potential because they are weakened by hunger or illness, basic nutrition and medical care can be seen as important ways of investing in human capital as well as direct contributions to well-being. This is particularly true in the case of children, whose future capabilities can be permanently stunted by deprivation at critical times. (See Box 14.2 for more on this issue.)

Box 14.2 Nutrition and School Performance

A growing body of scientific evidence demonstrates the importance of good nutrition for children's development and school performance. A 1998 research project at Tufts University found that:

Recent research provides compelling evidence that undernutrition during any period of childhood can have detrimental effects on the cognitive development of children and their later productivity as adults. In ways not previously known, undernutrition impacts the behavior of children, their school performance, and their overall cognitive development. These findings are extremely sobering in light of the existence of hunger among millions of American children.

Research on nutrition and education has especially focused on breakfast. According to Leia Kedem, a University of Illinois Extension nutrition and wellness educator:

Although any breakfast is better than no breakfast, making the extra effort to make it healthy might help your kids do better in school. Studies show that kids who eat a balanced breakfast have higher test scores and can concentrate better and solve problems more easily in class. The nutritional value of meals can also make a difference. A breakfast low in fiber and protein, like sugary toaster pastries, can lead to a midmorning energy crash. This is because the carbohydrates are digested and absorbed quickly, causing blood sugar levels to dive after an initial spike. Other than sudden fatigue, kids may also experience headaches and irritability.

Beyond just breakfast, overall diet sufficiency and quality are also related to academic performance. A 2008 study in Canada concluded that intake of fruit and vegetables were positively correlated with school performance, while fat intake was negatively correlated. The research validates the "importance of children's nutrition not only at breakfast but also throughout the day," with a recommendation for greater investment in school nutrition programs.

Sources: Center on Hunger, Poverty, and Nutrition, "The Link Between Nutrition and Cognitive Development in Children," Tufts University, School of Nutrition, Medford, MA, 1998; Michelle D. Florence, Mark Asbridge, and Paul J. V. Eugelers, "Diet Quality and Academic Performance," *Journal of School Health* 78(4) (2008): 209–215; "Good Nutrition Means Better School Performance," *Journal Gazette and Times Courier* (Illinois), August 6, 2013.

4.2 Intangible Human Capital

The dramatic rise in living standards since the Industrial Revolution started in the eighteenth century rests more than anything else on the remarkable rise in output of the average worker. This increase in productivity is based not on an increase in the human capacity for physical labor but on how technological innovations have been applied to productive processes. Sometimes, these innovations involved new ways of using the energy stored in natural resources, such as the use of coal to move trains and generate electricity. At other times, these innovations involved creating machines to perform tasks much more efficiently than was possible solely through human physical or mental effort. For example, computers are able to perform tasks in nanoseconds that would take a human a lifetime of work.

The development of such technologies makes it evident that the continuing increase in human productivity does not depend only on physical capital and sheer human effort. It also depends on intangible kinds of capital, including the knowledge, skills, and habits embodied in individuals.

Formal education, along with less formal ways of acquiring skills (e.g., early childhood education in homes and knowledge gained from on-the-job experience) are important contributors to human capital. As you read this paragraph, you are investing in your own human capital, in the form of an economics education.

Clearly, human capital has a way of accumulating over time. Scientific research is one good example of this. Scientists generally build upon the knowledge produced by previous scientists. Again, this accumulation of knowledge can be embodied in manufactured capital, indicating technological progress. For example, a worker at an automobile company may start with an existing engine design, and develop a new technique to make that engine more fuel efficient.

Discussion Questions

1. In what ways is it useful to think of human bodies and brains as if they were like productive machinery? What might be some drawbacks of this way of thinking?
2. One obvious way that you are increasing your human capital by going to school is that you can be more productive in a career. In what other ways do you believe that you are increasing your human capital through your education?

5. SOCIAL CAPITAL

The English poet John Donne penned the famous line that "no man is an island." Although the development of individual human capital is important for increasing productivity, nearly all economic activity involves the coordination of actions among numerous actors. Social capital consists of shared knowledge, ideas, and values, along with social organization and workplace relationships. These relationships and common understandings provide the social context for economic activity.

social organization: the ways in which human productive activities are structured and coordinated

Production possibilities depend on the ability to coordinate production among different people. Even with no change in machinery or technology, productivity can increase if coordination among workers improves or if workers become more motivated because of good management techniques. **Social organization** refers to the ways in which human productive activities are structured and coordinated.

Social capital also includes the cultural beliefs and goals that determine which knowledge is applied, which scientific questions are researched, and which technological possibilities are explored. A growing public awareness and acceptance of the hazards posed by global climate change, for example, could be considered a form of social capital, because it increases the ability of society to respond to a significant threat to its future well-being.

In contemporary industrialized economies, the term "social capital" is most often used to refer to characteristics of a society that encourage cooperation among groups of people (e.g., workers and managers) whose joint efforts are needed to achieve a common goal. This kind of capital is built up to the extent that a society is characterized by strong norms of reciprocity, which lead people to trust and help one another, and dense networks of civic participation, which encourage people to engage in mutually beneficial efforts rather than seeking only to gain individual advantage. Business accountants have led the way in recognizing one kind of social capital—good will—which they view as a significant business asset that makes a firm more valuable than one might think from looking at its physical assets alone. Good will includes a number of intangible factors, such as a firm's good reputation among its customers and creditors, good management, and good labor relations. It has become common practice to list good will among the assets of a firm that is for sale.

Social capital resembles other forms of capital in that it generates a service that enhances the output obtainable from other inputs, without being used up in the process of production.

Recognition of this concept by economists is fairly recent and has been strengthened by the observation that variation in social capital across societies can help to explain some of the differences in their economic development.

Discussion Questions

1. In what ways is it useful to think of knowledge, trust, motivation, and the like as though they were similar to productive machinery? What might be some drawbacks of this way of thinking?
2. Economic issues are often discussed in terms of money and prices, but it is difficult to quantify social capital in such terms. Can you think of topics, both within the category of social capital and in other categories, that have economic importance but are hard to express in terms of money?

6. FINANCIAL CAPITAL

For most production processes, you have to acquire inputs before you can create outputs. Before it can make its first sale, a start-up business needs to buy or rent a building and equipment, hire staff, and amass inventories of materials and supplies. You, as a student, must pay for tuition and textbooks either by using your savings or borrowing, in order to increase your human capital and eventually obtain a job. In a money economy financial capital is what allows all these productive activities to get going in advance of the returns that will flow from them.

Financial capital is a largely intangible form of capital. Its importance in the economy relies on the social beliefs that sustain the financial system, much more than on the physical paper or the electronic documents that record its existence. Economists distinguish between two different forms of financial capital: equity finance and debt finance.

6.1 EQUITY FINANCE

equity finance: an economic actor's use of its own funds to make productive investments

Suppose that you pay for a car completely in cash, as opposed to taking out a loan. This represents a form of **equity finance**, which means using your own money (i.e., wealth) to make a purchase. A business that uses its accumulated profits to purchase new computers or machinery is also undertaking equity finance. "Equity" means having an ownership right. Thus equity finance means using resources that an individual or business currently owns. (This use of the term "equity" should not be confused with another meaning of the same word, "justice or fairness.")

Like other forms of capital, financial capital can be thought of in terms of stocks that increase or decrease over time and that provide a flow of services. A farmer increases her financial capital stock by laying aside the proceeds from her last harvest. She will use (and, very often, use up) her equity financial capital as she spends it on supplies for the next productive season.

What are the commonest sources of equity finance? Individuals can finance their productive activities out of money that they have inherited or saved. Governments finance some programs out of accumulated past taxes. Businesses can accumulate funds by retaining some of their profits or by selling shares of the business in the form of stocks. People add to their stock of equity financial capital by saving, and they diminish their stock of equity financial capital by spending.

debt finance: borrowing others' funds to make productive investments

6.2 DEBT FINANCE

loan: money borrowed for temporary use, on the condition that it be repaid, usually with interest

Suppose instead that you need to take out a car loan, instead of paying all cash. As you do not have the ability to use equity finance to buy a car, you must rely upon **debt finance.** Debt finance means that you are able to gain access, temporarily, to the purchasing power of *other* actors' wealth.

One can think of taking out a **loan** as "renting" financial capital—renting the use of money. Just as an office can be rented and *used* productively by one enterprise while it is *owned* by another, the services of the financial capital are *used* by someone taking out a car loan while

principal: the original amount of money borrowed

interest: the charge for borrowing money

the financial capital is technically owned by a bank. Borrowers agree not only to repay the **principal** (the original amount) of the loan but also to give the lender **interest**, a charge for borrowing the funds, usually calculated as a percentage of the principal. (If the person taking out the car loan is not able to pay back the loan, the bank can usually take over ownership of the car in exchange for its lost funds.)

Banks and nonbank financial institutions, such as credit unions, are not the only providers of debt finance. Governments and large companies often raise financial capital directly by selling bonds, which are financial instruments that promise repayment of funds with interest.

Discussion Questions

1. Financial capital is important not only in the business and government spheres but also in the core sphere. What major purchases do families often finance through taking out a loan (i.e., debt finance)?
2. Explain how the concept of opportunity cost can influence the way in which you think about your use of financial capital.

7. SUSTAINING CAPITAL STOCKS

Only recently has the field of economics formally recognized that natural capital, human capital, and social capital are at least as critical to production as manufactured and financial capital—and sometimes more so. Along with this realization has come the recognition that all these forms of capital are subject to erosion as well as growth. Because all production begins with, and depends on, the availability of the necessary capital stocks—including, in most cases, all five kinds that we have discussed—it is important to consider how these capital stocks are produced and maintained, and what circumstances might endanger their quantity or quality. The necessity of attending to the basic economic activity of resource maintenance has become more evident in recent years.

For example, what happens if stocks of manufactured capital are not maintained? If our stocks of housing, roads, communication systems, factories, and equipment are wearing out without being replaced, our standard of living can decline. What about social and human capital? If formal education systems, norms of raising children, or patterns of behavior change in ways that cause a deterioration in the education and health of a population or in prevailing standards of honesty, reliability, and originality, then it is likely, again, that standards of living will decline in the future.

At this moment in history, the deterioration of natural capital stocks is an especially widely recognized problem. Only in recent decades have we encountered global limits on the capacity of nature to absorb the intended and unintended effects of our economic activity. Increasingly, humans have gone beyond harvesting the annual produce of seas and soils and have begun to deplete the natural capacity for regeneration.

It is possible for economic activity to augment stocks of manufactured and human capital continually, more than offsetting any decline associated with the depreciation of manufactured capital and the retirement of existing workers. In contrast, the impact of economic activity on the stock of natural capital is most often negative; either the existing stock is drawn down (when natural resource inputs are used) or the quality of the stock is diminished (as by the introduction of waste products).

The stock of renewable natural capital can be maintained or augmented using wise resource management, and the (apparent) stock of nonrenewable resources can be increased through new discoveries. Moreover, the problem of a deteriorating natural resource stock can be allayed or postponed by technological and production method changes that reduce the amount of natural resource depletion or waste product generation associated with a given amount of production. Yet the fact that the earth and its resources are finite suggests that sooner or later the limit to the size of the physical flow of production that can be maintained over time will be reached.

Many types of decline can be reversed, so these observations should not be taken as cause for despair. They do, however, point to the fact that economic policy and analysis are not simple matters. The economic health of a contemporary society depends on schools and family support systems as much as on factories and roads; it depends on workplace morale as well as on protection of air, soil, water, and species. And whether we are thinking about the long-term or the short-term health of the economy and the individuals in it, we must judge economic activities not only in relation to their intended effects but also in terms of their unplanned effects on the physical and social environments.

REVIEW QUESTIONS

1. What distinguishes a stock from a flow?
2. How can we distinguish a stock from a flow using a diagram?
3. What are the five major types of capital?
4. What are the two main types of natural capital?
5. What is a sustainable socioeconomic system?
6. What are the two main types of manufactured capital?
7. What are the two main types of human capital?
8. What is social capital?
9. What are the two main types of financial capital?

EXERCISES

1. Which of the following are flows? Which are stocks? If a flow, which of the five major kind(s) of capital does it increase or decrease? If a stock, what kind of capital is it?
   a. The fish in a lake
   b. The output of a factory during a year
   c. The income that you receive in a month
   d. The reputation of a business among its customers
   e. The assets of a bank
   f. The equipment in a factory
   g. A process of diplomatic negotiations
   h. The discussion in an economics class
2. Consider the case of a new computer antivirus software package.
   a. In a paragraph, briefly describe the capital stocks that provided the resource base for its creation.
   b. Which of the four economic activities is antivirus software designed to address? (Note: It may address more than one economic activity.)
3. A forest originally has 10,000 trees. Suppose that the forest naturally replenishes itself by 10 percent per year. That is, at the end of one year, if nothing else happened, it would have 10,000 + $(0.10 \times 10{,}000) = 11{,}000$ trees. (This assumption is not biologically accurate, but it keeps the math simple.) Suppose that 1,500 trees are harvested at the end of each year.
   a. How many trees will the forest have at the end of one year, after accounting for both natural replenishment and the effects of harvesting?
   b. Draw a stock–flow diagram illustrating the change in the forest stock from year 1 to year 2.
   c. How many trees will there be at the end of two years? (*Note:* Base the 10 percent replenishment amount on the number of trees that exist at the *beginning of the second year.*)
   d. How many trees will there be at the end of three years?
   e. For the harvest of trees to be sustainable, what is the largest number of trees that could be harvested each year (starting with the original stock of 10,000 trees)?
4. Match each concept in Column A with an example in Column B.

Column A	Column B
a. Equity finance	1. Fish in the ocean
b. Social capital	2. Starting a business by using money that you have saved
c. A renewable natural resource	3. Iron ore
d. Fixed manufactured capital	4. Spare parts at an auto repair shop
e. Human capital	5. A factory building
f. Inventories	6. A shared language within a community
g. A nonrenewable natural resource	7. Your own health

15 Production Costs

The United States is home to more than 30,000 businesses, ranging in size from the largest corporation in the world (in 2012, this was Walmart, which had revenues of nearly half a *trillion* dollars) to numerous businesses consisting of a single individual. Every day, many of these businesses are faced with decisions about what to produce, how to produce it, how to market it, and how much to sell it for. In this chapter, we focus on the economic activity of production: the conversion of resources into goods and services.

Although we focus on the production process of for-profit businesses, economic production takes places in all three spheres. According to published statistics, about 12 percent of economic production in the United States in 2012 was attributed to government, including federal, state, and local governments. Another 12 percent of economic production took place in households and institutions. However, these statistics understate the amount of production that occurs in the public purpose and core spheres, because it fails to include production that is not distributed through markets. We develop a model of production costs based on a for-profit firm, but many of the lessons of this model are applicable to public purpose and core production as well.

1. AN OVERVIEW OF PRODUCTION

Before we begin our analysis of production costs, we first consider the goals of production and define some important concepts.

1.1 THE GOALS OF PRODUCTION

In the business sphere, it is normally essential that one of the goals of production be to make a profit. This is not to say that the generation of profit is the only goal pursued by businesses. Many companies balance social and environmental objectives with profit-making. As one remarkable example, in 2011 the outdoor clothing and gear company Patagonia took out an ad in the *New York Times* advising readers: "Don't buy what you don't need. Think twice before buying anything," based on concern about the environmental impacts of all production.[1]

At the same time, every period of history provides examples of businesses that have behaved unethically in the pursuit of profits, including violence against workers. However, norms of what is generally acceptable change over time, sometimes swinging toward more social disapproval of harsh business practices, and at other times accepting—even celebrating—a "culture of greed," as seemed to be the case in the last quarter of the twentieth century and into the twenty-first century.

Economic analysis of production has tended to emphasize the objective of profit-making. Starting in the 1960s, some economists began to argue that business managers should *only* seek to maximize profits, without concern for any broader social or environmental objectives. The Nobel Prize–winning economist Milton Friedman once wrote:

[T]here is one and only one social responsibility of business—to use its resources and engage in activities designed to increase its profits so long as it stays within the rules of the game.[2]

But businesses are increasingly operating with a broader set of objectives, often referred to as the **triple bottom line.** This perspective reflects a commitment to social and environmental goals, as well as making profits.

triple bottom line: an assessment of the performance of a business according to social and environmental goals, as well as making profits

Looking farther back in history, before the Civil War in the United States, corporations were fully accountable to the public to ensure that they acted in a manner that served the public good. Corporate charters could be revoked for failing to serve the public interest and were valid for only a certain period of time. For example, in 1831 a Delaware constitutional amendment specified that all corporations were limited to a twenty-year life span.

More recently, an emphasis on externalities is giving renewed attention to the question of whether particular productive activities are consistent with social and environmental well-being. This question requires considering *all* costs and benefits of the production process. In Chapter 12 we focused on environmental externalities, but negative social externalities should also be considered. For example, a business that increases its profits by making its employees work overtime without pay is creating a negative social externality, not reflected in the prices of the products that it sells. Lawsuits have been brought against Walmart in several U.S. states that found the corporation guilty of forcing some employees to work without pay.[3] The negative social externality resulting from Walmart's minimizing what it pays workers extends to policies of hiring employees to work just below the number of hours that would qualify them for full-time benefits, including health insurance coverage. Lacking health-care benefits, and with salaries that leave them little spare money for regular doctor visits, such workers often use emergency rooms as their only venue for medical care. These costs are generally externalized onto states, which have to pay for emergency room visits that could easily have been avoided, at much less cost to society, if the workers had access to health insurance.

We can use the technique of cost-benefit analysis, also discussed in Chapter 12, to estimate the net social impacts of production decisions. One problem with implementing such an analysis, however, arises from the fact that some costs and benefits are easier to measure than others. It is relatively easy, for example, to determine how many jobs will be created if a large retailer builds a new store in an area. It may even be relatively easy to convert the number of jobs gained into a benefit that can be expressed in dollars. It is harder to quantify the costs to social well-being from any environmental damages associated with the store or the loss of community as people become less likely to shop at "mom and pop" competitors.

So, although much of our discussion about production costs and decisions is in the context of making profits, we also keep in mind the broader environmental and social context in which all production occurs.

1.2 An Economic Perspective on Production

As we have stated before, production involves the conversion of resources into goods and services. We define **inputs** as the resources that go into production, and **outputs** as the goods and services that result from production. In addition to desired goods and services, all production processes also generate waste, including pollution, waste materials, and waste heat.

inputs: the resources that go into production

outputs: the goods and services that result from production

We tend to think of production in terms of physical goods. For example, cotton goes into a textile mill as fiber and comes out as fabric. This fabric is then shipped to another location, printed with small red hearts, cut into pieces, sewn into boxer shorts, distributed through wholesalers, and eventually marketed by retailers. Or households may purchase cotton fabric and use it to produce homemade curtains or Halloween costumes. To most people, the various stages of manufacturing would be regarded as production, but the transport, distribution, and sale that are involved would not.

Economists think of production more broadly, including any activity involved in the conversion of resources into final goods and services. For example, Texas oil "producers" do not actually make oil; they merely transport it from its natural state under the ground to the nearest refinery. Yet this activity is still considered production in a broad economic sense. Similarly, such activities as storage, packaging, and retailing all can be interpreted as forms of production.

Nor is production confined to processes that involve tangible goods. Production also includes providing services. Accordingly, from an economist's point of view, physicians, child-care providers, mechanics, musicians, park rangers, lawyers, professors, house cleaners, tax auditors, and massage therapists are all engaged in production, even though they don't produce a physical product.

marginal analysis: analysis based on incremental changes, comparing marginal benefits to marginal costs

Another important concept in thinking about production from an economic perspective is **marginal analysis**, which involves thinking about incremental changes. We have already seen the importance of marginal thinking in Chapter 5. When we apply marginal analysis to production decisions, we ask whether it makes economic sense to produce one more unit of a good or service. In other words, we should compare the marginal benefits of a decision to its marginal costs.

As long as marginal benefits exceed marginal costs, it makes sense for a business to expand production. But after the marginal costs rise to the level of marginal benefits, the firm should stop increasing production. We spend much of the remainder of the chapter introducing an economic model of marginal production costs. We will then use this model in the next chapter to illustrate how a hypothetical firm can maximize its profits. But as we have discussed previously, a model is a simplification of the real world that focuses on some issues while ignoring others. So although this model is considered applicable to many production decisions, it is not intended to apply to every production situation.

Discussion Questions

1. What distinguishes the economic activity of production from the activity of resource maintenance? Of consumption? Of distribution?
2. Think about the processes involved in producing this textbook. Describe these processes, considering all the steps of production from an economic perspective. What inputs were required? What waste was generated?

2. Types of Production Costs

We begin our analysis by differentiating between different types of costs. As with several other topics explored here, economists view production costs from a perspective that differs somewhat from that of noneconomists.

2.1 Fixed Versus Variable Costs

Consider the production costs of farming. A farmer who grows corn, let's call her Gail, needs to purchase various inputs, such as seed, fertilizer, and fuel for machinery. To some extent, Gail can vary the amount of these inputs that she purchases. For example, she can use a little fertilizer or a lot. The amount that she spends on fertilizer will also depend on the type of fertilizer that she applies. Her options may include purchasing a chemical fertilizer, purchasing compost, or obtaining compost from her own farm residues.

variable costs: production costs that can be adjusted relatively quickly and that do not need to be paid if no production occurs

The production costs that Gail can easily adjust are called **variable costs**. Variable costs can be adjusted relatively quickly in response to changes in market conditions, production targets, or other circumstances. Another way to define variable costs is that these costs do not need to be paid if, for some reason, Gail decides not to produce corn.

fixed costs (sunk costs): production costs that cannot be adjusted quickly and that must be paid even if no production occurs

Gail has other costs to pay regardless of whether she decides to produce corn. These are called **fixed costs**, which include such expenses as a mortgage and monthly payments on machinery. Another term economists use for fixed costs is "sunk costs." Regardless of how much corn Gail produces, she cannot avoid paying these costs. The distinction between fixed and variable costs is not always clear. Gail could decide to sell all her farm machinery, so in this sense machinery becomes a variable cost, but it may take some time for her to find buyers. Given enough time, *all* production costs become variable as a business could decide to shut down entirely and sell off all its resources.

Differentiating between fixed and variable costs is important in order to analyze how producers will respond to changes in market conditions. By changing its variable costs, a business can normally change its output level. So, if corn prices rise, Gail may bring some new land into corn production, which will require greater expenses for seed, fertilizer, and fuel. But Gail cannot adjust her fixed costs in a relatively short period. If corn prices go down, she has the option of spending less on corn seed, but she still must pay the mortgage on her farm and other fixed costs. If corn prices stay down for an extended period, say several years, she may be forced to sell her farm and pursue a different career.

2.2 Accounting Versus Economic Costs

accounting costs: actual monetary costs paid by a producer as well as estimated reduction in the value of the producer's capital stock

The costs just discussed are all actual monetary costs paid by a producer. When Gail completes her tax return and calculates her farming profits, she (or her accountant) can list all these costs—both fixed and variable—as valid business expenses. **Accounting costs** can also include some items that are not actual out-of-pocket expenditures but that are understood to reduce the value of the stock of capital owned by the business; the most common example is depreciation of buildings or equipment. Table 15.1 presents an example of Gail's accounting costs.

We can take a broader perspective on Gail's costs of farming by considering other costs that, like depreciation, do not appear as monetary outflows. Perhaps the most obvious example is the value of Gail's time. If Gail is a full-time farmer, she is thus giving up the opportunity to work at a different job, say as an engineer or a teacher. The salary that she could obtain at her next-best option is the opportunity cost of Gail's decision to be a farmer. So if Gail's best alternative to farming is to be a teacher and earn $30,000 per year, this forgone salary also represents a production cost, as shown in Table 15.1.

Table 15.1   **Gail's Costs of Farming**

Accounting Costs		
Seeds	$20,000	
Fertilizer	$3,000	
Fuel	$5,000	
Interest on bank loan	$15,000	
Depreciation of equipment	$5,000	
Total accounting costs		$48,000
Opportunity Costs		
Forgone salary	$30,000	
Forgone return on equity capital	$12,000	
Total opportunity costs		$42,000
Total economic costs		$90,000
Externality Costs		
Pollution damage	$5,000	
Total social costs		$95,000

economic cost: the total cost of production, including both accounting and opportunity costs

Economic costs include accounting costs but also add in the value of forgone opportunities. In addition to a forgone salary, another economic cost would be the value of forgone investments. Suppose that, in addition to taking out a bank loan, Gail also uses her own equity capital to finance some of the costs of farming (recall our discussion of equity finance from Chapter 14). Her next-best alternative may have been to invest that money in the stock market and make a return on her investment. Her forgone investment returns are another economic cost, as shown in Table 15.1.

If Gail looks at the full economic costs of farming over this season—rather than just at the accounting costs—she will find that farming is more costly than she may have initially thought. Whereas her account books show costs of $48,000, it is really costing her $90,000 to farm for the season when we consider her opportunity costs.

The same concept applies to the costs of production in other spheres of the economy. For example, think about the government of an economically depressed county, which is considering whether to invest in building a new highway. The project will hire people and pay them a salary. The *accounting* costs for this labor, included in the project's budget, will be the actual salary paid. To calculate the *economic* costs of this labor, however, from the perspective of society's production possibilities, you have to think about how much this highway project pulls out of other productive activities that would otherwise have been undertaken. If the workers would otherwise have been unemployed and not productively engaged at home or in their communities, the answer might be that not very much is lost elsewhere. But if the workers could have otherwise been building needed new schools or hospitals, it may be that the economic costs are much higher than the accounting costs.

The advantage of considering economic costs, rather than just accounting costs, is that we have a more complete framework for making production decisions. Producers should always weigh the benefits of a decision against its costs, both its financial costs and the costs of what must be given up.

2.3 PRIVATE VERSUS EXTERNAL COSTS

Suppose that Gail's farming practices result in fertilizer runoff that pollutes a river, reducing downstream fishing and swimming opportunities and harming the ecosystem. As we saw in Chapter 12, this represents a negative externality. Gail is unlikely to take such costs into account when making production decisions. She will consider only her private costs—her accounting costs and perhaps her economic costs as well.

But the pollution represents a real cost imposed on society. Suppose that, using the techniques discussed in Chapter 12, we estimate the negative externality costs of Gail's farming at $5,000 per year. From the perspective of social welfare, this is an additional cost of farming, as shown in Table 15.1. The true social cost of farming would be the sum of the economic and externality costs. In an ideal world, there would be ways of ensuring that externality costs are internalized. For example, if Gail had to pay a "farming tax" of $5,000 per year to compensate society for the pollution damage, then the tax would be an accounting cost and thus enter directly into Gail's production decisions.

The distinction between private and external costs is important because a production process chosen by a producer that may appear to be the least expensive based on accounting, and perhaps economic, costs, may not be the least-cost option when externalities are considered. In the absence of any motivation to consider the social or environmental externalities, Gail may conclude that her optimal production decision is to rely on chemical fertilizers to grow corn. But the optimal production decision from the perspective of society may be that she should replace some chemical fertilizer with organic farming techniques. This exemplifies the fact that private production decisions may not always align with the best choice in terms of social well-being.

Discussion Questions

1. In order to take this course, you have paid tuition and bought this book. What other costs should be added in to calculate the *economic* costs of this course to you personally? (*Hint:* What is your best alternative to spending time taking this course? How are you financing your education?) Does your taking this course entail any externality costs, in addition to your private economic costs?

2. What fairness issues arise when producers are required to take social or environmental costs into account in their decision-making? For example, suppose that Gail is just barely making ends meet, using proceeds from the sale of her farm's output to feed and house her family—while the neighbors who are suffering the consequences of runoff from her fertilizer applications are mostly better off than she is. Should government policies take this into consideration? Who should make such a decision?

3. THE PRODUCTION FUNCTION

production function: an equation or graph that represents a relationship between types and quantities of inputs and the quantity of output

Actual production decisions are often a matter of trial and error. Firms might experiment with different levels of various inputs to determine which production processes are the least costly. Often the results will be difficult to predict in advance, and firms can make costly mistakes. But with our model of production, we assume for now that firms have accurate information about the relationship between the levels of various inputs and output. This enables us to define a **production function**, an equation or graph that represents the relationship between a set of inputs and the amount of output that a firm (or other economic actor) can produce over a given period. Production functions typically do not exist "out there" in the real-world economy, but this model can help us think about certain aspects of production in a very simple, and sometimes useful, way.

3.1 THINKING ABOUT INPUTS AND OUTPUTS

Many inputs go into real-world production processes. We continue to use the example of farming because it is relatively easy to produce fairly realistic, easy to comprehend, production functions for farms—and because there have been many studies of farming production functions. The normal inputs include land (a type of natural capital), machinery (manufactured capital), and labor (human capital). Human capital, as we have seen in earlier chapters, is more than just hours of labor; it also includes a component of formal education that has become increasingly important for modern farmers. Social capital can also be considered a farming input in terms of the strength and quality of relations among farm workers and managers. Financial capital is also needed by most farmers in terms of loans to finance the purchase of land, equipment, and other inputs.

In a very general sense, we can define a production function using the following mathematical equation:

$$Y = f \text{ (natural capital, manufactured capital, human capital, social capital, financial capital)}$$

where Y represents a quantity of output, $f()$ is read "is a function of," and the inputs include the levels of different types of capital discussed in Chapter 14. In the case of corn production, we can define a more specific production function as:

$$Y = f \text{ (seeds, fertilizer, pesticides, labor, land, equipment . . .)}$$

This means that the quantity of output (say bushels of corn) is a function of the number of seeds planted, the amount of fertilizer applied, the amount of pesticides applied, the amount of labor allocated to corn production, the amount of land used for corn production, the type of equipment used, and so on.

fixed input: a production input that is fixed in quantity, regardless of the level of production

variable input: a production input whose quantity can be changed relatively quickly, resulting in changes in the level of production

short run: (in terms of production processes) a period in which at least one production input has a fixed quantity

limiting factor: a fixed input that creates a constraint to increasing production

Extending our discussion about fixed and variable costs, we can correspondingly define various inputs as fixed or variable. **Fixed inputs** by definition are those for which the quantities do not change, regardless of the level of production. An example of a fixed input is a farmer who has leased a field for the growing season. If the farmer already signed a lease for the use of the field, she is not able *right now* to avoid paying for this input. By contrast, **variable inputs** are those for which the quantities can be changed quickly, resulting in changes in the level of production. In our farming example, fertilizers and pesticides are variable inputs because a farmer can change her use of these inputs relatively quickly.

As mentioned earlier, over a very long period all inputs might be considered variable. So economists try to make the distinction more specific by defining the **short run** as a period in which at least one production input is fixed in quantity. A farmer, for example, may be temporarily constrained by the size of her land holdings and by the amount of equipment she owns, but can vary many other inputs, such as seeds, fertilizers, and labor. In other production processes, an organization may be constrained by a lack of space, a shortage of materials, a dearth of suitably talented workers, or any other production input. The key aspect is that a **limiting factor** creates a constraint to increasing production. Even with access to unlimited amounts of all the *variable* inputs, production can go only so far, because of this one limiting factor.

In the **long run,** the quantities of all production inputs may be varied. In the case of farming, this means the amount of time (perhaps several months) in which more land can be purchased, more machinery purchased, and more labor hired. In other situations, it might take years for a business to increase or decrease (or eliminate) the quantities of all inputs.

3.2 GRAPHING PRODUCTION FUNCTIONS

long run: (in terms of production processes) a period in which all production inputs can be varied in quantity

As with supply and demand in Chapter 3, we can represent a production function using either a table or a graph. We keep our model simple by focusing on just one input at a time. One production relationship that has been studied by numerous researchers is the impact of different fertilizer levels on crop yields. Table 15.2 presents the results of one such study, showing the effect of applying various amounts of nitrogen fertilizer on corn yields over a season. The study was performed in Missouri in the late 1990s.[4] The researchers varied the amount of fertilizer used on different fields in increments of 20 pounds per acre. At harvest time, the corn yield was recorded in bushels per acre. For mathematical simplicity, we call each 20-pound increment a "bag" of fertilizer and express all values in per-acre terms. Nitrogen can be obtained from renewable, organic sources such as manure or alfalfa or from chemical fertilizer produced using nonrenewable natural gas. This study looked at nitrogen from chemical sources.

In this case, nitrogen fertilizer is a variable input, and corn is the output. Corn yields increase as more fertilizer is added. We can take the data in Table 15.2 and convert it to a

Table 15.2 **Corn Production Function**

Quantity of nitrogen fertilizer (bags per acre)	Corn yield (bushels per acre)
0	100
1	115
2	127
3	137
4	145
5	150
6	154
7	157
8	159

Figure 15.1   **Corn Production Function**

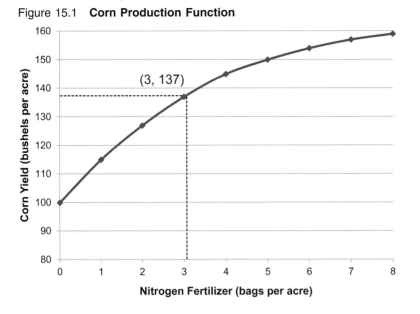

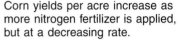

Corn yields per acre increase as more nitrogen fertilizer is applied, but at a decreasing rate.

graph, as shown in Figure 15.1. So, we can see, for example, that when 3 bags of fertilizer are applied per acre, corn yields are 137 bushels per acre. Note that we have started the vertical axes at 80 bushels per acre for graphical convenience, to focus on the range where corn yields occur in the study.

For this production function, we are only measuring the impact of one variable input—nitrogen fertilizer. The researchers in this case tried to keep all other variable inputs, such as the amount of seed applied, the amount of water, soil quality, and so on, unchanging across the various corn fields, to isolate the impact of one variable input. Recall that in economics, when we want to isolate the effect of one particular variable on another, we hope to study the particular relationship *ceteris paribus,* or "with all else constant." Remember, also, that a relationship in which an increase in one variable is accompanied by an increase in the other is called a "positive" or "direct" relationship. You can see in Figure 15.1 that nitrogen and crop yields have a positive relationship, though the curve goes upward less steeply as one moves to the right.

3.3 PRODUCTION IN THE SHORT RUN

total product curve: a curve showing the total amount of output produced with different levels of one variable input, holding all other inputs constant

marginal product: the additional quantity of output produced by increasing the level of a variable input by one, holding all other inputs constant

Another term that economists use to describe the production function in Figure 15.1 is a **total product curve**. A total product curve shows the total amount of product (i.e., output) as a function of one variable input, holding all other inputs constant. But as we mentioned earlier in the chapter, production decisions are based on marginal analysis. So, we focus on how much corn output changes with each additional bag of fertilizer. We call the additional corn output with each additional bag of fertilizer (holding all other inputs constant) the **marginal product**. We can take the data in Table 15.2 and calculate the marginal product for each additional bag of fertilizer, as shown in Table 15.3.

Table 15.3 shows that adding the first bag of fertilizer increases corn yields from 100 bushels per acre to 115 bushels per acre, for a marginal product of 15 bushels. The marginal product going from 1 to 2 bags of fertilizer is 12 bushels, as shown in the table as the difference between 127 and 115 bushels. You can calculate the marginal product for the fourth bag of fertilizer yourself for practice.

Table 15.3 indicates that the marginal product of additional fertilizer is constantly declining, referred to by economists as **diminishing marginal returns**. For each additional unit of an input, the marginal product (or return) increases by a smaller amount.

Table 15.3 **Calculating Marginal Product**

Quantity of nitrogen fertilizer (bags per acre)	Corn yield (bushels per acre)	Marginal product
0	100	—
1	115	= 115 – 110 = 15
2	127	= 127 – 115 = 12
3	137	10
4	145	??
5	150	5
6	154	4
7	157	3
8	159	2

diminishing marginal returns: a situation in which each successive unit of a variable input produces a smaller marginal product

constant marginal returns: a situation in which each successive unit of a variable input produces the same marginal product

increasing marginal returns: a situation in which each successive unit of a variable input produces a larger marginal product

We should not be surprised that the production function for corn displays diminishing marginal returns. If there were *not* diminishing marginal returns, you could feed the whole world from one farmer's field just by adding more and more nitrogen fertilizer forever. But, in reality, as more and more nitrogen is added to the same amount of land, eventually the corn plants become unable to make use of the extra amounts. Eventually, if excessive fertilizer were added, the graph would turn *downward,* with a negative slope, as the crop would suffer from fertilizer "burn."

In a case of diminishing marginal returns, as we have seen for corn production, the total product curve gets flatter as you move out to the right. Not all production functions display diminishing marginal returns, at least not throughout the entire production range. Suppose that we consider a production function for handmade shoes. Let's assume that one worker can make two shoes a day. So if we have only one worker (our variable input), two shoes per day can be produced. If we have two workers, then four shoes can be produced per day. Three workers means that six shoes can be produced. In this case, each additional unit of our variable input (workers) results in the same marginal product—two additional shoes per day. Economists refer to this as a case of **constant marginal returns**.

Finally, a production function can display **increasing marginal returns**. This can occur in our shoemaking example if adding workers allows for specialization and an overall increase in efficiency. For example, one worker might specialize in cutting leather, another might make only soles, and a third could focus on stitching. In this case, the total product curve would increase at an increasing rate, at least up to a certain number of workers.

Figure 15.2 illustrates production functions with constant and increasing marginal returns. For constant marginal returns, the total product curve is a straight line sloping upward. For increasing marginal returns, the total product curve becomes steeper as we move to the right.

Figure 15.2 **Total Product Curves with Constant and Increasing Marginal Returns**

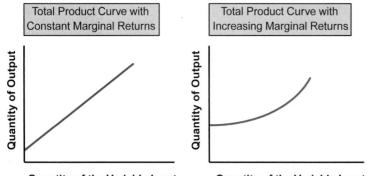

A total product curve with constant marginal returns is a straight line sloping upward. In the case of increasing marginal returns, the total product curve becomes steeper as we move to the right.

It is possible for a production process to exhibit *all* three patterns of marginal returns when we consider the entire range of production levels. Figure 15.3 shows increasing marginal returns at very low levels of the input, constant marginal returns for moderate levels of the input, and then decreasing marginal returns for high levels of the input. Such a production function may be common in the real world. Consider a restaurant. If there is only one worker to take orders, cook the food, and wash dishes, production is likely to be very inefficient. Adding more workers allows for specialization and increasing marginal returns. Once a restaurant has enough workers for each separate task, then perhaps doubling the number of workers (e.g., increasing from one cook to two cooks) might exactly double total production. However, eventually hiring more workers leads to decreasing marginal returns as the kitchen become too crowded to allow for effective production. As the old saying goes, too many cooks spoil the broth.

Figure 15.3   **A Total Product Curve with Increasing, Constant, and Decreasing Marginal Returns**

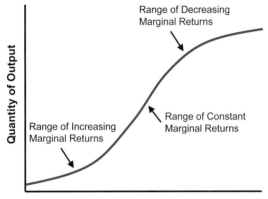

Many real-world production functions display increasing, constant, and decreasing marginal returns when we consider the full range of production levels.

4. PRODUCTION COSTS

In this last section, we combine information about production costs with a production function to determine the costs of different levels of production. We will differentiate between production in the short run and in the long run.

4.1 PRODUCTION COSTS IN THE SHORT RUN

Now that we understand the physical side of production, we can turn back to the topic of production costs. Our distinction between fixed and variable costs can be related to our discussion of fixed and variable inputs. Specifically, variable costs are costs that vary by changing the level of a variable input. So in order to apply more fertilizer, a farmer must increase her variable costs. Fixed costs are those that arise from fixed inputs. Gail's mortgage payments on her farm are fixed as she cannot vary the amount of land that she owns in the short run.

total cost: the sum of fixed and variable costs

Total cost is simply the sum of fixed and variable costs. We can apply this concept to our example of nitrogen fertilizer. Let's suppose that the cost of nitrogen fertilizer is $15 per bag. For simplicity, for now we assume that this is our only variable cost. All other costs of producing corn are considered fixed in the short run and total $500 per acre. Table 15.4 calculates the fixed and variable cost of applying different amounts of nitrogen fertilizer. For each additional bag of fertilizer, total costs increase by $15. In other words, the marginal cost of each additional bag of fertilizer is $15.

total cost curve: a graph showing the relationship between the total cost of production and the level of output

We can take the data in Table 15.4 and graph a **total cost curve**, which relates the total cost of production to the level of output, as shown in Figure 15.4. We see that the slope becomes steeper as we move to the right. This makes sense, as it becomes increasingly

Table 15.4   **Fixed, Variable, and Marginal Costs**

Quantity of nitrogen fertilizer (bags per acre)	Corn yield (bushels per acre)	Fixed costs ($)	Variable costs ($15 per bag of fertilizer)	Total costs ($)
0	100	500	0	500
1	115	500	15	515
2	127	500	30	530
3	137	500	45	545
4	145	500	60	560
5	150	500	75	575
6	154	500	90	590
7	157	500	105	605
8	159	500	120	620

Figure 15.4   **The Total Cost Curve for Corn**

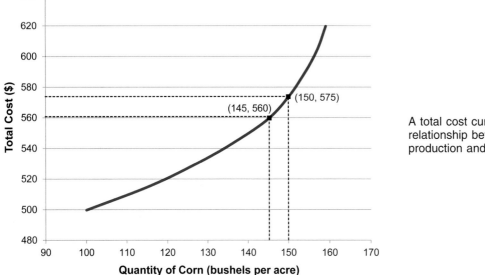

A total cost curve shows the relationship between the total cost of production and the level of output.

expensive to produce an additional bushel of corn per acre. In other words, the higher the level of corn production, the more fertilizer needs to be added to produce one more bushel per acre. This is consistent with a total product curve with diminishing marginal returns.

We can examine the total cost curve in more detail to determine the marginal cost of producing corn. Specifically, we can use the total cost curve, and the data in Table 15.4, to determine the marginal cost of producing one more bushel of corn. This will vary depending on the level of corn production. Note that this is fundamentally different from the marginal cost of a bag of nitrogen fertilizer, which is always $15 per bag.

Let's determine what the marginal cost of corn production is as we go from producing 145 bushels per acre to 150 bushels. We see in Table 15.4 that total costs increase from $560 to $575 as we go from adding 4 bags of fertilizer to 5 bags. As it costs an additional $15 to produce 5 more bushels of corn, the marginal cost *per bushel* is $3, obtained by dividing the additional cost of $15 by five bushels, as shown in Figure 15.5.

We can calculate the marginal cost of corn production for other levels of corn production, as shown in the last column of Table 15.5. You can test yourself by calculating the marginal cost of corn production going from 154 to 157 bushels per acre.

Table 15.5 **Marginal Cost of Corn Production**

Quantity of nitrogen fertilizer (bags per acre)	Corn yield (bushels per acre)	Marginal return of additional nitrogen (bushels of corn)	Cost of additional nitrogen ($ per bag)	Marginal cost (dollars per bushel of corn)
0	100	—	—	—
1	115	15	15	15 ÷ 15 = 1.00
2	127	12	15	15 ÷ 12 = 1.25
3	137	10	15	15 ÷ 10 = 1.33
4	145	8	15	15 ÷ 8 = 1.88
5	150	5	15	15 ÷ 5 = 3.00
6	154	4	15	15 ÷ 4 = 3.75
7	157	3	15	??
8	159	2	15	15 ÷ 2 = 7.50

We can see that the marginal cost of producing corn increases as production levels increase. Diminishing marginal returns to fertilizer application have resulted in **increasing marginal costs** for corn production. In other words, the cost of producing one more bushel of corn rises as more output is produced.

In computing the marginal costs, we ignored the fixed costs. This is correct, because we assumed that fixed costs would be paid regardless of whether any nitrogen fertilizer was used, and we were interested only in the cost of the "additional" or "marginal" bushel of corn production.

The important part of this discussion of diminishing marginal returns and increasing marginal costs is not so much the algebra involved, or even the graphs, though both can be helpful. The significant implication for producer behavior is that diminishing marginal returns and increasing marginal costs mean that, in the short run, the quantity of production will tend to be naturally limited.

Diminishing returns mean that it does not make sense for the farmer to try to feed the whole world from one plot. Increasing costs mean that at some point production will become too expensive relative to benefits received (e.g., revenue from sales of the harvest) to be worthwhile. In Chapter 16 we will see that diminishing returns are assumed in the case of the profit-maximizing competitive firm. Because marginal costs are increasing, whereas the price that the firm receives for its output is constant, the traditional microeconomic model gives a neat diagrammatic explanation of how a firm will choose a unique, profit-maximizing level of output.

What if marginal returns are constant, as illustrated in the left-hand graph in Figure 15.2? Then we will have **constant marginal costs**. In this case, each unit of the variable input (which has a constant price) adds exactly the same amount to output, so the cost for each additional unit of output is the same. The total cost curve will be a straight line.

What if marginal returns are increasing, as illustrated in the right-hand graph in Figure 15.2? Then we will have **decreasing marginal costs**. To portray a total cost curve with increasing marginal returns, you would draw a line that rises but also *flattens out* or curves toward the horizontal axis as you move to the right. Increasing marginal returns mean decreasing marginal costs, because additional production is getting *cheaper* as output increases.

Sometimes all these cost patterns are combined in one graph, such as Figure 15.5. Figure 15.5 shows the pattern of costs that corresponds to the pattern of returns that we saw in Figure 15.3, with decreasing marginal costs, followed by constant and then increasing marginal costs, as the quantity of output increases. In the lower part of the graph, the pattern of marginal costs is graphed explicitly.

For certain production processes, such as the application of fertilizer to corn, curves like these can actually be quite accurately graphed on the basis of real-world studies done by

increasing marginal costs: the situation in which the cost of producing one additional unit of output rises as more output is produced

constant marginal costs: the situation in which the cost of producing one additional unit of output stays the same as more output is produced

decreasing marginal costs: the situation in which the cost of producing one additional unit of output falls as more output is produced

Figure 15.5   **A Possible Pattern of Costs**

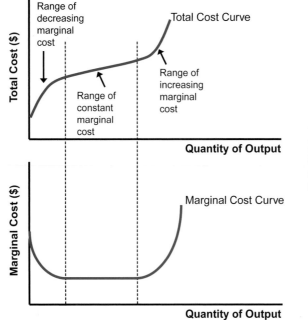

The graphs show the relationship between total and marginal cost curves. For many real-world enterprises, their marginal cost curve is U-shaped.

researchers. In most cases, however, these curves are only hypothetical. Rarely would lone producers, concerned with providing for a family or staying in business, have the luxury of being able to conduct such a study. While they were holding some inputs constant, and varying others from zero up to high amounts in order to find out what exactly their total product curve and total cost curve were, they could easily go out of business!

These graphs do, however, give us a visual image that can help us think about the many ways in which production and cost may be related, for many producers. We see that the concepts of diminishing returns and increasing returns, in particular, are important throughout the study of microeconomics.

4.2 PRODUCTION COSTS IN THE LONG RUN

In the long run, as we noted earlier, all inputs are variable. A farmer can buy or rent more land or equipment. A factory owner can build a new factory. More engineers can be trained in software development, if skilled engineers are a short-run fixed input. A business owner may be able to expand by hiring an assistant, if his or her own time for decision making is the limiting factor. A child-care enterprise can expand from a private home to a larger center, if space is the capacity constraint.

Given sufficient time to acquire the needed machines or other resources, or to make other necessary adjustments, a producer should be able to remove all obstacles to getting the highest net benefits (profits) from production. Although in the short run space, equipment, skills, or time present a constraint on capacity, in the long run these constraints can be loosened. Then a question arises: How big should an enterprise get?

Why do we observe, for example, small neighborhood child-care centers and single-worker locksmith businesses, but not small neighborhood steel foundries or hospitals? Many factors can contribute to the explanation of enterprise size, including factors related to history, culture, and the level of demand for a producer's output. Here we focus on technological and cost-related reasons that one size, or scale, may be more advantageous than another.

average cost (or average total cost): cost per unit of output, computed as total cost divided by the quantity of output produced

Because we are now looking at these issues with a long-term perspective, marginal cost—discussed above for the case of the short run, in which one input is fixed—is no longer the relevant concept, because now *all* inputs can be varied. It is, however, relevant to calculate the **average cost** (or **average total cost**) per unit of production. This can be done simply by dividing total cost by the quantity of output produced, at any production level. For example, if it costs $500 to produce 100 bushels of corn, the average cost per bushel at this level of production is simply $500/100 bushels = $5 per bushel.

long-run average cost: the cost of production per unit of output when all inputs can be varied in quantity

The relevant type of cost when the entire scale of production can be varied is the **long-run average cost**, which is the cost per unit of output when all inputs are variable. It is logical to think that, to whatever extent possible, enterprises will tend to grow to the size where the long-run average costs are lowest. Enterprises that are bigger or smaller than this optimal size would be unnecessarily expensive to run.

For example, to go into business, a locksmith needs primarily a set of tools and a van. To double the output of a single-locksmith enterprise would require a second locksmith, another set of tools, and another van. Except for perhaps some small savings in costs, such as advertising or billing, there is no reason to believe that the new, larger firm would be any cheaper to run, per unit of output, than the old, smaller one. In fact, if the new locksmith has to service customers who are farther away from the head office, it may be more expensive per unit of output. It may therefore make more sense for each neighborhood to have its own local locksmith (though perhaps a group of locksmiths might jointly hire advertising and billing services). Bigger is not necessarily better in this case.

economies of scale: situations in which the long-run average cost of production falls as the size of the enterprise increases

By contrast, a steel foundry requires a sizable investment in plant and equipment, and a hospital that has only a few beds would be either exceedingly expensive to run (as a consequence of underutilization of skilled labor and laboratory facilities) or exceedingly limited in its services. Enterprises in such industries tend to be big because of what economists call **economies of scale**. A process exhibits economies of scale when, in the long run, average production costs decline as the size of the enterprise increases. You could build a single foundry furnace to turn out a few pounds of iron a year—but it might cost its weight in gold to produce each pound of iron. A foundry reaches a stage of low costs per unit only when it is producing steel in much larger quantities.

constant returns to scale: situations in which the long-run average cost of production stays the same as the size of the enterprise increases

diseconomies of scale: situations in which the long-run average cost of production rises as the size of the enterprise increases

A production process exhibits **constant returns to scale** over the range where the long-run average cost is constant as the size of the enterprise changes. Finally, a process exhibits **diseconomies of scale** if the long-run average cost rises with the size of an enterprise. Similar to our previous discussion, a production process can display all three types of returns to scale. This is illustrated as a U-shaped long-run average cost curve in Figure 15.6.

What might cause diseconomies of scale? It is generally thought that no matter how many technical economies of scale there may be, for most enterprises there is a point at which

Figure 15.6   A Possible Pattern of Long-Run Average Costs

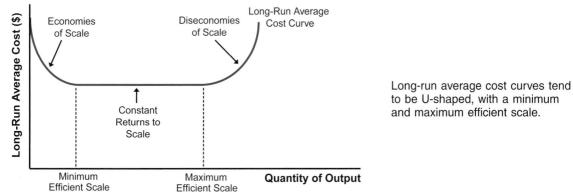

Long-run average cost curves tend to be U-shaped, with a minimum and maximum efficient scale.

minimum efficient scale: the lowest quantity of output at which a firm achieves its minimum per-unit production costs

maximum efficient scale: the highest quantity of output at which a firm achieves its minimum per-unit production costs

they are just too big for all the human beings and all the functions involved to be managed effectively. Some of the big business mergers in recent decades were inspired by hopes of reaping economies of scale (as well as market power or simply in the belief that bigger would be better). Such hopes were sometimes dashed, with the failure of such megamergers as AOL and Time Warner in 2001 and Sprint and Nextel in 2005.

Many production processes appear to have a **minimum efficient scale**. This is the point at which the long-run average cost curve begins to bottom out, as shown in Figure 15.6. For locksmiths, the minimum efficient scale might be the output level corresponding to a one-person shop; for an automobile company, it may be several thousand vehicles per year. Levels of output *less* than these may leave some resources underemployed, thus creating the downward-sloping portion of the long-run average cost curve. Given the problems of managing very large organizations, one can also posit the existence of a **maximum efficient scale**—which is the largest an enterprise can be and still benefit from low long-run average costs.

4.3 PRODUCTION PROCESS CHOICE

input substitution: increasing the use of some inputs, and decreasing that of others, while producing the same good or service

Another important issue in the economics of production is the choice of production process. If two or more processes exist that can make the same output, which should be chosen? Producers, to be economically efficient, should choose the process that entails the lowest cost.

Because various technologies are available, producers can engage in **input substitution**, using less of one input and more of another while producing the same good or service, as costs and availability change. As we mentioned earlier, in the case of corn farming, nitrogen can be obtained from renewable, organic sources such as manure and alfalfa or from chemical fertilizer produced using nonrenewable natural gas. Generally, whenever prices change, producers will want to substitute cheaper inputs for inputs that have become more expensive. From a public welfare perspective, input substitution will enhance well-being when the choices that are made take into account external as well as internal costs.

Of particular importance, historically, has been the process of substituting the use of machinery for human labor. This is dramatically exemplified in the American folk hero John Henry, the railway worker who pitted himself against the new steam drill that threatened to take jobs away from him and his fellows. In his heroic effort, John Henry fulfilled his promise to "die with a hammer in my hand."

Yet even with modern production methods that rely heavily on machines, labor remains an important input cost. Because of globalization and the possibility of moving production to any part of the world, an increasingly important question has been *where* to produce. Low wages in countries such as China, Vietnam, and Bangladesh have motivated many companies to locate production facilities in those countries. In general, the cost savings associated with production in a low-wage country outweigh the increased costs of transporting goods long distances to market. However, wage trends are beginning to reverse in some cases, and manufacturing in the United States may be making a comeback, as discussed in Box 15.1.

Discussion Questions

1. Explain in your own words why a firm's marginal cost curve may initially decline, but then increase, as the quantity of output increases.
2. Diminishing marginal returns is a valuable concept, not only in economics, but in many other areas of life: an obvious example (which we saw in Chapter 8, on consumption) was the diminishing pleasure received by eating successive units of the same food. Suggest two other areas in life that exhibit diminishing marginal returns. Can you also think of some examples in your own life where there are constant or increasing returns to scale (i.e., you get the same, or more, psychic or other "returns" from each additional increment of something)?

BOX 15.1 MADE IN THE USA AGAIN?

The production cost savings from low wages are a primary reason manufacturing has shifted from the United States and other developed countries to emerging countries such as China. But with rapid economic growth in China, the choice between "Made in China" and "Made in the USA" has become more difficult. Between 2005 and 2010 the average wage for factory workers in China increased by 69 percent. Meanwhile, wage growth in the United States has stagnated (recall our discussion of median wages in the United States in Chapter 9). Thus the relative wage advantage of producing in China is decreasing.

According to a study by Boston Consulting Group (BCG), the change in relative wage growth suggests the potential for an "American renaissance" in manufacturing. Hal Sirkin of BCG states, "Sometime around 2015, manufacturers will be indifferent between locating in America or China for production for consumption in America." He bases this prediction on the assumption that annual wage growth will continue to be a robust 17 percent per year in China but rather slow in the United States.

Firms are also finding that there are advantages to reducing the complexity of supply chains. When production occurs across several countries, an unexpected event in only one of those countries, such as an earthquake or a disease outbreak, can cause a costly supply disruption. Thus, keeping production domestic reduces overall risk.

BCG indicates that several companies have already brought overseas production back to the United States. The heavy equipment manufacturer Caterpillar has shifted some production from overseas to a factory in Texas. In 2010 Wham-O moved half its Frisbee and Hula Hoop production to the United States from China and Mexico.

But even if China's production cost advantage vanishes, other countries with even lower wages provide companies with viable options. For example, the manufacturing cost advantage of producing in India and Bangladesh is likely to persist for some time. Also, with rapid demand growth in emerging markets, production in China still makes economic sense for goods sold there.

Finally, shifting production back to the United States may not be feasible in some cases, at least in the short run. For example, the United States no longer has the supply base or the infrastructure to support consumer electronics manufacturing. While firms may not have realized it at the time, some production shifts will be very difficult to reverse.

Source: "Moving Back to America," *Economist,* May 12, 2011.

REVIEW QUESTIONS

1. What is the "triple bottom line" and how does it differ from the traditional economic assumption about the goal of production?
2. What is the difference between fixed costs and variable costs?
3. What is the difference between accounting costs and economic costs?
4. Name all the categories that comprise economic costs.
5. What is the difference between private costs and external costs?
6. What is a production function?
7. What is a limiting factor in production?
8. What distinguishes the short run from the long run?
9. How can we express a production function graphically?
10. What is marginal product?
11. Describe the meaning of diminishing returns, constant returns, and increasing marginal returns, and explain how each might come about.
12. Sketch a total product curve illustrating increasing returns, constant returns, and diminishing returns.
13. Distinguish among fixed cost, variable cost, total cost, and marginal cost.
14. Sketch a total cost curve illustrating fixed cost and decreasing, constant, and increasing marginal costs.
15. What are average costs?
16. What are economies of scale?
17. Sketch a long-run average cost curve illustrating economies of scale, constant returns to scale, and diseconomies of scale.
18. How do we define the efficient scale of production?

EXERCISES

1. Kai's records show that last month he spent $5,000 on rent for his shop, $3,000 on materials, $3,000 on wages and benefits for an employee, and $500 in interest on the loan that he used to start his business. He quit a job that had paid him $3,000 a month to devote himself full time to this business. Suppose that he has to pay the lease on his shop and the interest on the loan regardless of whether he produces. However, suppose that at any time he can change the amount of materials that he buys and the hours that his employee works and that he can also go back to his old job (perhaps part time).
   a. What are the accounting costs of operating his shop for the month?
   b. What are the economic costs?
   c. Which types of costs of running his business for a month are fixed? Which are variable?

2. A nonprofit organization dedicated to health care wants to open a new hospital near a residential neighborhood. A group of residents of that neighborhood protests this decision, claiming that traffic caused by the hospital will increase noise and auto emissions. The hospital rejects the idea of building a wall to contain the noise and fumes, claiming that this would be too expensive. Describe in a few sentences, using at least two terms introduced in this chapter, how an economist might describe this situation.

3. The production relationship between the number of chapters that Tiffany studies in her history book (the variable input) and the number of points that she will earn on a history exam (the output) is as follows:

Input: number of chapters studied	0	1	2	3
Output: test score	15	35	60	95

   a. Using graph paper or a computer spreadsheet or presentation program, graph the total product curve for exam points. Label clearly.
   b. What is the marginal return of the first chapter that Tiffany reads? And what is the marginal return of the third chapter that she reads?
   c. How would you describe, in words, this pattern of returns?

4. Match each concept in Column A with an example in Column B.

Column A	Column B
a. Fixed input	1. The more months that you work at consulting, the better you become at it
b. Variable input	2. The way that you irritate your roommate by working late at night
c. Opportunity cost	3. The lost salary that you could have had as an employee elsewhere
d. External cost	4. The more hours you work without a break, the less effectively you work
e. Increasing returns	5. The time that you spend consulting
f. Diminishing returns	6. The computer that you initially purchased when you started the business

5. Ramona designs Web pages and needs the jolt that she gets from the caffeine in cola drinks to keep herself awake and alert. The total product curve for the relationship between her cola consumption per day and the number of pages that she can design in one day is given in the following figure.

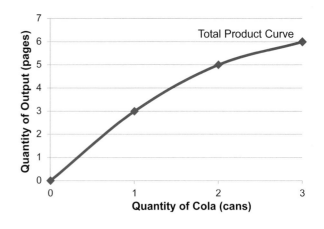

   a. Fill out Columns (2) and (3) of the table that follows, referring to the graph above.

Quantity of variable input (cans of cola)	(2) Quantity of output (pages)	(3) Marginal product (pages)	Fixed cost ($)	Variable cost ($)	Total cost ($)
0					
1					
2					
3					

b. Ramona's employer pays her $50 per day regardless of whether she is productive and provides her with all the cola that she wants to drink. Cola costs her employer $2 per can. Add to your table information on the fixed, variable, and total costs of Ramona's producing from 0 to 3 web pages.

c. Using graph paper or a spreadsheet or presentation program, graph the total cost curve. (What is measured on the horizontal axis? The vertical axis?)

d. Using information on the marginal product from your table above, calculate the marginal cost per page of output at each level of soda consumption.

6. Suppose that in her first hour of work, Lynn can hand-knit four pairs of mittens. During her second consecutive hour, Lynn can hand-knit three additional pairs of mittens, and during her third hour of work, as a consequence of fatigue, she can hand-knit only one additional pair. Suppose that she works for up to three hours and makes a wage of $15 per hour.

a. Create a table relating the number of hours worked to the *total* number of pairs of mittens produced, and graph the *total* product curve for the production of pairs of mittens. Label clearly.

b. Looking at labor costs only (ignoring, for the purposes of this exercise, the cost of the yarn that she uses and any fixed costs), make a table relating costs to the number of pairs of mittens produced. Graph the total (labor) cost curve for the production of mittens. Label clearly.

c. How would you describe in words the pattern of marginal returns? The pattern of marginal costs?

d. What is the marginal product, in pairs of mittens per hour, of her second hour of work? Of her third hour of work?

e. What is the marginal cost, in dollars per pairs of mittens, as she goes from an output of four pairs of mittens to an output of seven pairs of mittens? What is the marginal cost of the eighth pair of mittens?

NOTES

1. Patagonia, "Don't Buy This Jacket, Black Friday and the New York Times," www.thecleanestline.com/2011/11/dont-buy-this-jacket-black-friday-and-the-new-york-times.html.

2. Milton Friedman, "The Social Responsibility of Business Is to Increase Its Profits," *New York Times Magazine,* September 13, 1970.

3. See, for example, Amy Joyce, "Wal-Mart Workers Win Wage Suit," *Washington Post,* October 13, 2006.

4. Peter Scharf and Bill Wiebold, "Nitrogen Prices—How Do They Affect Optimum N Management?" *Integrated Pest & Crop Management Newsletter* 11(2) (2001).

16 Markets Without Power

Chances are that you have heard politicians or media commentators expound on the benefits of "free markets." One of the benefits claimed for free markets is that they result in economic efficiency—resources are allocated to their highest-valued uses, measured using welfare analysis. Behind this political argument is an economic model—a model of markets in which no one individual, company, or institution has power over the market. Economists call such markets "perfectly competitive." In this chapter, we discuss perfectly competitive markets and the implications of these markets for economic efficiency and equity.

1. UNDERSTANDING MARKET POWER AND COMPETITION

market power: the ability to control, or at least affect, the terms and conditions of a market exchange

Having power means having the ability to influence something. **Market power** is the ability to control, or at least affect, the terms and conditions of a market exchange. In this chapter and Chapter 17, we consider different types of markets based on the degree of market power held by sellers. In this chapter, we consider markets in which sellers, as well as buyers, possess *no market power*. In Chapter 17, we consider three types of markets in which sellers do possess a degree of market power.

Market power is related to the degree of competition in a market. In most markets, sellers compete with other sellers. A very general rule of thumb is that the more competitive a market is, the less market power is held by individual sellers. But what exactly do we mean by "competition"? As we have seen with other topics, economists' definition of competition differs from how people commonly use the term. So we briefly discuss four potential definitions of competition and how they relate to market power:

1. competition from the perspective of businesses
2. competition from the perspective of consumers
3. competition from the perspective of citizens
4. competition from the perspective of economists

1.1 THE BUSINESS PERSPECTIVE ON COMPETITION AND MARKET POWER

From the point of view of an individual business, competition is generally a bad thing—something to be reduced or eliminated. Competition means that other businesses are working to reduce your sales and profits. It also means that you have to be very aware of what your competitors are charging for their goods and services, and you may have to adjust your prices to reflect what your competitors are doing.

From the perspective of a business, market power is a good thing. You want to be able to influence people to buy what you are selling. You want to be able to command a high price for what you sell. You want to have the power to bargain for low prices for the resources that you buy. You want your business to grow, capturing a large share of the market in which you sell.

1.2 THE CONSUMER PERSPECTIVE ON COMPETITION AND MARKET POWER

To consumers, competition is generally a good thing. Competition among businesses tends to drive prices down, making goods and services more affordable to consumers. Many consumers like to "shop around" for the lowest prices. Having several competing stores (or Internet shopping sites) to choose from means that consumers are more likely to find bargains. (For more on competition from the perspective of both businesses and consumers, see Box 16.1.)

Consumers generally do not benefit when sellers possess market power. People who live in rural areas with just a single local gas station or grocery store will generally pay higher prices than people living in urban areas. While the higher prices may partly reflect higher wholesale costs to sellers, a seller that possesses market power can use that power to charge relatively high prices just because the seller knows that consumers must otherwise travel long distances to shop elsewhere.

1.3 THE CITIZEN PERSPECTIVE ON COMPETITION AND MARKET POWER

People are both consumers and citizens. Sometimes their goals as consumers may not align with their views as concerned citizens. Competition and market power is one such issue.

BOX 16.1 AMAZON AND MARKET COMPETITION

Amazon is the world's top online retailer, with 2012 global revenues of more than $60 billion. In the United States, Amazon accounted for 15 percent of all e-commerce in 2012. Amazon's founder, Jeff Bezos, has become one of the 20 richest people in the world, with a net worth of about $25 billion.

Amazon's success is based largely on its ability to offer a lower price than its competitors, especially "brick-and-mortar" competitors that must pay the cost of operating physical stores. Consumers benefit from Amazon's low prices, free shipping on many orders, and avoiding having to drive to stores.

But Amazon's price-based competitive advantage appears to be slipping. Amazon's competitors are increasingly willing to match, or even beat, Amazon's prices. For example, in July 2013 the online retailer Overstock announced that it would undercut Amazon's book prices by 10 percent. Amazon had no choice but to match the price discount. Best Buy has a policy of matching Amazon's price on similar items. Moreover, customers can pick up items at local Best Buy stores, so they do not have to wait days for delivery. In addition, Walmart is increasing its online shopping presence, looking to grab market share from Amazon.

Bed Bath & Beyond is another competitor that may be chipping away at Amazon's sales. A 2013 price survey found that the total cost of a basket of 30 items was 6.5 percent cheaper at Bed Bath & Beyond than at Amazon. For example, a shower curtain that sold for $32.39 at Amazon was priced at $24.99 at Bed Bath & Beyond. In addition, Bed Bath & Beyond frequently sends its customers coupons for a 20 percent discount, which makes their prices even lower.

Another factor that may hurt Amazon's ability to offer lower prices than its brick-and-mortar competitors is that Internet retailers may soon be required to collect state sales tax. Previously, Amazon did not charge its customers state sales taxes, even for orders delivered to states that levy them, giving Amazon a 5–10 percent price advantage in those states. However, Amazon began to collect state sales tax as early as 2008 for orders to New York, and now collects such taxes for orders delivered to 16 states. The Marketplace Fairness Act, which would require all Internet retailers to collect state sales taxes, has passed the U.S. Senate, but has not yet been voted on by the full Congress as of this book's publication. Because of changing laws and increasing competition, Amazon may no longer be the dominant retailing force that it has been in the past.

Source: Tom Gara, "Problem for Bezos: Mall Becoming Cheaper Than Amazon," *Wall Street Journal,* August 20, 2013; Greg Bensinger, "Amazon Passes Tax Milestone," *Wall Street Journal,* November 1, 2013; Amazon.com, "About Sales Tax on Items sold by Amazon.com," www.amazon.com/gp/help/customer/display.html?nodeId=468512; GovTrack.us, "S. 743: Marketplace Fairness Act of 2013," www.govtrack.us/congress/bills/113/s743#overview.

While consumers generally approve of competition because it tends to lead to lower prices, as concerned citizens they may perceive competition as the cause of undesirable social and environmental impacts. For example, consumers may support the construction of a new suburban "big box" store in their town because it will increase consumer choice and offer low prices. But others may oppose the store, on the basis that it will harm the environment, hurt "mom-and-pop" stores, and reduce the vitality of a downtown area.

Concerned citizens may also worry about businesses that cite the "need to stay competitive" as their reason for eliminating jobs, taking over smaller companies, refusing to implement voluntary pollution controls, or moving their production overseas, all of which are perceived as harmful. From the point of view of a concerned citizen, neither market power nor tooth-and-nail competition serves the interests of a peaceful and humane society. Many concerned citizens would prefer to see markets based on decentralized power, along with ethical and cooperative behavior that serves the common good.

Many citizens view market power primarily in terms of the size and financial clout of large corporations. They believe that "big business" disproportionately influences public policy to obtain tax breaks, subsidies, or exemption from environmental regulations. They cite examples of big businesses acting callously or unethically, raising prices on goods that people need, forcing workers to accept low wages, or intimidating people with lawsuits.

1.4 The Economists' Perspective on Competition and Market Power

Some economists view competition and market power through the lens of traditional welfare analysis. From this perspective, competition is generally a good thing (and market power can be a bad thing) because competition tends to increase the social welfare of a market. To an economist, the term "competitive market" does not imply the use of cutthroat or illegal policies. Instead, it is shorthand for the case in which so many buyers and sellers interact in a market that none are able to exercise significant market power. The fact that a competitor is always trying to take away your customers or your workers is what keeps you on your toes and makes you run your organization efficiently. Competition, to an economist, *means* decentralized power. The image of a self-regulating, "free" competitive market is at the core of traditional neoclassical economics.

As a social science, economics tends to make normative judgments from the point of view of social efficiency, not just from the perspective of one particular actor. The traditional neoclassical view, focused almost entirely on efficiency goals, notes that market power can create inefficiency. (We demonstrate this in Chapter 17.) Hence it considers market power largely harmful, except in certain unavoidable cases.

But as we have learned in other chapters, a complete economic analysis needs to consider all costs and benefits, not just those that accrue to market participants. In particular, we should consider social and environmental externalities. If competition drives businesses to treat their workers poorly or ignore environmental and safety regulations, these costs must be considered when we evaluate the extent to which an unregulated market leads to an efficient outcome. As economists, we may also be concerned about whether competitive markets lead to just outcomes, based on normative views of fairness.

Discussion Questions

1. To which of the four views of market power and competition do you most relate? Do you think all four views are valid, or is one particular view more worthwhile or "correct" than the others?
2. Can you think of an example of an economic actor that is *not* a business firm but that has "market power" in the sense defined in the text?

2. PERFECT COMPETITION

The economic model of perfect competition relies on particular assumptions and leads to certain conclusions about how firms will behave and what profits they can make.

2.1 THE CONDITIONS OF PERFECT COMPETITION

perfect competition: a market for the exchange of identical units of a good or service, in which there are numerous small sellers and buyers, all of whom have perfect information

The model of **perfect competition** is based on four key assumptions about a market:

1. There are *numerous small sellers and buyers.* Each buyer and seller is so small relative to the size of the relevant market that none can affect the market price.
2. Within any particular market, only one kind of good or service is traded and all units of the good or service offered for sale *are identical.* Therefore, buyers will not care which firm they buy from and will make purchasing decisions based solely on price.
3. Producers of the good or service can *freely enter or exit* the industry. There are no barriers preventing a new firm from joining the market or preventing an existing one from leaving the market.
4. Buyers and sellers all have *perfect information.* They all know where the good is available, at what prices it is offered, and whether profits are being made.

Another assumption is that the long-run minimum efficient scale (which we discussed in Chapter 15) of a producer in this industry is fairly small, relative to total demand in the market. In other words, production is characterized by constant returns to scale, not by economies of scale. This is important because, if it were *not* the case, the market might not be large enough for the many efficient firms assumed by the theory.

price taker: a seller that has no market power to set price. Price is determined solely by the interaction of market supply and market demand.

In a perfectly competitive market, every individual seller is a **price taker**, which means that each seller has no market power and price is determined by the interaction of market supply and demand. As each seller is relatively small, each can basically sell all they want to at the going price. But if they raise their price even just a little above the market-determined price, *no one* will buy from them because consumers can purchase identical items for a lower price from their competitors.

Being a price taker means that you face a perfectly elastic demand curve, as we discussed in Chapter 4. This is shown in Figure 16.1. A seller can sell all it wants at the market price of *P**. At any price above *P**, however, it will sell nothing. There is also no reason to sell at any price below *P** because it can sell as much as it wants at *P**.

Note that the *market* demand curve in a perfectly competitive market has the normal downward slope. Each individual seller faces a perfectly elastic demand curve, but the demand curve for the market as a whole will be less elastic, or perhaps inelastic.

Figure 16.1   **The Demand Curve for a Perfectly Competitive Seller**

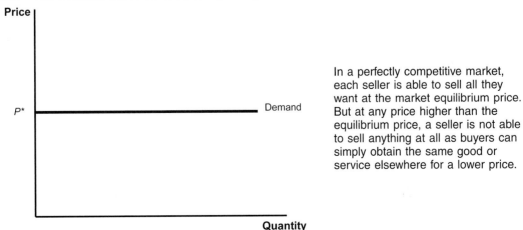

In a perfectly competitive market, each seller is able to sell all they want at the market equilibrium price. But at any price higher than the equilibrium price, a seller is not able to sell anything at all as buyers can simply obtain the same good or service elsewhere for a lower price.

2.2 EXAMPLES OF PERFECT COMPETITION?

Examples of perfectly competitive markets in the real world are hard to come by. In older text-books, agricultural commodities such as wheat were often given as examples of goods traded in perfectly competitive markets. It was argued that one farmer's wheat, of a given type, was nearly identical to the wheat of the same type sold by other farmers. Further, no individual farmer had any perceptible influence on the market price. However, in industrialized countries, agricultural markets today tend to be highly organized and regulated, with farmer-supported marketing boards, government-guaranteed minimum prices, long-term contracts, and the like deliberately influenc-ing the terms and conditions of the market. Further (as discussed in Chapter 17), some large agricultural corporations, such as Monsanto and Cargill, possess significant market power.

Perhaps the markets that most closely approach perfect competition today are not markets for goods but certain financial resale markets. For example, the conditions that prevail in the stock market often approximate those of perfect competition. The shares of stock of a particular company are all identical. Because this is a financial resale market, the cost of "production" is irrelevant, so there are no barriers to entry. Well-defined stock exchanges set up a structure under which the going price becomes common knowledge. When many shares of stock are outstanding, the trading of a few shares does not perceptibly affect the share price. If you own a few shares of stock and think about selling them, your broker will quote you a price—take it or leave it. The demand curve that you face, as an individual seller, is horizontal.

In some labor markets as well, conditions may approximate perfect competition. Workers with general skills, such as flipping burgers or sweeping floors, may provide nearly identical services from an employer's point of view. When there are many such "sellers," they may find that they have a choice of a job at "the going wage" or no job at all.

Discussion Questions

1. Suppose that you are thinking of starting your own business. Would you want to start a business in a perfectly competitive market? What do you think are the advantages and disadvantages of selling in a perfectly competitive market?
2. In addition to the markets mentioned in this section, can you think of any other markets that meet the assumptions of perfect competition?

3. PROFIT MAXIMIZATION UNDER PERFECT COMPETITION

We now consider the production decisions of perfectly competitive sellers. Although a perfectly competitive seller can *theoretically* sell all he wants, in practice a seller will limit production to maximize his profits. We illustrate profit maximization by building on the corn farming example that we developed in Chapter 15. We assume that corn farming occurs in a perfectly competi-tive market. Even though this may not be a totally realistic assumption, it allows us to illustrate the production decisions of a perfectly competitive seller. We present a more formal model of production decisions in a perfectly competitive market in the appendix to this chapter.

3.1 REVENUES

total revenues:
the total amount of money received by a seller, equal to price times quantity

In Chapter 15, we discussed production costs. We now consider revenues—the money that sellers receive from their sales. Assuming that all units sell for the same price, **total revenues** are simply equal to price multiplied by quantity. So if the price of corn were $4 per bushel and a farmer sold 1,000 bushels of corn, her total revenues would be $4,000.*

We can now define profits as the difference between total revenues and total costs. But recall from Chapter 15 that we have two different definitions of costs—accounting costs and economic costs. The difference is that economic costs include all opportunity costs,

---

*This was approximately the actual price of corn at the time that this book was written.

such as the wages that one could potentially earn doing something else. Comparably, we also have two definitions of profits. **Accounting profits** are calculated as the difference between total revenues and accounting costs. **Economic profits** are the difference between total revenues and economic costs. Accounting profits are higher than economic profits, because economic costs are higher than accounting costs. Note that it is entirely possible for a seller to make a positive accounting profit, but no economic profit, or even a negative profit (i.e., a loss).

accounting profits: the difference between total revenues and accounting costs

economic profits: the difference between total revenues and economic costs

The standard neoclassical model of perfect competition assumes that each seller seeks to maximize his or her profits. In the numerical model that we present here, we assume that costs mean economic costs, and thus profits are economic profits. We will see that economic profits are an important concept in the traditional model of perfect competition.

marginal revenue: the additional revenue obtained by selling one more unit. In a perfectly competitive market, marginal revenue equals price.

We also need to define **marginal revenue**, which is the *additional* revenue obtained by selling one more unit. In a perfectly competitive market, marginal revenue is simply the market price. So if the price of corn is $4 per bushel, the marginal revenue from selling one more bushel is simply $4. In Chapter 17, we consider markets in which the marginal revenue is not equal to price.

We can represent total revenues graphically, as shown in Figure 16.2. The total revenue curve is a straight line because marginal revenue is constant at $4 per bushel. So if a farmer sells 100 bushels of corn, for example, total revenues will be $400; if she sells 140 bushels of corn, total revenues will be $560.

Figure 16.2 **Total Revenues**

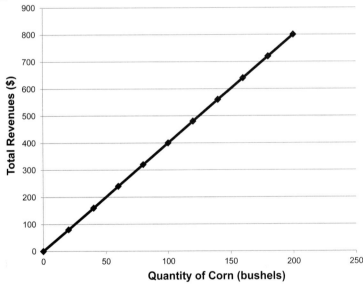

Total revenues increase linearly with the quantity sold given that the price for each unit (in this case, bushels of corn) is constant in a perfectly competitive market.

3.2 PROFIT MAXIMIZATION EXAMPLE

Continuing with our corn farming example, we need to determine the level of corn production that will result in the maximum profit. To compile Table 16.1, we can combine our information from Chapter 15 about production costs with the fact that corn sells for $4 per bushel. We have calculated the profit (or loss) of each level of corn production, based on different levels of fertilizer application. Note that Table 16.1 repeats the information from Table 15.4, but adds a total revenue and profit column. As discussed above, we assume that the fixed cost of $500 per acre is an economic cost, including both accounting and opportunity costs.

We see that the farmer's profits are maximized at a production level of 154 bushels per acre, applying 6 bags of fertilizer per acre. At this point, economic profits are $26 per acre. Any other level of production results in lower (or negative) profits.

Table 16.1 **Profit Maximization, Based on Analysis of Total Costs and Total Revenues**

Quantity of nitrogen fertilizer (bags/acre)	Corn yield (bushels per acre)	Fixed costs ($)	Variable costs ($15 per bag of fertilizer)	Total costs ($)	Total revenues ($)	Economic profit/loss ($)
0	100	500	0	500	400	−100
1	115	500	15	515	460	−55
2	127	500	30	530	508	−22
3	137	500	45	545	548	3
4	145	500	60	560	580	20
5	150	500	75	575	600	25
6	154	500	90	590	616	26
7	157	500	105	605	628	23
8	159	500	120	620	636	16

Profit maximization can be shown graphically as the difference between total revenues and total costs, as shown in Figure 16.3. In this figure we have combined Figure 16.2, showing total revenues, with our total cost curve from Figure 15.4. The vertical distance between the total revenue curve and the total cost curve represents profits. This vertical distance is greatest, and profits are maximized, at 154 bushels per acre.

In addition to determining the profit-maximizing level of production using a table or a graph of total revenues and total costs, we can also use marginal analysis. Recall that in Chapter 15 we calculated the marginal cost of producing one more bushel of corn at each level of fertilizer application (Table 15.5). We repeat this table here as Table 16.2, with the addition of one more column to the right indicating the marginal revenue from selling corn, which is constant at $4 per bushel.

Marginal analysis tells us that it makes economic sense to do something as long as the marginal benefits are greater than the marginal costs. So the farmer's question is whether it makes economic sense to add each bag of fertilizer. As long as the marginal revenues exceed

Figure 16.3 **Profit Maximization, Based on Analysis of Total Costs and Total Revenues**

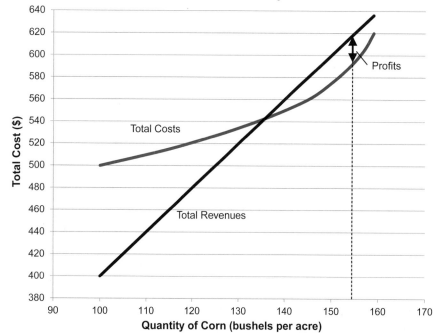

Profit maximization occurs at the level of production where the difference between total revenues and total costs is greatest.

Table 16.2 **The Marginal Cost and Marginal Revenue of Corn Production**

Quantity of nitrogen fertilizer (bags per acre)	Corn yield (bushels per acre)	Marginal return to additional nitrogen (bushels of corn)	Cost of additional nitrogen ($ per bag)	Marginal cost in dollars per bushel of corn	Marginal revenue in dollars per bushel of corn
0	100	—	—	—	4
1	115	15	15	15 ÷ 15 = 1.00	4
2	127	12	15	15 ÷ 12 = 1.25	4
3	137	10	15	15 ÷ 10 = 1.33	4
4	145	8	15	15 ÷ 8 = 1.88	4
5	150	5	15	15 ÷ 5 = 3.00	4
6	154	4	15	15 ÷ 4 = 3.75	4
7	157	3	15	15 ÷ 3 = 5.00	4
8	159	2	15	15 ÷ 2 = 7.50	4

the marginal costs the farmer should keeping adding fertilizer, because profits are increasing. So, for example, we can see that adding the third bag of fertilizer increases profits because the marginal cost, measured in dollars per bushel of corn, is $1.33 while the marginal revenues per bushel are $4.00.

Marginal revenues exceed marginal cost for every production level up to six bags of fertilizer. For the seventh bag of fertilizer, the marginal cost of $5 exceeds the marginal revenue of $4. By adding the seventh bag of fertilizer, the farmer loses money. So the profit-maximizing level of fertilizer application is six bags, at which the farmer produces 154 bushels of corn per acre. This is the same answer that we obtained previously based on tabular and graphical analysis of total costs and revenues.

We can also illustrate profit maximization using a graph of marginal costs and marginal revenues, shown in Figure 16.4. We see that marginal revenue is constant at $4 per bushel. The marginal cost of corn production is increasing, as we discussed in Chapter 15. The

Figure 16.4 **Profit Maximization, Based on Marginal Analysis**

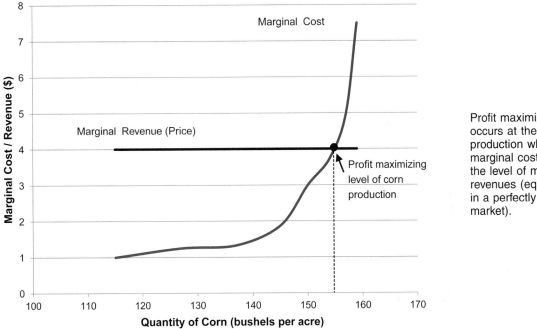

Profit maximization occurs at the level of production where the marginal cost rises to the level of marginal revenues (equal to price in a perfectly competitive market).

profit-maximizing level of corn production is 154 bushels, again up to the point where the marginal revenue equals marginal cost.

We can now state the general rule for **profit maximization under perfect competition**: A seller should increase production up to the point where marginal revenues equal marginal costs, commonly expressed as $MR = MC$. Given that marginal revenue is always equal to price under perfect competition, we can also state that profit maximizing means setting $P = MC$.

3.3 PROFITS UNDER PERFECT COMPETITION

profit maximization (under perfect competition): a seller should increase production up to the point where $MR = MC$. As $MR = P$ under perfect competition, we can also define the profit maximizing solution by setting $P = MC$.

In Table 16.1 we found that at the profit-maximizing level of production (154 bushels of corn per acre), the farmer is making $26 per acre in profits. Recall that this is an economic profit. Although this may not sound like much, a farmer may have many acres, perhaps hundreds, in corn production. Also, as an *economic* profit, this means that farming is providing a better income than *any other opportunity,* such as working as a police officer or an administrative assistant.

We now ask an important question: Can economic profits persist under perfect competition? The answer is no, based on the assumptions of perfect competition. Specifically:

- With free entry and exit, anyone can easily become a farmer, switching from any other profession.*
- With perfect information, everyone is aware that farming is providing higher profits than other opportunities.
- Another implication of perfect information is that everyone has access to information that will allow him or her to produce corn as efficiently as possible (i.e., at the lowest cost).
- All bushels of corn are identical, so anyone producing corn can sell as much as he or she wants at the market price.

Thus the existence of economic profits in our idealized picture of corn production will attract some people to switch what they are doing and take up corn farming. We assume that this will not affect the costs of corn farming—the costs remain the same as in Tables 16.1 and 16.2. However, the influx of new farmers increases the *market supply* of corn. In other words, at any given corn price, more corn will be supplied because more farmers are growing corn, as illustrated in Figure 16.5. The original market equilibrium, with a corn price of $4.00 per bushel, is E_0. As more farmers enter the market, the supply curve shifts to the right, moving from $Supply_0$ to $Supply_1$. With the increase in supply, the market price falls from $4.00 per bushel to a lower price, P_1.

Figure 16.5   The Impact of an Increase in Supply as Farmers Enter the Corn Market

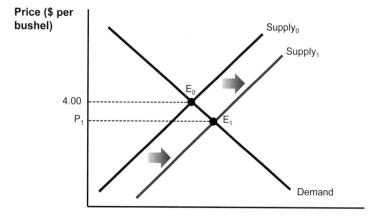

An increase in supply, as more farmers enter the market, will lower the equilibrium price (from $4.00 per bushel to P_1) and increase the quantity sold.

*Of course, becoming a corn farmer is not "free"—it normally requires training and significant investment in land and equipment. But, as in any economic model, we are abstracting from reality to illustrate a point.

Our next question becomes: How much will supply increase? Or, given that the equilibrium price will vary depending on how much supply shifts, what will P_1 eventually be?

Note that as the price of corn falls below $4.00 per bushel, each farmer's profits will fall. Thus the increase in supply reduces the amount of economic profits made by each farmer. But as long as economic profits exist, even if they are small, farming is still more attractive than all other opportunities. *Thus as long as economic profits exist, entry of new farmers into the market will continue.*

As each new farmer enters the market, three things will happen simultaneously:

1. The market supply curve shifts a little further to the right.
2. The market price falls a little further.
3. Economic profits for each farmer become a little lower.

We can illustrate what is happening in the market as a whole and for each individual farmer by putting the market supply and demand graph next to our graph of marginal costs and revenues for an individual farmer, as shown in Figure 16.6. Each farmer's marginal revenue curve is equal to price (a horizontal line), which is determined by market conditions (i.e., market supply and demand). When more farmers enter the market, shifting the supply curve from $Supply_0$ to $Supply_1$, each farmer's marginal revenue curve falls from MR_0 to MR_1. Each farmer's profit-maximizing level of production is still where $MR = MC$. So each farmer will respond to the decrease in price by shifting production from point A to point B. At the lower price, each farmer is making a smaller profit.

Figure 16.6   The Relationship between Market Conditions and Individual Production Decisions

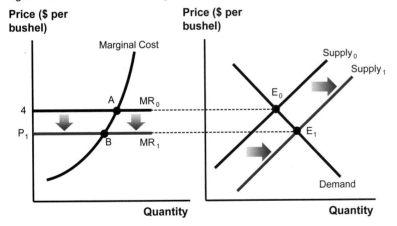

As more farmers enter the market, the equilibrium price will fall, and the economic profits of each individual farmer will decrease.

Eventually, we will reach a point where price falls enough that economic profits fall to zero. At this point, farming is equally attractive to the next best alternative, and there is no incentive for further entry to the market. In other words, under the assumptions of perfect competition, *economic profits will eventually fall to zero.* We call this the **perfectly competitive market equilibrium**. At this market equilibrium, there is no further incentive for entry or exit.

It is important to remember that even though economic profits are zero at the perfectly competitive market equilibrium, each farmer is still making an *accounting* profit. For every bushel of corn up to point B in Figure 16.6, marginal revenue is greater than marginal cost. So each farmer is making an accounting profit on every bushel of corn up to point B. Perfect competition drives economic profits to zero, but not accounting profits.

We can ask one final question based on our corn farming example: What is P_1, the price that will eventually drive economic profits to zero? Algebraically solving for P_1 requires more math than we cover in this book, but you can solve for P_1 with some trial and error. You would calculate total revenues in Table 16.1 based on successively lower corn prices until the maximum attainable

perfectly competitive market equilibrium: the market equilibrium in a perfectly competitive market in which the economic profits of each individual seller are zero, and there is no incentive for entry or exit

profit equals zero. For example, if the corn price were $3.90 per bushel instead of $4.00, 154 bushels of corn would sell for $600.60 (instead of $616.00). This is still higher than the total cost of $590, so an economic profit is still being made. Thus price at the perfectly competitive market equilibrium must be lower than $3.90. The solution for the perfectly competitive equilibrium price is slightly more than $3.83 per bushel. At this price, 154 bushels would sell for exactly $590, total revenues would equal total costs, and economic profits would be zero.*

Discussion Questions

1. Explain, in your words without a table or a graph, why economic profits fall to zero in a perfectly competitive market.
2. How useful do you think the model of a perfectly competitive market presented in this section is in explaining economic behavior in the real world? What do you think is the most relevant insight from the model?

4. LOSSES AND EXIT

In our corn example, each farmer is always making an accounting profit, even at the perfectly competitive market equilibrium. But in the real world, sometimes businesses do lose money and may even decide to shut down production and exit a market. In this section, we consider how a seller will behave when it is accruing losses rather than making a profit.**

4.1. LOSSES IN THE SHORT RUN

Let's suppose that the price of corn decreased to $3.60 per bushel, perhaps due to a decrease in the demand for corn. We can see how this affects an individual farmer by looking at Table 16.3. This is the same as Table 16.1 except that total revenues are now calculated based on a corn price of $3.60 per bushel instead of $4.00 per bushel. The fixed and variable costs of corn production have stayed the same.

We see that at the lower corn price, the "profit-maximizing" level of corn production, now at 150 bushels per acre with five bags of fertilizer, is actually a loss. The best that the farmer can do is to lose $35 per acre!

Table 16.3   **Impact of a Decrease in Corn Prices**

Quantity of nitrogen fertilizer (bags/acre)	Corn yield (bushels per acre)	Fixed costs ($)	Variable costs ($15 per bag of fertilizer)	Total costs ($)	Total revenues ($)	Economic profit/loss ($)
0	100	500	0	500	360	−140
1	115	500	15	515	414	−101
2	127	500	30	530	457	−73
3	137	500	45	545	493	−52
4	145	500	60	560	522	−38
5	150	500	75	575	540	−35
6	154	500	90	590	554	−36
7	157	500	105	605	565	−40
8	159	500	120	620	572	−48

---

*Note that in this particular example, the profit-maximizing level of production under the perfectly competitive market equilibrium remains 154 bushels of corn. However, as shown in Figure 16.6, the movement from point A to point B will generally result in a decrease in the optimal production level for each farmer. If we conducted this analysis such that farmers could add partial bags of fertilizer, then movement from point A to point B would result in a slight decrease in fertilizer application and thus a slight decrease in corn production per acre.

**In this section, we are still referring to economic, rather than accounting, losses.

Would it ever make sense for a farmer to stay in business when she is losing money? We know in the real world that businesses frequently lose money temporarily, only to make profits later. During the Great Recession in 2007–9, many businesses lost money, including banks and auto manufacturers. While some did go out of business, others survived and eventually returned to profitability.

Thus a farmer's decision comes down to whether she is willing and able to accept temporary losses, with the hope of making profits in the future, or quit farming. To understand how a rational farmer will behave, we have to recall, from Chapter 15, the distinction between the short run and the long run. In the short run, at least one input is fixed in quantity, and thus the cost of paying for any fixed inputs must be paid regardless of production levels. In the long run, all inputs are variable, and thus a seller can avoid paying all costs simply by leaving the market.

In our corn example, the fixed cost of $500 must be paid in the short term, regardless of the level of corn production. Even if the farmer decides to produce no corn, she must still pay this fixed cost. So the farmer's short-term production decision comes down to two options:

1. continue to produce some corn, even at a loss
2. produce no corn at all, and just pay the fixed costs

Table 16.3 shows that at 150 bushels of corn (the best the farmer can do), the farmer loses $35 per acre—total costs are $575, and total revenues are $540. Her other option is to not produce any corn. In this case, she will still have to pay her fixed cost of $500 per acre. She avoids having to pay any variable costs, but she also receives no revenues. So her losses will be $500 per acre if she produces no corn.

Obviously, it is better to lose only $35 per acre than to lose $500 per acre. By producing some corn, rather than none, she is able to more than cover her variable costs, recovering a large portion of her fixed costs as well. In other words, as long as she is able to cover her variable costs, in the short term it makes economic sense to continue production, even if losses are occurring.

A surprising implication of this conclusion is that *it does not matter how big the fixed costs are.* As long as there is something left over, after variable costs are paid, to go toward paying the fixed costs—*whatever they may be*—the farmer should continue to produce corn. Whether the fixed costs are $500 per acre or $5,000 per acre does not matter. You can prove this to yourself by calculating that the farmer does better by producing 150 bushels of corn and losing $4,535 per acre than by not producing and losing $5,000 per acre. The same would be true even if fixed costs were $1 million per acre!

sunk cost: an expenditure that was incurred or committed to in the past and is irreversible in the short run

This is a specific example of a more general economic principle concerning production decisions. *Sunk costs should not affect short-run production decisions.* A **sunk cost** is a cost that, in the short run, is the proverbial "water over the dam." The expense has already been incurred (or committed to) and cannot be reversed.

This principle often seems to contradict common sense. Humans seem to have an illogical but psychologically strong tendency to want to make past investments "pay off." And the larger the past investment, the more likely people are to be influenced by sunk costs. This is true not only of production decisions but of economic behavior in general. This is yet another example of seemingly irrational economic behavior, as we discussed in Chapter 7. Economics teaches us that when making decisions, we should focus on what is the best decision for us now and that past investment is irrelevant. (For some examples of how sunk costs can influence economic behavior, see Box 16.2.)

4.2 Losses in the Long Run

In the long run, all costs are variable. So in the long run the farmer can avoid having to pay the short-run fixed cost of $500 per acre simply by exiting the corn market. The farmer can

Box 16.2 Sunk Costs and Decision Making

Suppose that you have paid $50 in advance for a ticket to a concert. Assume that the ticket is nonrefundable and nontransferable. In other words, it is a sunk cost. But suppose that there is a blizzard the night of the concert, and traveling there would be miserable. Faced with a simple choice between relaxing at home and heading out into the blizzard to go to the concert, assume that you would prefer to stay home. But you have already paid $50 for the concert ticket. What do you do?

According to economic logic, the sunk cost of $50 should be irrelevant to your decision. What should matter is which option is the best choice for you now. But surveys show that many people are swayed by sunk costs and that the amount of the sunk cost matters. Now, suppose instead that you had won the concert ticket in a contest rather than paying $50 for it. Would that affect your decision? According to economic logic, it shouldn't.

It seems that people create "psychological accounts" in their heads about different expenditures, which can influence their decisions. Consider the following example from a paper published by Daniel Kahneman and his colleague Amos Tversky (recall that we discussed them in Chapter 7). First, suppose that you are going to see a play and the tickets cost $10. As you enter the theater, you discover that you have

lost a $10 bill. Do you still pay $10 for a ticket? Their survey results indicate that 82 percent of respondents would still buy a ticket. Most people viewed the loss of $10 as belonging to a different "account" than the one used to pay for the ticket.

However, imagine that you have already paid $10 for a ticket and you discover as you enter the theater that you have lost the ticket. Do you pay $10 for another ticket? In this case, only about half of respondents would buy another ticket. In this case, many people consider buying another ticket equivalent to paying $20 for a ticket, and thus overpaying.

In either case, $10 is a sunk cost—you either lost a $10 bill or you already paid $10 for a ticket. So the decision in either case as you enter the theater is whether you should pay a marginal $10 to see the play. But how the sunk cost is presented to people does have a significant influence on their answer. As usual, human behavior is complicated and context does matter.

Sources: Hal R. Arkes and Catherine Blumer, "The Psychology of Sunk Cost," *Organizational Behavior and Human Decision Processes* 35 (1985): 124–140; Amos Tversky and Daniel Kahneman, "The Framing of Decisions and the Psychology of Choice," *Science* 211 (4481) (1981): 453–458.

sell her land and machinery and take up a different profession. In a perfectly competitive market, or any market, short-term losses may be rational, but in the long run exit becomes preferable to losing money.

Again, human behavior may be more complicated than this, and exiting a market may be a difficult decision. For example, the decision to sell a farm that has been in a family for generations may involve more than financial factors. Selling the farm, say to a developer, may also create negative externalities, such as the loss of wildlife habitat. What is optimal for an individual seller may not be optimal for social welfare. In some cases where farms are losing money, it may be better from a social welfare perspective to subsidize the farmer so that she does not feel compelled to sell to a developer.

Discussion Questions

1. "Why would anyone run a business if he couldn't make a profit?" This is a frequent response to economists' idea that all firms in a particular market make zero "economic profits."
   a. In your own words, explain what economists mean by zero economic profits and why an entrepreneur would choose to operate a perfectly competitive business.
   b. Explain why perfectly competitive firms are assumed to make zero economic profits in the long run.
2. Suppose that you are halfway through a particular course and you decide that you are not learning anything useful and the rest of the course is not worth your effort (obviously we are not describing this course!). It is too late to drop the course and sign up for another one. Is this an example of a sunk cost? How does economics suggest that you decide whether to complete the course?

5. PRODUCTION, EFFICIENCY, AND EQUITY

One of the implications of the perfectly competitive market model is that each firm *must* act in an economically efficient manner. As economic profits are assumed to be zero in the long run, any firm that operates in an inefficient manner will make negative economic profits. In the long run, inefficient firms will thus be forced out of the market.

But in the real world, inefficiencies may be quite common, even in markets that approach the conditions of perfect competition. We next consider two types of inefficiencies that may exist in any market. Then we end this chapter with a discussion of efficiency and equity in perfectly competitive markets.

5.1 PATH DEPENDENCE

path dependence: a condition that exists when economic developments depend on initial conditions and past events— that is, when "history matters"

Path dependence, a term borrowed from mathematics, basically means that "history matters" in determining how production technologies—and even entire economies—develop. When a process is path dependent, the way in which it develops may depend crucially on "initial conditions" and past events. The present state of manufactured capital or human capital, for example, can be thought of as making up part of the initial conditions for current production decisions.

Agriculture offers a good example of path dependence. For example, in the western part of Germany farms tend to be relatively small, but in the eastern part of Germany farms tend to be much larger. The explanation has nothing to do with a difference in the minimum efficient scale in the two regions. Instead, it is a result of history—until 1990 Germany was split into two countries, and in East Germany farms were organized by the government as large collectives.[1]

Another agricultural example of path dependence concerns the allocation of water rights in the western United States.[2] To promote agricultural development in the West, water rights were allocated under the "prior appropriation doctrine," which states that the first person to establish any beneficial use of a given quantity of water obtains the right to that quantity of water in the future. Other water users who come later may also obtain water rights by establishing beneficial uses, but they are able to access water only after the demands of all "senior" water rights holders, who established rights before them, have been met.

The allocation of water under the prior appropriation doctrine is based on history, not economic efficiency. As water demands have increased in the West, economists have advocated for the establishment of water markets that would allow water rights holders to trade water, theoretically allocating water to more efficient uses. However, the efficiency gains from water trading have been much smaller than predicted, as many water rights holders have been concerned that if they do not put their water to beneficial uses, but trade it instead, they may lose their rights. Even worse, prior appropriation encourages inefficient water use because it basically means "use it or lose it." So, rather than adopt efficient irrigation techniques and risk losing some of their water rights, farmers may continue to rely on inefficient practices.

Historical evidence suggests that health care in the United States also developed in a path-dependent fashion, rather than an economically efficient manner.[3] As part of the New Deal legislation in the 1930s, President Franklin Roosevelt supported universal public health-insurance coverage, but it was defeated in Congress. Then during World War II wage controls were implemented that prevented businesses from increasing wages. To attract workers while being unable to offer higher wages, some firms began to offer health-insurance coverage as a fringe benefit. Labor unions then began to demand health-insurance coverage from employers. As employer-provided health insurance became more common, interest in universal health care faded. The United States now spends more than any other country on health care, as a percentage of GDP, yet many of its health outcomes are rather mediocre. We discuss health care in the United States in more detail in Chapter 17.

5.2 NETWORK EXTERNALITIES

**network external-
ity (in production):**
a situation in which a
particular technology
or production pro-
cess is more likely to
be adopted because
other economic ac-
tors have already
adopted it

In addition to taking place in a historical context, production decisions also take place within a rich social context. Many technologies, such as standards for computers, automobiles, and kitchen appliance sizes, are widely shared. A production technology is characterized by a **network eternality** if people are more likely to adopt it, the more *other* people have adopted it.

A common example of a network externality is the widespread use of Microsoft Windows operating systems on personal computers (PCs). Although other operating systems, such as Linux and Macintosh, exist and offer some advantages, the vast majority of users have a computer with a Windows operating system mainly because that is what other users have adopted. The dominance of Windows is also an example of path dependence, because of the history in which Microsoft was able to gain a strong initial position in the PC market after it established a partnership with IBM in the 1980s. (Another interesting question, likely explained in part due to network externalities, is why students are much more likely than professors to use Macs.)

A network externality is a type of "positive feedback" loop—the more that people adopt a given technology, the more likely it is that additional people will adopt that technology. In the case of Microsoft Windows, as it became more common, more software and computers were designed for Windows. This makes it even more difficult for a new operating system to gain market share, even if it is more efficient.

Suppose that you develop an alternative to Windows that is superior in many respects. Most users will not adopt your operating system until they believe that a lot of software that they need will be written for it, that upgrades will be available in the future, and that they will be able to communicate easily with others. But none of this can be assured until your invention has been widely adopted across a whole network of users. Your problem is that in order to *gain* widespread adoption, you must already *have* it! Unless you are in a position to create a widespread network out of nothing—perhaps, for example, by blanketing the country with free software and training—your technically superior invention will not be adopted broadly.

A similar problem exists for a city that is trying to increase the use of public transportation in order to decrease road congestion and pollution. If most of the people in the city use the public transportation system, as in New York City and many European cities, it will seem like a normal thing to do, residential and workplace location patterns will reflect the availability of public transportation, the buses and subways will run frequently, and service may be so good that people freely choose it over using a private car. By contrast, if few people use public transportation, it may be stigmatized, routes and services will (in the absence of massive subsidies) tend to be very limited and inconvenient, residences and workplaces will tend to sprawl, and thus ridership will be further discouraged.

Network externalities create another way in which rational decision making by individuals can lead to inefficient production processes and a failure to maximize long-run social welfare. (See Box 16.3 for another example of path dependence and network externalities.)

5.3 MARKETS, EFFICIENCY, AND EQUITY

A perfectly competitive market is, under certain assumptions, economically efficient according to welfare analysis (as discussed in Chapter 5). In theory, if nothing prevents a perfectly competitive market from reaching equilibrium then the sum of consumer and producer surplus is maximized. However, this equilibrium is economically efficient only if:

1. There are no positive or negative externalities associated with the production and consumption of the good or service, including externalities that might occur in the future. As we discussed in Chapter 12, externalities may be pervasive, in terms of environmental or social effects.
2. All buyers and sellers have perfect information, or at least the ability to correctly determine when the marginal benefits of acquiring additional information become smaller than the

BOX 16.3 THE QWERTY KEYBOARD

A classic example of path dependency is the layout of typewriters and computer keyboards. The conventional QWERTY layout, named for the first several letters in the top left row, was developed in the nineteenth century and rapidly became the norm throughout the English-speaking world. The QWERTY layout was actually designed to *slow down* typing in order to prevent the keys from jamming on old-fashioned typewriters!

Studies with modern typewriters and computer keyboards have shown that the QWERTY layout is far from the most efficient. Alternative keyboard designs have been developed that, with sufficient practice, increase typing speeds and reduce errors. For example, the "Dvorak Simplified Keyboard," patented in the 1930s, groups common letter combinations together to reduce awkward finger movements. Also, based on the usage rates of different letters, about 70 percent of key strokes occur on the row of letters where people commonly rest

their fingers, making it more ergonomic. However, efforts to market an alternative keyboard layout have consistently failed.

The major reason for the failure of alternatives to the QWERTY layout is that it has historically been built into an interlinked, economy-wide structure of equipment and training. Office equipment manufacturers are all set up to produce it. Keyboarding classes all teach it. A shift to a more efficient layout would entail substantial costs in time and money, even though long-run efficiency gains could be achieved.

In sum, you type on a QWERTY keyboard not because it is the most efficient layout but because of a historical quirk and the fact that everyone else is using it.

Source: Paul A. David, "Clio and the Economics of QWERTY," *American Economic Review* 75(2) (1985): 332–337.

marginal costs. As we discussed in Chapter 7, information is often lacking, even intentionally distorted to serve other economic interests, and economic actors often behave in ways that are inconsistent with the assumption of perfect information.

3. Consumer demand curves, based on willingness to pay, accurately reflect the benefits consumers obtain from their purchases. As we saw in Chapter 8, consumers often fail to accurately predict the benefits of goods and services.

So a market that meets all the conditions of perfect competition may still fail to maximize social and individual welfare if these additional conditions are not satisfied. Further, our analysis of perfect competition says nothing about whether the market outcome is considered equitable. An appealing feature of perfectly competitive markets to most economists is that they force firms to be efficient in their production decisions. As we mentioned at the start of this section, all perfectly competitive firms must be efficient or face going out of business. This production efficiency also ensures that consumers are offered the lowest possible prices. But the constant competitive pressure on firms can lead to job cuts and other cost-minimizing decisions that create social disruptions and externalities. For example, a perfectly competitive firm may try to temporarily capture positive economic profits by ignoring pollution regulations, increasing the negative externalities they impose on society.

Moving beyond a single perfectly competitive market, economists have proven that an entire economy that consists *only* of perfectly competitive markets will have an efficient allocation of all resources, without any government regulation.* This conclusion, which requires a complex mathematical proof, has been used by some economists to support limiting government involvement in markets.

Although no economy consists entirely of perfectly competitive markets, any movement toward the perfectly competitive ideal would seem to generally increase economic efficiency. However, this is not necessarily the case. In the 1950s the economists R.G. Lipsey and Kelvin

*This finding is known as the first fundamental theorem of welfare economics.

Lancaster demonstrated that *any* deviation from the perfectly competitive economy-wide ideal—even a slight deviation in a single market—may require government intervention in many markets to achieve the best possible outcome from the standpoint of economic efficiency.*

In the real world, the vast majority of markets in any economy are not perfectly competitive. Thus basing economic policy suggestions on an assumption of perfectly competitive markets is questionable, to say the least. Further, policy suggestions that focus exclusively on economic efficiency as a final goal, while ignoring other final goals such as environmental sustainability, fairness, and good social relations, are unlikely to be in the best interest of overall well-being.

So while our analysis of perfectly competitive markets is a useful tool in our economic toolbox, it does not say much about how the real world operates or what types of policies we should institute. More interesting and useful analyses concern what happens to markets when the conditions of perfect competition are not satisfied. But to understand these analyses, we first need to understand the perfectly competitive model presented in this chapter. In Chapter 17, the final chapter, we consider markets that are not perfectly competitive, including the implications of these markets for efficiency, fairness, and public policies.

Discussion Questions

1. Try to think of other examples, not mentioned in the text, of path dependence or network externalities. Do you think that these situations are inefficient? Do you think that government policy should play a role in eliminating path dependence and network externalities?

2. An interesting book published in the 1990s, titled *No Contest*, argues for the restructuring of society to promote cooperation rather than competition. The book contends that the pervasive existence of competition in society actually destroys social capital, creates anxiety, and lowers productivity. Do you think that there could be a viable alternative to an economy based on competitive pressures? Should government policies promote competition, cooperation, neither, or both?

REVIEW QUESTIONS

1. What is market power?
2. What is the business perspective on competition and market power?
3. What is the consumer perspective on competition and market power?
4. What is the citizen perspective on competition and market power?
5. What is the economists' perspective on competition and market power?
6. What are the four conditions of perfect competition?
7. What does the demand curve for a perfectly competitive seller look like?
8. What is the difference between accounting and economic profits?
9. How do we determine the profit-maximizing level of production using analysis of total costs and total revenues?
10. What is the rule for profit maximization using marginal analysis?
11. What happens to economic profits in a perfectly competitive market in the long run?
12. What is the graphical relationship between market conditions and an individual perfectly competitive seller's production decision?
13. What is the perfectly competitive market equilibrium?
14. What is a sunk cost? How does it influence production decisions, according to economic theory?
15. How should a producer decide whether to operate at a loss or shut down production in the short run?
16. Would a seller be expected to operate at a loss in the long run?
17. What is path dependence?
18. What are network externalities?
19. Under what conditions are perfectly competitive markets economically efficient?

---

*This finding is known as the theory of the second best.

EXERCISES

1. The Top Notch Grill's marginal costs of producing take-out meals are described below.

Quantity of meals	Marginal cost ($)
0	—
1	6
2	5
3	7
4	10
5	12
6	17

a. Assuming that the Grill has fixed costs of $7, what is its total cost at each level of production? (Add a column to the table.)

b. Assume that meals sell for $10 each and the Grill is a perfectly competitive firm. What are the Grill's total revenue (price × quantity), marginal revenue, and total profit (total revenue − total cost), at each level of production? (Add three more columns to the table.)

c. How many meals should the Grill produce, to maximize profits? Explain in a sentence or two how you arrived at your answer.

2. Suppose a firm that manufactures bicycles has the following cost structure:

Quantity of bicycles	Total cost ($)
0	50
1	100
2	200
3	400
4	800

a. How much does this firm have in fixed costs?

b. Using graph paper or a computer program, graph the total cost curve for this firm.

c. Suppose that bicycles sell for $200 each, and the firm is a price taker. Create a table showing the marginal cost, total cost, marginal revenue, total revenue (price × quantity), and total profit (total revenue − total cost) at each level of production.

d. Add a total revenue curve to the graph that you created in (b). Indicate with arrows the approximate quantity at which the vertical distance between the two curves is the greatest.

e. Would the firm make a profit by producing and selling only one bicycle? Would one bicycle be the best output level for the firm? What is the output level that maximizes profits?

3. Continuing with the bicycle firm described in the previous problem, consider how the firm's decision-making will change as the price of bicycles changes. For each of the following, make a new table.

a. If the price per bicycle were $100, what would the profit-maximizing level of output be? How much profit would the firm make?

b. If the price per bicycle were $20, what would the profit-maximizing level of output be? How much profit would the firm make?

4. Suppose that a perfectly competitive firm manufactures gizmos with the following cost structure (including all opportunity costs):

Quantity of gizmos	Total cost ($)
0	75
1	150
2	250
3	425
4	675

a. Calculate the marginal cost schedule for this firm in a table, and then graph the marginal cost curve.

b. If the price of gizmos on the market is $175 each, how many gizmos should the firm produce to maximize profits? What is the level of the firm's revenues at its chosen output level? How much does it make in profit?

c. Suppose that more firms start producing gizmos, and the market price drops to $125. How many gizmos should this firm now produce to maximize profits? (*Note:* In the case of discrete quantities such as these, interpret the $P = MC$ rule as "produce as long as price *is at least as great as* marginal cost.") What is this firm's new revenue level? How much does it make in profits?

d. When the price is $125, will more firms want to enter the market? Will existing firms want to exit?

5. Match each item in Column A with an example in Column B.

Column A	Column B
a. Condition for perfect competition	1. Accounting profits
b. Business perspective on competition	2. I buy an iPhone because everyone else has iPhones
c. Consumer perspective on competition	3. Competition drives prices lower, leading to bargain opportunities
d. Type of profit equal to zero at the perfectly competitive market equilibrium	4. History matters
e. Type of profit that is still positive at the perfectly competitive market equilibrium	5. Economic profits
f. Network externality	6. A lack of market power can lead to efficiency
g. Path dependence	7. The goal is to reduce or eliminate competition
h. Economists' perspective on competition	8. Each firm is a price taker

NOTES

1. Arlette Ostermeyer and Alfons Balmann, "Perception of Dairy Farming from Different Views—Results of a Stakeholder Discussion in the Region Altmark, Germany," paper presented at the EAAE 2011 Congress, Change and Uncertainty, Zurich, Switzerland, August 30–September 2, 2011.

2. Gary D. Libecap, "Institutional Path Dependence in Climate Adaptation: Coman's 'Some Unsettled Problems of Irrigation,' " *American Economic Review* 101 (2011): 1–19.

3. Scott E. Page, "Path Dependence," *Quarterly Journal of Political Science* 1 (2006): 87–115.

APPENDIX: A FORMAL MODEL OF PERFECT COMPETITION

In this appendix, we present a formal conceptual model of perfect competition. We start by introducing new material on production costs and then combine that with the production decisions of a price-taking firm.

Recall from Chapter 15 the definition of average total cost (*ATC*) as total cost divided by the quantity produced. For example, if the total cost of producing 200 bushels of corn were $800, the *ATC* would be $4.00 ($800 ÷ 200). *ATC* relates to marginal cost (*MC*) in the following manner:

- If $MC < ATC$, then *ATC* is decreasing
- If $MC > ATC$, then *ATC* is increasing
- When $ATC = MC$, *ATC* is at its lowest point

While this may seem difficult to grasp, consider the following analogy. Suppose that your current grade average in a class is a 90, and you get a new grade of 80 on a quiz. As your marginal grade (the quiz grade of 80) is lower than your average grade, your average grade will go down. However, if you instead score a 95 on the quiz, your marginal grade is higher than your average and your average will go up.

The relationship between *ATC* and *MC* is shown in Figure 16.7. We see that *ATC* starts out relatively high because fixed costs (which are often relatively large) are divided by a relative small quantity. As quantity increases, the average cost of production declines, even as marginal costs begin to rise (i.e., the reduction of *ATC* that is due to dividing by a larger

Figure 16.7 **The Relationship Between Average Total Costs and Marginal Costs**

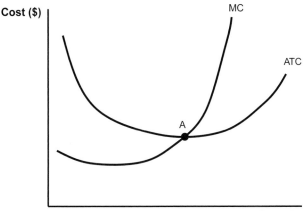

When average total cost is at its lowest point, it is equal to marginal cost.

average variable cost (AVC): total variable cost divided by the quantity produced

quantity more than offsets the rising marginal production costs). Eventually, the marginal cost rises above *ATC*, and then *ATC* rises. The minimum *ATC* is at point A.

Next we introduce a new cost variable, **average variable cost (AVC)**. *AVC* is equal to total variable cost divided by quantity. As *AVC* excludes fixed costs, it will always be less than *ATC*. Like *ATC*, the minimum *AVC* will occur where it intercepts the *MC* curve. Realize that all marginal costs are variable costs. So whenever $MC < AVC$, *AVC* is declining, and whenever $MC > AVC$, *AVC* will rise.

In Figure 16.8 we have added an *AVC* curve to the graph shown in Figure 16.7. Note that the distance between *ATC* and *AVC* is initially large because fixed costs are divided by a relatively small quantity. As quantity increases, fixed costs become less dominant in determining *ATC*, and *AVC* moves closer to *ATC*.

We can refer to this graph to determine the total costs of producing a given quantity and divide total costs into fixed and variable costs, as shown in Figure 16.9. Production is at Q_0. Total cost is the average per-unit cost (*ATC*) multiplied by Q_0, or the entire shaded area in the graph. The total variable costs are obtained by multiplying Q_0 by the average variable cost, which is the blue-shaded area in the graph. The difference is fixed costs, the gray-shaded area. Note that the area of fixed costs must be the same for any level of production, as it does not vary according to production levels.

Suppose that price is initially at P_0. A perfectly competitive firm would produce where $P = MC$, or at point X in Figure 16.10. Assuming the firm's costs include opportunity costs,

Figure 16.8 **The Relationship Between Average Total Costs, Marginal Costs, and Average Variable Costs**

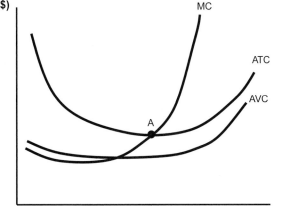

When average variable cost is at its lowest point, it is also equal to marginal cost.

Figure 16.9   **The Relationship Between Cost Curves and Areas of Total Costs, Fixed Costs, and Total Variable Costs**

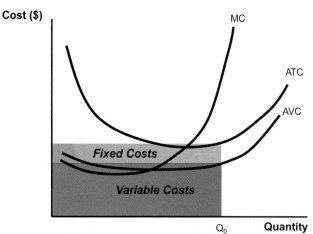

We can use the *ATC* and *AVC* curves to determine the areas of total costs, fixed costs, and variable costs for any level of production.

Figure 16.10 **Positive Economic Profits**

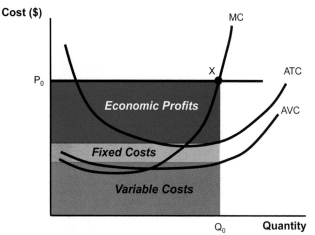

When price is greater than average total costs, a firm is making economic profits.

in this case the firm is making an economic profit, as shown in the graph as the blue-shaded area above the firm's total costs. Note that total revenues would be P_0 multiplied by Q_0, or the sum of all shaded areas.

As discussed in the chapter, the existence of economic profits creates an incentive for entry into the market. Assuming no barriers to entry, new firms will enter the market until economic profits are eliminated. This occurs when total revenues are just equal to total costs. As price falls, each perfectly competitive firm will reduce its production as the point where $P = MC$ moves to the left. The perfectly competitive market equilibrium is shown in Figure 16.11, with each firm producing at point Y (a quantity of Q_1 at a price of P_1). At this point, each firm is earning a zero economic profit—a profit just equal to what they could be making with their next-best alternative.

Finally, we consider the decision whether a firm should continue to produce in the short run while experiencing losses. As discussed in the chapter, perfectly competitive firms will continue to produce as long as they can recover their variable costs. So if price falls a little below P_1 in Figure 16.11, the firm will be making negative economic profits, but it will still be making enough revenues to cover its variable costs as well as pay some fixed costs—which is still better than shutting down production, earning no revenues, and having to pay all its fixed costs.

Figure 16.11 **Zero Economic Profits—The Perfectly Competitive Market Equilibrium**

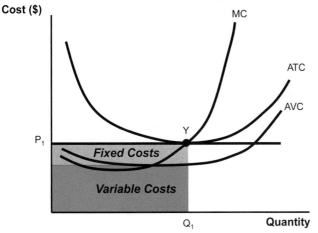

At the perfectly competitive market equilibrium, price equals *ATC* and each firm is making zero economic profits.

Eventually, the price will fall enough that the firm will not be able to cover its variable costs, and it is better off shutting down production and just paying its fixed costs, as illustrated in Figure 16.12. At a price of P_2 the firm produces at point Z (where $P = MC$) and makes just enough in revenues to cover its variable costs. However, if price falls below P_2, the firm will not be able to cover its variable costs and it is better off shutting down production and just paying its fixed costs.

Figure 16.12 **The Decision to Produce with Losses**

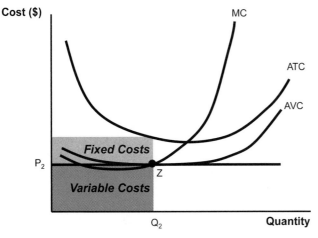

In the short run, a firm will continue to produce as long as revenues are sufficient to cover its variable costs.

17 Markets with Market Power

At the turn of the century, one of the ongoing big news stories concerned the lawsuits being brought against Microsoft—a company that had made its founder, Bill Gates, the richest person on the planet. At issue was the question of whether Microsoft had too much control over its market—in other words, whether its "market power" was excessive. As we will see, markets are rarely as competitive as described under the conditions of perfect competition from the last chapter. Indeed, many industries—from transportation and utilities to agriculture and health care—are characterized by a considerable degree of market power.

1. THE TRADITIONAL MODELS

Traditional neoclassical economics asks the question: "How do the number of firms in a product market and the characteristics of the good being sold affect the profit-maximizing decisions of the firm?" The four traditional types of market structure are perfect competition, pure monopoly, monopolistic competition, and oligopoly.

pure monopoly: the situation in which there is only one seller

monopolistic competition: the situation in which there are many sellers, but they sell slightly different things

oligopoly: the situation in which there are so few sellers that each needs to watch what the others are doing

- perfect competition: the situation in which there are many sellers, selling identical goods (see Chapter 16)
- **pure monopoly**: the situation in which there is only one seller
- **monopolistic competition**: the situation in which there are many sellers, but they sell slightly different things
- **oligopoly**: the situation in which there are so few sellers that each needs to watch what the others are doing

The first two are "idealized" types because they do rarely, if ever, exist in their "pure" form. In other words, although competition may exist to a significant degree, it is never "perfect"; and absolute monopolies also do not exist in the United States because they are prohibited by laws meant to encourage competitive behavior. These two "idealized types" are at opposite ends of a "competitiveness continuum," along which we find the other two types, monopolistic competition and oligopoly. Basically, the degree of competitiveness within an industry will inform whether the market more closely resembles monopolistic competition or oligopoly. In the latter case, markets are found to be truly complex, evolving social *organizations*. Arguably, oligopoly is the most important and prevalent type of market in contemporary industrialized economies.

Why model the first two types if they do not occur in the real world? As we have seen in earlier chapters, economists often sacrifice some realism in their analytical models in order to present simplified cases that can provide useful insights into economic behavior and decisions. The perfect competition and monopoly outcomes represent baseline cases to which we can then compare our conclusions about monopolistic competition and oligopoly.

2. PURE MONOPOLY: ONE SELLER

The case that is diametrically opposed to perfect competition is pure monopoly, in which there is only one seller. As in the case of perfect competition, the traditional model of profit maximization for monopoly leads to clear and definite predictions. But the predicted outcomes are, perhaps not surprisingly, very different from those of the perfect competition model.

2.1 THE CONDITIONS OF MONOPOLY

Monopoly is characterized by the following conditions:

1. There is only *one seller.*
2. The good being sold has *no close substitutes.* This means that buyers must buy from the monopolist or not at all.
3. *Barriers to entry* prevent other firms from starting to produce the good.

barriers to entry: economic, legal, or deliberate obstacles that keep new sellers from entering a market

Because the monopolist is the only seller in the market, it faces no competition from other firms. The condition of "no close substitutes" means that the good that the monopolist sells must be substantially different from anything else, so the monopolist does not have to worry about losing buyers to markets for similar, even if not identical, goods. If the monopolist made economic profits, other firms would, of course, want to enter the market. **Barriers to entry** are necessary to keep those other firms out. They come in three major kinds: economic barriers, legal barriers, and deliberate barriers.

Economic Barriers

Economic barriers derive primarily from the nature of the production technology. For example, the production technology may be characterized by high fixed costs, economies of scale, or network externalities.

High fixed costs prevent potential competitors from entering the industry on a small scale and expanding, because while they are small they cannot generate enough revenue to recover the sizable fixed costs. Competitors must therefore enter as very large-scale operations, which may be a difficult and risky thing to do. For example, the large initial investment required to build facilities that can produce specialized military aircraft make it difficult for any potential entrant to challenge existing firms.

natural monopoly: a monopoly that arises because the minimum efficient scale of the producing unit is large relative to the total market demand

The size of the market relative to the minimum efficient scale of a firm is also important (recall our discussion in Chapter 15). A monopoly will likely arise if the minimum efficient scale is large enough to correspond to the majority of a particular market. In such situations, any firm with less than the majority of the market will be producing at higher per-unit costs than a firm that is producing above the minimum efficient scale. Ultimately, these smaller competitors will be uncompetitive compared to a firm with monopoly power. A monopoly that emerges because of economies of scale is called a **natural monopoly**.

Network externalities (see Chapter 16) can also lead to monopolization. The fact that most PC users have come to use Windows operating systems and software written for those systems gives Microsoft an advantage that a competitor would find extremely hard to challenge.

Legal Barriers

Legal barriers include copyrights (which protect creative works), franchises and concessions (which directly prohibit entry), patents (which prevent other firms from using innovations), and trademarks (which protect brand names). Legal barriers provide the oldest and most secure foundations for monopoly. In times past, kings frequently granted monopoly rights as a reward for services rendered to them. In the United States, patent protection allows a firm exclusive use of an invention for an extended period of time, usually 17 to 20 years. If the invention produces a new and unique good or facilitates production at much lower costs than competitors incur, a monopoly can result.

How can one determine which type of enterprise, brand, or type of work deserves such legal protection? Critics often argue that the government is excessively generous in providing patents or trademarks, which can stifle market competition, noting that a well-endowed firm with market power has resources available to lobby the government to grant such concessions. When this occurs, it is another example of the rent-seeking behavior described in earlier chapters.

Deliberate Barriers

exclusionary practices: when a firm gets its suppliers or distributors to agree not to provide goods or services to potential competitors

A deliberate barrier involves the physical, financial, or political intimidation of potential competitors. Not surprisingly, many such "barriers" are illegal. For example, a monopolist might induce the supplier of an essential raw material not to supply potential competitors, or it might get a distributor to agree not to distribute products produced by a rival. Such deals, designed to exclude competitors from access to necessary goods and services, are called **exclusionary practices**.

predatory pricing: a powerful seller's temporary pricing of its goods or services below cost, in order to drive weaker competitors out of business

A powerful monopolist might also discourage potential competitors by engaging in **predatory pricing**. Whenever small competitors enter the market, the monopolist may temporarily lower the price of its product to a level so low that it does not cover costs, in order to drive its new rivals out of business. In international markets, selling output in another country at prices below the cost of domestic production is called **dumping**.

dumping: selling in foreign countries at prices that are below the firm's costs of production

A powerful monopolist might also threaten smaller potential competitors with unfounded (but very expensive) lawsuits, in attempts to intimidate or bankrupt them. In such cases, the size of the monopolist relative to potential competitors is clearly important: These strategies are possible only for relatively large, established firms with "deep pockets." Acts of violence are not unheard of as barriers to entry, most notably in monopolies run by organized crime.

2.2 EXAMPLES OF MONOPOLY

Although earlier we described monopoly as an "idealized" case, rarely if ever found in reality, examples of *near*-monopolies are fairly easy to find. For example, we have already mentioned Microsoft's dominance in PC operating systems. If a firm is the only supplier in a given geographic area, it is called a **local monopoly**. For example, a small, isolated town may have only one hardware store, which has a local monopoly for the sale of certain products. A university bookstore is another example of a local monopoly, in the provision of textbooks (although the store may face competition from online retailers).

local monopoly: a monopoly limited to a specific geographic area

Older textbooks often cited industries in transportation, communications, and public utilities as examples of natural monopolies. Until relatively recently, for example, the U.S. Postal Service had a monopoly on the delivery of letters and packages. Railroads, phone companies, and electric companies were traditionally operated either directly by the government or as **regulated monopolies**—that is, private companies run under government supervision. It would obviously have been inefficient, it was often argued, to have two mail carriers delivering to the same house, or two lines of railroad tracks, or multiple separate grids of electrical transmission wires.

regulated monopoly: a monopoly run under government supervision

In recent years, however, competition, deregulation, and privatization have complicated this picture. Nowadays, the U.S. Postal Service has competition in many markets from FedEx, UPS, and other firms, and it is not rare to see trucks with each of the three insignias delivering to the same business district or neighborhood on the same day. Market structure in communications and utilities has become more sophisticated; the aspects with large economies of scale (such as maintenance of the electrical grid) are separated from parts of the business where economies of scale are not so great (such as generation of electricity). What might once have seemed obvious (i.e., that utilities should be run as natural monopolies) may therefore no longer be so.

2.3 PROFIT MAXIMIZATION FOR A MONOPOLIST

In choosing what level of output to produce, a monopolistic firm follows the general pattern of behavior of a profit-maximizing firm as described in Chapter 16, seeking the level at which its marginal cost is equal to its marginal revenue ($MC = MR$). But although its costs are determined in the same way as those of a perfectly competitive firm, its revenues are significantly different.

A price-taking firm has such a small market share that it can sell however much of its product it chooses to at the going price. Because it is "small," no amount sold would, in theory, have any impact on the price determined by market conditions of supply and demand. In contrast, because a monopolistic firm is the sole supplier of a given product, it possesses enormous influence over the price of its product. Whereas the demand curve for the price-taking firm is horizontal, reflecting the firm's powerlessness over price, the demand curve for the monopolist's output is identical to the overall market demand curve for that product. In other words, it slopes downward.

The monopolistic firm is able to sell more only by inducing consumers as a group to buy more. That is, to sell more it must either mount an effective advertising campaign (to shift out the demand curve that it faces) or offer its product at a lower price. Another way to look at the difference is to note that the monopolist can raise its price, losing some sales but obtaining more revenue per unit for those remaining. In contrast, the price-taking firm will sell absolutely nothing if it raises its price above the existing market level. In short, a monopolist is a **price maker**, not a price taker. It can set both price and quantity, although the price-quantity combinations that it can choose are constrained by market demand.

price maker: a seller that can set the selling price, constrained only by demand conditions

Consider how a producer would behave if, instead of receiving a flat amount for each unit of output sold, it were a monopolist and faced the full schedule of market demand. Table 17.1 shows how the firm must, in order to sell more of its output, drop its selling price. It can sell 1 unit if it sets the price at $44, for example. But if it wants to sell 2 units, it must drop the price to $40 each in order to find another buyer. The first two columns of Table 17.1 thus describe the demand curve for this good.

The fourth column in Table 17.1 indicates how much *extra* revenue the monopolist would gain for producing and selling an additional unit. Although initial revenue for selling 1 unit is $44, if the monopolist wants instead to sell 2 units it must sell *both* units at the lower price of $40, receiving total revenue of $80. It thus gains $40 from selling the second unit but also loses the $4 (from the original $44) that it would have gotten from selling the first unit alone. Marginal revenue from the second unit, then, is only $36 (40 minus 4 or, what amounts to the same thing, 80 minus 44).

The remainder of Table 17.1 is calculated in the same fashion. Note that after the monopolist sells 6 units, total revenue starts to go *down* (from its peak at $144), and marginal revenue becomes negative. Recall from Chapter 4 that the upper regions of demand curves (where

Table 17.1 **Marginal Revenue for a Monopolist**

Quantity of output	Selling price ($)	Total revenue ($)	Marginal revenue ($)
1	44	44	44
2	40	80	36
3	36	108	28
4	32	128	20
5	28	140	12
6	24	144	4
7	20	140	−4
8	16	128	−12
9	12	108	−20

quantities are low and prices are high) tend to be elastic, meaning that reductions in price increase revenue. The lower regions tend to be inelastic, such that reductions in price *decrease* revenue. This is exactly what is illustrated numerically in Table 17.1.

We can use the data from Table 17.1 to construct a demand curve for the good, as well as a marginal revenue curve. These are shown in Figure 17.1. The marginal revenue curve lies below the demand curve (after the first unit) and falls off more steeply, entering the negative part of the graph after 6 units.

Figure 17.1 also shows the marginal cost curve for the good, which is similar to the cost curves we derived in Chapter 15. (The cost curves are independent of whether a producer is competitive or a monopolist; only the demand side of the market is different.) The monopolist will maximize profits by producing the quantity at which $MR = MC$, which occurs at point A in Figure 17.1. This is an output level of 5 units. Reading horizontally from the MC curve, you see that the marginal cost of producing the fifth unit is $12. The graph and table show that the marginal revenue from the fifth unit is also $12.

Figure 17.1 **Monopoly Profit Maximization**

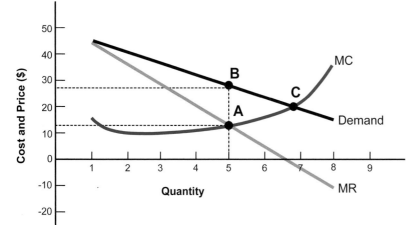

A monopolist decides how much to produce by setting marginal cost equal to marginal revenue (point A). The price that buyers are willing to pay for this quantity is read off the demand curve (point B). The monopolist produces less, and charges more, than would firms in a competitive equilibrium (point C).

The monopolist, however, will not charge its customers $12 per unit. Reading up from a quantity of 5 to the demand curve, we see that customers are willing to pay up to $28 each for the 5 units produced, as shown by point B on the demand curve in Figure 17.1 (see also the "Selling price" column in Table 17.1). The monopolist will produce at a marginal cost to itself of $12 per unit but will charge customers $28 per unit to maximize profits.

What level of profits will the monopolist make in the long run? Unlike in the competitive case, in which we assume that economic profits are driven to zero by the entrance of new producers, monopolists *can* make sustained positive economic profits, as long as barriers to entry keep potential competitors out. To determine the actual level of profits, you need to know more about the cost structure of the firm. This is investigated in the appendix to this chapter. If the monopolist's cost structure is such that it makes economic *losses*, presumably in the long run it will choose to exit the industry.

2.4 MONOPOLY AND INEFFICIENCY

Monopoly power generally leads to inefficiencies in the form of deadweight loss (discussed in Chapter 5), when compared to a competitive outcome. Because the monopolist produces at an output level at which the marginal willingness to pay (price) exceeds marginal cost, society could gain from increased output of the product. From the point of view of society, in other words, the cost of additional production is lower than the marginal benefits.

In the above example, buyers value the sixth unit at $24, whereas the cost of producing the sixth unit is less than $24 (as seen in Figure 17.1). The social benefit of producing the sixth unit is greater than the social marginal cost, and society would be better off if it were produced. The "curving triangle" ABC in Figure 17.1 represents the deadweight loss from the monopolist's decision, compared to a competitive situation in which marginal willingness to pay and marginal cost would be equal (at point C, where 7 units are produced).

Another way to examine the efficiency and distributional effects is to analyze producer surplus and consumer surplus. In Figure 17.2 the competitive equilibrium (price-taking) situation is portrayed by thinking of the MC curve as the sum of the MC curves of numerous competitive firms. The resulting competitive price and quantity are P_E and Q_E. The contrasting monopoly price and quantity are P_M and Q_M. As we have just noted, the fact that the monopolist will supply a lower quantity and charge a higher price creates deadweight loss. It also causes a distributional shift away from the buyers of the good and toward the monopolist. The rectangle labeled "transfer" would be part of consumer surplus in a competitive market, but the monopolist extracts the value represented by the rectangle from the consumer, thus *reducing overall consumer surplus*. Market power creates more benefit for the seller—which is why businesses like to get it—but at the expense of buyers of the good (lost consumer surplus) and of efficiency for society as a whole as it creates a deadweight loss relative to the competitive outcome.

Figure 17.2 **The Welfare Costs of Monopoly Power**

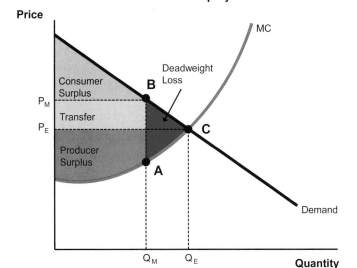

A monopolist imposes a deadweight loss on society relative to a situation of perfect competition and transfers surplus from consumers to itself.

Sometimes, people justify monopolies on the grounds that they create situations that foster innovation. Other justifications note that, in the 1950s and 1960s, the large U.S. firms in the steel and automotive industries shared some of their monopoly profits with their workers, providing levels of wages and benefits (especially pensions) that helped cast large firms with such market power in a positive light. Such benefits could not, however, be maintained when foreign competition forced them to cut such costs in order to remain profitable. But there are other economic objections to monopoly power. One of the most common is the claim that a lack of competition makes a monopolist lazy. A secure monopolist has less incentive to please customers, manage costs efficiently, and adopt new ideas than a firm that has its survival on the line. We should, moreover, consider what monopolists do with their positive economic profits. A monopolist may, in fact, need to spend most or all of the profits merely keeping entry barriers up. For instance, when monopolies are generated by exclusive concessions or licenses given out by governments, producers might spend much or all of their economic profits on rent-seeking activities of lobbying and bribing government officials in order to maintain their exclusive right to produce a good.

2.5 CAN MONOPOLY BE EFFICIENT?

However, in some situations the efficiency cost of monopoly may not be as negative as the foregoing analysis suggests. In some cases, monopoly may even be preferable to a competitive market.

Natural Monopoly

We have already mentioned one case in which a single big firm may be socially preferable to many small ones: natural monopoly. Competitive firms would face per-unit costs that were unnecessarily high, but a monopolist could exploit its economies of scale. Often, natural monopolies are regulated. The government allows only one firm to produce the good but mandates that it produce at higher levels, and sell at lower prices, than the firm would choose on its own. One prominent example is the Metropolitan Transportation Authority in greater New York. A private company that provides a variety of public transportation services, it is fundamentally a monopoly, but the local government regulates its pricing policy.

Regulated monopolies can, nonetheless, present the government with a dilemma, especially when substantial economies of scale are present. Often the marginal cost of production is very low. For example, on a passenger railroad line the marginal cost of transporting one more rider, assuming some seats are empty, is very low after the rails, engines, and schedules are all in place. Efficiently setting the price of a ticket equal to the marginal cost of providing a ride, however, would mean that the monopolist's revenues would not cover its costs, making its business untenable.

In some cases, the government subsidizes the monopolist to encourage socially beneficial price setting and levels of production. But although subsidies are a commonsense manner of persuading natural monopolists to increase production, they are politically very unpopular: Many taxpayers resent having their tax dollars go to private companies. Rather than regulating price, government might also regulate the company's profit rate or its output level. Alas, each comes with its own problem. Compelling companies not to exceed a specified profit rate creates an incentive to engage in wasteful spending (on, e.g., excess administration or perks for company executives), because higher costs permit the generation of greater absolute profits, whatever the maximum profit *rate*. And requiring companies to provide a minimum level of output to meet the needs of society creates an incentive to skimp on quality of service and materials used, in order to cut costs and thereby earn a higher profit. So although it is certainly true that natural monopolies make sense in certain industries and that such monopolies must be regulated, there is no single optimal method of regulation. It is likely to depend on the individual case.

Despite the economic case in favor of natural monopolies in some instances, many economists argue that *all* monopolies should be discouraged, if not abolished, because of their belief that competition always leads to a more efficient distribution and, invariably, lower prices. In recent decades, a significant deregulation of natural monopolies has taken place and not only in the United States. One well-publicized case was the privatization of municipal water supplies in Bolivia in the late 1990s. Such a move does not always deliver the expected benefits, namely, lower prices and greater availability of the commodity for consumers (see Box 17.1).

BOX 17.1   PRIVATIZATION OF MUNICIPAL WATER SUPPLIES

Municipal water supply is a common example of a natural monopoly. The significant fixed cost of water treatment facilities and supply pipes means that the minimum efficient scale is normally so large that it forms an effective barrier to entry for potential competitors. Municipal water has been traditionally supplied either by nonprofit public utilities or by highly regulated private companies that are limited in the prices that they can charge their customers.

In recent decades, some economists have proposed moving toward a greater degree of privatization of municipal water supplies, with fewer regulations on the prices that companies can charge. With water privatization, different companies bid for the right to become the monopoly provider. Under most privatization contracts, which commonly last for four to ten years, the water supply infrastructure remains publicly owned. However, proponents of privatization contend that for-profit companies will be motivated to operate water supply systems in a more efficient manner than public utilities.

Privatization of water supplies has been most controversial in developing countries. In the late 1990s, the World Bank pushed scores of poor countries to privatize their water supplies as a condition for receiving much-needed economic assistance. In several cases, most infamously Bolivia, private companies raised the price of water so much that poor families could not afford enough to meet basic needs.

The need for better water management is especially acute in China. With contracts to supply water becoming more lucrative, the number of private water utilities in China has skyrocketed. As water demands increase in Beijing, wells dug around the city must reach ever-greater depths to hit fresh water. But in China private water suppliers must pay the cost of constructing new wells. In order to recover investment costs, companies have dramatically raised the price of water. "It's more than most families can afford to pay," says Ge Yun, an economist with the Xinjiang Conservation Fund. "So as more water goes private, fewer people have access to it."

The World Bank continues to promote privatization, noting that higher water prices are necessary to induce conservation. Public utilities rarely charge enough to reflect the true economic and social costs of water; privatization advocates argue that this is the root cause of unsustainable water use. From the perspective of social welfare, market prices are too low if they fail to account for externalities. But economic efficiency may conflict with the goal of equity. Privatization may work best when combined with policies ensuring that the poorest can afford enough water to meet their basic needs, as in the South African system, which provides a minimum supply of water to all households free to ensure that basic needs can be met. Only water usage above this minimum amount is billed to households.

Source: Jennen Interlandi, "The New Oil: Should Private Companies Control Our Most Precious Natural Resource?" *Newsweek*, October 18, 2010.

Intellectual Property

The problem of covering costs arises again in the case of research costs for the development of new technologies. Patents, copyrights, and other protections of intellectual property are not granted simply to enrich inventors. The rationale for these forms of government-granted monopoly power is to *encourage* research and innovation. Development of new computer technologies, medical technologies, and drugs can be very expensive. Firms argue that they need a period of exclusive, high profits to finance their research and development. Without the ability to patent an innovation, it is argued, firms might find research unprofitable and so do less of it, to the detriment of all.

Of course, patents also have a social cost in that they restrict the production of some important and valuable goods while raising their price. The cost can be extremely high: In many cases, restricted access to certain indispensable medications results in unnecessary human suffering and premature death. Also, as societies become more concerned about climate change, there is concern that allowing new low-emission energy technologies to be patented could slow their rates of adoption, as the owner of the patent would produce such technologies based on maximum profit, not social need. Other forms of government action have been suggested as ways of encouraging invention that would not carry the patent system's harmful effect of restricting production and use. These include direct funding of research, offering research prizes, and buying patents from companies for a one-time fee.

Pressure to Appear Competitive

In the idealized case of pure monopoly, the seller is free to maximize profits. But do unregulated monopolists in the real world always maximize profits? Even if a monopolist faces neither a serious rival nor any meaningful government restriction, it may fear *potential* competitors or government action. If so, the monopolist might produce and price in a way that more closely resembles a competitive firm, out of fear that excessive monopoly profits would attract too much attention.

Often the barriers protecting a monopoly can be bypassed by producing a similar, though not identical, product. Monopolies held by American railroads in the early twentieth century, for example, were weakened not by competing railroads but by truck and airline competition that increased the elasticity of demand for railroad transportation. Textbooks written as recently as the 1970s sometimes asserted that competition between telephone companies and postal systems was impossible, because there was no way of sending documents by telephone—an idea that seems quaintly old-fashioned in an era of fax machines and e-mail. Microsoft has argued that even though it currently enjoys a near-monopoly, it is "competitive" in a dynamic sense because new technologies could arise at any time to upset its dominance in the market for PC operating systems.

Firms with market power might also be cautious out of fear of government action. Since the 1930s, most industrialized countries have created government agencies charged with investigating cases of monopoly power. Governments may take over monopolies, regulate them, or break them up into smaller companies if their existence is found to be socially harmful. The first ruling in the *United States vs. Microsoft* case (in which Microsoft was charged with violating antitrust statutes and engaging in abusive practices in its operating system and Web browser sales) mandated a breakup, although a federal appeals court ruling focused instead on changing its business practices. Some monopolists may refrain from fully exploiting their power in order to be less visibly irksome—hence less likely to be targeted for the sort of attention that Microsoft repeatedly receives.

Perfect Price Discrimination

Although we usually think of firms as charging the same price to all buyers, this need not be the case. An interesting—if rare—welfare result occurs in the case of what is called a "perfectly price-discriminating" monopolist.

price discrimination: a seller's charging different prices to different buyers, depending on their ability and willingness to pay

A **price-discriminating** seller is one that charges different prices to different buyers, depending on their ability and willingness to pay. How can a seller do this? One way is to keep its prices a secret. In the real world, car salespeople often carry out a version of price discrimination, offering a price that is closer to the list price and pressing more options on a buyer who comes into the showroom dressed in expensive clothing, while more rapidly offering discounts to a less–affluent-looking client. Airline companies characteristically do something similar, charging business travelers—who are generally quite inflexible about when they must fly—a higher price, on average, than vacationers. A clever way of doing this is by offering discounts for flights that require a weekend stay away (because doing so generally excludes business travelers).

Another way is to offer discounts structured so that some people, but—importantly—not others, will pass them up. Why do stores sometimes offer bulk discounts or "two for the price of one" sales or offer discounts only if you come on particular "sale days" or go to the trouble of bringing in a coupon? They are also trying to separate out the price-unresponsive

Figure 17.3 **Price Discrimination**

A price-discriminating seller can charge different prices to different people, thereby capturing what would otherwise be consumer surplus.

customers (who will buy anyway) from the price-responsive ones, who will take the time and trouble to find sales, mail in coupons for rebates, and so on.

This possibility is illustrated in the demand curve in Figure 17.3. Customer A does not care about getting a low price and would be willing to pay price P_A for the first few units (Q_A) of the good. The seller would like to be able to charge Customer A this high price and then drop the price a little for Customer B, who would not buy any of the good at price P_A but is happy to buy at price P_B, increasing the total quantity sold to Q_B. And so on. In this case, consumer surplus is whittled away—each customer is paying close to the maximum that he or she is willing to pay. The seller is reaping the benefits—extra revenue, represented by shaded rectangles on the graph, for each sale made above the price charged to the last buyer (P_D). Compare this to the "baseline" monopoly case discussed earlier. Remember that the monopolist faced the dilemma of undercutting itself by lowering the price on all goods sold by offering more to consumers; in the case of price discrimination, this problem is at least partially overcome.

If a monopolist could vary the price continuously—that is, not in discrete steps but over the entire demand curve, as shown in Figure 17.4—it would be engaging in "perfect" price discrimination. In such a hypothetical case, the monopolist captures the entire consumer surplus. Consumers therefore "gain" nothing from their purchases, because everyone spends exactly how much he or she is willing to pay—not a penny less. From a social point of view, a large transfer of benefit takes place from buyers to the monopolist. But the earlier deadweight efficiency

Figure 17.4 **Perfectly Price-Discriminating Monopolist**

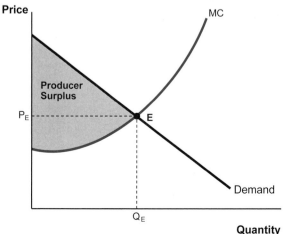

With perfect price discrimination, a monopolist has no reason to restrict output and will therefore create no deadweight loss.

loss would also be eliminated, in contrast to the case of a monopolist that is *not* perfectly price discriminating. This is because the seller in this case has no reason to restrict output and would produce until $P = MC$, which is no different from the outcome under perfect competition.

The equity consequences of price discrimination are interesting. In a case in which the monopolist reaps large profits at consumers' expense, price discrimination seems unfair to consumers. However, price discrimination may sometimes just allow a producer to break even. The only nonprofit mental health clinic in town, for example, may offer its services on a "sliding scale," in which the price charged to a client rises with his or her income. The care given to lower-income clients is thus subsidized by the higher prices paid by those with a higher ability to pay. If it were forced to charge only a single price, the clinic might have to close or turn away its poorest clients.

We can summarize the discussion of monopolies and efficiency in a few points:

- In cases in which a monopolist could be broken up into many cost-efficient, more competitive firms, the competitive option would generally be more socially beneficial.
- In cases of natural monopolies, in which competitive firms would not be cost efficient, the question is not one of "monopoly versus competition" but, rather, one of how best to structure and regulate a monopoly.
- When it comes to fostering innovation, a system of government-granted exclusive monopoly rights may bring about benefits. However, alternative methods of encouraging research and development might bring about even higher benefits.
- Monopolists that fear potential competition or government regulatory action might behave in a more socially efficient manner than otherwise (something not considered by the baseline monopoly model).
- Perfectly price-discriminating monopolists do not restrict output, and therefore cause no efficiency loss, but their actions may lead to concerns about negative distributional consequences.

As noted earlier, however, cases of *pure* monopoly happen extremely rarely—if at all—in the real world. Most goods have *some* reasonable substitutes. If railroads were monopolized, people might turn to trucks or cars, for example. Even if only one drug company produced the most effective drug for a medical condition, drugs produced by other companies can normally at least help. This brings us to a discussion of cases that are neither perfect competition nor pure monopoly.

Discussion Questions

1. On many campuses, the official college or university bookstores used to have monopoly power in selling textbooks to students. What would you call this kind of monopoly? Is it still the case at your institution? Why or why not?
2. Does it sometimes make sense to have just one company in charge of providing something? Some users of electronics are frustrated by the lack of compatibility among their gadgets and between their gadgets and those of their friends. Might it be better to have just one company manufacture computers, gaming machines, music players, cell phones, and the like in such a way that they all work smoothly with one another? What would be the advantages and disadvantages of such a situation?

3. MONOPOLISTIC COMPETITION

Monopolistic competition shares characteristics with both perfect competition and monopoly. Because of its name, however, many students confuse monopolistic competition with monopoly. It is important not to, because monopolistic competition is generally closer to the competitive end of the spectrum.

3.1 THE CONDITIONS OF MONOPOLISTIC COMPETITION

Monopolistic competition is generally characterized by the following conditions:

1. There are numerous small buyers and sellers.
2. The sellers produce goods that are close substitutes but are not identical. Products are often *differentiated,* which means that each seller's product is somewhat different from that offered by the other sellers.
3. Producers of the good or service can freely enter or exit the industry.
4. Buyers and sellers have perfect information.

The above conditions are identical to those of perfect competition, except that products are differentiated instead of identical. In this case, buyers care which producer they buy from.

3.2 EXAMPLES OF MONOPOLISTIC COMPETITION

How many different brands of blue jeans can you name? How many fast-food restaurants might you find in a large town or a city? Why might there be three different brands of gasoline offered at stations at the same busy intersection? These are all examples of differentiated products. McDonald's, Burger King, and Wendy's franchises all sell hamburgers, but they prepare them a little differently, and each franchise is located in a different spot. Different gas stations may offer slightly different products, different levels of service, or different complementary products or services (e.g., a convenience store or a car wash). Such differences in product offerings, however slight, often are sufficient to elicit a degree of brand loyalty on the part of the consumer, although its strength varies considerably across the population.

Situations of monopolistic competition seem to be ubiquitous in contemporary industrialized societies. In everyday life, we see many firms competing to sell us slightly different varieties of the same goods and services.

3.3 PROFIT MAXIMIZATION WITH MONOPOLISTIC COMPETITION

Product differentiation means that each seller is a miniature monopoly, the only producer of its particular good. Indeed, it is this fact that makes the firms *monopolistically* competitive. Starbucks coffee is a classic example. Although many argue that it produces superior coffee (and many others argue the contrary), it once had a virtual "monopoly" on the "amenities" that it offered along with its coffee—comfortable couches and Wi-Fi access, for example—as part of its "product line." These produced legions of loyal customers, and while many other smaller coffee outlets have mimicked Starbucks in this regard, Starbucks obtained an early enough start on the competition to secure for itself a sizable share of the coffee-drinking population.

We see similar brand loyalty in the fast-food industry. Some people, for example, might claim that McDonald's hamburgers are far superior to Wendy's and might be willing to continue to buy from McDonald's even if it raises its prices. You might be willing to pay a higher price for milk at a local convenience store, even though you know that the price is lower at the big supermarket miles away. Whereas perfectly competitive sellers will lose *all* their customers if they raise their prices above the prevailing market price, a firm that sells a differentiated product may have a little leeway. Firms in a situation of monopolistic competition face a downward-sloping demand curve for their particular product.

The fact that such firms face a downward-sloping demand curve means that their profit-maximization problem more closely resembles that of a monopolist (illustrated in Figure 17.1). They also face marginal revenue curves that lie below the demand curve. A sophisticated monopolistic competitor, with good information, or at least a good "feel" for market circumstances, will choose an output level by setting $MR = MC$ at point A in Figure 17.1 and will charge customers the price set by the demand curve, at point B.

Unlike what occurs in the case of monopoly, however, the demand for such a firm's good is affected by the availability of close substitutes. If a Wendy's restaurant shuts down, demand at McDonald's, Burger King, and other restaurants and franchises nearby is likely to rise. If a new Burger King opens up, demand for food provided by many existing nearby restaurants may fall. Even though no other firm produces an *identical* good, substitutes often are close enough to induce meaningful changes in the market.

The fact that entry and exit are easy means that if any monopolistically competitive firm is making positive economic profits, new producers will be attracted to the market and will begin to sell similar goods (e.g., other hamburgers). As new firms enter the market, the demand for the specific product in question (e.g., a McDonald's hamburger) will fall, as illustrated in Figure 17.5. Suppose the demand for a particular firm's products is D_1, and it is making positive economic profits. Other firms will enter the market, selling similar products, reducing the firm's demand to D_2. This will cut into the firm's revenues and profits. How many new firms will enter, and how much will demand fall for any one firm? In economists' approximation, it happens just up to the point where every firm is making zero economic profits. (See the appendix to this chapter for a graphical explanation.)

Figure 17.5 **The Effect of the Entry of New Firms on a Monopolistically Competitive Firm**

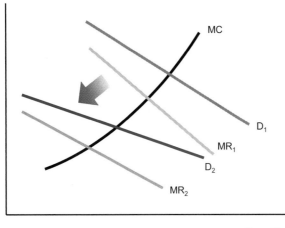

Price

MC

D_1

MR_1

D_2

MR_2

Quantity

A condition of easy entry and exit means that new firms can enter, driving down the demand experienced by any one monopolistically competitive firm.

Like the monopolist, the monopolistically competitive firm faces a downward-sloping demand curve and so produces less, and charges a higher price, than a perfectly competitive firm. As in the case of a perfectly competitive firm, however, free entry and exit in monopolistically competitive markets means that any positive economic profits to be gained should only be temporary, as new competitors move in to exploit new opportunities to earn money.

3.4 MONOPOLISTIC COMPETITION AND LONG-RUN EFFICIENCY

Compared to perfectly competitive firms, monopolistically competitive firms produce lower levels of output and charge higher prices. Like monopolies, they stop short of producing at levels where the social marginal benefit of production is just equal to the social marginal cost. It can also be shown (and *is* shown in the appendix to this chapter) that such firms have higher unit costs than would occur in a perfectly competitive market. In short, they operate inefficiently.

Monopolistically competitive firms may, like monopolists, expend considerable resources to protect their miniature monopoly. While perhaps unable to keep competitors from entering their general industry, they can try, increasingly, to differentiate their product. Firms in this

nonprice competition: competition through activities other than setting prices, such as advertising and location

kind of market structure are observed to engage in a great deal of **nonprice competition**. That is, they compete with other producers by advertising heavily in order to make buyers want *their* particular product (e.g., Gap jeans) and by using attractive signs and packaging, selecting better locations, varying their hours of operation, and so on.

In terms of social benefit, it seems evident that resources would be better spent producing fewer varieties of goods and services, at lower costs, and with less advertising. Yet some cast a more positive light on the problem, focusing instead on consumer preferences. They argue that inefficiencies in production are merely the price that must be paid to satisfy consumers' *desire* for variety (and, presumably, also for massive advertising and flashy packaging). Although probably not the whole story, it may very well be that the highest social benefit lies somewhere between dull, completely standardized products and the extreme proliferation of consumer goods that we currently observe.

Discussion Questions

1. Think of a somewhat differentiated good or service that you can buy locally in any number of different places—for example, a gallon of gasoline or a cup of coffee. Do you observe differences in prices? What differences might lead to these variations in prices? (Or is the assumption of perfect information violated? Does everyone know where the cheapest version can be found?) What examples of nonprice competition can you identify among the various sellers?
2. Do you think that the amount of variety in the goods and services that you are offered as a consumer is excessive? Just about right? Too limited? Do some forms of nonprice competition have consequences for long-term well-being and sustainability?

4. OLIGOPOLY

While oligopoly shares some characteristics of competitive markets, it is closer to monopoly in that a small number of firms possess a sizable share of the market. Oligopoly is similar to monopoly (and monopolistic competition) in that output is lower, and prices are higher, than would be the case under perfect competition. Oligopolists, like monopolists, may also possess significant political and economic clout on local or national levels.

4.1 MARKET STRUCTURE OF AN OLIGOPOLISTIC INDUSTRY

The oligopolistic market structure is characterized by the following conditions:

1. The market is dominated by *only a few* sellers, at least some of which control enough of the market to be able to influence the market price.
2. Entry is difficult.

The products produced by oligopolists may be either standardized or differentiated. Various assumptions may be made about how much information is available to producers and their customers in markets with oligopolies.

The most important implication of the condition that there are few firms is that the actions of each firm have effects on the market that rival firms cannot ignore. It means, among other things, that the rivals may respond in ways that, in turn, require a response from the original firm(s). In short, oligopoly exists if each firm must include, among the factors that it considers in deciding on its own actions, the possible reactions of rival firms.

Remember that in perfect competition the seller need not be concerned with the actions of others. All that such a seller needs to know is the market price. In the case of monopoly, of course, there are no other sellers to worry about. In the case of monopolistic competition, with many sellers, the effect of the action of any one seller is spread out over many other sellers. But in an oligopolistic situation, each firm needs to be keenly aware of what each of the (few) other firms is doing.

4.2 EXAMPLES OF OLIGOPOLY

industrial concentration ratio: the share of production, sales, or revenues attributable to the largest firms in an industry

An **industrial concentration ratio** is the share of total *production, sales,* or *revenues* attributable to the largest producers in an industry. The share of domestic *production* accounted for by the four largest firms is a traditional indicator of how oligopolistic an industry has become. Despite the absence of a precise definition, we say that an oligopoly exists wherever a "small" number of firms (perhaps between four and ten) possess something more than a majority of the market share (e.g., about two-thirds of the market share or more).

We presented some data on industrial concentration ratios in Chapter 0. In addition, according to the U.S. government's 2007 Economic Census (the most recent data available), the concentration ratio for credit card companies is 79 percent, for breakfast cereal manufacturing, 85 percent, and for glass container manufacturing, 86 percent. All three appear to satisfy even stringent criteria for oligopoly. The market for wireless telecommunications services is also dominated by just a few sellers. (See Box 17.2 for another example of oligopoly.)

4.3 OLIGOPOLY AND THE BEHAVIOR OF FIRMS

The behavior of oligopolistic firms is truly *social* in the sense of being interdependent with the behavior of other actors; hence it appears more complex than other market structures. Instead of one theory for oligopolies, economists have many, any of which might be helpful but none of which is definitive. We briefly describe two of them here: first, the theory of strategic interaction and game theory and, second, models of collusion, cartels, and price leadership.

BOX 17.2 OLIGOPOLY AND AIRLINE MERGERS

In February 2013, US Airways and American Airlines announced their intention to merge, an $11 billion deal that would create the world's largest airline. The proposed merger follows a trend of consolidation in the airline industry in the United States. Between 2001 and 2013, the top ten airline companies in the country had already combined to form five major carriers, including mergers of Northwest and Delta in 2008 and United and Continental in 2010. If approved by federal regulators, the US Airways and American Airlines merger would create four "megacarriers" that would control 83 percent of the U.S. air passenger market.

Initially it seemed that the merger would easily receive approval, as had been the case with previous airline mergers. But in August 2013, the U.S. Justice Department, joined by the attorneys general of seven states, filed a lawsuit to block the merger, arguing that it would cause "substantial harm" to passengers by raising fares and reducing competition. The government noted that the merger would eliminate competition on more than 1,000 routes. Assistant Attorney General Bill Baer said, "As we look at the

market today, it's not functioning as competitively as it ought to be, and if this deal goes through, it's going to be much worse."

"This is the best news that consumers could have possible gotten," said Charlie Leocha, director of the Consumer Travel Alliance. Leocha indicated that previous mergers have led to higher fares and reduced choices for travelers and that the proposed merger would have the same result.

One possible outcome is that the merger will still be approved, but only with some concessions by the two airlines. For example, they may be forced to give up some landing and take-off slots at busy Reagan National Airport outside Washington, DC, thus allowing for increased competition from other airlines. Meanwhile, the airlines contend that allowing them to merge will improve their ability to compete with other large carriers, such as United and Delta.

Sources: Chris Isidore, "American-US Air Deal Would Cut Passenger Choices," CNN Money, February 8, 2013; Pete Yost and David Koenig, "Government, States Challenge Proposed Airline Merger," Associated Press, August 13, 2013.

Strategic Interaction and Game Theory

One theory is that oligopolistic firms will act strategically against one another, plotting their moves as though they were generals planning a war or opponents in a game of chess. Oligopolistic sellers are often seen as engaging in "competition" in the active, aggressive sense in which business managers use this term. That is, oligopolistic firms choose prices, marketing strategies, and the like, with an eye to "beating out" specific rivals and gaining greater market share at their expense. A classic example is the rivalry between Coke and Pepsi.

duopoly: a market with only two sellers

payoff matrix: a table used in game theory to illustrate possible outcomes for each of two players, depending on the strategy that each chooses

Game theory, which has its origin in the work of mathematician John von Neumann (1903–1957) and economist Oskar Morgenstern (1902–1977), provides a framework for the formal analysis of some types of strategic behavior. For example, consider a market with two sellers, also known as a **duopoly**. Suppose that each is trying to decide whether to set a low or a high price for the good that they both sell. They need to pay attention to what the other one does, because if Firm 1 sets a high price, Firm 2 might set a low price and end up with all the customers (or vice versa). Using game theory, we can describe a **payoff matrix**, as shown in Figure 17.6.

Figure 17.6 **A Payoff Matrix**

Firm 2's Options

	Low Price	High Price
Low Price	low profit / low profit	loss / high profit
High Price	high profit / loss	moderate profit / moderate profit

Firm 1's Options

A payoff matrix shows what the profit outcomes will be for each of two oligopolistic firms, given their decisions about what price to charge.

The entries in the payoff matrix show the profit level that each firm can expect, given its choice and the choice of its rival. The combination "loss, high profit" in the bottom-left cell, for example, shows that if Firm 1 sets a high price while Firm 2 sets a low price, Firm 1 will make a loss, while Firm 2—which now has all the customers—will make high profits. (Test yourself: What does the upper-right-hand cell represent?) Clearly, each firm would find it to its own advantage to be the only low-price seller in the market. Recognition of this fact could lead to a **price war**, in which each firm progressively cuts its prices in order to try to be the low-price seller. Although a price war could, in some real-world cases, last until one party went out of business, in Figure 17.6 we have illustrated a case in which, when both firms set low prices, both keep a share of customers and make low profits. This is shown in the cell at the upper left. However, if both set high prices, as shown in the bottom-right cell, they could both make moderate profits while keeping a share of customers.

price war: a situation in which a firm cuts prices in order to try to undercut its rivals, and the rivals react by cutting prices even more

In this model, we assume that the firms are "noncooperative"—that is, that they are archrivals and do not communicate or cooperate with each other. Noncooperative game theory suggests that a rational firm will choose the option that will leave it best off (or least damaged) regardless of what its rival does. Looking at the payoff matrix in Figure 17.6, we can see that Firm 1 will choose to set a low price rather than a high price. If Firm 1 sets a low price and Firm 2 chooses "low," Firm 1 gets low, but positive, profits. If Firm 1 sets a low price and Firm 2 chooses "high," Firm 1 gets high profits. Regardless of what Firm 2 does, then, Firm 1 gets better outcomes than the corresponding loss or moderate profits than it would get by setting a high price. A similar analysis for Firm 2 shows that it also will choose to set its prices *low*. The "solution" to the game is the (low profit, low profit) cell. Yet in a certain sense it is not a solution at all, since what appears *individually* rational for each firm actually produces a perverse outcome that is suboptimal for both.

Scenarios such as this are often referred to as "prisoner's dilemmas" because of the well-known formulation in terms of prisoners who are held separately and asked to confess to a crime that they committed together. If neither confesses, they both go free after one year (call this situation a "plea bargain"). However, if only one confesses (ratting on the other), he goes free while the other goes to jail for 10 years. If both confess, they each are sentenced to jail for three years. The best strategy, for a prisoner who does not know what his partner in crime will do, is to confess. That way, he is assured of not having to go to jail for more than three years. (What outcome would be *best* for both? What would be necessary for them to achieve it?)

Strategic thinking can also be applied to nonprice competition, which oligopolists also frequently employ. For example, sellers may need to decide whether to spend a lot or a little on advertising, packaging, and booths at sales conventions. What they decide to do will, at least in part, depend on what their rivals do. Nonprice competition is most likely when each firm is selling a somewhat differentiated product.

Another form of game theory imagines that the parties do not make their decisions simultaneously, as in our example, but one after the other. The theory of "sequential games" covers situations in which one firm moves first and then the second chooses its strategy. Each firm's expectations about the reaction of the other are key to describing the probable outcomes of such a game. More recently, formal game theory has also been applied to "cooperative" games in which, for example, actors may bargain toward a mutually beneficial outcome.

Collusion, Cartels, and Price Leadership

Clearly, Firm 1 and Firm 2 in the above example (not to mention the prisoners) would do better if they got together and agreed on a joint strategy that gave them both their best outcomes. If the two firms could make a binding agreement to both keep their prices high, they could both make moderate profits instead of ending up at the noncooperative solution in which each makes low profits. Firms that cooperate in this way are said to engage in **collusion**. They get together and form a monopoly (at least a local one) for pricing purposes, even though they keep their production activities separate.

collusion: cooperation among potential rivals to gain market power as a group

Cartels such as the Organization of Petroleum Exporting Countries (OPEC) are examples of explicit collusion. OPEC did not try to keep its collusion a secret but instead announced its formation and its high prices.

Tacit collusion takes place when sellers collude more subtly, without creation of a cartel. Because cartels are by and large illegal in many industrialized countries, sellers must often pass information around on the sly. An industry association may collect information and post it on the Web so that all members will know what price the others are charging. Such flows of information make it easier to cooperate and to monitor compliance with tacit **price fixing**, in which all sellers implicitly agree to maintain a common price. One form of implicit collusion is **price leadership**, in which everyone in the industry looks to one firm, raising their prices when it does and lowering them likewise. Such price leadership, many believe, characterized the U.S. steel and airlines industries for years. Price leadership tends to be more common when the firms all sell identical, standardized products.

tacit collusion: collusion that takes place without creation of a cartel

price fixing: a form of collusion in which a group of sellers implicitly agrees to maintain a common price

price leadership: a form of collusion in which many sellers follow the price changes instituted by one particular seller

However, as members of OPEC discovered, collusion can be hard to sustain. Each seller has an incentive to undercut the set price privately, in order to sell a little more. Nevertheless, collusion has sometimes been persistent. Members may realize that it is in their greater long-term interest to stick with the collusive price rather than to risk losing everything by starting a price war.

4.4 HOW COMMON IS OLIGOPOLY?

Oligopolistic industries tend to be inefficient, for the same reasons that monopoly often is. In fact, oligopoly is often even less efficient. Because production decisions remain separate, there is less possibility of even reaping advantages of economies of scale.

Although oligopoly has traditionally been defined in terms of few sellers and difficult entry, the key feature that distinguishes the *behavior* of sellers is not so much the number of them as the existence of interdependence among them. A market can, in fact, display oligopolistic characteristics even with easy entry and hence many possible sellers. When four firms control 80 percent of the market, for example, it has little effect on their behavior whether the remaining 20 percent of the market is divided among 10 sellers or 1,000.

Oligopolies can also be local. Not all industries experience high concentration ratios at the national level. For example, the U.S. Census indicates that in 2007 the top four retail florists shared 2.1 percent of the total national market, and the top four credit unions shared 10.1 percent. Even when industries are not so concentrated at the national level, however, firms may behave in somewhat oligopolistic ways more locally. If there are two florists in a town, for example, you can bet that each keeps track of what the other is charging, where it is advertising, and how it adjusts its prices on Valentine's Day and Mother's Day!

Market structures in which sellers need to take into account the actions of other sellers, and then respond effectively and creatively, are possibly more prevalent in the real world than monopolistic competition (although certainty on this question would require precise definitions of each in terms of the respective concentration ratios). And even apparent monopolies are normally oligopolistic when one takes a closer look.

Take Microsoft, which is a good real-world example of a near-monopoly. Because computer users can still choose Macintosh or Linux operating systems, and because Microsoft can reasonably fear that the creation of a new technology could destroy its monopoly powers, it is not quite a pure monopoly. And we had mentioned McDonald's and Wendy's as monopolistic competitors, but you can be sure that they keep a watchful eye on each other's locations, pricing, and promotional strategies.

The need to take into account others' actions is important in traditional economics' narrowly defined (i.e., "few sellers") idea of oligopoly. But it is also of broader importance because rarely can *any* real-world company, of any size or in any industry, safely ignore the actions taken by others. Studies of economics, business, sociology, and politics share many common concerns when the prevalence of truly interdependent economic decision-making is taken into account.

Discussion Questions

1. What would it mean for two sellers to act noncooperatively, in a "prisoner's dilemma" manner? What real world examples can you think of? What, instead, would it mean for two sellers to collude? Which of the two outcomes is more common in the real world? Why?

2. Suppose that a seller in a duopoly needs to decide whether to spend a lot or a little on advertising. Assume that the consumers are already reasonably well informed about the product, so the purpose of a lot of advertising is to draw customers away from the rival. How could the payoffs from this situation resemble those in Figure 17.6? Draw a payoff matrix illustrating this case (with options "spend a lot" or "spend a little" and outcomes of low, moderate, or high profits) and describe the noncooperative solution. What if the government decided to ban advertising in this industry (as it has, in the past, banned advertising of cigarettes and alcohol in various media)? Would that help or hurt the companies' profits?

5. IMPERFECT COMPETITION IN AGRICULTURE AND HEALTH CARE

We now turn to a more in-depth discussion of two markets: agriculture and health care. These two markets are illustrative of many of the concepts we have been discussing in this chapter, as well as throughout the book, including economic efficiency, market failure, externalities, equity, and the role of government.

5.1 AGRICULTURE

On the face of it, markets for agricultural products should be a textbook case of perfect competition or at least something approaching it. Products are mostly undifferentiated—although this has changed in recent years, with growing attention to organic and locally produced food—and there exist a multitude of producers, many small and without market power. Yet U.S. agriculture has not been "competitive" for many years. Indeed, many economists find ironic the fact that, when they teach introductory economics, they often cite this market as a classic example of market *distortion.*

What types of distortion are present in agriculture, and how did the market get to be this way? Without going into great detail about the history, U.S. farmers struggled immensely during the Great Depression, when food prices dropped precipitously, because of both the forces of demand (a drop in demand from European countries) and supply (overproduction in response to price spikes during the 1920s). In order to keep many thousands of farmers from going bankrupt, the U.S. government embarked on an ambitious farm policy that, in many ways, continues to this day. What it entailed was basically the creation of a price floor in the agricultural markets (recall the discussion of price floors and price ceilings in Chapter 5), in which the government subsidized farmers for any difference between the food market price and what was deemed to be a "fair" price.

The problem with such a policy—and in 80 years it has never encountered a shortage of critics—is that it tends to "distort" markets for food. By setting a minimum price above the market price, the effect has been to stimulate overproduction—that is, production of food in an amount far greater than the quantity demanded at the market (i.e., unsubsidized) price.

We can see this in Figure 17.7. In the absence of any distortion, the market achieves equilibrium (point E) where the market price is P_m and the quantity produced, Q_m. When the government agrees to pay the subsidy to the farmer, the farmer now receives $P_m + s$. The "distortion" is the artificially produced surplus that, you will note, does not look the same as in the example from Chapter 5. The reason is that in this case the consumer *still pays* P_m (the whole purpose of the subsidy) and is therefore still motivated to buy Q_m. The surplus, or amount overproduced, is shown as $Q_P - Q_m$.

Figure 17.7   **Impact of Agricultural Subsidies**

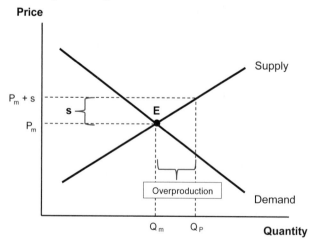

When the government provides a subsidy, it distorts the market. With the subsidy, farmers overproduce, and inefficiency results.

The manner in which the United States disposes of its surplus has varied over the years, and depending on crop type, but it usually has involved either selling it to other countries—as when the United States shipped vast amounts of surplus wheat to the Soviet Union in the early 1970s—providing it at low or no cost to very poor countries, or simply destroying it. The critics of the overall policy make the following points:

- U.S. farmland is being degraded faster than it would be with less incentive to overproduce.
- Rich farmers with large landholdings have received a disproportionately large share of the subsidies, making it all the harder for small farms to survive against this competition.
- Although in the short run the cheap or free food that poor countries receive from the United States may be essential to relieve a famine, in the long run it often drives farmers in those countries out of business, as they have to lower their prices to compete and often are unable to cover their production costs.

Taking another approach, the government has sometimes subsidized (i.e., paid) farmers to keep their land fallow (i.e., unplanted). In any case, what seems clear is that allocative efficiency was not the primary goal of U.S. agricultural policy. Instead, since the 1930s, the government has placed a great priority on protecting the U.S. farmer's livelihood.

In itself, this is a laudable objective. But aside from inefficiency, there is another consequence not visible in the above diagram. Figure 17.7, like many others in the book, presents a static interpretation of the problem—that is, viewed at a particular point in time. It does not provide any *dynamic* analysis or explanation of the likely response to the distortion in the market. That omission is critical, because herein lies one of the principal causes of the transformation of U.S. agriculture into an oligopolistic market. Whereas small family farms once dominated U.S. farming, today the majority of agricultural products are grown on a small number of (increasingly large) farms controlled by agribusiness giants like Cargill or Archer-Daniels Midland. As of 2010, the United States had 2.2 million farms, compared with 5.7 million in 1950, and the average farm size in 2010 was 418 acres, more than twice the average 60 years earlier (208 acres).

The growth in U.S average farm size since the 1930s has two main causes. The first, indeed, is a response to the original farm support policies, which both provoked new farming ventures and motivated consolidation of landholding, because the amount of the government subsidy was often tied to the size of the farm. The second was the self-perpetuating nature of scale economies. As farms became larger, they, like other industries, profited from economies of scale and were better able to shoulder rapidly increasing costs—especially after 1970—associated with the increasing mechanization of agriculture, increased price of petroleum, and higher interest rates on loans. A not-uncommon story, consequently, was the failure of smaller farms to compete and their sale to larger farms. The process, repeated many times across the country, only contributed to the concentration of land ownership.

Politics also played a role. Although the United States had been moving to limit overproduction in agriculture in earlier decades, in the early 1970s, U.S. Secretary of Agriculture Earl Butz took a very strident pro–big business approach. He is often credited with (or blamed for, depending on one's point of view) subsidizing the development of large commercial corn production and the growing use of inexpensive corn in prepared foods. It was not until 1996 that U.S. farm policy took a turn in the direction of a greater exposure to the market (with the Federal Agriculture Improvement and Reform Act), but stern opposition from politicians representing farming states in Congress led to a reversion to the earlier support policies.

As mentioned earlier in the section on monopoly, large companies with economies of scale have the potential to be very efficient if they produce large volumes at lower prices. This was Secretary Butz's argument in the early 1970s: Farms should be *big* in order to justify and support the mechanization and investment in new technology that would make farms much more efficient. Although the debate continues on whether large farms are more efficient than small ones, there are certainly disadvantages to excess market power in agriculture. As also noted earlier, lack of sufficient competition potentially makes oligopolistic firms complacent and less innovative. For those who believe that economics is not just about efficiency and production growth but also about people, output and price controls seemed to be the best way of dealing with the problem at the time.

The Great Depression was admittedly an exceptional period in our history, and the argument that farm policy has outlived its usefulness has its merits. Certainly, it has produced some unintended consequences, most of all the reduced number and viability of small farms. But many maintain that because food is a basic necessity, and because food prices are sometimes quite volatile, agricultural markets should continue to be regulated. Indeed, the main issue today might be not *whether* to regulate agriculture but the extent to which agricultural subsidies should favor the giant agricultural middlemen and the large producers who appear least to need them.

5.2 HEALTH CARE

The market for health care is remarkable in its complexity. It is, in fact, composed of numerous interrelated markets. For example, a variety of markets exist for different types of care—traditional medicine, allopathic medicine, homeopathy, herbal healers, and so forth—and markets for drugs and other pharmaceuticals. Moreover, there are markets for the insurance that in many cases pay for a variety of health-care services.

Classification of health care in terms of market structure depends on the specific market. The health insurance industry is oligopolistic because insurance premiums are more or less "set" by the relatively few insurers that control most of the market. Likewise, the relatively few pharmaceutical companies—or to be more precise, few *large* ones—have considerable market power, enhanced by generous patents granted by the government. Hospitals might also be reasonably considered regional oligopolies—or even monopolies, in more sparsely populated areas. Many attribute rapidly rising health-care costs in recent years to the substantial market power present in the industry (see Box 17.3).

The markets that connect individual health-care providers and "consumers" are, however, more difficult to classify. They would appear to have more of the attributes of competitive

---

BOX 17.3   RISING HEALTH-CARE COSTS AND MARKET POWER

A 2010 analysis by the Massachusetts Attorney General's office analyzed possible causes of rising health-care costs in the state. The report's conclusion is that higher costs can be attributed primarily to the exercise of market power by hospitals and physicians groups, rather than by improvements in the quality of care or the cost of providing care.

The analysis looked at the compensation that different health-care providers received from insurance companies. It found that the amount of compensation received by hospitals can vary by a factor of two for the same health-care services. In other words, some hospitals appear to be able to negotiate higher rates from insurance companies, not on the basis of providing better care but due to an ability to leverage their market power. Insurance companies, in turn, charge higher premiums to their customers.

The report found that "serious systemwide failings in the commercial health insurance marketplace" exist in the state. Massachusetts Attorney General Martha Coakley said, "Our review shows that the current system of health care payment is not always value-based, and health care providers throughout the state are compensated at widely different rates for providing similar quality and complexity of services."

Based on the report, the state is looking at evaluating ways to rein in rising health-care costs. One proposal is to move away from a "fee-for-service" system, in which hospitals and physicians are paid for each procedure that they perform, thus creating an incentive for unnecessary tests and operations. An alternative is a "capitated" system, in which hospitals and physicians receive a set payment from insurers for each patient they serve. Another cost-control option, favored by Governor Deval Patrick, is to give the state the authority to regulate "excessive or unreasonable" insurance premium rate increases. But Jim Klocke, executive vice president of the Greater Boston Chamber of Commerce, said that giving the state the power "to play a formal role in the price-setting process is not the right approach."

Source: Doug Trapp, "Cost Increases Tied to Market Power's Impact on Payment: Mass. Study," *American Medical News,* amednews.com, February 22, 2010.

markets, and it is certainly true that no providers control a substantial share of any mass market. Yet none of the individual markets are highly competitive either, for a number of reasons. Here we discuss four.

Heterogeneous Product

To begin with, recall that an important feature of perfect competition is that the product sold be identical or homogenous. This is clearly not the case in some markets in the health-care industry. One example is the quality of medical treatment. As countless online "reviews" attest, there is a great variety in quality, both of individual physicians and specialists and of hospitals. To the extent that the reviews accurately reflect reality, a doctor or a hospital judged "superior" might be justified in charging a higher price than other providers.

Even the "product" sold by the health insurance companies is highly variable. In contrast to the "single payer" insurance found in Canada and most European countries, for which coverage is more or less the same for all residents, there are numerous "tiers" of insurance in the United States. And each tier differs in the details, depending on the specific company offering the coverage. For example, most insurance companies today require a copayment, a way of ensuring that the consumer has some "skin in the game" so as to discourage overuse of health-care services. The size of this payment varies greatly as do the conditions under which it is paid—for example, for specialists only or for emergency care—and the restrictions on services covered (based on, e.g., if a provider is "signed up" with the insurance company). So we might almost consider meaningless the question of the "market price" of a particular health-care service.

Barriers to Entry

Another way in which health care differs from the idealized model of perfect competition is in the presence of barriers to entry. In the case of U.S. health insurance, the industry is oligopolistic, dominated by several fairly large companies that cover most of the market. As discussed earlier, it is exceedingly difficult to break into such a market as a small upstart. Providers of medical care face licensing requirements—medical school, licensing exams, and so on—that keep all but the most qualified from becoming doctors.

There certainly are good reasons for keeping unqualified individuals from practicing medicine. Yet the problem with such an entry barrier, many have argued, is that it grants undue protection to *existing* practitioners, potentially providing insufficient incentive to deliver the best possible quality. It is not our place to say whether these restrictions and protections are, on balance, for good or ill; certainly, both sides have valid arguments. But it is sufficient here to emphasize that entry barriers in health care can be substantial.

Information Asymmetry

Another basic attribute of a perfectly competitive market is the presence of "perfect information." In other words, classical economic theory presumes that both sides of the market— suppliers and "demanders"—have access to all the relevant information necessary to make an informed decision. This is decidedly not the case with health care.

What some economists call "information asymmetry"—a situation in which some market participants are more informed than others—is present, for example, when a doctor sees a patient. The patient is, in most cases, inadequately informed to make a proper judgment about whether a particular test or procedure that the doctor recommends is really necessary, so generally the doctor is simply trusted. Although the patient in many cases does not directly pay for most of what might be unnecessary procedures, the ultimate consequence—since the insurance companies end up financing an inefficiently high number of them—is that everyone's health insurance premiums go up.

Such asymmetry of information is also present between the patient and the insurance company. Most Americans have their health insurance company pay directly for a majority of their health-care expenses (in exchange for payment—usually monthly—of a fixed premium, privately or through an employer), and one can easily imagine how such a system could encourage overuse of medical services. As the marginal cost of many health-care services for insured individuals is zero, or very low, people have an incentive to demand services that may be unnecessary or very expensive. Further contributing to rising health-care costs, doctors are typically paid by insurance companies on the basis of each service performed, rather than actual health care outcomes.

Another issue is that individuals in poor health have a greater incentive to purchase insurance in the first place than those in relatively good health. This requires insurance companies to make more payments than they would expect if they were covering a random mix of sick and well, causing them to raise premiums to avoid losing money. This is a problem of **adverse selection**, in which the higher premiums further discourage healthy members of the population from signing up, and so on in a vicious cycle, eventually making the premiums so high as to jeopardize the system itself. While it is not actually as simple as this—to be sure, millions of healthy Americans have insurance, most because their employer helps pay for it—there is no question that premiums are inefficiently high due to disproportionate use of health-care services by the unhealthy.

The problem would easily be avoided by charging lower premiums to healthier people, not unlike what is done by life insurance companies. But this is, in practice, extremely difficult to do, because information asymmetry is much greater when it comes to determining the overall "healthiness" of an individual (e.g., one person might have a chronically bad back but be otherwise healthy, another might suffer from allergies, etc.) than for statistically assessing mortality based on a few critical health indicators. Also, even if feasible, it would imply that those who are already chronically ill would face prohibitively high premiums, an outcome that few people desire. Some insurance companies retain provisions for "pre-existing conditions" as a pretext for excluding new participants who are already sick, and these are precisely the people that the Affordable Care Act, or "Obamacare," is in part designed to protect.

adverse selection: a system that favors the weaker members of a given population, generally to the detriment of the system itself

Market Price

A final feature of a perfectly competitive market that is absent from health care is the presence of a clear and unambiguous market price. This is lacking even for basic medicines. Anyone who purchases pharmaceuticals has no doubt observed the significantly higher price charged for, say, the branded aspirin than for the generic (or "store brand") version—even though the two products are identical in their formulation. For another example, Walmart can sell some over-the-counter medicines (such as eye drops) at half the price set by other pharmacies due to a number of the store's outstanding characteristics: low costs due to efficiency, economies of scale, and low wages as well as enormous price-setting power, which allows it to negotiate prices with pharmaceutical companies. It is even harder to imagine a single, clear price for other health-care services, such as visits to doctor's offices or to hospitals, because there is so much variability among them.

Entry barriers, mentioned earlier, confound matters further. Lack of severe competition permits doctors, for instance, to discriminate based on price—familiar to most as having a "sliding scale." It is difficult to imagine the higher prices being sustained in the presence of greater competition. And information asymmetry plays perhaps the greatest role in failure to achieve a clear market price. Because insurance companies, health-care providers, and ordinary people all "trade" using different amounts—and quality—of information (about how necessary a procedure might be, its likelihood of success, its affordability, etc.), it might be surprising that prices are *ever* consistent.

Regarding price, another important consideration is that health care has an important "public good" dimension. The benefit of a vaccine, for example, is not only obtained by individuals, but also by everyone else living in a population of (mostly) vaccinated individuals (namely, a much lower chance of contracting the disease in question). Likewise, the benefits of psychiatric medications include the diminished likelihood, for everyone, of confronting an overabundance of mentally ill individuals. Because such indirect or residual benefits are "public"—that is, they do not enter into the private benefit-cost calculation of buyer and seller—they cannot be reflected in the market price.

Many have raised arguments about ways in which this sector of the economy could be made more competitive, with the goal of allocating resources more efficiently. Laudable as the goal no doubt is, there is something unique about health care—the fact that it is a fundamental human necessity *and* its provision is often plagued by market failure—that forces us to reconsider whether market-based approaches work best.

Another element to the problem is perhaps the most critical. Health insurance companies ultimately decide which claims they will pay. In most cases, then, they effectively decide whether a prescribed medical treatment will be undertaken, because most people would be unwilling (or, often, unable) to pay for it out of pocket. If the decisions of the insurers were based on their expertise in the area of medicine and their concern for the well-being of the insured, the present system would make a lot more sense. But the insurance company is fundamentally pursuing *profit,* which, of course, is not in itself a bad thing. The problem is when the pursuit of profit conflicts with the objective of ensuring patient health.

When compared to other countries, the United States does not perform well in terms of national health indicators. Although average life expectancy certainly is much higher in the country than in the far poorer countries of sub-Saharan Africa and South Asia, it is not as high as in most industrialized countries—that is, Western European countries, Canada, Japan, Australia, and New Zealand. And the United States also compares unfavorably, in terms of life expectancy and infant mortality, with a growing number of "middle-income" countries (e.g., Costa Rica, Cuba). None of this proves that other health-care systems—such as, most notably, a "single payer" system—are superior to one based on private profits and markets. But the evidence does call for research into the question of whether better systems might exist for delivering health care.

Discussion Questions

1. Select the topic of either agriculture or health, and answer the following questions:
   a. What do you think is the single biggest problem in this area of the economy?
   b. What kind of policy do you favor to help to overcome that problem?
   c. What makes it difficult to implement the policy that you favor?
2. Should the health-care industry become more like a competitive free market? Do you think that it would help bring costs down? How might such a change come about? What might be some potentially undesirable consequences?

6. SUMMARY AND A FINAL NOTE

The traditional four-way categorization of markets, summarized in Table 17.2, can be helpful in thinking about how market structure can affect the incentives facing firms. It is important to remember that the differences between these classifications are not always clear. In particular, in many real-world markets, sellers need to keep track of what others in their industry are doing and to plan strategically, whether there are few sellers or many. Such interdependent activity requires analysis that is beyond the scope of simple models of marginal thinking. Moreover, as we think about market power, we need to recognize that globalization, which has intensified in recent decades, has made dramatic changes in market conditions. Traditional categories may therefore no longer cover all of the most important situations.

Table 17.2 **Summary of Traditional Market Structures**

	Perfect competition	Pure monopoly	Monopolistic competition	Oligopoly
Number of sellers in the market	many	one	many	few
Type of item(s) sold	identical	unique	differentiated	varies
Market power of an individual seller	none	very high	some	substantial
Entry barriers	none	very high	none	some
Long-run economic profit	zero	positive	zero	varies
Profit-maximizing condition	MC = P	MC = MR	MC = MR	varies

The classical economic discussion of markets tends to focus on the benefits of "free" markets and competition. When the discussion turns to market power, economists mostly focus largely on *firms* that may have the power to affect *prices* in the markets where they *sell* goods that they have *produced.*

Market power, however, is much more widespread. For example,

- Governments, nonprofit organizations, and individuals can have market power. In some states and counties, for example, governments have a monopoly on liquor sales. An individual selling a unique work of art has market power.
- Nonprice terms and conditions of exchange such as delivery dates, quality standards, and length of contracts can be manipulated by economic actors with market power.
- Market power can exist in nonproduct markets, such as markets for resale of goods, markets for resources, and financial markets.
- Market power can occur on the buyers' side. That is, market power can be used to affect the prices paid by firms to their suppliers for *inputs,* including human labor. The cases of monopsony (one buyer) and oligopsony (few buyers) were discussed in Chapter 9 on labor markets.

Market power, therefore, refers to much more than the ability of firms to set prices above marginal cost. Although the classical analysis of market power tends to stress its detrimental consequences in terms of lost efficiency—an issue of concern from the point of view of the consumer—the consequences of market power in terms of fairness and distributional effects are often at least as important, if not more so, to human well-being. If, for example, market power allows a few large companies to force consumers to pay more for food while at the same time making earning a living increasingly difficult for small farmers, this could be at least as damaging to human well-being as the market power that allows a firm to set prices above marginal cost. A similar argument is easily made regarding the market power enjoyed by the pharmaceutical and the health insurance giants.

Market power is frequently used to impose externalities upon society. For example, a large manufacturer may lobby to gain an exemption from a pollution regulation. Thus instead of having the manufacturer pay the costs of pollution control, society pays costs in terms of poorer health and ecosystem damages.

The most important lesson here is to remember both the usefulness and limitations of textbook models. Abstract and admittedly simplified models of perfect competition and monopoly help us to understand the basics of how certain key ingredients of a market economy function. It is critically important to be able to generalize across many examples across the world, and over time, in order to gain general insight into how the economy works. But it is equally important—if not more so—not to idealize the models to the point that they come to be seen as reality itself.

Neither free markets nor monopolies exist in their purest sense; the world is far more complicated than this. The challenge is to learn to properly utilize the insights gained from economic models in the analysis of complex real-world problems. As should be clear from the examples in this book, it is often difficult to separate economic concepts of efficiency from issues of ethics, fairness, sustainability, and distribution. As the present chapter illustrates, market power often implies other forms of political power. The proper use of economic modeling and analysis recognizes both its usefulness and its limitations, in guiding us to a better understanding, and better policies, on agriculture, health, and many other issues that are critical for human well-being.

REVIEW QUESTIONS

1. List and briefly define the three market structure types in addition to perfect competition.
2. What market conditions characterize pure monopoly?
3. Describe three types of barriers to entry, giving examples of each.
4. How does a pure monopolist maximize profits?
5. In what ways are monopolies inefficient?
6. Explain, with a graph, how monopoly market power generally leads to inefficiency.
7. List and describe four cases in which monopolies might be efficient.
8. Explain, with a graph, how a price-discriminating seller behaves.
9. What market conditions characterize monopolistic competition?
10. How is a monopolistically competitive firm imagined to maximize profits?
11. Are monopolistically competitive markets efficient? Explain.
12. What market conditions characterize oligopoly?
13. Describe two theories used to describe the behavior of oligopolists.
14. Explain why the U.S. government would pay farmers to leave their land fallow.
15. Does present-day U.S. farm policy "protect" the farmer? Explain.
16. Is the health-care industry competitive? Explain.
17. What is "information asymmetry," and how does it lead to inefficiently high insurance premiums?

EXERCISES

1. When Braeburn Publishing priced its poetry book at $5, it sold 5 books, and when it priced the volume at $8, it sold 4 books. You can calculate that its revenues were higher with the higher price. Suppose that, from further test marketing, this firm determines that it faces the demand curve described by the following schedule.

Quantity of output (demanded)	Selling price ($)	Total revenue ($)	Marginal revenue ($)
1	17		—
2	14		
3	11		
4	8		
5	5		

a. Graph the demand curve for the poetry book, labeling carefully. (Compare your graph to Figure 4.1.)
b. Calculate total revenue and marginal revenue at each output level, and add a marginal revenue curve to your graph.
c. Can the $8 price be Braeburn's profit-maximizing choice? Why or why not?
d. Suppose that, thanks to computerized, on-demand publishing technology, Braeburn can produce any number of books at a constant cost of $5 each. (That is, average cost and marginal cost are both $5 for any quantity of books, and total costs are simply the number of books times $5.) Add a marginal cost curve to your graph. (It will *not* look like the "usual" *MC* curve—it will be horizontal.)

e. What are Braeburn's profit-maximizing price and output levels for the poetry book? State these, and label them on the graph.

f. What level of profit would Braeburn earn with the $8 price? (Recall that profits equal total revenue minus total cost.) What is the level of profit with the price you just found that maximizes profit?

2. Suppose that two oligopolistic retail chains are considering opening a new sales outlet in a particular town. The changes to each firm's profits, depending on the actions taken, are given in the following payoff matrix. If a chain does not open a new outlet, it earns no addition to profits. If one of the chains is the only one to open an outlet, it makes high additional profits. If they both open outlets, they have to split the available market, and they make only more moderate additional profits.

Firm 2's Options

	New Outlet	No New Outlet
Firm 1's Options		
New Outlet	moderate profit / moderate profit	no profit / high profit
No New Outlet	high profit / no profit	no profit / no profit

a. If Firm 1 decides to open a new outlet, but Firm 2 does *not* open a new outlet, how much additional profit does each firm make?

b. If Firm 1 decides to open a new outlet, what is the worst that can happen to it? If Firm 1 decides *not* to open a new outlet, what is the worst that can happen to it? Which option, then, should Firm 1 choose, if it wants to make the choice that leaves it best off, regardless of what the other firm does?

c. If the firms are noncooperative and each firm makes the choice that will leave it best off regardless of the other's choice, what will the outcome be?

d. Is this like the "prisoner's dilemma," in which both parties could get a better outcome by communicating and cooperating?

e. Now suppose that each firm is thinking of opening new outlets in a *number* of towns, and each town has a payoff matrix similar to this one. Would there be advantages in having the two chains communicate and cooperate in this case? If they decide to collude, what form do you think their collusion might take?

3. Match each concept in Column A with an example in Column B.

Column A	Column B
a. A legal barrier to entry	1. Lobbying to get a concession
b. Predatory pricing	2. Patent rights
c. Rent-seeking behavior	3. Electricity distribution
d. Nonprice competition	4. Cornflakes in different-colored boxes
e. Product differentiation	5. Cutting prices to below cost to drive out a rival
f. Price fixing	6. Cooperating with a rival to charge the same price
g. Natural monopoly	7. Advertising

APPENDIX: FORMAL ANALYSIS OF MONOPOLY AND MONOPOLISTIC COMPETITION

A1. THE ASSUMPTIONS

This appendix shows how monopoly and monopolistic competition market structures can be formally treated within a model of profit-maximizing firms.

A2. MONOPOLY

Suppose that our firm is a monopolist, with the marginal revenue schedule shown in Table 17.1 and Figure 17.1 and with the marginal cost curve shown in Figure 17.1. As described in this chapter, the monopolist maximizes profits by setting $MR = MC$. It produces 5 units, at a marginal cost of about $12, and sells them for a price of $28. Adding in the average total cost curve of the firm enables us to identify the area of economic profit, as shown in Figure

Figure 17.8 **Monopoly Profits**

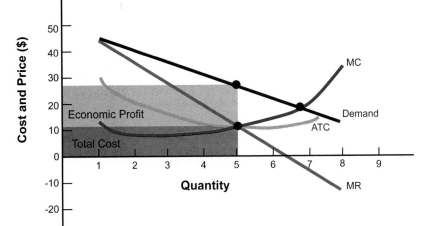

The monopolist sells its product at a per-unit price that is higher than its per-unit cost of production, thus reaping positive economic profits. Revenues are represented by the total shaded area. The part of revenues that goes to paying costs is represented by the darker shaded area. Thus the lighter area represents an excess of revenues over costs—the economic profit.

17.8. The firm's revenues include both shaded areas, whereas its costs are represented by the darker-shaded rectangle. The monopolist makes positive economic profit equal to the area of the lighter-shaded rectangle.

A3. MONOPOLISTIC COMPETITION

A monopolistically competitive firm faces a downward-sloping demand curve. Yet, like a perfectly competitive firm, it also makes zero economic profits in the long run.

This case is illustrated in Figure 17.9. Like a monopolist, the monopolistically competitive firm will choose to produce the quantity corresponding to point A, where $MR = MC$. It will charge a price corresponding to point B on the demand curve. Point B is also on the ATC curve in the long run. Thus the shaded rectangle represents both total revenue (price × quantity) and total cost (average total cost × quantity). The firm makes zero economic profits.

How does this come about? Look back at Figure 17.5. If the price were above the ATC curve, the firm would make positive economic profits, and (because there is free entry) new firms would enter the industry. This causes the demand curve for this firm's differentiated product to shift downward. The demand curve is imagined to shift downward until it just touches the ATC curve, as shown in Figure 17.9.

Figure 17.9 **Zero Economic Profits for a Monopolistically Competitive Firm**

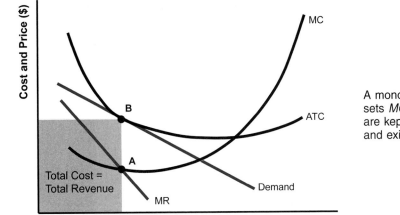

A monopolistically competitive firm sets $MC = MR$, but economic profits are kept at zero by the free entry and exit of firms.

Glossary

absolute deprivation: severe deprivation of basic human needs (8)

accounting costs: actual monetary costs paid by a producer as well as estimated reduction in the value of the producer's capital stock (15)

accounting profits: the difference between total revenues and accounting costs (16)

accurate: describes something that is correct (even if only in a general way) (3)

administrative obstacles: use of environmental, health, or safety regulations to prevent imports from other countries under the pretext of upholding higher standards (6)

adverse selection: a system that favors the weaker members of a given population, generally to the detriment of the system itself (17)

aggregate (or market) benefits: the benefits to all consumers in a market (5)

altruistic behavior: actions focused on the well-being of others, with no thought about oneself (7)

anchoring effect: overreliance on a piece of information that may or may not be relevant as a reference point when making a decision (7)

artificially scarce good: a good that is excludable but nonrival (13)

aspirational group: the group to which an individual aspires to belong (8)

auction market: a market in which an item is sold to the highest bidder (2)

availability heuristic: placing undue importance on particular information because it is readily available or vivid (7)

average cost (or average total cost): cost per unit of output, computed as total cost divided by the quantity of output produced (15)

average variable cost (AVC): total variable cost divided by the quantity produced (15)

backward-bending individual paid labor supply curve: a pattern that arises because, beyond some level of wages, income effects may outweigh substitution effects in determining individuals' decisions about how much to work (9)

bargaining: an activity in which a single buyer and a single seller negotiate the terms of their exchange (2)

barriers to entry: economic, legal, or deliberate obstacles that keep new sellers from entering a market (17)

behavioral economics: a subfield of microeconomics that studies how individuals and organizations make economic decisions (7)

bilateral monopoly: the situation in which there is only one buyer confronting only one seller (9)

bounded rationality: the hypothesis that people make choices among a somewhat arbitrary subset of all possible options due to limits on information, time, or cognitive abilities (7)

budget line: a line showing the possible combinations of two goods that a consumer can purchase (8)

business sphere: firms that produce goods and services for profitable sale (1)

capital: any resource that is valued for its potential economic contributions (14)

capital gains: increase in the value of an asset at the time it is sold compared to the price at which it was originally purchased by the same owner (10)

capital income: rents, profits, and interest (10)

capital-intensive production: production using methods that involve a high ratio of capital to labor (6)

ceteris paribus: a Latin phrase that means "other things equal" or "all else constant" (3)

change in demand: a shift of the entire demand curve in response to something changing other than price (3)

change in supply: a shift of the entire supply curve, in response to something changing other than price (3)

change in the quantity demanded: movement along a demand curve in response to a price change (3)

change in the quantity supplied: movement along a supply curve in response to a price change (3)

climate change: long-term changes in global climate, including warmer temperatures, changing precipitation patterns, more extreme weather events, and rising sea levels (13)

collusion: cooperation among potential rivals to gain market power as a group (17)

commodity market: a market for a raw material (2)

common good: the general well-being of society, including one's own well-being (7)

common property resource: a resource that is non-excludable and rival (13)

comparative advantage: the ability to produce some good or service at a lower opportunity cost than other producers (6)

compensating wage differentials: the theory that, all else being equal, workers will demand higher wages for jobs with unappealing characteristics, and be willing to accept lower wages for jobs with better characteristics (9)

complementary good: a good that is used along with another good (3)

congestion: the point at which the demand for a nonrival good results in a diminished benefit to each user, and thus it becomes rival (13)

constant marginal costs: the situation in which the cost of producing one additional unit of output stays the same as more output is produced (15)

constant marginal returns: a situation in which each successive unit of a variable input produces the same marginal product (15)

constant returns to scale: situations in which the long-run average cost of production stays the same as the size of the enterprise increases (15)

consumer society: a society in which a large part of people's sense of identity and meaning is found through the purchase and use of consumer goods and services (8)

consumer sovereignty: the idea that consumers' needs and wants determine the shape of all economic activities (8)

consumer surplus: the net benefits obtained from a purchase, equal to the difference between a consumer's maximum willingness to pay and the price (5)

consumerism: having one's sense of identity and meaning defined largely through the purchase and use of consumer goods and services (8)

consumption: the final use of a good or service (1)

contingent ranking: a stated preference method in which respondents are asked to rank various hypothetical scenarios (12)

contingent valuation: a stated preference method where survey respondents are asked about their willingness to pay for a hypothetical outcome (12)

core sphere: the economic activities of households, families, and communities (1)

cost-benefit analysis: a technique to analyze a policy or project proposal in which all costs and benefits are converted to monetary estimates, if possible, to determine the net social value (12)

cost of illness method: a nonmarket valuation technique that estimates the direct and indirect costs associated with illnesses with environmental causes (12)

deadweight loss: a reduction in social welfare as a result of a market regulation (5)

debt finance: borrowing others' funds to make productive investments (14)

decreasing marginal costs: the situation in which the cost of producing one additional unit of output falls as more output is produced (15)

defensive expenditures approach: a nonmarket valuation technique that obtains benefit estimates based on the cost of actions that people take to avoid environmental harm (12)

demand: the willingness and ability of purchasers to buy goods or services (3)

demand curve: a curve indicating the quantities that buyers are willing to purchase at various prices (3)

demand schedule: a table showing the relationship between price and the quantity demanded (3)

depreciation: decrease in the usefulness of a stock of capital due to wear and tear or obsolescence (14)

diminishing marginal returns: a situation in which each successive unit of a variable input produces a smaller marginal product (15)

diminishing marginal utility: the tendency for additional units of consumption to add less to utility than did previous units of consumption (8)

discount rate: the annual percentage rate at which future costs and benefits are discounted relative to current costs and benefits (12)

discounting: an approach in which costs and benefits that occur in the future are assigned less weight (i.e., discounted) relative to current costs and benefits (12)

diseconomies of scale: situations in which the long-run average cost of production rises as the size of the enterprise increases (15)

distribution: the sharing of products and resources among people (1)

double auction: an auction in which both the buyers and sellers state prices at which they are willing to make transactions (2)

dual labor markets: a situation in which *primary* workers enjoy high wages, opportunities for advancement, and job security, while *secondary* workers are hired with low wages, no opportunities for advancement, and no job security (9)

dumping: selling products at prices that are below the cost of production (6)

duopoly: a market with only two sellers (17)

Dutch auction: an auction in which the opening price is set high and then drops until someone buys (2)

ecolabeling: product labels that provide information about environmental impacts, or indicate certification (8)

ecological footprint: an estimate of how much land area a human society requires to provide all that the society takes from nature and to absorb its waste and pollution (8)

economic actor (economic agent): an individual or organization involved in the economic activities of resource maintenance or the production, distribution, or consumption of goods and services (1)

economic cost: the total cost of production, including both accounting and opportunity costs (15)

economic efficiency: the use of resources, or inputs, such that they yield the highest possible value of output or the production of a given output using the lowest possible value of inputs (1)

economic mobility: the potential for an individual or household to change its economic conditions (for better or worse) over time (10)

economic profits: the difference between total revenues and economic costs (16)

economics: the study of how people manage their resources to meet their needs and enhance their well-being (1)

economies of scale: situations in which the long-run average cost of production falls as the size of the enterprise increases (6)

ecosystem services: tangible benefits that humans obtain from natural processes, such as nutrient recycling, flood control, and pollination (12)

effective tax rate: one's taxes expressed as a percentage of total income (11)

efficiency wage theory: the theory that an employer can motivate workers to put forth more effort by paying them somewhat more than they could get elsewhere (9)

elasticity: a measure of the responsiveness of an economic actor to changes in market factors, including price and income (4)

employee morale: the attitude of workers toward their work and their employer (9)

employer-specific human capital: knowledge and skills that have been gained on a particular job and are useful only as long as a worker remains with the same employer (9)

equity finance: an economic actor's use of its own funds to make productive investments (14)

estate taxes: taxes on the transfers of large estates to beneficiaries (11)

exchange: the trading of one thing for another (1)

excise tax: a per-unit tax on a good or service (11)

excludable good: a good whose consumption by others can be prevented by its owner(s) (13)

exclusionary practices: when a firm gets its suppliers or distributors to agree not to provide goods or services to potential competitors (17)

explicit contract: a formal, often written agreement that states the terms of an exchange and may be enforceable through a legal system (2)

factor markets: markets for the services of land, labor, and capital (1)

factor-price equalization: the theory that trade should eventually lead to returns to factors of production that are equal across countries (6)

final goal: a goal that requires no further justification; it is an end in itself (2)

financial capital: funds of purchasing power available to purchase goods and services or facilitate economic activity (14)

financial market: a market for loans, equity finance, and financial assets (2)

fixed costs (sunk costs): production costs that cannot be adjusted quickly and that must be paid even if no production occurs (15)

fixed input: a production input that is fixed in quantity, regardless of the level of production (15)

fixed manufactured capital: manufactured goods that yield a flow of productive services over an extended period (14)

flow: something whose quantity is measured over a period of time (14)

framing: changing the way a particular decision is presented to people in order to influence their behavior (7)

free riders: those who obtain the benefits of a public good without paying anything for it (13)

free trade: exchange in international markets that is not regulated or restricted by government actions (6)

general human capital: knowledge and skills that workers can take with them as they move from one employer to another (9)

gift taxes: taxes on the transfer of large gifts to beneficiaries (11)

Gini ratio (or Gini coefficient): a measure of inequality, based on the Lorenz curve, that goes from 0 (absolute equality) up to 1 (absolute inequality). Greater inequality shows up as a larger area between the Lorenz curve and the diagonal line of absolute equality (10)

global public good: a public good available to the entire population of the planet (13)

globalization: the extension of free trade and communications across the entire world, leading to a great increase in the volume of traded goods and services, and in expanded interconnections among different regions (6)

green consumerism: making consumption decisions at least partly on the basis of environmental criteria (8)

greenhouse gases: gases such as carbon dioxide and methane whose atmospheric concentrations influence global climate by trapping solar radiation (13)

human capital: people's capacity for engaging in productive activities (14)

implicit contract: an informal agreement about the terms of a market exchange, based on verbal discussions or on traditions and normal expectations (2)

import substitution: a policy undertaken by governments seeking to reduce reliance on imports and encourage domestic industry. These often include the use of industry subsidies as well as protectionist policies (6)

inadequacy: a situation in which there is not enough of a good or service, provided at prices people can afford, to meet minimal requirements for human well-being (3)

income effect of a price change: the tendency of a price increase to reduce the quantity demanded of normal goods (and to increase the quantity demanded of any inferior goods) (4)

income elasticity of demand: a measure of the responsiveness of demand to changes in income, holding price constant (4)

increasing marginal costs: the situation in which the cost of producing one additional unit of output rises as more output is produced (15)

increasing marginal returns: a situation in which each successive unit of a variable input produces a larger marginal product (15)

indifference curve: a curve consisting of points representing combinations of various quantities of two goods, such that every such combination gives the consumer the same level of utility (8)

individual demand: the demand of one particular buyer (3)

individual supply: the supply of one particular seller (3)

individual transferable quota (ITQ): tradable rights to access or harvest a common property resource, such as the right to harvest a particular quantity of fish (13)

industrial concentration ratio: the share of production, sales, or revenues attributable to the largest firms in an industry (17)

infant industry: an industry that is relatively new to its region or country, and thus may be protected from international competition by tariffs and other trade barriers until it can better compete on world markets (6)

inferior goods: goods for which demand decreases when incomes rise and increases when incomes fall (4)

informal sphere: businesses operating outside government oversight and regulation. In less industrialized countries, it may constitute the majority of economic activity (2)

input substitution: increasing the use of some inputs, and decreasing that of others, while producing the same good or service (15)

inputs: the resources that go into production (15)

institutions: ways of structuring human activities based on customs, habits, and laws (2)

intangible capital: resources that cannot be seen or touched (14)

interest: the charge for borrowing money (14)

intermediate goal: a goal that is desirable because its achievement will bring you closer to your final goal(s) (1)

intermediate goods market: a market for an unfinished product (2)

internalizing negative externalities: bringing external costs into the market (for example, by instituting a Pigovian tax at a level equal to the externality damage), thus making market participants pay the true social cost of their actions (12)

intrinsic value: the value of something in an ecological or ethical sense, apart from any economic value based on willingness to pay (12)

inventories: stocks of raw materials or manufactured goods being stored until they can be used or sold (14)

investment: any activity intended to increase the quantity or quality of a resource over time (14)

labor force participation rate: the percentage of the adult, noninstitutionalized population that is either working at a paid job or seeking paid work (9)

labor income: payment to workers, including wages, salaries, and fringe benefits (10)

labor-intensive production: production using methods that involve a high ratio of labor to capital (6)

labor market: a market in which employers interact with people who wish to work (2)

labor market discrimination: a condition that exists when, among similarly qualified people, some are treated disadvantageously in employment on the basis of race, gender, age, sexual preference, physical appearance, or disability (9)

labor unions: legally recognized organizations that collectively bargain for their members (workers) regarding wages, benefits, and working conditions (9)

laissez-faire: the view that government intervention in markets should be limited to what is absolutely necessary. The term is French and means "leave alone." (5)

laissez-faire economy: an economy with little government regulation (2)

limiting factor: a fixed input that creates a constraint to increasing production (15)

living standard (or lifestyle) goals: goals related to satisfying basic needs and getting pleasure through the use of goods and services (8)

loan: money borrowed for temporary use, on the condition that it be repaid, usually with interest (14)

local monopoly: a monopoly limited to a specific geographic area (17)

long run: (in terms of production processes) a period in which all production inputs can be varied in quantity (15)

long-run average cost: the cost of production per unit of output when all inputs can be varied in quantity (15)

long-run elasticity: a measure of the response to a price change after economic actors have had time to make adjustments (4)

Lorenz curve: a line used to portray an income distribution, drawn on a graph with percentiles of households on the horizontal axis and the cumulative percentage of income on the vertical axis (10)

lower-bound estimate: an estimate that represents the minimum potential value of something. The actual value is thus greater than or equal to the lower-bound estimate (12)

macroeconomics: the subfield of economics that focuses on the economy as a whole (1)

manufactured (or produced) capital: all physical assets that have been made by humans using natural capital (14)

marginal analysis: analysis based on incremental changes, comparing marginal benefits to marginal costs (15)

marginal benefit (for consumers): the benefit of consuming one additional unit of something (5)

marginal benefits curve: a curve showing the additional benefit from each unit consumed. Another name for a demand curve, as applied to welfare economics (5)

marginal change: a change of one unit (either an increase or a decrease) (5)

marginal cost: the cost of producing one additional unit of something (5)

marginal factor cost of labor (MFC_L): the amount that a unit of additional labor adds to the firm's wage costs (9)

marginal physical product of labor (MPP_L): the amount that a unit of additional labor contributes to the physical product of a firm (9)

marginal product: the additional quantity of output produced by increasing the level of a variable input by one, holding all other inputs constant (15)

marginal propensity to consume: the tendency to spend, rather than save, an additional dollar of income (11)

marginal rate of substitution: how much of one good the consumer is willing to give up to get more of another (8)

marginal revenue: the additional revenue obtained by selling one more unit. In a perfectly competitive market, marginal revenue equals price (16)

marginal revenue product of labor (MRP_L): the amount that a unit of additional labor contributes to the revenues of the firm (9)

marginal tax rate: the tax rate applicable to an additional dollar of income (11)

market (first meaning): a place (physical or virtual) where there is a reasonable expectation of finding both buyers and sellers for the same product or service (2)

market (second meaning): an institution that facilitates economic interactions among buyers and sellers (2)

market (third meaning): an economic system (a "market economy") that relies on market institutions to conduct many economic activities (2)

market (or aggregate) demand: the demand from all buyers in a particular market (3)

market (or aggregate) supply: the supply from all sellers in a particular market (3)

market consumer surplus: the difference between aggregate costs and aggregate benefits, or net benefits obtained by all consumers in a market. On a supply-and-demand graph, it is equal to the area under a demand curve but above the price (5)

market disequilibrium: a situation of either shortage or surplus (3)

market equilibrium: a situation in which the quantity supplied equals the quantity demanded, and thus there is no pressure for changes in price or quantity bought or sold (3)

market failure: situations in which unregulated markets fail to produce the socially efficient outcome (5)

market power: the ability to control, or at least affect, the terms and conditions of a market exchange (16)

market price: the prevailing price for a specific good or service at a particular time in a given market (3)

market producer surplus: the net benefit (profits) obtained by all producers in a market. On a supply-and-demand graph, it is the area below price but above the supply curve (5)

market quantity sold: the number of "units" of a specific good or service sold in a given market during a particular period (3)

market-based approaches (to pollution regulation): policies that create an economic incentive for firms to reduce pollution without mandating that firms take any specific actions (12)

market value: the maximum amount that economic actors are willing and able to pay for a good or service (i.e., effective demand) (3)

markup (or cost-plus) pricing: a method of setting prices in which the seller adds a fixed percentage amount to his or her costs of production (3)

maximum efficient scale: the highest quantity of output at which a firm achieves its minimum per-unit production costs (15)

maximum willingness to pay (WTP): the maximum amount that a rational consumer will pay for a particular product. In welfare economics, consumers' maximum WTP represents the total benefits that they expect to obtain from a product, expressed in monetary terms (5)

meliorating: starting from the present level of well-being and continuously attempting to do better (7)

microeconomics: the subfield of economics that focuses on activities that take place within and among the major economic organizations of a society, including households, communities, governments, nonprofit organizations, and for-profit businesses (1)

minimum efficient scale: the lowest quantity of output at which a firm achieves it minimum per-unit production costs (15)

model: an analytical tool that highlights some aspects of reality while ignoring others (1)

money: a medium of exchange that is widely accepted, durable as a store of value, has minimal handling and storage costs, and serves as a unit of account (2)

monopolistic competition: the situation in which there are many sellers, but they sell slightly different things (17)

monopsony: a situation in which there is only one buyer but many sellers. This situation occurs in a labor market in which there are many potential workers but only one employer (9)

natural capital: physical assets provided by nature (14)

natural monopoly: a monopoly that arises because the minimum efficient scale of the producing unit is large relative to the total market demand (17)

negative (or inverse) relationship: the relationship between two variables if an increase in one is associated with a decrease in the other variable (3)

negative externalities: harmful side effects, or unintended consequences, of economic activity that affect those who are not directly involved in the activity (1)

neoclassical model: a model that portrays the economy as a collection of profit-maximizing firms and utility-maximizing households interacting through perfectly competitive markets (7)

net benefits: benefits minus any costs. Consumer surplus is a measure of net benefits because it is equal to the difference between the maximum willingness to pay and price (5)

network externality: (in production) a situation in which a particular technology or production process is more likely to be adopted because other economic actors have already adopted it (16)

nonexcludable good: a good whose benefits are freely available to all users (13)

nonmarket valuation techniques: economic valuation methods that obtain estimates for goods and services not directly traded in markets (12)

nonprice competition: competition through activities other than setting prices, such as advertising and location (17)

nonprice determinants of demand: any factor that affects the quantity demanded, other than the price of the good or service being demanded (3)

nonprice determinants of supply: any factor that affects the quantity supplied, other than the price of the good or service offered for sale (3)

nonrenewable resource: a resource that can only diminish over human time scales (14)

nonrival good: a good that can be consumed by more than one person at a time. The marginal cost of providing a nonrival good to an additional person is zero (13)

nonuse benefits: nontangible welfare benefits that people derive from ecosystems without physical interaction (i.e., psychological benefits) (12)

normal goods: goods for which demand increases when incomes rise and decreases when incomes fall (4)

normative questions: questions about how things should be (1)

occupational segregation: the tendency of men and women to be employed in different occupations (9)

oligopoly: the situation in which there are so few sellers that each needs to watch what the others are doing (17)

oligopsony: the case of a relatively small number of buyers (9)

open auction: an auction in which the opening price is set low and then buyers bid it up (2)

opportunity cost: the value of the best alternative that is forgone when a choice is made (1)

optimizing behavior: behavior that achieves an optimal (best possible) outcome (7)

outputs: the goods and services that result from production (15)

path dependence: a condition that exists when economic developments depend on initial conditions and past events—that is, when "history matters" (16)

payoff matrix: a table used in game theory to illustrate possible outcomes for each of two players, depending on the strategy that each chooses (17)

perfect competition: a market for the exchange of identical units of a good or service, in which there are numerous small sellers and buyers, all of whom have perfect information (16)

perfectly competitive market equilibrium: the market equilibrium in a perfectly competitive market in which the economic profits of each individual seller are zero, and there is no incentive for entry or exit (16)

perfectly inelastic demand: the quantity demanded does not change at all when price changes. The elasticity value is 0 (4)

physical capital: resources that are tangible (i.e., can be touched or seen) (14)

physical infrastructure: roads, ports, railroads, warehouses, and other tangible structures that provide the foundation for economic activity (2)

Pigovian tax: a tax levied on a product to reduce or eliminate the negative externality associated with its production (12)

pollution standards: policies that control pollution by setting allowable pollution standards or controlling the uses of a product or process (12)

positive (or direct) relationship: the relationship between two variables when an increase in one is associated with an increase in the other variable (3)

positive externalities: beneficial side effects, or unintended consequences, of economic activity that accrue to those who are not among the economic actors directly involved in the activity (1)

positive questions: questions about how things are (1)

posted prices: prices set by a seller (2)

precautionary principle: the notion that policies should err on the side of caution when there is a low-probability risk of a catastrophic outcome (12)

precise: describes something that is exact (though it may be unrealistic) (3)

predatory pricing: a powerful seller's temporary pricing of its goods or services below cost, in order to drive weaker competitors out of business (17)

present value: the current value of a future cost or benefit, obtained by discounting (12)

price ceiling: a regulation that specifies a maximum price for a particular product (5)

price discrimination: a seller's charging different prices to different buyers, depending on their ability and willingness to pay (17)

price-elastic demand: a relationship between price and quantity demanded characterized by relatively strong responses of buyers to price changes (4)

price-elastic demand (technical definition): the percentage change in the quantity demanded is larger than the percentage change in price. The elasticity value is more than 1 (4)

price elasticity of demand: the responsiveness of the quantity demanded to a change in price (4)

price elasticity of supply: a measure of the responsiveness of quantity supplied to changes in price (4)

price fixing: a form of collusion in which a group of sellers implicitly agrees to maintain a common price (17)

price floor: a regulation that specifies a minimum price for a particular product (5)

price-inelastic demand: a relationship between price and quantity demanded characterized by relatively weak responses of buyers to price changes (4)

price-inelastic demand (technical definition): the percentage change in the quantity demanded is smaller than the percentage change in price. The elasticity value is less than 1 (4)

price leadership: a form of collusion in which many sellers follow the price changes instituted by one particular seller (17)

price maker: a seller that can set the selling price, constrained only by demand conditions (17)

price taker: a seller that has no market power to set price. Price is determined solely by the interaction of market supply and market demand (16)

price war: a situation in which a firm cuts prices in order to try to undercut its rivals, and the rivals react by cutting prices even more (17)

principal: the original amount of money borrowed (14)

private good: a good that is excludable and rival (13)

private property: ownership of assets by nongovernment economic actors (2)

producer surplus: the net benefits that producers receive from selling products, equal to the difference between the selling price and the marginal costs (5)

product markets: markets for newly produced goods and services (1)

production: the conversion of resources into goods and services (1)

production function: an equation or graph that represents a relationship between types and quantities of inputs and the quantity of output (15)

production-possibilities frontier (PPF): a curve showing the maximum amounts of two outputs that society could produce from given resources, over a given period (1)

profit maximization (under perfect competition): a seller should increase production up to the point where $MR = MC$. As $MR = P$ under perfect competition, we can also define the profit maximizing solution by setting $P = MC$ (16)

progressive tax: a tax in which the percentage of one's income that is paid in taxes tends to increase with increasing income levels (11)

proportional tax: a tax in which all taxpayers pay the same tax rate, regardless of income (11)

public good: a good that is nonexcludable and non-rival (13)

public purpose sphere: governments as well as other organizations that seek to enhance well-being without making a profit (2)

pure monopoly: the situation in which there is only one seller (17)

race to the bottom: a situation in which countries or regions compete in providing low-cost business environments, resulting in deterioration in labor, environmental, or safety standards (6)

rationality axiom: the statement that "rational economic man maximizes his utility (or self-interest)" (7)

reference group: the group to which an individual compares himself or herself (8)

regressive tax: a tax in which the percentage of one's income paid in taxes tends to decrease with increasing income levels (11)

regulated monopoly: a monopoly run under government supervision (17)

relative deprivation: the feeling of lack that comes from comparing oneself with someone who has more (8)

renewable resource: a resource that regenerates through short-term natural processes (14)

rent: payments for the direct or indirect use of any capital assets (10)

replacement cost methods: nonmarket valuation techniques that estimate the value of ecosystem services based on the cost of actions that provide substitute services (12)

resale market: a market for an item that has been previously owned (2)

resource maintenance: preserving or improving the resources that contribute to the enhancement of well-being, including natural, manufactured, human, and social resources (1)

retail markets: markets where goods and services are purchased by consumers from businesses, generally in small quantities (2)

revealed preference methods: valuation techniques that infer the value of nonmarket goods and services based on people's decisions in related markets (12)

revenue-neutral (taxes): offsetting any tax increases with decreases in other taxes such that overall tax collections remain constant (12)

rival good: a good that can only be consumed by only one person at a time (13)

satisfice: to choose an outcome that would be satisfactory and then seek an option that at least reaches that standard (7)

scarcity: the concept that resources are not sufficient to allow all goals to be accomplished at once (1)

screening methods: approaches used by employers to limit their job search to specific candidates (9)

sealed-bid auction: an auction in which bids are given privately to the auctioneer (2)

short run: (in terms of production processes) a period in which at least one production input has a fixed quantity (15)

shortage: a situation in which the quantity demanded at a particular price exceeds the quantity that sellers are willing to supply (3)

short-run elasticity: a measure of the relatively immediate responsiveness to a price change (4)

signaling theory: a theory of the value of an education that suggests that an educational credential *signals* to an employer that a potential worker has desired character traits and work habits (9)

social capital: the stock of relationships, including trust and shared values, that facilitates economic activities (14)

social efficiency (in welfare economics): an allocation of resources that maximizes the net benefits to society (5)

social insurance taxes: taxes used to fund social insurance programs such as Social Security, Medicare, and Medicaid (11)

social organization: the ways in which human productive activities are structured and coordinated (14)

social value: the extent to which an outcome moves us toward our final goals (3)

social welfare: total benefits to society minus total costs, or total net benefits (5)

stated preference methods: nonmarket valuation techniques that directly ask survey respondents about their preferences in a hypothetical scenario (12)

stock: the quantity of something at a particular point in time (14)

stock-flow diagram: a diagram that shows how a stock changes over time, as flows add to it or subtract from it (14)

subjective well-being (SWB): a measure of welfare based on survey questions asking people about their own degree of life satisfaction (8)

subsidy: a per-unit payment to producers to lower production costs and encourage greater production (12)

substitutability: the possibility of using one resource instead of another (14)

substitute good: a good that can be used in place of another good (3)

substitution effect of a price change: the tendency of a price increase for a particular good to reduce the quantity demanded of that good, as buyers turn to relatively cheaper substitutes (4)

sunk cost: an expenditure that was incurred or committed to in the past and is irreversible in the short run (16)

supply curve: a curve indicating the quantities that sellers are willing to supply at various prices (3)

supply: the willingness of producers and merchandisers to provide goods and services (3)

supply schedule: a table showing the relationship between price and quantity supplied (3)

supply-side economics: the macroeconomic theory that low marginal tax rates lead to higher rates of economic growth by encouraging entrepreneurship and investment (11)

surplus: a situation in which the quantity that sellers are prepared to sell at a particular price exceeds the quantity that buyers are willing to buy at that price (3)

sustainable socioeconomic system: one that maintains its resources such that at least the same level of social well-being can be maintained over time (14)

tacit collusion: collusion that takes place without creation of a cartel (17)

tariffs: taxes (or duties) charged by national governments to the importers of goods from other countries (6)

tax incidence analysis: the study of who bears the ultimate burden of a tax (11)

taxable income: the portion of one's income that is subject to taxation after deductions and exemptions (11)

technological progress: the development of new methods of converting inputs (resources) into outputs (products or services) (1)

theory of market adjustment: the theory that market forces will tend to make shortages and surpluses disappear (3)

third-party effects: impacts of an economic transaction on those not involved in the transaction, such as the health effects of pollution (5)

time discount rate: an economic concept describing the relative weighting of present benefits or costs compared to future benefits or costs (7)

total cost: the sum of fixed and variable costs (15)

total cost curve: a graph showing the relationship between the total cost of production and the level of output (15)

total economic value: the sum of all the benefits for which people are willing to pay, with respect to an ecosystem or natural place (12)

total income: the sum of income that an individual or couple receives from all sources (11)

total product curve: a curve showing the total amount of output produced with different levels of one variable input, holding all other inputs constant (15)

total revenues: the total amount of money received by a seller, equal to price times quantity (16)

tradable pollution permits: a system of pollution regulation in which a government allocates permits that are required in order to produce pollution. After they are allocated, these permits may be traded among firms or other interested parties (12)

trade quota: a nationally imposed restriction on the quantity of a particular good that can be imported from another country (6)

trade-related subsidy: payments given to producers to encourage more production, either for export or as a substitute for imports (6)

tragedy of the commons: a situation in which an unregulated common property resource is seriously degraded due to overuse (13)

transfer: the giving of something, with nothing specific expected in return (1)

travel cost models: a revealed preference method used to obtain estimates of the recreation benefits of natural sites based on variations in the travel costs paid by visitors from different regions (12)

triple bottom line: an assessment of the performance of a business according to social and environmental goals as well as making profits (15)

underground market: a market in which illegal goods and services are sold or legal goods and services are sold in an illegal way (2)

unit-elastic demand: the percentage change in the quantity demanded is exactly equal to the percentage change in price. The elasticity value is 1 (4)

upstream taxes: taxes instituted as close as possible in a production process to the extraction of raw materials (12)

utility: the pleasure or satisfaction received from goods, services, or experiences (8)

utility function (or **total utility curve**): a curve showing the relation of utility levels to consumption levels (8)

value of a statistical life (VSL): society's willingness to pay to avoid one death, based on the valuation of relatively small changes in mortality risks (12)

variable costs: production costs that can be adjusted relatively quickly and that do not need to be paid if no production occurs (15)

variable input: a production input whose quantity can be changed relatively quickly, resulting in changes in the level of production (15)

voluntary simplicity: a conscious decision to live with limited or reduced level of consumption, in order to increase one's quality of life (8)

wealth: the net value of all the material and financial assets owned by an individual (1)

welfare economics: the branch of microeconomics that seeks to estimate the social welfare of different scenarios in order to determine how to maximize net social benefits (5)

well-being: a term used to broadly describe a good quality of life (1)

wholesale markets: markets where final goods are purchased by retailers from suppliers, normally in large quantities (2)

willingness-to-pay (WTP) principle: the economic value of something, such as an environmental benefit, is equal to the maximum amount people are willing to pay for it (12)

worker cooperatives: a labor arrangement in which the owners of an enterprise are the workers themselves (9)

World Trade Organization (WTO): an international organization that provides a forum for trade negotiations, creates rules to govern trade, and investigates and makes judgment on trade disputes (6)

Index

Note: Italicized locators indicate figures.

About the Authors

Neva R. Goodwin (PhD, Boston University) is co-director of the Global Development and Environment Institute (GDAE) at Tufts University.

Jonathan M. Harris (Ph.D., Boston University) is director of the Theory and Education Project at GDAE.

Julie A. Nelson (Ph.D., University of Wisconsin, Madison) is Professor of Economics at the University of Massachusetts Boston and Senior Research Fellow at GDAE.

Brian Roach (Ph.D, University of California, Davis) is Senior Research Associate at GDAE.

Mariano Torras (Ph.D., University of Massachusetts, Amherst) is Professor of Economics at Adelphi University and Senior Research Fellow at GDAE.